Men's Lives

◆ ◆ ◆

Men's Lives

◆ ◆ ◆

Second Edition

MICHAEL S. KIMMEL
STATE UNIVERSITY OF NEW YORK
AT STONY BROOK

MICHAEL A. MESSNER
UNIVERSITY OF SOUTHERN CALIFORNIA

MACMILLAN PUBLISHING COMPANY
NEW YORK

MAXWELL MACMILLAN CANADA
TORONTO

Editor: Bruce Nichols
Production Supervisor: George Carr
Production Manager: Jennifer Mallon
Cover Designer: Blake Logan
Cover Photograph: Picasso, *Footballeur*, Paris, 1961.
This book was set in Janson by TC Systems, Inc., and was printed and
bound by Book Press. The cover was printed by New England Book
Components.

Macmillan Publishing Company
866 Third Avenue, New York, New York 10022

Maxwell Macmillan Canada, Inc.
1200 Eglinton Avenue East
Suite 200
Don Mills, Ontario M3C 3N1

Library of Congress Cataloging-in-Publication Data
Men's lives / [compiled by] Michael S. Kimmel, Michael A. Messner.—
   2nd ed.
        p.   cm.
    ISBN 0-02-363870-2 (paper)
    1. Men—United States—Attitudes. 2. Masculinity (Psychology)—
United States. 3. Men—United States—Sexual behavior.
I. Kimmel, Michael S.   II. Messner, Michael A.
HQ1090.3.M465   1992
305.31—dc20   91-2586
                                                    CIP

Printing: 5 6 7   Year: 3 4 5 6 7 8

For our mothers,
Barbara Diamond
and Anita Messner-Voth

◆ ◆ ◆

Preface

◆ ◆ ◆

Over the past eight years we have been teaching courses on the male experience, or "men's lives." Our courses have reflected our own education and recent research of feminist scholars and profeminist men in American society. (By profeminist men we mean active supporters of women's claims against male violence and for equal opportunity, political participation, sexual autonomy, family reforms, and equal education.) Gender, these scholars have demonstrated, is a general feature of social life, one of the central organizing principles around which our lives revolve. In the social sciences, women's studies courses and courses about women in traditional disciplines have explored the experiences of women's lives. But what does it mean to be a man in contemporary American society?

This anthology is organized around specific themes that define masculinity and the issues that men confront over their lifetimes. In addition, we incorporate a social constructionist perspective that examines how men actively construct their masculinity within a social and historical context. Related to this construction and integrated in our examination are the variations that exist among men in relation to class, race, and sexual preference.

We begin Part One with issues and questions that unravel the "masculine mystique" and suggest various dimensions of men's position in society and their relationships with women and other men. Parts Two through Nine examine the different issues that emerge for men at different times of their lives and the ways in which their lives change over time. We touch on central moments related to boyhood and adolescence, sports, occupations, marriage, and fatherhood. Four of these parts deal with men's emotional and sexual relationships with women and with other men. The final part, "Men and the Future," explores some of the ways in which men are changing and some possible directions in which they might continue to change.

Although a major component of the traditional, normative definition of masculinity is independence, we are pleased to acknowledge those colleagues and friends whose criticism and support have been a constant help throughout our work on this project. Bruce Nichols, our editor at Macmillan, was handed our project and has adopted it as his own, facilitating our work at every turn. Chris Cardone, our original editor, was supportive from the start, and helped the project get going. Many other scholars who work on issues of masculinity, such as Bob Blauner, Robert Brannon, Harry Brod, Rocco Capraro, Bob Connell, James Harrison, Jeff Hearn, Martin Levine, David Morgan, Joe Pleck, Tony Rotundo, Don Sabo, and Peter Stein, have contributed to a supportive intellectual community in which to work.

We also thank the following reviewers for their helpful comments and suggestions for this edition: Margaret Andersen, University of Delaware; Judith Barker, Ithaca College; Bob Blauner, University of California, Berkeley; Chip Capraro, Hobart and William Smith Colleges; Don Sabo, D'Youville College; Roberta Seid, University of Southern California; Carol Wharton, University of Virginia; Diane Villwock, Morehead State University; and Tim Wernette, University of Arizona.

Colleagues at the State University of New York at Stony Brook and the University of Southern California have also been supportive of this work. We are especially grateful to Paul Attewell, Lois Banner, Ruth Schwartz Cowan, John Gagnon, Norman Goodman, Helen Lefkowitz-Horowtiz, Carol Jacklin, and Barrie Thorne. A teaching fellowship from the Lilly Endowment has generously supported Kimmel's work on pedagogical issues of teaching about men and masculinity.

This book is also a product of the profeminist men's movement, a loose network of men who support a feminist critique of traditional masculinity and support women's struggles to enlarge the scope of personal autonomy and public power for women. These men are engaged in a variety of efforts to transform masculinity in order to allow men to live fuller, richer, and healthier lives. The editors of *Changing Men* (with whom we have worked as Book Review Editor and Sports Editor), Mike Biernbaum and Rick Cote, have labored for a decade to provide a forum for antisexist men, and we acknowledge their efforts with gratitude and respect.

Finally, our wider circle of friends and colleagues has provided that rare atmosphere that combines intellectual challenge and emotional support. We are grateful to Judith Brisman, Barbara and Herb Diamond, Martin Duberman, Kate Ellis, Frances Goldin, Cathy Greenblat, Pam Hatchfield, Sandi Kimmel, David Levin, Mary Morris, Mitchell Tunick, and Nancy Young. We also acknowledge our fathers—Edwin H. Kimmel and Russell J. Messner—who provided such important models of masculinity for us as we were growing up. In addition, Pierrette Hondagneu-Sotelo and Iona Mara-Drita have lived with this project since its beginnings, and we are grateful that they share these men's lives. And we welcome Miles Hondagneu-Messner with hope and love, though we reserve judgment until we see his outside shot.

We have decided to dedicate this edition of *Men's Lives* to our mothers. As Bob Blauner points out, much of the prevailing "men's studies" theory stresses reconnection to fathers, and assumes the separation from mothers as essential and final. But separation is not antithetical to connection; they are two moments in intimately linked processes. We need both autonomy and community, and we thank our mothers for embodying both.

M. S. K.
M. A. M.

Contents

◆ ◆ ◆

PART EIGHT   *Male Sexualities*   *421*

PART NINE   *Men in Families*   *497*

PART TEN   *Men and the Future*   *549*

Men's Lives

◆ ◆ ◆

INTRODUCTION

This is a book about men. But, unlike other books about men, which line countless library shelves, this is a book about men *as men*. It is a book in which men's experiences are not taken for granted as we explore the "real" and significant accomplishments of men, but a book in which those experiences are treated as significant and important for themselves.

MEN AS "GENDERED BEINGS"

But what does it mean to examine men "as men"? Most courses in a college curriculum are about men, aren't they? But these courses routinely deal with men only in their public roles, so we come to know and understand men as scientists, politicians, military figures, writers, and philosophers. Rarely, if ever, are men understood through the prism of gender.

But listen to some male voices from some of these "ungendered" courses. Take, for example, composer Charles Ives, debunking "sissy" types of music; he said he used traditional tough guy themes and concerns in his drive to build new sounds and structures out of the popular musical idiom (cf. Wilkinson, 1986: 103). Or architect Louis Sullivan, describing his ambition to create "masculine forms": strong, solid, commanding respect. Or novelist Ernest Hemingway, retaliating against literary enemies by portraying them as impotent or homosexual.

Consider also political figures, such as Cardinal Richelieu, the seventeenth-century French First Minister to Louis XIII, who insisted that it was "necessary to have masculine virtue and do everything by reason" (cited in Elliott, 1984: 20). Closer to home, recall President Lyndon Baines Johnson's dismissal of a political adversary: "Oh him. He has to squat to piss!" Or his boast that during the Tet offensive in the Vietnam War, he "didn't just screw Ho Chi Minh. I cut his pecker off!"

Democrats have no monopoly on unexamined gender coloring their political rhetoric. Richard Nixon was "afraid of being acted upon, of being inactive, of being soft, or being thought impotent, of being dependent upon anyone else," according to his biographer, Bruce Mazlish. And don't forget Vice-President George Bush's revealing claim that in his television debate with Democratic challenger Geraldine Ferraro he had "kicked ass." (That few political pundits criticized such unapologetic glee concerning violence against women is again indicative of how invisible gender issues are in our culture.) Indeed, recent political campaigns have revolved, in part, around gender issues, as each candidate attempted to demonstrate that he was not a "wimp" but was a "real man." (Of course, the few successful female politicians face the double task of convincing the electorate that they are not the "weak-willed wimps" that their gender implies in the public mind while *at the same time* demonstrating that they are "real women.")

These are just a few examples of what we might call gendered speech, language that uses gender terms to make its case. And these are just a few of

1

the thousands of examples one could find in every academic discipline of how men's lives are organized around gender issues, and how gender remains one of the organizing principles of social life. We come to know ourselves and our world through the prism of gender. Only we act as if we didn't know it.

Fortunately, in recent years, the pioneering work of feminist scholars, both in traditional disciplines and in women's studies, and of feminist women in the political arena has made us aware of the centrality of gender in our lives. Gender, these scholars have demonstrated, is a central feature of social life, one of the central organizing principles around which our lives revolve. In the social sciences, gender has now taken its place alongside class and race as the three central mechanisms by which power and resources are distributed in our society, and the three central themes out of which we fashion the meanings of our lives.

We certainly understand how this works for women. Through women's studies courses and also in courses about women in traditional disciplines, students have explored the complexity of women's lives, the hidden history of exemplary women, and the daily experiences of women in the routines of their lives. For women, we know how gender works as one of the formative elements out of which social life is organized.

THE INVISIBILITY OF GENDER:
A SOCIOLOGICAL EXPLANATION

Too often, though, we treat men as if they had no gender, as if only their public personae were of interest to us as students and scholars, as if their interior experience of gender was of no significance. This became evident when one of us was in a graduate seminar on Feminist Theory several years ago. A discussion between a white woman and a black woman revolved around the question of whether their similarities as women were greater than their racial differences as black and white. The white woman asserted that the fact that they were both women bonded them, in spite of their racial differences. The black woman disagreed.

"When you wake up in the morning and look in the mirror, what do you see?" she asked.

"I see a woman," replied the white woman.

"That's precisely the issue," replied the black woman. "I see a black woman. For me, race is visible every day, because it is how I am not privileged in this culture. Race is invisible to you, which is why our alliance will always seem somewhat false to me."

Witnessing this exchange, Michael Kimmel was startled. When *he* looked in the mirror in the morning, he saw, as he put it, "a human being: universally generalizable. The generic person." What had been concealed—that he possessed both race and gender—had become strikingly visible. As a white man, he was able not to think about the ways in which gender and race had affected his experiences.

There is a sociological explanation for this blind spot in our thinking: the mechanisms that afford us privilege are very often invisible to us. What makes us marginal (unempowered, oppressed) are the mechanisms that we understand, because those are the ones that are most painful in daily life. Thus, white people rarely think of themselves as "raced" people, rarely think of race as a central element in their experience. But people of color are marginalized by race, and so the centrality of race is both painfully obvious and urgently needs study. Similarly, middle class people do not acknowledge the importance of social class as an organizing principle of social life, largely because for them class is an invisible force that makes everyone look pretty much the same. Working class people, on the other hand, are often painfully aware of the centrality of class in their lives. [Interestingly, upper class people are often more aware of class dynamics than are middle class people. In part, this may be the result of the emphasis on status within the upper class, as lineage, breeding, and family honor take center stage. In part, it may also be the result of a peculiar marginalization of the upper class in our society, as in the overwhelming number of television shows and movies that are ostensibly about just plain (i.e., middle class) folks.]

In this same way, men often think of themselves as genderless, as if gender did not matter in the daily experiences of our lives. Certainly, we can see the biological sex of individuals, but we rarely understand the ways in which *gender*—that complex of social meanings that is attached to biological sex—is enacted in our daily lives. For example, we treat male scientists as if their being men had nothing to do with the organization of their experiments, the logic of scientific inquiry, or the questions posed by science itself. We treat male political figures as if masculinity were not even remotely in their consciousness as they do battle in the political arena.

This book takes a position directly opposed to such genderlessness for men. We believe that men are also "gendered," and that this gendering process, the transformation of biological males into socially interacting men, is a central experience for men. That we are unaware of it only helps to perpetuate the inequalities based on gender in our society.

In this book, we will examine the various ways in which men are gendered. We have gathered together some of the most interesting, engaging, and convincing materials from the past decade that have been written about men. We believe that *Men's Lives* will allow readers to explore the meanings of masculinity in contemporary American culture in a new way.

EARLIER EFFORTS TO STUDY MEN

Certainly, researchers have been examining masculinity for a long time. Historically, there have been three general models that have governed social scientific research on men and masculinity. *Biological models* have focused on the ways in which innate biological differences between males and females programmed different social behaviors. *Anthropological models* have examined masculinity cross-culturally, stressing the variations in the behaviors and attributes associated with being a man. And, until recently, *sociological models* have stressed how socialization of boys and girls included accommodation to a "sex role" specific to one's biological sex. Although each of these perspectives helps to understand the meaning of masculinity and femininity, each is also limited in its ability to fully explain how gender operates in any culture.

Relying on differences in reproductive biology, some scholars have argued that the physiological organization of males and females makes the differences we observe in psychological temperament and social behaviors inevitable. One perspective holds that differences in endocrine functioning are the cause of gender difference, that testosterone predisposes males toward aggression, competition, and violence, whereas estrogen predisposes females toward passivity, tenderness, and exaggerated emotionality. Others insist that these observed behavioral differences derive from the differences between the size or number of sperm and eggs. Since a male can produce 100 million sperm with each ejaculation, whereas a female can produce less than 20 eggs capable of producing healthy offspring over the course of her life, these authors suggest that men's "investment" in their offspring is significantly less than women's investment. Other authors arrive at the same conclusion by suggesting that the different size of egg and sperm, and the fact that the egg is the source of the food supply, impels temperamental differences. Reproductive "success" to males means the insemination of as many females as possible; to females, reproductive success means carefully choosing one male to mate with and insisting that he remain present to care for and support their offspring. Still other authors argue that male and female behavior is governed by different halves of the brain; males are ruled by the left hemisphere, which controls rationality and abstract thought, whereas females are governed by the right hemisphere, which controls emotional affect and creativity. (For examples of these works, see Wilson, 1976; Trivers, 1972; Goldberg, 1975; and Goldberg et al., 1986.)

Observed normative temperamental differences between women and men that are assumed to be of biological origin are easily translated into political prescriptions. In this ideological sleight of hand, what is *normative* (i.e., what is prescribed) is translated into what is *normal*, and the mechanisms of this transformation are the assumed biological imperative. George Gilder, for example, assembles the putative biological differences between women and men into a call for a return to traditional gender roles. Gilder believes that male sexuality is, by nature, wild and lusty, "insistent" and incessant," careening out of control and threatening anarchic disorder, unless it can be controlled and constrained. This is the task of women. When women refuse to apply the brakes to male sexuality—by asserting their own or by choosing to pursue a life outside the domestic sphere—they abandon their "natural" function for illusory social gains. Sex education, abortion, and birth control are all condemned as facilitating women's escape from biological necessity. Similarly, he argues against women's employment, since the "unemployed man can contribute little to the community and will often disrupt it, but the woman may even do more good without a job than with one" (Gilder, 1986: 86).

The biological argument has been challenged by many scholars on several grounds. The implied causation between two observed sets of differences (biological differences and different behaviors) is misleading, since there is no logical reason to assume that one caused the other, or that the line of causation moves only from the biological to the social. The selection of biological evidence is partial, and generalizations from "lower" animal species to human beings are always suspect. One sociologist asks if these differences are "natural," why their enforcement must be coercive, why males and females have to be forced to assume the rules that they are naturally supposed to play (see Epstein, 1986:8). And one primatologist argues that the evidence adduced to support the current status quo might also lead to precisely the opposite conclusions, that biological differences would impel female promiscuity and male fragility (see Hrdy, 1981). Biological differences between males and females would appear to set some parameters for differences in social behavior, but would not dictate the temperaments of men and women in any one culture. These psychological and social differences would appear to be the result far more of the ways in which cultures interpret, shape, and modify these biological inheritances. We may be born males or females, but we become men and women in a cultural context.

Anthropologists have entered the debate at this point, but with different positions. For example, some anthropologists have suggested that the univerality of gender differences comes from specific cultural adaptations to the environment, whereas others describe the cultural variations of gender roles, seeking to demonstrate the fluidity of gender and the primacy of cultural organization. Lionel Tiger and Robin Fox argue that the sexual division of labor is universal because of the different nature of bonding for males and females. "Nature," they argue, "intended mother and child to be together" because she is the source of emotional security and food; thus, cultures have prescribed various behaviors for women that emphasize nurturance and emotional connection (Tiger and Fox, 1984: 304). The bond between men is forged through the necessity of "competitive cooperation" in hunting; men must cooperate with members of their own tribe in the hunt and yet compete for scarce resources with men in other tribes. Such bonds predispose men toward the organization of the modern corporation or governmental bureaucracy.

Such anthropological arguments omit as much as they include, and many scholars have pointed out problems with the model. Why did not intelligence become sex linked, as this model (and the biological model) would imply? Such positions also reveal a marked conservatism: the differences between women and men are the differences that nature or cultural evolution intended, and are therefore not to be tampered with.

Perhaps the best known challenge to this anthropological argument is the work of Margaret Mead. Mead insisted that the variations among cultures in their prescriptions of gender roles required the conclusion that culture was the more decisive cause of these differences. In her classic study, *Sex and Temperament in Three Primitive Societies* (1935), Mead observed such wide variability among gender role prescriptions—and such marked differences from our own—that any universality implied by biological or anthropological models had to be rejected. And although the empirical accuracy of Mead's work has been challenged in its specific arguments, the general theoretical arguments remain convincing.

Psychological theories have also contributed to the discussion of gender roles, as psychologists have specified the specific developmental sequences for both males and females. Earlier theorists observed psychological distancing from the mother as the precondition for independence and autonomy, or suggested a sequence that placed the capacity for abstract reason as the developmental stage beyond relational reasoning. Since it is normative for males to exhibit independence and the capacity for abstract reason, it was argued that males are more successful at negotiating these psychological passages, and implied that women somehow lagged behind men on the ladder of developmental success. (Such arguments may be found in Freud, Erikson, and Kohlberg.)

But these models, too, have been challenged, most recently by sociologist Nancy Chodorow, who argued that women's ability to connect contains a more fundamentally human trait than the male's need to distance, and by psychologist Carol Gilligan, who claimed that women's predisposition toward relational reasoning may contain a more humane strategy of thought than recourse to abstract principles. Regardless of our assessment of these arguments, Chodorow and Gilligan rightly point out that the highly ideological assumptions that make masculinity the normative standard against which the psychological development of *both* males and females was measured would inevitably make femininity problematic and less fully developed. Moreover, Chodorow explicitly insists that these "essential" differences between women and men are socially constructed and thus subject to change.

Finally, sociologists have attempted to synthesize these three perspectives into a systematic explanation of "sex roles." These are the collection of attitudes, attributes, and behaviors that is seen as appropriate for males and appropriate for females. Thus, masculinity is associated with technical mastery, aggression, competitiveness, and cognitive abstraction, whereas femininity is associated with emotional nurturance, connectedness, and passivity. Sex role theory informed a wide variety of prescriptive literature (self-help books) that instructed parents on what to do if they wanted their child to grow up as a healthy boy or girl.

The strongest challenge to all these perspectives, as we have seen, came from feminist scholars, who have specified the ways in which the assumptions about maturity, development, and health all made masculinity the norm against which both genders were measured. In all the social sciences, these feminist scholars have stripped these early studies of their academic facades to reveal the unexamined ideological assumptions contained within them. By the early 1970s, women's studies programs began to articulate a new paradigm for the study of gender, one that assumed nothing about men or women beforehand, and that made no assumptions about which gender was more highly developed. And by the mid-1970s, the first group of texts about men appeared that had been inspired by these pioneering efforts by feminist scholars.

THINKING ABOUT MEN: THE FIRST GENERATION

In the mid 1970s, the first group of works on men and masculinity appeared that was direcly influenced by these feminist critiques of the traditional explanations for gender differences. Some books underscored the costs to men of traditional gender role prescriptions, exploring how some aspects of men's lives and experiences are constrained and underdeveloped by the relentless pressure to exhibit other behaviors associated with masculinity. Books such as Marc Feigen-Fasteau's *The Male Machine* (1974) and Warren Farrell's *The Liberated Man* (1975) discussed the costs to men's health—both physical and psychological—and the quality of relationships with women, other men, and their children of the traditional male sex role.

Several anthologies explored the meanings of masculinity in the United States by adopting a feminist-inspired prism through which to view men and masculinity. For example, Deborah David and Robert Brannon's *The Forty-*

Nine Percent Majority (1976) and Joseph Pleck and Jack Sawyer's *Men and Masculinity* (1974) presented panoramic views of men's lives, from within a framework that accepted the feminist critique of traditional gender arrangements. Elizabeth Pleck and Joseph Pleck's *The American Man* (1980) suggested an historical evolution of contemporary themes. These works explored both the "costs" and the privileges of being a man in modern American society.

Perhaps the single most important book to criticize the normative organization of the male sex role was Joseph Pleck's *The Myth of Masculinity* (1981). Pleck carefully deconstructed the constituent elements of the male sex role, and reviewed the empirical literature for each component part. After demonstrating that the empirical literature did not support these normative features, Pleck argued that the male sex role model was incapable of describing men's experiences. In its place, he posited a male "sex role strain" model that specified the contemporary sex role as problematic, historically specific, and also an unattainable ideal.

Building on Pleck's work, a critique of the sex role model began to emerge. Sex roles had been cast as the static containers of behaviors and attitudes, and biological males and females were required to fit themselves into these containers, regardless of how ill-fitting these clusters of behaviors and attitudes felt. Such a model was ahistorical and suggested a false cultural universalism, and was therefore ill equipped to understand the ways in which sex roles change, and the ways in which individuals modify those roles through the enactments of gender expectations. Most telling, however, was the way in which the sex role model ignored the ways in which definitions of masculinity and femininity were based on, and reproduced, relationships of power. Not only do men as a group exert power over women as a group, but the definitions of masculinity and femininity reproduce those power relations. Power dynamics are an essential element in both the definition and the enactments of gender.

This first generation of research on masculinity was extremely valuable, particularly since it challenged the unexamined ideology that made masculinity the gender norm against which both men and women were measured. The old models of sex roles had reproduced the domination of men over women by insisting on the dominance of masculine traits over feminine traits. These new studies argued against both the definitions of either sex, and the social institutions in which those differences were embedded. A new model looked at "gender relations" and understood how the definition of either masculinity or femininity was relational, that is, how the definition of one gender depended, in part, on the understanding of the definition of the other.

In the early 1980s, the research on women again surged ahead of the research on men and masculinity. This time, however, the focus was not on the ways in which sex roles reproduce the power relations in society, but rather on the ways in which femininity is experienced differently by women in various social groups. Gradually, the notion of a single femininity—which was based on the white middle class Victorian notion of female passivity, langorous beauty, and emotional responsiveness—was replaced by an examination of the ways in which women differ in their gender role expectations by race, class, age, sexual orientation, ethnicity, region, and nationality.

The research of men and masculinity is now entering a new stage, in which the variations among men are seen as central to the understanding of men's lives. The unexamined assumption in earlier studies had been that one version of masculinity—white, middle age, middle class, heterosexual—was the sex role into which all men were struggling to fit in our society. Thus, working class men, men of color, gay men, and younger and older men were all observed as departing in significant ways from the traditional definitions of masculinity. Therefore, it was easy to see these men as enacting "problematic" or "deviant" versions of masculinity. Such theoretical assertions, however, reproduce precisely the power relationships that keep these men in subordinate positions in our society. It is not only that middle class, middle aged, heterosexual white masculinity becomes the standard against which all men are measured, but that this definition, itself, is used against those who do not fit as a way to keep them down. The normative definition of masculinity is not the "right" one, but it is the one that is dominant.

The challenge to the hegemonic definition of masculinity came from men whose masculinity was cast as deviant: men of color, gay men, and ethnic men. We understand now that we cannot speak of "masculinity" as a singular term, but must examine *masculinities:* the ways in which different men construct different versions of masculinity. Such a perspective can be seen in several recent works, such as Harry Brod's *The Making of Masculinities* (1987), Michael Kimmel's *Changing Men: New Directions in Research on Men and Masculinity* (1987), and Tim Carrigan, Bob Connell, and John Lee's "Toward a New Sociology of Masculinity" (1985). Bob Connell's *Gender and Power* (1987) and Jeff Hearn's *The Gender of Oppression* (1987) represent the most sophisticated theoretical statements of this perspective. Connell argues that the oppression of women is a chief mechanism that links the various masculinities, and that the marginalization of certain masculinities is an important component of the reproduction of male power over women. This critique of the hegemonic definition of masculinity as a perspective on men's lives is one of the organizing principles of our book, which is the first college-level text in this second generation of work on men and masculinities.

Now that we have reviewed some of the traditional explanations for gender relations, and have situated this book within the research on gender in general, and men in particular, let us briefly outline exactly the theoretical perspective we have employed in the book. Not only does our theoretical framework provide the organizing principle of the book as a whole, it also provided some of the criteria for the selection of the articles that are included.

THE SOCIAL CONSTRUCTION OF MASCULINITIES

Men are not born, growing from infants through boyhood to manhood, to follow a predetermined bilogical imperative, encoded in their physical organization. To be a man is to participate in social life as a man, as a gendered being. Men are not born; they are made. And men make themselves, actively contructing their masculinities within a social and historical context.

This book is about how men are made and how men make themselves in contemporary American society. It is about what masculinity means, about how masculinity is organized, and about the social institutions that sustain and eleborate it. It is a book in which we will trace what it means to be a man over the course of men's lives.

Men's Lives revolves around three important themes that are part of a social scientific perspective. First, we have adoped a *social contructionist* perspective. By this we mean that the important fact of men's lives is not that they are biological males, but that they become men. Our sex may be male, but our identity as men is developed through a complex process of interaction with the culture in which we both learn the gender scripts appropriate to our culture, and attempt to modify those scripts to make them more palatable. The second axis around which the book is organized follows from our social constructionist perspective. As we have argued, the experience of masculinity is not uniform and universally generalizable to all men in our society. Masculinity differs dramatically in our society, and we have organized the book to illustrate the *variations* among men in the construction of masculinity. Third, we have adopted a *life course* perspective, to chart the construction of these various masculinities in men's lives, and to examine pivotal developmental moments or institutional locations during a man's life in which the meanings of masculinity are articulated. These three perspectives—social constructionism, varitations among men, and the life course perspective—will define the organization of this book and the criteria we have used to select the articles included.

The Social Constructionist Model   The social constructionist perspective argues that the meaning of masculinity is neither transhistorical nor culturally universal, but rather varies from culture to culture and within any one culture over time. Thus, males become men in the United States in the late twentieth century in a way that is very different from men in Southeast Asia, or Kenya, or Sri Lanka. The meaning of masculinity varies from culture to culture.

Men's lives also vary within any one culture over time. The experience of masculinity in the contemporary United States is very different from that experience 150 years ago. Who would argue that what it meant to be a "real man" in seventeenth-century France (at least among the upper classes)—high-heeled patent leather shoes, red velvet jackets covering frilly white lace shirts, lots of rouge and white powder makeup, and a taste for the elegant refinement of ornate furniture—bears much resemblance to the meaning of masculinity among a similar class of French men today?

A perspective that emphasizes the social construction of gender is, therefore, both *historical* and *comparative*. It allows us to explore the ways in which the meanings of gender vary from culture to culture, and how they change within any one culture over historical time.

Variations Among Men   Masculinity also varies *within* any one society by the various types of cultural groups that compose it. Subcultures are organized around other poles, which are the primary way in which people organize themselves and by which resources are distributed. And men's experiences differ from one another in the ways in which social scientists have identified as the chief structural mechanisms along which power and resources are distributed. We cannot speak of masculinity in the United States as if it were a single, easily identifiable commodity. To do so is to risk positing one version of masculinity as normative, and making all other masculinities problematic.

In the contemporary United States, masculinity is constructed differently by class culture, by race and ethnicity, and by age. And each of these axes of masculinity modifies the others. Black masculinity differs from white masculinity, yet each of them is also further modified by class and age. A 30-year-old middle class black man will have some things in common with a 30-year-old middle class white man that he might not share with a 60-year-old working class black man, although he will share with him elements of masculinity that are different from the white man of his class and age. The resulting matrix of *masculinities* is complicated and often the elements are cross-cutting, but without understanding this, we risk collapsing all masculinities into one hegemonic version.

The challenge to a singular definition of masculinity as the normative definition is the second axis around which the readings in this book revolve.

The Life Course Perspective   The meaning of masculinity is not constant over the course of any man's life, but will change as he grows and matures. The issues confronting a man about proving himself, feeling successful, and the social institutions in which he will attempt to enact his definitions of masculinity will change throughout his life. Thus, we have adopted a *life course perspective* to discuss the ways in which different issues will emerge for men at different times of their lives, and the ways in which men's lives, themselves, change over time. The life course perspective we have employed will examine men's lives at various privotal moments in their development from young boys to adults. Like a slide show, these points will freeze the action for a short while, to afford us the opportunity to examine in more detail the ways in which different men in our culture experience masculinity at any one time.

The book's organization reflects these three concerns. The first two parts set the context through which we shall examine men's lives. Parts Three through Nine follow those lives through their full course, examining central moments experienced by men in the United States today. Specifically, Parts Two and Three touch on boyhood and adolescence, discussing some of the institutions organized to embody and reproduce American masculinities, such as fraternities, the Boy Scouts, and sports groups. Part Four, "Men and Work," explores the ways in which masculinities are constructed in relation to men's occupations. Part Five, "Men and Health: Body and Mind," deals with heart attacks, stress, AIDS, and other health problems among men. Part Six, "Men with Women: Intimacy and Power," describes men's emotional and sexual relationships. We deal with heterosexuality and homosexuality, mindful of the ways in which variations are based on specific lines (class, race, ethnicity). Part Seven, "Men with Men: Friendships and Fears," describes emotional and physical (but not necessarily sexual) relationships that men develop through their lives. Part Eight, "Male Sexualities," studies the normative elements of heterosexuality and probes the controversial political implications of pornography as a source of both straight and gay men's sexual information. Part Nine, "Men in Families," concentrates on masculinities within the family and the role of men as husbands, fathers, and senior citizens. Part Ten, "Men and the Future," examines some of the ways in which men are changing and points to some directions in which men might continue to change.

Our perspective, stressing the social construction of masculinities over the life course, will, we believe, allow a more comprehensive understanding of men's lives in the United States today.

REFERENCES

Brod, Harry, ed. *The Making of Masculinities*. Boston: Unwin, Hyman, 1987.

Carrigan, Tim, Bob Connell, and John Lee. "Toward a New Sociology of Masculinity" in *Theory and Society*, 1985, 5(14).

Chodorow, Nancy. *The Reproduction of Mothering*. Berkeley: University of California Press, 1978.

Connell, R. W. *Gender and Power*. Stanford, CA: Stanford University Press, 1987.

David, Deborah and Robert Brannon, eds. *The 49% Majority*. Reading, MA: Addison-Wesley, 1976.

Elliott, J. H. *Richelieu and Olivares*. New York: Cambridge University Press, 1984.

Epstein, Cynthia Fuchs. "Inevitability of Prejudice" in *Society*, Sept./Oct., 1986.

Farrell, Warren. *The Liberated Man*. New York: Random House, 1975.

Feigen-Fasteau, Marc. *The Male Machine*. New York: McGraw-Hill, 1974.

Gilligan, Carol. *In a Different Voice*. Cambridge, MA: Harvard University Press, 1982.

Gilder, George. *Men and Marriage*. Gretna, LA: Pelican Publishers, 1986.

Goldberg, Steven. *The Inevitability of Patriarchy*. New York: William Morrow & Co., 1975.

———. 1986. "Reaffirming the Obvious" in *Society*. Sept./Oct., 1986.

Hearn, Jeff. *The Gender of Oppression*. New York: St. Martin's Press, 1987.

Hrdy, Sandra Blaffer. *The Woman That Never Evolved*. Cambridge, MA: Harvard University Press, 1981.

Kimmel, Michael S., ed. *Changing Men: New Directions in Research on Men and Masculinity*. Newbury Park, CA: Sage Publications, 1987.

Mead, Margaret. *Sex and Temperament in Three Primitive Societies*. New York: McGraw-Hill, 1935.

Pleck, Joseph. *The Myth of Masculinity*. Cambridge, MA: M.I.T. Press, 1981.

——— and Elizabeth Pleck, eds. *The American Man*. Englewood Cliffs, NJ: Prentice-Hall, 1980.

——— and Jack Sawyer, eds. *Men and Masculinity*. Englewood Cliffs, NJ: Prentice-Hall, 1974.

Tiger, Lionel and Robin Fox. *The Imperial Animal*. New York: Holt, Rinehart & Winston, 1984.

Trivers, Robert. "Parental Investment and Sexual Selection" in *Sexual Selection and the Descent of Man* (B. Campbell, ed.). Chicago: Aldine Publishers, 1972.

Wilkinson, Rupert. *American Tough: The Tough Guy Tradition and American Character*. New York: Harper & Row, 1986.

Wilson, E. O. *Sociobiology: The New Synthesis*. Cambridge, MA: Harvard University Press, 1976.

◆ ◆ ◆

PART ONE

Perspectives on Masculinities

Jules Feiffer

"WHAT'S MANLY?"

A quick glance at any magazine rack or television talk show is enough to make you aware that these days, men are confused. What does it mean to be a "real man"? How are men supposed to behave? What are men supposed to feel? How are men to express their feelings? Who are we supposed to be like: Tootsie or Rambo? Clint Eastwood or Phil Donahue? Rhett Butler or Ashley Wilkes?

We are daily bombarded with images and handy rules to help us negotiate our way through a world in which all the rules seem to have suddenly vanished or changed. Some tell us to reassert traditional masculinity against all contemporary challenges. But a strength built only on the weakness of others hardly feels like strength at all. Others tell us that men are in power, the oppressor. But if men are in power as a group, why do individual men often feel so powerless? Can men change?

These questions will return throughout this book. In this section, several authors begin to examine some of the issues that define the depth of the question about men and masculinity. These articles begin to unravel the "masculine mystique" and suggest various dimensions of men's position in society, their power, their powerlessness and their confusion. Joseph Pleck, for example, explores contemporary definitions of masculinity, and the ways in which these definitions shape men's relations with women, with other men, and in society in general. Michael Kaufman takes men's problematic relationship to violence as a core theme in men's experience in society.

But we cannot speak of "men" as some universal category that is experienced in the same ways by each man. "All men are alike," runs a popular wisdom. But are they really? Are gay men's experiences with work, relationships, love, and politics similar to those of straight men? Do black and chicano men face the same problems and conflicts in their daily lives that white men face? Do middle class men have the same politicial interests as blue-collar men? The answers to these questions, as the articles in this part suggest, are not simple.

Although earlier studies of men and masculinity focused on the apparently universal norms of masculinity, recent work has attempted to demonstrate how different the worlds of various men are. Men are divided along the same lines that divide any other group: race, class, sexual orientation, ethnicity, age, and geographic region. Men's lives vary in crucial ways, and understanding these variations will take us a long way toward understanding men's experiences.

Earlier studies that suggested a single universal norm of masculinity reproduced some of the problems they were trying to solve. To be sure, *all* benefit from the inequality between women and men; for example, think of how rape jokes or male-exclusive sports cultures provide contexts for the bonding of men across class, race, and ethnic lines while denying full participation to women. But the single, seemingly universal masculinity obscured ways in which some men hold and maintain power over other men in our society, hiding the fact that all men do not share equally in the fruits of gender inequality.

Here is how sociologist Erving Goffman put it in his important book, *Stigma* (New York: Doubleday, 1963, p. 128):

> In an important sense there is only one complete unblushing male in America: a young, married, white, urban, northern, heterosexual Protestant father of college education, fully employed, of good complexion, weight, and height, and a recent record in sports. Every American male tends to look out upon the world from this perspective, this constituting one sense in which one can speak of a common value system in America. Any male who fails to qualify in any one of these ways is likely to view himself—during moments at least—as unworthy, incomplete, and inferior.

As Goffman suggests, the middle class, white, heterosexual masculinity is used as the marker against which other masculinities are measured, and by which standard they may be found wanting. What is *normative* (prescribed) becomes translated into what is *normal*. In this way, heterosexual men maintain their status by the oppression of gay men; middle aged men can maintain their dominance over older and younger men; upper class men can exploit working class men; and white men can enjoy privileges at the expense of men of color.

The articles by Jewelle Taylor Gibbs and Maxine Baca Zinn challenge popularly held negative sterotypes of black and chicano males as pathologically "macho." Instead, they suggest that an understanding of ethnic minority men must begin with a critical examination of how institutionalized racism, particularly (but not exclusively) in the economy, shapes and constrains the possibilities, choices, and personal life-styles of black and chicano men. Calls for "changing masculinities," these articles suggest, must involve an emphasis on *institutional* transformation, to which Gibbs's argument gives a special political urgency.

Michael Kimmel's article gives an illuminating glimpse into how ethnic identity informs our conceptions of masculinity in feminist politics. And Seymour Kleinberg's discussion of gay politics highlights the dangers in assuming a univeral "natural" heterosexuality when thinking about the politics of masculinities. Together, the articles in this section reveal that men's experiences vary enormously; students of men's lives must pay special attention to the richness of that diversity.

Joseph H. Pleck

MEN'S POWER WITH WOMEN, OTHER MEN, AND SOCIETY:
A MEN'S MOVEMENT ANALYSIS

My aim in this paper is to analyze men's power from the perspective afforded by the emerging antisexist men's movement. In the last several years, an antisexist men's movement has appeared in North America and in the Western European countries. While it is not so widely known as the women's movement, the men's movement has generated a variety of books, publications, and organizations,[1] and is now an established presence on the sex role scene. The present and future political relationship between the women's movement and the men's movement raises complex questions which I do not deal with here, though they are clearly important ones. Instead, here I present my own view of the contribution which the men's movement and the men's analysis make to a feminist understanding of men and power, and of power relations between the sexes. First, I will analyze men's power over women, particularly in relation to the power that men often perceive women have over them. Then I will analyze two other power relationships men are implicated in—men's power with other men, and men's power in society more generally—and suggest how these two other power relationships interact with men's power over women.

MEN'S POWER OVER WOMEN, AND WOMEN'S POWER OVER MEN

It is becoming increasingly recognized that one of the most fundamental questions raised by the women's movement is not a question about women at all, but rather a question about men: Why do men oppress women? There are two general kinds of answers to this question. The first is that men want power over women because it is in their rational self-interest to do so, to have the concrete benefits and privileges that power over women provides them. Having power, it is rational to want to keep it. The second kind of answer is

[1] See, for example, Deborah David and Robert Brannon, eds., *The Forty-Nine Percent Majority: Readings on the Male Role* (Reading, Mass.: Addison-Wesley, 1975); Warren Farrell, *The Liberated Man* (New York: Bantam Books, 1975); Marc Feigen-Fasteau, *The Male Machine* (New York: McGraw-Hill, 1974); Jack Nichols, *Men's Liberation: A New Definition of Masculinity* (Baltimore: Penguin, 1975); John Petras, eds., *Sex: Male/Gender: Masculine* (Port Washington, N.J.: Alfred, 1975); Joseph II. Pleck and Jack Sawyer, eds., *Men and Masculinity* (Englewood Cliffs, N.J.: Prentice-Hall, 1974). See also the *Man's Awareness Network (M.A.N.) Newsletter*, a regularly updated directory of men's movement activities, organizations, and publications, prepared by a rotating group of men's centers (c/o Knoxville Men's Resource Center, P.O. Box 8060, U.T. Station, Knoxville, Tenn. 37916); the Men's Studies Collection, Charles Hayden Humanities Library, Massachusetts Institute of Technology, Cambridge, Mass. 02139.

that men want to have power over women because of deep-lying psychological needs in male personality. These two views are not mutually exclusive, and there is certainly ample evidence for both. The final analysis of men's oppression of women will have to give attention equally to its rational and irrational sources.

I will concentrate my attention here on the psychological sources of men's needs for power over women. Let us consider first the most common and commonsense psychological analysis of men's need to dominate women, which takes as its starting point the male child's early experience with women. The male child, the argument goes, perceives his mother and his predominantly female elementary school teachers as dominating and controlling. These relationships *do* in reality contain elements of domination and control, probably exacerbated by the restriction of women's opportunities to exercise power in most other areas. As a result, men feel a lifelong psychological need to free themselves from or prevent their domination by women. The argument is, in effect, that men oppress women as adults because they experienced women as oppressing them as children.

According to this analysis, the process operates in a vicious circle. In each generation, adult men restrict women from having power in almost all domains of social life except child rearing. As a result, male children feel powerless and dominated, grow up needing to restrict women's power, and thus the cycle repeats itself. It follows from this analysis that the way to break the vicious circle is to make it possible for women to exercise power outside of parenting and parentlike roles and to get men to do their half share of parenting.

There may be a kernel of truth in this "mother domination" theory of sexism for some men, and the social changes in the organization of child care that this theory suggests are certainly desirable. As a general explanation of men's needs to dominate women, however, this theory has been quite overworked. This theory holds women themselves rather than men ultimately responsible for the oppression of women—in William Ryan's phrase, "blaming the victim" of oppression for her own oppression.[2] The recent film *One Flew over the Cuckoo's Nest* presents an extreme example of how women's supposed domination of men is used to justify sexism. This film portrays the archetypal struggle between a female figure depicted as domineering and castrating and a rebellious male hero (played by Jack Nicholson) who refuses to be emasculated by her. This struggle escalates to a climactic scene in which Nicholson throws her on the floor and nearly strangles her to death—a scene that was accompanied by wild cheering form the audience when I saw the film. For this performance, Jack Nicholson won the Academy Award as the best actor of the year, an indication of how successful the film is in seducing its audience to accept this act of sexual violence as legitimate and even heroic. The hidden moral message of the film is that because women dominate men, the most extreme forms of sexual violence are not only permissible for men, but indeed are morally obligatory.

To account for men's needs for power over women, it is ultimately more useful to examine some other ways that men feel women have power over

[2] William Ryan, *Blaming the Victim* (New York: Pantheon, 1970).

them than fear of maternal domination.[3] There are two forms of power that men perceive women as holding over them which derive more directly from traditional definitions of adult male and female roles, and have implications which are far more compatible with a feminist perspective.

The first power that men perceive women having over them is *expressive power*, the power to express emotions. It is well known that in traditional male-female relationships, women are supposed to express their needs for achievement only vicariously through the achievements of men. It is not so widely recognized, however, that this dependency of women on men's achievement has a converse. In traditional male–female relationships, men experience their emotions vicariously through women. Many men have learned to depend on women to help them express their emotions, indeed, to express their emotions for them. At an ultimate level, many men are unable to feel emotionally alive except through relationships with women. A particularly dramatic example occurs in an earlier Jack Nicholson film, *Carnal Knowledge*. Art Garfunkel, at one point early in his romance with Candace Bergen, tells Nicholson that she makes him aware of thoughts he "never even knew he had." Although Nicholson is sleeping with Bergen and Garfunkel is not, Nicholson feels tremendously deprived in comparison when he hears this. In a dramatic scene, Nicholson then goes to her and angrily demands: "You tell him his thoughts, now you tell me *my* thoughts!" When women withhold and refuse to exercise this expressive power for men's benefit, many men, like Nicholson, feel abject and try all the harder to get women to play their traditional expressive role.

A second form of power that men attribute to women is *masculinity-validating* power. In traditional masculinity, to experience oneself as masculine requires that women play their prescribed role of doing the things that make men feel masculine. Another scene from *Carnal Knowledge* provides a pointed illustration. In the closing scene of the movie, Nicholson has hired a call girl whom he has rehearsed and coached in a script telling him how strong and manly he is, in order to get him sexually aroused. Nicholson seems to be in control, but when she makes a mistake in her role, his desperate reprimands show just how dependent he is on her playing out the masculinity-validating script he has created. It is clear that what he is looking for in this encounter is

---

[3] In addition to the mother domination theory, there are two other psychological theories relating aspects of the early mother–child relationship in men's sexism. The first can be called the "mother identification" theory, which holds that men develop a "feminine" psychological identification because of their early attachment to their mothers and that men fear this internal feminine part of themselves, seeking to control it by controlling those who actually are feminine, i.e., women. The second can be called the "mother socialization" theory, holding that since boys' fathers are relatively absent as sex-role models, the major route by which boys learn masculinity is through their mothers' rewarding masculine behavior, and especially through their mothers' punishing feminine behavior. Thus, males associate women with punishment and pressure to be masculine. Interestingly, these two theories are in direct contradiction, since the former holds that men fear women because women make men feminine, and the latter holds that men fear women because women make men masculine. These theories are discussed at greater length in Joseph H. Pleck's "Men's Traditional Attitudes toward Women: Conceptual Issues in Research" in *The Psychology of Women: New Directions in Research*, ed. Julia Sherman and Florence Denmark (New York: Psychological Dimensions, 1978).

not so much sexual gratification as it is validation of himself as a man—which only women can give him. As with women's expressive power, when women refuse to exercise their masculinity-validating power for men, many men feel lost and bereft and frantically attempt to force women back into their accustomed role.

As I suggested before, men's need for power over women derives both from men's pragmatic self-interest and from men's psychological needs. It would be a mistake to overemphasize men's psychological needs as the sources of their needs to control women, in comparison with simple rational self-interest. But if we are looking for the psychological sources of men's needs for power over women, their perception that women have expressive power and masculinity-validating power over them is critical to analyze. These are the two powers men perceive women as having, which they fear women will no longer exercise in their favor. These are the two resources women possess which men fear women will withhold, and whose threatened or actual loss leads men to such frantic attempts to reassert power over women.

Men's dependence on women's power to express men's emotions and to validate men's masculinity has placed heavy burdens on women. By and large, these are not powers over men that women have wanted to hold. These are powers that men have themselves handed over to women, by defining the male role as being emotionally cool and inexpressive, and as being ultimately validated by heterosexual success.

There is reason to think that over the course of recent history—as male–male friendship has declined, and as dating and marriage have occurred more universally and at younger ages—the demands on men to be emotionally inexpressive and to prove masculinity through relating to women have become stronger. As a result, men have given women increasingly more expressive power and more masculinity-validating power over them, and have become increasingly dependent on women for emotional and sex-role validation. In the context of this increased dependency on women's power, the emergence of the women's movement now, with women asserting their right not to play these roles for men, has hit with a special force.

It is in this context that the men's movement and men's groups place so much emphasis on men learning to express and experience their emotions with each other, and learning how to validate themselves and each other as persons, instead of needing women to validate them emotionally and as men. When men realize that they can develop in themselves the power to experience themselves emotionally and to validate themselves as persons, they will not feel the dependency on women for these essential needs which has led in the past to so much male fear, resentment, and need to control women. Then men will be emotionally more free to negotiate the pragmatic realignment of power between the sexes that is underway in our society.

MEN'S POWER WITH OTHER MEN

After considering men's power over women in relation to the power men perceive women having over them, let us consider men's power over women in a second context: the context of men's power relationships with other men. In recent years, we have come to understand that relations between men and women are governed by a sexual politics that exists outside individual men's and women's needs and choices. It has taken us much longer to recognize that there is a systematic sexual politics of male–male relationships as well. Under patriarchy, men's relationships with other men cannot help but be shaped and patterned by patriarchal norms, though they are less obvious than the norms governing male–female relationships. A society could not have the kinds of power dynamics that exist between women and men in our society without certain kinds of systematic power dynamics operating among men as well.

One dramatic example illustrating this connection occurs in Marge Piercy's recent novel *Small Changes*. In a flashback scene, a male character goes along with several friends to gang rape a woman. When his turn comes, he is impotent; whereupon the other men grab him, pulling his pants down to rape *him*. This scene powerfully conveys one form of the relationship between male–female and male–male sexual politics. The point is that men do not just happily bond together to oppress women. In addition to hierarchy over women, men create hierarchies and rankings among themselves according to criteria of "masculinity." Men at each rank at masculinity compete with each other, with whatever resources they have, for the differential payoffs that patriarchy allows men.

Men in different societies choose different grounds on which to rank each other. Many societies use the simple facts of age and physical strength to stratify men. The most bizarre and extreme form of patriarchal stratification occurs in those societies which have literally created a class of eunuchs. Our society, reflecting its own particular preoccupations, stratifies men according to physical strength and athletic ability in the early years, but later in life focuses on success with women and ability to make money.

In our society, one of the most critical rankings among men deriving from patriarchal sexual politics is the division between gay and straight men. This division has powerful negative consequences for gay men and gives straight men privilege. But in addition, this division has a larger symbolic meaning. Our society uses the male heterosexual-homosexual dichotomy as a central symbol for *all* the rankings for masculinity, for the division on *any* grounds between males who are "real men" and have power and males who are not. Any kind of powerlessness or refusal to compete becomes imbued with the imagery of homosexuality. In the men's movement documentary film *Men's Lives*,[4] a high school male who studies modern dance says that others often think he is gay because he is a dancer. When asked why, he gives three reasons: because dancers are "free and loose," because they are "not big like football players," and because "you're not trying to kill anybody." The patriarchal connection: if you are not trying to kill other men, you must be gay.

Another dramatic example of men's use of homosexual derogations as weapons in their power struggle with each other comes from a document which provides one of the richest case studies of the politics of male–male relationships to yet appear: Woodward and Bernstein's *The Final Days*. Ehrlichman jokes that Kissinger is "queer," Kissinger calls an unnamed colleague a psychopathic homosexual, and Haig jokes that Nixon and Rebozo are having a homosexual relationship. From the highest ranks of male power to

---

[4] Available from New Day Films, P.O. Box 615, Franklin Lakes, N.J. 07417.

the lowest, the gay–straight division is a central symbol of all the forms of ranking and power relationships which men put on each other.

The relationships between the patriarchal stratification and competition which men experience with each other and men's patriarchal domination of women are complex. Let us briefly consider several points of interconnection between them. First, women are used as *symbols of success* in men's competition with each other. It is sometimes thought that competition for women is the ultimate source of men's competition with each other. For example, in *Totem and Taboo* Freud presented a mythical reconstruction of the origin of society based on sons' sexual competition with the father, leading to their murdering the father. In this view, if women did not exist, men would not have anything to compete for with each other. There is considerable reason, however, to see women not as the ultimate source of male–male competition, but rather as only symbols in a male contest where real roots lie much deeper.

The recent film *Paper Chase* provides an interesting example. This film combines the story of a small group of male law students in their first year of law school with a heterosexual love story between one of the students (played by Timothy Bottoms) and the professor's daughter. As the film develops, it becomes clear that the real business is the struggle within the group of male law students for survival, success, and the professor's blessing—a patriarchal struggle in which several of the less successful are driven out of school and one even attempts suicide. When Timothy Bottoms gets the professor's daughter at the end, she is simply another one of the rewards he has won by doing better than the other males in her father's class. Indeed, she appears to be a direct part of the patriarchal blessing her father has bestowed on Bottoms.

Second, women often play a *mediating* role in th patriarchal struggle among men. Women get men together with each other and provide the social lubrication necessary to smooth over men's inability to relate to each other noncompetitively. This function has been expressed in many myths, for example, the folk tales included in the Grimms' collection about groups of brothers whose younger sister reunites and reconciles them with their kingfather, who has previously banished and tried to kill them. A more modern myth, James Dickey's *Deliverance*, portrays what happens when men's relationships with each other are not mediated by women. According to Carolyn Heilbrun,[5] the central message of *Deliverance* is that when men get beyond the bounds of civilization, which really means beyond the bounds of the civilizing effects of women, men rape and murder each other.

A third function women play in male-male sexual politics is that relationships with women provide men a *refuge* for the dangers and stresses of relating to other males. Traditional relationships with women have provided men a safe place in which they can recuperate from the stresses they have absorbed in their daily struggle with other men, and in which they can express their needs without fearing that these needs will be used against them. If women begin to compete with men and have power in their own right, men are threatened by the loss of this refuge.

Finally, a fourth function of women in males' patriarchal competition with each other is to reduce the stress of competition by serving as an *underclass*. As

[5] Carolyn G. Heilbrun, "The Masculine Wilderness of the American Novel," *Saturday Review* 41 (January 29, 1972), pp. 41–44.

Elizabeth Janeway has written in *Between Myth and Morning*,[6] under patriarchy women represent the lowest status, a status to which men can fall only under the most exceptional circumstances, if at all. Competition among men is serious, but its intensity is mitigated by the fact that there is a lowest possible level to which men cannot fall. One reason men fear women's liberation, writes Janeway, is that the liberation of women will take away this unique underclass status of women. Men will now risk falling lower than ever before, into a new underclass composed of the weak of both sexes. Thus, women's liberation means that the stakes of patriarchal failure for men are higher than they have been before, and that it is even more important for men not to lose.

Thus, men's patriarchal competition with each other makes use of women as symbols of success, as mediators, as refuges, and as an underclass. In each of these roles, women are dominated by men in ways that derived directly from men's struggle with each other. Men need to deal with the sexual politics of their relationships with each other. Men need to deal with the sexual politics of their relationships with each other if they are to deal fully with the sexual politics of their relationships with women.

Ultimately, we have to understand that patriarchy has two halves which are intimately related to each other. Patriarchy is a *dual* system, a system in which men oppress women, and in which men oppress themselves and each other. At one level, challenging one part of patriarchy inherently leads to challenging the other. This is one way to interpret why the idea of women's liberation so soon led to the idea of men's liberation, which in my view ultimately means freeing men from the patriarchal sexual dynamics they now experience with each other. But because the patriarchal sexual dynamics of male–male relationships are less obvious than those of male–female relationships, men face a real danger: while the patriarchal oppression of women may be lessened as a result of the women's movement, the patriarchal oppression of men may be untouched. The real danger for men posed by the attack that the women's movement is making on patriarchy is not that this attack will go too far, but that it will not go far enough. Ultimately, men cannot go any further in relating to women as equals than they have been able to go in relating to other men as equals—an equality which has been so deeply disturbing, which has generated so many psychological as well as literal casualties, and which has left so many unresolved issues of competition and frustrated love.

MEN'S POWER IN SOCIETY

Let us now consider men's power over women in a third and final context, the context of men's power in the larger society. At one level, men's social identity is defined by the power they have over women and the power they can compete for against other men. But at another level, most men have very little power over their own lives. How can we understand this paradox?

The major demand to which men must accede in contemporary society is that they play their required role in the economy. But this role is not intrinsi-

---

[6] Elizabeth Janeway, *Between Myth and Morning* (Boston: Little, Brown, 1975); see also Elizabeth Janeway, "The Weak are the Second Sex," *Atlantic Monthly* (December 1973), pp. 91–104.

cally satisfying. The social researcher Daniel Yankelovich[7] has suggested that about 80 percent of U.S. male workers experience their jobs as intrinsically meaningless and onerous. They experience their jobs and themselves as worthwhile only through priding themselves on the hard work and personal sacrifice they are making to be breadwinners for their families. Accepting these hardships reaffirms their role as family providers and therefore as true men.

Linking the breadwinner role to masculinity in this way has several consequences for men. Men can get psychological payoffs from their jobs which these jobs never provide in themselves. By training men to accept payment for their work in feelings of masculinity rather than in feelings of satisfaction, men will not demand that their jobs be made more meaningful, and as a result jobs can be designed for the more important goal of generating profits. Further, the connection between work and masculinity makes men accept unemployment as their personal failing as males, rather than analyze and change the profit-based economy whose inevitable dislocations make them unemployed or unemployable.

Most critical for our analysis here, men's role in the economy and the ways men are motivated to play it have at least two negative effects on women. First, the husband's job makes many direct and indirect demands on wives. In fact, it is often hard to distinguish whether the wife is dominated more by the husband or by the husband's job. Sociologist Ralph Turner writes: "Because the husband must adjust to the demands of his occupation and the family in turn must accommodate to his demands on behalf of his occupational obligations, the husband appears to dominate his wife and children. But as an agent of economic institutions, he perceives himself as controlled rather than as controlling."[8]

Second, linking the breadwinner role to masculinity in order to motivate men to work means that women must not be allowed to hold paid work. For the large majority of men who accept dehumanizing jobs only because having a job validates their role as family breadwinner, their wives' taking paid work takes away from them the major and often only way they have of experiencing themselves as having worth. Yankelovich suggests that the frustration and discontent of this group of men, whose wives are increasingly joining the paid labor force, is emerging as a major social problem. What these men do to sabotage women's paid work is deplorable, but I believe that it is quite within the bounds of a feminist analysis of contemporary society to see these men as victims as well as victimizers.

One long-range perspective on the historical evolution of the family is that from an earlier stage in which both wife and husband were directly economically productive in the household economic unit, the husband's economic role has evolved so that now it is under the control of forces entirely outside the family. In order to increase productivity, the goal in the design of this new male work role is to increase men's commitment and loyalty to work and to reduce those ties to the family that might compete with it. Men's jobs are increasingly structured as if men had no direct roles or responsibilities in

---

[7] Daniel Yankelovich, "The Meaning of Work," in *The Worker and the Job*, ed. Jerome Rosow (Englewood Cliffs, N.J.: Prentice-Hall, 1974).

[8] Ralph Turner, *Family Interaction* (New York: Wiley, 1968), p. 282.

the family—indeed, as if they did not have families at all. But paradoxically, at the same time that men's responsibilities in the family are reduced to facilitate more efficient performance of their work role, the increasing dehumanization of work means that the satisfaction which jobs give men is, to an increasing degree, *only* the satisfaction of fulfilling the family breadwinner role. That is, on the one hand, men's ties to the family have to be broken down to facilitate industrial work discipline; but on the other hand, men's sense of responsibility to the family has to be increased, but shaped into a purely economic form, to provide the motivation for men to work at all. Essential to this process is the transformation of the wife's economic role to providing supportive services, both physical and psychological, to keep him on the job, and to take over the family responsibilities which his expanded work role will no longer allow him to fulfill himself. The wife is then bound to her husband by her economic dependency on him, and the husband in turn is bound to his job by his family's economic dependence on him.

A final example from the film *Men's Lives* illustrates some of these points. In one of the most powerful scenes in the film, a worker in a rubber plant resignedly describes how his bosses are concerned, in his words, with "pacifying" him to get the maximum output from him, not with satisfying his needs. He then takes back this analysis, saying that he is only a worker and therefore cannot really understand what is happening to him. Next, he is asked whether he wants his wife to take a paid job to reduce the pressure he feels in trying to support his family. In marked contrast to his earlier passive resignation, he proudly asserts that he will never allow her to work, and that in particular he will never scrub the floors after he comes home from his own job. (He correctly perceives that if his wife did take a paid job, he would be under pressure to do some housework.) In this scene, the man expresses and then denies an awareness of his exploitation as a worker. Central to his coping with repressing his incipient awareness of his exploitation is his false consciousness of his superiority and privilege over women. Not scrubbing floors is a real privilege, and deciding whether or not his wife will have paid work is a real power, but the consciousness of power over his own life that such privilege and power give this man is false. The relative privilege that men get from sexism and, more importantly, the false consciousness of privilege men get from sexism plays a critical role in reconciling men to their subordination in the larger political economy. This analysis does not imply that men's sexism will go away if they gain control over their own lives, or that men do not have to deal with their sexism until they gain this control. I disagree with both. Rather, my point is that we cannot fully understand men's sexism or men's subordination in the larger society unless we understand how deeply they are related.

To summarize, a feminist understanding of men's power over women, why men have needed it, and what is involved in changing it, is enriched by examining men's power in a broader context. To understand men's power over women, we have to understand the ways in which men feel women have power over them, men's power relationships with other men, and the powerlessness of most men in the larger society. Rectifying men's power relationship with women will inevitably both stimulate and benefit from the rectification of these other power relationships.

Michael Kaufman

THE CONSTRUCTION OF MASCULINITY AND THE TRIAD OF MEN'S VIOLENCE

The all too familiar story: a woman raped, a wife battered, a lover abused. With a sense of immediacy and anger, the women's liberation movement has pushed the many forms of men's violence against women—from the most overt to the most subtle in form—into popular consciousness and public debate. These forms of violence are one aspect of our society's domination by men that, in outcome, if not always in design, reinforce that domination. The act of violence is many things at once. At the same instant it is the individual man acting out relations of sexual power; it is the violence of a society—a hierarchical, authoritarian, sexist, class-divided, militarist, racist, impersonal, crazy society—being focused through an individual man onto an individual woman. In the psyche of the individual man it might be his denial of social powerlessness through an act of aggression. In total these acts of violence are like a ritualized acting out of our social relations of power: the dominant and the weaker, the powerful and the powerless, the active and the passive . . . the masculine and the feminine.

For men, listening to the experience of women as the objects of male violence is to shatter any complacency about the sex-based status quo. The power and anger of women's responses force us to rethink the things we discovered when we were very young. When I was eleven or twelve years old a friend told me the difference between fucking and raping. It was simple: with rape you tied the woman to a tree. At the time the anatomical details were still a little vague, but in either case it was something "we" supposedly did. This knowledge was just one part of an education, started years before, about the relative power and privileges of men and women. I remember laughing when my friend explained all that to me. Now I shudder. The difference in my responses is partially that, at twelve, it was part of the posturing and pretense that accompanied my passage into adolescence. Now, of course, I have a different vantage point on the issue. It is the vantage point of an adult, but more importantly my view of the world is being reconstructed by the intervention of that majority whose voice has been suppressed: the women.

This relearning of the reality of men's violence against women evokes many deep feelings and memories for men. As memories are recalled and recast, a new connection becomes clear: violence by men against women is only one corner of a triad of men's violence. The other two corners are violence against other men and violence against oneself.

On a psychological level the pervasiveness of violence is the result of what Herbert Marcuse called the "surplus repression" of our sexual and emotional desires.[1] The substitution of violence for desire (more precisely, the transmutation of violence into a form of emotionally gratifying activity) happens unequally in men and women. The construction of masculinity involves the construction of "surplus aggressiveness." The social context of this triad of

Reprinted from *Beyond Patriarchy: Essays on Pleasure, Power, and Change*, edited by Michael Kaufman. Toronto: Oxford University Press, 1987. Reprinted by permission.

violence is the institutionalization of violence in the operation of most aspects of social, economic, and political life.

The three corners of the triad reinforce one another. The first corner— violence against women—cannot be confronted successfully without simulta- neously challenging the other two corners of the triad. And all this requires a dismantling of the social feeding ground of violence: patriarchal, heterosexist, authoritarian, class societies. These three corners and the societies in which they blossom feed on each other. And together, we surmise, they will fall.

ORIGINS OF VIOLENCE

The most vexing question in the matter of men's violence is, of course, its biological roots. It would be very useful to know whether men in particular, or humans in general, are biologically (for example, genetically or hormon- ally) predisposed to acts of violence against other humans.

From the outset, feminism has been careful to draw a distinction between sex and gender. The strictly biological differences between the sexes form only the substrate for a society's construction of people with gender. Indeed, the appeal of feminism to many men, in addition to the desire to ally ourselves with the struggle of our sisters against oppression, has been to try to dissociate "male" from "masculine." While many of the characteristics associated with masculinity are valuable human traits—strength, daring, courage, rational- ity, intellect, sexual desire—the distortion of these traits in the masculine norm and the exclusion of other traits (associated with femininity) are oppres- sive and destructive. The process of stuffing oneself into the tight pants of masculinity is a difficult one for all men, even if it is not consciously experi- enced as such.

But the actual relation of sex and gender is problematic. For one thing, what might be called the "gender craft" of a society does its work on biological entities—entities whose ultimate source of pleasure and pain is their bodies.[2] What makes the relationship between sex and gender even more difficult to understand is that the production of gender is itself an incredibly complex and opaque process. As Michele Barrett and Mary McIntosh point out although stereotypical roles do exist, each individual is not "the passive victim of a monolithically imposed system."[3]

In recent years there has been a major attempt to reclaim for biology the social behaviour of human beings. Sociobiology aims at nothing less than the reduction of human social interaction to our genetic inheritance. The study of apes, aardvarks, and tapeworms as a means of discerning the true nature of humans is almost surprising in its naivete, but at times it is socially dangerous in its conception and execution. As many critics have pointed out, it ignores what is unique about human beings: our construction of ever-changing social orders.[4]

Indeed, humans are animals—physical creatures subject to the require- ments of genes, cells, organs, and hormones of every description. Yet we do not have a comprehensive understanding of how these things shape behavior and, even if we did, behavior is just a small, fragmented moment to be understood within the larger realm of human desire and motivation. Even if we did have a more comprehensive knowledge, what is important is that humans, unlike apes or even the glorious ant, live in constantly evolving and widely differing societies. Since the era when humans came into existence, our history has been a movement *away* from an unmediated, "natural," animal existence.

Even if we could ascertain that humans in general, or men in particular, are predisposed to building neutron bombs, this does not help us answer the much more important question of how each society shapes, limits, or accentuates this tendency. To take only the question of violence, why, as societies develop, does violence seem to move from something isolated and often ritualistic in its expression to a pervasive feature of everyday life? And why are some forms of physical violence so widely accepted (corporal punishment of children, for example) while others are not (such as physical attacks on pharoahs, presidents, and pontiffs)?

That much said let us also say this: there is no psychological, biological, or social evidence to suggest that humans are *not* predisposed to aggression and even violence. On the other hand, a predisposition to cooperation and peacefulness is also entirely possible. It is even possible that men—for reasons of hormones—are biologically more aggressive and prone to violence than women. We do not know the answer for the simple reason that the men we examine do not exist outside societies.[5]

But in any case, the important question is what societies do with the violence. What forms of violence are socially sanctioned or socially tolerated? What forms of violence seem built into the very structure of our societies? The process of human social development has been one of restraining, repressing, forming, informing, channeling, and transforming various biological tendencies. Could it not be that this process of repression has been a very selective one? Perhaps the repression of certain impulses and the denial of certain needs aggravate other impulses. I think of the man who feels he has no human connections in his life and who goes out and rapes a woman.

In spite of a general feminist rejection of sociobiology, this pseudoscience receives a strange form of support among some feminists. In her book, *Against Our Will. Men, Women and Rape*, Susan Brownmiller argues, not only that violent, male aggression is psychologically innate, but that it is grounded in male anatomy. And conversely, the view of female sexuality appears to be one of victimization and powerlessness. She argues, "By anatomical fiat—the inescapable construction of their genital organs—the human male was a natural predator and the human female served as his natural prey."[6] Alice Echols suggests that many cultural feminists also tend to repeat many traditional, stereotypical images of men and women.[7]

The essential question for us is, not whether men are predisposed to violence, but what society does with this violence. Why has the linchpin of so many societies been the manifold expression of violence perpetrated disproportionately by men? Why are so many forms of violence sanctioned or even encouraged? Exactly what is the nature of violence? And how are patterns of violence and the quest for domination built up and reinforced?

THE SOCIAL CONTEXT

For every apparently individual act of violence there is a social context. This is not to say there are no pathological acts of violence, but even in that case the "language" of the violent act, the way the violence manifests itself, can only be understood within a certain social experience. We are interested here in the manifestations of violence that are accepted as more or less normal, even if reprehensible: fighting, war, rape, assault, psychological abuse, and so forth. What is the context of men's violence in the prevalent social orders of today?

Violence has long been institutionalized as an acceptable means of solving conflicts. But now the vast apparati of policing and war making maintained by countries the world over pose a threat to the future of life itself.

"Civilized" societies have been built and shaped through the decimation, containment, and exploitation of other peoples: extermination of native populations, colonialism, and slavery. "I am talking," writes Aimé Césaire, "about societies drained of their essence, cultures trampled underfoot, institutions undermined, lands confiscated, religions smashed, magnificent artistic creations destroyed, extraordinary possibilities wiped out. . . . I am talking about millions . . . sacrificed."[8]

Our relationship with the natural environment has often been described with the metaphor of rape. An attitude of conquering nature, of mastering an environment waiting to be exploited for profit, has great consequences when we possess a technology capable of permanently disrupting an ecological balance shaped over hundreds of millions of years.

The daily work life of industrial, class societies is one of violence. Violence poses as economic rationality as some of us are turned into extensions of machines, while others become brains detached from bodies. Our industrial process becomes the modern-day rack of torture where we are stretched out of shape and ripped limb from limb. It is violence that exposes workers to the danger of chemicals, radiation, machinery, speedup, and muscle strain. It is violence that condemns the majority to work to exhaustion for forty or fifty years and then to be thrown into society's garbage bin for the old and used-up.

The racism, sexism, and heterosexim that have been institutionalized in our societies are socially regulated acts of violence.

Our cities themselves are a violation, not only of nature, but of human community and the human relationship with nature. As the architect Frank Lloyd Wright said, "To look at the plan of a great City is to look at something like the cross-section of a fibrous tumor."[9]

Our cities, our social structure, our work life, our relation with nature, our history, are more than a backdrop to the prevalence of violence. They are violence; violence in an institutionalized form encoded into physical structures and socioeconomic relations. Much of the sociological analysis of violence in our societies implies simply that violence is learned by witnessing and experiencing social violence: man kicks boy, boy kicks dog.[10] Such experiences of transmitted violence are a reality, as the analysis of wife battering indicates, for many batterers were themselves abused as children. But more essential is that our personalities and sexuality, our needs and fears, our strengths and weaknesses, our selves are created—not simply learned—through our lived reality. The violence of our social order nurtures a psychology of violence, which in turn reinforces the social, economic and political structures of violence. The ever-increasing demands of civilization and the constant building upon inherited structures of violence suggest that the development of civilization has been inseparable from a continuous increase in violence against humans and our natural environment.

It would be easy, yet ultimately not very useful, to slip into a use of the term "violence" as a metaphor for all our society's antagonisms, contradictions, and ills. For now, let us leave aside the social terrain and begin to unravel the nature of so-called individual violence.

THE TRIAD OF MEN'S VIOLENCE

The longevity of the oppression of women must be based on something more than conspiracy, something more complicated than biological handicap and more durable than economic exploitation (although in differing degrees all these may feature).

Juliet Mitchell[11]

It seems impossible to believe that mere greed could hold men to such a steadfastness of purpose.

Joseph Conrad[12]

The field in which the triad of men's violence is situated is a society, or societies, grounded in structures of domination and control. Although at times this control is symbolized and embodied in the individual father—patriarchy, by definition—it is more important to emphasize that patriarchal structures of authority, domination, and control are diffused throughout social, economic, political, and ideological activities and in our relations to the natural environment. Perhaps more than in any previous time during the long epoch of patriarchy, authority does *not* rest with the father, at least in much of the advanced capitalist and noncapitalist world. This has led more than one author to question the applicability of the term patriarchy.[13] But I think it still remains useful as a broad, descriptive category. In this sense Jessica Benjamin speaks of the current reign of patriarchy without the father. "The form of domination peculiar to this epoch expresses itself not directly as authority but indirectly as the transformation of all relationships and activity into objective, instrumental, depersonalized forms."[14]

The structures of domination and control form not simply the background to the triad of violence, but generate, and in turn are nurtured by, this violence. These structures refer both to our social relations and to our interaction with our natural environment. The relation between these two levels is obviously extremely complex. It appears that violence against nature—that is, the impossible and disastrous drive to dominate and conquer the natural world—is integrally connected with domination among humans. Some of these connections are quite obvious. One thinks of the bulldozing of the planet for profit in capitalist societies, societies characterized by the dominance of one class over others. But the link between the domination of nature and structures of domination of humans go beyond this. Various writers make provocative suggestions about the nature of this link.

Max Horkheimer and T. W. Adorno argue that the domination of humans by other humans creates the preconditions for the domination of nature.[15] An important subtheme of Mary O'Brien's book *The Politics of Reproduction* is that men "have understood their separation from nature and their need to mediate this separation ever since that moment in dark prehistory when the idea of paternity took hold in the human mind. Patriarchy is the power to transcend natural realities with historical, man-made realities. This is the potency principle in its primordial form."[16] Simone de Beauvoir says that the ambivalent feelings of men toward nature are carried over onto their feelings toward women, who are seen as embodying nature. "Now ally, now enemy, she appears as the dark chaos from whence life wells up, as this life itself, and as the over-yonder toward which life tends."[17] Violence against nature, like violence against women, violence against other men, and violence against oneself, is in part related to what Sidney Jourard calls the lethal aspects of masculinity.[18]

THE INDIVIDUAL REPRODUCTION OF MALE DOMINATION

No man is born a butcher.

Bertolt Brecht[19]

In a male-dominated society men have a number of privileges. Compared to women we are free to walk the streets at night, we have traditionally escaped domestic labor, and on average we have higher wages, better jobs, and more power. But these advantages in themselves cannot explain the individual reproduction of the relations of male domination, that is, why the individual male from a very early age embraces masculinity. The embracing of masculinity is not only a "socialization"into a certain gender role, as if there is a pre-formed human being who learns a role that he then plays for the rest of his life. Rather, through his psychological development he embraces and takes into himself a set of gender-based social relations: the person that is created through the process of maturation becomes the personal embodiment of those relations. By the time the child is five or six years old, the basis for lifelong masculinity has already been established.

Two factors, intrinsic to humans and human development, form the basis for the individual acquisition of gender. These conditions do not explain the existence of gender: they are simply preconditions for its individual acquisition.

The first factor is the malleability of human desires. For the infant all bodily activities—touch, sight, smell, sound, taste, thought—are potential sources of sexual pleasure. Or rather, they *are* sexual pleasure in the sense of our ability to obtain pleasure from our bodies. But this original polysexuality is limited, shaped, and repressed through the maturation process that is necessary to meet the demands of the natural and social world. Unlike other animals our sexuality is not simply instinct: it is individually and socially constructed. It is because of this, and because of the human's capacity to think and construct societies and ideologies, that gender can exist in differentiation from biological sex.

As Herbert Marcuse and, following him, Gad Horowitz have pointed out, the demands of societies of domination—of "surplus-repressive" societies— progressively narrow down sexuality into genital contact, with a heterosexual norm. (Marcuse argues that a certain "basic repression"—a damming up or deflection—of human desires is necessary for any conceivable human association. But in addition to this, hierarchical and authoritarian societies require a "surplus repression" to maintain structures of domination.)[20]

This narrowing down onto genital contact is not simply a natural genital preference but is the blocking of energy from a whole range of forms of pleasure (including "mental" activities). And for reasons discussed in my book *Beyond Patriarchy*, the acquisition of the dominant form of masculinity is an enhancement of forms of pleasure associated with activity and the surplus repression of our ability to experience pleasure passively.

We try to compensate for this surplus repression with the pleasures and preoccupations of work, play, sports, and culture. But these are not sufficient to offset the severe limits placed on love and desire. To put this crudely, a two-day weekend cannot emotionally compensate for five days of a deadening job. And what is more, these social activities are themselves sources of struggle and tension.

The second factor that forms the basis for the individual's acquisition of gender is that the prolonged period of human childhood results in powerful attachments to parental figures. The passionate bonding of the young child to the primary parental figures obtains its particular power and salience for our personal development in societies where isolated women have the primary responsibility for nurturing infants and children, where the child's relation with the world is mediated most strongly through a small family rather than through a small community as a whole, and in which traits associated with the "opposite" sex are suppressed.

This prolonged period of human childhood is a prolonged period of powerlessness. The intense love for one or two parents is combined with intense feelings of deprivation and frustration. This natural ambivalence is greatly aggravated in societies where the attention parents are able to provide the young is limited, where social demands place additional frustrations on top of the inevitable ones experienced by a tiny person, and where one or two isolated parents relive and repeat the patterns of their own childhood. As will be seen, part of the boy's acquisition of masculinity is a response to this experience of powerlessness.

By the time children are sufficiently developed physically, emotionally, and intellectually at five or six to have clearly defined themselves separately from their parents, these parental figures have already been internalized within them. In the early years, as in later ones, we identify with (or react against) the apparent characteristics of our love objects and incorporate them into our own personalities. This is largely an unconscious process. This incorporation and internalization, or rejection, of the characteristics of our love objects is part of the process of constructing our ego, our self.

This internalization of the objects of love is a selective one, and it is a process that takes place in specific social environments. The immediate environment is the family, which is a "vigorous agency of class placement and an efficient mechanism for the creation and transmission of gender inequality."[21] Within itself, to a greater or lesser extent, the family reflects, reproduces, and recreates the hierarchical gender system of society as a whole.[22]

As noted above, the child has ambivalent feelings toward his or her primary caring figures. Love combines with feelings of powerlessness, tension, and frustration. The child's experience of anxiety and powerlessness results not only from the prohibitions of harsh parents but also from the inability of even the most loving parents who cannot exist solely for their young, because of the demands of society, demands of natural reality, and demands of their own needs.

Both girls and boys have these ambivalent feelings and experiences of powerlessness. But the feelings toward the parents and the matter of power are almost immediately impregnated with social meaning. Years before the child can put words to it, she or he begins to understand that the mother is inferior to the father and that woman is inferior to man. That this inferiority is not natural but is socially imposed is beyond the understanding of the child and even beyond the understanding of sociobiologists, presidents, and popes. (Size itself might also feed into this perception of inferiority, or perhaps it is simply that in hierarchical, sexist society, size becomes a symbol of superiority.) In the end the biological fact of "otherness" becomes overlaced with a socially imposed otherness. The child is presented with two categories of humans: males, who embody the full grandeur and power of humanity, and females, who in Simone de Beauvoir's words, are defined as "other" in a phallocentric society.[23]

The human's answer to this powerlessness and to the desire to find pleasure is to develop an ego and a superego, that is, a distinct self and an internal mechanism of authority. An important part of the process of ego development is the identification with the objects of love. Progressively both sexes discover and are taught who the appropriate figures of identification are. But figures of identification are not equal.

Society presents the young boy with a great escape. He may feel powerless as a child, but there is hope, for as an adult male he will have privilege and (at least in the child's imagination) he will have power. A strong identification—that is, an incorporation into his own developing self—of his image of his father in particular and male figures in general is his compensation for his own sense of powerlessness and insecurity. It is his compensation for renouncing his first love.

In this process the boy not only claims for himself the activity represented by men and father. At the same time he steps beyond the passivity of his infantile relationship to the mother and beyond his overall sense of passivity (passivity, that is, in the sense of feeling overwhelmed by desires and a frustrating world). He embraces the project of controlling himself and controlling the world. He comes to personify activity. Masculinity is a reaction against passivity and powerlessness and, with it comes a repression of all the desires and traits that a given society defines as negatively passive or as resonant of passive experiences. The girl, on the other hand, discovers she will never possess male power and, henceforth, the most she can aspire to is to be loved by a man—that is, to actively pursue a passive aim.

Thus the achievement of what is considered the biologically normal male character (but which is really socially created masculinity) is one outcome of the splitting of human desire and human *being* into mutually exclusive spheres of activity and passivity. The monopoly of activity by males is not a timeless psychological or social necessity. Rather, the internalization of the norms of masculinity require the surplus repression of passive aims—the desire to be nurtured. The repression of passivity and the accentuation of activity constitute the development of a "surplus-aggressive" character type. Unfortunately, such a character type is the norm in patriarchal societies, although the degree of aggressiveness varies from person to person and society to society.

Part of the reason for this process is a response to the fear of rejection and of punishment. What does one fear? Loss of love and self-esteem. Why, in the child's mind, would it lose love and self-esteem? Because it does what is prohibited or degraded. In order to not do what is prohibited or degraded, during this process of identification the child internalizes the values and prohibitions of society. This is the shaping of the superego, our conscience, sense of guilt, and standards of self-worth. Through the internalization of social authority, aggressiveness is directed against oneself.[24]

This whole process of ego development is the shaping of a psychic realm that mediates between our unconscious desires, the world, and a punishing superego. But as should now be clear, the development of the ego is the development of masculine or feminine ego. In this sense, the ego is a definition of oneself formed within a given social and psychological environment and within what Gayle Rubin calls a specific sex-gender system.[25]

The boy is not simply *learning* a gender role but is becoming *part* of that gender. His whole self, to a greater or lesser extent, with greater or lesser conflict, will be masculine. Ken Kesey magnificently captured this in his decription of Hank, a central character in *Sometimes a Great Notion:* "Did it take that much muscle just to walk, or was Hank showing off his manly development? Every movement constituted open aggression against the very air through which Hank passed."[26]

THE REINFORCEMENT OF MASCULINITY

Masculinity is unconsciously rooted before the age of six, is reinforced as the child develops, and then positively explodes at adolescence. Beauvoir's comment about girls is no less true for boys: "With puberty, the future not only approaches; it takes residence in her body; it assumes the most concrete reality."[27]

It is particularly in adolescence that masculinity obtains its definitive shape for the individual. The masculine norm has its own particular nuances and traits dependent on class, nation, race, religion, and ethnicity. And within each group it has its own personal expression. Adolescence is important because it is the time when the body reawakens, when that long-awaited entrance into adulthood finally takes place, and when our culture makes the final socioeducational preparations for adult work life. In adolescence the pain and fear involved in repressing "femininity," and passivity, start to become evident. For most of us, the response to this inner pain is to reinforce the bulwarks of masculinity. The emotional pain created by obsessive masculinity is stifled by reinforcing masculinity itself.

The family, school, sports, friends, church, clubs, scouts, jobs, and the media all play a role as the adolescent struggles to put the final touches on himself as a real man. The expression of male power will be radically different from class to class. For the middle class adolescent, with a future in a profession or business, his own personal and social power will be expressed through a direct mastering of the world. Workaholism or at least a measuring of his value through status and the paycheck might well be the outcome. Fantasies of power are often expressed in terms of fame and success.

For a working class boy, the avenue of mastering the world of business, politics, the professions, and wealth is all but denied. For him male power is often defined in the form of working class machismo. The power to dominate is expressed in a direct physical form. Domination of the factors of production or of another person is achieved through sheer bravado and muscle power. In an excellent examination of the development of white male, working class identity in Britain, Paul Willis demonstrates that the acquisition of a positive working class identity is coterminous with the development of a particular gender identity. Though stigmatized by society as a whole, manual labor becomes the embodiment of masculine power. "Manual labor is suffused with masculine qualities and given certain sensual overtones for 'the lads.' The toughness and awkwardness of physical work and effort . . . takes on masculine lights and depths and assumes a significance beyond itself."[28]

Adolescence is also the time of our first intense courtships. Although so much of pre- and early-adolescent sexual experience is homosexual, those experiences tend to be devalued and ignored. Relations with young women are the real thing. This interaction furthers the acquisition of masculinity for boys because they are interacting with girls who are busy acquiring the complementary femininity. Each moment of interaction reinforces the gender acquisition of each sex.

THE FRAGILITY OF MASCULINITY

Masculinity is power. But masculinity is terrifyingly fragile because it does not really exist in the sense we are led to think it exists, that is, as a biological reality—something real that we have inside ourselves. It exists as ideology; it exists as scripted behavior; it exists within "gendered" relationships. But in the end it is just a social institution with a tenuous relationship to that with which it is supposed to be synonymous: our maleness, our biological sex. The young child does not know that sex does not equal gender. For him to be male is to be what he perceives as being masculine. The child is father to the man. Therefore, to be unmasculine is to be desexed—"castrated."

The tension between maleness and masculinity is intense because masculinity requires a suppression of a whole range of human needs, aims, feelings, and forms of expression. Masculinity is one half of the narrow, surplus-repressive shape of the adult human psyche. Even when we are intellectually aware of the difference between biological maleness and masculinity, the masculine ideal is so embedded within ourselves that it is hard to untangle the person we might want to become (more "fully human," less sexist, less surplus-repressed, and so on) from the person we actually are.

But as children and adolescents (and often as adults), we are not aware of the difference between maleness and masculinity. With the exception of a tiny proportion of the population born as hermaphrodites, there can be no biological struggle to be male. The presence of a penis and testicles is all it takes. Yet boys and men harbor great insecurity about their male credentials. This insecurity exists because maleness is equated with masculinity; but the latter is a figment of our collective, patriarchal, surplus-repressive imaginations.

In a patriarchal society being male is highly valued, and men value their masculinity. But everywhere there are ambivalent feelings. That the initial internalization of masculinity is at the father's knee has lasting significance. Andrew Tolson states that "to the boy, masculinity is both mysterious and attractive (in its promise of a world of work and power), and yet, at the same time, threatening (in its strangeness, and emotional distance). . . . It works both ways; attracts and repels in dynamic contradiction. This simultaneous distance and attraction is internalized as a permanent emotional tension that the individual must, in some way, strive to overcome."[29]

Although maleness and masculinity are highly valued, men are everywhere unsure of their own masculinity and maleness, whether consciously or not. When men are encouraged to be open, as in men's support and counselling groups, it becomes apparent that there exists, often under the surface, an internal dialogue of doubt about one's male and masculine credentials.

One need think only of anxieties about the penis, that incomparable scepter, that symbol of patriarchy and male power. Even as a child the boy experiences, more or less consciously, fearful fantasies of "castration." The child observes that the people who do not have penises are also those with less power. In the mind of a four- or five-year-old child who doesn't know about the power of advertising, the state, education, interactive psychological patterns, unequal pay, sexual harassment, and rape, what else can he think bestows the rewards of masculinity than that little visible difference between men and women, boys and girls?

Of course at this early age the little penis and testicles are not much defense against the world. Nor can they measure against the impossibly huge genitals of one's father or other men. I remember standing in the shower when I was five or six years old, staring up in awe at my father. Years later I realized a full circle had turned when I was showering with my five-year-old son and saw the same crick in his neck and the same look in his eyes. This internalized image of the small, boyish self retains a nagging presence in each man's unconscious. This is so much so that, as adults, men go to war to prove themselves potent, they risk their lives to show they have balls. Expressions such as these, and the double meaning of the word impotent, are no accident.

Just the presence of that wonderfully sensitive bit of flesh, as highly valued as it is in patriarchal culture, is not enough to guarantee maleness and masculinity. But if there are indeed such great doubts in adolescence and beyond about one's masculine credentials, how is it that we combat these doubts? One way is by violence.

MEN'S VIOLENCE AGAINST WOMEN

In spite of the inferior role which men assign to them, women are the privileged objects of their aggression.

Simone de Beauvoir[30]

Men's violence against women is the most common form of direct, personalized violence in the lives of most adults. From sexual harassment to rape, from incest to wife battering to the sight of violent pornographic images, few women escape some form of male aggression.

My purpose here is not to list and evaluate the various forms of violence against women, nor to try to assess what can be classed as violence per se.[31] It is to understand this violence as an expression of the fragility of masculinity and its place in the perpetuation of masculinity and male domination.

In the first place, men's violence against women is probably the clearest, most straightforward expression of relative male and female power. That the relative social, economic, and political power can be expressed in this manner is, to a large part, because of differences in physical strength and in a lifelong training (or lack of training) in fighting. But it is also expressed this way because of the active/passive split. Activity as aggression is part of the masculine gender definition. That is not to say this definition always includes rape or battering, but it is one of the possibilities within a definition of activity that is ultimately grounded in the body.

Rape is a good example of the acting out of these relations of power and of the outcome of fragile masculinity in a surplus-repressive society. In the testimonies of rapists one hears over and over again expressions of inferiority, powerlessness, anger. But who can these men feel superior to? Rape is a crime that not only demonstrates physical power, but that does so in the language of male–female sex-gender relations. The testimonies of convicted rapists collected by Douglas Jackson in the late 1970s are chilling and revealing.[32] Hal: "I felt very inferior to others. . . . I felt rotten about myself and by committing rape I took this out on someone I thought was weaker than me, someone I could control." Carl: "I think that I was feeling so rotten, so low, and such a creep . . . " Len: "I feel a lot of what rape is isn't so much sexual desire as a person's feelings about themselves and how that relates to sex. My fear of relating to people turned to sex because . . . it just happens to be the fullest area to let your anger out on, to let your feelings out on."

Sometimes this anger and pain are experienced in relation to women but just as often not. In either case they are addressed to women who, as the Other in a phallocentric society, are objects of mystification to men, the objects to whom men from birth have learned to express and vent their feelings, or simply objects with less social power and weaker muscles. It is the crime against women par excellence because, through it, the full weight of a sexually based differentiation among humans is played out.

This anger and pain are sometimes overlayed with the effects of a class hierarchy. John: "I didn't feel too good about women. I felt that I couldn't pick them up on my own. I took the lower-class woman and tried to make her look even lower than she really was, you know. 'Cause what I really wanted was a higher-class woman but I didn't have the finesse to actually pick these women up."

Within relationships, forms of male violence such as rape, battering, and what Meg Luxton calls the "petty tyranny" of male domination in the household[33] must be understood both "in terms of violence directed against women as women and against women as wives."[34] The family provides an arena for the expression of needs and emotions not considered legitimate elsewhere.[35] It is the one of the only places where men feel safe enough to express emotions. As the dams break, the flood pours out on women and children.[36] The family also becomes the place where the violence suffered by individuals in their work lives is discharged. "At work men are powerless, so in their leisure time they want to have a feeling that they control their lives."[37]

While this violence can be discussed in terms of male aggression, it operates within the dualism of activity and passivity, masculinity and femininity. Neither can exist without the other. This is not to blame women for being beaten, nor to excuse men who beat. It is but an indication that the various forms of men's violence against women are a dynamic affirmation of a masculinity that can only exist as distinguished from femininity. It is my argument that masculinity needs constant nurturing and affirmation. This affirmation takes many different forms. The majority of men are not rapists or batterers, although it is probable that the majority of men have used superior physical strength or some sort of physical force or threat of force against a woman at least once as a teenager or an adult. But in those who harbor great personal doubts or strongly negative self-images, or who cannot cope with a daily feeling of powerlessness, violence against women can become a means of trying to affirm their personal power in the language of our sex-gender system. That these forms of violence only reconfirm the negative self-image and the feeling of powerlessness shows the fragility, artificiality, the precariousness of masculinity.

VIOLENCE AGAINST OTHER MEN

At a behavioral level, male violence against other men is visible throughout society. Some forms, such as fighting, the ritualized display violence of teenagers and some groups of adult men, institutionalized rape in prisons, and attacks on gays or racial minorities are very direct expressions of this violence. In many sports, violence is incorporated into exercise and entertainment. More subtle forms are the verbal putdown or, combined with economic and other factors, the competition in the business, political, or academic world. In its most frightening form, violence has long been an acceptable and even preferred method of addressing differences and conflicts among different groups and states. In the case of war, as in many other manifestations of violence, violence against other men (and civilian women) combines with autonomous economic, ideological, and political factors.

But male violence against other men is more than the sum of various activities and types of behavior. In this form of violence a number of things are happening at once, in addition to the autonomous factors involved. Sometimes mutual, sometimes one-sided, there is a discharge of aggression and hostility. But at the same time as discharging aggression, these acts of violence and the ever-present potential for male violence against other men reinforce the reality that relations between men, whether at the individual or state level, are relations of power.[38]

Most men feel the presence of violence in their lives. Some of us had fathers who were domineering, rough, or even brutal. Some of us had fathers who simply were not there enough; most of us had fathers who either consciously or unconsciously were repelled by our need for touch and affection once we had passed a certain age. All of us had experiences of being beaten up or picked on when we were young. We learned to fight, or we learned to run; we learned to pick on others, or we learned how to talk or joke our way out of a confrontation. But either way these early experiences of violence caused an incredible amount of anxiety and required a huge expenditure of energy to resolve. That anxiety is crystallized in an unspoken fear (particularly among heterosexual men): all other men are my potential humiliators, my enemies, my competitors.

But this mutual hostility is not always expressed. Men have formed elaborate institutions of male bonding and buddying: clubs, gangs, teams, fishing trips, card games, bars, and gyms, not to mention that great fraternity of Man. Certainly, as many feminists have pointed out, straight male clubs are a subculture of male privilege. But they are also havens where men, by common consent, can find safety and security among other men. They are safe houses where our love and affection for other men can be expressed.

Freud suggested that great amounts of passivity are required for the establishment of social relations among men but also that this very passivity arouses a fear of losing one's power. (This fear takes the form, in a phallocentric, male-dominated society, of what Freud called "castration anxiety.") There is a constant tension of activity and passivity. Among their many functions and reasons for existence, male institutions mediate this tension between activity and passivity among men.

My thoughts take me back to grade six and the constant acting out of this drama. There was the challenge to fight and a punch in the stomach that knocked my wind out. There was our customary greeting with a slug in the shoulder. Before school, after school, during class change, at recess, whenever you saw another one of the boys whom you hadn't hit or been with in the past few minutes, you'd punch each other on the shoulder. I remember walking from class to class in terror of meeting Ed Skagle in the hall. Ed, a hefty young football player a grade ahead of me, would leave a big bruise with one of his friendly hellos. And this was the interesting thing about the whole business; most of the time it was friendly and affectionate. Long after the bruises have faded, I remember Ed's smile and the protective way he had of saying hello to me. But we couldn't express this affection without maintaining the active/passive equilibrium. More precisely, within the masculine psychology of surplus aggression, expressions of affection and of the need for other boys had to be balanced by an active assault.

But the traditional definition of masculinity is not only surplus aggression. It is also exclusive heterosexuality, for the maintenance of masculinity requires the repression of homosexuality.[39] Repression of homosexuality is one thing, but how do we explain the intense fear of homosexuality, the homophobia, that pervades so much male interaction? It isn't simply that many men may choose not to have sexual relations with other men; it is rather that they will find this possibility frightening or abhorrent.

Freud showed that the boy's renunciation of the father—and thus men—as an object of sexual love is a renunciation of what are felt to be passive sexual desires. Our embrace of future manhood is part of an equation:

male = penis = power = active = masculine.

The other half of the equation, in the language of the unconscious in patriarchal society, is

female = castrated = passive = feminine.

These unconscious equations might be absurd, but they are part of a socially shared hallucination of our partriarchal society. For the boy to deviate from this norm is to experience severe anxiety, for what appears to be at stake is his ability to be active. Erotic attraction to other men is sacrificed because there is no model central to our society of active, erotic love for other males. The emotionally charged physical attachments of childhood with father and friends eventually breed feelings of passivity and danger and are sacrificed. The anxiety caused by the threat of losing power and activity is "the motive power behind the 'normal' boy's social learning of his sex and gender roles." Boys internalize "our culture's definition of 'normal' or 'real' man: the possessor of a penis, therefore loving only females and that actively; the possessor of a penis, therefore 'strong' and 'hard,' not 'soft,' 'weak,' 'yielding,' 'sentimental,' 'effeminate,' passive. To deviate from this definition is not to be a real man. To deviate is to arouse [what Freud called] castration anxiety."[40]

Putting this in different terms, the young boy learns of the sexual hierarchy of society. This learning process is partly conscious and partly unconscious. For a boy, being a girl is a threat because it raises anxiety by representing a loss of power. Until real power is attained, the young boy courts power in the world of the imagination (with superheroes, guns, magic, and pretending to be grown-up). But the continued pull of passive aims, the attraction to girls and to mother, the fascination with the origin of babies ensure that a tension continues to exist. In this world, the only thing that is as bad as being a girl is being a sissy, that is, being like a girl.[41] Although the boy doesn't consciously equate being a girl or sissy with homosexual genital activity, at the time of puberty these feelings, thoughts, and anxieties are transferred onto homosexuality per se.

For the majority of men, the establishment of the masculine norm and the strong social prohibitions against homosexuality are enough to bury the erotic desire for other men. The repression of our bisexuality is not adequate, however, to keep this desire at bay. Some of the energy is transformed into derivative pleasures—muscle building, male comradeship, hero worship, religious rituals, war, sports—where our enjoyment of being with other men or admiring other men can be expressed. These forms of activity are not enough to neutralize our constitutional bisexuality, our organic fusion of passivity and activity, and our love for our fathers and our friends. The great majority of men, in addition to those men whose sexual preference is clearly homosexual, have, at some time in their childhood, adolescence, or adult life, had sexual or quasi-sexual relations with other males, or have fantasized or dreamed about such relationships. Those who don't (or don't recall that they have), invest a lot of energy in repressing and denying these thoughts and feelings. And to make things worse, all those highly charged male activities in the sportsfield, the meeting room, or the locker room do not dispel eroticized relations with other men. They can only reawaken those feelings. It is, as Freud would have said, the return of the repressed.

Nowhere has this been more stunningly captured than in the wrestling scene in the perhaps mistitled book, *Women in Love*, by D. H. Lawrence. It was late at night. Birkin had just come to Gerald's house after being put off following a marriage proprosal. They talked of working, of loving, and fighting, and in the end stripped off their clothes and began to wrestle in front of the burning fire. As they wrestled, "they seemed to drive their white flesh deeper and deeper against each other, as if they would break into a oneness." They entwined, they wrestled, they pressed nearer and nearer. "A tense white knot of flesh [was] gripped in silence." The thin Birkin "seemed to penetrate into Gerald's more solid, more diffuse bulk, to interfuse his body through the body of the other, as if to bring it subtly into subjection, always seizing with some rapid necromantic foreknowledge every motion of the other flesh, converting and counteracting it, playing upon the limbs and trunk of Gerald like some hard wind. . . . Now and again came a sharp gasp of breath, or a sound like a sigh, then the rapid thudding of movement on the thickly-carpeted floor, then the strange sound of flesh escaping under flesh."[42]

The very institutions of male bonding and patriarchal power force men to constantly reexperience their closeness and attraction to other men, that is, the very thing so many men are afraid of. Our very attraction to ourselves, ambivalent as it may be, can only be generalized as an attraction to men in general.

A phobia is one means by which the ego tries to cope with anxiety. Homophobia is a means of trying to cope, not simply with our unsuccessfully repressed, eroticized attraction to other men, but with our whole anxiety over the unsuccessfully repressed passive sexual aims, whether directed toward males or females. But often, Otto Fenichel writes, "individuals with phobias cannot succeed in avoiding the feared situations. Again and again they are forced to experience the very things they are afraid of. Often the conclusion is unavoidable that this is due to an unconscious arrangement of theirs. It seems that unconsciously they are striving for the very thing of which they are consciously afraid. This is understandable because the feared situations origi- nally were instinctual aims. It is a kind of 'return of the repressed'."[43]

In the case of homophobia, it is not merely a matter of an individual phobia, although the strength of homophobia varies from individual to individual. It is a socially constructed phobia that is essential for the imposition and mainte- nance of masculinity. A key expression of homophobia is the obsessive denial of homosexual attraction; this denial is expressed as violence against other men. Or to put it differently, men's violence against other men is one of the chief means through which patriarchal society simultaneously expresses and discharges the attraction of men to other men.[44]

The specific ways that homophobia and men's violence toward other men are acted out varies from man to man, society to society, and class to class. The great amount of *directly expressed* violence and violent homophobia among some groups of working class youth would be well worth analyzing to give clues to the relation of class and gender.

This corner of the triad of men's violence interacts with and reinforces violence against women. This corner contains part of the logic of surplus aggression. Here we begin to explain the tendency of many men to use force as a means of simultaneously hiding and expressing their feelings. At the same time the fear of other men, in particular the fear of weakness and passivity in relation to other men, helps create our strong dependence on women for meeting our emotional needs and for emotional discharge. In a surplus- repressive patriarchal and class society, large amounts of anxiety and hostility are built up, ready to be discharged. But the fear of one's emotions and the fear of losing control mean that discharge only takes place in a safe situation. For many men that safety is provided by a relationship with a woman where the commitment of one's friend or lover creates the sense of security. What is more, because it is a relationship with a woman, it unconsciously resonates with that first great passive relation of the boy with his mother. But in this situation and in other acts of men's violence against women, there is also the security of interaction with someone who does not represent a psychic threat, who is less socially powerful, probably less physically powerful, and who is herself operating within a pattern of surplus passivity. And finally, given the fragility of masculine identity and the inner tension of what it means to be masculine, the ultimate acknowledgement of one's masculinity is in our power over women. This power can be expressed in many ways. Violence is one of them.

When I speak of man's violence against himself I am thinking of the very structure of the masculine ego. The formation of an ego on an edifice of surplus repression and surplus aggression is the building of a precarious structure of internalized violence. The continual conscious and unconscious blocking and denial of passivity and all the emotions and feelings men associate with passivity—fear, pain, sadness, embarrassment—is a denial of part of what we are. The constant psychological and behavioral vigilance against passivity and its derivatives is a perpetual act of violence against oneself.

The denial and blocking of a whole range of human emotions and capacities are compounded by the blocking of avenues of discharge. The discharge of fear, hurt, and sadness, for example (through crying or trembling), is necessary because these painful emotions linger on even if they are not consciously felt. Men become pressure cookers. The failure to find safe avenues of emotional expression and discharge means that a whole range of emotions are transformed into anger and hostility. Part of the anger is directed at oneself in the form of guilt, self-hate, and various physiological and psychological symptoms. Part is directed at other men. Part of it is directed at women.

By the end of this process, our distance from ourselves is so great that the very symbol of maleness is turned into an object, a thing. Men's preoccupation with genital power and pleasure combines with a desensitization of the penis. As best he can, writes Emmanuel Reynaud, a man gives it "the coldness and the hardness of metal." It becomes his tool, his weapon, his thing. "What he loses in enjoyment he hopes to compensate for in power; but if he gains an undeniable power symbol, what pleasure can he really feel with a weapon between his legs?"[45]

Beyond Men's Violence   Throughout Gabriel Garcia Marquez's *Autumn of the Patriarch*, the ageless dictator stalked his palace, his elephantine feet dragging forever on endless corridors that reeked of corruption. There was no escape from the world of terror, misery, and decay that he himself had created. His tragedy was that he was "condemned forever to live breathing the same air which asphyxiated him."[46] As men, are we similarly condemned, or is there a road of escape from the triad of men's violence and the precarious structures of masculinity that we ourselves recreate at our peril and that of women, children, and the world?

Prescribing a set of behavioral or legal changes to combat men's violence against women is obviously not enough. Even as more and more are convinced there is a problem, this realization does not touch the unconscious structures of masculinity. Any man who is sympathetic to feminism is aware of the painful contradiction between his conscious views and his deeper emotions and feelings.

The analysis in this article suggests that men and women must address each corner of the triad of men's violence and the socioeconomic, psycho-sexual orders on which they stand. Or to put it more strongly, it is impossible to deal successfully with any one corner of this triad in isolation from the others.

The social context that nurtures men's violence and the relation between socioeconomic transformation and the end of patriarchy have been major themes of socialist feminist thought. This framework, though it is not without controversy and unresolved problems, is one I accept. Partriarchy and systems of authoritarianism and class domination feed on each other. Speaking of the relation of capitalism and the oppression of women, Michele Barrett says that male–female divisions

> are systematically embedded in the structure and texture of capitalist social relations . . . and they play an important part in the political and ideological stability of this society. They are constitutive of our subjectivity as well as, in part, of capitalist political and cultural hegemony. They are interwoven into a fundamental relationship between the wage-labour system and the organization of domestic life and it is impossible to imagine that they could be extracted from the relations of production and reproduction of capitalism without a massive transformation of those relations taking place.[47]

Radical socioeconomic and political change is a requirement for the end of men's violence. But organizing for macrosocial change is not enough to solve the problem of men's violence, not only because the problem is so pressing here and now, but because the continued existence of masculinity and surplus aggressiveness works against the fundamental macrosocial change we desire.

The many manifestations of violence against women have been an important focus of feminists. Women's campaigns and public education against rape, battering, sexual harassment, and more generally for control by women of their bodies are a key to challenging men's violence. Support by men, not only for the struggles waged by women, but in our own workplaces and among our friends is an important part of the struggle. There are many possible avenues for work by men among men. These include: forming counselling groups and support services for battering men (as in now happening in different cities in North American); championing the inclusion of clauses on sexual harassment in collective agreements and in the constitutions or bylaws of our trade unions, associations, schools, and political parties; raising money, campaigning for government funding, and finding other means of support for rape crisis centers and shelters for battered women; speaking out against violent and sexist pornography; building neighborhood campaigns of wife and child abuse; and personally refusing to collude with the sexism of our workmates, colleagues, and friends. The latter is perhaps the most difficult of all and requires patience, humor, and support from other men who are challenging sexism.

But because men's violence against women is inseparable from the other two corners of the triad of men's violence, solutions are very complex and difficult. Ideological changes and an awareness of problems are important but insufficient. While we can envisage changes in our child-rearing arrangements (which in turn would require radical economic changes) lasting solutions have to go far deeper. Only the development of non–surplus-repressive societies (whatever these might look like) will allow for the greater expression of human needs and, along with attacks on patriarchy per se, will reduce the split between active and passive psychological aims.[48]

The process of achieving these long-term goals contains many elements of economic, social, political, and psychological change each of which requires a fundamental transformation of society. Such a transformation will not be created by an amalgam of changed individuals; but there *is* a relationship between personal change and our ability to construct organizational, political, and economic alternatives that will be able to mount a successful challenge to the status quo.

One avenue of personal struggle that is being engaged in by an increasing number of men has been the formation of men's support groups. Some groups focus on consciousness raising, but most groups stress the importance of men talking about their feelings, their relations with other men and with women, and any number of problems in their lives. At times these groups have been criticized by some antisexist men as yet another place for men to collude against women. The alternatives put forward are groups whose primary focus is either support for struggles led by women or the organization of direct, antisexist campaigns among men. These activities are very important, but so too is the development of new support structures among men. And these structures must go beyond the traditional form of consciousness raising.

Consciousness raising usually focuses on manifestations of the oppression of women and on the oppressive behavior of men. But as we have seen, masculinity is more than the sum total of oppressive forms of behavior. It is deeply and unconsciously embedded in the structure of our egos and superegos; it is what we have become. An awareness of oppressive behavior is important, but too often it only leads to guilt about being a man. Guilt is a profoundly conservative emotion and as such is not particularly useful for bringing about change. From a position of insecurity and guilt, people do not change or inspire others to change. After all, insecurity about one's male credentials played an important part in the individual acquisition of masculinity and men's violence in the first place.

There is a need to promote the personal strength and security necessary to allow men to make more fundamental personal changes and to confront sexism and heterosexism in society at large. Support groups usually allow men to talk about our feelings, how we too have been hurt growing up in a surplus-repressive society, and how we, in turn, act at times in an oppressive manner. We begin to see the connections between painful and frustrating experiences in our own lives and related forms of oppressive behavior. As Sheila Rowbotham notes, "the exploration of the internal areas of consciousness is a political necessity for us."[49]

Talking among men is a major step, but it is still operating within the acceptable limits of what men like to think of as rational behavior. Deep barriers and fears remain even when we can begin to recognize them. As well as talking, men need to encourage direct expression of emotions—grief, anger, rage, hurt, love—within these groups and the physical closeness that has been blocked by the repression of passive aims, by social prohibition, and by our own superegos and sense of what is right. This discharge of emotions has many functions and outcomes: like all forms of emotional and physical discharge it lowers the tension within the human system and reduces the likelihood of a spontaneous discharge of emotions through outer- or inner-directed violence.

But the expression of emotions is not an end in itself; in this context it is a means to an end. Stifling the emotions connected with feelings of hurt and pain acts as a sort of glue that allows the original repression to remain. Emotional discharge, in a situation of support and encouragement, helps unglue the ego structures that require us to operate in patterned, phobic, oppressive, and surplus-aggressive forms. In a sense it loosens up the repressive structures and allows us fresh insight into ourselves and our past. But if this emotional discharge happens in isolation or against an unwitting victim, it only reinforces the feelings of being powerless, out of control, or a person who must obsessively control others. Only in situations that contradict these feelings—that is, with the support, affection, encouragement, and backing of other men who experience similar feelings—does the basis for change exist.[50]

The encouragement of emotional discharge and open dialogue among men also enhances the safety we begin to feel among each other and in turn helps us to tackle obsessive, even if unconscious, fear of other men. This unconscious fear and lack of safety are the experience of most heterosexual men throughout their lives. The pattern for homosexual men differs, but growing up and living in a heterosexist, patriarchal culture implants similar fears, even if one's adult reality is different.

Receiving emotional support and attention from a group of men is a major contradiction to experiences of distance, caution, fear, and neglect from other men. This contradiction is the mechanism that allows further discharge, emotional change, and more safety. Safety among even a small group of our brothers gives us greater safety and strength among men as a whole. This gives us the confidence and sense of personal power to confront sexism and homophobia in all its various manifestations. In a sense, this allows us each to be a model of a strong, powerful man who does not need to operate in an oppressive and violent fashion in relation to women, to other men, or to himself. And that, I hope, will play some small part in the challenge to the oppressive reality of partriarchal, authoritarian, class societies. It will be changes in our own lives inseparably intertwined with changes in society as a whole that will sever the links in the triad of men's violence.

NOTES

My thanks to those who have given me comments on earlier drafts of this paper, in particular my father. Nathan Kaufman and to Gad Horowitz. As well I extend my appreciation to the men I have worked with in various counselling situations who have helped me develop insights into the individual acquisition of violence and masculinity.

[1] Herbert Marcuse. *Eros and Civilization* (Boston: Beacon Press. 1975; New York: Vintage, 1962): Gad Horowitz. *Repression* (Toronto: University of Toronto Press, 1977).

[2] Part of Freud's wisdom was to recognize that, although the engendered psychology of the individual was the product of the maturation of the individual within an evolving social environment, the body was in the last analysis the subject and the object of our desires.

[3] Michele Barrett and Mary McIntosh. *The Anti-Social Family* (London: Verso/New Left Books. 1982). 107.

[4] See the critical remarks on biological determinism by Carmen Schifellite elsewhere in this volume.

[5] On the range of societies, see the article by Richard Lee and Richard Daly in this volume.

[6] Susan Brownmiller. *Against Our Will: Men, Women and Rape* (New York: Bantam Books, 1976). 6.

[7] Alice Echols, "The New Feminism of Yin and Yang" in Ann Snitow et al., eds., *Powers of Desire* (New York: Monthly Review Press. 1983) 439–59; and Alice Echols, "The Taming of the Id;: Feminist Sexual Politics, 1968–83," in Carol Vance, ed., *Pleasure and Danger* (London: Routledge and Kegan Paul, 1984), 50–72. The two articles are essentially the same.

[8] Aimé Césaire, *Discourse on Colonialism* (New York: Monthly Review Press, 1972), 21–2; first published in 1955 by Editions Présence Africaine.

[9] C. Tunnard, *The City of Man* (New York: Scribner, 1953), 43. Quoted in N. O. Brown, *Life Against Death* (Middletown: Wesleyan University Press, 1959), 283.

[10] This is the approach, for example, of Suzanne Steinmetz. She says that macrolevel social and economic conditions (such as poverty, unemployment, inadequate housing, and the glorification and acceptance of violence) lead to high crime rates and a tolerance of violence that in turn leads to family aggression. See her *Cycle of Violence* (New York: Praeger, 1977), 30.

[11] Juliet Mitchell, *Psychoanalysis and Feminism* (New York: Vintage, 1975), 362.

[12] Joseph Conrad, *Lord Jim*, (New York: Bantam Books, 1981), 146; first publsihed 1900.

[13] See for example Michele Barrett's thought-provoking book, *Women's Oppression Today* (London: Verso/New Left Books, 1980), 10–19, 250–1.

[14] Jessica Benjamin, "Authority and the Family Revisited: or, A World Without Fathers?". *New German Critique* (Winter 1978), 35.

[15] See *ibid.*, 40, for a short discussion of Adorno's and Horkheimer's *Dialectic of Enlightenment*.

[16] Mary O'Brien, *The Politics of Reproduction* (London: Routledge and Kegan Paul, 1981), 54–5.

[17] Simone de Beauvoir, *The Second Sex* (New York: Vintage, 1974), 162; first published 1949. Dorothy Dinnerstein pursues a similar line of argument but, in line with the thesis of her book, points to mother-raised-children as the source of these ambivalent feelings toward women. See Dinnerstein, *op. cit.*, especially, 109–10.

[18] Sidney Jourard, "Some Lethal Aspects of the Male Role" in Joseph H. Pleck and Jack Sawyer, eds., *Men and Masculinity* (Englewood Cliffs: Prentice-Hall, 1974), 21–9.

[19] Bertolt Brecht, *Three Penny Novel*, trans. Desmond I. Vesey (Harmondsworth: Penguin, 1965). 282.

[20] Marcuse, *op. cit.*, and Horowitz, *op. cit.*

[21] Barrett and MacIntosh, *op. cit.*, p. 29.

[22] This is true not only because each socioeconomic system appears to create corresponding family forms, but because in turn, that family structure plays a large role in shaping the society's ideology. In Barrett's and McIntosh's words, in our society a family perspective and family ideology have an "utterly hegemonic status" within society as a whole. And there is a dialectical interaction between family form and the organization of production and paid work (*ibid.*, 78, 130).

[23] De Beauvoir, *op. cit.*, *passim*.

[24] Sigmund Freud, *Civilization and Its Discontents* (New York: W. W. Norton, 1962), 70, 72.

[25] Gayle Rubin, "The Traffic in Women: Notes on the 'Political Economy' of Sex" in Rayna R. Reiter, ed., *Toward an Anthropology of Women* (New York: Monthly Review Press, 1975), 157–210.

[26] Ken Kesey, *Sometimes a Great Notion* (New York: Bantam, 1965), 115. (One is eerily reminded of St. Augustine's statement, "Every breath I draw in is a sin." Quoted in Horowitz, *op. cit.*, 211.)

[27] De Beauvoir, *op. cit.*, 367.

[28] Paul Willis, *Learning to Labor* (New York: Columbia University Press, 1981), 150. And see Stan Gray's article elsewhere in this volume.

[29] Andrew Tolson, *The Limits of Masculinity* (London: Tavistock, 1977), 25.

[30] Simone de Beauvoir, in the *Nouvel Observateur*, Mar. 1, 1976. Quoted in Diana E. H. Russell and Nicole Van de Ven, eds., *Crimes Against Women* (Millbrae, Calif.: Les Femmes, 1976), xiv.

[31] Among the sources on male violence that are useful, even if sometimes problematic, see Leonore E. Walker, *The Battered Woman* (New York: Harper Colophon, 1980); Russell and Van de Ven, *op. cit.*; Judith Lewis Herman, *Father-Daughter Incest* (Cambridge, Mass.: Harvard University Press, 1981); Suzanne K. Steinmetz, *The Cycle of Violence* (New York: Praeger, 1977); Sylvia Levine and Joseph Koenig, *Why Men Rape* (Toronto: MacMillan, 1980); Susan Brownmiller, *op. cit.*, and Connie Guberman and Margie Wolfe, eds., *No Safe Place* (Toronto: Women's Press, 1985).

[32] Levine and Koenig, *op. cit.*, pp. 28, 42, 56, 72.

[33] Meg Luxton, *More Than a Labour of Love* (Toronto: Women's Press, 1980), 66.

[34] Margaret M. Killoran, "The Sound of Silence Breaking: Toward a Metatheory of Wife Abuse" (M.A. thesis, McMaster University, 1981), 148.

[35] Barrett and MacIntosh, *op. cit.*, 23.

[36] Of course, household violence is not monopolized by men. In the United States roughly the same number of domestic homicides are committed by each sex. In 1975, 8.0% of homicides were committed by husbands against wives and 7.8% by wives against husbands. These figures, however, do not indicate the chain of violence, that is, the fact that most of these women were reacting to battering by their husbands. (See Steinmetz, *op. cit.*, p. 90.) Similarly, verbal and physical abuse of children appears to be committed by men and women equally. Only in the case of incest is there a near monopoly by men. Estimates vary greatly, but between one-fifth and one-third of all girls experience some sort of sexual contact with an adult male, in most cases with a father, stepfather, other relative, or teacher. (See Herman, *op. cit.*, 12 and *passim*.)

[37] Luxton, *op. cit.*, p. 65.

[38] This was pointed out by I. F. Stone in a 1972 article on the Vietnam war. At a briefing about the U.S. escalation of bombing in the North, the Pentagon official described U.S. strategy as two boys fighting: "If one boy gets the other in an arm lock, he can probably get his adversary to say 'uncle' if he increases the pressure in sharp, painful jolts and gives every indication of willingness to break the boy's arm" ("Machismo in Washington," reprinted in Pleck and Sawyer, *op. cit.*, 131). Although women are also among the victims of war, I include war in the category of violence against men because I am here referring to the causality of war.

[39] This is true both of masculinity as an institution and masculinity for the individual. Gay men keep certain parts of the self-oppressive masculine norm intact simply because they have grown up and live in a predominantly heterosexual, male-dominated society.

[40] Horowitz, *op. cit.*, 99.

[41] This formulation was first suggested to me by Charlie Kreiner at a men's counseling workshop in 1982.

[42] D. H. Lawrence, *Women in Love* (Harmondsworth: Penguin, 1960). 304–5; first published 1921.

[43] Fenichel, *op. cit.*, 212.

[44] See Robin Wood's analysis of the film *Raging Bull* in this volume.

[45] Emmanuel Reynaud, *Holy Virility*, translated by Ros Schwartz (London: Plato Press, 1983), 41–2.

[46] Gabriel Garcia Marquez. *Autumn of the Patriarch*, trans. Gregory Rabassa (Harmondsworth: Penguin, 1972). 111: first published 1967.

[47] Barrett, *op. cit.*, pp. 254–5. Willis follows a similar line of thought in his discussion of the development of the male working class. He says that patriarchy "helps to provide the real human and cultural conditions which . . . actually allow subordinate roles to be taken on 'freely' within liberal democracy" (Willis, *op. cit.*, 151). But then in turn, this reinforces the impediments to change by the maintenance of a division within the working class. As an article in the early 1970s in *Shrew* pointed out, "the tendency of male workers to think of themselves as men (i.e., powerful) rather than as workers (i.e., members of an oppressed group), promotes a false sense of privilege and power, and an identification with the world of men, including the boss," *Shrew* 3, no. 5 (June 1971): 1–2, quoted by Sheila Rowbotham *Woman's Consciousness, Men's World* (Harmondsworth, Penguin 1973).

[48] For a discussion on non–surplus-repressive societies, particularly in the sense of being complementary with Marx's notion of communism, see Horowitz, *op. cit.*, particularly chapter 7, and also Marcuse, *op. cit.*, especially chaps. 7, 10, and 11.

[49] Rowbotham, *op. cit.*, 36.

[50] As is apparent, although I have adopted a Freudian analysis of the unconscious and the mechanisms of repression, these observations on the therapeutic process—especially the importance of a supportive counseling environment, peer-counseling relations, emotional discharge, and the concept of contradiction—are those developed by forms of co-counseling, in particular, Reevaluation Counselling. But unlike the latter, I do not suppose that any of us can discharge all of our hurt, grief, and anger and uncover an essential self simply because our "self" is created

through that process of frustration, hurt, and repression. Rather I feel that some reforming of the ego can take place that allows us to integrate more fully a range of needs and desires, which in turn reduces forms of behavior that are oppressive to others and destructive to ourselves. Furthermore, by giving us greater consciousness of our feelings and the means of discharge, and by freeing dammed-up sources of energy, these changes allow us to act more successfully to change the world.

Jewelle Taylor Gibbs

YOUNG BLACK MALES IN AMERICA
ENDANGERED, EMBITTERED, AND EMBATTLED

An endangered species is, according to Webster, "a class of individuals having common attributes and designated by a common name . . . [which is] in danger or peril of probable harm or loss." This description applies in a metaphorical sense, to the current status of young black males in contemporary American society. They have been miseducated by the educational system, mishandled by the criminal justice system, mislabeled by the mental health system, and mistreated by the social welfare system. All the major institutions of American society have failed to respond appropriately and effectively to their multiple needs and problems. As a result, they have become—in an unenviable and unconscionable sense—rejects of our affluent society and misfits in their own communities (Gibbs, 1984).

Who are these black youth who are increasingly subjected to the belated scrutiny of social scientists, educators, policymakers, and the mass media? They are black males in the 15–24-year-old age group who live predominantly in urban inner-city neighborhoods but can also be found in rural areas, working-class suburbs, and small towns all over America. They are the teenagers and young adults from families at the lower end of the socioeconomic spectrum, many of whom are welfare-dependent and live below the poverty line. They are the black youth who are seen when one drives through inner-city ghetto neighborhoods, hanging out on dimly lit street corners, playing basketball on littered school lots, selling dope in darkened alleys, and "rapping" in front of pool halls and bars. The media refer to them by a variety of labels: "dropouts," "delinquents," "dope addicts," "street-smart dudes," "welfare pimps," and, even more pejoratively, as members of the "underclass." They refer to themselves as "home boys," "hardheads," "bloods," and "soul brothers." Labels are powerful clues to the ways in which groups are perceived, valued, and treated, but labels cannot convey the feelings of frustration, humiliation, and anger of these black youth who experience daily doses of failure, rejection, and discrimination. From the brutal lynching of Emmett Till in Mississippi in 1955 to the "justifiable" police killing of Michael Stewart on a New York City subway in 1983, young black males in America have been the primary victims of mob violence, police brutality, legal executions, and ghetto homicide.

Abridged from Jewelle Taylor Gibbs, *Young, Black and Male in America* (Auburn House, an imprint of Greenwood Publishing Group, Inc., Westport, CT, 1988), pp. 1–35. Copyright © 1988 by Auburn House. Abridged and reprinted with permission of the author and Greenwood Publishing Group, Inc.

Black males are portrayed by the mass media in a limited number of roles, most of them deviant, dangerous, and dysfunctional. This constant barrage of predominantly disturbing images inevitably contributes to the public's negative stereotypes of black men, particularly of those who are perceived as young, hostile, and impulsive. Even the presumably positive images of blacks as athletes and entertainers project them as animal-like or childlike in their aggressiveness, sensuality, "natural rhythm," and uninhibited expressiveness. Clearly, the message says: If they entertain you, enjoy them (at a safe distance); if they serve you, patronize them (and don't forget to leave a tip); if they threaten you, avoid them (don't ride on the subway). Thus young black males are stereotypes by the five "d's": dumb, deprived, dangerous, deviant, and disturbed. There is no room in this picture for comprehension, caring, or compassion of the plight of these young black men.

A few vignettes illustrate the impact of these stereotypes on community attitudes and behaviors toward this group:

- Just five days before Christmas 1986, three young black men (ages 19, 23, and 37) stopped at a pizza parlor to call for help when their car broke down in the predominantly white neighborhood of Howard Beach, Queens. While there, they ordered pizza and chatted briefly with the counterman, but became apprehensive when a crowd of white youth gathered outside and began chanting: "Niggers, go home." As they left the restaurant, they were beaten and chased by the angry youth in various directions. One of the black youth, 23-year-old Michael Griffith, after pleading to an onlooker for help, ran onto the nearby freeway to escape his assailants and was killed by an oncoming car. Subsequently, four white teenagers, none older than 18, were arrested and charged with manslaughter. In their defense, neighbors were quoted as saying that they were "just average boys from respectable families," and that they probably thought that the three black men were "up to no good."
- In October 1986, the *Washington Post* inaugurated a new Sunday magazine section with a feature story on the problems of operating small businesses in the downtown areas of the capital city, where merchants customarily installed bars on their windows and frequently refused to open their doors to young black males whom they viewed as potential assailants. Although the *Post* was heavily criticized by local black leaders for this inflammatory article, the paper was only revealing a practice that is common in central city shopping areas of New York, Chicago, Los Angeles, and many others.
- The sheriff of Jefferson Parish, Louisiana, a predominantly white suburb of New Orleans, called a news conference on December 2, 1986 to announce that his deputies would henceforth arrest any young black males seen in the residential areas of his community after dark. When civil rights groups objected to this policy, the sheriff defended his position on the grounds that most of the crime in the New Orleans area was committed by young black men and, therefore, it seemed perfectly reasonable and justifiable to arrest anyone fitting that description, as a preventive measure.
- In Liberty City, Florida, a riot broke out in the predominantly black area after a young black male died in police custody in May 1980. The police claimed that his death was an accident, but witnesses swore that he had been subdued with a choke hold and brutally beaten by the police. This incident was one of a series of confrontations between blacks and the local police, with black males consistently complaining of police brutality and discrimination.
- In December 1984, a young black man approached a white man riding on a New

York City subway, asking him for five dollars. Three of the black youth's friends sitting nearby were watching, perhaps planning to join in the panhandling, as the white man pulled out a gun and shot all four of them. One youth is paralyzed for life, but Bernhard Goetz, a 37-year-old electrical engineer, was hailed as a hero by many New Yorkers and was treated as a celebrity by the mass media. In his defense, Goetz's lawyer claimed that he felt his life was threatened because of the "gleam in their eyes." Nearly two and a half years later, in June 1987, a jury of his peers found him "not guilty" of attempted murder and assault.

In 1985 there were 8.5 million black youth in the 10–24-year-old age range, with nearly 3 million each in the 15–19 and 20–24-year-old age groups. Black males accounted for nearly 3 million in the 15–24 category, or 50 percent of the total group. Since nearly half of the total black population is composed of children and youth, the median age for blacks is 25.8 years compared to a median age of 31.8 for whites (U.S. Census Bureau, 1987). Thus, any social and economic problems in the black community will have a disproportionate impact on black youth under the age of 25, and more particularly on the additional unenumerated black males (Gibbs, 1985).

Nearly half (42.7 percent) of black youth under 18 live in families who are below the poverty line, while two-thirds (67.1 percent) of those living in female-headed families are classified as poor. Two of every five (42 percent) black youth live in female-headed families (U.S. Census Bureau, 1987). Clearly, this type of family structure tends to have a negative impact on the economic status and opportunities for all black youth, and it may have particularly negative effects on black males (CDF, 1986c).

Children in black female-headed families are five times as likely to be welfare-dependent than those in intact black families. Thus, males in female-headed families are not only reared without fathers as role models, but are also reared in families triply stigmatized by being black, single-parent, and on welfare. Furthermore, youth in these families are more likely to live in substandard housing, to attend inferior schools, to have inadequate health and dental care, to have higher rates of chronic illnesses, to have more behavioral problems, and to live in deteriorating neighborhoods with high crime rates, poor services, and inadequate public transportation (CDF, 1985a and 1986a).

Even for those black youth who live in intact nuclear families, economic stability and quality of life are much less predictable and permanent than for comparable white youth (CDF, 1985b). For such youth, total family income is more likely to depend on both parents working, but their fathers are 2.5 times more likely than adult white males to be unemployed. Both parents are more likely than parents of white youth to be employed in lower-status, lower-income jobs in the white-collar, blue-collar, and unskilled sectors of the economy. In 1986, the median black family income of $17,604 was only 57 percent of white family income of $30,809, a decrease from 61 percent in 1970. Thus, it is an illusion that the gap between black and white family income has narrowed in the past 15 years. In fact, black family income is lower than it was in 1978, and its modest gains since 1980 remain heavily dependent on two parents working, a stable economy, and the security of government employment (U.S. Census Bureau, 1987).

Just as the modest economic gains experiences by the black family in the late 1960s and early 1970s have largely been offset by the increasing rate of poverty among single-parent families, black youth have also lost ground on five out of six social indicators. What is particularly dramatic and demoralizing is that, while all other groups (including women and recent immigrants) have made progress since 1960 in all of these areas, young black males in particular are now more likely than they were in 1960 to be unemployed, to be addicted to drugs, to be involved in the criminal justice system, to be unwed fathers, and to die from homicide or suicide. The educational statistics indicate a reduction in high school drop-out rates among black males during this period, but this improved high school completion rate has been offset by a decline in the college enrollment rates of black high school graduates and a continuing high rate of illiteracy among 18–21-year-old black youth, both of which are more characteristic of black males. . . .

SOCIAL INDICATORS FOR YOUNG BLACK MALES

Education   A surface familiarity with the statistics on the educational attainment of black youth suggests that there has been some improvement in the past 25 years. For example, the proportion of high school dropouts among black youth in the 14–24 age group steadily declined from 23.8 percent in 1960 to 13.2 percent in 1984, and for 16–17-year-olds, from 22.3 percent to 5.2 percent in the same period (College Entrance Examination Board, 1985). In recent years the gap between black and white overall drop-out rates in the high school age group has reached parity, in spite of disproportionately high rates for inner-city black youth. However, these figures do not reveal the number of black high school graduates who were functionally illiterate or barely able to fill out a job application. While an earlier survey estimated that more than 20 percent of black male adolescents in the 12–17 age group were unable to read at the fourth-grade level (Brown, 1979), more recent statistics indicated that 21 percent of all 18- and 19-year-old and 25 percent of all 20- and 21-year-old black youth had neither completed nor were presently enrolled in high school in 1980 (U.S. Census Bureau, 1981). Thus, more than one out of five black youth in the 18–21 age group currently do not have either the basic certificate or basic skills which in our society are necessary for most entry-level jobs, apprenticeship programs, military service, or postsecondary education.

While reasons for dropping out of high school are varied, a recent Urban League Study pointed out that many black male teenagers leave because of family economic problems, academic difficulties, or disciplinary problems, and females often drop out due to pregnancy (Williams, 1982). This study also reported that nearly one-third of black families with incomes below $6,000 and 18 percent of black families with incomes above $20,000 had at least one child suspended from school. These figures suggest that black students have attitudes or behaviors which school administrators and teachers define as problematic and which they are either unwilling or unable to deal with effectively. On the other hand, inner-city students are confronted with nearly insurmountable barriers to learning and achievement in schools which are characterized by poorly prepared teachers, inadequate educational facilities, low teacher expectations, ineffective administrators, and chronic violence. Lack of communication between parents and school authorities, as well as prevailing community attitudes toward the schools, probably contribute to bureaucratic inflexibility, student alienation, and hostility in a continuously escalating cycle of mistrust and maladaptive behaviors. Whether black teenagers drop out of school or obtain a meaningless high school diploma based on "social promotion," the consequences are higher rates of unemployment, fewer options for jobs, greater welfare dependency, and long-range limitations on their social and economic mobility (see Bane and Ellwood, 1983; McLanahan, 1985). . . .

Employment/Unemployment   In November 1987, the U.S. Labor Department announced a national unemployment rate of 6.0 percent. Unemployment among black youth, however, was 34.0 percent—twice the rate of 17.4 percent among all teenagers. This national rate is nearly three times higher than the 12.1 percent employment rate among 16–19-year-old black youth in 1960, but lower than the local unemployment rates in many large metropolitan areas of the country, which have consistently ranged between 40 and 50 percent in the past decade. Since 1960, unemployment rates of black male youth have consistently been higher than black females by a ratio of 2 to 1.

Unemployment statistics obviously reflect the labor force participation rates of black youth, which have fallen dramatically since 1960. At that time, 82.0 percent of black males 20–24 participated in the labor force, but in 1980 only 73.5 percent of this group participated (Wilson and Neckerman, 1984). Labor force participation rates for black males 16–19 also dropped from 42.4 percent in 1960 to 36.5 percent in 1980. In the early 1960s, over half of the black high school graduates 16–24 were employed, but by 1980 fewer than one-third were able to find jobs. In 1983 black high school dropouts were twice as likely to be unemployed, with only 26 percent in the labor force (U.S. Dept. of Labor, 1987). Ironically, employment rates increased for all white youth, including high school dropouts, during this same period from 67 to 71 percent.

A recent study found that in 1984 nearly half of the black youth in the 16–24 age group had no work experience at all (Larson, 1986). These extremely high unemployment rates, affecting from over one-third to one-half of the nation's young black males, have significant implications for these young people and for the society at large in the next few decades (Sum, Harrington, and Goedicke, 1987). If black youth are unable to find jobs, they will not develop the work skills, attitudes, and habits that are appropriate and necessary in a competitive, highly technological economy. Moreover, recent studies have indicated that chronically unemployed black males constitute a disproportionately high percentage of those workers who become "discouraged" and completely drop out of the job-seekers' market (Auletta, 1982). Without gainful employment, black youth are increasingly tempted to participate in the underground alternative economy of the urban ghettos—that is, the illegal system of barter in stolen goods, drugs, gambling, and prostitution (Glasgow, 1981; Clark, 1965). The prospect of a rapidly increasing cadre of unemployed and unemployable urban youth, socialized to a nonproductive life-style on the streets, has major implications in terms of the development of a permanent urban underclass with the accompanying sociopolitical consequences (Glasgow, 1981; Wilson and Aponte, 1985). . . .

Delinquency and Crime   The rate of delinquency among black youth has increased from 19.6 percent of all juvenile arrests in 1960 to 23.2 percent in 1985; thus 407,807, or approximately 7 percent of all black adolescents in the 10–19 age group, were arrested in 1985 (FBI, 1986).

Black juveniles were arrested more frequently than whites for robbery, rape, homicide, and aggravated assault. They were also more likely than white juveniles to be arrested for other violent personal crimes, disorderly conduct, sexual misbehavior, and handling stolen property. National data, compiled from 1977 to 1982 by the FBI on juvenile arrests by race for Part I offenses (violent crimes against persons and property), indicate that blacks accounted for nearly one-third of all arrests; yet black juveniles represent less than one-fifth of the total youth population (Krisberg et al., 1986). During that same period, over half of the juvenile arrests for the most violent crimes were among black youth. However, arrest rates tend to give a biased view of the actual prevalence of delinquent behavior in black youth.

Another perspective on black youth crime rates is provided by the National Youth Survey (NYS), a longitudinal study of self-reported delinquency and substance use among a probability sample of 11–17-year-olds in the United States. Data collected from 1976 to 1983 indicate that black youth reported a slightly higher rate of general delinquency, index offenses, and felony offenses than white youth, but few of these offense differences were consistent or statistically significant across age subgroups and over the seven-year period (Krisberg et al., 1986). Despite official statistics indicating that black youth are disproportionately represented among violent and high-frequency offenders, Huizinga and Elliott (1985) analyzed the NYS data for 1976-1980 and found no statistically significant racial differences in high-rate offenders except for one year (1976). These researchers conclude:

> *Overall, these findings suggest that there are few if any substantial and consistent differences between the delinquency involvement of different racial groups. This finding is not unique. Other large scale self-report studies of delinquency have reached similar conclusions.—As a result*, it does not appear that differences in delinquent behavior can provide an explanation for the observed race differential in incarceration rates. *(p. 13) (emphasis supplied)*

These authors assume that self-report surveys of delinquency are equally valid for black and white youth, which may be arguable, particularly since the most violent offenders are least likely to remain subjects in a longitudinal study. However, given their well-documented conclusion, it is particularly disturbing to note that black youth are significantly more likely than any other ethnic group to be incarcerated in public juvenile facilities for both overall delinquency and for Part I offenses (Krisberg et al., 1986). Further, these authors note that, while 71 percent of incarcerated black youth are confined in public facilities, only 54 percent of whites are in these facilities. In 1979 black males had the highest rate of incarceration for all sex/race subgroups (587.9 per 100,000) and black females were highest among females incarcerated (76.9 per 100,000) in public juvenile facilities. By 1982, these incarceration rates had increased dramatically to 810 per 100,000 for black males and 98.4 per 100,000 for black females, more than double the rate of increase among whites of either gender.

By 1982, when black males comprised about 14 percent of youth under the jurisdiction of the juvenile court, they represented 39 percent of all incarcerated male juveniles, a ratio of 44 to 1 compared to the rate of white male juvenile incarceration. Further, the rate of black youth incarceration for Part I offenses in 1982 was 8.6 per 100, which was 69 percent higher than the 5.1 per 100 rate of incarceration for white youth for the same offense category (Krisberg et al., 1986).

The proportion of minority youth in public correctional facilities increased 26 percent from 1977 to 1982, with nearly two-thirds of this increase due to black youth. Of even greater concern, a recent report noted that on any given day the state prison population contains more than 5 percent of all black males in their 20s. Projected lifetime rates predict that up to 15 percent of all black males will spend some time in an adult prison, while only 2 to 3 percent of white males are expected to do so (Krisberg et al., 1986).

Some studies have suggested that black teens are more likely to be arrested, booked, and remanded for trial and to receive harsher dispositions than whites. It has also been suggested that the more frequent arrests of black youth for minor offenses occur both because inner-city neighborhoods are patrolled more intensively and because police tend to overreact to the perceived negative attitudes and "anti-authority demeanor" of black youth (Piliavin and Briar, 1964; Thornton, James, and Doerner, 1982). Whether or not these factors can reasonably account for the widespread discrepancy between arrest rates of black and white youth, the fact remains that black youth are disproportionately involved in the juvenile justice system, resulting in severe limitations on their educational and occupational opportunities and creating a vicious cycle of delinquency, incarceration, recidivism, and chronic criminal careers—or unemployment and marginal social adaptation in adulthood (Tolmach, 1985).

Moreover, the primary victims of black juvenile crime are the juveniles themselves and the black community. In addition, the rate of victimization for crimes of violence is generally greater for blacks than whites at all income levels, and the victimization rate of residents of central cities was roughly twice that of residents of urban and suburban areas (FBI, 1981). In 1980, 95 percent of those who committed crimes against blacks were themselves black, and the majority of these crimes were committed by youth under the age of 24. Inner-city neighborhoods are increasingly becoming brutalized by youth who burglarize stores and homes, vandalize schools and churches, and terrorize those who are old, sick, and vulnerable. The major victims of these antisocial youth are black females, age 25 and older, black males in the 50–64 age group, and other black male teenagers in the 12–15 age group (FBI, 1981). . . .

Substance Abuse   Recent data from the National Institute on Drug Abuse indicate that nonwhite youth in the 18–25 age group have higher or equal rates of drug abuse than white youth in every major drug category except for inhalants and hallucinogens (NIDA, 1979). For the younger age group, 12–17, 31 percent of black teens reported they had used marijuana, and 29 percent said they had used alcohol in this 1979 NIDA survey. Although a number of recent studies have indicated that in early adolescence the overall rate of drug and alcohol use is actually lower among black than white youth, the rates of heroin and cocaine (including the recent derivative "crack") are disproportionately high among older black male youth (Brunswick, 1979). Reliable estimates of drug use in this population are difficult to obtain due to sampling problems and other methodological issues, but studies of selected samples of young black inner-city males in major metropolitan areas suggest high lifetime rates of these drugs. For example, a study of drug use in a Harlem sample of black males in the mid-1970s found that heroin and cocaine rates were three times higher than reported by a national sample of selective service registrants (Brunswick, 1979).

The issue is not simply a legal or moral issue. Society's concern should be focused on the damage these young people are inflicting on themselves physically, psychologically, and socially (Brunswick and Messeri, 1986). Drug use among black youth is highly correlated to low school achievement, delinquency, and accidental deaths. Moreover, drug addiction inevitably involves teenagers in activities that will increase access to drugs, whether these involve stealing, dealing, or hustling sex in order to "get high" (Beschner and Friedman, 1979; Gandossy, Williams, and Harwood, 1980; Thornton, James, and Doerner, 1982). Addicts lose interest in school, work, and gradually deteriorate so that "getting high" becomes the major motivation of each day; eventually, they become walking zombies, worthless to themselves, their families, and their communities. Drug addiction among black youth also substantially increases the risk of arrest and imprisonment, physical and mental illness, and death by overdosing (Gandossy, Williams, and Harwood, 1980; Nelson et al., 1974).

The newest drug-related threat to young black males is the spectre of AIDS (acquired immunodeficiency syndrome), which is increasing rapidly among intravenous drug users in the inner cities. In 1986, the Centers for Disease Control (1986b) reported that black males accounted for nearly one of four (23 percent) of all males with AIDS. The rate of infection of the AIDS virus is also reported to be higher among blacks than whites in samples of military recruits and potential blood donors (Centers for Disease Control, 1986a). Since few of these young black men practice preventive health care or engage in drug treatment programs, they are virtually unreachable for public health education campaigns (CDF, 1986b). The implications of AIDS among young black male drug addicts, especially those who are sexually active and adamantly opposed to any form of male contraception, are truly frightening for the black community, furtively ticking away with the insidious danger of a time bomb primed to explode in the 21st century. . . .

Unwed Teenage Parenthood In 1985, the Guttmacher Institute published a startling report that the pregnancy rate for American teenagers in the 15–19-year-old age group was the highest of all industrialized nations at 96 per 1,000 pregnancies per year. In 1980, America was also the only country where the rate was increasing and, contrary to popular stereotypes, it was increasing more rapidly among white than black adolescent females. Despite the decreasing birth trend among black teenagers, pregnancy rates are still twice as high among blacks as whites (163 per 1,000 vs. 83 per 1,000), and out-of-wedlock pregnancy is a major problem in the black community (CDF, 1986d). In 1980, for example, nearly one out of ten black teenage females gave birth (9.5 percent) compared to one out of 25 white females (4.5 percent). Black teens are more likely to have their babies, while white teens are more likely to terminate their pregnancies by abortions. In 1983, 85.7 percent of babies born to black females under age 19 were out-of-wedlock compared to 39.7 percent born to white teenage mothers (CDF, 1986d).

These are children having children, with profound physical and psychosocial consequences for the girls themselves, as well as negative implications for their babies and their families (Family Impact Seminar, 1979). Teenage mothers are more likely to drop out of high school, more likely to go on welfare, and more likely to experience complications in pregnancy and associated physical and psychological problems than adult women who bear their first child (Chilman, 1983; Furstenberg, Lincoln, and Menken, 1981). Moreover, teen mothers are more likely than adult women to have larger families, to experience less occupational stability and economic mobility, and to be less competent and effective as parents.

Babies born to teenage mothers are more likely to have low birth weight and other perinatal and postnatal problems, to have poor health, and to experience abuse or neglect. Infant mortality rates are highest among teen mothers and nearly twice as high among blacks as among whites (19.2 v. 9.7 per 1,000 live births in 1983). If they survive, these children tend to be less healthy, less academically successful in school, more likely to grow up in a single-parent, welfare-dependent family, and more likely than children born to adult women to become single parents themselves.

The effects of premature fatherhood on the youthful male partners of these teenage mothers has only recently been of interest to researchers. Several studies have found that, compared with their peers who have not fathered children, these young men are more likely to attain a lower educational level and lower occupational status, to have larger faimilies, and to experience unstable marriages (Chilman, 1983; Furstenberg, Lincoln, and Menken, 1981).

Much less is known about the male partners who father these out-of-wedlock children. Contrary to popular belief, one study suggests that a significant number of these men are young adults and older men who become sexually involved with younger women. The typical profile of the teenage/young adult unwed father, drawn from ethnographic studies and reports of teenage parenting programs, is a high school dropout who is unemployed, low-skilled, and lives with his family. Such a characterization may be both inaccurate and biased, however, because it is based on small samples of young men willing to participate in studies or motivated to cooperate in parenting programs with the teenage mothers of their children.

Several studies have indicated that young black males not only have negative attitudes toward using contraception, but also discourage their female sexual partners from using any contraceptive measures (Shapiro, 1980; CDF, 1986a; Gibbs, 1986). Ethnographic studies suggest that black males are very interested in having children to demonstrate their virility, yet many do not exhibit a similar level of commitment to supporting them after they arrive. More recently, however, there is some evidence that these young fathers often do have continuing involvment with their children, contribute to their support when their financial status permits, and play a significant role in their lives over an extended period of time (CDF, 1986c). Thus, the stereotype of the "irresponsible teenage father" may be more of a myth than a reality, based on false assumptions and inadequate empirical data from nonrepresentative samples.

Nonetheless, the impact of these illegitimate births on black families has yet to be fully understood and documented. Some sociological studies suggest that children reared in single-parent homes have fewer competent role models and fewer social supports, which, in turn, limits their ability to grow up in successfully functioning families, to develop satisfactory heterosexual relationships, and to form stable family units of their own (Ladner, 1971; Williams, 1982). The recent prediction that 94 percent of all black children born in 1980 will spend part of their lives before age 18 in a single-parent family (predominantly female-headed) has very serious implications for the stability of black families and for the health and welfare of black youth (Hofferth, 1985). . . .

Homicide and Suicide   The final and most alarming social indicator is the increase in mortality rates among young black males, particularly from homicide and suicide. Homocide is now the leading cause of death for black male teenagers and young adults.

In 1960 the homicide rate for black males 15–24 was 46.4 per 100,000 (DHHS, 1986). This rate increased through the next two decades, reaching a peak of 102.5 per 100,000 in 1970 and then declining to 61.5 per 100,000 in 1984. However, the current rate is still 33 percent higher than it was 25 years ago, a level unacceptable in a civilized society. A young black male has a 1 in 21 chance of being murdered before he reaches the age of 25. In 1985 alone, more than 1,900 black youth 15–24 were murdered—over 90 percent of them by other black youth (NCHS, 1986).

While white youth die primarily from accidents, black youth die primarily from homicide. With the increase in drug trifficking in the inner cities, drug dealers employ violence with impunity in cities like New York, Detroit, Oakland, and Washington, D. C., where they now use Uzi machine guns to protect their turf and to terrorize their neighborhoods, often killing innocent bystanders.

Despite the recent decline in the homicide rate, it is still unacceptably high and represents a clear and present danger to the black community. This wanton violence suggests a pervasive disregard for human life and a profound alienation from shared community norms and values. What factors can account for this violent behavior among young black males? What are the psychological, physical, and sociodemographic factors which place young black males at such high risk for a homicidal death? Is there any relationship between the increased rates of homicide and suicide for this population group? An analysis of suicide rates may shed some light on these questions, but leaves unanswered the more troubling question of the underlying causes of the overall increase in mortality rates among young black males.

In 1960 the suicide rate for black males was 4.1 per 100,000, and for black females it was 1.3 per 100,000 in the 15–24 age group. After peaking in 1971 and 1976, the suicide rate in this age group declined slightly but by 1982 had nearly tripled to 11.0 per 100,000 for black males and nearly doubled to 2.2 per 100,000 for black females (NCHS, 1986). Even though suicide rates among black males are still lower than whites of the same age, it has been suggested that the figures would be much higher if causes of death among blacks, in general, were reported as reliably as are causes of death among whites. For example, if suspected cases of suicide by single-car accidents, deliberate drug overdoses, victim-precipitated homicides, and other violent accidents were included in these statistics, the suicide rates would be significantly higher, particularly since the rates of homicide and other types of violent accidents are higher among nonwhite youth (Holinger, 1979).

In an analysis of long-term trends in adolescent suicide, Holinger and Offer (1982) demonstrated the correlation between adolescent population changes and adolescent suicide rates in the United States and suggested that higher rates may reflect increased peer competition—for colleges, jobs, and access to services—that occurs during periods of adolescent population growth. Since young black males are clearly in a more disadvantaged competitive position compared with whites, this may very well contribute to their feelings of hopelessness and thereby increase their vulnerability to suicidal behavior.

In spite of the increase in suicide rates among young black males, their rates are consistently lower than the rates of white males and higher than those of black females. . . .

In summary these six social indicators—education, unemployment, delinquency, drug abuse, teenage parenthood, and mortality rates from homicide and suicide—are bellwethers of the serious problems experienced by many black youth in American society, but particularly afflicting young black males. Like the biological food chain, each problem contributes to a larger problem and, in turn, is encompassed by it. None of these problems can or should be viewed in a vacuum—they are all inextricably connected. For a young black male, dropping out of school increases the probability of unemployment, which increases the risk of delinquency and criminal behavior, which in turn, increases the vulnerability to drug abuse. Young black men who are unemployed and involved in a delinquent or addictive life-style are more likely to be sexually irresponsible and less likely to marry if their partners become pregnant. Finally, suicide may be perceived as the only option for a young black man who has no skills, no options, and no future. In order to improve the status of young black males, it is first necessary to understand the complex set of factors which have contributed to these problems. . . .

CONTRIBUTING FACTORS TO THE DETERIORATING STATUS OF YOUNG BLACK MALES

Four major sets of factors can account for this downward spiral of black youth, and particularly black males, since 1960: historical, sociocultural, economic, and political. These factors are briefly discussed below.

Historical Factors   Black youth today are the ultimate victims of a legacy of nearly 250 years of slavery, 100 years of legally enforced segregation, and decades of racial discrimination and prejudice in every facet of American life. Countless authors have documented the brutality of slavery, the cruelty of segregation, and the injustice of discrimination. Generations of blacks have endured inferior schools, substandard housing, menial jobs, and the indignities of poverty. Yet, through all of these travails, each generation of blacks made some progress and believed that their children would eventually merge into the mainstream of American society. These beliefs were infused with new life by the New Deal programs of the 1930s, nurtured by the economic opportunities of World War II, and fostered by the postwar policies of the Truman administration. By 1960, many blacks were optimistic that "Jim Crow" was in a terminal stage, theat opportunities were increasing for minorities, and that black youth would finally be able to share in the American dream. No one could have anticipated that the tremendous civil rights and economic gains of the 1960s would have been seriously eroded and ideologically challenged by the mid-1980s, leaving black youth in a worse economic and social situation than they had experienced since before President John F. Kennedy initiated his New Frontier.

The past two and one-half decades since 1960 have been one of the most turbulent periods in American history, encompassing the rise of the civil rights movement, the urban riots, the women's movement, the Vietnam War, the war on poverty, and major political and economic changes in the society. The era began with a liberal Democratic administration committed to increasing opportunities for minorities, but it has gradually evolved into a conservative Republican administration which has aggressively dismantled or diluted many of the most effective civil rights and social welfare programs.

Black youth, who lived through a period of heightened expectations and increased opportunities in the 1960s and early 1970s, began to see their dreams of major social change gradually fade as the economy stopped expanding and other groups (e.g., women, immigrants) began competing for the same limited resources. While much of the civil rights legislation and many of the anti-poverty programs primarily benefited working and middle-class blacks (who were in a better position to take advantage of them), the unanticipated effect of these changes was to create a wider gap between middle-class and poor blacks. Middle-class blacks moved out of the inner cities into integrated urban and suburban areas, leaving poor blacks behind in blighted neighborhoods without effective leadership, successful role models, or the supportive institutions and social networks that provided social stability, economic diversity, and traditional values to the community (see Clark, 1965; Glasgow, 1981). Thus, with increased isolations from the black middle class and alienation from the white community, black inner-city ghettos have gradually become "welfare reservations" where black youth have few, if any, positive role models; where they lack access to high-quality educational, recreational, and cultural facilities; where they do not have job opportunities or adequate transportation to locate jobs; and where they are confronted daily with adult role models who are openly involved in drugs, prostitution, gambling, and other forms of deviant behavior.

Sociocultural Factors   These recent historical and demographic developments have undoubtedly contributed to sociocultural changes in the black community. As the black middle class has drifted away from the inner cities, it has left a vacuum not only in terms of leadership but also in terms of values and resources. For example, in these transformed ghettos, the black church, which had formerly been the center of activity in the black community, has lost much of its central function as a monitor of norms and values. The power of political organizations has been diminished, as their constituencies no longer include the better educated and wealthier blacks who are more likely to participate actively in the political process. In cities with shrinking tax bases, civic and social organizations have fewer resources to improve neighborhoods, initiate youth programs, or provide incentives to attract external sources of support.

With the breakdown or weakening of these traditional institutions within inner-city communities, there has been a parallel breakdown of the traditional black community values of the importance of family, religion, education, self-improvement, and social cohesion through extensive social support networks. Many blacks in inner cities no longer seem to feel connected to each other, responsible for each other, or concerned about each other. Rather than a sense of shared community and a common purpose, which once characterized black neighborhoods, these inner cities now reflect a sense of hopelessness, alienation, and frustration. It is exactly this kind of frustration that exploded in the urban riots of the 1960s from Watts, California, to Detroit, Michigan, to Washington, D.C.

It is also this kind of frustration that erupts into urban crime and violence, family violence, and self-destructive violence. Thus, we see situations in which young black men sell drugs openly on major throughfares without fear of apprehension; teenage girls have multiple out-of-wedlock pregnancies without fear of ostracism; youthful gangs terrorize neighborhoods without fear of retaliation; and young teenagers loiter aimlessly at night on street corners without fear of reprobation.

The poverty and the powerlessness of black youth are inextricably linked to the safety and security of the rest of the society, since the frustration-bred violence will ultimately spill over the invisible walls of the ghetto. The violence which young black males now direct mainly against the black community (black-on-black crime), against relatives and friends (homicide), and against themselves (suicide), will inevitably erupt and spread throughout urban and suburban America, leaving behind damage, destruction, and distrust in its wake. In anxious anticipation of this rising tide of black rage, urban dwellers now put bars on their doors and windows, shopkeepers turn their stores into fortresses, and politicians build new prisons. The causes of these antisocial behaviors are ignored, denied, or blamed on the black youth, who are written off as being intellectually deficient, culturally deprived, and pathologically deviant. Short-term remedies are devised for the consequences of their behaviors, with little understanding that these band-aid solutions are very temporary, very perishable, and very ineffective to cure the underlying causes of frustration and anger in these black youth.

Economic Factors   The post-World War II economic revolution in the United States is the third major factor contributing to the problems of black youth. Two parallel developments created chronic unemployment among black males, both young and old: the structural change in the economy from a predominantly manufacturing and industrial base to a predominantly high-technology and service base, and the movement of these newer jobs from the central cities to the suburbs and peripheral areas (Kasarda, 1985; Sum, Harrington, and Goedicke, 1987). Black youth did not have the skills to compete in the new industries; nor did they have the transportation to follow the jobs to the suburbs. As these jobs moved away from the central cities to the suburbs and exurbs, new services were developed to supply the needs of employers in these industrial and technical companies. These new employment opportunities were increasingly filled by white women and young immigrant workers.

After the urban riots of the 1960s, many of the "Mom-and Pop" stores were forced to close or moved away from the inner cities, removing another source of employment for black youth. As these convenience stores have gradually been replaced, the new owners are predominantly Asian, Hispanic, and Middle-Eastern immigrants who tend to employ family members rather than black youth from the community. Some black leaders have accused these immigrant shopkeepers of commercial exploitation of the black community without returning any economic benefits to the community by hiring black youth.

Black youth, who once had the monopoly on menial service and domestic jobs in restaurants, airports, and department stores, are increasingly being displaced by Asian and Hispanic youth. Although there is some controversy about the displacement theory, statistics indicate that black youth employment rates have decreased as the employment rates of other nonwhite youth have increased. In any case, whether the competition for jobs between black and immigrant youth is perceived or actual, interethnic tensions have increased between blacks and these other minority groups in many urban areas. However, some employers have suggested that immigrant youth are more cooperative, less aggressive, and willing to work for lower wages than black youth. In their analysis of the employment problems of poor youth in America, Sum and his colleagues (1987) conclude that "it is poor black teens who were experiencing the most severe employment problems in March 1985 in both an absolute sense and relative to whites and Hispanics in similar family income positions" (p. 217). Clearly, there are some "noneconomic" factors operating in the severe employment problems of young black males— problems which reflect discriminatory hiring practices as much as they reflect economic and technological changes. . . .

Political Factors   The fourth major factor which has exacerbated already existing problems for black youth is the conservative political climate in this country, which began with the election of Richard Nixon in 1968 and has been strongly reinforced by the Reagan administration. Many political analysts interpret this growing conservatism as a backlash to the antipoverty programs and affirmative action policies of the Johnson and Carter administrations, a not-so-subtle protest of the "middle-American majority" to the civil rights and economic gains of minority groups (Omi and Winant, 1986). Threatened with the loss of their special status, these "middle Americans" have been manipulated by politicians and lobbyists for their own self-serving goals. Framing their rationale in neoconservative dogma, these policymakers have shifted the emphasis from the goal of providing all citizens with a decent standard of living through federally subsidized health and welfare programs to the need to blame the poor and disadvantaged for their perceived lack of motivation, their "dysfunctional" family systems, and their dependency on welfare programs. By shifting the focus from society's responsibility for its most vulnerable citizens to an emphasis on the so-called "social pathology" of minority youth and their families, advocates of this view (such as Murray, 1984) have quite deliberately and effectively transformed the national debate from a proactive emphasis on policies of prevention and early intervention to a reactive emphasis on retrogressive policies and punitive programs. As a result, politicians who support cuts in social programs aimed primarily at disadvantaged and minority families have found increasing favor with the voters in the past 20 years; thus programs with a direct inmpact on black youth, such as CETA, the Job Corps, federally subsidized loans for college, and youth employment programs, all have been severely cut back or eliminated.

The impact of these political and economic changes has resulted in direct negative consequences of fewer educational and employment opportunities for young black males. It has also affected their perceptions of opportunity and their access to the American dream of social and economic mobility. Several national surveys and opinion polls have shown that black families believe they are worse off economically and politically in the 1980s than they were in the 1970s. Consequently, black youth have responded by withdrawing from the labor market, reducing their applications to four-year colleges, and increasing their inolvement in self-destruction and deviant behavior. . . . Peak suicide rates of black youth are also correlated with periods of political conservatism in the past two decades. Thus, there is a reciprocal relationship between the political backlash against minority gains and the social indicators for black youth; that is, these youth respond in a *rational manner* to perceived prejudice and socioeconomic barriers to their mobility by dropping out of the labor market and choosing not to attend college. This reciprocal relationship suggests a self-fulfilling prophecy, which could be reversed if policies and programs were to change, as suggested in later chapters of this book.

This summary of the major social and economic problems of young black males clearly demonstrates that they are an endangered group and a population "at risk" for an escalating cycle of deviance, dysfunction, and despair. . . .

While today's young black males may not be enumerated in the census, may not achieve in the classroom, and may not be counted in the labor force, they are still far from invisible. They cannot be dismissed by the rhetoric of politicians or the analysis of social scientists. They intrude on the nation's consciousness and appeal to the nation's conscience. Their plight is worsening, their pain is growing, and their anger is escalating. Our society must make "the invisible visible" and must bring these black youth into the social, economic, and political mainstream. . . .

REFERENCES

Allen, W. R. (1978). The search for applicable theories of Black family life. *Journal of Marriage and the Family* 40: 117–29.

American Public Welfare Association (APWA). (1986). *One child in four*. New York: APWA.

Auletta, K. (1982). *The underclass*. New York: Random House.

Bane, M. J., and Elwood, D. (1983). Slipping into and out of poverty: The dynamics of spells. Working Paper 1199. Washington, D. C.: National Bureau of Economic Research.

Barret, R., and Robinson, B. (1982). Teenage fathers: Neglected too long. *Social Work* 27: 484–88.

Becshner, G., and Friedman, A., eds. (1979). *Youth and drug abuse*. Lexington, Mass.: Lexington Books.

Brown, S. (1979). The health needs of adolescents. In *Healthy people: The surgeon general's report on mental health promotion and disease prevention*. Publication 79-55071A. Washington, D.C.: U.S. DHEW.

Brunswick, A. (1979). Black youths and drug-use behavior In *Youth and drug abuse*, edited by G. Beschner and A. Friedman. Lexington, Mass.: Lexington Books.

Brunswick, A., and Messeri, P. (1986). Drugs, lifestyle and health: A longitudinal study of urban black youth. *American Journal of Public Health* 76:52–57.

Carson, E. (1983). Possible approaches for social science research on the underclass. Paper presented at the Population Association of America, Pittsburgh.

CDF. See Children's Defense fund.

Census Bureau, See U.S. Bureau of the Census.

Centers for Disease Control (1986a). Acquired immunodeficiency syndrome (AIDS) among blacks and Hispanics—United States. *Morbidity and Mortality Weekly Report* 35: 656–58.

———.(1986b). Update—Acquired immunodeficiency syndrome—United States. *Morbidity and Mortality Weekly Report* 35:757–65.

Children's Defense Fund. (1985a). *A children's defense budget*. Washington, D.C.: CDF.

———.(1985b). *Black and white children in America*. Washington, D.C.: CDF.

———.(1986a). *A children's defense budget*. Washinton, D.C.: CDF.

———(1986b). *Building health programs for teenagers*. Washington, D.C.: CDF.

———.(1986c). *Declining earnings of young men: Their relation to poverty, teen pregnancy and family formation*. Washington, D.C.: CDF.

———.(1986d). *Welfare and teen pregnancy: What do we know? What do we do?* Washington, D.C.: CDF.

Chilman, C. (1983). *Adolescent sexuality in a changing American society*. New York: John Wiley & Sons.

Clark, K. B. (1965). *Dark ghetto: Dilemmas of social power*. New York: Harper & Row.

College Entrance Examination Board. (1985). *Equality and excellence:* The educational status of Black Americans. New York: The College Board.

Congressional Budget Office. (1982). *Improving youth employment prospects: Issues and options*. Washington, D.C.: Congress of the United States.

Deal, T. (1975). An organizational explanation of the failure of alternative secondary schools. *Educational Researcher* 4:10–16.

Department of Health and Human Services (DHHS). (1981). Statistical series, annual data, 1980, Ser. E-21, Washington, D.C.

Edmonds, R. (1979). Effective schools for the urban poor. *Educational Leadership* 37: 15–24.

Family Impact Seminar. (1979). *Teenage pregnancy and family impact: New perspectives on policy*. Washington, D.C.: George Washington University.

FBI (1986). Crime in the U.S., 1985 *Uniform Crime Reports*, Washington, D.C.

Furstenberg, F., Jr., Lincoln, R., and Menken, J. (1981). *Teenage sexuality, pregnancy and childbearing*. Philadelphia: University of Pennsylvania Press.

Gandossy, R., Williams, J., and Harwood, H. (1980). *Drugs and crime: A survey and analysis of the literature*. Washington, D.C.: U.S. Dept. of Justice.

Gibbs, J. T. (1984). Black adolescents and youth: An endangered species. *American Journal of Orthopsychiatry* 54: 6–21.

———.(1985). Young black males: An endangered species. Invited lecture at Annual Civil Rights Institute, NAACP Legal Defense and Educational Fund, Inc., New York (May).

———.(1986). Psychosocial correlates of sexual attitudes and behaviors in urban early adolescent females: Implications for intervention. *Journal of Social Work and Human Sexuality* 5: 81–97.

Glasgow, D. (1981). *The black underclass*. New York: Vintage Books.

Hofferth, S. L. (1985). Updating children's life course. *Journal of Marriage and the Family* 47: 93–115.

Holinger, P. (1979). Violent deaths among the young: Recent trends in suicide, homicide, and accidents. *American Journal of Psychiatry* 136: 1144–47.

Holinger, P., and Offer, D. (1982). Prediction of adolescent suicide: A population model. *American Journal of Psychiatry* 139: 302–07.

Huizinga, D., and Elliott, D. (1985). *Juvenile offenders' prevalence, offender incidence and arrest rates by race*. Boulder, Colo.: Institute of Behavioral Science.

Kasarda, J. (1985). Urban change and minority opportunities. In *The new urban reality*, edited by P. E. Peterson. Washington, D.C.: The Brookings Institute.

Krisberg, B., Schwartz, I., Fishman, G., Eiskovits, Z., and Guttman, E. (1986). *The incarceration of minority youth.* Minneapolis: H. H. Humphrey Institute of Public Affairs, University of Minnesota.

Ladner, J. (1971). *Tomorrow's tomorrow: The black woman.* Garden City, N.Y.: Doubleday.

Larson, T. (1986). Employment and unemployment of young black men. Unpublished paper, Berkeley, Calif.

Marshall, R. (1986). Economic change and education. Address at the Carnegie Forum on Education and the Economy, May 14–16 San Diego.

McAndrew, G. (1986). Turning dropouts into graduates. *Youth Policy* 9: 3–4.

McFate, K. (1987). Defining the underclass. *Focus* 15: 8–12 (Newsletter of the Joint Center for Political Studies, Washington, D.C.).

McLanahan, S. (1985). Family structure and the reproduction of poverty. *American Journal of Sociology* 90: 873–901.

Murray, C. (1984). *Losing ground: American social policy 1950–1980.* New York: Basic Books.

National Center for Health Statistics (NCHS). (1986). *Monthly vital statistics report.* Washington, D.C.

National Institute of Drug Abuse (NIDA). (1979). *National survey on drug abuse, 1979.* Washington, D.C.: NIDA.

New York Times, National Edition. (1987a). Big city mayors ask census change. July 24, p. 7.

———. (1987b). U.S. rejects pleas to adjust 1990 census for undercount. October 31, p. 1.

———. (1987c). Louisiana leads U.S. in a surge of executions. August 9, p. 7.

Omi, M., and Winant, H. (1986). *Racial formation in the United States: From the 1960s to the 1980s.* New York: Routledge & Kegan.

Ozawa, M. (1986). Nonwhites and the demographic imperative in social welfare spending. *Social Work* 31: 440–46.

Piliavin, I., and Briar, S. (1964). Police encounters with juveniles. *American Journal of Sociology* 70: 206–214.

Shapiro, C. (1980). Sexual learning: The short-changed adolescent male. *Social Work* 25: 489–93.

Snowdon, L. R. (editor). (1982). *Reaching the underserved: Mental health needs of neglected populations.* Beverly Hills, Calif.: Sage Publications.

Solomon, I. D. (1987). Blacks in the military. *The Crisis* 94: 15–26.

Stack, C. (1974). *All our kin.* New York: Harper & Row.

Sum, A., Harrington, P., and Goedicke, W. (1987). One-fifth of the nation's teenagers: Empolyment problems of poor youth in America, 1981–1985. *Youth and Society* 18: 195–237.

Thornton, W., James, J., and Doerner, W. (1982). *Delinquency and justice.* Glenview, Ill.: Scott, Foresman.

Tolmach, J. (1985). There ain't nobody on my side. *Journal of Child Clinical Psychology* 14: 214–19.

U.S. Bureau of the Census. (1981). School enrollment: Social and economic characteristics of students, 1980 (advance report). *Current population reports, ser.* P-20. Washington, D.C.

———. (1987). *Statistical abstract of the United States, 1987.* 107th ed. Washington, D.C.: U.S. Government Printing Office.

———. (1987). *Money income and poverty status of families and persons in the United States: 1986. Current population reports, ser.* P-60, 157. Washington, D.C.

———. (1986). *Report of the Secretary's Task Force on Black and Minority Health*, vol. V. Washington, D.C.

U.S. Dept. of Labor. (1987). *Youth 2000: Challenge and opportunity.* Washington, D.C.

Williams, J., ed. (1982). *The state of black America, 1982.* New York: National Urban League.

Wilson, W. J., and Aponte, R. (1985). Urban poverty. *Annual Review of Sociology* 11: 231–58.

Wilson, W. J., and Neckerman, K. M. (1984). Poverty and family structure: The widening gap between evidence and public policy issues. Paper prepared for conference on Poverty and Policy: Retrospect and Prospects, 6–8 December, Williamsburg, Virginia.

Maxine Baca Zinn
CHICANO MEN AND MASCULINITY

Only recently have social scientists begun to systematically study the male role. Although men and their behavior had been assiduously studied (Pleck and Brannon, 1978), masculinity as a specific topic had been ignored. The scholar's disregard of male gender in the general population stands in contrast to the preoccupation with masculinity that has long been exhibited in the literature on minority groups. The social science literature on Blacks and Chicanos specifically reveals a long-standing interest in masculinity. A common assumption is that gender roles among Blacks are less dichotomous than among Whites, and more dichotomous among Chicanos. Furthermore, these differences are assumed to be a function of the distinctive historical and cultural heritage of these groups. Gender segregation and stratification, long considered to be a definitive characteristic of Chicanos, is illustrated in Miller's descriptive summary of the literature:

> Sex roles are rigidly dichotomized with the male conforming to the dominant-aggressive archetype, and the female being the polar opposite—subordinate and passive. The father is the unquestioned patriarch—the family provider, protector and judge. His word is law and demands strict obedience. Presumably, he is perpetually obsessed with the need to prove his manhood, oftentimes through excessive drinking, fighting, and/or extramarital conquests (1979:217).

The social science image of the Chicano male is rooted in three interrelated propositions: (1) That a distinctive cultural heritage has created a rigid cult of masculinity, (2) That the masculinity cult generates distinctive familial and socialization patterns, and (3) That these distinctive patterns ill-equip Chicanos (both males and females) to adapt successfully to the demands of modern society.

The machismo concept constitutes a primary explanatory variable for both family structure and overall subordination. Mirandé critically outlines the reasoning in this interpretation:

> The macho male demands complete deference, respect and obedience not only from the wife but from the children as well. In fact, social scientists maintain that this rigid male-dominated family structure has negative consequences for the personality development of Mexican American children. It fails to engender achievement, independence, self-reliance or self worth—values which are highly esteemed in American society. . . . The authoritarian Mexican American family constellation then produces dependence and subordination and reinforces a present time orientation which impedes achievement (1977:749).

In spite of the widely held interpretation associated with male dominance among Chicanos, there is a growing body of literature which refutes past

M. Baca Zinn, "Chicano Family Research: Conceptual distortions and alternative directions" appeared in the *JES* 7:3. Reprinted from *The Journal of Ethnic Studies* 10:2.

images created by social scientists. My purpose is to examine empirical challenges to machismo, to explore theoretical developments in the general literature on gender, and to apply both of these to alternative directions for studying and understanding Chicano men and masculinity. My central theme is that while ethnic status may be associated with differences in masculinity, those differences can be explained by structural variables rather than by references to common cultural heritage.

THEORETICAL CHALLENGES TO CULTURAL INTERPRETATIONS: THE UNIVERSALITY OF MALE DOMINANCE

The generalization that culture is a major determinant of gender is widely accepted in the social sciences. In the common portrayal of Chicanos, exaggerated male behavior is assumed to stem from inadequate masculine identity.

> The social science literature views machismo as a compensation for feelings of inadequacy and worthlessness. This interpretation is rooted in the application of psychoanalytic concepts to explain both Mexican and Chicano gender roles. The widely accepted interpretation is that machismo is the male attempt to compensate for feelings of internalized inferiority by exaggerated masculinity. "At the same time that machismo is an expression of power, its origin is ironically linked to powerlessness and subordination." The common origins of inferiority and machismo are said to lie in the historical conquest of Mexico by Spain involving the exploitation of Indian women by Spanish men thus producing the hybrid Mexican people having an inferiority complex based on the mentality of a conquered people (Baca Zinn, 1980:20).

The assumption that male dominance among Chicanos is rooted in their history and embedded in their culture needs to be critically assessed against recent discussions concerning the universality of male dominance. Many anthropologists consider all known societies to be male dominant to a degree (Stockard and Johnson 1980:4). It has been argued that in all known societies male activities are more highly valued than female activities, and that this can be explained in terms of the division of labor between domestic and public spheres of society (Rosaldo, 1973). Women's child-bearing abilities limit their participation in public sphere activities and allow men the freedom to participate in and control the public sphere. Thus in the power relations between the sexes, men have been found to be dominant over women and to control economic resources (Spence 1978:4).

While differing explanations of the cause of male dominance have been advanced, recent literature places emphasis on networks of social relations between men and women and the status structures within which their interactions occur. This emphasis is crucial because it alerts us to the importance of structural variables in understanding sex stratification. Furthermore, it casts doubt on interpretations which treat culture (the systems of shared beliefs and orientations unique to groups) as the cause of male dominance. If male dominance is universal, then it cannot be reduced to the culture of a particular category of people.

CHALLENGES TO MACHISMO

Early challenges to machismo emerged in the protest literature of the 1960s and 1970s and have continued unabated. Challenges are theoretical, empirical, and impressionistic. Montiel, in the first critique of machismo, set the stage for later refutations by charging that psychoanalytic constructs resulted in indiscriminate use of machismo, and that this made findings and interpretations highly suspect (1970). Baca Zinn (1975:25) argued that viewing machismo as a compensation for inferiority (whether its ultimate cause is seen as external or internal to the oppressed), in effect blames Chicanos for their own subordination. Sosa Riddell proposed that the machismo myth is exploited by an oppressive society which encourages a defensive stance on the part of Chicano men (1974). Delgado (1974:6) in similar fashion, wrote that stereotyping acts which have nothing to do with machismo and labeling them as such was a form of societal control.

Recent social science literature on Chicanos has witnessed an ongoing series of empirical challenges to the notion that machismo is the norm in marital relationships (Grebler, Moore and Guzman, 1970; Hawkes and Taylor, 1975; Ybarra, 1977; Cromwell and Cromwell, 1978; Cromwell and Ruiz, 1979; Baca Zinn, 1980a). The evidence presented in this research suggests that in the realm of marital decision making, egalitarianism is far more prevalent than macho dominance.

Cromwell and Ruiz find that the macho characterization prevalent in the social science literature is "very compatible with the social deficit model of Hispanic life and culture" (1979:355). Their re-analysis of four major studies on marital decision making (Cromwell, Corrales and Torsellio, 1973; Delchereo, 1969; Hawkes and Taylor, 1975 and Cromwell and Cromwell, 1978) concludes that "the studies suggest that while wives make the fewest unilateral decisions and husbands make more, joint decisions are by far the most common in these samples . . ." (1979:370).

Other studies also confirm the existence of joint decision making in Chicano families and furthermore they provide insights as to factors associated with joint decision making, most importantly that of wives' employment. For example, Ybarra's survey of 100 married Chicano couples in Fresno, California found a range of conjugal role patterns with the majority of married Chicano couples sharing decision making. Baca Zinn (1980a) examined the effects of wives' employment outside of the home and level of education through interviews and participation in an urban New Mexico setting. The study revealed differences in marital roles and marital power between families with employed wives and nonemployed wives. "In all families where women were not employed, tasks and decision making were typically sex segregated. However, in families with employed wives, tasks and decision making were shared" (1980a:51).

Studies of the father role in Chicano families also called into question the authoritative unfeeling masculinized male figure (Mejia, 1976; Luzod and Arce, 1979). These studies are broadly supportive of the marital role research which points to a more democratic egalitarian approach to family roles. Luzod and Arce conclude:

> It is not our contention to say that no sex role differences occur within Chicano families, but rather demonstrate the level of importance which

both the father and mother give to respective duties as parents as well as the common hopes and desires they appear to share equally for their progeny than was commonly thought. It therefore appears erroneous to focus only on maternal influences in the Chicano family since Chicano fathers are seen as being important to the children and moreover may provide significant positive influences on the development of their children (1979:19).

Recent empirical refutations of super-masculinity in Chicano families have provided the basis of discussions of the Chicano male role (Valdez, 1980; Mirandé, 1979, 1981). While these works bring together in clear fashion impressionistic and empirical refutations of machismo, they should be considered critical reviews rather than conceptual refutations. In an important essay entitled, "Machismo: Rucas, Chingasos, y Chingaderas" (1981), Mirandé critically assesses the stereotypic components of machismo, yet he asserts that it also has authentic components having to do with the resistance of oppression. While this is a significant advance, it requires conceptual focus and analysis.

UNANSWERED QUESTIONS, UNRESOLVED ISSUES AND UNRECOGNIZED PROBLEMS

The works discussed above provide a refutation of the simplistic, one-dimensional model of Chicano masculinity. As such they constitute important contributions to the literature. My own argument does not contradict the general conclusion that machismo is a stereotype, but attempts to expand it by posing some theoretical considerations.

In their eagerness to dispute machismo and the negative characteristics associated with the trait, critics have tended to neglect the phenomenon of male dominance at societal, institutional, and interpersonal levels. While the cultural stereotype of machismo has been in need of critical analysis, male dominance does exist among Chicanos. Assertions such as the following require careful examination:

> There is sufficient evidence to seriously question the traditional male dominant view (Mirandé, 1979:47).

Although male dominance may not typify marital decision making in Chicano families, it should not be assumed that it is nonexistent either in families or in other realms of interaction and organization.

Research by Ybarra (1977) and Baca Zinn (1980) found both egalitarian and male dominant patterns of interaction in Chicano families. They found these patterns to be associated with distinct social conditions of families, most notably wives' employment. The finding that male dominance can be present in some families but not in others, depending on specific social characteristics of family members, is common in family research.

The important point is that we need to know far more than we do about which social conditions affecting Chicanos are associated with egalitarianism and male dominance at both micro and macro levels of organization. Placing the question within this framework should provide significant insights by enlarging the inquiry beyond that of the culture stereotype of machismo. It is necessary to guard against measuring and evaluating empirical reality against this stereotype. The dangers of using a negative ideal as a normative guide are raised by Eichler (1980). In a provocative work, she raises the possibility that the literature challenging gender stereotypes, while explicitly attempting to overcome past limitations of the gender roles research may operate to reinforce the stereotype. Thus, it could be argued that energy expended in refuting machismo may devote too much attention to the concept, and overlook whole areas of inquiry. We have tended to assume that ethnic groups vary in the demands imposed on men and women. "Ethnic differences in sex roles have been discussed by large numbers of social scientists" (Romer and Cherry, 1980:246). However, these discussions have treated differences as cultural or subcultural in nature. Davidson and Gordon are critical of subcultural explanations of differences in gender roles because they "fail to investigate the larger political and economic situations that affect groups and individuals. They also fail to explain how definition of the roles of women and men, as well as those associated with ethnicity, vary over time and from place to place" (1979:124).

1. What specific social conditions are associated with variation in general roles among Chicanos?
2. If there are ethnic differences in gender roles, to what extent are these a function of shared beliefs and orientations (culture) and to what extent are they a function of men's and women's place in the network of social relationships (structure)?
3. To what extent are gender roles among Chicanos more segregated and male dominated than among other social groups?
4. How does ethnicity contribute to the subjective meaning of masculinity (and femininity)?

STRUCTURAL INTERPRETATIONS OF GENDER ROLES

There is a good deal of theoretical support for the contention that masculine roles and masculine identity may be shaped by a wide range of variables having less to do with culture than with common structural position. Chafetz calls into question the cultural stereotype of machismo by proposing that it is a socioeconomic characteristic:

> . . . more than most other Americans, the various Spanish speaking groups in this country (Mexican American, Puerto Rican, Cuban), . . . stress dominance, aggressiveness, physical prowess and other stereotypical masculine traits. Indeed the masculine sex role for this group is generally described by reference to the highly stereotyped notion of machismo. In fact, a strong emphasis on masculine aggressiveness and dominance may be characteristic of most groups in the lower ranges of the socioeconomic ladder (1979:54).

Without discounting the possibility that cultural differences in male roles exist, it makes good conceptual sense to explain these differences in terms of sociostructural factors. Davidson and Gordon suggest that the following social conditions affect the development of gender roles in ethnic groups: (1) the position of the group in the stratification system, (2) the existence of an ethnic community, (3) the degree of self identification with the minority group (1978:120). Romer and Cherry more specifically propose that ethnic or subcultural sex role definitions can be viewed as functions of the specific and multiple role demands made on a given subgroup such as skilled or unskilled workers, consumers, etc., and the cultural prism through which these role expectations are viewed (1980:246). Both of these discussions underscore the importance of the societal placement of ethnics in the shaping of gender roles. This line of reasoning should not be confused with "culture of poverty" models which posit distinctive subcultural traits among the lower class. However, it can be argued that class position affects both normative and behavioral dimensions of masculinity.

The assumption that Chicanos are more strongly sex typed in terms of masculine identity is called into question by a recent study. Senour and Warren conducted research to question whether ethnic identity is related to masculine and feminine sex role orientation among Blacks, Anglos and Chicanos. While significant sex differences were found in all categories, Senour and Warren concluded that Mexican American males did not emerge as super masculine in comparison to Black and Anglo males (1976:2).

There is some support for this interpretation. In roles dealing with masculinity among Black males, Parker and Kleiner (1977) and Staples (1978) find that role performance must be seen in light of the structurally generated inequality in employment, housing, and general social conditions. Staples writes:

> . . . men often define their masculinity in terms of the ability to impregnate women and to reproduce prolifically children who are extensions of themselves, especially sons. For many lower income black males there is an inseparable link between their self image as men and their ability to have sexual relations with women and the subsequent birth of children from those sexual acts. At the root of this virility cult is the lack of role fulfillment available to men of the underclass. The class factor is most evident here, if we note that middle class black males sire fewer children than any other group in this society (1978:178).

What is most enlightening about Staples' discussion of masculinity is that it treats male behavior and male identity not as a subcultural phenomenon, but as a consequence of social structural factors associated with race and class.

A thoughtful discussion of inequality, race, and gender is provided by Lewis (1977). Her analysis enlarges upon Rosaldo's model of the domestic public split as the source of female subordination and male dominance discussed earlier. It has pertinent structural considerations. Lewis acknowledges the notion of a structural opposition between the domestic and public spheres which offers useful insights in understanding differential participation and evaluation of men and women. Nevertheless, she argues that its applicability to racial minority men and women may be questionable since historically Black men (like Black women) have been excluded from participation in public sphere institutions. Lewis asserts:

> What the black experience suggests is that differential participation in the public sphere is a symptom rather than a cause of structural inequal-

ity. While inequality is manifested in the exclusion of a group from public life, it is actually generated in the groups' unequal access to power and resources in a hierarchically arranged social order. Relationships of dominance and subordination, therefore, emerge from a basic structural opposition between groups which is reflected in exclusion of the subordinate group from public life (1977:342).

Lewis then argues that among racially oppressed groups, it is important to distinguish between the public life of the dominant and the dominated societies. Using this framework we recognize a range of male participation from token admittance to the public life of the dominant group to its attempts to destroy the public life within a dominated society. She points to the fact that Mexican American men have played strong public roles in their own dominated society, and as Mexican Americans have become more assimilated to the dominating society, sex roles have become less hierarchical. The significant feature of this argument has to do with the way in which attention is brought to shifts in power relationships between the dominant society and racial minorities, and how these shifts effect changes in relationships between the sexes. Lewis' analysis makes it abundantly clear that minority males' exclusion from the public sphere requires further attention.

CHICANO MASCULINITY AS A RESPONSE TO STRATIFICATION AND EXCLUSION

There are no works, either theoretical or empirical, specifically devoted to the impact of structural exclusion on male roles and male identity. However, there are suggestions that the emphasis on masculinity might stem from the fact that alternative roles and identity sources are systematically blocked from men in certain social categories. Lillian Rubin, for example, described the martial role egalitarianism of middle class professional husbands as opposed to the more traditional authoritarian role of working class husbands in the following manner:

> . . . the professional male is more secure, has more status and prestige than the working class man, factors which enable him to assume a less overtly authoritarian role within the family. There are, after all, other places, other situations where his authority and power are tested and accorded legitimacy. At the same time, the demands of his work role for a satellite wife require that he risk the consequences of a more egalitarian family ideology. In contrast, for the working class men, there are few such rewards in the world outside the home. The family is usually the only place where he can exercise power, demand obedience to his authority. Since his work role makes no demands for wifely participation, he is under fewer and less immediate external pressures to accept the egalitarian ideology (Rubin, 1976:99).

Of course, Rubin is contrasting behaviors of men in different social classes, but the same line of thinking is paralleled in Ramos' speculation that for some Chicanos what has been called "machismo" may be a "way of feeling capable in a world that makes it difficult for Chicanos to demonstrate their capabilities" (Ramos, 1979:61).

We must understand that while maleness is highly valued in our society, it interacts with other categorical distinctions in both manifestation and meaning. As Stoll (1974:124) presents this idea, our society is structured to reward some categories in preference to others (e.g., men over women) but the system is not perfectly rational. First the rewards are scarce, second, other categories such as race, ethnicity and other statuses are included in the formula. Furthermore, the interaction of different categories with masculinity contributes to multiple societal meanings of masculinity, so that "one can never be sure this aspect of one's self will not be called into dispute. One is left having to account for oneself, thus to be on the defensive" (Stoll, 1974:124). It is in light of the societal importance attributed to masculinity that we must assess Stoll's contention that "gender identity is a more profound personal concern for the male in our society than it is for women, because women can take it for granted that they are female" (Stoll, 1974:105). This speculation may have implications for Chicanos as well. Perhaps it will be found that ethnic differences in the salience of gender are not only one of degree but that their relative significance has different meanings. In other words, gender may not be a problematic identifier for women if they can take if for granted, though it may be primary because many still participate in society through their gender roles. On the other hand, men in certain social categories have had more roles and sources of identity open to them. However, this has not been the case for Chicanos or other men of color. Perhaps manhood takes on greater importance for those who do not have access to socially valued roles. Being male is one sure way to acquire status when other roles are systematically denied by the workings of society. This suggests that an emphasis on masculinity is not due to a collective internalized inferiority, rooted in a subcultural orientation. To be "hombre" may be a reflection of both ethnic and gender components and may take on greater significance when other roles and sources of masculine identity are structurally blocked. Chicanos have been excluded from participation in the dominant society's political–economic system. Therefore, they have been denied resources and the accompanying authority accorded men in other social categories. My point that gender may take on a unique and greater significance for men of color is not to justify traditional masculinity, but to point to the need for understanding societal conditions that might contribute to the meaning of gender among different social categories. It may be worthwhile to consider some expressions of masculinity as attempts to gain some measure of control in a society that categorically denies or grants people control over significant realms of their lives.

Turner makes this point about the male posturing of Black men: "Boastful, or meek, these performances are attempts by black men to actualize control in some situation" (Turner, 1977:128). Much the same point is made in discussions of Chicanos. The possibility has been raised that certain aggressive behaviors on the part of Chicano men was "a calculated response to hostility, exclusion, and racial domination," and a "conscious rejection of the dominant society's definition of Mexicans as passive, lazy, and indifferent" (Baca Zinn, 1975:23). Mirandé (1981:35) also treats machismo as an adaptive characteristic, associated with visible and manifest resistance of Chicano men to racial oppression. To view Chicano male behavior in this light is not to disregard possible maladaptive consequences of overcompensatory masculinity, but rather to recast masculinity in terms of responses to structural conditions.

Differences in normative and behavioral dimensions of masculinity would be well worth exploring. Though numerous recent studies have challenged macho male dominance in the realm of family decision making, there is also evidence that patriarchal *ideology* can be manifested even in Chicano families where decision making is not male dominant. Baca Zinn's findings of *both* male dominant and egalitarian families revealed also that the ideology of patriarchy was expressed in all families studied:

> Patriarchal ideology was expressed in statements referring to the father as the "head" of the family, as the "boss," as the one "in charge." Informants continually expressed their beliefs that it "should be so." Findings confirmed that while male dominance was a cultural ideal, employed wives openly challenged that dominance on a behavioral level (1979:15).

It is possible that such an ideology is somehow associated with family solidarity. This insight is derived from Michel's analysis of family values (cited in Goode, 1963:57). Drawing on cross cultural studies, she reports:

> . . . the concept of the strength or solidarity of the family is viewed as being identical with the father . . . the unity of the family is identified with the prerogatives of the father.

If this is the case, it is reasonable to suggest that the father's authority is strongly upheld because family solidarity is important in a society that excludes and subordinates Chicanos. The tenacity of patriarchy may be more than a holdover from past tradition. It may also represent a contemporary cultural adaptation to the minority condition of structural discrimination.

CONCLUSION

The assumption that male dominance among Chicanos is exclusively a cultural phenomenon is contradicted by much evidence. While many of the concerns raised in this paper are speculative in nature, they are nevertheless informed by current conceptualization in relevant bodies of literature. They raise the important point that we need further understanding of larger societal conditions in which masculinity is embedded and expressed. This forces us to recognize the disturbing relationship between the stratification axes of race, class and sex. To the extent that systems of social inequality limit men's access to societally valued resources, they also contribute to sexual stratification. Men in some social categories will continue to draw upon and accentuate their masculinity as a socially valued resource. This in turn poses serious threats to sexual equality. We are compelled to move the study of masculinity beyond narrow confines of subcultural roles, and to make the necessary theoretical and empirical connections between the contingencies of sex and gender and the social order.

REFERENCES

Baca Zinn, Maxine.
1975 "Political Familism: Toward Sex Role Equality in Chicano Families," *International Journal of Chicano Studies Research*. 6:13–26.

1980a "Employment and Education of Mexican American Women: The Interplay of Modernity and Ethnicity in Eight Families." *Harvard Educational Review* 50:47–62.
1980b "Gender and Ethnic Identity Among Chicanos." *Frontiers:* V(2)18–24.
    Chafetz, Janet Saltzman.
1974 *Masculine/Feminine or Human.* E. E. Ithica, Ill.: Peacock Publishers, Inc.
    Cromwell, Vicky L. and Ronald E. Cromwell.
1978 "Perceived Dominance in Decision-Making and Conflict Resolution Among Anglo, Black and Chicano Couples." *Journal of Marriage and the Family.* 40(Nov):749–759.
    Cromwell, Ronald E. and Rene E. Ruiz.
1979 "The Myth of Macho Dominance in Decision Making Within Mexican and Chicano Families." *Hispanic Journal of Behavioral Sciences.* 1:355–373.
    Davidson, Laurie and Laura Kramer Gordon
1979 "The Sociology of Gender." Rand McNally College Publishing Co.
    Delgado, Abelardo.
1974 "Machismo." *La Luz.* (Dec.):6.
    Eichler, Margrit.
1980 *The Double Standard: A Feminist Critique of Feminist Social Science.* St. Martin's Press.
    Grebler, Leo, Joan W. Moore and Ralph C. Guzman.
1970 *The Mexican American People: The Nation's Second Largest Minority.* The Free Press.
    Hawkes, Glenn R. and Minna Taylor.
1975 "Power Structure in Mexican and Mexican-American Farm Labor Families." *Journal of Marriage and the Family.* 37:807–811.
    Hyde, Janet Shibley and B. G. Rosenberg.
1976 Half the Human Experience. *The Psychology of Women.* D. C. Heath and Company.
    Lewis, Diane K.
1977 "A Response to Inequality: Black Women, Racism, and Sexism." *SIGNS: Journal of Women in Culture and Society.* 3:339–361.
    Luzod, Jimmy A. and Carlos H. Arce.
1979 "An Exploration of the Father Role in the Chicano Family." Paper presented at the National Symposium on the Mexican American Child. Santa Barbara, California.
    Mejia, Daniel P.
1976 Cross-Ethnic Father Role: Perceptions of Middle Class Anglo American Parents, Doctoral Dissertation, University of California, Irvine.
    Miller, Michael V.
1975 "Variations in Mexican-American Family Life: A Review Synthesis." Paper presented at Rural Sociological Society, San Francisco, California.
    Mirandé, Alfredo.
1977 "The Chicano Family: A Reanalysis of Conflicting Views." *Journal of Marriage and the Family.* 39:747–756.
1979 "A Reinterpretation of Male Dominance in the Chicano Family." *Family Coordinator.* 28(4), 473–497.
1981 "Machismo: Rucas, Chingasos, y Chingaderas." *De Colores,* Forthcoming.
    Montiel, Miguel.
1970 "The Social Science Myth of the Mexican American Family." *El Grito.* 3:56–63.
    Parker, Seymour and Robert J. Kleiner.
1977 "Social and Psychological Dimensions of the Family Role Performance of the Negro Male." Pp. 102–117 in Doris Y. Wilkinson and Ronald L. Taylor (editors), *The Black Male in America.* Nelson Hall.
    Pleck, Joseph H. and Robert Brannon.
1978 "Male Roles and the Male Experience: Introduction." *Journal of Social Issues.* 34:1–4.
    Ramos, Reyes.
1979 "The Mexican American: Am I Who They Say I Am?" Pp. 49–66 in Arnulfo D. Trejo (editor), *The Chicanos as We See Ourselves.* The University of Arizona Press.
    Riddell, Adaljiza Sosa.
1974 "Chicanas and El Movimiento." *Aztlan.* 5(1 and 2):155–165.
    Romer, Nancy and Debra Cherry.

1980 "Ethnic and Social Class Differences in Children's Sex-Role Concepts." *Sex Roles.* 6:245–263.

Rosaldo, Michelle and Louise Lamphere.
1974 *Woman, Culture, and Society.* Stanford: Stanford University Press.

Rubin, Lillian.
1976 *Worlds of Pain.* Basic Books.

Senour, Maria Neito and Lynda Warren.
1976 "Sex and Ethnic Differences in Masculinity, Femininity and Anthropology." Paper presented at the meeting of the Western Psychological Association, Los Angeles, California.

Spence, Janet T. and Robert L. Helmreich.
1978 *Masculinity and Femininity: The Psychological Dimensions, Correlates and Antecedents.* University of Austin Press.

Staples, Robert.
1978 "Masculinity and Race: The Dual Dilemma of Black Men." *Journal of Social Issues.* 34:169–183.

Stockard, Jean and Miriam M. Johnson.
1980 *Sex Roles.* Englewood Cliffs, New Jersey: Prentice-Hall.

Stoll, Clarice Stasz.
1974 *Male and Female: Socialization, Social Roles, and Social Structure.* William C. Brown Publishers.

Taylor, Ronald L.
1977 "Socialization to the Black Male Role." Pp. 1–6 in Doris Y. Wilkinson and Ronald L. Taylor (editors), *The Black Male in America.* Nelson Hall.

Turner, William H.
1977 "Myths and Stereotypes: The African Man in America." Pp. 122–144 in Doris Y. Wilkinson and Ronald L. Taylor (editors), *The Black Male in America.* Nelson Hall.

Valdez, Ramiro.
1980 "The Mexican American Male: A Brief Review of the Literature." *Newsletter of the Mental Health Research Project*, I.D.R.A. San Antonio: 4–5.

Ybarra-Soriano, Lea.
1977 *Conjugal Role Relationships in the Chicano Family.* Ph.D. diss. University of California at Berkeley.

Michael S. Kimmel

JUDAISM, MASCULINITY AND FEMINISM

In the late 1960s, I organized and participated in several large demonstrations against the war in Vietnam. Early on—it must have been 1967 or so—over 10,000 of us were marching down Fifth Avenue in New York urging the withdrawal of all U.S. troops. As we approached one corner, I noticed a small but vocal group of counter-demonstrators, waving American flags and shouting patriotic slogans. "Go back to Russia!" one yelled. Never being particularly shy, I tried to engage him. "It's my duty as an American to oppose

Reprinted from *Changing Men*, Summer/Fall 1987.

This essay was originally prepared as a lecture on "Changing Roles for the American Man" at the 92nd Street Y in November, 1983. I am grateful to Bob Brannon and Harry Brod for comments and criticisms of an earlier draft.

policies I disagree with. This is patriotism!" I answered. "Drop dead, you commie Jew fag!" was his reply.

Although I tried not to show it, I was shaken by his accusation, perplexed and disturbed by the glib association of communism, Judaism, and homosexuality. "Only one out of three," I can say to myself now, "is not especially perceptive." But yet something disturbing remains about that linking of political, religious, and sexual orientations. What links them, I think, is a popular perception that each is not quite a man, that each is less than a man. And while recent developments may belie this simplistic formulation, there is, I believe, a kernel of truth to the epithet, a small piece I want to claim, not as vicious smear, but proudly. I believe that my Judaism did directly contribute to my activism against that terrible war, just as it currently provides the foundation for my participation in the struggle against sexism.

What I want to explore here are some of the ways in which my Jewishness has contributed to becoming an anti-sexist man, working to make this world a safe environment for women (and men) to fully express their humanness. Let me be clear that I speak from a cultural heritage of Eastern European Jewry, transmuted by three generations of life in the United States. I speak of the culture of Judaism's effect on me as an American Jew, not from either doctrinal considerations—we all know the theological contradictions of a biblical reverence for women, and prayers that thank God for not being born one—nor from an analysis of the politics of nation states. My perspective says nothing of Middle-Eastern machismo; I speak of Jewish culture in the diaspora, not of Israeli politics.

The historical experience of Jews has three elements that I believe have contributed to this participation in feminist politics. First, historically, the Jew is an *outsider*. Wherever the Jew has gone, he or she has been outside the seat of power, excluded from privilege. The Jew is the symbolic "other," not unlike the symbolic "otherness" of women, gays, racial and ethnic minorities, the elderly and the physically challenged. To be marginalized allows one to see the center more clearly than those who are in it, and presents grounds for alliances among marginal groups.

But the American Jew, the former immigrant, is "other" in another way, one common to many ethnic immigrants to the United States. Jewish culture is, after all, seen as an ethnic culture, which allows it to be more oppressive and emotionally rich than the bland norm. Like other ethnic subgroups, Jews have been characterized as emotional, nurturing, caring. Jewish men hug and kiss, cry and laugh. A little too much. A little too loudly. Like ethnics.

Historically, the Jewish man has been seen as less than masculine, often as a direct outgrowth of this emotional "respond-ability." The historical consequences of centuries of laws against Jews, of anti-Semitic oppression, are a cultural identity and even a self-perception as "less than men," who are too weak, too fragile, too frightened to care for our own. The cruel irony of ethnic oppression is that our rich heritage is stolen from us, and then we are blamed for having no rich heritage. In this, again, the Jew shares this self-perception with other oppressed groups who, rendered virtually helpless by an infantilizing oppression, are further victimized by the accusation that they are, in fact, infants and require the beneficence of the oppressor. One example of this cultural self-hatred can be found in the comments of Freud's colleague and friend Weininger (a Jew) who argued that "the Jew is saturated with femininity. The most feminine Aryan is more masculine than the most manly Jew. The Jew lacks the good breeding that is based upon respect for one's own individuality as well as the individuality of others."

But, again, Jews are also "less than men" for a specific reason as well. The traditional emphasis on literacy in Jewish culture contributes in a very special way. In my family, at least, to be learned, literate, a rabbi, was the highest aspiration one could possibly have. In a culture characterized by love of learning, literacy may be a mark of dignity. But currently in the United States literacy is a cultural liability. Americans contrast egghead intellectuals, divorced from the real world, with men of action—instinctual, passionate, fierce, and masculine. Senator Albert Beveridge of Indiana counseled in his 1906 volume *Young Man and the World* (a turn of the century version of *Real Men Don't Eat Quiche*) to "avoid books, in fact, avoid all artificial learning, for the forefathers put America on the right path by learning from completely natural experience." Family, church and synagogue, and schoolroom were cast as the enervating domains of women, sapping masculine vigor.

Now don't get me wrong. The Jewish emphasis on literacy, on mind over body, does not exempt Jewish men from sexist behavior. Far from it. While many Jewish men avoid the Scylla of a boisterous and physically harassing misogyny, we can often dash ourselves against the Charybdis of a male intellectual intimidation of others. "Men with the properly sanctioned educational credentials in our society," writes Harry Brod, "are trained to impose our opinions on others, whether asked for or not, with an air of supreme self-confidence and aggressive self-assurance." It's as if the world were only waiting for our word. In fact, Brod notes, "many of us have developed mannerisms that function to intimidate those customarily denied access to higher educational institutions, especially women."[1] And yet, despite this, the Jewish emphasis on literacy has branded us, in the eyes of the world, less than "real" men.

Finally, the historical experience of Jews centers around, hinges upon our sense of morality, our ethical imperatives. The preservation of a moral code, the commandment to live ethically, is the primary responsibility of each Jew, male or female. Here, let me relate another personal story. Like many other Jews, I grew up with the words "Never Again" ringing in my ears, branded indelibly in my consciousness. For me they implied a certain moral responsibility to bear witness, to remember—to place my body, visibly, on the side of justice. This moral responsibility inspired my participation in the anti-war movement, and my active resistance of the draft *as a Jew*. I remember family dinners in front of the CBS Evening News, watching Walter Cronkite recite the daily tragedy of the war in Vietnam. "Never again," I said to myself, crying myself to sleep after watching napalm fall on Vietnamese villagers. Isn't this the brutal terror we have sworn ourselves to preventing when we utter those two words? When I allowed myself to feel the pain of those people, there was no longer a choice; there was, instead, a moral imperative to speak out, to attempt to end that war as quickly as possible.

In the past few years, I've become aware of another war. I met and spoke with women who had been raped, raped by their lovers, husbands, and fathers, women who had been beaten by those husbands and lovers. Some were even Jewish women. All those same words—Never Again—flashed across my mind like a neon meteor lighting up the darkened consciousness.

Hearing that pain and that anger prompted the same moral imperative. We Jews say "Never Again" to the systematic horror of the Holocaust, to the cruel war against the Vietnamese, to Central American death squads. And we must say it against this war waged against women in our society, against rape and battery.

So in a sense, I see my Judaism as reminding me every day of that moral responsibility, the *special* ethical imperative that my life, as a Jew, gives to me. Our history indicates how we have been excluded from power, but also, as men, we have been privileged by another power. Our Judaism impels us to stand against any power that is illegitimately constituted because we know only too well the consequences of that power. Our ethical vision demands equality and justice, and its achievement is our historical mission.

NOTE

1 Harry Brod, "Justice and a Male Feminist" in *The Jewish Newspaper* (Los Angeles) June 6, 1985, p. 6.

Seymour Kleinberg

THE NEW MASCULINITY OF GAY MEN, AND BEYOND

WHERE HAVE ALL THE SISSIES GONE: A VIEW FROM THE 1970S

One week after Labor Day 1977, I made a trip to the Anvil Bar, a gay club in New York City. For a long time I had wanted to know whether the legends of debauchery one heard with some skepticism were accurate. No one I knew was a member, and I had been told by those who claimed to be informed that I was not a likely type to crash successfully. I presumed they meant that my only leather jacket, tailored like a blazer, would not pass muster. Then a close friend became enamored of a go-go boy who danced there, joined the Anvil, and took me along to meet Daniel.

The bar nearly lived up to its fame. The boys do dance continually on top of the four-sided bar, they do strip naked, not counting construction shoes or cock rings. There is a back room where no-nonsense, hard-core porno films silently and continually flicker, shown by a mesmerized projectionist wearily perched on the ledge of the back wall. A small pitch-dark cubicle called the fuck room opens off the rear wall. In the middle of the front-room bar is

"The New Masculinity of Gay men," written in 1978, was originally published as a chapter of Kleinberg's book *Alienated Affections* (New York: St. Martin's Press, 1980). "Life After Death: A View From the Late 1980s" is excerpted from an article in the *New Republic*, 11 and 18 Aug., 1986.

a stage raised five feet where fist-fucking demonstrations used to be held at 3 a.m. if the crowd was enthusiastic, but those spontaneous shows were stopped when they began to draw tourists from the uptown discos. Now it is used by the dancers, who take turns exhibiting their specialities in the lime-light. The boys range from extraordinary to middling, from high-schoolers to forty-year-olds, from professionals (everything) to amateurs who move awk-wardly but who are graceful and stunning when they don't move at all. There are types for every taste and some for none. Hispanic and black, WASP and Italian, the boys dance three hours of a six-hour stint for $25 a night, three or four times a week. There are always new faces, and the management is liberal about letting anyone with a good body try out. Usually, there is one dancer who has had some ballet training and is naive enough to make that clear; he is invariably the least favored by the clientele.

My friend's Daniel is unusual. He is one of the few boys who can use the trapeze bars bolted to the ceiling with real expertise. Without breaking the rhythm of his dance, he leaps for a trapeze and spends four or five minutes on or swinging from one bar to another in the most daring manner. When he alights, it is with a sure flip back onto the bar, where he continues to dance with an unbroken stride. Daniel has never fallen, as some of the boys have (a broken nose or a fractured arm is not unheard of), nor has he crashed into a customer since he holds his drugs well.

His other specialty is his ability to grab with his buttocks the folded one-dollar or five-dollar tips the men at the bar hold between their teeth, a variation on the skill of the Cotton Club girls of Harlem in the twenties and thirties. His perfect behind descends in time to the music over the customer's uplifted face, and there is a round of applause when the money disappears into those constricted rosy cheeks.

Like most of the clientele, Daniel looks like a college athlete or construction worker, two favored images these recent seasons. Clothed, he wears the uniform of the moment: cheap plaid flannel shirts and jeans, or if it is really warm just overalls, and boots or construction worker's shoes no matter what the weather is. With the first signs of frost, boots and heavy leather bomber jackets are *de rigueur*.

Daniel is also typical of one type of club client in that he is a masochist, a "slave" who sleeps with other men with the permission of his master (who instructs him to charge a hefty fee). While Daniel's masochism has taken a pecuniary turn, he is not really a whore, for he is indifferent to money, keeping only what he needs for his uppers and poppers, his grass and coke. He dances frenetically four nights a week and does what he is told because he finds that exciting. There is little that he has not experienced sexually, and at twenty-two, his tastes are now as perverse as any possibilities Western civili-zation has devised.

To look at him, one would hardly suspect that this Irish kid from Queens with his thatch of reddish hair, cowlick and all, this sweet-faced boy built like a swimmer in his blue-collar uniform, lives a life more sexually extreme than anything described by the Marquis de Sade. When he discusses his life, it appears to be an endless dirty movie, but the anecdotes tend to leave his listeners in a moral vacuum. While it is possible to become erotically excited hearing his adventures, it is difficult to judge them without feeling prudish. Conventional moral standards are tangential, psychological ones almost as irrelevant. One is not really shocked; rather, one feels adrift, puzzled, perhaps bemused. Most of all, this nice boy seems very remote.

The values of his generation, acted out as theater of the absurd, are even more histrionic in Daniel's life. Just as one does not expect experimental theater or avant-garde art to live up to the standards of naturalism, one does not try to understand Daniel's life from the lessons of one's own experience: the collective sanity of the past is momentarily dumb.

What one struggled to learn and call "adult" as the final approbation now looks somewhat priggish. If one wanted to use such standards, why go to the Anvil at all? But once one *is* there or at the Mine Shaft or any of half a dozen bars just like them, what does one use to understand this spectacle of men? Some, like me, are clearly audience at a drama where only the actors understand the play. Intuition is not trustworthy, and easy judgments make one feel like a tourist. But whether or not one wishes to refrain from judgment, one thing is clear, if not glaring. The universal stance is a studied masculinity. There are no limp wrists, no giggles, no indiscreet hips swiveling. Walk, talk, voice, costume, grooming are just right: this is macho country. It is a rigorous place where one destroys oneself in drugs and sexual humiliation.

The same impulses are evident in other scenes. Fire Island Pines is as besotted and extreme as the leather and Levis world, and often they overlap, but the Pines is playful. Like its shabbier neighbor, Cherry Grove, the Pines enjoys the long legacy of camp. It loves to dictate next year's chic to café society, for novelty, flair, and sophistication are as paramount in this scene as they are in the world of women's fashion. For a time, the place seemed to veer toward egalitarianism: only youthful beauty was required if one were not rich. But with inflation, the freeloading beauty has to be spectacular indeed. The dance halls of the Pines and the Grove, like the waterfront bars, are filled with handsome men posing in careful costumes, and no matter how elegant or expensive, they are all butch.

As a matter of fact, young gay men seem to have abjured effeminacy with universal success. Muscular bodies laboriously cultivated all year round are standard; youthful athletic agility is everyone's style. The volleyball game on the beach is no longer a camp classic; now it takes itself as seriously as the San Francisco gay softball team. Hardness is in.

But talk to these men, sleep with them, befriend them, and the problems are the old familiar ones: misery when they are in love, loneliness when they are not, frustration and ambitiousness at work, and a monumental self-centeredness that exacerbates the rest. These have been the archetypes of unhappiness in homosexual America for as long as I can remember.

What is different from anything else I remember, however, is the relentless pursuit of masculinity. There are no limits; the most oppressive images of sexual violence and dominance are adopted unhesitatingly. Though the neo-Nazi adorations—fascinating fascism as Susan Sontag terms them—are more sinister than the innocuous ideals of the weight-lifting room, they are equally mindless. The offense is not aesthetic; it is entirely political. The homosexuals who adopt images of masculinity, conveying their desire for power and their belief in its beauty, are in fact eroticizing the very values of straight society that have tyrannized their own lives. It is the tension between this style and the content of their lives that demands the oblivion of drugs and sexual libertinism. In the past, the duplicity of closeted lives found relief in effemi-

nate camping; now the suppression of denial of the moral issue in their choice
is far more damaging. The perversity of imitating their oppressors guarantees
that such blindness will work itself out as self-contempt.

Sex and Sexual Politics   This is the central message of the macho bar world:
manliness is the only real virtue; other values are contemptible. And manliness is not some philosophical notion or psychological state; it is not even
morally related to behavior. It lies exclusively in the glamorization of physical
strength.

This idea of masculinity is so conservative it is almost primitive. That
homosexuals are attracted to it and find it gratifying is not a total surprise. Gay
male sexual preference has always favored a butch boyish beauty and only in
artistic or intellectual circles has beauty been allowed a certain feyness.
Butchness is always relative; the least swishy man in the room is the most
butch. It usually meant one looked straight, one could pass. In the past, an
over-enthusiasm for butchness translated itself into a taste for rough trade.
Those who were too frightened or sane to pursue that particular quarry could
always find a gay partner who would accommodatingly act the part.

There is a special eroticism in the experience of pretending to be degraded
that is by no means rare in adult sexual behavior of whatever persuasion. The
homosexual whose erotic feelings are enhanced by the illusion that his partner
holds him in contempt, who is thrilled when told his ass or mouth is just like a
cunt, is involved in a complicated self-deception. What appears to be happening is a homosexual variation of masochism: the contempt of the "straight"
partner emblazes gay self-contempt, which in turn is exploited as an aphro-
disiac. Why this process works is less clear than how it does.

The complex tie between the need for degradation and sexual excitement
has never been satisfactorily explored, though Freud began the effort over
eighty years ago and writers and artists have always intuitively understood it.
It seems to be prominent in societies that are advanced, where sexual mores
are liberal or ambivalent, and where intellectual life is very sophisticated. In
times like ours, when women are redefining their roles and images, men must
also redefine theirs. As women forgo in dress and appearance the *style* of their
oppression (it is the easiest to abandon and thus one of the first aspects to go),
and as glamor falls under a suspicious light, men, increasingly accused of
being the symbol of sexism, are forced to confront their own ideas of masculinity.

While straight men define their ideas from a variety of sources (strength,
achievement, success, money), two of those sources are always their attitudes
toward women and toward paternity. It is no coincidence that the same
decade that popularized liberation for women and announced that the nuclear
family was a failure also saw men return to a long-haired, androgynous style.
If straight men are confused about their maleness, what is the dilemma for gay
men, who rarely did more than imitate these ideas?

It is no accident that the macho gesture is always prominent in those gay
bars and resorts where women are entirely absent. Certain gay locales have
always catered exclusively to one sex: porno movie houses and bookstores,
baths, public toilets. The new bars are often private clubs as much for the sake
of legally barring women as for screening male customers. Their atmosphere
is eerily reminiscent of the locker room. And, of course, while they are there,

the men live as if there were no women in the world. This is a useful illusion. It allows some of them to get gang-banged in the back rooms and still evade the self-reproach that derives from the world's contempt for homosexual men who behave sexually like women. If there are no women in the world, some men simply must replace them. With women absent, whether one is sexually active or passive is no longer the great dividing issue.

In fact, some of the men who look most butch are the most liberated in bed, the least role-oriented. While there is still much role preference for passivity, it no longer has the clear quality it had in the past. Then, gay men made unmistakable announcements: those who liked to be fucked adopted effeminate mannerisms; those who were active tried to look respectable.

Quentin Crisp in his autobiography, *The Naked Civil Servant*, epitomized these attitudes. He documents the anger of an acquaintance railing at the misfortune of having picked up a young soldier who wanted to be fucked: "All of a sudden, he turned over. After all I'd done—flitting about the room in my wrap . . . camping myself silly. My dear, I was disgusted."[1] Today, to replace the usually reliable information that straight or campy behavior conveyed in the past, gay men at the leather bars have taken to elaborate clothing signals: key chains or handkerchiefs drooping from left or right pocket in blue or yellow or red all have coded meanings. Occasionally, some of the *cognoscenti* lie and misalliances occur. Of course, one could ask a prospective partner what his preferences are, but that is the least likely behavior between strangers.

If I am critical of the present style, it is not because I advocate a return to the denigrations of the past. Quentin Crisp's rebelliousness testifies to the hourly misery of gay life when all the sexual roles are petrified. He considered all his friends "pseudo men in search of pseudo women." That is not an improvement on pseudo men in search of nothing. Nor is his sense of inferiority: "I regard all heterosexuals, however low, as superior to any homosexual, however noble." Such estimates were commonplace for men subjected to lifelong ridicule because they could not or would not disguise their effeminacy.

But camping for Crisp and for the entire homosexual world until the end of the 1950s was not just the expression of self-contempt by men pretending to be women and feeling pseudo as both. Camping also gave homosexual men an *exclusive* form of behavior that neither women nor straight men could adopt. Some women and straight men are camp, but that is another story.

Camping in the gay world did not mean simply behaving in a blatantly effeminate manner; that was camp only when performed in the presence of those it irritated or threatened or delighted. Swishing is effective only if someone else notices, preferably registering a sense of shock, or ideally, outrage. In discreet bars like the Blue Parrot in 1950, men impeccably Brooks Brothers and as apparently WASP as one's banker could, in a flicker, slide into limpness. They had available a persona that mixed ironic distance, close observation, and wit, all allies of sanity.

Camping did express self-denigration, but it was a complex criticism. For example, the women whom these men imitated were themselves extraordinary; androgynous idols like Garbo or Dietrich symbolized an ambiguous and amoral sexuality. But more important, in their campy behavior, gay men revealed an empathic observation of women and feminine interests.

When camping also released for gay men some of their anger at their closeted lives, it became a weapon as well as a comment. The behavior chosen for imitation or ridicule was usually evidence of sexist attitudes, of positions women had taken or were forced to take that had effeminized them out of their humanity. It is for this reason that feminists object to drag queens who still try to resemble the slavish emblems of the past, and their criticism would be valid if the imitations were sincere. But men in drag are not swept up in the delusion that they are women; only insane men in drag believe that. The rest are committed to ambiguity; they are neither men nor women and are only rarely androgynous—the aura of the drag is neuter.

When a gay man said, "Oh, Mary, come off it," he was sneering at pretension, self-deceit, or prudery. That it took the form of reminding one's fellow faggot that he was in reality no better than a woman, and often not as good with his "pseudo" sexual equipment, is not politically commendable, but why should gay men have had a special consciousness about sexism? At least they had a sure recognition of it: they imitated women because they understood that they were victims in sisterhood of the same masculine ideas about sexuality. Generations of women defined themselves entirely in men's terms, and homosexual men often seemed to accept the same values.

But there was also a chagrined recognition that they just could not live up to expectations. They could not be men as heterosexuals defined manhood; most of all they could not be men because they did not sleep with women or beget children. No amount of manliness could counterbalance that. Between the values of virility that they did not question and their rage at having no apparent alternatives, gay men would camp out their frustration. It was not a particularly effective means of ending oppression, but it was a covert defiance of a society that humiliated them.

With the political and social changes of the sixties, a new androgyny seemed to be on the verge of life. Heterosexual and homosexual suddenly became less interesting than just sexual. Getting out of the closet was more than announcing one was gay; it was a pronouncement that one was free of sexual shame. The new mood fostered this; even straight boys looked prettier than girls. The relief at seeing male vanity in the open, surrendered to and accepted, made it possible for homosexuals to reconsider some of their attitudes toward themselves. It was not longer extraordinary to look effeminate in a world where most sexual men looked feminine and where sexually liberated women were the antithesis of the glamorous and fragile.

Sexual style had become a clear political issue. Conventional manliness was properly identified with reaction and repression. The enemy had a crewcut, was still posturing in outmoded chivalric stances, while his wife and daughter and son embraced the revolutionary notion of rolelessness. To some extent, this is where American society still is: searching for a sense of what roles, if any, are appropriate for adult men and women. Only the betrayed patriarch still refuses to acknowledge the permanence of these changes, since for him they are pure deprivations, erosions of his long, long, privilege.

Homosexuality and Masculinity   "Feminist" is a term that increasing numbers of gay men apply to themselves as they come to recognize the common oppression of homosexuals and women. The empathy of gay men in the past is the foundation for this newer understanding, and it is heartening to discover that a mutual sense of victimization need not always lead to self-denigration. If in the past women were less likely to self-contempt at being women than gay men felt at being homosexual, it was partly because women were rewarded for their acquiescence and partly because they did not have to experience the sense of having betrayed their birthright. Homosexual men usually gave up paternity as well as other prerogatives for their gayness and too often felt gypped for what they got. They exchanged the simplicity of being phallic oppressors for advantages much more dubious, and the sense that they had betrayed their best interests was haunting. As more gays come to realize the bankruptcy of conventional ideas of masculinity, it is easier for them to forgo the sexism they shared with heterosexual men.

Unfortunately, heterosexuals cling to their sexual definitions with even greater tenacity. For example, the Save Our Children slogan is not as banal as it sounds; the phobic hostility behind it expresses a genuine fear that some children will be lost, lost to patriarchy, to the values of the past, to the perpetuation of conventional ideas of men and women. There is a fear of homosexuality that is far beyond what the surface can explain.

Many gays, especially apolitical ones, are dismissive of Anita Byrant and what she represents. Remarks like "Straights will just have to hope that heterosexuality can hold its own on the open market" express a contempt for the fears, but not much understanding of them. It *is* puzzling: where does this idea of the frailty of heterosexuality come from, the assumption that a mere knowledge that teachers or ordinary people are gay will automatically seduce children? It comes from the panic about new sexual ideas, but most of all, about the identity of women.

It often sounds absurd when conservatives accuse feminist women of attempting to destroy the family, though it does not stop them from making the accusation. It is easier to appear sensible talking about the seduction of children by homosexuals. I suggest that much of the recent vehemence about the children is deflected from a much more central rage against women who are redefining their ideas about child rearing. The political issue is always hottest when women's connection with motherhood is raised. Thus, the issues of child rearing and anti-abortion gather a conservative support that puzzles liberal America. What these issues have in common is the attempt of women to free themselves from conventional roles, crucially their roles as mothers. That liberation is the first wave; the secondary one, far more perilous, lies beneath the surface: it demands that men liberate themselves from their notions as well, since the central ideas about masculinity have always been related to the unquestioned responsibilities of men as husbands and fathers.

It is curious that lesbians are never mentioned when child molestation is raised as an issue, and when lesbians are attacked, as they were at Houston, it is in relation to their militant feminism, not in relation to their being school teachers. Lesbians have usually been exempt from heterosexual fears about seduction, partly because they are women and, like all women, traditionally powerless. When they are attacked, when the press notices lesbian issues, it is often in connection with custody cases. There the issue of saving the children for heterosexuality and precisely for patriarchy is clear. These lesbians who once lived as straight women, who married and had children, as objects of the most extreme wrath, and one that has used the judicial system as its instrument to punish them.

But most lesbians are not mothers, and most lesbian mothers do not end up, fortunately, as victims in custody hearings. Lesbians are usually dismissed as unimportant, as nuisances. It is the lowest rung on the ladder of social contempt. But gay men who have abdicated their privileges, who have made sexual desire a higher priority than power over women, are indeed not men at all.

Bryant's keynote is that homosexuals should return to the closet. That would solve the problem for straights, since it is *visibility* that is terrifying. To be openly gay without contrition or guilt or shame is to testify that there are viable alternative sexual styles. But the real alternative for the children is not necessarily homosexuality; it is to reject the old verities of masculine and feminine.

Ironically, the men at the Anvil have not rejected those verities at all. Their new pseudo-masculinity is a precise response to the confusions of a society venturing toward sexual redefinition. But it is in its way as reactionary as the hysteria that Anita Bryant's campaign consolidated.

The men of the macho bars will not buy Quentin Crisp's book, or if they do, they will not read it sympathetically, whereas they *are* part of the audience that made the story of football player David Kopay a best seller.[2] I do not want to belittle Kopay's modest effort, but its success depends more on his image than on his courage. Effeminate men like Crisp who have the courage to defy society are eccentric; butch men are heroic. Of course, what is left unsaid is that Kopay could have passed: no one would have known if he hadn't told them, and having once announced it, he can still pass. What could sissies like Crisp do even if they didn't flaunt it? Crisp's *life* is an act of courage.

Ex-soldier Leonard Matlovich is also a respectable image.[3] When media reporters treat him and Kopay just like the mainstream Americans they have always been, they make a point many gays approve of: homosexual men are really like everyone else. If beneath Matlovich's conservative, bemedalled chest beat aberrant yearnings, the public, if not the army, can accommodate them. What makes Kopay and Matlovich seem acceptable to gays and straights alike, while the Quentin Crisps remain pitiful?

Crisp was defiant and miserable, and acknowledged victim, and unrepentant: it was all agony, but it couldn't have been any other way. Even more, Crisp made his sexuality the obsession of his life. His whole existence was devoted to proclaiming his homosexuality; it is the meaning of his life. Today, his heir is Daniel, who is as absorbed in the same singular definition of himself. Daniel's life seems consecrated to pleasure while Crisp's was miserable, and that is an enormous difference. But the source of his pleasure in sexuality is as extreme, as dangerous and defiant as the quest for pleasure in Crisp's life. I may feel that Crisp is morally superior because he has suffered and Daniel refuses to, but that is only a sentimental notion. What is stunning in both their lives is the exclusivity of sexuality, and while Daniel is not heroic, his life demands that one refrain from easy judgment. The drama of such displays is filled with meaning for them and us. These lives are not like others'.

Kopay and Matlovich are fighting to be like everyone else. They claim that they are just like other football players or professional soldiers, and I do not dispute them. Compared to their conventionality, their homosexuality is almost incidental. Neither of them has gotten off quite free, nor have they seemed to expect to. For reasons they articulate with unquestionable credibility, they could not tolerate the duplicity of being conservative, rather ordinary men and secret homosexuals. Ironically, to some extent they have now become extraordinary men if somewhat commonplace homosexuals.

The men in leather watching naked go-go boys and having sex in back-room bars are not like Crisp or Daniel whom they regard as a kind of erotic theater; they are much closer to Kopay and Matlovich with whom they can identify. The rock-bottom premise of such sympathy is that all forms of traditional masculinity are respectable; all symptoms of effeminacy are contemptible. Real sexual extremism, like Daniel's, belongs to a netherworld; it is not regarded as liberated but as libertine. Daniel is the complete sexual object, and his presence makes the bar world the psychological equivalent of the brothel for the men who watch him. He turns them on, and then they can play whore or client or both.

Most men who are ardent for leather defend it as play. Dressing butch is another version of the gay uniform. What is the harm of walking through the world dressed like a construction worker? What does it matter what costume you wear to the ball? Go as Cinderella's fairy godmother, and you may break the law. But go as Hell's Angels, and you risk breaking your own spirit.

It is no coincidence that in the macho bar world and the libertine baths the incidence of impotence is so high that it is barely worth remarking, or that gay men increasingly rely on the toys and trappings of sadomasochism. It is not irrelevant that the new gay image of virility is most often illustrated in pornography.

Manly means hot, and hot is everything. Why then isn't it working better? Men tell me that I do not appreciate this new celebration of masculinity, that I am overlooking the important "fact": "We fell for masculinity when we were twelve; there must be something to it because it made us gay. Most of us didn't become gay because we fell in love with sissies; we became sissies because we fell in love with men, usually jocks."

It sounds familiar. And so what if one chooses to make one's life pornographic? Isn't that only the most recent version of sexual devotion, of incarnating Eros in one's life? Besides, it's too late to be a dogooder. Obviously, as soon as one sets up notions of propriety, no matter how well intended, they will be preempted by the worst, most coercive forces in our society. One is then forced to accept all choices of style; the alternative is to find oneself allied with oppression. In the arena of sexual politics, there is the left and the right. Those who think they are in the middle will ultimately discover that the center is the right.

But my feelings tell me that there is another version; that macho is somehow another closet, and not a new one—many have suspected that it's the oldest closet in the house. Macho cultures have always had more covert homosexuality. Without belaboring the analogy, there is one consistency. In those cultures, homosexuality is not a sexual identity; it is defined as role. Only the passive partner, which means anally passive or orally active, is homosexual; the other role is reserved for men, because one either is a man or one is not; that is, one is a woman, and a woman who cannot bear a child and attest to a man's virility is beneath contempt, at best a whore.

The men in the macho bars are not like this. They have adopted a style and abandoned its psychic origin in sexual role playing. Apparently they have rescued the best and discarded the worst. But it is an appearance that resonates with unexamined yearnings. It says I am strong and I am free, that gay no longer means the contemptibleness of being nelly, which is the old powerless *reactiveness* to oppression. Insofar as it does that—strong is better than weak, free is always good—it is an improvement on the past. But it claims more: it says that this is a choice, a proper fulfillment of those initial desires that led us to love men, and even at its oddest, it is only playful.

But it is not free, not strong, and it is dangerous play. It is dangerous to dress up like one's enemy, and worse, it can tie one to him as helplessly as ever. It still says that he, the powerful brute, is the definer, to which we then react. It is the other side of nelly, and more helpless because it denies that one is helpless at all. Effeminacy acknowledged the rage of being oppressed in defiance; macho denies that there *is* rage and oppression. The strength of those new bodies is a costume designed for sexual allure and for the discotheque. Passing for the enemy does not exempt one from the wrath. Men in leather are already the easiest marks for violent teenagers on a drunken rampage in Greenwich Village or on Mission Street on a Saturday night. Macho is another illusion. The lessons of Negroes who disliked blackness, or Jews who insisted they were assimilated, really *German*, are ignored. To some whites, everything not white is black; to Nazis, Jews are Jews, sidelocks or no. Telling the enemy one is as good as he is because one is like him does not appease him; often it makes him more vicious, furious because somehow his victim seems to approve his scorn. And the freedom—that too is illusory except as sexual taste. In that area alone, there has been real change. Compared to their counterparts in the past gay men today have found a freedom to act out their erotic tastes. But taste is not a choice; usually, it is a tyrant.

Homosexuals at their most oppressed have not been in love with men; they have been in love with masculinity. The politics of the New Left and the sexual aesthetics of androgyny have not lasted, but they seemed to be offering alternatives that were authentic, better choices than the ones we had. The new style seems both inauthentic and barely better than the old options. Sometimes it seems worse.

That is what is disturbing and enraging: to find it the growing choice in the 1980s. Does it seriously matter that some men choose to imitate their worst enemies? What is remarkable about such an old story? For one, it is so unnecessary. For the first time in modern history, there are real options for gays. The sissies in the Blue Parrot had little choice other than to stay home. They could only pretend their lives were ordinary. That pretense was survival, but one that led fatally to rage and self-contempt. The theatricality of camping helped to keep some sanity and humanity because it was an awareness of one's helplessness. Macho values are the architects of closeted lives, and adopting that style is the opposite of awareness. Whatever its ironies, they are not critical ones.

Fortunately, gay men are less helpless than they have ever been before, and because of that they are more threatened. What is worth affirming is not bravura, but political alliance with women and with a whole liberal America that is dedicated to freedom of personal choice. *That* is worth celebrating.

LIFE AFTER DEATH: A VIEW FROM THE LATE 1980S

These days the mood of the gay community ranges from cloudy optimism to crystal-clear despair, depending on whom you talk to. I've been talking to gay activists, journalists, academics, therapists and medical doctors, businessmen, poets and painters, working-class men, and men who don't work, either because they don't need to or because they can't find a job. Some are Marxists, some lesbian feminists, and some have no politics but sexual politics. the term "gay community" refers partly to a discernible group of homosexual men and lesbians in large cities, and partly to a political idea. The media made it a term to reckon with long before anyone could say what it was. In 1969 "gay community" was largely a political idea and a myth. Even then there was a community in the simplest sense of the word, but what it looked like, as in the case of the blind men describing the elephant, depended on what you touched.

Seventeen years later, there are listings in the Yellow Pages. Coherent and representative groups have emerged, particularly in San Francisco, Los Angeles, and New York. They differ enough to be unable to provide a national leadership, and persistent closetry makes estimates of their numbers and their members rough at best, but a gay man or woman would likely feel at home in any of those three cities. The real differences are geographical, not political or social, and there is no single lifestyle or even a dominant one. The promiscuous one that became the hallmark of urban gay life in the early seventies—newsworthy because it was commercial and outrageous and because it gradually became the self-defining image of so many gay men—no longer prevails as it once did.

Today the general mood is grim. Everyone is either melancholy or anxious, afraid not only of AIDS but of the growing signs of hostility toward gay men and women. It is chilling when the *New York Times*, purportedly in the interests of balanced journalism, publishes William F. Buckley in support of tatooing homosexual men and intravenous-drug users, while the word "quarantine" quivers between the lines of the article. (I naively waited for letters of protest from both the Jewish and gay communities. Wouldn't Jews be disgusted by the parodic horror of the suggestion?) Though Buckley is absurd, the fears he touches are not.

Helplessness about AIDS and uncertainty about the social future are exacerbated for gay men and women by their memories of the past. This is one reason so many are eager to be involved with gay organizations, to be tangibly connected to a real, not an ideological community. To be passive again is to stress one's helplessness, to be waiting for the next blow and wondering if the humiliation will be bearable.

Most of society is less concerned about who is responsible for the AIDS epidemic than with how gay men are going to behave in order to inhibit its spread. That issue, it should be said at once, arose in the gay community almost as soon as it was clear that AIDS was regarded as a gay disease. The closing of the bathhouses in San Francisco and New York was the occasion for raising the question in public. Publicly and privately it was admitted that the issue of accountability and social responsibility would have to be addressed. Obviously, this meant altering sexual behavior and style of life. Efforts were made in every large North American city with a gay community to inform and educate gay men about "safe sex," hoping that would be enough to halt the spread of AIDS. It is not yet clear how much deprivation this entails or how successful the educational campaign has been. History does not offer much ground for optimism: venereal epidemics of the past ended not with altered sexual behavior but with the discovery of penicillin.

But another issue, internal and not yet explored in any public way, has now arisen and needs attention, an issue that the symptoms of the crisis sometimes hint at: what does it mean to be homosexual in the modern world? This question is not about grievances and injustices, and it cannot be answered on the barricades, especially the barricade of rhetoric. As long as the subject of gay identity is argued in terms of whether it is good or bad, legitimate or illegitimate, there is no energy left to address the question of what it is. The new activism cannot address the more important internal questions the crisis has raised. The sources of change are elsewhere, in behavior and in thought about the homosexual condition that most men and women are reluctant to embrace.

Promiscuity and Liberation   Some have refused to change; they search for safe places to practice old pleasures. Latin America and the Caribbean have long accommodated homosexual men with their informal bordellos, their "muchachos" who are partners to passive men but who do not think of themselves as homosexual. It is only a question of time before these gay men spread AIDS to other islands near Haiti, from which they probably first brought it to the mainland. It is hard to gauge the state of mind of such men. They may be filled with rage and seeking revenge. They may fatalistically believe that their behavior doesn't matter. They don't feel they are doing anything wrong, or they don't care. They have no moral sense, or they are immoral. It's bad enough to live in dread of dying an awful premature death. Yet to be filled with desire for revenge, or to be without desire at all, even for ordinary dignity, is a terrible way to live or die. I assume that such men act less from conscious indecency than from pure evasion. To emphasize sexual desire and desirability is a very effective way to mask anxiety. The habit of promiscuity doesn't allow much room for introspection.

Promiscuity is a broad term. For some men, it means serial affairs or brief erotic relationships. For others, there are no relationships at all; sexual encounters begin and end with momentary arousal. And for some men, promiscuity is all of these—having a lover, and having someone else, and having anyone else. Promiscuity is time consuming and repetitious. Still, it also has another history and meaning for gay men; and it is that history, and that meaning, with which gay men in the shadow of AIDS must grapple.

In the last fifteen years or so, until AIDS appeared, promiscuity had been a rich if not invaluable experience for gay men, uniting a sense of liberation with a politics of resentment, a feeling of living at the modern edge with an outlet for aggressions created by long-held grievances. Such a combination is explosive, of course, and antiintellectual. But gay men did not invent sexual liberation. They merely stamped it with their hallmark of aggressive display. Casual sex, freed from commercialism, seemed a glamorous portent of a society free from sexism. After "Stonewall," the riot at a New York bar in which gay men successfully resisted arrest and inadvertently inaugurated gay liberation, gay activists felt they were going to redefine the old terms, junk the guilt and the remorse. They were already discarding with contempt the shrinks and the moralists, paying some of them back for the years of misery they had helped to create, the self-dislike they had urged gays to internalize for the sake of what now seemed merely propriety. Out the window went "sick" and "bad." Many could hardly believe they were jettisoning that dismal baggage.

Those years of sexual opportunism were a time of indifference to psychological inquiry. Description was a higher priority. After so much silence, the need to explain and the desire to shock were first on the agenda of gay writers and intellectuals, while the majority of gay men were exploring an exhilarating sense of relief in discos, bars with back room, and the baths. The politics of that eroticism had as much to do with ego as with eros: gay men said that sexuality did not diminish social status, to say nothing of intellectual or professional stature—no matter how vividly it was practiced.

In the early seventies, when movement politics was at the zenith of its popularity, the values it promoted were very seductive. It said the old romantic pieties were a slavish imitation of straight society, where they were already undergoing vigorous scrutiny from feminists. If women and blacks could use politics to demand that society acknowledge thay had been unjustly treated, why not gay men? If the acknowledgment of that injustice took the form of striking down old laws and replacing them with better ones, then that, obviously, was the agenda. But for the most part, neither the victories nor the defeats changed the daily lives of gay men and women very much. With or without sodomy laws, most lived without concern for legality. It was understood that the principal struggle was psychological, a demand first for recognition, then for acceptance; the bold terms in which that demand was couched guaranteed the right to pursue a sexual lifestyle of their own choosing. After Stonewall, gays chose to be very visible.

Before Stonewall, promiscuous sex was illegal, but it was no particular threat to health. If the heart and heat of gay politics has been to ensure the right to fuck who, when, and where one pleases, then the consequences now for the movement have a rough poetic justice. The more that sex dominated the style of life, from discos to parades, with rights secured or not, the less need most men felt they had for politics—and the less others, such as lesbians, feminists, and minorities, felt the gay movement offered them. For gay men sexual politics became something oddly literal. Both before and after the movement, promiscuity was honored as the sign of an individual's aggressiveness (no matter how passive he was in bed). To fuck was to defy, as bad girls of the past did, dismantling some of society's dearest notions about virtue. But most homosexuals want to be conventional. They are no more imaginative, courageous, or innovative than their neighbors. They want a good life on the easiest terms they can get. Many regard as uninteresting the activism that a handful of men and women are devoted to.

By the late seventies, movement politics displaced flamboyant effeminacy. The piece of trade (a man who is fellated by another but pretends to be heterosexual) whose very pose of masculinity ensured his contempt for his homosexual partner, had been replaced by that formerly groveling queen himself, now looking more virile than his proletarian idol. The dominant image of rebellion was no longer the defiant queens with their merciless ironies but powerful, strong bodies modeled on working-class youth. This new image exposed the erotic ideal of gay male life more clearly and responsively than anything since classical Greece. It was a vast improvement. Liberation freed gays from a lot of burdens, and one of the biggest was to end the search for masculinity among the enemy.

But paralleling the rise of the macho body has been the decline of the health of the male community—a nasty coincidence, if you believe in coincidence. The deeper truth, however, is that the very values that motivated us to look strong rather than be strong are the same values that elevated promiscuity as the foundation of a social identity. AIDS is mobilizing many to work in agencies caring for the ill, allowing them opportunities for sympathy and generosity—but that, too, is not the basis of an identity. What is killing you is not likely to give you a sense of self.

Even if AIDS were cured tomorrow, the style and identity of gay life in the seventies and mid-eighties would be as dated as the sexual mores of closeted homosexual life are now. Many men may rush back to the baths, but it can no longer be the liberating experience it once was. AIDS has nullified promiscuity as politically or even psychologically useful and has replaced one set of meaning with another. It has now become mythic as the dark side of sexuality, Thanatos to Eros. The life force that is the sexual drive has always had its counterpart, and AIDS is the most dramatic juxtaposition of the need for another and the fear of the other, of pain and pleasure, of life and death, in modern medical history. From the ancient Greeks on down, without a moment's interruption, the interpretation has been the same: unfettered sexuality means death, whether through dishonor, the wrath of the gods, or nature itself. We are the heirs of those legends. AIDS, like a blotter, has absorbed those old meanings.

Life after Death   There is much, then, that gay men must give up. The loss of sexual life, nearly as much as the grief and fear, is a deprivation for which no amount of civic work or marching to banners of Gay Pride can compensate. The most dramatic changes have occurred among those large numbers of men who have become abstinent, assuming a sense of responsibility to themselves if not to others. Not only must gay men refrain from what alone gave them a powerful enough identity to make a mark on the consciousness of society, a behavior that replaced society's contempt with the much more respectable fear and anger, but they must cease to think of themselves as unloved children. They must do both before they can have social acceptance or before their own behavior can have meaning for each other more nurturing than it has been. It is very hard to give up a sense of deprivation when little that created it has disappeared, and worse, when one is beset with fear.

One thing, however, is clear: gay men are not acting in concert. If gay men sensed they belonged to a recognized community, instead of struggling still to assert their legitimacy, the task would be simpler. If they felt the larger society was no longer so adamantly adversarial, they could give up the sense of injustice that makes talk of social responsibility seem hypocritical. And if their own experiences with each other had provided them with bonds deeper than momentary pleasure, they could trust themselves to act as a group in which members assumed responsibility for each other.

As long as the larger society continues to prefer the old homosexual invisibility, the nice couple next door to whom anyone can condescend, as long as that society fails to express its responsibilities to gay men, the harder it will be for gay men to give up their seductive sense of grievance. Those men who act irresponsibly in the midst of this crisis betray their isolation, their failure to feel they belong either to a gay community or to a larger one. They perceive the demand for accountability as a demand from strangers. Society has not acted as the surrogate family in which we all develop our loyalties and moral sense. In fact, too often it acts just like the family of gay men: filled with contempt or indifference.

Many gays are now relieved that sex is no longer a banner issue. It is not even so important that we all stand up to be counted; enough of us have stood up to satisfy the curious. Instead, much as other groups in U.S. society have done, the gay community has had to reassess more profoundly its relationship to the larger society. Customarily, that relationship has been adversarial. Now, for the first time in my memory, the gay community expects help. It hopes for sympathy from heterosexual society. It expects that those who are ordinarily silent will be uncomfortable with such neutrality when orthodox religious leaders proclaim AIDS the scourge of God upon homosexuals, or when politicians exploit and promote fear.

AIDS has made it necessary for gay men to begin questioning themselves. For too long we have lived as if we were driven, too impelled to know what we were doing and what, consequently, was happening to us. It takes perhaps half a lifetime before one is capable of the introspection (not self-absorption) necessary to make sense of the past and thus act as a morally free adult. The same is true of groups. There are moments in history when groups, too, must tell the truth about themselves.

NOTES

1. Quentin Crisp, *The Naked Civil Servant* (New York: New American Library, 1983).
2. David Kopay and Perry D. Young, *The David Kopay Story* (New York: Arbor House, 1980).
3. Leonard Matlovich was formerly a sergeant in the U.S. Army.

PART TWO

◆ ◆ ◆

From Boys to Men

Matt Groening

THE ROAD TO MANHOOD

"One is not born, but rather becomes, a woman," wrote the French feminist thinker, Simone de Beauvoir in her ground-breaking book, *The Second Sex* (NY: Vintage, 1958). The same is true for men. And the social processes by which boys become men are complex and important. How does early childhood socialization differ for boys and girls? What specific traits are emphasized for boys that mark their socialization as different? What types of institutional arrangements reinforce those traits? How do the various institutions in which boys find themselves—school, family, and friends—influence their development? What of the special institutions that promote "boy's life" or an adolescent male subculture?

During their childhood and adolescence, masculinity becomes a central theme in a boy's life. *New York Times* editor A. M. Rosenthal put the dilemma this way: "So there I was, 13 years old, the smallest boy in my freshman class at DeWitt Clinton High School, smoking a White Owl cigar. I was not only little, but I did not have longies—long trousers—and was still in knickerbockers. Obviously, I had to do something to project my fierce sense of manhood" (*New York Times*, 26 April 1987). That the assertion of manhood is part of a boy's natural development is suggested by Roger Brown, in his text book, *Social Psychology* (NY: Free Press, 1965, p. 161):

> In the United States, a *real* boy climbs trees, disdains girls, dirties his knees, plays with soldiers, and takes blue for his favorite color. When they go to school, real boys prefer manual training, gym, and arithmetic. In college the boys smoke pipes, drink beer, and major in engineering or physics. The real boy matures into a "man's man" who plays poker, goes hunting, drinks brandy, and dies in the war.

The articles in this section address the question of a boy's development. Joseph H. Pleck provides an interesting discussion of how the rules of traditional masculinity shape the kinds of behaviors that we expect of boys. Barrie Thorne discusses the consequences of separate and same-sex play for boys and girls.

The next four articles examine some distinctly male institutions. Jeffrey P. Hantover gives an historical account of the creation of the Boy Scouts of America as an attempt to develop an institution to rescue boys from the dangers of "feminization," and Richard Majors describes the black male style of "cool pose" as a strategy to counter the way racism "emasculates black men. If the Boy Scouts have historically been a "boy's liberation movement," preadolescent play culture continues this socialization, as Gary Alan Fine shows in his essay on "dirty play." Finally, the contemporary collegiate fraternity, as Peter Lyman shows, continues to provide a homosocial haven for young men, an island of brotherhood, with serious consequences for women.

Joseph H. Pleck
PRISONERS OF MANLINESS

TRUE OR FALSE?
—Boys need a father figure when they are growing up in order to become secure men.
—Boys are harmed academically and psychologically because so many teachers in the early grades are women.
—Male homosexuality reflects a man's confusion over his masculine role.
—Men who have not developed a secure masculine identity are more likely than other men to be violent, hostile to women, and irrationally afraid of homosexuality.
—Black men are especially vulnerable to problems with masculinity.

The macho image of the male may have softened recently; many men now realize that they can express tender feelings without jeopardizing their performance in business or in bed. However, the belief that it is essential for men to acquire a "sex-role identity"—expressed by masculine traits, attitudes, and interests—remains firmly entrenched. So does the belief that it is hard for men to develop this secure sense of masculinity, especially now that women are becoming more assertive.

If you answered true to all or most of the above statements, the chances are that you still hold to the belief that a strong sex role identity is crucial to male psychological health. The notion is not just a popular prejudice. It is the creation of decades of research in psychology, including the work of some of the most prominent investigators—among them Alfred Adler, Lewis Terman, Talcott Parsons, Jerome Kagan, and E. Mavis Hetherington. It has been disseminated by other writers, notably by Benjamin Spock and by the psychologist Fitzhugh Dodson, who advised fathers in his 1974 book, *How to Father:* "Your preschool boy needs contact with you so that he can imitate you and stabilize his gender identity as a male."

Psychologists have been preoccupied with masculinity over the past several decades. Research on sex roles actually has focused primarily on men and has been dominated by two insistent questions: what makes males less masculine than they should be and what can we do about it? The answers given, both by psychologists and by other social scientists, are based on the theory of male sexrole identity, whose key assertions are summarized in the true/false statements that appear above.

My own examination of the evidence suggests that the theory is unsubstantiated and has damaging consequences for men, women, and society as a whole. The conventional expectations of what it means to be a man are difficult to live up to for all but a lucky few and lead to unnecessary self-deprecation in the rest when they do not measure up. Even for those who do, there is a price; they may be forced, for example, to inhibit the expression of many emotions.

The emergence of male-identity theory since the 1930s can best be interpreted as a response to the gradual breakdown of social and institutional structures that supported traditional sex roles—for example, the decline of the large family, which kept a woman home having babies. With industrialization and ubanization, these structures waned, leaving doubts about just what it meant to be female or male. The vacuum was neatly filled by the "discovery" that masculinity and femininity had deep psychological bases. It is no accident that the work that founded male-identity theory, *Sex and Personality*, by the Stanford psychologists Lewis Terman and Catherine Miles, was published in 1936, at the depths of the Depression, which posed the single greatest threat to the male role in U.S. history by taking away men's ability to support their families, traditionally their most important responsibility. If holding a job could no longer be counted on to define manhood, perhaps a masculinity/femininity test could.

To understand how poorly substantiated the theory of male sex-role identity is, it is important to examine the psychological research underlying each of the five basic assertions above.

BOYS NEED A FATHER FIGURE WHEN THEY ARE GROWING UP IN ORDER TO BECOME SECURE MEN

At issue here is not *whether* it is good for a boy to have positive relationships with his father or other adult males, but *why*. This notion implies that the most important result of a boy's contact with his father is the boy's sex-role identity—and that view raises several problems.

The research that people most often think demonstrates the point above has examined the effects on boys of having fathers who were not present. Between 1945 and 1975, this topic was more popular than almost any other in sex-role research. Many studies found no differences. Others produced conflicting results. In one experiment, Mavis Hetherington of the University of Virginia compared boys with fathers and boys without them by giving them a test in which children guessed the preferences for toys of an imaginary child named "It" (represented by a stick figure), who was supposed to be sexually neutral. Hetherington found that boys whose fathers were absent beginning in the first four years of life made fewer "masculine" choices, saying that "It" liked to play with a necklace rather than a dumptruck, for example. She interpreted this as a sign that they were having difficulty in thinking of themselves as male. Another study, by psychologists David Lynn and William Sawrey, found that the sons of Norwegian sailors who were away at least nine months a year were *more* masculine than average. The investigators interpreted the boys' behavior as indication that they were overcompensating—trying to make up for inner sexual insecurities.

These findings may indicate that father absence causes identity problems, but they may also indicate that researchers stack the deck in favor of the hypothesis: they interpret both *low* and *high* masculinity as signs of sexual insecurity. Proponents of the boys-need-male-models hypothesis explain these inconsistent results by claiming that father absence can make boys either more or less masculine depending on their personalities and circumstances.

In my view, these arguments are feeble attempts to make recalcitrant data fit the theory.

In their 1971 report, *Boys in Fatherless Families*, Elizabeth Herzog and Cecilia Sudia of the federal Office of Child Development concluded that the evidence "offers no firm basis for assuming that boys who grow up in father-less homes are more likely, as men, to suffer from inadequate masculine identity as a result of lacking a resident male model." In school performance, Herzog and Sudia also found that if factors like class and education were equal, boys with absent fathers appeared to turn out as well as boys whose fathers were present. They did show slightly more delinquent be-havior.

Other research on fathers and sons concerns the impact on a son's masculin-ity of variations in the father's characteristics, especially his power, his warmth, and his own degree of masculinity. Some important studies, such as the 1965 work *Identification and Child Rearing* by Stanford psychologists Robert Sears, Lucy Rau, and Richard Alpert, have found that almost no relationship exists. Other research, such as the studies conducted by Paul Mussen in the Berkeley psychology department of the 1950s and 1960s, for example, has found some relationship. However, Mussen's studies require a greater degree of faith in his measures than is usually the case in psychological research. His oft-cited findings of relationships between fathers' warmth and sons' mas-culinity assume, for example, that a father is friendly if a boy depicts a male character in a doll-play game as friendly and that a boy is mascu-line if he declares that the stick figure named "It" likes to play with a dump-truck rather than a necklace. (Those who cite Mussen's studies also usu-ally fail to report his further finding that males who were ranked high on masculinity scales as youths displayed considerable maladjustment in adult-hood.)

Today, a new generation of research is focusing on a broader range of questions: when a father is close to his children, how does his presence affect his children's thinking, how does childrearing affect his feelings about him-self? As part of the contemporary reappraisal, many people now believe that if fathers are more involved in raising children than they were, children, and sons in particular, will learn that men can be warm and supportive of others as well as be high achievers. Thus, fathers' involvement may be beneficial not because it will help *support* traditional male roles, but because it will help break them down.

BOYS ARE HARMED ACADEMICALLY AND
PSYCHOLOGICALLY BECAUSE SO MANY TEACHERS IN
THE EARLY GRADES ARE WOMEN

Most current attention to sex role issues in education concerns the disadvantages that girls seem to face in schools. But an older elaboration of the boys-need-male-models hypothesis is still around: the theory that boys are damaged by the predominance of women in the educational system.

In her 1969 study, *The Femininized Male*, New York University sociologist Patricia C. Sexton argued: "Though run at the top by men, schools are essentially feminine institutions, from nursery school through graduate school. In the school, women set the standards for adult behavior, and many favor students, male and female, who most conform to their own behavior norms—polite, clean, obedient, neat, and nice." Sexton concluded, then, that "if the boy absorbs school values, he may become feminized himself."

The "feminization" argument involves three hypotheses: (1) boys do better with male teachers, (2) teachers "reinforce" (respond to and/or encourage) femininity in boys, and (3) boys perceive school as feminine. The evidence for all three is weak.

Studies of academic performance do not show that boys with male teachers do any better academically than boys with female teachers. On measures of social adjustment, many studies find no differences and others find only weak or inconsistent ones. For example, Dorothy J. Sciarra, now a professor of child development at the University of Cincinnati, hypothesized that male models in the early years of school would enhance boys' self-esteem, thereby decreasing both their aggression and their susceptibility to peer-group influence. When she compared boys with adult males in the classrooms and boys without, however, she found a tendency for boys with male models to be *more* susceptible to peer-group influences, although statistical tests showed that the result could have been due to change.

Sciarra handily transformed the trend disconfirming the feminization thesis into one confirming it by redefining, after the fact, the meaning of what she measured: she argued that susceptibility to peer-group pressure (a negative characteristic) was actually peer-group *cooperation* (a desirable one) and thus showed the positive effect that male models had on boys.

Reviewing the research on boys with male teachers, psychologists Dolores Gold of Concordia University and Myrna Reis of the Jewish Vocational Service of Montreal concluded that "increasing the number of male teachers in the early school grades is a proposed panacea to alleviate boys' school difficulties which . . . appeals to common sense as well as to widespread bias. However, it is an alternative which likely will not be effective."

The evidence that teachers encourage femininity in boys is also weak. Researchers often cite a 1969 study by Beverly Fagot and Gerald Patterson, psychologists at the University of Oregon, showing that teachers reinforce feminine behaviors in boys more often than masculine ones. Detailed examination of this study—which includes only two nursery school classes and four teachers—reveals, however, that the major "feminine" behaviors being reinforced were art activities and listening to stories. Perhaps more interesting than the finding that teachers reinforced those behaviors is the psychologists' interpretation of art and listening to stories as feminine.

A study that may be closer to the truth is a 1973 survey of preschool through second-grade teachers by developmental psychologist Patrick Lee and Annie Wolinsky at Columbia Teachers College. They classified only 14 percent of the activities that female teachers reinforced as female-typed; 17 percent were male-typed, and the vast majority were neutral.

Another study that is widely cited as showing teachers' alleged reinforcement of femininity was done in 1972 by psychologists Teresa Levitin and David Chananic at the University of Michigan. It found that teachers approved more of obedient and dependent fifth-grade boys than of disobedient and aggressive ones (though they reported liking the disobedient boys no less). But there too, the cards were stacked by selecting male traits that are socially undesirable and female ones that are desirable. Given such a bias, it comes as no surprise that teachers disapproved of the undesirable ones—but they disapproved of them regardless of the child's sex and because they are socially undesirable, not because they are masculine.

The idea that boys perceive school as feminine originated in an ingenuous study done in the 1960s by developmental psychologist Jerome Kagan at Harvard. Kagan's second and third graders were taught to pair sexually neutral nonsense syllables with objects pertaining to men and women—"DEP" with men's trousers and a baseball bat, "ROV" with a women's shoe and lipstick. After learning the associations, the children were then asked to guess the category, whether DEP or ROV, of each of a new set of objects, including eight related to schools, for example, a pencil, a school building, a blackboard, a page of arithmetic.

It is by no means clear from the results of Kagan's study that boys perceive school as feminine. Of the eight school-related objects, the second-grade boys rated only two (blackboard, page of arithmetic) as feminine significantly more often than masculine, but they saw two others (map, book) as masculine more often than feminine—and more strongly so. In the third grade, the boys perceived the arithmetic page as masculine, the blackboard as neutral. Thus, far from demonstrating that boys see school as feminine, Kagan's study actually found that second-grade boys perceived a minority of school objects as feminine, but they viewed an equal minority of other objects as even more strongly masculine, and that only one grade later they had discarded or even reversed their perceptions of the feminine school objects.

MALE HOMOSEXUALITY REFLECTS A MAN'S CONFUSION OVER HIS MASCULINE ROLE

As psychologist Donald Brown of the U.S. Air Force Academy put it in 1957, "The male invert psychologically perceives himself as a female, and accordingly looks to the 'opposite' sex for sexual gratification. . . . Inversion has its roots in the earliest years of life when the child forms, at first involuntarily and later consciously, an identification attachment to the parent of the opposite sex and thereby internalizes the sex role of the opposite sex."

Homosexuality has always been a central preoccupation of those concerned about male identity. A major portion of Terman and Miles's *Sex and Personality* is devoted to studies of homosexuals—primarily male homosexuals. When people say they are concerned about how "male identity" is affected by whatever it is they see it threatened by (single parent families, a mother's employment, girls in school sports, and so forth), very often what they have in mind is an increased rate of male homosexuality. Homosexuality, especially in men, is thus viewed as the quintessential failure in development of normal sex-role identity.

One kind of evidence that might support this interpretation is data showing that male homosexuals emerge as more feminine than heterosexuals on tests of masculinity and femininity. The tests place people on a scale ranging from masculine to feminine according to their answers to such questions as "I prefer a shower to a bath" (Yes = masculine); "I would like to be a singer" (Yes = feminine); and "I like artichokes" (Yes = feminine). These items have distinguished men from women in at least some samples.

Data showing male homosexuals as more feminine than heterosexuals on these tests exist, but whatever they mean, much of the research is based on prisoners, who are hardly typical of all heterosexuals and homosexuals. One study actually used heterosexual rapists as the control group against whose masculinity the masculinity of homosexuals was compared!

A second problem with interpreting homosexuality as a failure to develop a masculine identity is that many studies completely fail to find significant differences in masculinity between male homosexuals and male heterosexuals. Three recent studies, with samples of college students and improved measures that assess masculinity and femininity as separate dimensions that can coexist in anyone, yield completely inconsistent results.

In response to the empirical failings, male-identity theorists like Donald Brown and British psychiatrist D. J. West now argue that there are actually two kinds of male homosexuals: "passive" ones, who are psychologically feminine and therefore fit the original theory, and "active" ones, who are not and therefore don't. This interpretation assumes a distinction that most authorities now reject. It also has the interesting implication, quite troubling for a larger theory of male identity, that there are no differences in sex-role identity between heterosexual males and "active" homosexual males. Such intellectual surgery may reconcile the theory with the data, but it amputates a vital spot in the patient. In short, whatever does cause homosexuality, there is little evidence to show that the factors involve an inadequate sense of a masculine identity.

MEN WHO HAVE NOT DEVELOPED A SECURE MASCULINE IDENTITY ARE MORE LIKELY THAN OTHER MEN TO BE VIOLENT, HOSTILE TO WOMEN, AND IRRATIONALLY AFRAID OF HOMOSEXUALITY

Weakness in sex-role identity may be reflected in too much masculinity as well as too little. The notion is that male crime, misogyny, and homophobia represent overcompensations for underlying male insecurity. To describe that phenomenon, Alfred Adler in 1927 coined the term "masculine protest." Harvard sociologist Talcott Parsons proposed in 1947 that the Western pattern of close mother–child relationships causes boys to have an unresolved feminine identification against which they psychologically defend themselves through aggression and delinquency. The idea has been further developed by numerous theorists and researchers.

In the 1950 study *The Authoritarian Personality*, Theodor Adorno and other psychologists at Berkeley suggested that this character type was, in part, the result of male insecurity. The researchers interpreted authoritarianism, which included rigidity, contempt for weakness, and intolerance of deviance—especially sexual deviance—as the underlying psychological basis of World War II fascism. (Adorno and one of his coinvestigators, Else Frenkel-Brunswick, had earlier fled from Hitler.) Nevitt Sanford, another of the investigators, wrote later that the researchers "became convinced that one of the main sources of this personality syndrome was ego-alien femininity— that is to say, underlying femininity that had to be countered by whatever defenses the subject had at his disposal." In effect, they linked men's insecure sex-role identities to the rise of Hitler and to the Holocaust.

Researchers have applied the "hypermasculinity" hypothesis most often to the relationship between delinquency and father absence, especially in black males. There, too, the evidence is thin. Herzog and Sudia concluded that in studies in which social class is controlled (a relative rarity), father absence may have a weak effect on delinquency, but that the effect is too small to have any practical significance. For example, in a 1969 study, Lawrence Rosen, a sociologist at Temple University, surveyed a probability sample of 1,098 black male youths in a 10-square-mile area of Philadelphia and found that having an absent father was connected to only 1.2 percent of the variation in the amount of delinquency among the youths. More intensive studies examining variations among delinquents, such as those conducted in 1970 by Charles Harrington at Columbia Teachers College and in 1974 by Ohio State University sociologists Ira Silverman and Simon Dinitz, find few differences among subgroups of delinquents and other institutionalized males, with or without fathers, in hypermasculinity and sex-role identity. Harrington concludes that his study "throws into some question the view of aggression as 'protest masculinity.'"

The idea that many men fear women, a fear rooted in insecure masculinity, has attracted a number of feminist scholars. Nancy Chodorow, a psychoanalytic sociologist at the University of California, Berkeley, argued in 1974 that "in his attempt to gain an elusive masculine identification . . . the boy tries to reject his mother and deny the deep personal identification with her that has developed during his early years. He does this by repressing whatever he takes to be feminine inside himself, and, importantly, by denigrating whatever he considers to be feminine in the outside world (that is, women)."

It is unclear what kind of data might provide a definitive test of this theory. Some studies find that men who say they have the closest relationships with their mothers report the most favorable attitude toward women—not the least favorable, as the theory predicts. Or do those data actually *support* the theory, because the men's profemale attitudes prove how much they are identified with their mothers? The theory's protean ability to interpret both profeminist and antifeminist attitudes as signs that a man is identified with his mother makes it possible to interpret any data as supporting the hypothesis.

There are, no doubt, some men who hate and fear women because of complex psychological dynamics deriving from their relationship with their mothers. But it is questionable whether those dynamics in the few should be invoked as the basis of the far more common, garden-variety male sexism so evident in our culture. Simpler theories can account for much, if not most, male antipathy to women: for example, negative male attitudes toward women may justify male social privilege.

Male dispositions to crime and violence, fear of women, and extreme fear of homosexuality are profoundly undesirable and cause serious social problems. Many men do indeed try to act "masculine." The question is how best to interpret their behavior. The hypermasculinity approach assumes that men have a natural inner urge to learn the male role, that many fail to attain it and therefore overcompensate, and that they—and their mothers—are ultimately at fault.

An alternative view is that people are not born with an inner psychological need to take on roles or traits different from those of the other sex, but that their culture strongly inculcates this need. If they do not spontaneously fit the cultural mold, they may try to force themselves into it. Thus, exaggerated masculinity, rather than being a reaction to inner insecurities, may reflect an overlearning of the externally prescribed role or an overconformity to it. The alternative interpretation, part of the emerging new theory of sex-role strain, puts the burden of responsibility for destructive, extreme male behavior on society's unrealistic male-role expectations—where it belongs—and not on the failings of individual men and their mothers.

Hypermasculinity arguments narrowmindedly ignore the direct role psychology has played in fostering hypermasculinity. After decades of psychological pronouncements about the deficiencies of women and the psychopathology of homosexuals, it seems a self-serving evasion of moral responsibility for psychologists to claim that the real reason that men dislike women and homosexuals is because of a sex-role identity problem caused by identifying too closely with their mothers.

BLACK MEN ARE ESPECIALLY VULNERABLE TO PROBLEMS WITH MASCULINITY

According to this idea, acquiring a secure sense of masculinity is more difficult for blacks than for whites because black fathers are absent more often and because many of them, even when present, are poor role models for their children.

Identity problems are then supposedly compounded in adulthood by higher rates of unemployment and overrepresentation in low-paying, low-prestige jobs among black men, especially such "feminine" service jobs as waiting on tables. As Harvard's social psychologist and race-relations expert Thomas F. Pettigrew expressed it in 1964, among black males "the sex-identity problems created by the fatherless home are perpetuated in adulthood." In their 1968 best-seller, *Black Rage*, psychiatrists William Grier and Price Cobbs assert that "whereas the white man regards his manhood as an ordained right, the black man is engaged in a never-ending struggle for its possession."

Pettigrew based his conclusions about blacks' greater sex-role identity problems (as shown by masculinity/femininity measures) on only two studies—one involving a sample of Alabama convicts, the other a sample of tubercular working-class veterans in Wisconsin—hardly a broad base of evidence. More recent studies, with both more representative samples and better sex-role measures, have not found the same differences between blacks and whites.

The "black emasculation" hypothesis was in vogue in the late 1960s and early 1970s. Its appeal to liberals arguing for equal rights is obvious: it holds that the racial oppression of blacks, in addition to producing the obvious consequences of poverty, shorter life expectancy, and so forth, has an even more insidious and subtle effect—the destruction of black men's masculinity. That apparently radical critique of racism conceals a patronizing view of blacks as psychological cripples and masks as well a deeply conservative notion of what proper sex roles ought to be.

Nowhere is that more evident than in Daniel Patrick Moynihan's 1967 work, *The Negro Family: The Case for National Action*, the famous "Moynihan Report." Moynihan argued for the worthy objective of a federal policy to promote full employment targeted especially at black males. But his justification for it hinged on the hypothetically devastating consequences of unemployment on black males' sex-role identities. In Moynihan's view, "the very essence of the male animal, from the bantam rooster to the four-star general, is to strut." Writing as America mobilized for a war in Vietnam, he praised military service as an almost ideal solution to black men's frustrated masculinity: "Given the strains of the disorganized and matrifocal family life in which so many Negro youth come of age, the Armed Forces are a dramatic and desperately needed change: a world away from women, a world run by strong men of unquestioned authority."

Another example of the patronization inherent in the black-emasculation hypothesis occurred in a popular book on fatherhood, *Father Power*, published in 1965 by University of Rhode Island psychologist Henry Biller and journalist Dennis Meredith. Material on black fathers appears in a chapter titled "Fathers with Special Problems." The only other example given there is the physically handicapped father.

Like the hypermasculinity hypothesis, the black-emasculation hypothesis ultimately blames the victim of a social problem for having it. Many critics have responded to this idea in narrow terms, arguing that black men have other role models, that their sexual identities are not impaired, or even that they actually are more masculine than white men. Few critics, unfortunately, have questioned the concept of sex-role identity itself. Few have asked just how much the notion of sex-role identity really does add to our understanding of the more basic issues—issues involving the negative impact of poverty, unemployment, or unsatisfying jobs on black (or any other) men.

On the basis of the evidence, we cannot go so far as to say that these five assertions have been proven false; in research, negative findings can never conclusively prove that a relationship does not exist, but can only show that a relationship has not been confirmed. We can say, however, that many popular ideas about masculinity that are widely thought to be backed up by decades of research have not been substantiated.

Unsubstantiated theories of masculinity have negative consequences for both sexes. In making women responsible for male insecurity and hostility, traditional male sex-role identity theory has made women both villains and victims in a male struggle for masculinity. The theory also holds that sex roles cannot change substantially because male identity is so fragile, a belief that leads to policies and strategies for imprisoning men in traditional roles, just as exaggerated ideas of women's fragility support restrictions on them. When a school district in West Virginia introduced a home economics curriculum that included homemaking skills for boys, members of the community opposed it on the grounds that it would turn their sons into homosexuals. The argument, typical of many, implies that the only way to make a man secure in his sex-role identity is to lock him up within it.

At last, a new approach to understanding masculinity and femininity is emerging, based on quite different assumptions—the theory of sex-role strain. In this view, there is no special need to encourage men and women to take different roles. If women and men do differ biologically in ways that cause different psychological traits (researchers are still debating), this approach says these differences will express themselves without help from parents and psychologists anxious about their children's sex-role identity. The point is not that we have to make men and women the same, but rather, that we do not have to strive so hard to make them different.

Researchers taking the new approach are investigating how traditional cultural standards for men and women create feelings of inadequacy if those standards are not achieved and other problems if they are. For example, what are the consequences of raising women to inhibit their achievement and men to inhibit their emotions? How does perceiving a difference between oneself and a cultural ideal for one's sex impair well-being? In the new view, the problem of sex roles is not how to learn a predetermined sex-role identity but rather how to avoid the strain built into traditional roles.

The feminist journalist Letty Cottin Pogrebin recently noted that feminist parents often find it easier to understand what nonsexist childrearing means for their daughters than for their sons. They support nontraditional activities and interests for daughters, but are often concerned if their sons are not aggressive and competitive or are sensitive or artistic ("They eventually have to face the real world, don't they?"). The journalists Lindsy Van Gelder and Carrie Carmichael reported in *Ms.* magazine in 1975 that when they asked a sample of feminist parents what they were doing to make their sons less like typical males, parents either had no response or expressed fears that any changes in traditional childrearing would make their sons homosexual. Van Gelder and Carmichael suggest that unless something is done to support change in men's roles, when today's daughters "reach womanhood in the 1990s, they will be confronted with a new generation of perfectly preserved 1960s males." So, indeed, they will—unless we demystify psychological myths of masculinity.

FURTHER READINGS

Gold, Dolores, and Myrna Reis, *Do Male Teachers in the Early School Years Make a Difference?* ERIC Clearinghouse, 1978.

Herzog, Elizabeth and Cecilia Sudia, "Children in Fatherless Families," in *Review of Child Development Research*, Vol. 3. Bettye Caldwell and Henry N. Ricciult, eds., University of Chicago Press, 1973.

Pogrebin, Letty Cottin, *Growing Up Free.* McGraw-Hill, 1980.

Barrie Thorne

GIRLS AND BOYS TOGETHER . . . BUT MOSTLY APART:
GENDER ARRANGEMENTS IN ELEMENTARY SCHOOLS

Throughout the years of elementary school, children's friendships and casual encounters are strongly separated by sex. Sex segregation among children, which starts in preschool and is well established by middle childhood, has been amply documented in studies of children's groups and friendships (e.g., Eder & Hallinan, 1978; Schofield, 1981) and is immediately visible in elementary school settings. When children choose seats in classrooms or the cafeteria, or get into line, they frequently arrange themselves in same-sex clusters. At lunchtime, they talk matter-of-factly about "girls' tables" and "boys' tables." Playgrounds have gendered turfs, with some areas and activities, such as large playing fields and basketball courts, controlled mainly by boys, and others—smaller enclaves like jungle-gym areas and concrete spaces for hopscotch or jumprope—more often controlled by girls. Sex segregation is so common in elementary schools that it is meaningful to speak of separate girls' and boys' worlds.

Studies of gender and children's social relations have mostly followed this "two worlds" model, separately describing and comparing the subcultures of girls and of boys (e.g., Lever, 1976; Maltz & Borker, 1983). In brief summary: Boys tend to interact in larger, more age-heterogeneous groups (Lever, 1976; Waldrop & Halverson, 1975; Eder & Hallinan, 1978). They engage in more rough and tumble play and physical fighting (Maccoby & Jacklin, 1974). Organized sports are both a central activity and a major metaphor in boys' subcultures; they use the language of "teams" even when not engaged in sports, and they often construct interaction in the form of contests. The shifting hierachies of boys' groups (Savin-Williams, 1976) are evident in their more frequent use of direct command, insults, and challenges (Goodwin, 1980).

Fewer studies have been done of girls' groups (Foot, Chapman, & Smith, 1980; McRobbie & Garber, 1975), and—perhaps because categories for description and analysis have come more from male than female experience—researchers have had difficulty seeing and analyzing girls' social relations. Recent work has begun to correct this skew. In middle childhood, girls' worlds are less public than those of boys; girls more often interact in private places and in smaller groups or friendship pairs (Eder & Hallinan, 1978; Waldrop & Halverson, 1975). Their play is more cooperative and turn-taking (Lever, 1976). Girls have more intense and exclusive friendships, which take shape around keeping and telling secrets, shifting alliances, and indirect ways of expressing disagreement (Goodwin, 1980; Lever, 1976; Maltz & Borker, 1983). Instead of direct commands, girls more often use directives which merge speaker and hearer, e.g., "let's" or "we gotta" (Goodwin, 1980).

Although much can be learned by comparing the social organization and

Reprinted from Willard W. Hartup and Zick Rubin, eds., *Relationships and Development.* Hillsdale, NJ: Lawrence Erlbaum Associates, 1986. Volume sponsored by the Social Science Research Center, Copyright © 1986 by Lawrence Erlbaum Associates, Inc.

subcultures of boys' and of girls' groups, the separate worlds approach has eclipsed full, contextual understanding of gender and social relations among children. The separate worlds model essentially involves a search for group sex differences, and shares the limitations of individual sex difference research. Differences tend to be exaggerated and similarities ignored, with little theoretical attention to the integration or similarity and difference (Unger, 1979). Statistical findings of difference are often portrayed as dichotomous, neglecting the considerable individual variation that exists; for example, not all boys fight, and some have intense and exclusive friendships. The sex difference approach tends to abstract gender from its social context, to assume that males and females are qualitatively and permanently different (with differences perhaps unfolding through separate developmental lines). These assumptions mask the possibility that gender arrangements and patterns of similarity and difference may vary by situation, race, social class, region, and subculture.

Sex segregation is far from total, and is a more complex and dynamic process than the portrayal of separate worlds reveals. Erving Goffman (1977) has observed that sex segregation has a "with-then-apart" structure; the sexes segregate periodically, with separate spaces, rituals, groups, but they also come together and are, in crucial ways, part of the same world. This is certainly true in the social environment of elementary schools. Although girls and boys do interact as boundaried collectivities—an image suggested by the separate worlds approach—there are other occasions when they work or play in relaxed and integrated ways. Gender is less central to the organization and meaning of some situations than others. In short, sex segregation is not static, but is a variable and complicated process.

To gain an understanding of gender which can encompass both the "with" and the "apart" of sex segregation, analysis should start not with the individual, nor with a search for sex differences, but with social relationships. Gender should be conceptualized as a system of relationships rather than as an immutable and dichotomous given. Taking this approach, I have organized my research on gender and children's social relations around questions like the following: How and when does gender enter into group formation? In a given situation, how is gender made more or less salient or infused with particular meanings? By what rituals, processes, and forms of social organization and conflict do "with-then-apart" rhythms get enacted? How are these processes affected by the organization of institutions (e.g., different types of schools, neighborhoods, or summer camps), varied settings (e.g., the constraints and possibilities governing interaction on playgrounds vs. classrooms), and particular encounters?

METHODS AND SOURCES OF DATA

This study is based on two periods of participant observation. In 1976–1977 I observed for 8 months in a largely working-class elementary school in California, a school with 8% Black and 12% Chicana/o students. In 1980 I did fieldwork for 3 months in a Michigan elementary school in similar size (around 400 students), social class, and racial composition. I observed in several classrooms—a kindergarten, a second grade, and a combined fourth-fifth grade—and in school hallways, cafeterias, and playgrounds. I set out to follow the round of the school day as children experience it, recording their interactions with one another, and with adults, in varied settings.

Participant observation involves gaining access to everyday, "naturalistic" settings and taking systematic notes over an extended period of time. Rather than starting with preset categories for recording, or with fixed hypotheses for testing, participant-observers record detail in ways which maximize opportunities for discovery. Through continuous interaction between observation and analysis, "grounded theory" is developed (Glaser & Strauss, 1967).

The distinctive logic and discipline of this mode of inquiry emerges from: (1) theoretical sampling—being relatively systematic in the choice of where and whom to observe in order to maximize knowledge relevant to categories and analysis which are being developed; and (2) comparing all relevant data on a given point in order to modify emerging propositions to take account of discrepant cases (Katz, 1983). Participant observation is a flexible, open-ended and inductive method, designed to understand behavior within, rather than stripped from, social context. It provides richly detailed information which is anchored in everyday meanings and experience.

DAILY PROCESSES OF SEX SEGREGATION

Sex segregation should be understood not as a given, but as the result of deliberate activity. The outcome is dramatically visible when there are separate girls' and boys' tables in school lunchrooms, or sex-separated groups on playgrounds. But in the same lunchroom one can also find tables where girls and boys eat and talk together, and in some playground activities the sexes mix. By what processes do girls and boys separate into gender-defined and relatively boundaried collectivities? And in what contexts, and through what processes, do boys and girls interact in less gender-divided ways?

In the school settings I observed, much segregation happened with no mention of gender. Gender was implicit in the contours of friendship, shared interest, and perceived risk which came into play when children chose companions—in their prior planning, invitations, seeking-of-access, saving-of-places, denials of entry, and allowing or protesting of "cuts" by those who violated the rules for lining up. Sometimes children formed mixed-sex groups for play, eating, talking, working on a classroom project, or moving through space. When adults or children explicitly invoked gender—and this was nearly always in ways which separated girls and boys—boundaries were heightened and mixed-sex interaction became an explicit arena of risk.

In the schools I studied, the physical space and curricula were not formally divided by sex, as they have been in the history of elementary schooling (a history evident in separate entrances to old school buildings, where the words "Boys" and "Girls" are permanently etched in concrete). Nevertheless, gender was a visible marker in the adult-organized school day. In both schools, when the public address system sounded, the principal inevitably opened with: "Boys and girls . . . ," and in addressing clusters of children, teachers and aides regularly used gender terms ("Heads down, girls"; "The girls are ready and the boys aren't"). These forms of address made gender visible and salient, conveying an assumption that the sexes are separate social groups.

Teachers and aides sometimes drew upon gender as a basis for sorting children and organizing activities. Gender is an embodied and visual social category which roughly divides the population in half, and the separation of girls and boys permeates the history and lore of schools and playgrounds. In both schools—although through awareness of Title IX, many teachers had changed this practice—one could see separate girls' and boys' lines moving, like caterpillars, through the school halls. In the 4th-5th grade classroom the teacher frequently pitted girls against boys for spelling and math contests. On the playground in the Michigan school, aides regarded the space close to the building as girls' territory, and the playing fields "out there" as boys' territory. They sometimes shooed children of the other sex away from those spaces, especially boys who ventured near the girls' area and seemed to have teasing in mind.

In organizing their activities, both within and apart from the surveillance of adults, children also explicitly invoked gender. During my fieldwork in the Michigan school, I kept daily records of who sat where in the lunchroom. The amount of sex segregation varied: It was least at the first grade tables and almost total among sixth graders. There was also variation from classroom to classroom within a given age, and from day to day. Actions like the following heightened the gender divide:

> In the lunchroom, when the two second grade tables were filling, a high-status boy walked by the inside table, which had a scattering of both boys and girls, and said loudly, "Oooo, too many girls," as he headed for a seat at the far table. The boys at the inside table picked up their trays and moved, and no other boys sat at the inside table, which the pronouncement had effectively made taboo.

In the end, that day (which was not the case every day), girls and boys ate at separate tables.

Eating and walking are not sex-typed activities, yet in forming groups in lunchrooms and hallways children often separated by sex. Sex segregation assumed added dimensions on the playground, where spaces, equipment, and activities were infused with gender meanings. My inventories of activities and groupings on the playground showed similar patterns in both schools: Boys controlled the large fixed spaces designated for team sports (baseball diamonds, grassy fields used for football or soccer); girls more often played closer to the building, doing tricks on the monkey bars (which, for 6th graders, became an area for sitting and talking) and using cement areas for jumprope, hopscotch, and group games like four-square. (Lever, 1976, provides a good analysis of sex-divided play.) Girls and boys most often played together in kickball, and in group (rather than team) games like four-square, dodgeball, and handball. When children used gender to exclude others from play, they often drew upon beliefs connecting boys to some activities and girls to others:

> A first grade boy avidly watched an all-female game of jump rope. When the girls began to shift positions, he recognized a means of access to the play and he offered, "I'll swing it." A girl responded, "No way, you don't know how to do it, to swing it. You gotta be a girl." He left without protest.

Although children sometimes ignored pronouncements about what each sex could or could not do, I never heard them directly challenge such claims.

When children had explicitly defined an activity or a group as gendered, those who crossed the boundary—especially boys who moved into female-marked space—risked being teased. ("Look! Mike's in the girls' line!" "That's a girl over there, a girl said loudly, pointing to a boy sitting at an otherwise all-female table in the lunchroom.") Children, and occasionally adults, used teasing—especially the tease of "liking" someone of the other sex, or of "being" that sex by virtue of being in their midst—to police gender boundaries. Much of the teasing drew upon heterosexual romantic definitions, making cross-sex interaction risky, and increasing social distance between boys and girls.

RELATIONSHIPS BETWEEN THE SEXES

Because I have emphasized the "apart" and ignored the occasions of "with," this analysis of sex segregation falsely implies that there is little contact between girls and boys in daily school life. In fact, relationships between girls and boys—which should be studied as fully as, and in connection with, same-sex relationships—are of several kinds:

1. "Borderwork," or forms of cross-sex interaction which are based upon and reaffirm boundaries and asymmetries between girls' and boys' groups;
2. Interactions which are infused with heterosexual meanings;
3. Occasions where individuals cross gender boundaries to participate in the world of the other sex; and
4. Situations where gender is muted in salience, with girls and boys interacting in more relaxed ways.

Borderwork   In elementary school settings boys' and girls' grouped are sometimes spatially set apart. Same-sex groups sometimes claim fixed territories such as the basketball court, the bars, or specific lunchroom tables. However, in the crowded, multifocused, and adult-controlled environment of the school, groups form and disperse at a rapid rate and can never stay totally apart. Contact between girls and boys sometimes lessens sex segregation, but gender-defined groups also come together in ways which emphasize their boundaries.

"Borderwork" refers to interaction across, yet based upon and even strengthening gender boundaries. I have drawn this notion from Fredrik Barth's (1969) analysis of social relations which are maintained across ethnic boundaries without diminishing dichotomized ethnic status.[1] His focus is on more macro, ecological arrangements; mine is on face-to-face behavior. But the insight is similar: Groups may interact in ways which strengthen their borders, and the maintenance of ethnic (or gender) groups can best be understood by examining the boundary that defines the group, "not the cultural stuff that it encloses" (Barth, 1969, p. 15). In elementary schools there are several types of borderwork: contests or games where gender-defined teams

1. I am grateful to Frederick Erickson for suggesting the relevance of Barth's analysis.

compete; cross-sex rituals of chasing and pollution; and group invasions. These interactions are asymmetrical, challenging the separate-but-parallel model of "two worlds."

Contests   Boys and girls are sometimes pitted against each other in classroom competitions and playground games. The 4th–5th grade classroom had a boys' side and a girls' side, an arrangement that re-emerged each time the teacher asked children to choose their own desks. Although there was some within-sex shuffling, the result was always a spatial moiety system—boys on the left, girls on the right—with the exception of one girl (the "tomboy" whom I'll describe later), who twice chose a desk with the boys and once with the girls. Drawing upon and reinforcing the children's self-segregation, the teacher often pitted the boys against the girls in spelling and math competitions, events marked by cross-sex antagonism and within-sex solidarity:

> The teacher introduced a math game; she would write addition and subtraction problems on the board, and a member of each team would race to be the first to write the correct answer. She wrote two score-keeping columns on the board: 'Beastly Boys'. . . 'Gossipy Girls.' The boys yelled out, as several girls laughed, 'Noisy girls! Gruesome girls!' The girls sat in a row on top of their desks; sometimes they moved collectively, pushing their hips or whispering 'pass it on.' The boys stood along the wall, some reclining against desks. When members of either group came back victorious from the front of the room, they would do the 'giving five' handslapping ritual with their team members.

On the playground a team of girls occasionally played against a team of boys, usually in kickball or team two-square. Sometimes these games proceeded matter-of-factly, but if gender became the explicit basis of team solidarity, the interaction changed, becoming more antagonistic and unstable:

> Two fifth-grade girls against two fifth-grade boys in a team game of two-square. The game proceeded at an even pace until an argument ensued about whether the ball was out or on the line. Karen, who had hit the ball, became annoyed, flashed her middle finger at the other team, and called to a passing girl to join their side. The boys then called out to other boys, and cheered as several arrived to play. 'We got five and you got three!' Jack yelled. The game continued, with the girls yelling, 'Bratty boys! Sissy boys!' and the boys making noises—'weee haw' 'ha-ha-ha'—as they played.

Chasing   Cross-sex chasing dramatically affirms boundaries between girls and boys. The basic elements of chase and elude, capture and rescue (Sutton-Smith, 1971) are found in various kinds of tag with formal rules, and in informal episodes of chasing which punctuate life on playgrounds. These episodes begin with a provocation (taunts like "You can't get me!" or "Slobber monster!"; bodily pokes or the grabbing of possessions). A provocation may be ignored, or responded to by chasing. Chaser and chased may then alternate roles. In an ethnographic study of chase sequences on a school playground, Christine Finnan (1982) observes that chases vary in number of chasers to chased (e.g., one chasing one, or five chasing two); form of provocation (a taunt or a poke); outcome (an episode may end when the chased outdistances the chaser, or with a brief touch, being wrestled to the ground, or the recapturing of a hat or a ball); and in use of space (there may or may not be safety zones).

Like Finnan (1982), and Sluckin (1981), who studied a playground in England, I found that chasing has a gendered structure. Boys frequently chase one another, an activity which often ends in wrestling and mock fights. When girls chase girls, they are usually less physically aggressive; they less often, for example, wrestle one another to the ground.

Cross-sex chasing is set apart by special names—"girls chase the boys"; "boys chase the girls"; "the chase"; "chasers"; "chase and kiss'; "kiss chase"; "kissers and chasers"; "kiss or kill"—and by children's animated talk about the activity. The names vary by region and school, but contain both gender and sexual meanings (this form of play is mentioned, but only briefly analyzed, in Finnan, 1981; Sluckin, 1981; Parrott, 1972; and Borman, 1979).

In "boys chase the girls" and "girls chase the boys" (the names most frequently used in both the California and Michigan schools) boys and girls become, by definition, separate teams. Gender terms override individual identities, especially for the other team ("Help, a girl's chasin' me!"; "C'mon Sarah, let's get that boy"; "Tony, help save me from the girls"). Individuals may call for help from, or offer help to, others of their sex. They may also grab someone of their sex and turn them over to the opposing team: "Ryan grabbed Billy from behind, wrestling him to the ground. 'Hey, girls, get 'im,' Ryan called."

Boys more often mix episodes of cross-sex with same-sex chasing. Girls more often have safety zones, places like the girls' restroom or an area by the school wall, where they retreat to rest and talk (sometimes in animated postmortems) before new episodes of cross-sex chasing begin.

Early in the fall in the Michigan school, where chasing was especially prevalent, I watched a second grade boy teach a kindergarten girl how to chase. He slowly ran backwards, beckoning her to pursue him, as he called, "Help, a girl's after me." In the early grades chasing mixes with fantasy play, e.g., a first-grade boy who played, "sea monster," his arms outflung and his voice growling, as he chased a group of girls. By third grade, stylized gestures—exaggerated stalking motions, screams (which only girls do), and karate kicks—accompany scenes of chasing.

Names like "chase and kiss" mark the sexual meanings of cross-sex chasing, a theme I return to later. The threat of kissing—most often girls threatening to kiss boys—is a ritualized form of provocation. Cross-sex chasing among sixth graders involves elaborate patterns of touch and touch avoidance, which adults see as sexual. The principal told the sixth graders in the Michigan school that they were not to play "pom-pom," a complicated chasing game, because it entailed "inappropriate touch."

Rituals of Pollution   Cross-sex chasing is sometimes entwined with rituals of pollution, as in "cooties," where specific individuals or groups are treated as contaminating or carrying "germs." Children have rituals for transfering cooties (usually touching someone else and shouting "You've got cooties!"), for immunization (e.g., writing "CV" for "cootie vaccination" on their arms), and for eliminating cooties (e.g., saying "no gives" or using "cootie catchers" made of folded paper) described in Knapp & Knapp, 1976). While girls may give cooties to girls, boys do not generally give cooties to one another (Samuelson, 1980).

In cross-sex play, either girls or boys may be defined as having cooties, which they transfer through chasing and touching. Girls give cooties to boys more often than vice versa. In Michigan, one version of cooties is called "girl stain"; the fourth-graders whom Karkau, 1973, describes, used the phrase "girl touch." "Cootie queens," or "cootie girls" (there are no "kings" or "boys") are female pariahs, the ultimate school untouchables, seen as contaminating not only by virtue of gender, but also through some added stigma such as being overweight or poor.[2] That girls are seen as more polluting than boys is a significant asymmetry, which echoes cross-cultural patterns, although in other cultures female pollution is generally connected to menstruation, and not applied to prepubertal girls.

Invasions   Playground invasions are another asymmetric form of border-work. On a few occasions I saw girls invade and disrupt an all-male game, most memorably a group of tall sixth-grade girls who ran onto the playing field and grabbed a football which was in play. The boys were surprised and frustrated, and, unusual for boys this old, finally tattled to the aide. But in the majority of cases, boys disrupt girls' activities rather than vice versa. Boys grab the ball from girls playing four-square, stick feet into a jumprope and stop an ongoing game, and dash through the area of the bars, where girls are taking turns performing, sending the rings flying. Sometimes boys ask to join a girls' game and then, after a short period of seemingly earnest play, disrupt the game:

> Two second-grade boys begged to "twirl" the jumprope for a group of second-grade girls who had been jumping for some time. The girls agreed, and the boys began to twirl. Soon, without announcement, the boys changed from "seashells, cockle bells' to "hot peppers" (spinning the rope very fast), and tangled the jumper in the rope. The boys ran away laughing.

Boys disrupt girls' play so often that girls have developed almost ritualized responses: They guard their ongoing play, chase boys away, and tattle to the aides. In a playground cycle which enhances sex segregation, aids who try to spot potential trouble before it occurs sometimes shoo boys away from areas where girls are playing. Aides do not anticipate trouble from girls who seek to join groups of boys, with the exception of girls intent on provoking a chase sequence. And indeed, if they seek access to a boys' game, girls usually play with boys in earnest rather than breaking up the game.

A close look at the organization of borderwork—or boundaried interactions between the sexes—shows that the worlds of boys and girls may be separate but they are not parallel, nor are they equal. The worlds of girls and boys articulate in several asymmetric ways:

1. On the playground, boys control as much as ten times more space than girls, when one adds up the area of large playing fields and compares it with the

---

2. Sue Samuelson (1980) reports that in a racially mixed playground in Fresno, California, Mexican-American, but not Anglo children gave cooties. Racial, as well as sexual inequality may be expressed through these forms.

much smaller areas where girls predominate. Girls, who play closer to the building, are more often watched over and protected by the adult aides.

2. Boys invade all-female games and scenes of play much more than girls invade boys. This, and boys' greater control of space, correspond with other findings about the organization of gender, and inequality, in our society: compared with men and boys, women and girls take up less space, and their space, and talk, are more often violated and interrupted (Greif, 1982; Henley, 1977; West & Zimmerman, 1983).

3. Although individual boys are occasionally treated as contaminating (e.g., a third grade boy who [to] both boys and girls was "stinky" and "smelled like pee"), girls are more often defined as polluting. This pattern ties to themes that I discuss later: It is more taboo for a boy to play with (as opposed to invade) girls, and girls are more sexually defined than boys.

A look at the boundaries between the separated worlds of girls and boys illuminates within-sex hierarchies of status and control. For example, in the sex-divided seating in the 4th–5th grade classroom, several boys recurringly sat near "female space": their desks were at the gender divide in the classroom, and they were more likely than other boys to sit at a predominantly female table in the lunchroom. These boys—two nonbilingual Chicanos and an overweight "loner" boy who was afraid of sports—were at the bottom of the male hierarchy. Gender is sometimes used as a metaphor for male hierarchies; the inferior status of boys at the bottom is conveyed by calling them "girls":

> Seven boys and one girl were playing basketball. Two younger boys came over and asked to play. While the girl silently stood, fully accepted in the company of players, one of the older boys disparagingly said to the younger boys, 'You girls can't play.'[3]

In contrast, the girls who more often travel in the boys' world, sitting with groups of boys in the lunchroom or playing basketball, soccer, and baseball with them, are not stigmatized. Some have fairly high status with other girls. The worlds of girls and boys are assymetrically arranged, and spatial patterns map out interacting forms of inequality.

Heterosexual Meanings   The organization and meanings of gender (the social categories "woman/man," "girl/boy") and of sexuality vary cross-culturally (Ortner & Whitehead, 1981)—and, in our society, across the life course. Harriet Whitehead (1981) observed that in our (Western) gender system, and that of many traditional North American Indian cultures, one's choice of a sexual object, occupation, and one's dress and demeanor are closely associated with gender. However, the "center of gravity" differs in the two gender systems. For Indians, occupational pursuits provide the primary imagery of gender; dress and demeanor are secondary, and sexuality is least important. In our system, at least for adults, the order is reversed: heterosexuality is central to our definitions of "man" and "woman" ("masculinity"/"femininity"), and

---

3. This incident was recorded by Margaret Blume, who, for an undergraduate research project in 1982, observed in the California school where I earlier did fieldwork. Her observations and insights enhanced my own, and I would like to thank her for letting me cite this excerpt.

the relationships that obtain between them, whereas occupation and dress/ demeanor are secondary.

Whereas erotic orientation and gender are closely linked in our definitions of adults, we define children as relatively asexual. Activities and dress/ demeanor are more important than sexuality in the cultural meanings of "girl" and "boy." Children are less heterosexually defined than adults, and we have nonsexual imagery for relations between girls and boys. However, both children and adults sometimes use heterosexual language—"crushes," "like," "goin' with," "girlfriends," and "boyfriends"—to define cross-sex relationships. This language increases through the years of elementary school; the shift to adolescence consolidates a gender system organized around the institution of heterosexuality.

In everyday life in the schools, heterosexual and romantic meanings infuse some ritualized forms of interaction between groups of boys and girls (e.g., "chase and kiss") and help maintain sex segregation, "Jimmy likes Beth" or "Beth likes Jimmy" is a major form of teasing, which a child risks in choosing to sit by or walk with someone of the other sex. The structure of teasing, and children's sparse vocabulary for relationships between girls and boys, are evident in the following conversation which I had with a group of third-grade girls in the lunchroom:

> Susan asked me what I was doing, and I said I was observing the things children do and play. Nicole volunteered, 'I like running, boys chase all the girls. See Tim over there? Judy chases him all around the school. She likes him.' Judy, sitting across the table, quickly responded, 'I hate him. I like him for a friend.' 'Tim loves Judy,' Nicole said in a loud, sing-song voice.

In the younger grades, the culture and lore of girls contain more heterosexual romantic themes than that of boys. In Michigan, the first-grade girls often jumped rope to a rhyme which began: "Down in the valley where the green grass grows, there sat Cindy (name of jumper), as sweet as a rose. She sat, she sat, she sat so sweet. Along came Jason, and kissed her on the cheek . . . first comes love, then comes marriage, then along comes Cindy with a baby carriage . . ." Before a girl took her turn at jumping, the chanters asked her "Who do you want to be your boyfriend?" The jumper always proffered a name, which was accepted matter-of-factly. In chasing a girl's kiss carried greater threat than a boy's kiss; "girl touch," when defined as contaminating, had sexual connotations. In short, starting at an early age, girls are more sexually defined than boys.

Through the years of elementary school, and increasing with age, the idiom of heterosexuality helps maintain the gender divide. Cross-sex interactions, especially when children initiate them, are fraught with the risk of being teased about "liking" someone of the other sex. I learned of several close cross-sex friendships, formed and maintained in neighborhoods and church, which went underground during the school day.

By the fifth grade a few children began to affirm, rather than avoid, the charge of having a girlfriend or a boyfriend; they introduced the heterosexual courtship rituals of adolescence:

> In the lunchroom in the Michigan school, as the tables were forming, a

high-status fifth-grade boy called out from his seat at the table: 'I want Trish to sit by me.' Trish came over, and almost like a king and queen, they sat at the gender divide—a row of girls down the table on her side, a row of boys on his.

In this situation, which inverted earlier forms, it was not a loss, but a gain in status to publically choose a companion of the other sex. By affirming his choice, the boy became unteasable (note the familiar asymmetry of heterosexual courtship rituals: the male initiated). This incident signals a temporal shift in arrangements of sex and gender.

Traveling in the World of the Other Sex   Contests, invasions, chasing, and heterosexually-defined encounters are based upon and reaffirm boundaries between girls and boys. In another type of cross-sex interaction, individuals (or sometimes pairs) cross gender boundaries, seeking acceptance in a group of the other sex. Nearly all the cases I saw of this were tomboys—girls who played organized sports and frequently sat with boys in the cafeteria or classroom. If these girls were skilled at activities central in the boys' world, especially games like soccer, baseball, and basketball, they were pretty much accepted as participants.

Being a tomboy is a matter of degree. Some girls seek access to boys' groups but are excluded; other girls limit their "crossing" to specific sports. Only a few—such as the tomboy I mentioned earlier, who chose a seat with the boys in the sex-divided fourth–fifth grade—participate fully in the boys' world. That particular girl was skilled at the various organized sports which boys played in different seasons of the year. She was also adept at physical fighting and at using the forms of arguing, insult, teasing, naming, and sports-talk of the boys' subculture. She was the only Black child in her classroom, in a school with only 8% Black students; overall that token status, along with unusual athletic and verbal skills, may have contributed to her ability to move back and forth across the gender divide. Her unique position in the children's world was widely recognized in the school. Several times, the teacher said to me, "She thinks she's a boy."

I observed only one boy in the upper grades (a fourth grader) who regularly played with all-female groups, as opposed to "playing at" girls' games and seeking to disrupt them. He frequently played jumprope and took turns with girls doing tricks on the bars, using the small gestures—for example, a helpful push on the heel of a girl who needed momentum to turn her body around the bar—which mark skillful and earnest participation. Although I never saw him play in other than an earnest spirit, the girls often chased him away from their games, and both girls and boys teased him. The fact that girls seek, and have more access to boys' worlds than vice versa, and the fact that girls who travel with the other sex are less stigmatized for it, are obvious asymmetries, tied to the asymmetries previously discussed.

Relaxed Cross-Sex Interactions   Relationships between boys and girls are not always marked by strong boundaries, heterosexual definitions, or by interacting on the terms and turfs of the other sex. On some occasions girls and boys interact in relatively comfortable ways. Gender is not strongly salient nor explicitly invoked, and girls and boys are not organized into boundaries collectively. These "with" occasions have been neglected by those studying gender and children's relationships, who have emphasized either the model of separate worlds (with little attention to their articulation) or heterosexual forms of contact.

Occasions where boys and girls interact without strain, where gender wanes, rather than waxes in importance, frequently have one or more of the following characteristics:

1. The situations are organized around an absorbing task, such as a group art project or creating a radio show, which encourages cooperation and lessens attention to gender. This pattern accords with other studies finding that cooperative activities reduce group antagonism (e.g., Sherif & Sherif, 1953, who studied divisions between boys in a summer camp; and Aronson et al., 1978, who used cooperative activities to lessen racial divisions in a classroom).
2. Gender is less prominent when children are not responsible for the formation of the group. Mixed-sex play is less frequent in games like football, which require the choosing of teams, and more frequent in games like handball or dodgeball which individuals can join simply by getting into a line or a circle. When adults organize mixed-sex encounters—which they frequently do in the classroom and in physical education periods on the playground—they legitimize cross-sex contact. This removes the risk of being teased for choosing to be with the other sex.
3. There is more extensive and relaxed cross-sex interaction when principles of grouping other than gender are explicitly involved—for example, counting off to form teams for spelling or kickball, dividing lines by hot lunch or cold lunch, or organizing a work group on the basis of interests or reading ability.
4. Girls and boys may interact more readily in less public and crowded settings. Neighborhood play, depending on demography, is more often sex and age integrated than play at school, partly because with fewer numbers, one may have to resort to an array of social categories to find play partners or to constitute a game. And in less crowded environments there are fewer potential witnesses to "make something of it" if girls and boys play together.

Relaxed interactions between girls and boys often depend on adults to set up and legitimize the contact.[4] Perhaps because of this contingency—and the other, distancing patterns which permeate relations between girls and boys—the easeful moments of interaction rarely build to close friendship. Schofield (1981) makes a similar observation about gender and racial barriers to friendship in a junior high school.

IMPLICATIONS FOR DEVELOPMENT

I have located social relations within an essentially spatial framework, emphasizing the organization of children's play, work, and other activities within specific settings, and in one type of institution, the school. In contrast, frameworks of child development rely upon temporal metaphors, using im-

---

4. Note that in daily school life, depending on the individual and the situation, teachers and aides sometimes lessened, and at other times heightened sex segregation.

ages of growth and transformation over time. Taken alone, both spatial and temporal frameworks have shortcomings; fitted together, they may be mutually correcting.

Those interested in gender and development have relied upon conceptualizations of "sex role socialization" and "sex differences." Sexuality and gender, I have argued, are more situated and fluid than these individualist and intrinsic models imply. Sex and gender are differently organized and defined across situations, even within the same institution. This situational variation (e.g., in the extent to which an encounter heightens or lessens gender boundaries, or is infused with sexual meanings) shapes and constrains individual behavior. Features which a developmental perspective might attribute to individuals, and understand as relatively internal attributes unfolding over time, may, in fact, be highly dependent on context. For example, children's avoidance of cross-sex friendship may be attributed to individual gender development in middle-childhood. But attention to varied situations may show that this avoidance is contingent on group size, activity, adult behavior, collective meanings, and the risk of being teased.

A focus on social organization and situation draws attention to children's experiences in the present. This helps correct a model like "sex role socialization" which casts the present under the shadow of the future, or presumed "endpoints" (Speier, 1976). A situated analysis of arrangements of sex and gender among those of different ages may point to crucial disjunctions in the life course. In the fourth and fifth grades, culturally defined heterosexual rituals ("goin' with") begin to suppress the presence and visibility of other types of interaction between girls and boys, such as nonsexualized and comfortable interaction, and traveling in the world of the other sex. As "boyfriend/girlfriend" definitions spread, the fifth-grade tomboy I described had to work to sustain "buddy" relationships with boys. Adult women who were tomboys often speak of early adolescence as a painful time when they were pushed away from participation in boys' activities. Other adult women speak of the loss of intense, even erotic ties with other girls when they entered puberty and the rituals of dating, that is, when they became absorbed into the institution of heterosexuality (Rich, 1980). When Lever (1976) describes best-friend relationships among fifth-grade girls as preparation for dating, she imposes heterosexual ideologies onto a present which should be understood on its own terms.

As heterosexual encounters assume more importance, they may alter relations in same-sex groups. For example, Schofield (1981) reports that for sixth- and seventh-grade children in a middle school, the popularity of girls with other girls was affected by their popularity with boys, while boys' status with other boys did not depend on their relations with girls. This is an asymmetry familiar from the adult world; men's relationships with one another are defined through varied activities (occupations, sports), while relationships among women—and their public status—are more influenced by their connections to individual men.

A full understanding of gender and social relations should encompass cross-sex as well as within-sex interactions. "Borderwork" helps maintain separate, gender-linked subcultures, which, as those interested in development have begun to suggest, may result in different milieux for learning. Daniel Maltz and Ruth Borker (1983) for example, argue that because of different interactions within girls' and boys' groups, the sexes learn different rules for creating and interpreting friendly conversation, rules which carry into adulthood and help account for miscommunication between men and women. Carol Gilligan (1982) fits research on the different worlds of girls and boys into a theory of sex differences in moral development. Girls develop a style of reasoning, she argues, which is more personal and relational; boys develop a style which is more positional, based on separateness. Eleanor Maccoby (1982), also following the insight that because of sex segregation, girls and boys grow up in different environments, suggests implications for gender differentiated prosocial and antisocial behavior.

This separate worlds approach, as I have illustrated, also has limitations. The occasions when the sexes are together should also be studied, and understood as contexts for experience and learning. For example, asymmetries in cross-sex relationships convey a series of messages: that boys are more entitled to space and to the nonreciprocal right of interrupting or invading the activities of the other sex; that girls are more in need of adult protection, and are lower in status, more defined by sexuality, and may even be polluting. Different types of cross-sex interaction—relaxed, boundaried, sexualized, or taking place on the terms of the other sex—provide different contexts for development.

By mapping the array of relationships between and within the sexes, one adds complexity to the overly static and dichotomous imagery of separate worlds. Individual experiences vary, with implications for development. Some children perfer same-sex groupings; some are more likely to cross the gender boundary and participate in the world of the other sex; some children (e.g., girls and boys who frequently play "chase and kiss") invoke heterosexual meanings, while others avoid them.

Finally, after charting the terrain of relationships, one can trace their development over time. For example, age variation in the content and form of borderwork, or of cross and same-sex touch, may be related to differing cognitive, social, emotional, or physical capacities, as well as to age-associated cultural forms. I earlier mentioned temporal shifts in the organization of cross-sex chasing, for mixing with fantasy play in the early grades to more elaborately ritualized and sexualized forms by the sixth grade. There also appear to be temporal changes in same and cross-sex touch. In kindergarten, girls and boys touch one another more freely than in fourth grade, when children avoid relaxed cross-sex touch and instead use pokes, pushes, and other forms of mock violence, even when the touch clearly couches affection. This touch taboo is obviously related to the risk of seeming to *like* someone of the other sex. In fourth grade, same-sex touch begins to signal sexual meanings among boys, as well as between boys and girls. Younger boys touch one another freely in cuddling (arm around shoulder) as well as mock violence ways. By fourth grade, when homophobic taunts like "fag" become more common among boys, cuddling touch begins to disappear for boys, but less so for girls.

Overall, I am calling for more complexity in our conceptualization of gender and of children's social relationships. Our challenge is to retain the temporal sweep, looking at individual and group lives as they unfold over time, while also attending to social structure and context, and to the full variety of experiences in the present.

ACKNOWLEDGMENT

I would like to thank Jane Atkinson, Nancy Chodorow, Arlene Daniels, Peter Lyman, Zick Rubin, Malcolm Spector, Avril Thorne, and Margery Wolf for comments on an earlier version of this paper. Conversations with Zella Luria enriched this work.

REFERENCES

Aronson, F., et al. (1978). *The jigsaw classroom.* Beverly Hills, CA: Sage.

Barth, F. (Ed.). (1969). *Ethnic groups and boundaries.* Boston: Little, Brown.

Borman, K. M. (1979). Children's interactions in playgrounds. *Theory into Practice, 18,* 251–257.

Eder, D., & Hallinan, M. T. (1978). Sex differences in children's friendships. *American Sociological Review, 43,* 237–250.

Finnan, C. R. (1982). The ethnography of children's spontaneous play. In G. Spindler (Ed.), *Doing the ethnography of schooling* (pp. 358–380). New York: Holt, Rinehart & Winston.

Foot, H. C., Chapman, A. J., & Smith, J. R. (1980). Introduction. *Friendship and social relations in children* (pp. 1–14). New York: Wiley.

Gilligan, C. (1982). *In a different voice: Psychological theory and women's development.* Cambridge, MA: Harvard University Press.

Glaser, B. G., & Strauss, A. L. (1967). *The discovery of grounded theory.* Chicago: Aldine.

Goffman, E. (1977). The arrangement between the sexes. *Theory and Society, 4,* 301–336.

Goodwin, M. H. (1980). Directive-response sequences in girls' and boys' task activities. In S. McConnell-Ginet, R. Borker, & N. Furman (Eds.), *Women and language in literature and society* (pp. 157.–173). New York: Praeger.

Grief, E. B. (1980). Sex differences in parent-child conversations. *Women's Studies International Quarterly, 3.* 253–258.

Henley, N. (1977). *Body politics: Power, sex, and nonverbal communication.* Englewood Cliffs, NJ: Prentice-Hall.

Karkau, K. (1973). *Sexism in the fourth grade.* Pittsburgh: KNOW, Inc. (pamphlet)

Katz, J. (1983). A theory of qualitative methodology: The social system of analytic fieldwork. In R. M. Emerson (Ed.), *Contemporary field research* (pp. 127–148). Boston: Little, Brown.

Knapp, M., & Knapp, H. (1976). *One potato, two potato: The secret education of American children.* New York: W. W. Norton.

Lever, J. (1976). Sex differences in the games children play. *Social Problems, 23,* 478–487.

Maccoby, E. (1982). *Social groupings in childhood: Their relationship to prosocial and antisocial behavior in boys and girls.* Paper presented at conference on The Development of Prosocial and Antisocial Behavior. Voss, Norway.

Maccoby, E., & Jacklin, C. (1974). *The psychology of sex differences.* CA: Stanford University Press.

Maltz, D. N., & Borker, R. A. (1983). A cultural approach to male-female miscommincation. In J. J. Gumperz (Ed.), *Language and social identity* (pp. 195–216). New York: Cambridge University Press.

McRobbie, A., & Garber, J. (1975). Girls and subcultures. In S. Hall and T. Jefferson (Eds.), *Resistance through rituals* (pp. 209–223). London: Hutchinson.

Ortner, S. B., & Whitehead, H. (1981). *Sexual meanings.* New York: Cambridge University Press.

Parrott, S. (1972). Games children play: Ethnography of a second-grade recess. In J. P. Spradley & D. W. McCurdy (Eds.), *The cultural experience* (pp. 206–219). Chicago: Science Research Associates.

Rich, A. (1980). Compulsory heterosexuality and lesbian existence. *Signs, 5,* 631–660.

Samuelson, S. (1980). The cooties complex. *Western Folklore, 39,* 198–210.

Savin-Williams, R. C. (1976). An ethological study of dominance formation and maintenance in a group of human adolescents. *Child Development, 47,* 972–979.

Schofield, J. W. (1981). Complementary and conflicting identities: Images and interaction in an interracial school. In S. R. Asher & J. M. Gottman (Eds.), *The development of children's friendships* (pp. 53–90). New York: Cambridge University Press.

Sherif, M., & Sherif, C. (1953). *Groups in harmony and tension.* New York: Harper.

Jeffrey P. Hantover

THE BOY SCOUTS AND THE VALIDATION OF MASCULINITY

The Boy Scouts of America was formally incorporated in 1910 and by 1916 had received a federal charter, absorbed most of the organizations which had claimed the Scouting name, and was an accepted community institution. The President of the United States was the organization's honorary president, and Scouting courses were offered in major universities. At the end of its first decade, the Boy Scouts was the largest male youth organization in American history with 358,573 scouts and 15,117 scoutmasters.

The Boy Scouts' rapid national acceptance reflected turn-of-the-century concern over the perpetuation and validation of American masculinity. The widespread and unplanned adoption of the Scout program prior to 1916 suggests that Scouting's message, unadorned by organizational sophistication, spoke to major adult concerns, one of which was the future of traditional conceptions of American masculinity.

This paper will argue that the Boy Scouts served the needs of adult men as well as adolescent boys. The supporters of the Scout movement, those who gave their time, money, and public approval, believed that changes in work, the family, and adolescent life threatened the development of manliness among boys and its expression among men. They perceived and promoted Scouting as an agent for the perpetuation of manliness among adolescents; the Boy Scouts provided an environment in which boys could become "red blooded" virile men. Less explicitly, Scouting provided men an opportunity to counteract the perceived feminizing forces of their lives and to act according to the traditional masculine script.

THE OPPORTUNITY TO BE A MAN:
RESTRICTION AND ITS CONSEQUENCES

Masculinity is a cultural construct and adult men need the opportunity to perform normatively appropriate male behaviors. Masculinity is not affirmed once and for all by somatic change; physical development is but a means for the performance of culturally ascribed behaviors. American masculinity is

Reprinted from *Journal of Social Issues* Volume 34, Number 1, 1978.
The author wishes to thank Joseph Pleck and Mayer Zald for their constructive comments.

continually affirmed through ongoing action. What acts a man performs and how well he does them truly make a male a man.

However, the availability of opportunites is not constant. Anxiety about the integrity and persistence of the male role can result from a restriction of opportunities experienced by the individual and the groups with which he identifies. Adult experiences produce adult anxieties. Masculine anxiety can arise when adult men know the script and wish to perform according to cultural directions but are denied the opportunity to act: The fault lies in social structuring of opportunities and not in individual capabilities and motivations.

The anxiety men increasingly exhibited about the naturalness and substance of manliness in the period 1880 to World War I flowed from changes in institutional spheres traditionally supportive of masculine definitional affirmation. Feminism as a political movement did raise fears of feminization but, as Filene (1975) suggests, in relation to preexistent anxiety about the meaning of manliness. Changes in the sphere of work, the central institutional anchorage of masculinity, undercut essential elements in the definition of manliness. Men believed they faced diminishing opportunites for masculine validation and that adolescents faced barriers to the very development of masculinity.

Masculine anxiety at the turn of the century was expressed in the accentuation of the physical and assertive side of the male ideal and in the enhanced salience of gender in social life. The enthronement of "muscularity" is evident in leisure activities, literary tastes, and cultural heroes. In the early nineteenth century, running and jumping were not exercises befitting a gentleman (Rudolph, 1962), but now men took to the playing fields, gyms, and wilderness in increasing numbers. Football, baseball, hiking, and camping became popular and were defended for their contribution to the development of traditional masculine character. Popular magazine biographies of male heroes in the period 1894 to 1913 shifted from an earlier idealization of passive traits such as piety, thrift, and industry to an emphasis on vigor, forcefulness, and mastery (Greene, 1970). Literary masculinization extended beyond mortals like Teddy Roosevelt to Christ who was portrayed as "the supremely manly man": attractive to women, individualistic, athletic, self-controlled, and aggressive when need be—"he was no Prince of Peace-at-any-price" (Conant, 1915, p. 117).

Sex-role distinctions became increasingly salient and rigid. The birth control issue became enmeshed in the debate over women's proper role; diatribes against expanded roles for women accompanied attacks on family limitation. The increased insistence on sexual purity in fiction and real life was a demand for women to accept the traditional attributes of purity, passivity, and domesticity. The emphasis on the chivalric motif in turn-of-the-century youth organizations (Knights of King Arthur, Order of Sir Galahad, Knights of the Holy Grail) can be interpreted as an expression of the desire to preserve male superordination in gender relations.

PERCEIVED FORCES OF FEMINIZATION

Men in the period 1880 to World War I believed that opportunities for the development and expression of masculinity were being limited. They say forces of feminization in the worlds of adults and adolescents. I will concentrate on changes in the adult opportunity structure. However, the forces of feminization that adolescents were thought to face at home and school should be mentioned, for they contributed to the anxiety of men worried about the present and wary of the future.

For the expanding urban middle class, the professionalization and sanctification of motherhood, the smaller family size, the decline in the number of servants who could serve as buffers between mother and son, and the absence of busy fathers from the home made the mother–son relationship appear threatening to proper masculine socialization. The expansion of the public high school took sons out of the home but did not allay fears of feminization. Female students outnumbered males, the percentage of female staff rose steadily between 1880 and World War I, and the requirements of learning demanded "feminine" passivity and sedentariness. Education would weaken a boy's body and direct his mind along the "psychic lines" of his female instructors. Finally, let me suggest that G. Stanley Hall's concept of adolescence may have generated sexrole anxiety by extending and legitimating dependency as a natural stage in the developmental cycle. A cohort of men who had reached social maturity before the use and public acceptance of adolescence as an age category, who had experienced the rural transition to manhood at an early age, and who had fought as teenagers in the Civil War or knew those who had were confronted with a generation of boys whose major characteristics were dependency and inactivity.

Changes in the nature of work and in the composition of the labor force from 1880 to World War I profoundly affected masculine self-identity. From 1870 to 1910 the number of clerical workers, salespeople, government employees, technicians, and salaried professionals increased from 756 thousand to 5.6 million (Hays, 1957). The dependency, sedentariness, and even security of these middle-class positions clashed with the active mastery, independence, self-reliance, competitiveness, creativity, and risk-taking central to the traditional male ideal (Mills, 1951). In pre-Civil War America, there were opportunities to approach that ideal: It is estimated that over 80% of Americans were farmers or self-employed businessmen (Mills, 1951). They owned the property they worked; they produced tangible goods; and they were not enmeshed in hierarchical systems of "command and obedience."

Industrialization and bureaucratization reduced opportunities to own one's business, to take risks, exercise independence, compete, and master men and nature. The new expanded middle class depended on others for time, place, and often pace of work. The growth of chain stores crowded out independent proprietors, made small business ventures shortlived, and reduced the income of merchants frequently below the level of day laborers (Anderson & Davidson, 1940). Clerical positions were no longer certain stepping stones to ownership; and clerical wages were neither high enough to meet standards of male success nor appreciably greater than those of less prestigious occupations (Filene, 1975; Douglas, 1930).

This changed occupational landscape did not go unnoticed. College graduates were told not to expect a challenging future:

> The world is steadily moving toward the position in which the individual is to contribute faithfully and duly his quota of productive or protective social effort, and to receive in return a modest, certain, not

greatly variable stipend. He will adjust his needs and expenses to his income, guard the future by insurance or some analogous method, and find margin of leisure and opportunity sufficient to give large play to individual tastes and preferences. (Shaw, 1907, p. 3)

Interestingly for this paper's thesis, graduates were to seek fulfillment in activities outside work.

The increased entry of women into the labor force raised the specter of feminization as did the changed character of work. In terms of masculine anxiety, the impact was two-fold: the mere fact of women working outside the home in larger numbers and their increased participation in jobs which demanded nonmasculine attributes. From 1870 to 1920, there was a substantial increase in the percentage of women aged 16 and over in nonagricultural occupations—from 11.8% to 21.3% (Hill, 1929). Men expressed concern over the entrance of women into a previously exclusive domain of masculine affirmation. (Women's occupations were not enumerated in the federal census until 1860.) Magazine and newspaper cartoons showed women in suits, smoking cigars, and talking business while aproned men were washing dishes, sweeping floors, and feeding babies (Smuts, 1959). Sex-role definition, not simple income, was at stake. Only one-third of employed men in 1910 worked in occupations where women constituted more than 5% of the work force (Hill, 1929). The actual threat posed by working women was more cultural than economic. Women doing what men did disconfirmed the naturalness and facticity of sex-role dichotomization.

Imposed on this general concern was the anxiety of men in white-collar positions. It was into these "nonmasculine" jobs that women entered in large numbers. Women were only 3% of the clerical work force in 1870, but 35% in 1910 (U.S. Department of Commerce, 1870; Hill, 1929). The increase for specific occupations between 1910 and 1920 is even more dramatic, especially for native white women of native parentage: female clerks increased 318%; bookkeepers, accountants, and cashiers, 257%; stenographers and typists, 121%; and sales personnel, 66% (Hill, 1929). It is to be argued that men in these occupations, feminine in character and composition, sought nonoccupational means of masculine validation, one of which was being a scoutmaster.

SCOUTING AND THE CONSTRUCTION OF MANLINESS

The Boy Scouts of America responded explicitly to adult sex-role concerns. It provided concerned men the opportunity to support "an organized effort to make big men of little boys . . . to aid in the development of that master creation, high principled, clean and clear thinking, independent manhood" (Burgess, 1914, p. 12). At the turn of the century, manliness was no longer considered the inevitable product of daily life; urbanization appeared to have removed the conditions for the natural production of manliness. Scouting advertised itself as an environmental surrogate for the farm and frontier:

The Wilderness is gone, the Buckskin Man is gone, the painted Indian has hit the trail over the Great Divide, the hardships and privations of pioneer life which did so much to develop sterling manhood are now but a legend in history, and we must depend upon the Boy Scout Movement to produce the MEN of the future. (Daniel Carter Beard in Boy Scouts of America, 1914, p. 109)

Scouting's program and structure would counter the forces of feminization and maintain traditional manhood. Following the dictates of Hall's genetic psychology, boys were sexually segregated in a primary group under the leadership of an adult male. The gang instinct, like all adolescent instincts, was not to be repressed but constructively channeled in the service of manhood. By nature boys would form gangs, and the Boy Scouts turned the gang into a Scout patrol. The gang bred virility, did not tolerate sissies, and would make a boy good but not a goody-goody; in short, he would "be a real boy, not too much like his sister" (Puffer, 1912, p. 157; also see Page, 1919).

The rhetoric and content of Scouting spoke to masculine fears of passivity and dependence. Action was the warp and woof of Scouting, as it was the foundation of traditional American masculinity. After-school and summer idleness led to and was itself a moral danger, and scouts were urged to do "anything rather than continue in dependent, and enfeebling, and demoralizing idleness" (Russell, 1914, p. 163). "Spectatoritis" was turning "robust, manly, self-reliant boyhood into a lot of flat-chested cigarette smokers with shaky nerves and doubtful vitality" (Seton, 1910, p. xi). So Scout activities involved all members, and advancement required each boy to compete against himself and nature. Scouting stands apart from most nineteenth-century youth organizations by its level of support for play and its full acceptance of outdoor activities as healthy for boys.

The Scout code, embodied in the Scout Oath, Law, Motto, and requirements for advancement, was a code for conduct, not moral contemplation. It was "the code of red blooded, moral manly men" (Beard, Note 1, p. 9). The action required by the code, not one's uniform or badges, made a boy a scout and differentiated a scout from a non-scout. The British made a promise to act, but the Americans made a more definite commitment to action: they took an oath. More than the British, Americans emphasized that theirs was a "definite code of personal purposes," whose principles would shape the boy's total character and behavior.

The Scout code would produce that ideal man who was master of himself and nature. The American addition to the Scout oath, "To keep myself physically strong, mentally awake, and morally straight," was a condition for such mastery. In pre-Civil War America, "be prepared" meant being prepared to die, having one's moral house in order (Crandall, 1957). The Scout motto meant being prepared to meet and master dangers, from runaway horses to theater fires and factory explosions. In emergencies, it was the scout who "stood firm, quieted those who were panic stricken and unobtrusively and efficiently helped to control the crowds" (Murray, 1937, p. 492). American Scouting added the tenth law: "A Scout is Brave." Bravery meant self-mastery and inner direction, having the courage "to stand up for the right against the coaxing of friends or the jeers or threats of enemies."

The linchpin of the Scout code was the good deed. Boys active in community service reassured males that the younger generation would become manly men. To Scout supporters, the movement provided a character building "moral equivalent to war." The phrase was used by William James in 1910 to suggest a kind of Job Corps for gilded youths. They would wash windows, build roads, work on fishing boats, and engage in all types of manual labor. This work would knock the childishness out of the youth of the luxurious classes and would produce the hardiness, discipline, and manliness that previously only war had done (James, 1971). As a result, young men would walk with their heads higher, would be esteemed by women, and be better fathers and teachers of the next generation. Scouts would not accept payment for their good deeds. To take a tip was un-American, un-masculine, and made one a "bit of a boot lick" (Eaton, 1918, p. 38). Adherence to the Scout code would produce traditional manliness in boy's clothing:

> The REAL Boy Scout is not a "sissy." He is not a hothouse plant, like little Lord Fauntleroy. There is nothing "milk and water" about him; he is not afraid of the dark. He does not do bad things because he is afraid of being decent. Instead of being a puny, dull, or bookish lad, who dreams and does nothing, he is full of life, energy, enthusiasm, bubbling over with fun, full of ideas as to what he wants to do and knows how he wants to do it. He has many ideals and many heroes. He is not hitched to his mother's apronstrings. While he adores his mother, and would do anything to save her from suffering or discomfort, he is self-reliant, sturdy and full of vim. (West, 1912, p. 448)

THE SCOUTMASTER AND MASCULINE VALIDATION

Scouting assuaged adult masculine anxiety not only by training boys in the masculine virtues. The movement provided adult men a sphere of masculine validation. Given the character and composition of their occupations and the centrality of occupation to the male sex role, young men in white-collar positions were especially concerned about their masculine identity. They were receptive to an organization which provided adult men the opportunity to be men as traditionally defined.

At the core of the image of the ideal scoutmaster was assertive manliness. Scoutmasters were "manly" patriots with common sense and moral character who sacrificially served America's youth (Boy Scouts of America, 1920). Scouting wanted "REAL, live men—red blooded and righthearted men— BIG men"; "No Miss Nancy need apply" (Boy Scouts of America, n.d., p. 9). Scoutmasters by the force of their characters, not by their formal positions (as in a bureaucracy), would evoke respect. They were portrayed as men of executive ability who took decisive action over a wide range of problems and were adroit handlers of men and boys. An analysis of the social characteristics and motivation of all the Chicago scoutmasters for whom there are records— original applications—through 1919 ($N = 575$) raises questions about the veracity of this portrayal (Hantover, 1976).

The first scoutmasters were men of educational, occupational, and ethnic status, but they did not serve solely from a sense of *noblesse oblige* and a disinterested commitment to all boys. They were more concerned about saving middle-class boys from the effeminizing forces of modern society than with "civilizing" the sons of the lower classes. Only four scoutmasters singled out the lower class for special mention; just 8% of the over 700 experiences with youth listed by scoutmasters were with lower-class youth. The typical Chicago scoutmaster was white, under 30, native born, Protestant, college educated, and in a whitecollar or professional/semi-professional occupation. Scoutmasters were more Protestant, better educated, and in higher prestige occupations than the adult male population of Chicago. Many teachers, clergymen, and boys' workers were scoutmasters because Scouting was part of their job, was good training for it, or at least was congruent with their vocational ideology. If we exclude those men drawn to Scouting by the requirements of their occupations, Scouting disproportionately attracted men who had borne longer the "feminine" environment of the schools and now were in occupations whose sedentariness and dependence did not fit the traditional image of American manliness.

Though the motivational data extracted from the original scoutmaster applications are limited, there does emerge from the number and quality of responses a sense that clerical workers were concerned about the development of masculinity among adolescents and its expression by adults. Clerical workers were more concerned than other occupations unrelated to youth and service about training boys for manhood, filling a boy's time with constructive activities so he would not engage in activities detrimental to the development of manhoood, and about the sexual and moral dangers of adolescence.

It is not simply chance, I believe, that clerical workers gave elaborate and individualistic responses which evince a sense of life's restrictedness and danger. A 26-year-old stenographer, "always having lived in Chicago and working indoors," felt Scouting was a way to get outdoors for himself, not the scouts. A 21-year-old clerk, implying that his career had reached its apogee, praised Scouting for its development of initiative and resourcefulness and admitted that lack of these qualities had handicapped him greatly. A draftsman, only 27, thought "association with the boys will certainly keep one from getting that old and retired feeling." Another young clerk evokes a similar sense of life's restrictedness when he writes that Scouting "affords me an opportunity to exercise control over a set of young men. I learn to realize the value of myself as a force as a personality."

The masculine anxiety that clerical workers felt may not have been generated by their occupations alone. They brought to the job achievements and attributes which at the turn of the century could have exacerbated that anxiety. Clerical workers had the highest percentage of high school educated scoutmasters of any occupational group. They were subject to the perceived feminine forces of high school without the status compensation of a college education and a professional position. With education controlled, Protestants and native Americans were more likely to be clerical workers. It was the virility and reproductive powers of the native American stock which were being questioned after the Civil War. Women in the better classes (native and Protestant) denied men the opportunity to prove their masculinity through paternity. Albion Small complained, "In some of the best middle-class social strata in the United States a young wife becomes a subject of surprised comment among her acquaintances if she accepts the burdens of maternity! This is a commonplace" (Small, 1915, p. 661). The fecundity and alleged sexuality of the immigrants raised turn-of-the-century fears about the continued dominance of the native Protestant stock. The experiences of key reference groups as well as one's own individual experiences were factors contributing to a sense of endangered masculinity.

CONCLUSION

Adult sex-role anxiety is rooted in the social structure; and groups of men are differentially affected, depending on their location in the social system and the opportunity structure they face. Critics of men's supposed nature can be dismissed as misguided by medical and religious defenders. But when the opportunity structure underlying masculinity begins to restrict, questioning may arise from the ranks of the men themselves. When taken-for-granted constructs become the objects of examination, anxiety may arise because elements in a cultural system are defended as natural, if not transcendant, rather than convenient or utilitarian. Under the disconfirming impact of social change, men may at first be more likely to reassert the validity of traditional ends and seek new avenues for their accomplishment than to redefine their ends.

"Men not only define themselves, but they actualize these definitions in real experience—*they live them*" (Berger, Berger, & Kellner, 1974, p. 92). Social identities generate the need for self-confirming action. The young men in the scoutmaster ranks were the first generation to face full force the discontinuity between the realities of the modern bureaucratic world and the image of masculine autonomy and mastery and the rhetoric of Horatio Alger. They found in the Boy Scouts of America an institutional sphere for the validation of masculinity previously generated by the flow of daily social life and affirmed in one's work.

NOTE

[1]Beard, D. C. Untitled article submitted to *Youth Companion*. Unpublished manuscript, Daniel Carter Beard Collection, Library of Congress, 1914. (See pp. 126–127 of this book.)

REFERENCES

Anderson, H. D., & Davidson, P. E. *Occupational trends in the United States.* Stanford: Stanford University Press, 1940.

Berger, P., Berger, B., & Kellner, H. *The homeless mind.* New York: Vintage Press, 1974.

Boy Scouts of America. Fourth annual report. *Scouting*, 1914, 1.

Boy Scouts of America. *Handbook for scoutmasters* (2nd ed.). New York: Boy Scouts of America, 1920.

Boy Scouts of America. *The scoutmaster and his troop.* New York: Boy Scouts of America, no date.

Burgess, T. W. Making men of them. *Good Housekeeping Magazine*, 1914, 59, 3–12.

Conant, R. W. *The virility of Christ.* Chicago: no publisher, 1915.

Crandall, J. C., Jr. *Images and ideals for young Americans: A study of American juvenile literature, 1825–1860.* Unpublished doctoral dissertation, University of Rochester, 1957.

Douglas, P. *Real wages in the United States, 1890–1926.* New York: Houghton Mifflin, 1930.

Eaton, W. P. *Boy Scouts in Glacier Park.* Boston: W. A. Wilde, 1918.

Filence, P. G. *Him, her, self: Sex roles in modern America.* New York: Harcourt Brace Jovanovich, 1975.

Greene, T. P. *America's heroes: The changing models of success in American magazines.* New York: Oxford University Press, 1970.

Hantover, J. P. *Sex role, sexuality, and social status: The early years of the Boy Scouts of America.* Unpublished doctoral dissertation, University of Chicago, 1976.

Hays, S. P. *The response to industrialism: 1885–1914*. Chicago: University of Chicago Press, 1957.

Hill, J. A. *Women in gainful occupations 1870 to 1920* (Census Monograph No. 9, U.S. Bureau of the Census). Washington, D.C.: U.S. Government Printing Office, 1929.

James, W. The moral equivalent of war. In J. K. Roth (Ed.), *The moral equivalent and other essays*. New York: Harper Torchbook, 1971.

Mills, C. W. *White collar*. New York: Oxford University Press, 1951.

Murray, W. D. *The history of the boy scouts of America*. New York: Boy Scouts of America, 1937.

Page, J. F. *Socializing for the new order of educational values of the juvenile organization*. Rock Island, Ill.: J. F. Page, 1919.

Puffer, J. A. *The boy and his gang*. Boston: Houghton Mifflin, 1912.

Rudolph, F. *The American college and university*. New York: Knopf, 1962.

Russell, T. H. (Ed.). *Stories of boy life*. No location: Fireside Edition, 1914.

Seton, E. T. *Boy Scouts of America: A handbook of woodcraft, scouting, and life craft*. New York: Doubleday, Page, 1910.

Shaw, A. *The outlook for the average man*. New York: Macmillan, 1907.

Small, A. The bonds of nationality. *American Journal of Sociology*, 1915, *10*, 629–83.

Smuts, R. W. *Women and work in America*. New York: Columbia University Press, 1959.

U.S. Department of Commerce. *Ninth census of the United States, 1870: Population and social statistics* (Vol. I). Washington, D.C.: U.S. Government Printing Office, 1870.

West, J. E. The real boy scout. *Leslie's Weekly*, 1912, 448.

Richard Majors

COOL POSE:
THE PROUD SIGNATURE OF BLACK SURVIVAL

Just when it seemed that we black males were beginning to recover from past injustices inflicted by a dominant white society, we find once again that we are being revisited in a similar vein. President Reagan's de-emphasis of civil rights, affirmative action legislation and social services programs; the rise of black neoconservatives and certain black feminist groups; harshly critical media events on television (e.g., the CBS documentary "The Vanishing Family—Crisis in Black America") and in films (e.g., *The Color Purple*); and the omnipresent problems of unemployment and inadequate health care, housing, and education—all have helped to shape a negative political and social climate toward black men. For many black men this period represents a *New Black Nadir*, or lowest point, and time of deepest depression.

Black people in general, and the black man in particular, look out on a world that does not positively reflect their image. Black men learned long ago that the classic American virtues of thrift, perseverance and hard work would not give us the tangible rewards that accrue to most members of the dominant society. We learned early that we would not be Captains of Industry or builders of engineering wonders. Instead, we channeled our creative energies into construction of a symbolic universe. Therefore we adopted unique poses and postures to offset the externally imposed "zero" image. Because black men

Copyright © 1986. *Changing Men: Issues in Gender, Sex, and Politics* 17 (Winter 1986).

were denied access to the dominant culture's acceptable avenues of expression, we created a form of self-expression—the "Cool Pose."[1-3]

Cool Pose is a term that represents a variety of attitudes and actions that serve the black man as mechanisms for survival, defense and social competence. These attitudes and actions are performed using characterizations and roles as facades and shields.

COOL CULTURE

Historically, coolness was central to the culture of many ancient African civilizations. The Yorubas of Western Nigeria (900 B.C. to 200 A.D.) are cited as an example of an African civilization where cool was integrated into the social fabric of the community.[4] Uses of cool ranged from the way a young man carried himself before his peers to the way he impressed his elders during the initiation ritual. Coolness helped to build character and pride for individuals in such groups and is regarded as a precolonial cultural adaptation. With the advent of the modern African slave trade, cool became detached from its indigenous cultural setting and emerged equally as a survival mechanism.

Where the European saw America as the promised land, the African saw it as the land of oppression. Today, reminders of Black America's oppressive past continue in the form of chronic underempolyment, inadequate housing, inferior schools, and poor health care. Because of these conditions many black men have become frustrated, angry, confused and impatient.

To help ease the pain associated with these conditions, black men have taken to alcoholism, drug abuse, homicide, and suicide. In learning to mistrust the words and actions of dominant white people, black males have learned to make great use of "poses" and "postures" which connote control, toughness, and detachment. All these forms arise from the mistrust that the black males feel towards the dominant society.

For these black males, particular poses and postures show the white man that "although you may have tried to hurt me time and time again, I can take it (and if I am hurting or weak, I'll never let you know). They are saying loud and clear to the white establishment, "I am strong, full of pride, and a survivor." Accordingly, any failures in the real world become the black man's secret.

THE EXPRESSIVE LIFE STYLE

On the other hand, those poses and postures that have an expressive quality or nature have become known in the literature as the "expressive life style."[5] The expressive life style is a way in which the black male can act cool by actively displaying particular performances that emphasize creative expression. Thus, while black people historically have been forced into conciliatory and often demeaning positions in American culture, there is nothing conciliatory about the expressive life style.

This dynamic vitality will not be denied even in limited stereotypical roles—as demonstrated by Hattie McDaniel, the maid in *Gone With the Wind* or Bill "Bojangle" Robinson as the affable servant in the Shirley Temple movies. This abiding need for creative self-expression knows no bounds, and asserts itself whether on the basketball court or in dancing. We can see it in black athletes—with their stylish dunking of the basketball, their spontaneous dancing in the end zone, and their different styles of handshakes (e.g., "high fives")—and in black entertainers with their various choreographed "cool" dance steps. These are just a few examples of black individuals in their professions who epitomize this creative expression. The expressive life style is a dynamic—not a static—art form, and new aesthetic forms are always evolving (e.g., "rap-talking" and breakdancing). The expressive life style, then, is the passion that invigorates the demeaning life of blacks in White America. It is a dynamic vitality that transforms the mundane into the sublime and makes the routine spectacular.

A CULTURAL SIGNATURE

Cool Pose, manifested by the expressive life style, is also an aggressive assertion of masculinity. It emphatically says, "White man, this is my turf. You can't match me here." Though he may be impotent in the political and corporate world, the black man demonstrates his potency in athletic competition, entertainment and the pulpit with a verve that borders on the spectacular. Through the virtuosity of a performance, he tips the socially imbalanced scales in his favor. "See me, touch me, hear me, but, white man, you can't copy me." This is the subliminal message which black males signify in their oftentimes flamboyant performance. Cool Pose, then, becomes the cultural signature for such black males.

Being cool is a unique response to adverse social, political and economic conditions. Cool provides control, inner strength, stability and confidence. Being cool, illustrated in its various poses and postures, becomes a very powerful and necessary tool in the black man's constant fight for his soul. The poses and postures of cool guard, preserve and protect his pride, dignity and respect to such an extent that the black male is willing to risk a great deal for it. One black man said it well: "The white man may control everything about me—that is, except my pride and dignity. That he can't have. That is mine and mine alone."

THE COST

Cool Pose, however, is not without its price. Many black males fail to discriminate the appropriate uses of Cool Pose and act cool much of the time, without regard to time or space.[6] Needless to say, this can cause severe problems. In many situations a black man won't allow himself to express or show any form of weakness or fear or other feelings and emotions. He assumes a facade of strength, held at all costs, rather than "blow his fronts" and thus his cool. Perhaps black men have become so conditioned to keeping up their guard against oppression from the dominant white society that this particular attitude and behavior represent for them their best safeguard against further mental or physical abuse. However, this same behavior makes it very difficult for these males to let their guard down and show affection, even for people that they actually care about or for people that may really care about them (e.g., girlfriends, wives, mothers, fathers, "good" friends, etc.).

When the art of being cool is used to put cool behaviors ahead of emotions or needs, the result of such repression of feelings can be frustration. Such frustrations sometimes cause aggression which often is taken out on those individuals closest to such men—other black people. It is sadly ironic, then, that the same elements of cool that allow for survival in the larger society may hurt black people by contributing to one of the more complex problems facing black people today—black-on-black crime.

Further, while Cool Pose enables black males to maintain stability in the face of white power, it may through inappropriate use render many of them unable to move with the mainstream or evolve in healthy ways. When misused, cool can suppress the motivation to learn, accept or become exposed to stimuli, cultural norms, aesthetics, mannerisms, values, etiquette, information or networks that could help them overcome problems caused by white racism. Finally, in a society which has as its credo, "A man's home is his castle," it is ironic that the masses of black men have no castle to protect. Their minds have become their psychological castle, defended by impenetrable cool. Thus, Cool Pose is the bittersweet symbol of a socially disesteemed group that shouts, "We are" in face of a hostile and indifferent world that everywhere screams, "You ain't."

COOL AND THE BLACK PSYCHE

To be fully grasped, Cool Pose must be recognized as having gained ideological consensus in the black community. It is not only a quantitatively measured "social reality" but a series of equally "real" rituals of socialization. It is a comprehensive, officially endorsed cultural myth that became entrenched in the black psyche with the beginning of the slave experience. This phenomenon has cut across all socioeconomic groups in the black community, as black men fight to preserve their dignity, pride, respect and masculinity with the attitudes and behaviors of Cool Pose. Cool Pose represents a fundamental structuring of the psyche of the black male and is manifested in some way or another in the daily activities and recreational habits of most black males. There are few other social or psychological constructs that have shaped, directed or controlled the black male to the extent that the various forms of coolness have. It is surprising, then, that for a concept that has the potential to explain problems in black male and black female relationships, black-on-black crime, and black-on-black pregnancies, there is such limited research on this subject.

In the final analysis, Cool Pose may represent the most important yet least researched area with the potential to enhance our understanding and study of black behavior today.

NOTES

1. Majors, R. G., Nikelly, A. G., "Serving the Black Minority: A New Direction for Psychotherapy." *J. for Non-white Concerns*, 11:142–151 (1983).

2. Majors, R. G., "The Effects of 'Cool Pose': What Being Cool Means." *Griot*, pp. 4–5 (Spring, 1985).

3. Nikelly, A. G. & Majors, R. G. "Techniques for Counseling Black Students," *Techniques: J. Remedial Educ. & Counseling*, 2:48–54 (1986).

4. Bascom, W., *The Yoruba of Southwestern Nigeria*. (New York: Holt, Rinehart & Winston, 1969).

5. Rainwater, L., *Behind Ghetto Walls*. (Chicago: Aldine, 1970).
6. Majors, R. G., "Cool Pose: A New Hypothesis in Understanding Anti-Social Behavior in Lower SES Black Males," unpublished manuscript.

Gary Alan Fine

THE DIRTY PLAY OF LITTLE BOYS

The tormented Earl of Gloster moaned in *King Lear:* "As flies to wanton boys, are we to gods; they kill us for their sport." These mordant lines may tell us more about the interests of boys than gods. Why do boys kill flies for their sport? Why, as Plutarch noted, do they throw stones at frogs; or why, as Swift depicted, do they pour salt on sparrows' tails? What are boys like or, more to the point, what do boys do? While mountains of tomes have been devoted to scientific, development studies of boys, few researchers have spent time with them on their own turf.

My chosen site was around the world of sport. For three years I spent springs and summers observing ten Little League baseball teams in Minnesota, Rhode Island, and Massachusetts as they went through their seasons. I observed at practice fields and in dugouts, remaining with the boys after the games and arriving early to learn what they did when adults were not present. As I came to know these boys better, I hung out with them when they were "doing nothing."

My goal was to elucidate the process by which the rich veins of preadolescent male culture are developed—particularly those areas considered morally unacceptable by adults. In sport and in informal male activity, sex role development and display are crucial—certainly in the view of the participants. If we hope to understand how adult sex roles are shaped, we must observe the blossoming of these roles in childhood peer groups.

Preadolescence is a difficult period to define, covering the twilight zone between the perils of the Oedipus complex and the *Stürm und Drang* of puberty. Yet preadolescence is more than a way station to puberty. Child psychologists Fritz Redl once cleverly suggested that preadolescence is the period in which "the nicest children begin to behave in the most awful way." This pithy description captures the basic split personality of this period. By preadolescence, the boy is a part of several social worlds: same-sex groups, cross-sex interaction, school, and family life. Each of these settings requires a different standard of behavior. Because there is not total segregation of the child's life with friends from that with parents, parents tend to be aware of boys' awfulness, even if they are unaware of the details.

The conflict derives from the fact that the preadolescent has neither the right nor the ability to keep these two spheres of social life separate. When removed from peers, juveniles may be sweet, even considerate, and sometimes tender. Yet, placed in a social situation in which they do not have to be on their best behavior and given situational constraints which militate against proper behavior, they may engage in aggressive sexuality, prejudice, and

Published by permission of Transaction Publishers, from "The Dirty Play of Little Boys," *Society*, Vol. 24, No. 1, November 1986. Copyright © 1986 Transaction Publishers.

destructiveness. These are "good boys" engaging in "dirty play." These patterns of behavior reflect both biological and social factors, and provide internal and external constraints on a child's behavior. These factors constitute the child's imperatives of development.

In examining the social lives of these middle-class, suburban white preadolescent baseball players, I focused on their friendships. For these boys, as for most of us, friendship constitutes a staging area in which activities improper elsewhere can be tested in a supportive environment. The moral choices children are experimenting with are played out with their chums. Boys are "boys" only when they are with their peers.

How is it that these boys are willing to engage in activities so abhorrent to adults—what I have called "dirty play." The concept of dirty play is borrowed loosely from sociologist Everett Hughes's discussion of "dirty work." Hughes asked how it is that some in our society become involved [in and] become satisfied with what the rest of society consider[s] to be dirty work— those activities that no "decent" person would do. Hughes's focus was on the occupational order, but the issue applies equally to the world of preadolescent play. Why do our children do these things? Hughes noted that some people had to engage in some very unpleasant behaviors to keep the social order functioning, and that other members of the society did not wish to know about this in order to "keep their hands clean." In some of Hughes's formulations these dirty work activities were behaviors no decent person should agree to, such as the behavior of Nazi SS officers. But Hughes recognized that some dirty workers (grave diggers, janitors) are necessary for all smoothly functioning social systems. Because of the "pollution" of the work, the rest of society closes its eyes and the dirty workers remain a closed society. A membrane protects the rest of society from contamination from these dirty workers.

The same membrane may be necessary in regard to children's dirty play. Dirty play may well be necessary for effective socialization (at least to our society as it currently exists), but it may be best for adults not to know what their offspring are doing. Children's play, perhaps, should remain in the closet. The dirty play of children seems to be a natural outpouring of some of the developmental imperatives of growing up, but how it is handled depends very much on the situations in which children and the adult guardians find themselves. I begin my analysis by describing some forms that this preadolescent dirty play takes. Specifically I focus on: aggressive pranks, sexual talk and activity, and racist remarks.

Some children's pranks can, on occasion, be elaborate and distressing. Consider the following: A group of boys wraps dog feces in newspaper, lights the newspaper on fire, rings a homeowner's doorbell, and runs away to watch. When the victim comes to the door, he stomps on the flaming package. At that point another boy rings the back doorbell and the man, not thinking, rushes through the house, tracking it with dog excrement.

AGGRESSIVE PRANKS

Such accounts suggest that children are continually engaging in troublesome behavior. However, we need to be careful not to overgeneralize this behavior. Talk about these legendary pranks is far more common than their doing. After their original occurrence, the story is told and retold. Talking about the prank conveys the meaning of the event with far less danger to the participants. Pranks represent an attempt by preadolescents to explore the boundaries of moral propriety. In their talk, preadolescents place a premium on daring behavior as expressed through what they term "mischief."

Pulling a prank is a form of social behavior, both in that pranks vary from community to community and because preadolescents who play these pranks invariably do them with those closest to them. In one suburb, "mooning" cars (pulling down one's trousers while facing away from the traffic) was the most common prank; in another "egging" cars and houses was most common, and in the others the most frequent prank was to ring doorbells and run away. Virtually all of the boys who play these pranks do so in the company of their best friends. In one community, of the forty-eight boys who named their prank partners, 89 percent of these were described as "best" or "close" friends. Friendship, therefore, serves as the staging area in which this type of ritualized dirty play occurs. Given the value placed on taking chances, the co-presence of friends is likely to promote the performance of aggressive pranks in defining the action as legitimate, providing status for the boy if he succeeds, and goading him if his fear of adults threatens to stand in his way.

Rather than defining pranks as expressions of an aggressive instinct directed at those who control them—the traditional psychiatric approach—I see pranks as social action designed to shape a boy's public identity. The dirty play has something of a status content about it, where the goal is not to do harm, but to gain renown for being daring. The prank is but the set-piece that provides the basis of identity attributions—not an aggressive end in itself.

SEXUAL TALK

Whatever latency might have been during Freud's childhood, in contemporary America preadolescence is a period of much sexual talk and some sexual behavior. This sexual talk, among boys in particular, with its aggressive overtones is worrying to parents who are unable to understand how their sons could possibly talk that way about each other and about girls. Yet, however much we might object, boys strive to be "masculine" and they talk about girls in terms both unflattering and too explicit for what their parents expect them to know.

Males maturing in our sexualized society quickly recognize the value of being able to talk about sexual topics in ways that bring them credit. As with pranks, sexual talk is a social activity and is a form of presenting oneself in desirable ways. In fact, given the reality that many of the talkers have not reached puberty, we can assume that their sexual interests are more social than physiological. Boys wish to convince their peers that they are sexually mature, active, and knowledgeable.

One means by which a person can convince others that he has an appropriate sexualized self is through sexualized behavior. This can include behavior among same-sex peers (mutual masturbation, homosexual experimentation, or autosexual activities such as measuring the length of one's penis) or behavior with girls. These behaviors, like pranks, although not frequent for any one child, may be notable and remembered. One public kiss, if done well, can serve for a thousand private caresses. The second "proof" of sexuality is talk—both talk that has a behavioral referent and talk that is in itself an indication of a sexualized self. In the first instance, the talk presents behavior that should, by rights, remain private ("kiss and tell"), and must be convincing as narrative; the latter serves as an end in itself—such as sexualized insults and talk about biological and physiological processes. This indicates that the child knows, in the words of one preadolescent, "What's a poppin'." These expectations are primarily social, and are based on the desire to reveal what preadolescents consider adult competences, although adults will consider these same things to be dirty when performed by preadolescents.

A boy must walk a narrow line between not showing enough involvement with girls, in which case he may be labeled effeminate, immature, or gay, and showing too much serious, tender attention, in which case he may be labeled "girl crazy." For these reasons, much talk indicates that boys are interested in girls sexually, but they are not so interested that they find any to their liking. While preadolescent boys have girlfriends, they must be careful about what they say about them to other boys. Girls can easily break the bonds of brotherhood among boys.

A related fear among boys is that of being tarred as homosexual or gay. During my research (in the late 1970s) boys attempted to define their sexualized selves in contrast to "improper" sexual activity. To be sure, most of these boys have never met anyone whom they believe really is a homosexual, and they have, at best, a foggy vision of gay sexual behaviors. Despite this, it is common to hear boys saying things like "You're a faggot," "What a queer," and "Kiss my ass."

Being gay has little to do with homosexual behavior; rather it suggests that the target is immature. Indeed, some homosexual behavior (for example, mutual masturbation) occurs among high-status boys who would never be labeled gay. Being gay is synonymous with being a baby and a girl. In each instance the target has not comported himself in accord with the traditional male sex role. Homosexual rhetoric has an additional benefit for the speaker in that its use suggests that the speaker is mature himself, and can be differentiated from the boy who is scorned.

RACIST INVECTIVE

When I inform white audiences that I found considerable racial invective in the middle-class suburban communities I studied, many are surprised; most of the blacks I tell are not. These boys had little direct contact with blacks, but as they lived near major metropolitan areas, they were well aware of racial tensions.

One of the Little League teams, a team in southern Rhode Island, was particularly notable for the racial epithets uttered by players. The team was lily-white, but there were four black children on other teams in the league and this team had a black coach two seasons before. The talk by one of the star players was particularly virulent, and his hatred was particularly reserved for two of the black children in the league, Roger and Bill Mott: "I was talking with some players about the best home-run hitters in the League, and I mentioned that Billy Mott was pretty good. Justin replies with disgust: 'That dumb nigger.' He immediately described how 'two niggers tried to jump me.'" Most racial talk was not serious in intent, but was joking. In driving some boys home one day in a Massachusetts suburb we passed two black youths walking quietly through town. One boy leaned out of my car window and yelled "Get out of here, you jungle bunnies." The other boys broke up in gales of laughter. Or: "One of the groundskeeper's helpers is a swarthy adolescent. Justin playfully tells his friends Harry and Whitney that the boy is a Puerto Rican and, therefore, is 'half nigger and half white.' Justin calls him a 'punk' and Justin and Whitney both call him 'half and half.' The boy, within earshot, is becoming angry: Justin, Harry, and Whitney run away laughing."

Remember that most times this rhetoric occurs it is not spoken in anger, but in play—although play of a rather nasty disposition. Preadolescents, emphasizing status and position among peers, are very concerned about group boundaries. It should be no surprise that they draw lines between those who are part of the group and those who must remain outsiders. This explains some of the concerns about sexuality and gender at this period and also explains the concern with race, class, nationality, and geographical affiliation (school, town, etc.). Further, during preadolescence children learn the adult significance of these boundary issues. Even if parents do not tell white children that blacks are inferior, the children still learn that race is a crucial division in our society, and preadolescents will assume that those who are not "us" are suitable subjects for attack. Although such an analysis does not work equally well for all children with regard to each demographic or social category, it is fair to emphasize that social differentiation is common to the period and is reflected in remarks adults find disquieting and offensive.

WHY DIRTY PLAY?

The prevalence of dirty play in the lives of children, and their evident enjoyment of it, should give pause to all adults. Rarely do children behave fully in accord with adult moral standards. This is particularly dramatic in societies such as our own in which adults believe in the innocence of children. The existence of these forms of play suggests either that children are not really innocent or that they have been corrupted. Either charge is troubling.

I suggest four rationales for these "disturbing" behaviors: (1) control, (2) status, (3) social differentiation, and (4) socialization to perceived adult norms. These four themes do not apply equally well to all examples of play. If asked, most preadolescents would admit to engaging in these activities because they are "fun," but this sidesteps the question of why these sorts of things are seen as fun. Thus, we must go beyond this simple explanation.

Dirty play can be seen as a claim-making behavior. Each instance attempts implicitly to make a statement about the rights of preadolescents to engage in a set of activities and have a set of opinions in the face of adult counter-pressures. When children behave in accord with adult prescriptions, which they often do, their play causes little comment, but when a preadolescent chooses to play in a way contrary to adult authority the play becomes an issue. Preadolescents recognize this problem and are typically sophisticated enough to engage in their dirty play out of the eyesight and earshot of their adult guardians. They are claiming for themselves the right to make public statements about race, sex, or authority. This play is remarkably sophisticated in that it deals with those areas of adult social structure adults typically wish to preserve for themselves.

These acts are sociopolitical, although playful. While the content of this dirty play is troubling to many, it is also troubling that our children feel competent to make judgments and act on them. They reflect a judgment on adult social order and, typically, one different from that which adults officially put forward, although one that (especially in the case of racial and sexual remarks) they may privately believe.

The adult emphasis on decorum and politeness is significant in light of the age-graded power structure. Politeness is a tactic used by those in power to keep those without power subservient. Politeness and decorum structure collective action so as to preserve order and process. If all that children can do to "get their way" is to request things politely from adults, then adults have full power to make their own decisions without consequences from those who are asking. Once a request has been rejected by the authorities there is nothing the requester can do, under this model, other than accept this decision gracefully. The implicit benefit for those without power is that on the next polite request the authority might be more willing to accede. However, there is not certainty of this and, even so, authority still remains unchallenged.

It may be apt to speak of these examples of dirty play that question the adult authority structure through the metaphor of playful terrorism. Ultimately such "terrorism" is politically impotent because of the lack of organization of the "terrorist groups," their lack of commitment and uniformity of beliefs, the tight control adults have over them, and the rewards that can be offered to those who conform. Still, it is hard to miss the potential threat to the authority structure inherent in some of this play which tests boundaries and legitimacy.

The dirty play I have described is important in shaping relationships within the group, as well as outside. Its performance is a technique for gaining status within a peer group. Preadolescent interaction can be seen, in part, as a status contest at an age at which status really matters. Status matters at all ages, but during preadolescence, with its change in orientation toward adult status symbols and a social world outside of the eyes of adults, the evaluation of peer position is of particular importance.

Boys gain renown from participating in these actions. There is a premium on being willing to do things that other boys wish to do but are afraid to. If there is some consensus that the prank is desirable, the boy who performs it or leads the group gains status for breaking through the barrier of fear in which others are enveloped. There is risk involved in throwing eggs at houses or at moving cars; one could get caught, beaten, grounded, or even arrested.

The costs, coupled with the lack of status rewards, suggest why it is apparently so rare for preadolescents to engage in these behaviors when alone. It is not that they have a personal, destructive impulse but, rather, they want to show off in the presence of friends. To think of these children as bad misses the point; they are, more or less, amoral—in that enforcing the dictates of morality is not one of their primary goals; rather, their aim is to get by with as much interpersonal smoothness as possible. The concern with those wonderful Goffmanlike images of "presentation of self," "teamwork," and "impression management" is omnipresent.

One of the collective tasks of preadolescents is to define themselves in contrast to other groups that share some characteristics. In my empirical discussion of dirty play among white middle-class boys I focused on racial and sexual differentiation. Whites are not blacks, and boys are not girls. Also, there is the belief held to fiercely by many of those whom I have studied that whites are better than blacks, and that boys are better than girls. Given the stance of today's tolerant, egalitarian society and particularly those social scientists who choose to write about it, such beliefs are heresy, morally repugnant, and represent a social problem. Yet, from the standpoint of the preadolescent white boy they seem perfectly natural. Ethnocentrism always does. Indeed, when we look over the lengthy landscape of human history we see that social differentiation has been more the rule than the exception. People always wish to make their own group special and distinct. This basic need of humanity is sometimes (particularly) overcome, but surely the desire for differentiation is not a mark of Cain.

When boys torment girls or jeer at blacks, we may see this as a kind of dirty play that does not necessarily adhere to the moral selves of these social actors. The positive side of such group actions is that the preadolescents are learning some measure of communal feeling, even though it is directed at another group. It is significant that much of what we consider to be dirty or cruel play is at the expense of some other group or members of another group. Even disagreeable play that is internally directed typically is focused on a boy who is to be differentiated from the group in some significant way: such as because of some physical handicap or because of the belief that he can be morally differentiated (for example, as "gay").

Preadolescent dirty play does not simply appear from nowhere. It is a transformation of things that boys see enacted by older boys or by adults, or learn about through the media. The content does matter. Yet, this is often material that many adults sincerely wish they had not communicated. Unfortunately we cannot shield preadolescents from that which we do not want them to learn. They are information vacuum cleaners and, of the information gained, will selectively use that which fits their purposes.

The themes of preadolescent dirty play are far from unrecognizable. Aggression, sexism, and racism are found in adult activity. These themes are also indicated in dramatic media representations, even when the themes are ostensibly being disparaged. Still, audiences can choose to select whatever information they wish from a media production, even if this material is incompatible with the official morality of the society. The best example of this during the research project was the reaction to the film, *The Bad News Bears*. Although the film ostensibly warned against the dangers of over-competition and excessive adult involvement in youth sports, the images that preadolescents took from the film were techniques of talking dirty and acting grossly ("stick this where the sun never shines").

We all know that often a moral message is but the sugar coating for sexual or aggressive doings that the producers use to capture an audience. This technique is as applicable to media productions aimed at adults as those aimed at children. In the case of children this may be compounded by the fact that preadolescents often attempt to act mature. Maturity does not have a clearly defined meaning; however, maturity as a concept implies a change in behavior. To validate that we are acting maturely, we need to act differently from the ways we have acted before. This typically takes the form of doing those things we had not known about or had not been allowed to do under the watchful eyes of adults. As a consequence, many of these markers of maturity will be precisely those things that adults see as dirty play. It is not that the children are being childish or immature in their view, but the contrary. They are attempting to live up to adult standards of behavior, and address adult issues from which they had previously been excluded.

Socialization to society's expectations has been well established as one important feature of children's play; yet, what is learned through play is diverse and some of what is learned may be formally offensive to those given the task of guiding children's development. The agenda for children's development is not always set by adults, although it typically is based on a reflection of what they do.

TAMING DIRTY PLAY?

Each of these four component motivations of dirty play should help us understand that playing dirty, by adult standards, is not identical to being morally bad. The issue, as Everett Hughes raised it in light of adult "dirty work," is the extent to which a person can get away with doing dirty work without that dirtiness adhering to his public self. In some cases that would appear to be relatively easy; in other cases, almost impossible.

The connection of a boy's dirty play with his moral self is a matter of negotiation, with different ideologies prevailing at different times, places, among different groups, and depending on the relationship of the judger to the person judged. The likely intention of the actor, the presence of others supporting the action, the social supports for the action, and the actual expected outcome influence the way in which children's dirty play will be evaluated.

Children's dirty play is virtually inevitable. There are so many needs and traditions connected with the doing of these actions that we would be hard pressed to visualize a serious program that would eradicate these behaviors. These are play forms we must live with. We do have one weapon—a long-term weapon, but a dramatically effective one as many of us can testify: guilt. In planting the seeds that this type of behavior is morally objectionable, we may recognize that these teachings will not work when given. Yet, often they will eventually be effective when reward structures change and when social needs alter. The seed of morality will (imperfectly) bloom at some later date and in some other place. As children grow older, and their needs for presentation of self change, they come to believe that such behaviors they used to delight in are morally offensive. While we object to children playing concentration camp guards, holding mock lynchings, or simply torturing their peers in the name of fun, we should recognize that this too may pass. Although sometimes morality does not change, if the new "improved" morality is supported by the subtle reward structures of adult society, we can say with a fair measure of confidence that dirty players emerge into saintly adults—at least adequately saintly adults. Children, in dealing with a transformed version of the raw, emotional issues of life, distress adults but they need not permanently smudge the very core of their angelic souls.

SUGGESTED READINGS

Glassner, B. "Kid Society." *Urban Education* 11 (1976):5–22.
Hughes, E. "Good People and Dirty Work." *Social Problems* 10 (1962):3–11.
Knapp, M. and Knapp, H. *One Potato, Two Potato. . . . :The Secret Education of American Children*. New York: Norton, 1976.
Sutton-Smith, B. *A History of Children's Play*. Philadelphia: University of Pennsylvania Press, 1981.

Peter Lyman

THE FRATERNAL BOND AS A JOKING RELATIONSHIP
A CASE STUDY OF THE ROLE OF SEXIST JOKES IN MALE GROUP BONDING

One evening during dinner, 45 fraternity men suddenly broke into the dining room of a nearby campus sorority, surrounded the 30 women residents, and forced them to watch while one pledge gave a speech on Freud's theory of penis envy as another demonstrated various techniques of masturbation with a rubber penis. The women sat silently, staring downward at their plates, and listened for about 10 minutes, until a woman law student who was the graduate resident in charge of the house walked in, surveyed the scene and demanded, "Please leave immediately!" As she later described that moment, "There was a mocking roar from the men, 'It's tradition.' I said, 'That's no reason to do something like this, please leave!' And they left. I was surprised. Then the women in the house started to get angry. And the guy who made the penis-envy speech came back and said to us, 'That was funny to me. If that's not funny to you I don't know what kind of sense of humor you have, but I'm sorry.' "

That night the women sat around the stairwell of their house discussing the event, some angry and others simply wanting to forget the whole thing. They finally decided to ask the university to require that the men return to discuss the event. When university officials threatened to take action, the men agreed to the meeting. I had served as a faculty resident in student housing for two years and had given several talks in the dorm about humor and gender, and was asked by both the men and the women involved to attend the discussion as a facilitator, and was given permission to take notes and interview the participants later, provided I concealed their identities.

The penis-envy ritual had been considered a successful joke in previous years by both "the guys and the girls," but this year it failed, causing great tension between two groups that historically had enjoyed a friendly joking relationship. In the women's view, the joke had not failed because of its subject; they considered sexual jokes to be a normal part of the erotic joking relationship between men and women. They thought it had failed because of

From *Changing Men*, edited by Michael Kimmel. Newbury Park, CA: Sage Publications, 1987. Reprinted by permission.

its emotional structure, the mixture of sexuality with aggression and the atmosphere of physical intimidation in the room that signified that the women were the object of a joking relationship between the men. A few women argued that the failed joke exposed the latent domination in men's relation to women, but this view was labelled "feminist" because it endangered the possibility of reconstituting the erotic joking relationship with the men. Although many of the men individually regretted the damage to their relationship with women friends in the group, they argued that the special male bond created by sexist humor is a unique form of intimacy that justified the inconvenience caused the women. In reinterpreting these stories as social constructions of gender, I will focus upon the way the joke form and joking relationships reveal the emotional currents underlying gender in this situation.

THE SOCIOLOGY OF JOKES

Although we conventionally think of jokes as a meaningless part of the dramaturgy of everyday life, this convention is part of the way that the social function of jokes is concealed and is necessary if jokes are to "work." It is when jokes fail that the social conflicts that the joke was to reconstruct or "negotiate" are uncovered, and the tensions and emotions that underlie the conventional order of everyday social relations are revealed.

Joking is a special kind of social relationship that suspends the rules of everyday life in order to preserve them. Jokes indirectly express the emotions and tensions that may disrupt everyday life by "negotiating" them (Emerson, 1979, 1970), reconstituting group solidarity by shared aggression and cathartic laughter. The ordinary consequences of forbidden words are suspended by meta-linguistic gestures (tones of voice, facial expressions, catch phrases) that send the message "this is a joke," and emotions that would ordinarily endanger a social relationship can be spoken safely within the micro-world created by the "the joke form" (Bateson, 1955).

Yet jokes are not just stories, they are a theater of domination in everyday life, and the success or failure of a joke marks the boundary within which power and aggression may be used in a relationship. Nearly all jokes have an aggressive content, indeed shared aggression toward an outsider is one of the primary ways by which a group may overcome internal tension and assert its solidarity (Freud, 1960, p. 102). Jokes both require and renew social bonds; thus Radcliffe-Brown pointed out that "joking relationships" between mothers-in-law and their sons-in-law provide a release for tension for people structurally bound to each other but at the same time feeling structural conflict with each other (Radcliffe-Brown, 1959). Joking relationships in medicine, for example, are a medium for the indirect expression of latent emotions or taboo topics that if directly expressed would challenge the physician's authority or disrupt the need to treat life and death situations as ordinary work (see Coser, 1959; Emerson, 1969, 1970).

In each of the studies cited above, the primary focus of the analysis was upon the social function of the joke, not gender, yet in each case the joke either functioned through a joking relationship between men and women, such as in Freud's or Radcliffe-Brown's analysis of mother-in-law jokes, or through the joking relationship between men and women. For example, Coser describes the role of nurses as a safe target of jokes: as a surrogate for the male doctor in patient jokes challenging medical authority; or as a surrogate for the patient in the jokes with which doctors expressed anxiety. Sexist jokes, therefore, should be analyzed not only in general terms of the function of jokes as a means of defending social order, but in specific terms as the mechanism by which the order of gender domination is sustained in everyday life. From this perspective, jokes reveal the way social organizations are gendered, namely, built around the emotional rules of male bonding. In this case study, gender is not only the primary content of men's jokes, but the emotional structures of the male bond is built upon a joking relatiohship that "negotiates" the tension men feel about their relationship with each other, and with women.

Male bonding in everyday life frequently takes the form of a group joking relationship by which men create a serial kind of intimacy to "negotiate" the latent tension and aggression they feel toward each other. The humor of male bonding relationships generally is sexual and aggressive, and frequently consists of sexist or racist jokes. As Freud (1960, p. 99) observed, the jokes that individual men direct toward women are generally erotic, tend to clever forms (like the double entendre), and have a seductive purpose. The jokes that men tell about women in the presence of other men are sexual and aggressive rather than erotic and use hostile rather than clever verbal forms; and, this paper will argue, have the creation of male group bonding as their purpose. While Freud analyzed jokes in order to reveal the unconscious, in this chapter, relationships will be analyzed to uncover the emotional dynamics of male friendships.

The failed penis-envy joke reveals two kinds of joking relationships between college men and women. First, the attempted joke was part of an ongoing joking relationship between "the guys and the girls," as they called each other. The guys used the joking relationship to negotiate the tension they felt between sexual interest in the girls and fear of commitment to them. The guys contrasted their sense of independence and play in male friendships to the sense of dependence they felt in their relationships with women, and used hostile joking to negotiate their fear of the "loss of control" implied by intimacy. Second, the failure of the joke uncovered the use of sexist jokes in creating bonds between men; through their own joking relationships (which they called friendship), the guys negotiated the tension between their need for intimacy with other men and their fear of losing their autonomy as men to the authority of the work world.

THE GIRLS' STORY

The women frequently had been the target of fraternity initiation rites in the past, and generally enjoyed this joking relationship with the men, if with a certain ambivalence. "There was a naked Christmas Carol event, they were singing 'We wish you a Merry Christmas,' and 'Bring on the hasty pudding' was the big line they liked to yell out. And we had five or six pledges who had to strip in front of the house and do naked jumping jacks on the lawn, after all the women in the house were lined up on the steps to watch." The women did not think these events were hostile because they had been invited to watch, and the men stood with them watching, suggesting that the pledges, not the women, were the targets of the joke. This made the joke sexual, not sexist, and part of the normal erotic joking relation between the guys and girls. Still, these jokes were ritual events, not real social relationships; one woman said, "We were just supposed to watch, and the guys were watching us watch. The men set up the stage and the women are brought along to observe. They were the controlling force, then they jump into the car and take off."

At the meeting with the men, two of the women spoke for the group while 11 others sat silently in the center, surrounded by about 30 men. Each tried to explain to the men why the joke had not been funny. The first began, "I'm a feminist, but I'm not going to blame anyone for anything. I just want to talk about my feelings." When she said, "these guys pile in, I mean these huge guys," the men exploded in loud cathartic laughter, and the women joined in, releasing some of the tension of the meeting. She continued, "Your humor was pretty funny as long as it was sexual, but when it went beyond sexual to sexist, then it became painful. You were saying 'I'm better than you.' When you started using sex as a way of proving your superiority it hurt me and made me angry."

The second woman speaker criticized the imposition of the joke form itself, saying that the men's raid had the tone of a symbolic rape. "I admit we knew you were coming over, and we were whispering about it. But it went too far, and I felt afraid to say anything. Why do men always think about women in terms of violating them, in sexual imagery? You have to understand that the combination of a sexual topic with the physical threat of all of you standing around terrified me. I couldn't move. You have to realize that when men combine sexuality and force it's terrifying to women." This woman alluded to having been sexually assaulted in the past, but spoke in a nonthreatening tone that made the men listen silently.

The women spoke about feeling angry about the invasion of their space, about the coercion of being forced to listen to the speeches, and about being used as the object of a joke. But they reported their anger as a psychological fact, a statement about a past feeling, not an accusation. Many began by saying, "I'm not a feminist, but . . .," to reassure the men that although they felt angry, they were not challenging traditional gender relations. The women were caught in a double-bind; if they spoke angrily to the men they would violate the taboo against the expression of anger by women (Miller, 1976, p. 102). If they said nothing, they would internalize their anger, and traditional feminine culture would encourage them to feel guilty about feeling angry at all (Bernardez, 1978; Lerner, 1980). In part they resolved the issue by accepting the men's construction of the event as a joke, although a failed joke; accepting the joke form absolved the men of responsibility, and transformed a debate about gender into a debate about good and bad jokes.

To be accepted as a joke, a cue must be sent to establish a "frame" [for] the latent hostility of the joke content in a safe context; the men sent such a cue when they stood next to the women during the naked jumping jacks. If the cue "this is a joke" is ambiguous, or is not accepted, the aggressive content of the joke is revealed and generally is responded to with anger or aggression, endangering the relation. In part the women were pointing out to the men that the cue "this is a joke" had not been given in this case, and the aggressive content of the joke hurt them. If the cue is given properly and accepted, the everyday rules of social order are suspended and the rule "this is fun" is imposed on the expression of hostility.

Verbal aggression mediated by the joke form generally will be [accepted] without later consequences in the everyday world, and will be judged in terms of the formal intention of jokes, shared play marked by laughter in the interest of social order. By complaining to the university, the women had suspended the rules of joke culture, and attempted to renegotiate them by bringing in an observer; even this turned out to be too aggressive, and the women retreated to traditional gender relationships. The men had formally accepted this shift of rules in order to avoid punishment from the university, however their defense of the joke form was tacitly a defense of traditional gender rules that would define male sexist jokes toward women as erotic, not hostile.

In accepting the construction of the event as "just a joke" the women absolved the men of responsibility for their actions by calling them "little boys." One woman said, "It's not wrong, they're just boys playing a prank. They're little boys, they don't know what they're doing. It was unpleasant, but we shouldn't make a big deal out of it." In appealing to the rules of the joke form the men were willing to sacrifice their relationship to the women to protect the rules. In calling the men "little boys" the women were bending the rules trying to preserve the relationship through a patient nurturing role (see Gilligan, 1982, p. 44).

In calling the guys "little boys," the girls had also created a kind of linguistic symmetry between "the boys and the girls." With the exception of the law student, who called the girls "women," the students called the men "guys" and the women "girls." Earlier in the year the law student had started a discussion about this naming practice. The term "women" had sexual connotations that made "the girls" feel vulnerable, and "gals," the parallel to "guys," connoted "older women" to them. While the term "girls" refers to children, it was adopted because it avoided sexual connotations. Thus the women had no term like "the guys," which is a bonding term that refers to a group of friends as equals; the women often used the term "the guys" to refer to themselves in a group. As the men's speeches were to make clear, the term "guys" refers to a bond that is exclusively male, which is founded upon the emotional structure of the joke form, and which justifies it.

THE GUYS' STORY

Aside from the roar of laughter when a woman referred to their intimidating size, the men interrupted the women only once. When a woman began to say that the men obviously intended to intimidate them, the men loudly protested that the women couldn't possibly judge their intentions, that they intended the whole event only as a joke, and the intention of a joke is, by definition, just fun.

At this point the two black men in the fraternity intervened to explain the rules of male joke culture to the women. The black men said that in a sense they understood what the women meant, it is painful being the object of aggressive jokes. In fact, they said, the collective talk of the fraternity at meals and group events was made up of nothing but jokes, including many racist jokes. One said, "I know what you mean. I've had to listen to things in the house that I'd have hit someone for saying if I'd heard them outside." There was again cathartic laughter among the guys, for the male group bond consisted almost entirely of aggressive words that were barely contained by the responsibility absolving rule of the joke form. A woman responded, "Maybe people should be hit for saying those things, maybe that's the right thing to do." But the black speaker was trying to explain the rules of male joke culture to the women, "if you'd just ignored us, it wouldn't have been any fun." To ignore a joke, even though it makes you feel hurt or angry, is to show strength or coolness, the two primary masculine ideals of the group.

Another man tried to explain the failure of the joke in terms of the difference between the degree of "crudeness" appropriate among the guys and between "guys and girls." He said, "As I was listening at the edge of the room, near the door, and when I looked at the guys I was laughing but when I looked at the girls I was embarrassed. I could see both sides at the same time. It was too crude for your sense of propriety. We have a sense of crudeness you don't have. That's a cultural aspect of the difference between girls and guys."

The other men laughed as he mentioned "how crude we are at the house," and one of the black men added, "you wouldn't believe how crude it gets." Many of the men said privately that while they individually found the jokes about women vulgar, the jokes were justified because they were necessary for the formation of the fraternal bond. These men thought the mistake had been to reveal their crudeness to the women, this was "in bad taste."

In its content, the fraternal bond was almost entirely a joking relationship. In part, the joking was a kind of "signifying" or "dozens," a ritual exchange of insults that functioned to create group solidarity. "If there's one theme that goes on, it's the emphasis on being able to take a lot of ridicule, of shit, and not getting upset about it. Most of the interaction we have is verbally abusing each other, making disgusting references to your mother's sexuality, or the women you were seen with, or your sex organ, the size of your sex organ. And you aren't cool unless you can take it without trying to get back." Being cool is an important male value in other settings as well, such as sports or work; the joke form is a kind of male pedagogy in that, in one guys' words, it teaches "how to keep in control of your emotions."

But the guys themselves would not have described their group as a joking relationship or even as a male bond; they called it friendship. One man said he had found perhaps a dozen guys in the house who were special friends, "guys I could cry in front of." Yet in interviews, no one could recall any of the guys actually crying in front of each other. One said, "I think the guys are very close, they would do nearly anything for each other, drive each other places, give each other money. I think when they have problems about school, their car, or something like that, they can talk to each other. I'm not sure they can talk to each other about problems with women though." The image of crying in front of the other guys was a moving symbol of intimacy to the guys, but in fact crying would be an admission of vulnerability, which would violate the ideals of "strength" and "being cool."

Although the fraternal bond was idealized as a unique kind of intimacy upon which genuine friendship was built, the content of the joking relationship was focused upon women, including much "signifying" talk about mothers. The women interpreted the sexist jokes as a sign of vulnerability. "The thing that struck me the most about our meeting together," one said, "was when the men said they were afraid of trusting women, afraid of being seen as jerks." According to her, this had been the women's main reaction to the meeting by the other women, "How do you tell men that they don't have to be afraid, and what do you do with women who abuse that kind of trust?" One of the men on the boundary of the group remarked that the most hostile misogynist jokes came from the men with the fewest intimate relationships with women. "I think down deep all these guys would love to have satisfying relationships with women. I think they're scared of failing, of having to break away from the group they've become comfortable with. I think being in a fraternity, having close friendships with men is a replacement for having close relationships with women. It'd be painful for them because they'd probably fail."

Joking mobilized the commitment of the men to the group by policing the individual men's commitments to women and minimized the possibility of dyadic withdrawal from the group (see Slater, 1963). "One of the guys just acquired a girlfriend a few weeks ago. He's someone I don't think has had a woman to be friends with, maybe ever, at least in a long time. Everybody has been ribbing him intensely the last few weeks. It's good natured in tone. Sitting at dinner they've invented a little song they sing to him. People yell questions about his girlfriend, the size of her vagina, does she have big breasts."

Since both the jokes and the descriptions of the parties have strong homoerotic overtones, including the exchange of women as sexual partners, jokes were also targeted at homosexuality, to draw an emotional line between the homosocial male bond and homosexual relationships. Being called "queer," however, did not require a sexual relationship with another man, but only visible signs of vulnerability or nurturing behavior.

MALE BONDING AS A JOKING RELATIONSHIP

Fraternal bonding is an intimate kind of male group friendship that suspends the ordinary rules and responsibilities of everyday life through joking relationships. To the guys, dyadic friendship with a woman implied "loss of control," namely, responsibility for work and family. In dealing with women, the group separated intimacy from sex, defining the male bond as intimate but not sexual (homosocial), and relationships with women as sexual but not intimate (heterosexual). The intimacy of group friendship was built upon shared spontaneous action, "having fun," rather than the self-disclosure that marks women's friendships (see Rubin, 1983, p. 13). One of the men had been inexpressive as he listened to the discussion, but spoke about fun in a voice filled with emotion, "The penis-envy speech was a hilarious idea, great college fun. That's what I joined the fraternity for, a good time. College is a stage in my life to do crazy and humorous things. In 10 years when I'm in the business world I won't be able to carry on like this [again cathartic laughter from the men]. The initiation was intended to be humorous. We didn't think through how sensitive you women were going to be."

This speech gives the fraternal bond a specific place in the life cycle. The joking relationship is a ritual bond that creates a male group bond in the transition between boyhood and manhood, after the separation from the family, where the authority of mothers limits fun, but before becoming subject to the authority of work. One man later commented on the transitional nature of the male bond, "I think a lot of us are really scared of losing total control over our own lives. Having to sacrifice our individuality. I think we're scared of work in the same way we're scared of women." In this sense individuality is associated with what the guys called "strength," both the emotional strength suggested by being cool, and the physical strength suggested by facing the risks of sports and the paramilitary games they liked to play.

The emotional structure of the joking relationship is built upon the guys' latent anger about the discipline that middle-class male roles imposed upon them, both marriage rules and work rules. The general relationship between organization of men's work and men's domination of women was noted by Max Weber (1958, pp. 345–346), who described "the vocational specialist" as a man mastered by the rules of organization that create an impersonal kind of dependence, and who therefore seeks to create a feeling of independence through the sexual conquest of women. In each of the epochs of Western history, Weber argues, the subordination of men at work has given rise to a male concept of freedom based upon the violation of women. Although Weber tied dependence upon rules to men's need for sexual conquest through seduction, this may also be a clue to the meaning of sexist jokes and joking relationships among men at work. Sexist jokes may not be simply a matter of recreation or a means of negotiating role stress, they may be a reflection of the emotional foundations of organizational life for men. In everyday work life, sexist jokes may function as a ritual suspension of the rules of responsibility for men, a withdrawal into a microworld in which their anger about dependence upon work and women may be safely expressed.

In analyzing the contradictions and vulnerabilities the guys felt about relationships with women and the responsibilities of work, I will focus upon three dimensions of the joking relationship: (1) the emotional content of the jokes; (2) the erotic of rule breaking created by the rules of the joke form; and (3) the image of strength and "being cool" they pitted against the dependence represented by both women and work.

The Emotional Dynamic of Sexist Jokes   When confronted by the women, the men defended the joke by asserting the formal rule that the purpose of jokes is play, then by justifying the jokes as necessary in order to create a special male bond. The defense that jokes are play defines aggressive behavior as play. This defense was far more persuasive to the men than to the women, since many forms of male bonding play are rule-governed aggression, as in sports and games. The second defense, asserting the relation between sexist jokes and male bonds, points out the social function of sexist jokes among the guys, to control the threat that individual men might form intimate emotional bonds with women and withdraw from the group. Each defense poses a puzzle about the emotional dynamics of male group friendship, for in each case male group friendship seems more like a defense against vulnerability than a positive deal.

In each defense, intimacy is split from sexuality in order to eroticize the male bond, thereby creating an instrumental sexuality directed at women. The separation of intimacy from sexuality transforms women into "sexual objects," which both justifies aggression at women by suspending their relationships to the men and devalues sexuality itself, creating a disgust at women as the sexual "object" unworthy of intimate attention. What is the origin of this conjunction between the devaluation of sexuality and the appropriation of intimacy for the male bond?

Chodorow (1978, p. 182) argues that the sense of masculine identity is constructed by an early repression of the son's erotic bond with his mother; with this repression the son's capacity for intimacy and commitment is devalued as feminine behavior. Henceforth men feel ambivalent about intimate relationships with women, seeking to replicate the fusion of intimacy and sexuality that they had experienced in their primal relationships to their mothers, but at the same time fearing engulfment by women in heterosexual relationships, like the engulfment of their infant selves by their mothers (Chodorow, 1976). Certainly the content of the group's joke suggests this repression of the attachment to the mother, as well as hostility to her authority in the family. One man reported, "There're an awful lot of jokes about people's mothers. If any topic of conversation dominates the conversation it's 'heard your mother was with Ray [one of the guys] last night.' The guys will say incredibly vulgar things about their mothers, or they'll talk about the anatomy of a guy's girlfriends, or women they'd like to sleep with." While the guys' signifying mother jokes suggest the repression Chodorow describes, the men realized that their view of women made it unlikely that marriage would be a positive experience. One said, "I think a lot of us expect to marry someone pretty enough that other men will think we got a good catch, someone who is at least marginally interesting to chat with, but not someone we'd view as a friend. But at the same time, a woman who will make sufficient demands that we won't be able to have any friends. So we'll be stuck for the rest of our lives without friends."

While the emotional dynamic of men's "heterosexual knots" may well begin in this primordial separation of infant sons from mothers, its structure is replicated in the guys' ambivalence about their fathers, and their anger about the dependence upon rules in the work world. Yet the guys themselves described the fraternal bond as a way of creating "strength" and overcoming dependence, which suggests a positive ideal of male identity. In order to explore the guys' sense of the value of the male bond, their conception of strength and its consequences for the way they related to each other and to women has to be taken seriously.

STRENGTH

Ultimately the guys justified the penis-envy joke because it created a special kind of male intimacy, but while the male group is able to appropriate its members' needs for intimacy and commitment, it is not clear that it is able to satisfy those needs, because strength has been defined as the opposite of intimacy. "Strength" is a value that represents solidarity rather than intimacy, the solidarity of a shared risk in rule-governed aggressive competition; its value is suggested by the cathartic laughter when the first woman speaker said, "These guys poured in, these huge guys."

The eros detached from sexuality is attached to rules, not to male friends; the male bond consists of an erotic toward rules, and yet the penis-envy joke expresses most of all the guys' ambivalence about rules. Like "the lads," the male gangs who roam the English countryside, "getting in trouble" by enforcing social mores in unsocial ways (Peters, 1972), "the guys" break the rules in rule-governed ways. The joke form itself suggests this ambivalence about rules and acts as a kind of pedagogy about the relationship between rules and aggression in male work culture. The joke form expresses emotions and tensions that might endanger the order of the organization, but that must be spoken lest they damage social order. Jokes can create group solidarity only if they allow dangerous things to be said; allow a physical catharsis of tension through laughter; or create the solidarity of an "in group" through shared aggression against an "out group." In each case there is an erotic in joke forms: an erotic of shared aggression, of shared sexual feeling, or an erotic of rule breaking itself.

It has been suggested that male groups experience a high level of excitement and sexual arousal in public acts of rule breaking (Thorne & Luria, 1986). The penis-envy speech is precisely such an act, a breaking of conventional moral rules in the interest of group arousal. In each of the versions of the joking relationship in this group there is such an erotic quality: in the sexual content of the jokes, in the need for women to witness dirty talk or naked pledges, in the eros of aggression of the raid and jokes themselves. The penis-envy speech, a required event for all members of the group, is such a collective violation of the rules, and so is the content of their talk, a collective dirty talking that violates moral rules. The cathartic laughter that greeted the words, "You wouldn't believe what we say at the house," testifies to the emotional charge invested in dirty talk.

Because the intimacy of the guys' bond is built around an erotic of rule breaking, it has the serial structure of shared risk rather than the social structure of shared intimacy. In writing about the shared experience of suffering and danger of men at war, J. Glenn Gray (1959, pp. 89–90) distinguishes two kinds of male bonding, comradeship and friendship. Comradeship is based upon an erotic of shared danger, but is based upon the loss of an individual sense of self to a group identity, while friendship is based upon an individual's intellectual and emotional affinity to another individual. In the eros of friendship one's sense of self is heightened; in the eros of comradeship a sense of self is replaced by a sense of group membership. In this sense the guys were seeking comradeship, not friendship, hence the group constructed its bond through an erotic of shared activities with an element of risk, shared danger, or rule breaking: in sports, in paramilitary games, in wild parties, in joking relations. The guys called the performance of these activities "strength," being willing to take risks as a group and remaining cool.

Thus the behavior that the women defined as aggressive was seen by the men as a contest of strength governed by the rules of the joke form, to which the proper response would have been to remain "cool." To the guys, the masculine virtue of "strength" has a positive side, to discover oneself and to discover a sense of the other person through a contest of strength that is governed by rules. To the guys, "strength" is not the same as power or aggression because it is governed by rules, not anger; it is anger that is "uncool."

"BEING COOL"

It is striking that the breaking of rules was not spontaneous, but controlled by the rules of the joke form: that aggressive talk replaces action; that talk is framed by a social form that requires the consent of others; that talk should not be taken seriously. This was the lesson that the black men tried to teach the women in the group session: In the male world, aggression is not defined as violent if it is rule governed rather than anger governed. The fraternal bond was built upon this emotional structure, for the life of the group centered upon the mobilization of aggressive energies in rule-governed activities (in sports, games, jokes, parties), in each arena aggression was highly valued (strength) only when it was rule governed (cool). Getting angry was called "losing control" and the guys thought they were most likely to lose control when they experienced themselves as personally dependent, as in relationships with women and at work.

Rule-governed aggression is a conduct that is very useful to organizations, in that it mobilizes aggressive energies but binds them to order by rules (see Benjamin, 1980, p. 154). The male sense of order is procedural rather than substantive because the male bond is formal (rule governed), rather than personal (based upon intimacy and commitment). Male groups in this sense are shame cultures, not guilt cultures, because the male bond is a group identity that subordinates the individual to the rules, and because social control is imposed through collective judgments about self-control, such as "strength" and "cool." The sense of order within such male groups is based upon the belief that all members are equally dependent upon the rules and that no personal dependence is created within the group. This is not true of the family or of relations with women, both of which are intimate, and, from the guys' point of view, are "out of control" because they are governed by emotion.

The guys face contradictory demands from work culture about the use of aggressive behavior. Aggressive conduct is highly valued in a competitive society when it serves the interests of the organization, but men also face a strong taboo against the expression of anger at work when it is not rule governed. "Competition" imposes certain rules upon aggressive group processes: Aggression must be calculated, not angry; it must be consistent with the power hierarchy of the organization, serving authority and not challenging it; if expressed, it must be indirect, as in jokes; it must serve the needs of group solidarity, not of individual autonomy. Masculine culture separates anger from aggression when it combines the value "strength" with the value "being cool." While masculine cultures often define the expression of anger as "violent" or "loss of control," anger, properly defined, is speech, not action; angry speech is the way we can defend our sense of integrity and assert our sense of justice. Thus it is anger that challenges the authority of the rules, not aggressive behavior in itself, because anger defends the self, not the organization.

The guys' joking relationship taught them a pedagogy for the controlled use of aggression in the work world, to be able to compete aggressively without feeling angry. The guys recognized the relationship between their male bond and the work world by claiming that "high officials of the university know about the way we act and they understand what we are doing." While this might be taken as evidence that the guys were internalizing their fathers' norms and thus inheriting the mantle of patriarchy, the guys described their fathers as slaves to work and women, not as patriarchs. The guys also asserted themselves against the authority of their fathers by acting out against the authority of rules in the performance of "strength."

The guys clearly benefited from the male authority that gave them the power to impose the penis-envy joke upon the women with essentially no consequences. Men are allowed to direct anger and aggression toward women because social norms governing the expression of anger or humor generally replicate the power order of the group. It is striking, however, that the guys would not accept the notion that men have more power than women do; to them it is not men who rule, but rules that govern men. These men had so internalized the governing of male emotions by rules that their anger itself could emerge only indirectly through rule-governed forms, such as jokes and joking relationships. In these forms their anger could serve only order, not their sense of self or justice.

REFERENCES

Bateson, G. (1972). A theory of play and fantasy, In *Steps toward an ecology of mind* (pp. 177–193). New York: Ballantine.

Benjamin, J. (1978). Authority and the family revisited, or, A world without fathers. *New German Critique, 4*(3), 13, 35–57.

Benjamin, J. (1980). The bonds of love: Rational violence and erotic domination. *Feminist Studies, 6*(1), 144–174.

Berndardez, T. (1978). Women and anger. *Journal of the American Medical Women's Association, 33*(5), 215–219.

Bly, R. (1982). What men really want: An interview with Keith Thompson. *New Age*, pp. 30–37, 50–51.

Chodorow, N. (1976). Oedipal asymmetries, heterosexual knots. *Social Problems, 23*, 454–468.

Chodorow, N. (1978). *The reproduction of mothering.* Berkeley: University of California Press.

Coser, R. (1959). Some social functions of laughter: A study of humor in a hospital setting. *Human Relations, 12*, 171–182.

Emerson, J. (1969). Negotiating the serious import of humor. *Sociometry, 32*, 169–181.

Emerson, J. (1970). Behavior in private places. In H. P. Dreitzel (Ed.), *Recent sociology: Vol. 2. Patterns in communicative behavior.* New York: Macmillan.

Freud, S. (1960). *Jokes and their relation to the unconscious.* New York Norton.

Gilligan, C. (1982). *In a different voice.* Cambridge, MA: Harvard University Press.

Gray, G. J. (1959). *The warriors: Reflections on men in battle.* New York: Harper & Row.

Lerner, H. E. (1980). Internal prohibitions against female anger. *American Journal of Psychoanalysis, 40*, 137–148.

Miller, J. B. (1976). *Toward a new psychology of women.* Boston: Beacon.

Peters, E. L. (1972). Aspects of the control of moral ambiguities. In M. Gluckman (Ed.), *The allocation of responsibility* (pp. 109–162). Manchester: Manchester University Press.

Radcliffe-Brown, A. (1959). *Structure and function in primitive society.* Glencoe, IL: Free Press.

Rubin, L. (1983). *Intimate strangers.* New York: Harper & Row.

Slater, P. (1963). On social regression. *American Sociological Review, 28*, 339–364.

Thorne, B., & Luria, Z. (1986). Sexuality and gender in children's daily worlds. *Social Problems.*

Weber, M. (1958). Religions of the world and their directions. In H. Gerth & C. W. Mills (Eds.), *From Max Weber.* New York: Oxford University Press.

◆ ◆ ◆

PART THREE

Sports and War: Rites of Passage in Male Institutions

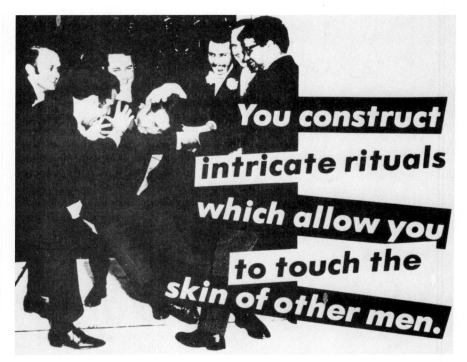

Photo courtesy of Barbara Kruger.

LA Times 11-16-89

Are men naturally more competitive, aggressive, and violent than women? Why are so many cultural heroes males who have been victors on the playing fields or the battle fields? Why do men so often feel that their closest relationships with other men are those that developed "in the heat of battle?" And how do men's battles with each other connect to men's domination of women? The articles in this section shed light on these questions by focusing our attention on two very male-dominated institutions: organized sports and the military.

Recently, largely because of the women's movement, sport sociologists and historians have begun to reconceptualize the meaning of sport as a social institution. Clearly, a major role of sports in the twentieth century has been to provide an institutional context for "masculinity-validation" in a rapidly changing world. Much of the experiential and ideological prominence of sports can be attributed to the fact that it is a male-created homosocial world that provides dramatic symbolic "proof" of the "natural superiority" of men over women. But as the first few articles in this section show, there is nothing "natural" about the connection between sports and what we think of as masculinity. In fact, as the first article by Don Sabo shows, organized sports is an important institutional context in which certain types of masculinity are produced and "naturalized." Here boys learn to overvalue competition and winning, to take physical pain and control their emotions, to view aggression and violence as legitimate means to achieve one's goals, to uncritically accept authority and hierarchy, and to devalue women as well as any "feminine" qualities in males. The next article by Michael Messner suggests how the narrow definitions of masculinity that boys learn in sports connect with other forms of social domination.

The athletic experience can act as a training ground for the construction of an even narrower form of masculinity: the soldier. The article by Connell demonstrates that violent aggression is not *the* "natural" form of masculinity. In fact, it takes a very intense process of socialization to make killers out of most men. Levy shows how racism, misogyny, and homophobia are utilized by the military to dehumanize the enemy in order to rationalize killing him or her. Together, these articles show how, in patriarchal society, values concerning militarism and war have permeated the very fabric of social life. Challenging the form of masculinity that so dominates our society (and that brings us wars) will involve more than simply changing the ways we raise young boys—it must involve a basic rethinking of many of our most fundamental social institutions.

Don Sabo

PIGSKIN, PATRIARCHY AND PAIN

I am sitting down to write as I've done thousands of times over the last decade. But today there's something very different. I'm not in pain.

A half-year ago I underwent back surgery. My physician removed two disks from the lumbar region of my spine and fused three vertebrate using bone scrapings from my right hip. The surgery is called a "spinal fusion." For seventy-two hours I was completely immobilized. On the fifth day, I took a few faltering first steps with one of those aluminum walkers that are usually associated with the elderly in nursing homes. I progressed rapidly and left the hospital after nine days completely free of pain for the first time in years.

How did I, a well-intending and reasonably gentle boy from western Pennsylvania ever get into so much pain? At a simple level, I ended up in pain because I played a sport that brutalizes men's (and now sometimes women's) bodies. *Why* I played football and bit the bullet of pain, however, is more complicated. Like a young child who learns to dance or sing for a piece of candy, I played for rewards and payoffs. Winning at sport meant winning friends and carving a place for myself within the male pecking order. Success at the "game" would make me less like myself and more like the older boys and my hero, Dick Butkus. Pictures of his hulking and snarling form filled my head and hung above my bed, beckoning me forward like a mythic Siren. If I could be like Butkus, I told myself, people would adore me as much as I adored him. I might even adore myself. As an adolescent I hoped sport would get me attention from girls. Later, I became more practical-minded and I worried about my future. What kind of work would I do for a living? Football became my ticket to a college scholarship which, in western Pennsylvania during the early 'sixties, meant a career instead of getting stuck in the steel-mills.

THE ROAD TO SURGERY.

My bout with pain and spinal "pathology" began with a decision I made in 1955 when I was eight years old. I "went out" for football. At the time, I felt uncomfortable inside my body—too fat, too short, too weak. Freckles and glasses too! I wanted to change my image, and I felt that changing my body was one place to begin. My parents bought me a set of weights, and one of the older boys in the neighborhood was solicited to demonstrate their use. I can still remember the ease with which he lifted the barbell, the veins popping through his bulging biceps in the summer sun, and the sated look of strength and accomplishment on his face. This was to be the image of my future.

That fall I made a dinner-table announcement that I was going out for football. What followed was a rather inauspicious beginning. First, the initiation rites. Pricking the flesh with thorns until blood was drawn and having hot peppers rubbed in my eyes. Getting punched in the gut again and again.

Being forced to wear a jockstrap around my nose and not knowing what was funny. Then came what was to be an endless series of proving myself: calisthenics until my arms ached; hitting hard and fast and knocking the other guy down; getting hit in the groin and not crying. I learned that pain and injury are "part of the game."

I "played" through grade school, co-captained my high school team, and went on to become an inside linebacker and defensive captain at the NCAA Division I level. I learned to be an animal. Coaches took notice of animals. Animals made first team. Being an animal meant being fanatically aggressive and ruthlessly competitive. If I saw an arm in front of me, I trampled it. Whenever blood was spilled, I nodded approval. Broken bones (not mine of course) were secretly seen as little victories within the bigger struggle. The coaches taught me to "punish the other man," but little did I suspect that I was devastating my own body at the same time. There were broken noses, ribs, fingers, toes and teeth, torn muscles and ligaments, bruises, bad knees, and busted lips, and the gradual pulverizing of my spinal column that, by the time my jock career was long over at age thirty, had resulted in seven years of near-constant pain. It was a long road to the surgeon's office.

Now surgically freed from its grip, my understanding of pain has changed. Pain had gnawed away at my insides. Pain turned my awareness inward. I blamed myself for my predicament; I thought that I was solely responsible for every twinge and sleepless night. But this view was an illusion. My pain, each individual's pain, is really an expression of a linkage to an outer world of people, events, and forces. The origins of our pain are rooted *outside*, not inside, our skins.

THE PAIN PRINCIPLE

Sport is just one of many areas in our culture where pain is more important than pleasure. Boys are taught that to endure pain is courageous, to survive pain is manly. The principle that pain is "good" and pleasure is "bad" is crudely evident in the "no pain, no gain" philosophy of so many coaches and athletes. The "pain principle" weaves its way into the lives and psyches of male athletes in two fundamental ways. It stifles men's awareness of their bodies and limits our emotional expression. We learn to ignore personal hurts and injuries because they interfere with the "efficiency" and "goals" of the "team." We become adept at taking the feelings that boil up inside us—feelings of insecurity and stress from striving so hard for success—and channeling them in a bundle of rage which is directed at opponents and enemies. This posture toward oneself and the world is not limited to "jocks." It is evident in the lives of many nonathletic men who, as "workaholics" or success-strivers or tough guys, deny their authentic physical or emotional needs and develop health problems as a result.

Today, I no longer perceive myself as an *individual* ripped off by athletic injury. Rather, I see myself as just *one more man among many men* who got swallowed up by a social system predicated on male domination. Patriarchy has two structural aspects. First, it is an hierarchical system in which men dominate women in crude and debased, slick and subtle ways. Feminists have made great progress exposing and analyzing this dimension of the edifice of sexism. But it is also a system of *intermale dominance*, in which a minority of men dominates the masses of men. This intermale dominance hierarchy exploits the majority of those it beckons to climb its heights. Patriarchy's mythos of heroism and its morality of power-worship implant visions of ecstasy and masculine excellence in the minds of the boys who ultimately will defend its inequities and ridicule its victims. It is inside this institutional framework that I have begun to explore the essence and scope of "the pain principle."

TAKING IT

Patriarchy is a form of social hierarchy. Hierarchy breeds inequity and inequity breeds pain. To remain stable, the hierarchy must either justify the pain or explain it away. In a patriarchy, women and the masses of men are fed the cultural message that pain is inevitable and that pain enhances one's character and moral worth. This principle is expressed in Judeo-Christian beliefs. The Judeo-Christian god inflicts or permits pain, yet "the Father" is still revered and loved. Likewise, as chief disciplinarian in the patriarchal family, the father has the right to inflict pain. The "pain principle" also echoes throughout traditional western sexual morality; it is better to experience the pain of *not* having sexual pleasure than it is to have sexual pleasure.

Most men learn to heed these cultural messages and take their "cues for survival" from the patriarchy. The Willie Lomans of the economy pander to the prophets of profit and the American Dream. Soldiers, young and old, salute their neo-Hun generals. Right-wing Christians genuflect before their idols of righteousness, affluence, and conformity. And male athletes adopt the visions and values that coaches are offering: to take orders, to take pain, to "take out" opponents, to take the game seriously, to take women, and to take their place on the team. And if they can't "take it," then the rewards of athletic comraderie, prestige, scholarships, pro contracts, and community recognition are not forthcoming.

Becoming a football player fosters conformity to male-chauvinistic values and self-abusing lifestyles. It contributes to the legitimacy of a social structure based on patriarchal power. Male competition for prestige and status in sport and elsewhere leads to identification with the relatively few males who control resources and are able to bestow rewards and inflict punishment. Male supremacists are not born, they are made, and traditional athletic socialization is a fundamental contribution to this complex social-psychological and political process. Through sport, many males, indeed, learn to "take it"—that is, to internalize patriarchal values which, in turn, become part of their gender identity and conception of women and society.

My high school coach once evoked the pain principle during a pre-game peptalk. For what seemed an eternity, he paced frenetically and silently before us with fist clenched and head bowed. He suddenly stopped and faced us with a smile. It was as though he had approached a podium to begin a long-awaited lecture. "Boys," he began, "people who say that football is a 'contact sport' are dead wrong. Dancing is a contact sport. Football is a game of pain and violence! Now get the hell out of here and kick some ass." We practically ran through the wall leaving the locker room, surging in unison to fight the coach's war. I see now that the coach was right but for all the wrong reasons. I should have taken him at his word and never played the game!

Michael Messner

BOYHOOD, ORGANIZED SPORTS, AND THE CONSTRUCTION OF MASCULINITIES

The rapid expansion of feminist scholarship in the past two decades has led to fundamental reconceptualizations of the historical and contemporary meanings of organized sport. In the nineteenth and twentieth centuries, modernization and women's continued movement into public life created widespread "fears of social feminization," especially among middle-class men (Hantover, 1978; Kimmel, 1987). One result of these fears was the creation of organized sport as a homosocial sphere in which competition and (often violent) physicality was valued, while "the feminine" was devalued. As a result, organized support has served to bolster a sagging ideology of male superiority, and has helped to reconstitute masculine hegemony (Bryson, 1987; Hall, 1988; Messner, 1988; Theberge, 1981).

The feminist critique has spawned a number of studies of the ways that women's sport has been marginalized and trivialized in the past (Greendorfer, 1977; Oglesby, 1978; Twin, 1978), in addition to illuminating the continued existence of structural and ideological barriers to gender equality within sport (Birrell, 1987). Only recently, however, have scholars begun to use feminist insights to examine men's experiences in sport (Kidd, 1987; Messner, 1987; Sabo, 1985). This article explores the relationship between the construction of masculine identity and boyhood participation in organized sports.

I view gender identity not as a "thing" that people "have," but rather as a *process of construction* that develops, comes into crisis, and changes as a person interacts with the social world. Through this perspective, it becomes possible to speak of "gendering" identities rather than "masculinity" or "femininity" as relatively fixed identities or statuses.

There is an agency in this construction; people are not passively shaped by their social environment. As recent feminist analyses of the construction of feminine gender identity have pointed out, girls and women are implicated in the construction of their own identities and personalities, both in terms of the ways that they participate in their own subordination and the ways that they resist subordination (Benjamin, 1988; Haug, 1987). Yet this self-construction is not a fully conscious process. There are also deeply woven, unconscious motivations, fears, and anxieties at work here. So, too, in the construction of masculinity. Levinson (1978) has argued that masculine identity is neither fully "formed" by the social context, nor is it "caused" by some internal dynamic put into place during infancy. Instead, it is shaped and constructed

Reprinted from *Journal of Contemporary Ethnography*, Vol. 18 No. 4, January 1990, 416–444. © 1990 Sage Publications, Inc.

through the interaction between the internal and the social. The internal gendering identity may set developmental "tasks," may create thresholds of anxiety and ambivalence, yet it is only through a concrete examination of people's interactions with others within social institutions that we can begin to understand both the similarities and differences in the construction of gender identities.

In this study I explore and interpret the meanings that males themselves attribute to their boyhood participation in organized sport. In what ways do males construct masculine identities within the institution of organized sports? In what ways do class and racial differences mediate this relationship and perhaps lead to the construction of different meanings, and perhaps different masculinities? And what are some of the problems and contradictions within these constructions of masculinity?

DESCRIPTION OF RESEARCH

Between 1983 and 1985, I conducted interviews with 30 male former athletes. Most of the men I interviewed had played the (U.S.) "major sports"— football, basketball, baseball, track. At the time of the interview, each had been retired from playing organized sports for at least five years. Their ages ranged from 21 to 48, with the median, 33; 14 were black, 14 were white, and two were Hispanic; 15 of the 16 black and Hispanic men had come from poor or working-class families, while the majority (9 of 14) of the white men had come from middle-class or professional families. All had at some time in their lives based their identities largely on their roles as athletes and could therefore be said to have had "athletic careers." Twelve had played organized sports through high school, 11 through college, and seven had been professional athletes. Though the sample was not randomly selected, an effort was made to see that the sample had a range of difference in terms of race and social class backgrounds, and that there was some variety in terms of age, types of sports played, and levels of success in athletic careers. Without exception, each man contacted agreed to be interviewed.

The tape-recorded interviews were semistructured and took from one and one-half to six hours, with most taking about three hours. I asked each man to talk about four broad eras in his life: (1) his earliest experiences with sports in boyhood, (2) his athletic career, (3) retirement or disengagement from the athletic career, and (4) life after the athletic career. In each era, I focused the interview on the meanings of "success and failure," and on the boy's/man's relationships with family, with other males, with women, and with his own body.

In collecting what amounted to life histories of these men, my overarching purpose was to use feminist theories of masculine gender identity to explore how masculinity develops and changes as boys and men interact within the socially constructed world of organized sports. In addition to using the data to move toward some generalizations about the relationship between "masculinity and sport," I was also concerned with sorting out some of the variations among boys, based on class and racial inequalities, that led them to relate differently to athletic careers. I divided my sample into two comparison groups. The first group was made up of 10 men from higher-status backgrounds, primarily white, middle-class, and professional families. The second group was made up of 20 men from lower-status backgrounds, primarily minority, poor, and working-class families.

BOYHOOD AND THE PROMISE OF SPORTS

Zane Grey once said, "All boys love baseball. If they don't they're not real boys" (as cited in Kimmel, 1990). This is, of course, an ideological statement; In fact, some boys do *not* love baseball, or any other sports, for that matter. There are millions of males who at an early age are rejected by, become alienated from, or lose interest in organized sports. Yet all boys are, to a greater or lesser extent, judged according to their ability, or lack of ability, in competitive sports (Eitzen, 1975; Sabo, 1985). In this study I focus on those males who did become athletes—males who eventually poured thousands of hours into the development of specific physical skills. It is in boyhood that we can discover the roots of their commitment to athletic careers.

How did organized sports come to play such a central role in these boy's lives? When asked to recall how and why they initially got into playing sports, many of the men interviewed for this study seemed a bit puzzled: after all, playing sports was "just the thing to do." A 42-year-old black man who had played college basketball put it this way:

> It was just what you did. It's kind of like, you went to school, you played athletics, and if you didn't, there was something wrong with you. It was just like brushing your teeth: it's just what you did. It's part of your existence.

Spending one's time playing sports with other boys seemed as natural as the cycle of the seasons: baseball in the spring and summer, football in the fall, basketball in the winter—and then it was time to get out the old baseball glove and begin again. As a black 35-year-old former professional football star said:

> I'd say when I wasn't in school, 95% of the time was spent in the park playing. It was the only thing to do. It just came as natural.

And a black, 34-year-old professional basketball player explained his early experiences in sports:

> My principal and teacher said, "Now if you work at this you might be pretty damned good." So it was more or less a community thing—everybody in the community said, "Boy, if you work hard and keep your nose clean, you gonna be good." Cause it was natural instinct.

"It was natural instinct." "I was a natural." Several athletes used words such as these to explain their early attraction to sports. But certainly there is nothing "natural" about throwing a ball through a hoop, hitting a ball with a bat, or jumping over hurdles. A boy, for instance, may have amazingly dexterous inborn hand-eye coordination, but this does not predispose him to a career of hitting baseballs any more than it predisposes him to a life as a brain surgeon. When one listens closely to what these men said about their early experiences in sports, it becomes clear that their adoption of the self-definition of "natural athlete" was the result of what Connell (1990) has called "a collective practice" that constructs masculinities. The boyhood development of masculine identity and status—truly problematic in a society that offers no official rite of passage into adulthood—results from a process of interaction with people and social institutions. Thus, in discussing early motivations in sports, men commonly talk of the importance of relationships with family members, peers, and the broader community.

FAMILY INFLUENCES

Though most of the men in this study spoke of their mothers with love, respect, even reverence, their descriptions of their earliest experiences in sports are stories of an exclusively male world. The existence of older brothers or uncles who served as teachers and athletic role models—as well as sources of competition for attention and status within the family—was very common. An older brother, uncle, or even close friend of the family who was a successful athlete appears to have acted as a sort of standard of achievement against whom to measure oneself. A 34-year-old black man who had been a three-sport star in high school said:

> My uncles—my Uncle Harold went to the Detroit Tigers, played pro ball—all of 'em, everybody played sports, so I wanted to be better than anybody else. I knew that everybody in this town knew them—their names were something. I wanted my name to be just like theirs.

Similarly, a black 41-year-old former professional football player recalled:

> I was the younger of three brothers and everybody played sports, so consequently I was more or less forced into it. 'Cause one brother was always better than the next brother and then I came along and had to show them that I was just as good as them. My oldest brother was an all-city ballplayer, then my other brother comes along he's all-city and all-state, and then I have to come along.

For some, attempting to emulate or surpass the athletic accomplishments of older male family members created pressures that were difficult to deal with. A 33-year-old white man explained that he was a good athlete during boyhood, but the constant awareness that his two older brothers had been better made it difficult for him to feel good about himself, or to have fun in sports;

> I had this sort of reputation that I followed from the playgrounds through grade school, and through high school. I followed these guys who were all-conference and all-state.

Most of these men, however, saw their relationships with their athletic older brothers and uncles in a positive light; it was within these relationships that they gained experience and developed motivations that gave them a competitive "edge" within their same-aged peer group. As a 33-year-old black man describes his earliest athletic experiences:

> My brothers were role models. I wanted to prove—especially to my brothers—that I had heart, you know, that I was a man.

When asked, "What did it mean to you to be 'a man' at that age?" he replied:

> Well, it meant that I didn't want to be a so-called scaredy-cat. You want to hit a guy even though he's bigger than you to show that, you know, you've got this macho image. I remember that at that young an age, that feeling was exciting to me. And that carried over, and as I got older, I got better and I began to look around me and see, well hey! I'm competitive with these guys, even though I'm younger, you know? And then of course all the compliments come—and I began to notice a change, even in my parents—especially in my father—he was proud of that, and that was very important to me. He was extremely important . . . he showed me more affection, now that I think of it.

As this man's words suggest, if men talk of their older brothers and uncles mostly as role models, teachers, and "names" to emulate, their talk of their relationships with their fathers is more deeply layered and complex. Athletic skills and competition for status may often be learned from older brothers, but it is in boys' relationships with fathers that we find many of the keys to the emotional salience of sports in the development of masculine identity.

RELATIONSHIPS WITH FATHERS

The fact that boys' introductions to organized sports are often made by fathers who might otherwise be absent or emotionally distant adds a powerful emotional charge to these early experiences (Osherson, 1986). Although playing organized sports eventually came to feel "natural" for all of the men interviewed in this study, many needed to be "exposed" to sports, or even gently "pushed" by their fathers to become involved in activities like Little League baseball. A white, 33-year-old man explained:

> I still remember it like it was yesterday—Dad and I driving up in his truck, and I had my glove and my hat and all that—and I said, "Dad, I don't want to do it." He says, "What?" I says, "I don't want to do it." I was nervous. That I might fail. And he says, "Don't be silly. Lookit: There's Joey and Petey and all your friends out there." And so Dad says, "You're gonna do it, come on." And in my memory he's never said that about anything else; he just knew I needed a little kick in the pants and I'd do it. And once you're out there and you see all the other kids making errors and stuff, and you know you're better than those guys, you know: Maybe I *do* belong here. As it turned out, Little League was a good experience.

Some who were similarly "pushed" by their fathers were not so successful as the aforementioned man had been in Little League baseball, and thus the experience was not altogether a joyous affair. One 34-year-old white man, for instance, said he "inherited" his interest in sports from his father, who started playing catch with him at the age of four. Once he got into Little League, he felt pressured by his father, one of the coaches, who expected him to be the star of the team:

> I'd go O-for-four sometimes, strike out three times in a Little League game, and I'd dread the ride home. I'd come home and he'd say, "Go in the bathroom and swing the bat in the mirror for an hour," to get my swing level . . . It didn't help much, though, I'd go out and strike out three or four times again the next game too [laughs ironically].

When asked if he had been concerned with having his father's approval, he responded:

> Failure in his eyes? Yeah, I always thought that he wanted me to get some kind of [athletic] scholarship. I guess I was afraid of him when I was a kid. He didn't hit that much, but he had a rage about him—he'd rage, and that voice would just rattle you.

Similarly, a 24-year-old black man described his awe of his father's physical power and presence, and his sense of inadequacy in attempting to emulate him:

> My father had a voice that sounded like rolling thunder. Whether it was intentional on his part or not, I don't know, but my father gave me a sense, an image of him being the most powerful being on earth, and that no matter what I ever did I would never come close to him . . . There were definite feelings of physical inadequacy that I couldn't work around.

It is interesting to note how these feelings of physical inadequacy relative to the father lived on as part of this young man's permanent internalized image. He eventually became a "feared" high school football player and broke school records in weigh-lifting, yet,

> As I grew older, my mother and friends told me that I had actually grown to be a larger man than my father. Even though in time I required larger clothes than he, which should have been a very concrete indication, neither my brother nor I could ever bring ourselves to say that I was bigger. We simply couldn't conceive of it.

Using sports activities as a means of identifying with and "living up to" the power and status of one's father was not always such a painful and difficult task for the men I interviewed. Most did not describe fathers who "pushed" them to become sports stars. The relationship between their athletic strivings and their identification with their fathers was more subtle. A 48-year-old black man, for instance, explained that he was not pushed into sports by his father, but was aware from an early age of the community status his father had gained through sports. He saw his own athletic accomplishments as a way to connect with and emulate his father:

> I wanted to play baseball because my father had been quite a good baseball player in the Negro leagues before baseball was integrated, and so he was kind of a model for me. I remember, quite young, going to a baseball game he was in—this was before the war and all—I remember

being in the stands with my mother and seeing him on first base, and being aware of the crowd . . . I was aware of people's confidence in him as a serious baseball player. I don't think my father ever said anything to me like "play sports" . . . [But] I knew he would like it if I did well . . . His admiration was important . . . he mattered.

Similarly, a 24-year-old white man described his father as a somewhat distant "role model" whose approval mattered:

My father was more of an example . . . he definitely was very much in touch with and still had very fond memories of being an athlete and talked about it, bragged about it . . . But he really didn't do that much to teach me skills, and he didn't always go to every game I played like some parents. But he approved and that was important, you know. That was important to get his approval. I always knew that playing sports was important to him, so I knew implicitly that it was good and there was definitely a value on it.

First experiences in sports might often come through relationships with brothers or older male relatives, and the early emotional salience of sports was often directly related to a boy's relationship with his father. The sense of commitment that these young boys eventually made to the development of athletic careers is best explained as a process of development of masculine gender identity and status in relation to same-sex peers.

MASCULINE IDENTITY AND EARLY COMMITMENT TO SPORTS

When many of the men in this study said that during childhood they played sports because "it's just what everybody did," they of course meant that it was just what *boys* did. They were introduced to organized sports by older brothers and fathers, and once involved, found themselves playing within an exclusively male world. Though the separate (and unequal) gendered worlds of boys and girls came to appear as "natural," they were in fact socially contructed. Thorne's observations of children's activities in schools indicated that rather than "naturally" constituting "separate gendered cultures," there is considerable interaction between boys and girls in classrooms and on play-grounds. When adults set up legitimate contact between boys and girls, Thorne observed, this usually results in "relaxed interactions." But when activites in the classroom or on the playground are presented to children as sex-segregated activities and gender is marked by teachers and other adults ("boys line up here, girls over there"), "gender boundaries are heightened, and mixed-sex interaction becomes an explicit arena of risk" (Thorne, 1986; 70). Thus sex-segregated activities such as organized sports as structured by adults, provide the context in which gendered identities and separate "gen-dered cultures" develop and come to appear natural. For the boys in this study, it became "natural" to equate masculinity with competition, physical strength, and skills. Girls simply did not (could not, it was believed) partici-pate in these activities.

Yet it is not simply the separation of children, by adults, into separate activities that explains why many boys came to feel such a strong connection with sports activities, while so few girls did. As I listened to men recall their earliest experiences in organized sports, I heard them talk of insecurity, loneliness, and especially a need to connect with other people as a primary motivation in their early sports strivings. As a 42-year-old white man stated, "The most important thing was just being out there with the rest of the guys—being friends." Another 32-year-old interviewee was born in Mexico and moved to the United States at a fairly young age. He never knew his father, and his mother died when he was only nine years old. Suddenly he felt rootless, and threw himself into sports. His initial motivations, however, do not appear to be based on a need to compete and win:

> Actually, what I think sports did for me is it brought me into kind of an instant family. By being on a Little League team, or even just playing with all kinds of different kids in the neighborhood, it brought what I really wanted, which was some kind of closeness. It was just being there, and being friends.

Clearly, what these boys needed and craved was that which was most problematic for them: connection and unity with other people. But why do these young males find *organized sports* such an attractive context in which to establish "a kind of closeness" with others? Comparative observations of young boys' and girls' game-playing behaviors yield important insights into this question. Piaget (1965) and Lever (1976) both observed that girls tend to have more "pragmatic" and "flexible" orientations to the rules of games; they are more prone to make exceptions and innovations in the middle of a game in order to make the game more "fair." Boys, on the other hand, tend to have a more firm, even [in] flexible orientation to the rules of a game; to them, the rules are what protects any fairness. This difference, according to Gilligan (1982), is based on the fact that early developmental experiences have yielded deeply rooted differences between males' and females' developmental tasks, needs, and moral reasoning. Girls, who tend to define themselves primarily through connection with others, experience highly competitive situations (whether in organized sports or in other hierarchical institutions) as threats to relationships, and thus to their identities. For boys, the development of gender identity involves the construction of positional identities, where a sense of self is solidified through separation from others (Chodorow, 1978). Yet feminist psychoanalytic theory has tended to oversimplify the internal lives of men (Lichterman, 1986). Males do appear to develop positional iden- tities, yet despite their fears of intimacy, they also retain a human need for closeness and unity with others. This ambivalence toward intimate relation- ships is a major thread running through masculine development throughout the life course. Here we can conceptualize what Craib (1987) calls the "elective affinity" between personality and social structure: For the boy who both seeks and fears attachment with others, the rule-bound structure of organized sports can promise to be a safe place in which to seek nonintimate attachment with others within a context that maintains clear boundaries, distance, and separation.

COMPETITIVE STRUCTURES AND
CONDITIONAL SELF-WORTH

Young boys may initially find that sports gives the the opportunity to experience "some kind of closeness" with others, but the structure of sports and athletic careers often undermines the possibility of boys learning to transcend their fears of intimacy, thus becoming able to develop truly close and intimate relationships with others (Kidd, 1990; Messner, 1987). The sports world is extremely hierarchical, and an incredible amount of importance is placed on winning, on "being number one." For instance, a few years ago I observed a basketball camp put on for boys by a professional basketball coach and his staff. The youngest boys, about eight years old (who could barely reach the basket with their shots) played a brief scrimmage. Afterwards, the coaches lined them up in a row in front of the older boys who were sitting in the grandstands. One by one, the coach would stand behind each boy, put his hand on the boy's head (much in the manner of a priestly benediction), and the older boys in the stands would applaud and cheer, louder or softer, depending on how well or poorly the young boy was judged to have performed. The two or three boys who were clearly the exceptional players looked confident that they would receive the praise they were due. Most of the boys, though, had expressions ranging from puzzlement to thinly disguised terror on their faces as they awaited the judgments of the older boys.

This kind of experience teaches boys that it is not "just being out there with the guys—being friends," that ensures the kind of attention and connection that they crave; it is being *better* than the other guys—*beating* them—that is the key to acceptance. Most of the boys in this study did have some early successes in sports, and thus their ambivalent need for connection with others was met, at least for a time. But the institution of sport tends to encourage the development of what Schafer (1975) has called "conditional self-worth" in boys. As boys become aware that acceptance by others is contingent upon being good—a "winner"—narrow definitions of success, based upon performance and winning become increasingly important to them. A 33-year-old black man said that by the time he was in his early teens:

> It was expected of me to do well in all my contests—I mean by my coaches, my peers, and my family. So I in turn expected to do well, and if I didn't do well, then I'd be very disappointed.

The man from Mexico, discussed above, who said that he had sought "some kind of closeness" in his early sports experiences began to notice in his early teens that if he played well, was a *winner*, he would get attention from others:

> It got to the point where I started realizing, noticing that people were always there for me, backing me all the time—sports got to be really fun because I always had some people there backing me. Finally my oldest brother started going to all my games, even though I had never really seen who he was [laughs]—after the game, you know, we never really saw each other, but he was at all my baseball games, and it seemed like we shared a kind of closeness there, but only in those situations. Off the field, when I wasn't in uniform, he was never around.

By high school, he said, he felt "up against the wall." Sports hadn't delivered what he had hoped it would, but he thought if he just tried harder, won one more championship trophy, he would get the attention he truly craved. Despite his efforts, this attention was not forthcoming. And, sadly, the pressures he had put on himself to excel in sports had taken most of the fun out of playing.

For many of the men in this study, throughout boyhood and into adolescence, this conscious striving for successful achievement became the primary means through which they sought connection with other people (Messner, 1987). But it is important to recognize that young males' internalized ambivalences about intimacy do not fully determine the contours and directions of their lives. Masculinity continues to develop through interaction with the social world—and because boys from different backgrounds are interacting with substantially different familial, educational, and other institutions, these differences will lead them to make different choices and define situations in different ways. Next, I examine the differences in the ways that boys from higher- and lower-status families and communities related to organized sports.

STATUS DIFFERENCES AND COMMITMENTS TO SPORTS

In discussing early attractions to sports, the experiences of boys from higher- and lower-status backgrounds are quite similar. Both groups indicate the importance of fathers and older brothers in introducing them to sports. Both groups speak of the joys of receiving attention and acceptance among family and peers for early successes in sports. Note the similarities, for instance, in the following descriptions of boyhood athletic experiences of two men. First, a man born in a white, middle-class family:

> I loved playing sports so much from a very early age because of early exposure. A lot of the sports came easy at an early age, and because they did, and because you were successful at something, I think that you're inclined to strive for that gratification. It's like, if you're good, you like it, because it's instant gratification. I'm doing something that I'm good at and I'm gonna keep doing it.

Second, a black man from a poor family:

> Fortunately I had some athletic ability, and, quite naturally, once you start doing good in whatever it is—I don't care if it's jacks—you show off what you do. That's your ability, that's your blessing, so you show it off as much as you can.

For boys from both groups, early exposure to sports, the discovery that they had some "ability," shortly followed by some sort of family, peer, and community recognition, all eventually led to the commitment of hundreds and thousands of hours of playing, practicing, and dreaming of future stardom. Despite these similarities, there are also some identifiable differences that begin to explain the tendency of males from lower-status backgrounds to develop higher levels of commitment to sports careers. The most clear-cut difference was that while men from higher-status backgrounds are likely to describe their earliest athletic experiences and motivations almost exclusively in terms of immediate family, men from lower-status backgrounds more commonly describe the importance of a broader community context. For instance, a 46-year-old man who grew up in a "poor working class" black family in a small town in Arkansas explained:

> In that community, at the age of third or fourth grade, if you're a male, they expect you to show some kind of inclination, some kind of skill in football or basketball. It was an expected thing, you know? My mom and my dad, they didn't push at all. It was the general environment.

A 48-year-old man describes sports activities as a survival strategy in his poor black community:

> Sports protected me from having to compete in gang stuff, or having to be good with my fists. If you were an athlete and got into the fist world, that was your business, and that was okay—but you didn't have to if you didn't want to. People would generally defer to you, give you your space away from trouble.

A 35-year-old man who grew up in "a poor black ghetto" described his boyhood relationship to sports similarly:

> Where I came from, either you were one of two things: you were in sports or you were out on the streets being a drug addict, or breaking into places. The guys who were in sports, we had it a little easier, because we were accepted by both groups . . . So it worked out to my advantage, cause I didn't get into a lot of trouble—some trouble, but not a lot.

The fact that boys in lower-status communities faced these kinds of realities gave salience to their developing athletic identities. In contrast, sports were important to boys from higher-status backgrounds, yet the middle-class environment seemed more secure, less threatening, and offered far more options. By the time most of these boys got into junior high or high school, many had made conscious decisions to shift their attentions away from athletic careers to educational and (nonathletic) career goals. A 32-year-old white college athletic director told me that he had seen his chance to pursue a pro baseball career as "pissing in the wind," and instead, focused on education. Similarly, a 33-year-old white dentist who was a three-sport star in high school, decided not to play sports in college, so he could focus on getting into dental school. As he put it,

> I think I kind of downgraded the stardom thing. I thought it was small potatoes. And sure, that's nice in high school and all that, but on a broad scale, I didn't think it amounted to all that much.

This statement offers an important key to understanding the construction of masculine identity within a middle-class context. The status that this boy got through sports had been *very* important to him, yet he could see that "on a broad scale," this sort of status was "small potatoes." This sort of early recognition is more than a result of the oft-noted middle-class tendency to raise "future-oriented" children (Rubin, 1976; Sennett and Cobb, 1973).

Perhaps more important, it is that the *kinds* of future orientations developed by boys from higher-status backgrounds are consistent with the middle-class context. These men's descriptions of their boyhoods reveal that they grew up immersed in a wide range of institutional frameworks, of which organized sports was just one. And—importantly—they could see that the status of adult males around them was clearly linked to their positions within various professions, public institutions, and bureaucratic organizations. It was clear that access to this sort of institutional status came through educational achievement, not athletic prowess. A 32-year-old black man who grew up in a professional-class family recalled that he had idolized Wilt Chamberlain and dreamed of being a pro basketball player, yet his father discouraged his athletic strivings:

> He knew I liked the game. I *loved* the game. But basketball was not recommended; my dad would say, "That's a stereotyped image for black youth . . . When your basketball is gone and finished, what are you gonna do? One day, you might get injured. What are you gonna look forward to?" He stressed education.

Similarly, a 32-year-old man who was raised in a white, middle-class family, had found in sports a key means of gaining acceptance and connection in his peer group. Yet he was simultaneously developing an image of himself as a "smart student," and becoming aware of a wide range of nonsports life options:

> My mother was constantly telling me how smart I was, how good I was, what a nice person I was, and giving me all sorts of positive strokes, and those positive strokes became a self-motivating kind of thing. I had this image of myself as smart, and I lived up to that image.

It is not that parents of boys in lower-status families did not also encourage their boys to work hard in school. Several reported that their parents "stressed books first, sports second." It's just that the broader social context—education, economy, and community—was more likely to *narrow* lower-status boys' perceptions of real-life options, while boys from higher-status backgrounds faced an expanding world of options. For instance, with a different socioeconomic background, one 35-year-old black man might have become a great musician instead of a star professional football running back. But he did not. When he was a child, he said, he was most interested in music:

> I wanted to be a drummer. But we couldn't afford drums. My dad couldn't go out and buy me a drum set or a guitar even—it was just one of those things; he was just trying to make ends meet.

But he *could* afford, as could so many in his socioeconomic condition, to spend countless hours at the local park, where he was told by the park supervisor

> that I was a natural—not only in gymnastics or baseball—whatever I did, I was a natural. He told me I shouldn't waste this talent, and so I immediately started watching the big guys then.

In retrospect, this man had potential to be a musician or any number of things, but his environment limited his options to sports, and he made the best of it. Even within sports, he, like most boys in the ghetto, was limited:

> We didn't have any tennis courts in the ghetto—we used to have a lot of tennis balls, but no racquets. I wonder today how good I might be in tennis if I had gotten a racquet in my hands at an early age.

It is within this limited structure of opportunity that many lower-status young boys found sports to be *the* place, rather than *a* place, within which to construct masculine identity, status, the relationships. A 36-year-old white man explained that his father left the family when he was very young and his mother faced a very difficult struggle to make ends meet. As his words suggest, the more limited a boy's options, and the more insecure his family situation, the more likely he is to make an early commitment to an athletic career:

> I used to ride my bicycle to Little League practice—if I'd waited for someone to pick me up and take me to the ball park I'd have never played. I'd get to the ball park and all the other kids would have their dad bring them to practice or games. But I'd park my bike to the side and when it was over I'd get on it and go home. Sports was the way for me to move everything to the side—family problems, just all the embar-rassments—and think about one thing, and that was sports . . . In the third grade, when the teacher went around the classroom and asked everybody, "What do you want to be when you grow up?," I said, "I want to be a major league baseball player," and everybody laughed their heads off.

This man eventually did enjoy a major league baseball career. Most boys from lower-status backgrounds who make similar early commitments to ath-letic careers are not so successful. As stated earlier, the career structure of organized sports is highly competitive and hierarchical. In fact, the chances of attaining professional status in sports are approximately 4:100,000 for a white man, 2:100,000 for a black man, and 3:1 million for a Hispanic man in the United States (Leonard and Reyman, 1988). Nevertheless, the immediate rewards (fun, status, attention), along with the constricted (nonsports) struc-ture of opportunity, attract disproportionately large numbers of boys from lower-status backgrounds to athletic careers as their major means of construct-ing a masculine identity. These are the boys who later, as young men, had to struggle with "conditional self-worth," and, more often than not, occupa-tional dead ends. Boys from higher-status backgrounds, on the other hand, bolstered their boyhood, adolescent, and early adult status through their athletic accomplishments. Their wider range of experiences and life chances led to an early shift away from sports careers as the major basis of identity (Messner, 1989).

CONCLUSION

The conception of the masculinity-sports relationship developed here begins to illustrate the idea of an "elective affinity" between social structure and personality. Organized sports is a "gendered institution"—an institution constructed by gender relations. As such, its structure and values (rules, formal organization, sex composition, etc.), reflect dominant conceptions of masculinity and femininity. Organized sports is also a "gendering institution"—an institution that helps to construct the current gender order. Part of this construction of gender is accomplished through the "masculinizing" of male bodies and minds.

Yet boys do not come to their first experiences in organized sports as "blank slates," but arrive with already "gendering" identities due to early developmental experiences and previous socialization. I have suggested here that an important thread running through the development of masculine identity is males' ambivalence toward intimate unity with others. Those boys who experience early athletic successes find in the structure of organized sport an affinity with this masculine ambivalence toward intimacy: The rule-bound, competitive, hierarchical world of sport offers boys an attractive means of establishing an emotionally distant (and thus "safe") connection with others. Yet as boys begin to define themselves as "athletes," they learn that in order to be accepted (to have connection) through sports, they must be winners. And in order to be winners, they must construct relationships with others (and with themselves) that are consistent with the competitive and hierarchical values and structure of the sports world. As a result, they often develop a "conditional self-worth" that leads them to construct more instrumental relationships with themselves and others. This ultimately exacerbates their difficulties in constructing intimate relationships with others. In effect, the interaction between the young male's preexisting internalized ambivalence toward intimacy with the competitive, hierarchical institution of sport has resulted in the construction of a masculine personality that is characterized by instrumental rationality, goal-orientation, and difficulties with intimate connection and expression (Messner, 1987).

This theoretical line of inquiry invites us not simply to examine how social institutions "socialize" boys, but also to explore the ways that boys' already-gendering identities interact with social institutions (which, like organized sport, are themselves the product of gender relations). This study has also suggested that it is not some singular "masculinity" that is being constructed through athletic careers. It may be correct, from a psychoanalytic perspective, to suggest that all males bring ambivalences toward intimacy to their interactions with the world, but "the world" is a very different place for males from different racial and socioeconomic backgrounds. Because males have substantially different interactions with the world, based on class, race, and other differences and inequalities, we might expect the construction of masculinity to take on different meanings for boys and men from differing backgrounds (Messner, 1989). Indeed, this study has suggested that boys from higher-status backgrounds face a much broader range of options than do their lower-status counterparts. As a result, athletic careers take on different meanings for these boys. Lower-status boys are likely to see athletic careers as *the* institutional context for the construction of their masculine status and identities, while higher-status males make an early shift away from athletic careers toward other institutions (usually education and nonsports careers). A key line of inquiry for future studies might begin by exploring this irony of sports careers: Despite the fact that "the athlete" is currently an example of an exemplary form of masculinity in public ideology, the vast majority of boys who become most committed to athletic careers are never well-rewarded for their efforts. The fact that class and racial dynamics lead boys from higher-status backgrounds, unlike their lower-status counterparts, to move into nonsports careers illustrates how the construction of different kinds of masculin*ities* is a key component of the overall construction of the gender order.

REFERENCES

Birrell, S. (1987) "The woman athlete's college experience; knowns and unknowns." J. of Sport and Social Issues 11: 82–96.

Benjamin, J. (1988) The Bonds of Love: Psychoanalysis, Feminism, and the Problem of Domination. New York: Pantheon.

Bryson, L. (1987) "Sport and the maintenance of masculine hegemony." Women's Studies International Forum 10: 349–360.

Chodorow, N. (1978) The Reproduction of Mothering. Berkeley: Univ. of California Press.

Connell, R. W. (1987) Gender and Power. Stanford, CA: Stanford Univ. Press.

Connell, R. W. (1990) "An iron man: the body and some contradictions of hegemonic masculinity," In M. A. Messner and D. F. Sabo (eds.) Sport, Men and the Gender Order: Critical Feminist Perspectives. Champaign, IL: Human Kinetics.

Craib, I. (1987) "Masculinity and male dominance." Soc. Rev. 38: 721–743.

Eitzen, D. S. (1975) "Athletics in the status system of male adolescents: a replication of Coleman's *The Adolescent Society*." Adolescence 10: 268–276.

Gilligan, C. (1982) In a Different Voice: Psychological Theory and Women's Development. Cambridge, MA: Harvard Univ. Press.

Greendorfer, S. L. (1977) "The role of socializing agents in female sport involvement." Research Q. 48: 304–310.

Hall, M. A. (1988) "The discourse on gender and sport: from femininity to feminism." Sociology of Sport J. 5: 330–340.

Hantover, J. (1978) "The boy scouts and the validation of masculinity." J. of Social Issues 34: 184–195.

Haug, F. (1987) Female Sexualization. London: Verso.

Kidd, B. (1987) "Sports and masculinity," pp. 250–265 in M. Kaufman (ed.) Beyond Patriarchy: Essays by Men on Pleasure, Power, and Change. Toronto: Oxford Univ. Press.

Kidd, B. (1990) "The men's cultural centre: sports and the dynamic of women's oppression/men's repression," In M. A. Messner and D. F. Sabo (eds.) Sport, Men and the Gender Order: Critical Feminist Perspectives. Champaign, IL: Human Kinetics.

Kimmel, M. S. (1987) "Men's responses to feminism at the turn of the century." Gender and Society 1: 261–283.

Kimmel, M. S. (1990) "Baseball and the reconstitution of American masculinity: 1880–1920," In M. A. Messner and D. F. Sabo (eds.) Sport, Men and the Gender Order: Critical Feminist Perspectives. Champaign, IL: Human Kinetics.

Leonard, W. M. II and J. M. Reyman (1988) "The odds of attaining professional athlete status: refining the computations." Sociology of Sport J. 5: 162–169.

Lever, J. (1976) "Sex differences in the games children play." Social Problems 23: 478–487.

Levinson, D. J. et al. (1978) The Seasons of a Man's Life. New York: Ballantine.

Lichterman, P. (1986) "Chodorow's psychoanalytic sociology: a project half-completed." California Sociologist 9: 147–166.

Messner, M. (1987) "The meaning of success: the athletic experience and the development of male identity," pp. 193–210 in H. Brod (ed.) The Making of Masculinities: The New Men's Studies. Boston: Allen & Unwin.

Messner, M. (1988) "Sports and male domination: the female athlete as contested ideological terrain." Sociology of Sport J. 5: 197–211.

Messner, M. (1989) "Masculinities and athletic careers." Gender and Society 3: 71–88.

Oglesby, C. A. (Ed.) (1978) Women and Sport: From Myth to Reality. Philadelphia: Lea & Farber.

Osherson, S. (1986) Finding our Fathers: How a Man's Life is Shaped by His Relationship with His Father. New York: Fawcett Columbine.

Piaget, J. H. (1965) The Moral Judgement of the Child. New York: Free Press.

Rubin, L. B. (1976) Worlds of Pain: Life in the Working Class Family. New York: Basic Books.

Sabo, D. (1985) "Sport, patriarchy and male identity: new questions about men and sport." Arena Rev. 9: 2.

Schafer, W. E. (1975) "Sport and male sex role socialization." Sport Sociology Bull. 4: 47–54.

Sennett, R. and J. Cobb (1973) The Hidden Injuries of Class. New York: Random House.

Theberge, N. (1981) "A critique of critiques: radical and feminist writings on sport." Social Forces 60: 2.

Thorne, B. (1986) "Girls and boys together . . . but mostly apart: gender arrangements in elementary schools," pp. 167–184 in W. W. Hartup and Z. Rubin (eds.) Relationships and Development. Hillsdale, NJ: Lawrence Erlbaum.

Twin, S. L. [ed.] (1978) Out of the Bleachers: Writings on Women and Sport. Old Westbury, NY: Feminist Press.

Bob Connell

MASCULINITY, VIOLENCE, AND WAR

ONE

In 1976 there were 22 million people under arms in the world's 130-odd standing armies. The figure today may be a little higher. Probably 20 million of them are men. I have not seen any global totals by sex, but there are figures for particular countries which serve as pointers. In the major NATO forces in 1979–80, for instance, 92% of the US military forces were men; 95% of the French and British; 99.93% of the German. From what is commonly known about other countries, these are not likely to be exceptional figures. The vast majority of the world's soldiers are men. So are most of the police, most of the prison warders, and almost all the generals, admirals, bureaucrats and politicians who control the apparatus of coercion and collective violence. Most murderers are men. Almost all bandits, armed robbers, and muggers are men; all rapists, most domestic bashers; and most people involved in street brawls, riots and the like.

The same story, then, appears for both organised and unorganised violence. It seems there is some connection between being violent and being male. What is it? And what light can an analysis of masculinity, apparently a question of individual psychology, throw on the question of violence on a world scale?

Reprinted from *War/Masculinity*, P. Patton and R. Poole, eds. Melbourne, Australia: Intervention Publishers.

There is surprisingly widespread belief that this is all "natural." Human males are genetically programmed to be hunters and killers, the argument runs. The reason is that ape-man aggression was a survival need in the prehistoric dawn, while the ape-women clustered passively round their campfires suckling and breeding.

Right-wing inflections of this argument thus explain and justify aggression, competition, hierarchy, territoriality, patriarchy, and by inference private property, national rivalry, armies and war. Crude versions of this doctrine are part of the stock rhetoric of modern fascism. More sophisticated versions are developed by "sociobiologists" in the universities.

Remarkably, there is now a feminist version of this argument too. The line of thought is that human males are naturally predatory and violent; patriarchal power is thus an expression of men's inner nature. Rape and war become synonymous. A poster slogan reads: RAPE IS WAR, WAR IS RAPE. Even serious and thoughtful attempts to reckon with the connection between sexual dominance and war, like Penny Strange's pamphlet *It'll Make a Man of You*, talk freely of "male cosmology," "male violence," "male values" and so on.

Two things have gone wrong here. One is that biological speculation has substituted for hard analysis. A critical examination shows practically no grounding in evidence. The sociobiologists' pre-history is speculative, their anthropology highly selective, and their mechanisms of selection and inheritance simply imaginary. By equally convincing evolutionary speculation one can "prove" that men are naturally co-operative and peaceful. In fact it has been done, by Kropotkin in *Mutual Aid*.

More important, perhaps, is the confusion of concepts in phrases like "male power," "male violence," "male culture," "malestream thought," "male authority." In each of these phrases a social fact or process is coupled with, and implicitly attributed to, a biological fact. The result is not only to collapse together a rather heterogeneous group (do gays suffer from "male cosmology," for instance; or boys?). It also, curiously, takes the heat off the open opponents of feminism. The hard-line male chauvinist is now less liable to be thought personally responsible for what he says or does in particular circumstances, since what he says or does is attributable to the general fatality of being male.

That this is a point where argument and emotion have got tangled is not accidental. There is a basic theoretical problem here. The social categories of gender are quite unlike other categories of social analysis, such as class, in being firmly and visibly connected to biological difference. It is therefore both tempting and easy to fall back on biological explanation of any gender pattern. This naturalisation of social processes is without question the commonest mechanism of sexual ideologies. That biological difference underpins and explains the social supremacy of men over women is the prized belief of enormous numbers of men, and a useful excuse for resisting equality. Academic or pseudo-academic versions of this argument, male-supremacist "sociobiology" from Tiger's *Men in Groups* through Goldberg's *The Inevitability of Patriarchy* to the present, find a never-failing audience.

If we cannot do better than this in getting to grips with the connection between masculinity and violence, then the left might as well pack its bags and go home, turn on the VCR and play *Threads* until the missiles arrive. For if it all stems from the biological fact of maleness, there is nothing that can be done.

We can do better, and the basis for doing so is well known. It is to recognise that war, murder, rape and masculinity are social and cultural facts, not settled by biology. The patterns we have to deal with as issues of current politics have been produced within human society by the processes of history. It is the shape of social relations, not the shape of genes, that is the effective cause. "Male" and "masculine" are very different things. Masculinity is implanted in the male body, it does not grow out of it.

This argument implies a very different approach to the nature of gender from the natural categories appealed to by both sociobiology and cultural (or eco-) feminism. Such an understanding has been emerging from the work of other groups of feminists (in Australia, research such as Game and Pringle's *Gender at Work* and Burton's *Subordination*), theorists of gay liberation (such as Fernbach's *The Spiral Path*), and others. Broadly, gender is seen as a structure of social practice, related in complex ways to biological sex but with a powerful historical dynamic of its own.

That general framework suggests two lines of approach to the question of masculinity and war. One is to investigate the social construction of masculinity. The other is to undertake a social analysis of war. In what follows I'll suggest some points about both.

TWO

Given a framework of social analysis, we can look at the familiar images and archetypes of manliness in a clearer light. They are parts of the cultural process of producing particular types of masculinity. What messages they convey are important because they help to shape new generations.

One of the central images of masculinity in the Western cultural tradition is the murderous hero, the supreme specialist in violence. A string of warrior-heroes—Achilles, Siegfried, Lancelot and so on—populate European literature from its origins. The twentieth century has steadfastly produced new fictional heroes of this type: Tarzan, Conan, James Bond, the Jackal, the Bruce Lee characters. If you walk into a shop selling comics you will find a stunning array of violent heroes: cops, cowboys, supermen, infantry sergeants, fighter pilots, boxers and so on. The best of the Good Guys, it seems, are those who pay evil-doers back in their own coin.

This connection between admired masculinity and violent response to threat is a resource that governments can use to mobilise support for war. The most systematic case in modern history was the Nazis' cult of Nordic manhood, reaching its peak in the propaganda image of the SS-man during World War II. In a different context, a cult of masculinity and toughness flourished in the Kennedy and Johnson administrations in the USA, and helped commit that country to war in Vietnam. Fasteau documents this in one of the early books to come out of the American "men's movement," *The Male Machine*. I can remember the process operating on young men of my generation in Australia, whose conservative government sent troops to support the Americans in Vietnam. Involvement in the war was presented as standing up to threat, and opponents were smeared as lily-livered effeminates. In the fullness of time support for napalm raids and carpet bombing by B-52s became the test of manliness. In the aftermath of the TWA jet hijacking, Regan has been playing this tune again, trying to rouse American feeling against the threat of terrorism to provide a cover for his own military operations in central America.

Yet there is a good deal of scepticism in response to Reagan. And in the previous case, Western opposition to the Vietnam war did grow. Together with the Vietnamese resistance it eventually forced the American military to withdraw. The cult of masculine toughness is not all-powerful. This should alert us to some complexities in masculinity and its cultural images.

It is striking that the *Iliad* centres not on Achilles' supremacy in violence, but on his refusal to use it. And what changes his mind is not his reaction to threat, but his tenderness—his love for his friend Patroclus. Siegfried and Lancelot, not exactly gentle characters, are likewise full of hesitations, affection, and divided loyalties.

The image of heroism in modern figures like Tarzan and James Bond is a degraded one. The capacity for tenderness, emotional complexity, aesthetic feeling and so on has been deleted. More exactly, they are split off and assigned only to women, or to other, inferior types of men—such as the wimps, poofters and effeminates who evaded the Vietnamese war. (Part of the legend of Achilles was that he put on a dress and lived among women in order to evade the Trojan war.)

We know very little of the history of masculinity as distinct from the history of men; the detailed research has not been done. We know enough to understand that such changes in images of heroism are part of the historical process by which different kinds of masculinity are separated from each other, some exalted and some spurned. A crucial fact about men is that masculinity is not all of a piece. There have always been different kinds, some more closely associated with violence than others. This is why one should not talk of "male violence" or of "males" doing this and that—phrasing which smuggles back in the idea of a biological uniformity of social behaviour.

At any given moment some forms of masculinity will be hegemonic—that is, most honoured and most influential—and other forms will be marginalized or subordinated. The evidence about these forms is very scattered, as the question is only just coming into focus as a research issue. Some points are clear. Modern hegemonic masculinity is defined as heterosexual (not true of all societies or all periods of history), and sharply contrasted with homosexual masculinity (in our society the type case of subordinated masculinity). Some other forms of subordinated masculinity are temporary—like that of apprentices in a strongly-masculinized trade. There are kinds of masculinity that are not directly subordinated but rather marginalized by a process of social change that undermines their cultural presuppositions—the patriarchal masculinity of many immigrant men from Mediterranean countries is an important case in Australia at present. And there are struggles about what form of masculinity should be hegemonic—for instance the contest going on in the ruling classes of the capitalist world between professional/managerial and enterpreneurial/authoritarian masculinities. (The victory of Reaganism in the US is an important shift in the style of American patriarchy as well as in the precise locus of class power.)

THREE

In some civilisations the hegemonic forms of masculinity stress restraint and responsibility rather than violence. I believe that was true, for instance, of Confucian China. In contemporary Western society, hegemonic masculinity is strongly associated with aggressiveness and the capacity for violence. Modern feminism has shown us one of the bases for this: the assertion of men's power over women. This relationship itself has a strong component of violence. Wife-bashing, intimidation of women in the street, rape, jealousy-murder, and other patterns of violence against women are not accidental or incidental. They are widespread and systematic, arising from the tensions of a power struggle. This struggle has many turns and twists. Even in a society that defines a husband as the "head of the household," there are many families where wives actually run the show. Bashings may then result from an attempt to re-assert a damaged masculine ego. In other cases domestic violence is a direct expression of the husband's power, his belief that he can get away with anything, and his contempt for women in general or his wife in particular.

So there are many complexities and contradictions. The main axis, however, remains the social subordination of women, and men's general interest in maintaining it. The masculinity built on that bedrock is not necessarily violent—most men in fact do not bash women—but it is constructed, so to speak, with a door open towards violence.

Gay liberation has shown us another dimension: hegemonic masculinity is aggressively heterosexual. It defines itself in part by a vehement rejection of homosexuality. This rejection very often takes violent forms: arrests, frequent bashings, and occasional murders. Homosexual men seem to arouse particular fear and loathing among tough "macho" men. This fact has led many to think the violence is an attempt to purge the world of what one suspects in oneself. In psychoanalytic terms, there is a current of repressed homosexual feeling buried somewhere in hegemonic masculinity. This, again, suggests the importance of the tensions and contradictions within masculinity. It is by no means a neat package.

In much of the writing about men produced by the "men's liberation movement" of the 1970s it was assumed that violence was simply an expression of conventional masculinity. Change the macho image, stop giving little boys toy guns, and violence would be reduced. We can now see that the connection of masculinity and violence is both deeper and more complex than that. Violence is not just an expression; it is a part of the process that divides different masculinities from each other. There is violence within masculinity; it is constitutive. Once again, this is not to imply that it is universal. Real men don't necessarily bash three poofters before breakfast every day. For one thing, TV does it for them. Part of the pattern of contemporary masculinity is the commercial production of symbolic violence on an unprecedented scale, from Tarzan movies to Star Wars, Space Invaders, World Series Cricket, and now Rambo.

FOUR

It is very important that much of the actual violence is not isolated and individual action, but is institutional. Much of the poofter-bashing is done by the police; much of the world's rape is done by soldiers. These actions grow readily out of the "legitimate" violence for which police forces and armies are set up. The state is an instrument of coercion; this remains true whatever else about it varies. It uses one of the great discoveries of modern history, rational bureaucratic organization, to have policy-making centralized and execution down the line fairly uniform. Given this, the state can become the vehicle of calculated violence based on and using hegemonic masculinity. Armies are a kind of hybrid between bureaucracy and masculinity.

But to make this connection with an undifferentiated "masculine violence"—as, say, Fernbach does in *The Spiral Path*—is to misunderstand the way armies work. Generals, notoriously, die in bed. They are not themselves "violent men," and would be bad generals if they were. Of course they need violent men under their command as front-line troops, or at least as organisers of front-line troops—men like the grim Sergeant Croft of *The Naked and the Dead* (a novel that strikingly makes the point about different masculinities).

It is the *relationship* between forms of masculinity—physically violent but subordinate to orders on the one hand, dominating and organisationally competent on the other—that is the basis of military organisation. The two need not overlap at all. Heinrich Himmler, the commander of one of the most brutal military organisations in recent history, never killed anyone personally. When present at any execution where some brains splattered on his neat SS uniform, he threw a screaming fit.

Even this is to understate the matter. In modern armies the majority of soldiers are not combatants at all. Most are in support services, as transport workers, administrators, technicians, maintenance workers, cooks, etc., and have no competence as fighters at all. The proportion of this kind of worker in armies has grown markedly over the last century and a half with the increasing technologisation of warfare, as several major developments have reduced the need for cannon-fodder and increased the need for supply workers. The US made two great contributions to the art of war in the 1940s—nuclear weapons and logistics. Logistics was certainly more militarily effective at the time. And you don't want Rambo types driving your jeeps and supply trucks.

Automatic weapons (machine-guns and quick-firing artillery), self-propelled military vehicles (tanks and aircraft), and ultimately long-distance weapons that eliminate the 'front' (strategic bombers, nuclear missiles) have successively intensified the trend. They have made more and more important in military organisations a third kind of masculinity, the professionalised, calculative rationality of the technical specialist.

The first stage of this was the rise of the "General Staff" to a central position in European military organisation by the early twentieth century. The idea of a General Staff was a group of planners, separate from the command of combat units, who worked out overall strategies as well as technical issues of supply. The "Schlieffen Plan" for the German attack on France in 1914 marked the ascendancy of staff over line commanders. In no sense did this mean a shift away from violence—the violence of war was growing on an unprecedented scale. The man who was the 20th century's most successful general, the Soviet Chief of Staff Georgi Zhukov, was notorious for his disregard for human life. He accepted huge casualties in order to gain advantage in battles of attrition at Moscow, Stalingrad and Kursk (the battles responsible for the ultimate defeat of Hitler).

The second stage was the mobilisation of physical scientists on a large scale into weapons research, culminating in the Manhattan Project. The friction within the Manhattan Project, and the crisis of conscience suffered by the nuclear physicists immediately after the explosion of the Hiroshima and Nagasaki bombs, are measures of the difficulty of the integrating this kind of worker into the military. But the huge growth of nuclear weapons research establishments in the USA and USSR since then shows that the initial difficulties have been overcome. The end of the world has been made technically possible by this achievement in human relations.

FIVE

In the past, as well as being the main actors of war, men have also been the main victims. Napoleon's wars killed mainly soldiers. The harnessing of high technology to the bureaucratic state has steadily changed this. Hitler's mass extermination campaigns, and the Anglo-American firebombing of Hamburg, Dresden and Tokyo, were an organized turning of conventional weapons to the killing of whole populations. The nuclear arsenal has been directed against whole populations from the start.

It has thus become a matter of urgency for humans as a group to undo the tangle of relationships that sustains the nuclear arms race. Masculinity is part of this tangle. It will not be easy to alter. The pattern of an arms race, i.e., mutual threat, itself helps sustain an aggressive masculinity.

Nor can the hegemonic pattern of masculinity be rejected totally. To achieve disarmament in reality means conducting a long and difficult struggle against an entrenched power structure. This calls for some of the qualities hegemonic masculinity exalts—toughness, endurance, determination and the like. It is no accident tht hegemonic masculinity has been important in radical movements in the past: in unionism, in national liberation movements, and in socialist parties.

Yet we know masculinity is not fixed. It is at least conceivable that we can re-work masculinity in a way that sustains a struggle without reproducing the enemy. In much this sense feminism has been re-working femininity. In doing this it will be useful to remember the hidden riches of masculinity, as well as its horrors. There are cultural resources in subordinated masculinities, and in patterns lost or bypassed in recent history.

REFERENCES

Burton, C., *Subordination: Feminism and Social Theory*, Sydney, Allen and Unwin, 1985.

Carrigan, T., Connell, R. W. & Lee, J. "Hard and Heavy Phenomena: the Sociology of Masculinity," *Theory & Society*, 1985.

Chapkis, W., Ed., *Loaded Questions: Women in the Military*, Amsterdam, Transnational Institute, 1981.

Clark, A., *Barbarossa: The Russian-German Conflict 1941–1945*, Harmondsworth, Penguin, 1966.

Connell, R. W., "Men's bodies" in *Which Way Is Up?*, Sydney, Allen and Unwin, 1983.

Fernbach, D., *The Spiral Path: A Gay Contribution to Human Survival*, London, Gay Mens' Press, 1981.

Fasteau, M. F., *The Male Machine*, New York, McGraw-Hill, 1974.

Game, A. & Pringle, R., *Gender at Work*, Sydney, Allen and Unwin, 1983.

Goldberg, S., *The Inevitability of Patriarchy*, New York, William Morrow, 1973.

Irving, D. J. C., *The Destruction of Dresden*, London, Kimber, 1963.

Kropotkin, P., *Mutual Aid* (1902), Boston, Extending Horizons, n.d.

Mailer, N., *The Naked and the Dead* (1949), London, Deutsch, 1964.

Strange, P., *It'll Make a Man of You: A Feminist View of the Arms Race*, Nottingham, Peace News/Mushroom, 1983.

Tiger, L., *Men in Groups*, New York, Random House, 1969.

Zhukov, G. K., *Marshal Zhukov's Greatest Battles*, London, Sphere, 1971.

Charles J. Levy

ARVN AS FAGGOTS:
INVERTED WARFARE IN VIETNAM

The way in which civilians often view Vietnam from the United States suggests that too much perspective can be just as distorting as too little. For it seems to be popularly believed that the actions of American troops there have resulted from racism and depersonalization of the enemy. But racism would not explain why there has been a high regard for the Viet Cong and North Vietnamese Army (VC/NVA) who are racially indistinguishable from the Army of the Republic of (South) Vietnam (ARVNs) for whom there has been a low regard. Nor would depersonalization of the enemy explain why there was substantial hostility directed against the ARVNs with whom there was personal contact, and little or no hostility toward the more remote VC/NVA.

In the case of American marines, the beginning of an explanation could be found in boot camp. Homosexuality appeared in two contradictory themes of basic training. On the one hand, homosexuals were the enemy. Referring to navy corpsmen in general, and one in particular, a former marine explained:

> A lot of them were like prissy. I mean looked on the faggoty-type side. You could tell they were corpsmen. But I mean if that guy was in marine boot camp he'd of got bounced out. Or he'd have so many problems within the system that he fucking wouldn't be able to hack it. He'd go out of his mind. He'd be called "a faggot."

On the other hand, marine recruits were called "faggots" by their drill instructors during boot camp. By compelling these men to accept such labels, the drill instructors achieved on a psychological level the same control that they had on a physical level when, for example, the men were not permitted a bowel movement for the first week of boot camp.

As defined by the boot camp experience, homosexuality was only incidentally a sexual condition. More important, it represented a lack of all the aggressive characteristics that were thought to comprise masculinity. The connection between passivity and homosexuality was made vivid to the marines in boot camp inasmuch as they were unable to combat either the label or the activities surrounding it. When a recruit mentioned that he and a friend had been separated in violation of the "buddy system" under which they joined, the drill instructor is reported to have asked, "Do you like Private R?" the next question is, "Do you want to fuck him?"

After sending six men into a small shower room, the drill instructor, in another account, shouted, "Everybody on your back."

> We're all nude. So you fall on top of each other. You get assholes in your face. And then they turn on cold water and they make you run out and stand there.

This ritual, like most others in boot camp, was coupled with violence. As the men left the showers, the drill instructors "beat your fucking head in."

The violence towards trainees was merged with their learning how to do violence, so that "We used to be disgusted with the other services because we considered them unaggressive." Aggression meant learning how to protect not only their lives, but also their masculinity. Accordingly, after boot camp they referred to the Marine Corps as "the crotch," while the other military branches were called "the sister services."

The overreaching lesson of boot camp had been that combat must be on the marines' terms. This point was made by the drill instructors in a way that led one veteran to recall: "You just get shit on all the time if you don't live by their rules. If you don't they'll screw you any way they can." One of these accepted rules involved the rationale for this training, "They have to do it to protect your lives if you're going in combat." Boot camp training was continually linked to Vietnam by such means as reminding the recruits of the date they would be arriving there and by indicating the number of casualties that would result "if you don't take the training seriously." It was made clear that submission to the drill instructors would provide the recruits with the training that was necessary to in turn make the VC/NVA submit.

Yet, in Vietnam, the marines discovered that the VC/NVA "fight on their fucking terms, not on ours," according to another veteran. Much effort was aimed at getting the VC/NVA to fight on the marine terms. "What we tried to do is fucking chase them around so they don't know what's going on. But it's never that way." The VC/NVA not only refused to fight on the marines' terms, by fighting on their own terms they made the marines' terms inoperable. The link that was established between boot camp and Vietnam reappeared to hinder rather than help morale. For instead of the promised discontinuity between the two settings, the marines vis-á-vis the VC/NVA bore an unexpected similarity to the recruits who were called "girl" by the drill instructors.

The ascendance of the VC/NVA's terms was possible in large part because these terms were unknown to the marines. Even after locating the VC/NVA, their intentions were unclear:

> It depends on where they want to fight. You never know if they want to fight there and get that one company and consider it a day. Or if they want to just really get out of there. You can't tell. Or if they're just sucking you into one big mob scene.

The last of these possibilities, that there were other VC/NVA waiting in ambush, was the governing one. It meant that the marines were never able to assume a correspondence between the VC/NVA they saw and the ones that saw them.

Because the marines were seen in their totality, their intentions were open. Their terms were correspondingly weakened. For the VC/NVA were given an opportunity to develop counter-terms: "They know every map square where they can hold a good defense. Where there's a lot of heavy brush that would be tough for us to move our heavy equipment in."

Some of the problems that arose from trying to prepare men who were still in the United States for Vietnam were inherent to using a low risk artificial setting to anticipate the high risk real one. Training in the United States did not pass for combat in Vietnam: "When they used to send us out we used to go make believe. We set up an ambush and make believe someone walked by. You knew when all this shit was over you got to get to bed. So I mean it's not good." Just as combat in Vietnam does not pass for training in the United States: "You're not sitting there in 'Nam saying to yourself: 'Let me think now, the instructor told me to do it this way.' What the hell!"

The deeper problems that arose had less to do with training for wars in general than with this war in particular. Booby traps caused a majority of deaths in Vietnam. But booby trap training was regarded as a contradiction in terms:

> They show you all the booby traps and stuff. What's good showing you the booby trap. I mean, if you find a booby trap, the odds are good you ain't going to see it 'til after it blows up.

Efforts to simulate a Vietnam in the United States suffered from a more general handicap: "How can you train a person to fight someone that they've been fighting for so long that they haven't done good enough a job to find out anything about them?" Training in the United States, then, was futile for the same principal reason that combat in Vietnam was to be futile for the marines. So the difficulty of anticipating the VC/NVA through training in the United States was at least one authentic reconstruction of the setting to be found in Vietnam. Also the apparent unreality of training in the United States may not have been entirely inappropriate preparation for Vietnam. The above example of marines setting ambushes for other marines was said to be "make believe." But it anticipated the internecine character of the war.

The military techniques of the VC/NVA compelled the marines to violate their own traditions. These traditions were not abstractions. They were reasons for being. They also provided a set of expectations for Vietnam. But after arriving there, it turned out they had no application when "You can't go in and kick ass like you could in other wars." Here is the process of discovery:

> When I first got there, Two VC held down the whole platoon just by firing over our heads. Then word was passed out, 'Stay down. Don't waste rounds. They'll just do this for fifteen minutes and leave.' And being a new guy and thinking how the marines are supposed to be so tough, I said, 'Why don't we go get them?' But, of course, they [the experienced marines] knew what they were doing. We probably

would've went and got them, there probably would've been booby traps all over the place and we would've probably lost another 20 guys getting two. So we just sit there and stay for 15 minutes, 20 minutes, until they got tired.

When they arrived in Vietnam, these men had belonged to the Marine Corps for about eight months. This is a short time to become deeply involved in traditions—even allowing for the intensity of the boot camp experience. The commitment to the traditions of the Marine Corps was largely a result of their coinciding with the traditions of the street corners to which these men had belonged before their enlistment. The interchangeability of the traditions could be seen when the same marine who was "thinking how the marines are supposed to be so tough" later described his Vietnam experience through a street corner analogy: "That's like some guy walking up to you and punching you in the face every night and then before you have time to turn around or put up your hands he's gone."

ORIENTAL SMILES

The previously clear and central distinction between aggressiveness and passivity was lost for the marines when they arrived in Vietnam. They found themselves using aggressive means which had passive results. Meantime, the VC/NVA used passive means which had aggressive results.

The passive aspects of the VC/NVA took a variety of forms. To begin with, the VC/NVA did not fit any of the traditional American notions of what a formidable adversary should look like. They were the wrong size. Sometimes they were the wrong sex. They wore the wrong clothes, since the VC and occasionally the NVA lacked uniforms. They even wore the wrong expression: "It's hard to look through an Oriental person. They could probably hate your guts and stab you in the back, but they'll always smile at you." As it turned out, the more passive they appeared, the more difficult it was to defend against their aggression.

The marines heard lectures about Vietnamese men expressing friendship among themselves and with other men through physical contact. But this behavior became all the more inexplicable as a result of the lectures. For if handholding between men was a custom, it meant—as far as the marines were concerned—that these gestures were not aberrations within the Vietnamese society: rather the whole society was an aberration. A marine recalled that

> we had classes before we went over: that's just their way of life. Like them holding their arm on another guy means they're friends. It don't mean—that's what we were told anyways.

Nevertheless, in Vietnam, "most of us" believed it did mean they were homosexuals.

The marines needed an explanation that would enable them to relate these male gestures to their own culture, not that of the Vietnamese. This was possible by defining it as homosexuality, since it was a familiar category to marines. By placing the ARVN in it, his behavior ceased to be strange.

Equally important, the marines understood what their own behavior ought to be in response:

> I had been in the country a year by this time. We were going back to regiment in Danang. We pulled the truck over and the ARVN engineer stopped us at a roadblock. And they bore you to death. They make you sick. They're trying to be military. So they've got this roadblock up. And they stopped the truck. And the driver is saying, "Get out of our way, you little slopes." And they come out and they said, "We have a wounded veteran." We said, "So what?" They said, "He doesn't have one leg. Could you give him a ride up to the hospital?" So everybody's saying, "Let him hop." I was in charge of the detail so I said, "Let him on." I was in the back of the truck. It was a PC three-quarter. So he comes over on his crutches. I said, "Throw your crutches up." So he passed up the crutches. And I grabbed him under the arms and I pick him up and I set him in the seat. The little slope grabbed me by the leg. And I had been in the country long enough to know that most of them are queer. They hold hands and stuff. And this sort of irks most marines and soldiers. And we're told that it's a Vietnamese custom, when you're really friendly you should hold hands. So they try to hold a lot of guys' hands. So they end up getting beat bloody. The guy grabbed my leg. So I got mad. I wasn't in a good mood that morning and I whacked him. And my buddies grabbed his crutches. And I said "Go!" So we took off. We threw his crutches in the rice paddy one time and went about another 150 yards and threw the other crutch and then out he went. He was screaming and crying and begging us. "Out you go." We all had a good laugh about that.

In more important ways, the classification of ARVNs as homosexuals was not based on their presumed sexual activity. The fact that ARVNs were living at bases with their wives contributed to the belief that they were homosexuals. For the presence of wives meant the ARVNs led a soft life. Hence they were not, to use a common marine term, "hard."

In the same way, the fact that ARVNs did not attempt to engage in homosexual activity with the marines was taken as proof that the ARVNs were homosexual. For it was thought that fear, a sign of homosexuality, kept them from making advances: "They wouldn't fool around with us anyway. They wouldn't even look at us the wrong way. 'Cause they knew how good we were, which I thought we were."

A literal interpretation of the war by the marines, among other results, would have made them allies of the ARVNs. But the ARVNs provided the model for a less literal approach that released the marines from whatever obligations remained to define them as allies. It was thought they interpreted the war out of existence: "They don't want nothing to do with the war, but yet it's their war."

The reluctance of the ARVNs to engage in combat was treated as interchangeable with fighting on the side of the VC/NVA. A marine who regarded the ARVNs as homosexuals, "every one of them," cited as evidence: "They're just too scared where there is gooks. Where the gooks are, they go in the opposite direction. They don't want to go out and make contact with them at all." A related assumption was expressed by another marine who considered it just as likely they would go in the same direction as the VC/NVA: "I heard if you get a patrol of ARVNs with you, and if they're getting beat, they'll just go right on the opposite side. And they'll shoot at you instead of with you. They kind of get scared."

UNRELIABLE ALLIES

The marines considered the ARVNs to be so far removed from the war that in the process of preventing their lives from being disrupted they were able to augment them. As one former marine observed "I think they got a good thing going for them because of the black market." Further, this remoteness from the war while in the midst of it often meant that the marines saw themselves being made more vulnerable to attacks from the VC/NVA:

> The ARVNs felt that being in the army was great. They used to wear starched utilities. Everything was so nice. And like the marines were all slobs, because we had our clothes washed in rice paddy water and everything else. Nothing starched. And they looked like they should be in recruiting posters all the time. We had ARVN security and it started to rain. They went in houses—into their buddy's house—until the rain stopped, so they wouldn't get their uniforms wet. And left us out there with no security.

Official ethnology was the response of the Marine Corps to a feeling among the marines that "We didn't like the idea of us fighting for an army of faggots." Specifically,

> You hear the propaganda report, you know, our bullshit, like public relations between us and the Vietnamese. Well our public relations give us propaganda material telling us how the Vietnamese are a proud, simple people and courageous. And give us history of the country and how they fought the Chinese and everybody. And the Vietnamese war heroes and all this other shit. To impress upon us the fact that they're really not fucking gutless bastards. But we all knew better and we used to just hate them all the more. The more they tried to justify the Vietnamese the more we didn't like them.

The troops were not in a situation that they thought lent itself to this or any other form of intellectualizing. What did matter was that where the marines were vulnerable to attack from the VC/NVA they became the passive party, and the ARVNs were seen contributing to this vulnerability. In at least one sense, moreover, the marines were more passive vis-à-vis the VC/NVA than the ARVN were. The marines had their passivity imposed upon them by the VC/NVA, while the ARVNs acted passively through their own volition.

At times, the marines worked almost as hard at making themselves the enemy of the ARVNs as they did at making the ARVN their enemy. The first process recreated the theme of boot camp that violence should be done *for* one group so that they might do violence *to* a second group. There was a consensus among marines that ARVNs had nothing to fight for: "They didn't give a shit." The marines tried to give them something to fight against by making themselves the foremost enemy of the ARVNs.

As the marines found it increasingly difficult to establish a direct link between means and intended ends, they resorted to these indirect links. The assumption was that a marine offense against the VC/NVA required an offense against the ARVN that would result in an ARVN defense against the marines that would take the form of an ARVN offense against the VC/NVA. The mechanics of this sequence appear in the following episode:

> The marines were in there putting out the fire but unbeknownst to them, they were stomping to death a three-week-old baby. So this caused uncontrollable laughter among the marines when they found they had accidentally killed a baby. There's nothing else they could do. And they've got to keep up this pretense of being fucking raving maniacs in order to keep the respect of the Montagnards. The gooks think that we're fucking lunatics. And you've got to keep this. As long as they're afraid of us, they won't give you a hard time. If they're afraid you'll shoot them in any minute and you don't find anything wrong in killing. So the guys start laughing. First, it was sort of a nervous laugh and then they just had a fucking grand time.

However, it soon became clear to these marines that an indirect linkage of means and ends was at least as unattainable as a direct one. When they were ambushed soon afterwards, the marine squad leader

> yelled to the commander of the Vietnamese to bring on line assaults. So the four marines get up and they're pumping away. And all the eight gooks just sat theire and watched them. And then they withdrew in disorganized retreat. What they do is they ran like hell while the marines were on line shooting. What they [marines] had to do is pull some escape and evasion maneuvers to get away. They were pissed.

In other words, the sequence that materialized consisted of a VC offense that resulted in an ARVN defense that resulted in a marine defense.

In short, one reason the ARVNs became the enemy was that the marines were, after all, bound to them as allies. For the ineffectiveness of the ARVNs in combat meant the task of the marines was that much greater and more dangerous: "Most of the time when they did get into contact they always got their ass kicked. And we usually had to come in and help them out."

The marines were bound to the ARVNs in a more immediate way. They provided the marines with a means of trying to salvage a disrupted frame-of-reference. For the ARVNs were proof that there was, after all, a connection between passivity and homosexuality. The marines were not only able to focus on them as passive targets, they could act against them aggressively.

Locating homosexual ARVNs was a welcome relief from having to cope with an often unrecognizable and always evasive VC/NVA. There were no problems identifying the homosexuality of the readily available ARVNs. The identification was based on criteria that did not require interrogation or scrutiny. The proof was an impression:

> We thought a lot of them were queer, because of the way they act. They were so I don't know, prissy like, and awkward. And just the way they laughed and looked at you.

This imprecise definition is appropriate considering that "prissy" owes its first two letters to precise.

However, the assualts agaisnt assumed homosexuals were in no sense a charade. They were more a form of warfare than an alternative to it. All that kept the beatings from escalating was a lack of resistance. The exceptions illuminated the usual case:

> They'll come up to you and they'll rub your leg and you sucker them. Because as far as we're concerned, they're queer. So the ARVN lieutenant told his men, "The next time a marine hits you, I want you to shoot him." So our lieutenant heard about it and he says, "As soon as you see an ARVN pick up a weapon, first I want you to kill the lieutenant, and then I want you to wipe out all his men." We continued to beat them up and nobody shot anybody.

Meantime, the VC/NVA imposed the ultimate passivity on marines by making them the instruments of their own death. For the VC/NVA were "good at skills that we didn't even know—like booby traps." Most booby traps are arranged to have the victim act as his own executioner. And there is a mockery involved which accounts for the term. It is a trap for the booby. The only aggression permitted the marine was against himself. The more aggressive the marine tried to be, the more susceptible he was to booby traps.

Marines continued to be their own victims when they tried to fight on the terms of the VC/NVA. The marines began using a highly sophisticated mine called the Claymore that they expected to be far more effective than the relatively crude booby traps of the VC/NVA. The Claymore has pellets in the front that are fired by an explosive in the back. However, the VC/NVA were able to carry the Claymore one step further:

> They can sneak right up and turn your Claymore around. And then you start moving around there so you'll hit the Claymore and it's turned around. You'll be the one that gets it.

Booby trapped by their own booby traps. As the marines sought a new means of becoming more aggressive, they were made still more passive.

The invisibility of the VC/NVA and the visibility of the marines were the underlying reasons for the success of one and the failure of the other with booby traps. For there are two condiitons that must be met if a booby trap is to operate successfully. First, the hunter must know where his prey will be. Second, the prey must not know where the hunter has been.

There is an interval between planting and detonating a booby trap. The aggressor is removed in both time and space from his aggression. But the marines (and the corner boys before them) were unaccustomed to aggression that was not spontaneous. This was another reason they had both a problem setting booby traps and a propensity for tripping them.

The ambush is closely related to the booby trap. It relies on one's own invisibility and the other's visibility. There are, in addition, elaborate preparations that require deferred aggression. For these reasons, the ambushes prepared by marines were subject to the same problems as the booby traps they set:

> Every night these NVA or VC used to come down and they used to
> screw up marine ambushes. And they always used to get away. They'd
> know where the ambush was set up and killer teams were set up. They'd
> sneak by them when they go into the village to get their rice and what
> they needed and leave. And then they'd screw them up on the way back.
> They'd fire on the ambush. And they'd take off up into the mountains.
> They did this every night. And they [marines] never got any of them.

Hiding entails actively seeking invisibility. It is ordinarily considered a passive act, because it is seen as the avoidance of action. More important, it is seen
as the avoidance of being acted upon. But in the context of Vietnam, both
these components were redefined when they became the means by which the
VC/NVA were able to act aggressively. To speak of a means and end suggests
a break that did not exist. Instead, the means and end were part of the same
process. When the VC/NVA hid, it was not only a way to avoid disadvan-
tageous encounters with the marines, it was preparation for engaging the
marines on advantageous terms:

> A lot of times you don't see them. They suck you into some type of
> ambush situation where there's a lot of them and a lot of you's. And
> they've already preregistered the area. Like two weeks before that
> they'll lie in the same position and fire their weapons for effect.

Not only was the means not entirely passive because it was part of an
aggressive end, but the end was not entirely aggressive because it was part of a
passive means. That is, the VC/NVA strategy was all the more difficult for
the marines to sort out because it was cyclical. The marines found that the
VC/NVA "aren't staying and fighting." Instead, "they hit you and run." But
the running could not be classified as passive, because in addition to being the
last stage of an aggressive act, it was the first stage of the next aggressive act.
The confusion that resulted from trying to classify the tactics of the VC/NVA
is reflected in the following account where the VC are shuttled between
categories of offense and defense:

> The VC was more or less on a defense all the time. Always hiding and
> coming out at night. but he still had to move around, unless he was in a
> large group. But he always had to be the aggressor. And he was always
> under cover and stuff. So when he did come out and you did get in
> contact with him, he was determined that either he was going to die or
> he was going to get one of us.

When the VC/NVA hid, it was an aggressive act even if it did not lead to an
engagement with the marines. For the marines had an aggressive mission in
Vietnam. They were there to eliminate the VC/NVA. A status quo meant
failure. The objective of the Marine Corps was summed up by the name given
their "search and destroy missions." The VC/NVA could thwart these missions simply by hiding.

> You'd go in there for three days; you'd pull out. And if they were there
> anyways, they weren't there when we got there. I imagine they must
> have come back after we left. So those are the most useless operations I
> ever heard of. If they seen a hole they'd start saying, "Oh, I bet there's

weapons down there. I bet there's rice down there." We'd dig it up and there'd be nothing there. We never found nothing. I went on three of those, never found nothing.

The only result of these operations would be "carrying a couple of dead guys back—our own," men who encountered booby traps.

Catching those who hide is a form of aggressiveness, except in Vietnam. The contradiction of being permitted by the enemy to take the intiative was described by a former marine: "You catch them when they want you to catch them. They have all their bunkers and everything all set for you."

Traditionally, setting the time and place of battle has been another aggressive characteristic. The marines found themselves helping to set these terms because the VC/NVA "just wait 'til I guess they think they have you at your weakest, then they hit you." Another veteran provides an illustration:

> Usually they'll hit the areas that are most secure. The lines are never checked. There won't be much bother about falling to sleep on watch. The platoon commander didn't care because we were never hit. Everyone gets to not caring.

Here too the apparent passivity of the VC/NVA was the means to an aggressive act. For they were able to make the camp vulnerable by not attacking it.

The marines had a sense of being objects that comes from being continually visible while those viewing them remain for the most part invisible. But they had not adapted to the dangers that follow from this condition. It was only in retrospect, that the marine veteran just quoted saw that the more secure they felt, the less secure they were in fact. In Vietnam, when the VC/NVA abstained from an attack it was regarded as security not as a forewarning. There was less stress for the marines in facing a disaster that would be observable than in admitting to themselves that they were living with an unseen threat.

Telescoped examples of this dilemma could occur several times a day to the same men. A former marine tells of walking at the head of a patrol along a trail:

> You see a shell case. So you start to step over this way. But you think: "Maybe it was put there on purpose so I'd step over that way." So it really screws your head up. The hell with it. I'd step over this way. And if it blows, it'll blow.

The weakness of the marines was maximized by not only the behavior but more particularly through the attitudes with which they were provided by the VC/NVA. The invisibility of the VC/NVA provided them with a safe view of marines as a prelude to safe action against them: "They could be hiding under a rock or in a tunnel. We could walk right over them so they could see everything you have. What the hell can you do? They're watching you all the time, you never see them."

All this means that the marines were less visible to themselves than they were to the VC/NVA. Until the marines set off a mine or walked into an ambush, they did not usually know where they were in relation to the VC/NVA. In one way or another, "You wait to get hit; wait for them to come to you." But there was more involved than the VC/NVA seeing precisely what dangers the marines were exposed to. For the VC/NVA saw into the operations of the marines as well as the context in which they were held. It amounted to the marines having to rely on the VC/NVA in order to view themselves. The VC made this reliance explicit:

> They talked to us all the time and shit—loud-speakers. In fact they told us one night, before anyone that was with us knew it, that we were going to move up to Phu Bai. Imagine that! They told us over a loud-speaker that they were pulling us out, because they knew if we stayed there that the VC were going to annihilate us. So the squad leader went to the CO and they checked on it and we *were* going to move out about three weeks later. So they knew it before we did. That kind of fucked up your mind a little, you know.

(The announcement by the VC was in English—which served to tell the marines that their language, too, was visible.) Even a formal statement of defeat by the VC/NVA could be made into an aggressive act by them:

> One day eight of them [NVA] turned themselves in. You could see their white flag. They had me walking up. I felt like an asshole. They're fucking clean. New uniforms. Spotless. Their boots were shined. Haircuts. And they're supposed to be living in the mud? They're doing better than we are. And they're walking up. They're clean as a whistle. They had tailored uniforms. So everyone's there wondering: What's going on out there?

In describing the episode, this former marine wonders if "they just sent them out there to turn themselves in to make us look like they were doing good out there." But he dismisses this possibility. It is a reassuring one insofar as it indicates the prisoners were not typical. Yet, to accept this explanation would be an acknowledgment that the NVA were capable of deliberately redefining the terms of war by turning surrender on its head. Further, it would mean that the marines had accommodated the NVA.

Where the marines did succeed in killing, they often discovered that this could not be considered a form of domination, particularly when the victims were civilians. These deaths were both a cause and effect of the marines' passivity. For killing civilians usually meant the marines had lost control. The particular kind of control varied, but every case included a loss of control over the VC/NVA. When the marines were acting in rage, the civilians they killed served as surrogates for elusive VC/NVA. They were acting spontaneously at the time, but afterwards the marines saw their action as a loss of control over themselves:

> You see a guy you're really tight with for a period of months getting killed. We got really pissed off about it. You don't just say, "Well, fuck it." You go like kind of nutty. Anybody that even looked at you the wrong way you'd probably shoot. I think the American fighting man can be the most vicious ever. People don't realize this.

When civilians were killed through mistaken identity, it was a more direct reminder that the VC/NVA were beyond control, to the point of being unidentifiable. The misplaced aggressiveness of these acts sometimes resulted in ridicule, as when a marine shot a village elder one night and was afterwards nicknamed "killer" by his fellow marines. His death was the outcome of a curfew rule that required the shooting of any violators. The curfew was imposed as a means of assuring that the VC/NVA would be identifiable.

Whatever the circumstances, killing civilians weakened the position of the marines. For it meant the villagers became still more dedicated to the VC/NVA, as seen in the following episode about the death of another elder:

> There's a killer team out one night. They were outside this village. This old man, he was a villager, was going out to do a crap in the rice paddy. And he was killed. That was right at the edge of the village. He was mistaken for a VC. Immediately after that happened the villagers turned VC sympathizers. After that, there was always a build up of VC coming in. Along Highway 1, on the other side of the village, it was always mined. After this happened there was like a triple amount of mines planted in the road. And there was a road going up to the top of the hill. It was never really combed for any mines. Two days later a jeep went over a mine and blew up. That never happened before. But I imagine it was the villagers.

There were other ways in which the marines discovered that killing might not be the ultimate measurement of domination after all. For example, the VC/NVA were seen demonstrating a greater control of the situation when they abstained from killing. This realization by the marines made the control of the VC/NVA over them still greater:

> This [NVA soldier] goes "Good morning, marines." A lot of shit they did just to fuck up your head. I mean, they must have had a chance before that to really fucking zap someone. They did this shit just to fucking scare the fuck out of you. Just to let you know that they were on the ball and they weren't fucking around. Everyone fucking flies out of the trenches with their rifles. They're expecting attack. Fucking gook is probably laughing his ass off in the bushes. That's fucked up though.

The marines had finally recognized hiding as a means of killing. But here it was seen as a more subtle form of aggression—a means of killing morale. The VC/NVA directed the attention of marines to the importance of a psychological assault through their constant practice of it. However, the marines were as unable to cope with this sophisticated approach as they were with an apparently unsophisticated agrarian approach to combat.

The marines found that more than themselves was being relegated to passivity. The same thing was happening to the previously inviolate technology that had permitted the United States to maintain an aggressive stance in the world. Here, too, the victim brought on his own undoing, for the aggressiveness of this technology in Vietnam was often self-destructive. The following episode is typical of what could happen when technological superiority was invoked instead of dealing with the VC/NVA on equal terms:

> Say you had 30 gooks in the open. And you were too far away from them. Instead of losing men over them, artillery was the best bet. But we had too many restrictions on us. Like when we had to call an artillery mission. They had to get air clearance which is make sure there wasn't any helicopters flying around in the area or any jets, any Phantoms,

flying over the area. So by the time we got that clearance then we'd have to get a ground clearance making sure that there wasn't any friendly troops around that area. So by the time the clearance came in, they were walking away. I mean they were just gone.

This failure had much to do with the characteristics of technology that were expedient or tolerated when they appeared in the United States. Its massiveness was inappropriate for the intimacy of combat in Vietnam where no one group was at a great distance from any other group. The bureaucracy attached to the technology was intended to make it manageable, but in the fluidity of this combat the bureaucracy made it all the more unmanageable.

Moreover, the futility of technology was carefully engineered by the VC/NVA. They were skilled at bringing out its limitations. Just as they made the visibility of marines a disadvantage by emphasizing the opposite characteristic among themselves, so they were able to turn technology into a disadvantage by not trying to fight it with technology. Again they stressed an opposite; this time, nature. It was a matter of building a strategy out of both their strength and the marines' weaknesses. Americans were unaccustomed to nature being used aggressively. When necessary, the land was used as a weapon:

> In valleys where you're pinned down—a lot of times we've had jets come in over the top of us, when it was hard to hit them any other way. They couldn't come across because of the mountains and stuff. They release the bombs right over our heads. And you can see the bombs. They'd be going towards us. And we're saying, "Ooh, fucking things just don't drop." But they like carried on the momentum of the speed they're going. They go in front of you. They blow up. That takes a lot of skill on an estimate. And a lot of fucking luck. The gooks choose this type of thing because they know that our jets can't come into a valley this way and make it, because there's a mountain there and they can't get up. So they set up their defenses so they can shoot down the planes as they're coming in.

The rationale for much of American technology had been the conquest of nature. But in Vietnam, the VC/NVA used nature for the conquest of technology.

Technological futility led to occasional attempts at de-emphasizing technology. But this only made way for problems that were more subtle and therefore less predictable. It brought out the other levels on which American culture was not transferable. These problems were subtle to the Americans, but they were obvious to everyone else. For example, a program was established to work with the villagers in a manner that minimized technology.

> We had an outfit that was called CAC—Combined Action Company. But *cac* in Vietnamese means *prick*. So they had to change it to Combined Action Platoons. They called it CAP. It was a laughing stock of the villages. And the VC played it to the hilt.

The extent to which the ethos of this war disoriented the marines was reflected in their way of trying to cope with it. For they engaged in a classification of the VC/NVA that was in itself disorienting. While the ARVNs represented what the marines feared they were becoming, the VC/

NVA represented what the marines would like to have been. It was typically thought that in contrast to the ARVNs, the VC "have a lot of balls." Such metaphors of courage assisted in linking cowardice to a lack of masculinity, which is a short conceptual distance from homosexuality.

Through relating to the VC/NVA, the marines were seeking a way to offset their inability to relate to the terms of the war. Their approval of the VC/NVA was reflected in the narrative of a former marine whose unit had suffered heavy casualties on several occasions, leading to its being known as "the walking dead." Eventually they found themselves at Khe Sanh. The NVA had them surrounded and were again inflicting substantial damage without being damaged. The siege was so thorough that the NVA were tunneling underneath the marine positions. During the excavation, a marine used a stethoscopic device to overhear the conversation of the NVA digging below:

> Scared as everybody was, you had to fucking laugh hearing them swearing and shit. 'Cause they were like us really. I figured the grunts [NVA] were there exactly like us. They didn't like the fucking shit more than we did. They're probably down there swearing about their fucking officers and fucking shit like that. It was funny. We were really laughing.

There was another way in which the marines benefited from thinking of the VC/NVA in personal terms. It made them visible—only to a slight degree—but it was that much of an improvement over invisibility. The contrasting visibility of the marines was indicated when "They'd shoot at you at midnight. You'd light up a smoke and he'd shoot at you." The unseen sniper was made visible insofar as he received a name from the mariens: "Bed-Check Charley."

While the personalization of the VC/NVA operated in a way that introduced positive feelings, the impersonalization of the VC/NVA was invoked to prevent negative feelings. The fact that the NVA were trying to kill marines was explained away by one former marine who recalled that "you don't dislike them, because no one NVA ever did anything to you."

In other words, the marines did not suppose that the VC/NVA, on such occasions, were acting personally toward them. Clearly, the same could not be said about the ARVNs. The marines had no trouble relating specific grievances to specific ARVNs. Moreover, they had a sense that homosexuality was more personal than death.

HOW THE MARINE VETERANS' STUDY WAS MADE

In a working class Irish neighborhood of Boston, the community boasts of having the highest proportion of marine enlistees in the country. This claim, repeated to the point of being a cliché, is characteristic of the community's intensely patriotic attitudes. This preoccupation with patriotism became the subject of research three years ago when the study reported in the accompanying article was undertaken. As the marines from the neighborhood began arriving home from Vietnam the following year, the researcher concentrated on getting acquainted with them in order to explore the process of becoming a veteran. Over a period of several years he gradually got to know 60 marine veterans who represented a cross section of the neighborhood to the extent that there are economic and educational variations in such a homogeneous community.

Since the veterans' frame of reference was still the war, it was necessary to reconstruct as far as possible their experiences in Vietnam. The most formal part of this reconstruction was extensive tape-recorded interviews. However, the interviews did not occur until the researcher had established an informal relationship with the men during a year spent on their corners, at their bars and wherever else they "hung." The veterans guided the interviews. Although they were held individually, the interviews produced recurring themes. It was these themes that guided the writing of the essay.

Some of the same themes have reappeared in the veterans' civilian life, particularly in connection with the violence that now characterizes their lives. In its broadest terms, this dependence on violence reflects their having fought an unrequited war. Not only had the war not been won, but the men had been unable to establish a satisfactory working relationship with it. Because they are still trying to achieve the dominance that had been denied them in Vietnam (without any of this necessarily being a conscious process), the war remains alive for them in civilian life. Their threshold for feeling threatened is markedly lower that in the case of men whose civilian life was uninterrupted by the war.

This is not to say that these veterans were nonviolent before their enlistment. But in the past, there were informal rules that limited the amount of damage to the other party. These limits no longer bind them. Another difference, also related to Vietnam, is that this violence is likely to be directed at those who are nominally allies. For example, a group that some veterans rejoined was particularly known for its mutual assistance. But one night there was a fire fight between these veterans. The casualties included one dead. As a consequence, the formerly cohesive group reappeared as two factions, led by veterans, that have been involved in additional combat against each other—resulting in another murder.

The connection with Vietnam may be camouflaged when the victim is a veteran's mother and his weapon is a hurled television set. But the underlying parallels remain, beyond her being a nominal ally. Here, in common with most cases, the violence is spontaneous. For the veterans are still responding to the initiatives of others. And the intentions of these others are still likely to be misperceived. There are times when the continuity with Vietnam is more explicit, as when a veteran destroyed a restaurant in Boston's Chinatown after attacking the waiter who put a hand on his shoulder.

For every boy aged 5 - 12 in the U.S.,
2 G.I. Joe products are sold yearly.

DEMILITARIZE THE PLAYGROUND

PART FOUR

◆ ◆ ◆

Men and Work

Building the Golden Gate Bridge, 1937.

In what ways is work tied to male identity? Do men gain a sense of fulfillment from their work, or do they view it as necessary drudgery? How might the organization of workplaces play on, reinforce, or sometimes threaten the types of masculinity that males have already learned as youngsters? How does the experience of work (or of not having work) differ for men of different social classes, ethnic, and sexual preference groups? And how do recent structural changes in society impact upon the masculinity–work relationship? The articles in this section address these issues and more.

As Jesse Bernard points out, the rise of urban industrial capitalism saw the creation of separate "public" and "domestic" spheres of social life. As women were increasingly relegated to working in the home, men were increasingly absent from the home, and the male "breadwinner role" was born. The sexual division of labor, this gendered split between home and workplace, has led to a variety of problems and conflicts for women and for men. Since World War II, as Anthony Astrachan points out in his article, profound structural changes —among them, women's continued movement into the paid labor force, higher levels of structural unemployment, and the rise of a more service-oriented economy—have led to dramatic shifts in the quality and quantity of men's experiences in the paid labor force.

These economic changes have had a different impact on various groups of men. Ian Harris, for example, describes the poor fit between media images of men and the realities of men's working experiences. David Collinson explores the ways that various forms of oppression (racism, sexism, homophobia) are reproduced in the joking of British working class men. Ben Fong-Torres and Martin P. Levine each documents the impact of inequality on Asian men and gay men, both in the types of positions available to them and their experiences on the job.

Photograph by Serge Sohier of a painting by Greg Dasler.

Jessie Bernard

THE GOOD-PROVIDER ROLE:
ITS RISE AND FALL

The Lord is my shepherd, I shall not want. He sets a table for me in the very sight of my enemies; my cup runs over (23rd Psalm). And when the Israelites were complaining about how hungry they were on their way from Egypt to Canaan, God told Moses to rest assured: There would be meat for dinner and bread for breakfast the next morning. And, indeed, there were quails that very night, enough to cover the camp, and in the morning the ground was covered with dew that proved to be bread (Exodus 16:12–13). In fact, in this role of good provider, God is sometimes almost synonymous with Providence. Many people, like Micawber, still wait for him, or Providence, to provide.

Granted, then, that the first great provider for the human species was God the Father, surely the second great provider for the human species was Mother, the gatherer, planter, and general factotum. Boulding (1976), citing Lee and deVore, tells us that in hunting and gathering societies, males contribute about one fifth of the food of the clan, females the other four fifths (p. 96). She also concludes that by 12,000 B.C. in the early agricultural villages, females provided four fifths of the human subsistence (p. 97). Not until large trading towns arose did the female contribution to human subsistence decline to equality with that of the male. And with the beginning of true cities, the provisioning work of women tended to become invisible. Still, in today's world it remains substantial.

Whatever the date of the virtuous woman described in the Old Testament (Proverbs 31:10–27), she was the very model of a good provider. She was, in fact, a highly productive conglomerate. She woke up in the middle of the night to tend to her business; she oversaw a multiple-industry household; *her* candles did not go out at night; there was no ready market for the high-quality linen girdles she made and sold to the merchants in town; and she kept track of the real estate market and bought good land when it became available, cultivating vineyards quite profitably. All this time her husband sat at the gates talking with his cronies.

A recent counterpart to the virtuous woman was the busy and industrious shtetl woman:

> The earning of a livelihood is sexless, and the large majority of women . . . participate in some gainful occupation if they do not carry the chief burden of support. The wife of a "perennial student" is very apt to be the sole support of the family. The problem of managing both a business and a home is so common that no one recognizes it as special. . . . To bustle about in search of a livelihood is merely another form of bustling about managing a home; both are aspects of . . . health and livelihood. (Zborowski & Herzog, 1952, p. 131)

From *American Psychologist*, Vol. 36, No. 1 (January 1981), pp. 1–12. Copyright 1981 by the American Psychological Association. Reprinted by permission of the publisher and author.

In a subsistence economy in which husbands and wives ran farms, shops, or businesses together, a man might be a good, steady worker, but the idea that he was *the* provider would hardly ring true. Even the youth in the folk song who listed all the gifts he would bestow on his love if she would marry him—a golden comb, a paper of pins, and all the rest—was not necessarily promising to be a good provider.

I have not searched the literature to determine when the concept of the good provider entered our thinking. The term *provider* entered the English language in 1532, but was not yet male sex typed, as the older term *purveyor* already was in 1442. Webster's second edition defines the good provider as "one who provides, especially, colloq., one who provides food, clothing, etc. for his family; as, he is a good or an adequate provider." More simply, he could be defined as a man whose wife did not have to enter the labor force. The counterpart to the good provider was the housewife. However the term is defined, the role itself delineated relationships within a marriage and family in a way that added to the legal, religious, and other advantages men had over women.

Thus, under the common law, although the husband was legally head of the household and as such had the responsibility of providing for his wife and children, this provision was often made with help from the wife's personal property and earnings, to which he was entitled:

> He owned his wife's and children's services, and had the sole right to collect wages for their work outside the home. He owned his wife's personal property outright, and had the right to manage and control all of his wife's real property during marriage, which included the right to use or lease property, and to keep any rents and profits from it. (Babcock, Freedman, Norton, & Ross, 1975, p. 561)

So even when she was the actual provider, the legal recognition was granted the husband. Therefore, whatever the husband's legal responsibilities for support may have been, he was not necessarily a good provider in the way the term came to be understood. The wife may have been performing that role.

In our country in Colonial times women were still viewed as performing a providing role, and they pursued a variety of occupations. Abigail Adams managed the family estate, which provided the wherewithal for John to spend so much time in Philadelphia. In the 18th century "many women were active in business and professional pursuits. They ran inns and taverns; they managed a wide variety of stores and shops; and, at least occasionally, they worked in careers like publishing, journalism and medicine" (Demos, 1974, p. 430). Women sometimes even "joined the menfolk for work in the fields" (p. 430). Like the household of the proverbial virtuous woman, the Colonial household was a little factory that produced clothing, furniture, bedding, candles, and other accessories, and again, as in the case of the virtuous woman, the female role was central. It was taken for granted that women provided for the family along with men.

The good provider as a specialized male role seems to have arisen in the transition from subsistence to market—especially money—economies that accelerated with the industrial revolution. The good-provider role for males emerged in this country roughly, say, from the 1830s, when de Tocqueville was observing it, to the late 1970s, when the 1980 census declared that a male was not automatically to be assumed to be the head of the household. This gives the role a life span of about a century and a half. Although relatively short-lived, while it lasted the role was a seemingly rock-like feature of the national landscape.

As a psychological and sociological phenomenon, the good-provider role had wide ramifications for all our thinking about families. It marked a new kind of marriage. It did not have good effects on women: The role deprived them of many chips by placing them in a peculiarly vulnerable position. Because she was not reimbursed for her contribution to the family in either products or services, a wife was stripped to a considerable extent of her access to cash-mediated markets. By discouraging labor force participation, it deprived many women, especially affluent ones, of opportunities to achieve strength and competence. It deterred young women from acquiring productive skills. They dedicated themselves instead to winning a good provider who would "take care of" them. The wife of a more successful provider became for all intents and purposes a parasite, with little to do except indulge or pamper herself. The psychology of such dependence could become all but crippling. There were other concomitants of the good-provider role.

EXPRESSIVITY AND THE GOOD-PROVIDER ROLE

The new industrial order that produced the good provider changed not so much the division of labor between the sexes as it did the site of the work they engaged in. Only two of the concomitants of this change in work site are selected for comment here, namely, (a) the identification of gender with work site as well as with work itself and (b) the reduction of time for personal interaction and intimacy within the family.

It is not so much the specific kinds of work men and women do—they have always varied from time to time and place to place—but the simple fact that the sexes do different kinds of work, whatever it is, which is in and of itself important. The division of labor by sex means that the work group becomes also a sex group. The very nature of maleness and femaleness becomes embedded in the sexual division of labor. One's sex and one's work are part of one another. One's work defines one's gender.

Any division of labor implies that people doing different kinds of work will occupy different work sites. When the division is based on sex, men and women will necessarily have different work sites. Even within the home itself, men and women had different work spaces. The woman's spinning wheel occupied a different area from the man's anvil. When the factory took over much of the work formerly done in the house, the separation of work space became especially marked. Not only did the separation of the sexes become spatially extended, but it came to relate work and gender in a special way. The work site as well as the work itself became associated with gender; each sex had its own turf. This sexual "territoriality" has had complicating effects on efforts to change any sexual division of labor. The good provider worked primarily in the outside male world of business and industry. The homemaker worked primarily in the home.

Spatial separation of the sexes not only identifies gender with work site and work but also reduces the amount of time available for spontaneous emotional give-and-take between husbands and wives. When men and women work in an economy based in the home, there are frequent occasions for interaction.

(Consider, for example, the suggestive allusions made today to the rise in the birth rate nine months after a blackout.) When men and women are in close proximity, there is always the possibility of reassuring glances, the comfort of simple physical presence. But when the division of labor removes the man from the family dwelling for most of the day, intimate relationships become less feasible. De Tocqueville was one of the first to call our attention to this. In 1840 he noted that

> almost all men in democracies are engaged in public or professional life; and . . . the limited extent of common income obliges a wife to confine herself to the house, in order to watch in person and very closely over the details of domestic economy. All these distinct and compulsory occupations are so many natural barriers, which, by keeping the two sexes asunder, render the solicitations of the one less frequent and less ardent—the resistance of the other more easy. (de Tocqueville, 1840, p. 212)

Not directly related to the spatial constraints on emotional expression by men, but nevertheless a concomitant of the new industrial order with the same effect, was the enormous drive for achievement, for success, for "making it" that escalated the provider role into the good-provider role. De Tocqueville (1840) is again our source:

> The tumultuous and constantly harassed life which equality makes men lead [becoming good providers] not only distracts them from the passions of love, by denying them time to indulge in it, but it diverts them from it by another more secret but more certain road. All men who live in democratic ages more or less contract ways of thinking of the manufacturing and trading classes. (p. 221)

As a result of this male concentration on jobs and careers, much abnegation and "a constant sacrifice of her pleasures to her duties" (de Tocqueville, 1840, p. 212) were demanded of the American woman. The good-provider role, as it came to be shaped by this ambience, was thus restricted in what it was called upon to provide. Emotional expressivity was not included in the role. One of the things a parent might say about a man to persuade a daughter to marry him, or a daughter might say to explain to her parents why she wanted to, was not that he was a gentle, loving, or tender man but that he was a good provider. He might have many other qualities, good or bad, but if a man was a good provider, everything else was either gravy or the price one had to pay for a good provider.

Lack of expressivity did not imply neglect of the family. The good provider was a "family man." He set a good table, provided a decent home, paid the mortgage, bought the shoes, and kept his children warmly clothed. He might, with the help of the children's part-time jobs, have been able to finance their educations through high school and, sometimes, even college. There might even have been a little left over for an occasional celebration in most families. The good provider made a decent contribution to the church. His work might have been demanding, but he expected it to be. If in addition to being a good provider, a man was kind, gentle, generous, and not a heavy drinker or gambler, that was all frosting on the cake. Loving attention and emotional involvement in the family were not part of a woman's implicit bargain with the good provider.

By the time de Tocqueville published his observations in 1840, the general outlines of the good-provider role had taken shape. It called for a hard-working man who spent most of his time at his work. In the traditional conception of the role, a man's chief responsibility is his job, so that "by definition any family behaviors must be subordinate to it in terms of significance and [the job] has priority in the event of a clash" (Scanzoni, 1975, p. 38). This was the classic form of the good-provider role, which remained a powerful component of our social structure until well into the present century.

COSTS AND REWARDS OF THE GOOD-PROVIDER ROLE FOR MEN

There were both costs and rewards for those men attached to the good-provider role. The most serious cost was perhaps the identification of maleness not only with the work site but especially with success in the role. "The American male looks to his breadwinning role to confirm his manliness" (Brenton, 1966, p. 194).[1] To be a man one had to be not only a provider but a *good* provider. Success in the good-provider role came in time to define masculinity itself. The good provider had to achieve, to win, to succeed, to dominate. He was a bread*winner*. He had to show "strength, cunning, inventiveness, endurance—a whole range of traits henceforth defined as exclusively 'masculine' " (Demos, 1974, p. 436). Men were judged as men by the level of living they provided. They were judged by the myth "that endows a money-making man with sexiness and virility, and is based on man's dominance, strength, and ability to provide for and care for 'his' woman" (Gould, 1974, p. 97). The good provider became a player in the male competitive macho game. What one man provided for his family in the way of luxury and display had to be equaled or topped by what another could provide. Families became display cases for the success of the good provider.

The psychic costs could be high:

> By depending so heavily on his breadwinning role to validate his sense of himself as a man, instead of also letting his roles as husband, father, and citizen of the community count as validating sources, the American male treads on psychically dangerous ground. It's always dangerous to put all of one's psychic eggs into one basket. (Brenton, 1966, p. 194)

The good-provider role not only put all of a man's gender-identifying eggs into one psychic basket, but it also put all the family-providing eggs into one basket. One individual became responsible for the support of the whole family. Countless stories portrayed the humiliation families underwent to keep wives and especially mothers out of the labor force, a circumstance that would admit to the world the male head's failure in the good-provider role. If a married woman had to enter the labor force at all, that was bad enough. If she made a good salary, however, she was "co-opting the man's passport to masculinity" (Gould, 1974, p. 98) and he was effectively castrated. A wife's

[1] Rainwater and Yancey (1967), critiquing current welfare policies, note that they "have robbed men of their manhood, women of their husbands, and children of their fathers. To create a stable monogamous family we need to provide men with the opportunity to be men, and that involves enabling them to perform occupationally" (p. 235).

earning capacity diminished a man's position as head of the household (Gould, 1974, p. 99).

Failure in the role of a good provider, which employment of wives evidenced, could produce deep frustration. As Komarovsky (1940, p. 20) explains, this is "because in his own estimation he is failing to fulfill what is the central duty of his life, the very touchstone of his manhood—the role of family provider."

But just as there was punishment for failure in the good-provider role, so also were there rewards for successful performance. A man "derived strength from his role as provider" (Komarovsky, 1940, p. 205). He achieved a good deal of satisfaction from his ability to support his family. It won kudos. Being a good provider led to status in both the family and the community. Within the family it gave him the power of the purse and the right to decide about expenditures, standards of living, and what constituted good providing. "Every purchase of the family—the radio, his wife's new hat, the children's skates, the meals set before him—all were symbols of their dependence upon him" (Komarovsky, 1940, pp. 74–75). Such dependence gave him a "profound sense of stability" (p. 74). It was a strong counterpoise vis-à-vis a wife with a stronger personality. "Whether he had considerable authority within the family and was recognized as its head, or whether the wife's stronger personality . . . dominated the family, he nevertheless derived strength from his role as provider" (Komarovsky, 1940, p. 75). As recently as 1975, in a sample of 3,100 husbands and wives in 10 cities, Scanzoni found that despite increasing egalitarian norms, the good provider still had "considerable power in ultimate decision-making" and as "unique provider" had the right "to organize his life and the lives of other family members around his occupation" (p. 38).

A man who was successful in the good-provider role might be freed from other obligations to the family. But the flip side of this dispensation was that he could not make up for poor performance by excellence in other family roles. Since everything depended on his success as provider, everything was at stake. The good provider played an all-or-nothing game.

DIFFERENT WAYS OF PERFORMING THE GOOD-PROVIDER ROLE

Although the legal specifications for the role were laid out in the common law, in legislation, in legal precedents, in court decisions, and, most importantly, in custom and convention, in real-life situations the social and social-psychological specifications were set by the husband or, perhaps more accurately, by the community, alias the Joneses, and there were many ways to perform it.

Some men resented the burdens the role forced them to bear. A man could easily vent such resentment toward his family by keeping complete control over all expenditures, dispensing the money for household maintenance, and complaining about bills as though it were his wife's fault that shoes cost so much. He could, in effect, punish his family for his having to perform the role. Since the money he earned belonged to him—was "his"—he could do with it what he pleased. Through extreme parsimony he could dole out his money in a mean, humiliating way, forcing his wife to come begging for pennies. By his reluctance and resentment he could make his family pay emotionally for the provisioning he supplied.

At the other extreme were the highly competitive men who were so involved in outdoing the Joneses that the fur coat became more important than the affectionate hug. They "bought off" their families. They sometimes succeeded so well in their extravagance that they sacrificed the family they were presumably providing for to the achievements that made it possible (Keniston, 1965).[2]

The Depression of the 1930s revealed in harsh detail what the loss of the role could mean both to the good provider and to his family, not only in the loss of income itself—which could be supplied by welfare agencies or even by other family members, including wives—but also and especially in the loss of face.

The Great Depression did not mark the demise of the good-provider role. But it did teach us what a slender thread the family hung on. It stimulated a whole array of programs designed to strengthen that thread, to ensure that it would never again be similarly threatened. Unemployment insurance was incorporated into the Social Security Act of 1935, for example, and a Full Employment Act was passed in 1946. But there proved to be many other ways in which the good-provider role could be subverted.

ROLE REJECTORS AND ROLE OVERPERFORMERS

Recent research in psychology, anthropology, and sociology has familiarized us with the tremendous power of roles. But we also know that one of the fundamental principles of role behavior is that conformity to role norms is not universal. Not everyone lives up to the specifications of roles, either in the psychological or in the sociological definition of the concept. Two extremes have attracted research attention: (a) the men who could not live up to the norms of the good-provider role or did not want to, at one extreme, and (b) the men who overperformed the role, at the other. For the wide range in between, from bluecollar workers to professionals, there was fairly consistent acceptance of the role, however well or poorly, however grumblingly or willingly, performed.

First the noncomformists. Even in Colonial times, desertion and divorce occurred:

> Women may have deserted because, say, their husbands beat them; husbands, on the other hand, may have deserted because they were unable or unwilling to provide for their usually large families in the face of the wives' demands to do so. These demands were, of course, backed by community norms making the husband's financial support a sacred duty. (Scanzoni, 1979, pp. 24–25)

[2] Several years ago I presented a critique of what I called "extreme sex role specialization," including "work-intoxicated fathers." I noted that making success in the provider role the only test for real manliness was putting a lot of eggs into one basket. At both the blue-collar and the managerial levels, it was dysfunctional for families. I referred to the several attempts being made even then to correct the excesses of extreme sex role specialization: rural and urban communes, leaving jobs to take up small-scale enterprises that allowed more contact with families, and a rebellion against overtime in industry (Bernard, 1975, pp. 217–239).

Fiedler (1962) has traced the theme of male escape from domestic responsibilities in the American novel from the time of Rip Van Winkle to the present:

> The figure of Rip Van Winkle presides over the birth of the American imagination; and it is fitting that our first successful home-grown legend should memorialize, however playfully, the flight of the dreamer from the shrew—into the mountains and out of time, away from the drab duties of home . . . anywhere to avoid . . . marriage and responsibility. One of the factors that determine theme and form in our great books is this strategy of evasion, this retreat to nature and childhood which makes our literature (and life) so charmingly and infuriatingly "boyish." (pp. xx–xxi)

Among the men who pulled up stakes and departed for the West or went down to the sea in ships, there must have been a certain proportion who, like their mythic prototype, were simply fleeing the good-provider role.

The work of Demos (1974), a historian, offers considerable support for Fiedler's thesis. He tells us that the burdens thrust on men in the 19th century by the new patterns of work began to show their effects in the family. When "the [spatial] separation of the work lives of the husbands and wives made communication so problematic," he asks, "what was the likelihood of meaningful communication?" (Demos, 1974, p. 438). The answer is, relatively little. Divorce and separation increased, either formally or by tacit consent—or simply by default, as in the case of a variety of defaulters—tramps, bums, hoboes—among them.

In this connection, "the development of the notorious 'tramp' phenomenon is worth noticing," Demos (1974, p. 438) tells us. The tramp was a man who just gave up, who dropped out of the role entirely. He preferred not to work, but he would do small chores or other small-scale work for a handout if he had to. He was not above begging the housewife for a meal, hoping she would not find work for him to do in repayment. Demos (1974) describes the type:

> Demoralized and destitute wanderers, their numbers mounting into the hundreds of thousands, tramps can be fairly characterized as men who had run away from their wives. . . . Their presence was mute testimony to the strains that tugged at the very core of American family life. . . . Many observers noted that the tramps had created a virtual society of their own [a kind of counterculture] based on a principle of single-sex companionship. (p. 438)

A considerable number of them came to be described as "homeless men" and, as the country became more urbanized, landed ultimately on skid row. A large part of the task of social workers for almost a century was the care of the "evaded" women they left behind.[3] When the tramp became wholly demoral-

---

[3] In one department of a South Carolina cotton mill early in the century, "every worker was a grass widow" (Smuts, 1959, p. 54). Many women worked "because their husbands refused to provide for their families. There is no reason to think that husbands abandoned their duties more often than today, but the woman who was burdened by an irresponsible husband in 1890 usually had no recourse save taking on his responsibilities herself. If he deserted, the law-enforcement agencies of the time afforded little chance of finding and compelling him to provide support" (Smuts, 1959, p. 54). The situation is not greatly improved today. In divorce child support is allotted in only a small number of cases and enforced in even fewer. "Roughly half of all families with an absent parent don't have awards at all. . . . Where awards do exist they are usually for

ized, a chronic alcoholic, almost unreachable, he fell into a category of his own—he was a bum.

Quite a different kettle of fish was the hobo, the migratory worker who spent several months harvesting wheat and other large crops and the rest of the year in cities. Many were the so-called Wobblies, or Industrial Workers of the World, who repudiated the good-provider role on principle. They had contempt for the man who accepted it and could be called conscientious objectors to the role. "In some IWW circles, wives were regarded as the 'ball and chain.' In the West, IWW literature proclaimed that the migratory worker, usually a young, unmarried male, was 'the finest specimen of American manhood . . . the leaven of the revolutionary labor movement' " (Foner, 1979, p. 400). Exemplars of the Wobblies were the nomadic workers of the West. They were free men. The migratory worker, "unlike the factory slave of the Atlantic seaboard and the central states, . . . was most emphatically 'not afraid of losing his job.' No wife and family cumbered him. The worker of the East, oppressed by the fear of want for wife and babies, dared not venture much" (Foner, 1979, p. 400). The reference to fear of loss of job was well taken; employers preferred married men, disciplined into the good-provider role, who had given hostages to fortune and were therefore more tractable.

Just on the verge between the area of conformity to the good-provider role—at whatever level—and the area of complete noncomformity to it was the nongood provider, the marginal group of workers usually made up of "the under-educated, the under-trained, the under-employed, or part-time employed, as well as the under-paid, and of course the unemployed" (Snyder, 1979, p. 597). These included men who wanted—sometimes desperately—to perform the good-provider role but who for one reason or another were unable to do so. Liebow (1966) has discussed the ramifications of failure among the black men of Tally's corner: The black man is

> under legal and social constraints to provide for them [their families], to be a husband to his wife and a father to his children. The chances are, however, that he is failing to provide for them, and failure in this primary function contaminates his performance as father in other respects as well. (p. 86)

In some cases, leaving the family entirely was the best substitute a man could supply. The community was left to take over.[4]

At the other extreme was the overperformer. De Tocqueville, quoted earlier, was already describing him as he manifested in the 1830s. And as late as 1955 Warner and Ableggden were adding to the considerable literature on

---

small amounts, typically ranging from $7 to $18 per week per child" (Jones, 1976, abstract). A summary of all the studies available concludes that "approximately 20 percent of all divorced and separated mothers receive child support regularly, with an additional 7 percent receiving it 'sometimes'; 8 percent of all divorced and separated women receive alimony regularly or sometimes" (Jones, 1976, p. 23).

[4] Even though the annals of social work agencies are filled with cases of runaway husbands, in 1976 only 12.6% of all women were in the status of divorce and separation, and at least some of them were still being "provided for." Most men were at least trying to fulfill the good-provider role.

industrial leaders and tycoons, referring to their "driving concentration" on their careers and their "intense focusing" of interests, energies, and skills on these careers, "even limiting their sexual activity" (pp. 48–49). They came to be known as workaholics or work-intoxicated men. Their preoccupation with their work even at the expense of their families was, as I have already noted, quite acceptable in our society.

Poorly or well performed, the good-provider role lingered on. World War II initiated a challenge, this time in the form of attracting more and more married women into the labor force, but the challenge was papered over in the 1950s with an "age of togetherness" that all but apotheosized the good provider, his house in the suburbs, his homebody wife, and his third, fourth, even fifth, child. As late as the 1960s most housewives (87%) still saw breadwinning as their husband's primary role (Lopata, 1971, p. 91).[5]

INTRINSIC CONFLICT IN THE GOOD-PROVIDER ROLE

Since the good-provider role involved both family and work roles, most people believed that there was no incompatibility between them or at least that there should not be. But in the 1960s and 1970s evidence began to mount that maybe something was amiss.

De Tocqueville had documented the implicit conflict in the American businessman's devotion to his work at the expense of his family in the early years of the 19th century; the Industrial Workers of the World had proclaimed that the good-provider role which tied a man to his family was an impediment to the great revolution at the beginning of the 20th century; Fiedler (1962) had noted that throughout our history, in the male fantasy world, there was freedom from the responsibilities of this role; about 50 years ago Freud (1930/1958) had analyzed the intrinsic conflict between the demands of women and the family on one side and the demands of men's work on the other:

> Women represent the interests of the family and sexual life, the work of civilization has become more and more men's business; it confronts them with ever harder tasks, compels them to sublimations of instinct which women are not easily able to achieve. Since man has not an unlimited amount of mental energy at his disposal, he must accomplish his tasks by distributing his libido to the best advantage. What he employs for cultural [occupational] purposes he withdraws to a great extent from women, and his sexual life; his constant association with men and his dependence on his relations with them even estrange him from his duties as husband and father. Woman finds herself thus forced into the background by the claims of culture [work] and she adapts an inimical attitude towards it. (pp. 50–51)

In the last two decades, researchers have been raising questions relevant to Freud's statement of the problem. They have been asking people about the

---

[5] Although all the women in Lopata's (1971) sample saw breadwinning as important, fewer employed women (54%) than either nonemployed urban (63%) or suburban (64%) women assigned it first place (p. 91).

relative satisfactions they derive from these conflicting values—family and work. Among the earliest studies comparing family–work values was a Gallup poll in 1940 in which both men and women chose a happy home over an interesting job or wealth as a major life value. Since then there have been a number of such polls, and a considerable body of results has now accumulated. Pleck and Lang (1979) and Hesselbart (Note 1) have summarized the findings of these surveys. All agree that there is a clear bias in the direction of the family. Pleck and Lang conclude that "men's family role is far more psychologically significant to them than is their work role" (p. 29), and Hesselbart—however critical she is of the studies she summarizes—believes they should not be dismissed lightly and concludes that they certainly "challenge the idea that family is a 'secondary' valued role" (p. 14).[6] Douvan (Note 2) also found in a 1976 replication of a 1957 survey that family values retained priority over work: "Family roles almost uniformly rate higher in value production than the job role does" (p. 16).[7]

The very fact that researchers have asked such questions is itself interesting. Somehow or other both the researchers and the informants seem to be saying that all this complaining about the male neglect of the family, about the lack of family involvement by men, just is not warranted. Neither de Tocqueville nor Freud was right. Men do value family life more than they value their work. They do derive their major life satisfactions from their families rather than from their work.

It may well be true that men derive the greatest satisfaction from their family roles, but this does not necessarily mean they are willing to pay for this benefit. In any event, great attitudinal changes took place in the 1960s and 1970s.

Douvan (Note 2), on the basis of surveys in 1957 and 1976, found, for example, a considerable increase in the proportion of both men and women who found marriage and parenthood burdensome and restrictive. Almost three fifths (57%) of both married men and married women in 1976 saw marriage as "all burdens and restrictions," as compared with only 42% and 47%, respectively, in 1957. And almost half (45%) also viewed children as "all burdens and restrictions" in 1976, as compared with only 28% and 33% for married men and married women, respectively, in 1957. The proportion of working men with a positive attitude toward marriage dropped drastically

---

[6] Pleck and Lang (1979) found only one serious study contradicting their own conclusions: "Using data from the 1973 NORC [National Opinion Research Center] General Social Survey, Harry analyzed the bivariate relationship of job and family satisfaction to life happiness in men classified by family life cycle stage. In three of the five groups of husbands . . . job satisfaction had a stronger association than family satisfaction to life happiness" (pp. 5–6).

[7] In 1978, a Yankelovich survey on "The New Work Psychology" suggested that leisure is now becoming a strict competitor for both family and work as a source of life satisfactions: "Family and work have grown less important than leisure; a majority of 60 percent say that although they enjoy their work, it is not their major source of satisfaction" (p. 46). A 1977 survey of Swedish men aged 18 to 35 found that the proportion saying the family was the main source of meaning in their lives declined from 45% in 1955 to 41% in 1977; the proportion indicating work as the main source of satisfaction dropped from 33% to 17%. The earlier tendency for men to identify themselves through their work is less marked these days. In the new value system, the individual says, in effect, "I am more than my role. I am myself" (Yankelovich, 1978). Is the increasing concern with leisure a way to escape the dissatisfaction with both the alienating relations found on the work site and the demands for increased involvement with the family?

over this period, from 68% to 39%. Working women, who made up a fairly small number of all married women in 1957, hardly changed attitudes at all, dropping only from 43% to 42%. The proportion of working men who found marriage and children burdensome and restrictive more than doubled, from 25% to 56% and from 25% to 58%, respectively. Although some of these changes reflected greater willingness in 1976 than in 1957 to admit negative attitudes toward marriage and parenthood—itself significant—profound changes were clearly in process. More and more men and women were experiencing disaffection with family life.[8]

"ALL BURDENS AND RESTRICTIONS"

Apparently, the benefits of the good-provider role were greater than the costs for most men. Despite the legend of the flight of the American male (Fiedler, 1962), despite the defectors and dropouts, despite the tavern habitué's "ball and chain" cliché, men seemed to know that the good-provider role, if they could succeed in it, was good for them. But Douvan's (Note 2) findings suggest that recently their complaints have become serious, bone-deep. The family they have been providing for is not the same family it was in the past.

Smith (1979) calls the great trek of married women into the labor force a subtle revolution—revolutionary not in the sense of one class overthrowing a status quo and substituting its own regime, but revolutionary in its impact on both the family and the work roles of men and women. It diluted the prerogatives of the good-provider role. It increased the demands made on the good provider, especially in the form of more emotional investment in the family, more sharing of household responsibilities. The role became even more burdensome.

However men may now feel about the burdens and restrictions imposed on them by the good-provider role, most have, at least ostensibly, accepted them. The tramp and the bum had "voted with their feet" against the role; the hobo or Wobbly had rejected it on the basis of a revolutionary ideology that saw it as enslaving men to the corporation; tavern humor had glossed the resentment habitués felt against its demands. Now the "burdens-and-restrictions" motif has surfaced both in research reports and, more blatantly, in the male liberation movement. From time to time it has also appeared in the clinician's notes.

Sometimes the resentment of the good provider takes the form of simply wanting more appreciation for the life-style he provides. All he does for his family seems to be taken for granted. Thus, for example, Goldberg (1976), a psychiatrist, recounts the case of a successful businessman:

> He's feeling a deepening sense of bitterness and frustration about his wife and family. He doesn't feel appreciated. It angers him the way they seem to take the things his earnings purchase for granted. They've come to expect it as their due. It particularly enrages him when his children put him down for his "materialistic middle-class trip." He'd like to tell

---

[8] Men seem to be having problems with both work and family roles. Veroff (Note 3), for example, reports an increased "sense of dissatisfaction with the social relations in the work setting" and a "dissatisfaction with the affiliative nature of work" (p. 47). This dissatisfaction may be one of the factors that leads men to seek affiliative-need satisfaction in marriage, just as in the 19th century they looked to the home as shelter from the jungle of the outside world.

them to get someone else to support them but he holds himself back. (p. 124)

Brenton (1966) quotes a social worker who describes an upper-middle-class woman: She has "gotten hold of a man who'll drive himself like mad to get money, and [is] denigrating him for being too interested in money, and not interested in music, or the arts, or in spending time with the children. But at the same time she's subtly driving him—and doesn't know it" (p. 226). What seems significant about such cases is not that men feel resentful about the lack of appreciation but that they are willing to justify their resentment. They are no longer willing to grin and bear it.

Sometimes there is even more than expressed resentment; there is an actual repudiation of the role. In the past, only a few men like the hobo or Wobbly were likely to give up. Today, Goldberg (1976) believes, more are ready to renounce the role, not on theoretical revolutionary grounds, however, but on purely selfish ones:

> Male growth will stem from openly avowed, unashamed, self-oriented motivations. . . . Guilt-oriented "should" behavior will be rejected because it is always at the price of a hidden build-up of resentment and frustration and alienation from others and is, therefore, counterproductive. (p. 184)

The disaffection of the good provider is directed to both sides of his role. With respect to work, Lefkowitz (1979) has described men among whom the good-provider role is neither being completely rejected nor repudiated, but diluted. These men began their working lives in the conventional style, hopeful and ambitious. They found a job, married, raised a family, and "achieved a measure of economic security and earned the respect of . . . colleagues and neighbors" (Lefkowitz, 1979, p. 31). In brief, they successfully performed the good-provider role. But unlike their historical predecessors, they in time became disillusioned with their jobs—not jobs on assembly lines, not jobs usually characterized as alienating, but fairly prestigious jobs such as aeronautics engineer and government economist. They daydreamed about other interests. "The common theme which surfaced again and again in their histories, was the need to find a new social connection—to reassert control over their lives, to gain some sense of freedom" (Lefkowitz, 1979, p. 31). These men felt "entitled to freedom and independence." Middle-class, educated, self-assured, articulate, and for the most part white, they knew they could talk themselves into a job if they had to. Most of them did not want to desert their families. Indeed, most of them "wanted to rejoin the intimate circle they felt they had neglected in their years of work" (p. 31).

Though some of the men Lefkowitz studied sought closer ties with their families, in the case of those studied by Sarason (1977), a psychologist, career changes involved lower income and had a negative impact on families. Sarason's subjects were also men in high-level professions, the very men least likely to find marriage and parenthood burdensome and restrictive. Still, since career change often involved a reduction in pay, some wives were unwilling to accept it, with the result that the marriage deteriorated (p. 178). Sometimes it looked like a no-win game. The husband's earlier career brought him feelings of emptiness and alienation, but it also brought financial rewards for the family. Greater work satisfaction for him in lower paying work meant reduced satisfaction with life-style. These findings lead Sarason to raise a number of points with respect to the good-provider role. "How much," he asks, "does an individual or a family need in order to maintain a satisfactory existence? Is an individual being responsible to himself or his family if he provides them with little more than the bare essentials of living?" (p. 178). These are questions about the good-provider role that few men raised in the past.

Lefkowitz (1979) wonders how his downwardly mobile men lived when they left their jobs. "They put together a basic economic package which consisted of government assistance, contributions from family members who had not worked before and some bartering of goods and services" (p. 31). Especially interesting in this list of income sources are the "contributions from family members who had not worked before" (p. 31). Surely not mothers and sisters. Who, of course, but wives?

WOMEN AND THE PROVIDER ROLE

The present discussion began with the woman's part in the provider role. We saw how as more and more of the provisioning of the family came to be by way of monetary exchange, the woman's part shrank. A woman could still provide services, but could furnish little in the way of food, clothing, and shelter. But now that she is entering the labor force in large numbers, she can once more resume her ancient role, this time, like her male counterpart the provider, by way of a monetary contribution. More and more women are doing just this.

The assault on the good-provider role in the Depression was traumatic. But a modified version began to appear in the 1970s as a single income became inadequate for more and more families. Husbands have remained the major providers, but in an increasing number of cases the wife has begun to share this role. Thus, the proportion of married women aged 15 to 54 (living with their husbands) in the labor force more than doubled between 1950 and 1978, from 25.2% to 55.4%. The proportion for 1990 is estimated to reach 66.7% (Smith, 1979, p. 14). Fewer women are now full-time housewives.

For some men the relief from the strain of sole responsibility for the provider role has been welcome. But for others the feeling of degradation resembles the feelings reported 40 years earlier in the Great Depression. It is not that they are no longer providing for the family but that the role-sharing wife now feels justified in making demands on them. The good-provider role with all its prerogatives and perquisites has undergone profound changes. It will never be the same again.[9] Its death knell was sounded when, as noted above, the 1980 census no longer automatically assumed that the male member of the household was its head.

---

[9] Among the indices of the waning of the good-provider role are the increasing number of married women in the labor force; the growth in the number of female-headed families; the growing trend toward egalitarian norms in marriage; the need for two earners in so many middle-class families; and the recognition of these trends in the abandonment of the identification of head of household as a male.

THE CURRENT SCENE

Among the new demands being made on the good-provider role, two deserve special consideration, namely, (a) more intimacy, expressivity, and nurturance—specifications never included in it as it originally took shape—and (b) more sharing of household responsibility and child care.

As the pampered wife in an affluent household came often to be an economic parasite, so also the good provider was often, in a way, a kind of emotional parasite. Implicit in the definition of the role was that he provided goods and material things. Tender loving care was not one of the requirements. Emotional ministrations from the family were his right; providing them was not a corresponding obligation. Therefore, as de Tocqueville had already noted by 1840, women suffered a kind of emotional deprivation labeled by Robert Weiss "relational deficit" (cited in Barnard, 1976). Only recently has this male rejection of emotional expression come to be challenged. Today, even blue-collar women are imposing "a host of new role expectations upon their husbands or lovers. . . . A new role set asks the blue-collar male to strive for . . . deep-coursing intimacy" (Shostak, Note 4, p. 75). It was not only vis-à-vis his family that the good provider was lacking in expressivity. This lack was built into the whole male role script. Today not only women but also men are beginning to protest the repudiation of expressivity prescribed in male roles (David & Brannon, 1976; Farrell, 1974; Fasteau, 1974; Pleck & Sawyer, 1974).

Is there any relationship between the "imposing" on men of "deep-coursing intimacy" by women on one side and the increasing proportion of men who find marriage burdensome and restrictive on the other? Are men seeing the new emotional involvements being asked of them as "all burdens and restrictions"? Are they responding to the new involvements under duress? Are they feeling oppressed by them? Fearful of them?

From the standpoint of high-level pure-science research there may be something bizarre, if not even slightly absurd, in the growing corpus of serious research on how much or how little husbands of employed wives contribute to household chores and child care. Yet it is serious enough that all over the industrialized world such research is going on. Time studies in a dozen countries—communist as well as capitalist—trace the slow and bungling process by which marriage accommodates to changing conditions and by which women struggle to mold the changing conditions in their behalf. For everywhere the same picture shows up in the research: an image of women sharing the provider role and at the same time retaining responsibility for the household. Until recently such a topic would have been judged unworthy of serious attention. It was a subject that might be worth a good laugh, for instance, as when an all-thumbs man in a cartoon burns the potatoes or finds himself bumbling awkwardly over a diaper, demonstrating his—proud—male ineptness at such female work. But it is no longer funny.

The "politics of housework" (Mainardi, 1970) proves to be more profound than originally believed. It has to do not only with tasks but also with gender—and perhaps more with the site of the tasks than with their intrinsic nature. A man can cook magnificently if he does it on a hunting or fishing trip; he can wield a skillful needle if he does it mending a tent or a fishing net; he can even feed and clean a toddler on a camping trip. Few of the skills of the homemaker are beyond his reach so long as they are practiced in a suitably male environment. It is not only women's work in and of itself that is degrading but any work on female turf. It may be true, as Brenton (1966) says, that "the secure man can wash a dish, diaper a baby, and throw the dirty clothes into the washing machine—or do anything else women used to do exclusively—without thinking twice about it" (p. 211), but not all men are that secure. To a great many men such chores are demasculinizing. The apron is shameful on a man in the kitchen; it is all right at the carpenter's bench.

The male world may look upon the man who shares household responsibilities as, in effect, a scab. One informant tells the interviewer about a conversation on the job: "What, are you crazy?" his hard-hat fellow workers ask him when he speaks of helping his wife. "The guys want to kill me. 'You son of a bitch! You are getting us in trouble.' . . . The men get really mad" (Lein, 1979, p. 492). Something more than persiflage is involved here. We are fairly familiar with the trauma associated with the invasion by women of the male work turf, the hazing women can be subjected to, and the male resentment of admitting them except into their own segregated areas. The corresponding entrance of men into the traditional turf of women—the kitchen or the nursery—has analogous but not identical concomitants.

Pleck and Lang (1979) tell us that men are now beginning to change in the direction of greater involvement in family life. "Men's family behavior is beginning to change, becoming increasingly congruent with the long-standing psychological significance of the family in their lives" (p. 1). They measure this greater involvement by way of the help they offer with homemaking chores. Scanzoni (1975), on the basis of a survey of over 3,000 husbands and wives, concludes that at least in households in which wives are in the labor force, there is the "possibility of a different pattern in which responsibility for households would unequivocally fall equally on husbands as well as wives" (p. 38). A brave new world indeed. Still, when we look at the reality around us, the pace seems intolerably slow. The responsibilities of the old good-provider role have attenuated far faster than have its prerogatives and privileges.

A considerable amount of thought has been devoted to studying the effects of the large influx of women into the work force. An equally interesting question is what the effect will be if a large number of men actually do increase their participation in the family and the household. Will men find the apron shameful? What if we were to ask fathers to alternate with mothers in being in the home when youngsters come home from school? Would fighting adolescent drug abuse be more successful if fathers and mothers were equally engaged in it? If the school could confer with fathers as often as with mothers? If the father accompanied children when they went shopping for clothes? If fathers spent as much time with children as do mothers?

Even as husbands, let alone as fathers, the new pattern is not without trauma. Hall and Hall (1979), in their study of two-career couples, report that the most serious fights among such couples occur not in the bedroom, but in the kitchen, between couples who profess a commitment to equality but who find actually implementing it difficult. A young professional reports that he is philosophically committed to egalitarianism in marriage and tries hard to practice it, but it does not work. He even feels guilty about this. The stresses involved in reworking roles may have an impact on health. A study of engineers and accountants finds poorer health among those with employed wives than among those with nonemployed wives (Burke & Wier, 1976). The processes involved in role change have been compared with those involved in deprogramming a cult member. Are they part of the increasing sense of marriage and parenthood as "all burdens and restrictions"?

The demise of the good-provider role also calls for consideration of other questions: What does the demotion of the good provider to the status of senior provider or even mere coprovider do to him? To marriage? To gender identity? What does expanding the role of housewife to that of junior provider or even coprovider do to her? To marriage? To gender identity? Much will of course depend on the social and psychological ambience in which changes take place.

A PARABLE

I began this essay with a proverbial woman. I close it with a modern parable by William H. Chafe (Note 5), a historian who also keeps his eye on the current scene. Jack and Jill, both planning professional careers, he as doctor, she as lawyer, marry at age 24. She works to put him through medical school in the expectation that he will then finance her through law school. A child is born during the husband's internship, as planned. But in order for him to support her through professional training as planned, he will have to take time out from his career. After two years, they decide that both will continue their training on a part-time basis, sharing household responsibilities and using day-care services. Both find part-time positions and work out flexible work schedules that leave both of them time for child care and companionship with one another. They live happily ever after.

That's the end? you ask incredulously. Well, not exactly. For, as Chafe (Note 5) points out, as usual the personal is also political:

> Obviously such a scenario presumes a radical transformation of the personal values that today's young people bring to their relationships as well as a readiness on the part of social and economic institutions to encourage, or at least make possible, the development of equality between men and women. (p. 28)

The good-provider role may be on its way out, but its legitimate successor has not yet appeared on the scene.

NOTES

[1] Hesselbart, S. *Some underemphasized issues about men, women, and work.* Unpublished manuscript, 1978.

[2] Douvan, E. *Family roles in a twenty-year perspective.* Paper presented at the Radcliffe Pre-Centennial Conference, Cambridge, Massachusetts, April 2–4, 1978.

[3] Veroff, J. *Psychological orientations to the work role: 1957–1976.* Unpublished manuscript, 1978.

[4] Shostak, A. *Working class Americans at home: Changing expectations of manhood.* Unpublished manuscript, 1973.

[5] Chafe, W. *The challenge of sex equality: A new culture or old values revisited?* Paper presented at the Radcliffe Pre-Centennial Conference, Cambridge, Massachusetts, April 2–4, 1978.

REFERENCES

Babcock, B., Freedman, A. E., Norton, E. H., & Ross, S. C. *Sex discrimination and the law: Causes and remedies.* Boston: Little, Brown, 1975.

Bernard, J. *Women, wives, mothers.* Chicago: Aldine, 1975.

Bernard, J. Homosociality and female depression. *Journal of Social Issues,* 1976, *32,* 207–224.

Boulding, E. Familial constraints on women's work roles. *SIGNS: Journal of Women in Culture and Society,* 1976, *1,* 95–118.

Brenton, M. *The American male.* New York: Coward-McCann, 1966.

Burke, R. & Wier, T. Relationship of wives' employment status to husband, wife and pair satisfaction and performance. *Journal of Marriage and the Family,* 1976, *38,* 279–287.

David, D. S. & Brannon, R. (Eds.). *The forty-nine percent majority: The male sex role.* Reading, Mass.: Addison-Wesley, 1976.

Demos, J. The American family in past time. *American Scholar,* 1974, *43,* 422–446.

Farrell, W. *The liberated man.* New York: Random House, 1974.

Fasteau, M. F. *The male machine.* New York: McGraw-Hill, 1974.

Fiedler, L. *Love and death in the American novel.* New York: Meredith, 1962.

Foner, P. S. *Women and the American labor movement.* New York: Free Press, 1979.

Freud, S. *Civilization and its discontents.* New York: Doubleday-Anchor, 1958. (Originally published, 1930.)

Goldberg, H. *The hazards of being male.* New York: New American Library, 1976.

Gould, R. E. Measuring masculinity by the size of a paycheck. In J. H. Pleck & J. Sawyer (Eds.). *Men and masculinity.* Englewood Cliffs, N.J.: Prentice-Hall, 1974. (Also published in *Ms.,* June 1973, pp. 18ff.)

Hall, D. & Hall, F. *The two-career couple.* Reading, Mass.: Addison-Wesley, 1979.

Jones, C. A. *A review of child support payment performance.* Washington, D.C.: Urban Institute, 1976.

Keniston, K. *The uncommitted: Alienated youth in American society.* New York: Harcourt, Brace & World, 1965.

Komarovsky, M. *The unemployed man and his family.* New York: Dryden Press, 1940.

Lefkowitz, B. Life without work. *Newsweek,* May 14, 1979, p. 31.

Lein, L. Responsibility in the allocation of tasks. *Family Coordinator,* 1979, *28,* 489–496.

Liebow, E. *Tally's corner.* Boston: Little, Brown, 1966.

Lopata, H. *Occupation housewife.* New York: Oxford University Press, 1971.

Mainardi, P. The politics of housework. In R. Morgan (Ed.), *Sisterhood is powerful.* New York: Vintage Books, 1970.

Pleck, J. H. & Lang, L. Men's family work: Three perspectives and some new data. *Family Coordinator,* 1979, *28,* 481–488.

Pleck, J. H. & Sawyer, J. (Eds.), *Men and masculinity.* Englewood Cliffs, N.J.: Prentice-Hall, 1974.

Rainwater, L. & Yancy, W. L. *The Moynihan report and the politics of controversy.* Cambridge, Mass.: M.I.T. Press, 1967.

Sarason, S. B. *Work, aging, and social change.* New York: Free Press, 1977.

Scanzoni, J. H. *Sex roles, life styles, and childbearing: Changing patterns in marriage and the family.* New York: Free Press, 1975.

Scanzoni, J. H. An historical perspective on husband-wife bargaining power and marital dissolution. In G. Levinger & O. Moles (Eds.), *Divorce and separation in America.* New York: Basic Books, 1979.

Smith, R. E. (Ed.), *The subtle revolution.* Washington, D.C.: Urban Institute, 1979.

Smuts, R. W. *Women and work in America.* New York: Columbia University Press, 1959.

Snyder, L. The deserting, non-supporting father: Scapegoat of family non-policy. *Family Coordinator,* 1979, *38,* 594–598.

Tocqueville, A. de. *Democracy in America.* New York: J. & H. G. Langley, 1840.

Warner, W. L. & Ablegglen, J. O. *Big business leaders in America.* New York: Harper, 1955.

Yankelovich, D. The new psychological contracts at work. *Psychology Today*, May 1978, pp. 46–47; 49–50.

Zborowski, M. & Herzog, E. *Life is with people.* New York: Schocken Books, 1952.

Anthony Astrachan
MEN AND THE NEW ECONOMY

Pete used to be proud of the work he did as a machinist in an auto parts factory. Now he's just tired—and scared. Half the workers in his plant have been laid off because carmakers have been buying parts from Japan. On top of that, his company is automating in order to compete. "That means they only need a quarter of the workers they used to." Pete says, "and if they move the plant or write new job descriptions that get around the union and seniority, they can hire women. With the computer running the operation they don't need my muscle. And they don't need my skill with the lathe and the drill presses anymore. Work gets simple enough and they turn it over to the girls."

Pete is one of the many men in the United States who see themselves as casualties of the changes occurring in the workplace over the past 30 years. Some, like Pete, string together complaints about imports, automation, and women as though they were all part of the same great shift.

In fact, men are facing very different kinds of change. One thing these changes have in common, however: They alter the nature of work itself. In the United States more than in other countries, and for men more than for women, what you do defines who you are. A man's work is an important part of his identity as a man.

ECONOMICS VS. MAN THE PROVIDER

Historically, men grew up expecting to provide for themselves and for their family. Providing was a man's job—whether he did it as doctor or lawyer, merchant or corporate executive, cop or soldier, auto worker or miner.

Today the role of man as provider is being transformed, and economic change is the main force responsible. Note the measure of the shift: In 1960, 83.3 percent of all men over the age of 16 were in the labor force; in 1985, it was 76.2 percent. By contrast, 37.7 percent of women 16 and over were in the labor force in 1960, but the figure had risen to 54.4 percent by 1985.

Men are no longer the sole providers for their families. The traditional family—a husband who goes out to work while his wife stays home and raises children—now accounts for only 10.7 percent of U.S. households. Now, more than 32 percent of all households are two-earner families in which the wife shares the role of provider.

There are two reasons for these changes. First, the cycle of inflation and recession and the shift from manufacturing to services have produced an economy in which the family needs more than one income to live decently or even survive. Second, rising competition from imports, dwindling jobs in manufacturing, the high Reagan budget, and growing trade deficits occurring over the past five years have helped to destroy thousands of the jobs that enabled men to provide.

IMPORTS AND JOBS

The boom in imports has had so much impact in everyday life and in the media recently that we may forget it's part of a broader decline in manufacturing and connected with the switch from smokestack to high-tech industry over the past 20 years. Economists estimate that we have lost about 2 million jobs, 30,000 of them in the textile industry alone, since the U.S. dollar and U.S. imports started to climb in 1981. The rise in imports and the fall in manufacturing seem like statistical abstractions, but the abstract soon becomes concrete: Brown Shoe Company of St. Louis closed eight of its 30 domestic shoe plants and bought a company that imports Italian shoes; Caterpillar Tractor cut its total work force by a third; Dixie Yarns in Chattanooga spun 45 percent less yarn in 1985 than the year before.

Then the statistics hit home: Theodore McBryar, a 43-year-old Dixie Yarns dye-machine operator, made only half as much in 1985 as he did the year before and couldn't afford to replace his 1973 Chevrolet, which had 213,000 miles on it when *U.S. News* reported his plight. Kevin Englert, 30, a roving tender at the same mill, couldn't buy his three children new clothes for last school year. That kind of hardship undermines a man's faith in himself. A man unable to "do his job" as provider has lost more than just money.

Ironically, the economic policies that have hurt traditional men (and traditional corporations) by bringing on the import crisis came from the conservative administration of Ronald Reagan, whose supporters labor so hard—and most fruitlessly—in behalf of traditional values in both personal and economic life.

TECHNOLOGY VS. A "MAN'S JOB"

Automation, like economics, brings losses beyond jobs or money. "A man's job" once required skill, strength, and the ability to work long hours—all admirable qualities that used to be thought of as exclusively male. Thanks to technological advances, many such jobs now require less and less skill in the use of a worker's hands, eyes, and judgment. Pride and craftsmanship become irrelevant.

This seems brand new, something very modern. In fact, it's the latest stage in a long historical process that began with the Industrial Revolution and the development of factories 200 years ago and gathered force with the invention of the assembly line in the early years of this century.

Today's jobs require more and more obedience to company rules and the tyranny of electronic monitoring. Management often translates these new conditions to mean that the work has become suitable for women, whom they see as reliable, punctual workers who like repetitive work and believe that they profit when the company does. Male managers, in fact, do not try to hide this. Most technological changes in one factory "were of a type that would tend to increase the percentage of women. For example, we have broken down the alignment of components and simplified [the] job, and as the jobs called for less skill, they became women's work." That was one New Jersey executive quoted in Georgina Smith's study of the job market, which cited many more.

WOMEN IN MEN'S JOBS

The arrival of women in the workplace, particularly in what were once labeled masculine occupations, is a social and psychological shift that is more significant and far reaching than the economic changes caused by the five-year boom in imports or by automation, though these may have higher and more visible immediate costs.

A woman employed in what was once called a man's job is a more radical departure from tradition because she violates a division of labor that goes back millennia. She is also more universal. Imports hurt some industries, automation primarily affects factory workers, but we all meet this working woman, whether or not we are employed. She is in every kind of work and from every racial and ethnic group.

The idea that a woman can and should do "a man's job" is the product of social and psychological forces that are reshaping both the male role as provider and the male monopoly on certain occupations.

These powerful traditions deprived women of independence and equality, confining them to low-paid work that brought few of the satisfactions of mastery and achievement that many of us find so necessary for happiness. For the past 20 years women have been fighting to do away with these restrictions on equality and power. Their struggle has produced changes in U.S. politics, culture, and psychology. They have shown that the old strengths and skills and the ability to work long hours that were needed for what used to be seen as a man's job are not exclusively male—or even often required now. The number of women has increased in many occupations, from factory worker to police officer to corporate manager to physician—18 percent of blue-collar workers and 16 percent of doctors and lawyers, for example, are now women.

Frequently overlooked, however, is the part economic forces have played in these changes. Women have been pushed in this direction by the same shifts that have done so much to change the role of work in men's lives.

This affects both men's acceptance of change and their resistance to it. Most men recognize the injustice of the old division of labor and have learned to live with some of the ways women are changing that division. Our acceptance reflects recognition of many realities—a family needs two incomes to survive; women perform as well as men in many jobs; women have the right to equal opportunity in any occupation they choose.

But for most men, I believe, resistance is still stronger than acceptance. The very economic necessities that bring women into "a man's job" underline the erosion of the male role as provider and thus produce conflict. Polls that show acceptance must be seen in this context. It appears that many men give pollsters views that they think are socially acceptable, but behave differently. A recent survey by the *Harvard Business Review*, for instance, shows that only 5 percent of male executives have an unfavorable view of female executives, compared to 41 percent in 1965. But more than half the men surveyed made $100,000 or more a year, while only 10 percent of the women did. However low the expressed bias, many women attribute such measurable discrimination to male resistance.

Most men can't accept that a woman no longer devotes herself primarily to housekeeping and childcare, even though they know it's true and still value her as a partner. It is hard to welcome change when the myths and emotions of the traditional system remain strong. It's especially hard when men are confronted at the same time with such economic and technological changes, just described, that damage or destroy many of the satisfactions of work that might otherwise survive the introduction of women into the workplace. Generally, men find it more difficult to feel support for the women they work with than a wife or daughter going out to face a similar situation.

My own research indicates that most men also feel some combination of anger, fear, and anxiety toward women in traditionally masculine jobs, often treating women co-workers in any or all of three ways. They show *hostility;* *deny* their competence, sometimes their very presence; or *transform* them in fantasy—into nuns, whores, lovers, mothers, wives, daughters, sisters—any role that allows them to treat women as traditional females rather than peers.

These behaviors take different forms in different occupations. Hostility is often expressed sexually. Some factory workers, for instance, put porn pictures in their tool chests and display them when women workers walk by. Suggestive propositions and other forms of sexual harassment directed at women are common occurrences in offices. Recruiters from the investment banking firm Goldman, Sachs asked women at Stanford University if they would have an abortion rather than jeopardize their careers, thus attacking both their right and their ability to combine motherhood and career.

Denial is what's being expressed by the committee of men who direct all their comments to the man from the ad agency, though the woman on the team, sitting next to him at the table, is his boss and the designer of the campaign. It's denial also when men insist that most women are not as career-oriented as men, despite statistics showing that in many industries women in technical, professional, supervisory, and managerial positions have the same rate of turnover as men.

Transformation can take forms as nasty as a sexual assault on a woman coal miner or as "innocent" as a request by a male executive that his female colleague sew on an errant button for him, thus transforming her into a mother.

THE BRIGHT SIDE

The fearsome changes discussed here are changes in work that alter the shape of society and of individual lives, that change the very way we see ourselves as men. The answer to these threats isn't to block imports, stop automation, or deny women the right to work. It's to find ways that government, corporations, and individuals can cushion the effects of change.

One way is to remember that in every change there's a bright side as well as a dark side. In every case, the promise can alter our lives as much as the threat does.

On the economic front, for instance, the threat of imports has been accompanied by the arrival of foreign firms to build factories here that may make up for some of the jobs lost, like Komatsu, the Japanese manufacturer of earth-moving machines, in Chattanooga.

Technology has improved living standards for everyone and working conditions for the people who master new tools. It can lead to increased responsibility and demand higher skills in operators, as Paul Adler points out in his book *Dollars and Sense*. Responsibility increases because machines cost more and produce more. Operators need higher skills because they must understand the control program logic well enough to correct errors on the line or help write new programs. When the Communications Workers of America polled members in 1979, about 78 percent said technological change had increased the skill requirements of their jobs.

A woman in "a man's job" constitutes a more personal challenge to a man than economic or technological change. It's a challenge he meets at home as well as at work, in his gut, often in his crotch, as well as in his head. Despite or because of the challenge she represents, a man can probably enrich his life more by learning to work with women in his kind of job than by switching jobs to escape the threat of imports or mastering automation.

Men can start by seeking the positive emotions that are generated by the arrival of women in the workplace, and by their assertion of equality. These emotions are admiration, identification, and pleasure. Such feelings produce positive behavior—acceptance, support, and association.

I also believe a man can work with a woman in "her kind" of job. A small but increasing number of men are now sharing the work of raising their children. They find it enriches both their own and their children's lives.

Few men, however, even those who welcome women as peers, do literally half the household work. There will always be economic crises and technological changes that alter our work patterns, but society will truly be transformed only when men do half the work of childcare and take half the responsibility for it from the moment of birth. Unhappily, we can't take more than a small step toward this day until individuals and trade unions, government and corporations, change the way work is organized.

Ian Harris

MEDIA MYTHS AND THE REALITY OF MEN'S WORK

The dominant image of the American male portrayed on television, in film, and in magazines depicts a white collar gentleman living in the suburbs in affluent circumstances. These individuals own American Express credit cards and buy the latest model cars. Images of these men occupy a powerful place in the American psyche and set standards for male behavior. They run the media and the large corporations. They speak to us through radios and television. They teach our children. They care for us when we are sick. They are not only standard bearers but also the image makers who provide a model for male expectations.

Reprinted from *Media and Values*, Spring 1990.

Advertising campaigns used to promote American products create the deceptive myth that the majority of men enjoy the privileges of white collar professional status. However, few men actually achieve the images of success provided by American media industries. As indicated by the accompanying table, the vast majority of men do not occupy white collar professional jobs. Men wishing to build a broad based men's movement with men from all different social classes must dispel the myth of the successful white collar professional and understand the varied life experiences of men in the United States.

Occupational Categories of Men in the United States*

Total Male Population in 1980	110,032,000	
Non-institutionalized Men over Age 16	79,642,000	
Men in Active Labor Force**	62,088,000	
Unemployed Men	4,157,000	
Employed Men	55,988,000	(100%)
Blue Collar Occupations	25,110,000	(45%)
Non-Professional/Technical Occupations	15,049,000	(27%)
Professional White Collar Occupations	8,692,000	(15%)
Service and Farm Occupations	7,137,000	(13%)

* Taken from *Statistical Abstract of the U.S.*, 1981, pp. 380–383.
** This category does not include 866,400 men who are in the armed forces, retired, discouraged workers, or in institutions.

THE REALITY OF MEN'S WORK

Of those men fortunate enough to be employed at all, most work in jobs where they cannot live out "the American dream" as portrayed by the media. The individuals who fit the category "Males in Professional White Collar Occupations" in the table account for only 15% of all employed men, or 8% of the total male population. Nonetheless, it would be overly simplistic to conclude that only this small percentage of men consider themselves successful. The non-professional technical occupations, representing an additional 27% of employed men, include engineers, skilled craftsmen, and other technicians who experience relatively high status and success. Some men in blue collar occupations and service and farm occupations also earn good salaries and, by their own accounts, feel successful in their work and in their lives. Yet men in all classes are affected by white collar professional images broadcast through the media and may strive for the affluence and perceived success of white collar men.

That few actually achieve the status of white collar professionals has severe consequences. Raised in a society that honors the Horatio Alger myth, most men believe that a man who works hard will get ahead. Sex role standards for men describe a life where American men are supposed to be good fathers, contribute to their communities, and occupy positions of power. The reality of men's lives, however, is very different from these expectations. A 1984 U.S. Bureau of Census publication calculates a median income of $15,600 for men fifteen years or older,[1] which is not so far above the poverty threshold of $10,609 for a family of four in 1984.[2] With half the men in the United States earning less than $15,600, it is evident that millions of males do not enjoy the status popularly ascribed to American men in the media. Indeed, only twenty-nine percent of men in the United States make $25,000 or more, an amount that would allow some to approach the standards of consumerism expected of successful men.

The media myth that most men enjoy or have access to the material benefits of the successful white collar professional is obviously a hoax. Most men will never get status jobs. As indicated in the table, the vast majority of men either work in occupations other than white collar, are institutionalized, are unemployed or have dropped out of the active work force. However, their stories are not told in the media, and their plight is ignored.

The forty-five percent of working men in blue collar jobs 'man' the factories and other skilled and unskilled trades. Many do not have college educations. They constitute what sociologists refer to as the working class. Stuck in positions that offer little or no opportunities for advancement, these men labor in jobs that are often dull, repetitive, and dangerous. They usually have little or no control over their work conditions. This group is increasingly threatened when corporate leaders modernize plants with labor saving devices, move industrial production to third world countries, and close down factories in those parts of the United States that have heavily unionized work forces. From the 1950s until approximately 1978 this group of men enjoyed some economic security, and media images of the happy, beer-drinking blue collar worker abounded. However, the current recession has eliminated millions of their jobs and threatened their emotional health and economic well being. Most of these men feel inadequate in the face of a dominant media culture which venerates executives in three piece suits.[3] They blame themselves for their failure to live up to standards set forth in the culture, while envying other men for achieving success when they cannot achieve their goals.

The thirteen percent of working men in service and farm occupations are suffering acutely in the current U.S. economy. Farm employment has been reduced drastically over the years because mechanization has required less labor on American farms. Those farmers who have been able to keep working are currently having dreams of economic security eroded as high interest rates and competition from abroad catches them in desperate economic circumstances they can't control. Life on the farm is fast becoming a nightmare in an epidemic of farm foreclosures where men have to abandon lifestyles they have struggled to establish.

Current economic statistics indicate that the service sector is expanding. However, these jobs, many of which are located in convenience fast food industries and janitorial positions, are not unionized and pay far less than the jobs men used to have on farms and in blue collar occupations. Without unions to support them, men in service occupations have few benefits such as health care or pensions and enjoy little job security.

Even though men in blue collar, service and farm occupations are excluded from achieving "the American dream," it is not correct to assume that men in professional white-collar occupations (or nonprofessional technical jobs, for that matter) lead more fulfilling lives. Identifying with the goals of the various institutions they work for—corporations, law firms, universities, government agencies, and social service organizations—they see themselves advancing up a career ladder to achieve greater security and power. However, the number of positions at the top are very limited. Rather than fulfilling their dreams of success, most of these men fall far short. They don't get into prestigious schools. They don't land a job with a large agency. They don't receive promotions. And as they get older, they often are dismissed and replaced by younger men who receive lower salaries. Far from leading successful careers, the majority of white collar men spend their lives battling within highly competitive organizations that are so stressful that working within them predisposes them to cancer, heart attacks, and other stress related diseases.

Some men who were trained to occupy white collar occupations have "dropped out" and are working in low paying jobs to support themselves and pursue nonmaterialistic goals. Many in leadership positions in the antisexist men's movement come from this class of white collar workers. Most are college graduates, working in helping professions as social workers, community organizers, therapists, or educators. Most do not earn the glamorous salaries depicted on television and their understanding of the reality of men's lives leads them to seek solutions to the problems that characterize men's and women's lives.

THE UNDERCLASS

Of special concern are men in the underclass.[4] Underclass men lead desperate lives. They do not really "belong" in regular labor force statistics at all. They are migrant workers, prisoners, welfare recipients, homeless street people, and patients in mental hospitals. Seventy percent of these men belong to minority groups. They exist in violent worlds where they have to fight—often unsuccessfully—to survive.

Underclass men do not have regular work. Their hustles for survival include robbery, pimping, drug pushing and other illegal activities. Many end up in prison when they break the law to earn their livelihood. In fact, prison becomes a sort of brutal haven to escape the viciousness of the street. After a prison term many try desperately to get low paying unskilled work, where they slave in poverty for the rest of their lives. For the thousands of men who live in this class, life has no future, few possessions and little purpose. As children, some may dream of becoming professional sports stars, but most stop working in school because they see that striving to "do better" is a waste of time.[5] The stresses of living in substandard circumstances without decent health care and economic security create a situation where these men have higher death rates, higher rates of major fatal diseases, and higher levels of institutionalization than any other sector of the population.[6] In a recent interview Claude Brown, the author of *Manchild in the Promised Land*, indicated that youth on the streets of Harlem feel they have nothing to lose. And with an unemployment rate of 50% for minority youth, this feeling is understandable. Therefore they go for broke and have few qualms about committing violent crimes. He quoted a young man as saying, "If I get caught or maimed, I become the state's responsibility; if I'm killed, my problems are really over.[7] Many of these men are filled with anger at a system that denies them access to the cultural norm of success for American males.

ALIENATION FROM WORK

Whether employed or unemployed, whether blue or white collar, men in the United States share a common alienation regarding the conditions of their employment. This alienation is rooted in the realization that a man's work (or lack of work) is at odds with fulfilling personal goals and becoming the sort of person he wishes to be. For middle class men this alienation is mostly psychological and is derived from stress on the job and/or frustrations in personal life. For men in the lower classes (including the underclass) male alienation is compounded by economic oppression: men are denied employment opportunities, access to services, retirement incomes, etc. The problems these men face also include a lack of civil rights, justice, safety, and decent housing. These fundamental inequalities manifest psychologically as a sense of alienation from the cultural norms of society.

Male frustration and alienation result in part from the discrepancy between the norms of success expected of men as fathers and heads-of-households and the reality of their personal lives which falls far short of the affluent circumstances depicted by the media. In 1984 the median family income in the United States was approximately $24,000.[8] Although a disproportionate number of female-headed households fall below the median, this statistic indicates that millions of men and their families can't live up to media images of success and affluence. Even if these men earn an income close to the median, they probably can't afford a house, a new car, or a vacation that allows them to escape. They can't fulfill the traditionally masculine "provider" role by paying for their children's education or allowing their spouses to stay home. Current economic pressures have forced most families into situations where both husband and wife work. This has had severe consequences for the traditional nuclear family, as evidenced by the increased rate of divorce. In a society with such high economic demands, many men have to borrow large amounts of money. They spend their lives struggling to pay off debts with little or no sense of comfort about their economic circumstances. Feeling constantly overwhelmed contributes to men's sense of inadequacy about their role as providers and their inability to achieve standards so abundantly displayed in the American culture.

The hierarchical structure and requirements of most men's work places severe demands on men and their families and friends. In modern industrial society men who are employed sell their labor power to others who determine the conditions of employment. Thus, they are totally dependent upon a wage for living. To accede to the demands of the workplace, men alienate themselves from supportive networks, such as family life. As a result of the all-consuming emphasis placed on work, most men neither spend time with children, nor participate equally in domestic chores. When women have primary responsibility for raising children, both boys and girls learn to turn to women and not men for emotional support, and men do not develop nurturing aspects of their personalities.

Unfortunately, male socialization does not help men cope with the realities of the modern workplace. Indeed, male training is designed to create good workers, not full human beings. The proscriptions against emotional expressiveness, sharing personal problems with others, or working cooperatively rather than competitively all exacerbate the sense of alienation men feel in their lives. To cope with deep felt insecurities from lack of job security, status, stable relationships and income, men learn to put up a facade that they are competent and in charge of their destiny. As a result of their learned inability to express feelings, men disclose less about themselves than women do; they are less insightful and empathic, less competent at loving, and more prone than women to manifest these tensions in stress-related illnesses.[9] The intense competitiveness of the workplace causes men to be distrustful and suspicious of their peers, preventing real communication and empathy with others on the job.

IMPLICATIONS FOR THE MEN'S MOVEMENT

Largely in response to the anger and frustration about the conditions most men find themselves in, some men have been organizing recently to address the problems stated above. Men concerned about these issues have joined support groups, questioned the validity of male sex roles, challenged the oppressive nature of pornography, promoted father's role in parenting, and created a movement to shatter masculine myths that set sex role expectations. However, the men's movement currently lacks a clear focus and a broad base. The leadership of this movement has come from the very narrow sector of the population that is college educated and holds white collar professional jobs ("the helping professions"). Most of the men active in the men's movement were raised in the middle class.[10] They are largely ignorant of the problems of most men in the United States, in part because the media seldom, if ever, realistically present underclass and working class existence. Because these men do not experience the problems of men in other occupational categories, their programs and demands do not relate to the complexity and variety of lifestyles of the vast majority of men in the United States.

Men from the professional managerial class represent a small proportion of the society that is perceived to benefit from the existing social order. If the men's movement wants to change the oppressive nature of the social system, it must support the struggles of working class men, minority men and under- class men. Men's movement activists must build coalitions with blue collar workers, with members of the underclass and with men whose struggles to survive create an urgency in their lives that makes it hard for them to relate to the "touchy-feely" environment of many men's movement gatherings. The men's movement must support the creation of institutions such as alternative schools, day care centers, worker owned industries, health care centers, community organizations, and labor unions where men from the underclass and working class will have leadership roles in decision-making and collective action.

Men working to improve American society need to identify the sources of male alienation and use these frustrations to build a political agenda that will draw support from the vast majority of men unable to achieve the myth of male success. Consciousness-raising groups are a useful organizing tool in providing supportive environments for men to seek personal solutions for their frustrations and sense of alienation. However, these consciousness- raising groups are inadequate for challenging social norms and political insti- tutions that place unreal demands on men in the United States.

What is required is an articulated political program for the men's movement that speaks to men's economic insecurities while challenging traditional male stereotypes. In order for a men's political agenda to have wide appeal, it will have to argue for full employment and address the need for better jobs. It will have to challenge the current economic trend to create jobs in the deadly defense sector at the expense of jobs in the social service sector. Underclass and working class men who are to join this movement will have to see the real benefits it offers them. These men will have to be convinced that the men's movement has developed a political agenda that will allow men and women to have some say over their work conditions; provide social services; provide jobs with livable wages and decent benefits; realize standards of justice and protect civil rights.

Those concerned with the limitations of traditional sex roles must realize that neither men nor women will attain any real liberation until the millions of men and women in the underclass and working class can enjoy economic security and social services to provide for their basic needs. The struggle to change sex role stereotypes has been hard. The growing men's movement must not be sidetracked by the notion that male liberation is a personal—not political—goal. We need to bury the popular myth that male success consists of making money. Let's create a new American myth where men are concerned human beings promoting a better life for all creatures on this planet. Liberation is a long and difficult struggle that requires the economic transformation of society as well as altering personal relationships. It will succeed only when men and women act together to attack the structures of class that dominate social living and to create new relationships and institutions that will command the respect of a desperate, alienated, and lonely population.

NOTES

[1] U.S. Department of Commerce. "Money Income and Poverty Status of Families and Persons in the United States, 1984." Series P-60, No. 149, August, 1985. (Washington, D.C.: U.S. Government Printing Office), p. 16.

[2] Ibid., p. 1.

[3] Jonathan Cobb and Richard Sennett, *The Hidden Injuries of Class* (New York: Knopf, 1972).

[4] It is very hard to know how many men exist in the underclass. Ken Auletta in his book, *The Underclass* (New York: Random House, 1982) says that the number varies from 2 million to 18 million depending on how the underclass is defined.

[5] See John Ogabu, *Minority Education and Caste: The American System in Cross Cultural Perspective*, (New York: Harcourt, Brace, Jovanovich, 1978).

[6] For an informative discussion of these problems see *Black Men*, Lawrence E. Gary, ed. (Beverley Hills: Sage Publications, 1984).

[7] " 'Manchild' of Today Has Become an 'Urban Monster'," *Milwaukee Journal*. March 23, 1986.

[8] *U.S. Statistical Abstract*, 1981, p. 471.

[9] Sidney Jourard, *The Transparent Self*, (New York: D. Van Nostrand Company, 1971).

[10] In 1983 I distributed a survey to the entire membership of the Great Lakes Men's Network. Forty percent of the membership of this organization responded. All of them were college graduates. Seventy percent worked in professional jobs. Twenty percent had graduate degrees.

David L. Collinson

'ENGINEERING HUMOUR':
MASCULINITY, JOKING AND CONFLICT IN SHOP-FLOOR RELATIONS

This article examines the interrelationship between humour and masculinity in the social relations of an all-male, shop-floor workforce. The analysis seeks not only to highlight the collective elements of this joking culture, but also to explore the contradictions and divisions which also characterized shop-floor relations.

It could be argued that the recurrent research finding of employee 'light-heartedness' demonstrates either that workers are generally satisfied with their fragmented tasks in the labour process or that they are able to 'let off steam' and so dissipate their frustration with deskilled and routinized jobs. For example, Roy (1958) describes how four machinists avoided 'going nuts' in the face of the 'beast of monotony' by constructing an informal group culture characterized by mock aggression and incessant teasing. Humour may also be the means by which *social* frustration and conflict can be expressed in ways that reduce hostility and maintain social order. Burawoy (1979) discovered that racial prejudice between blacks and whites was articulated in jokes on the shop-floor. Since the production process demanded a degree of worker co-operation, overt racial hostility had to be minimized and was therefore diluted in humour. Yet there is also a substantial amount of evidence suggesting that joking does not always constitute a shortcut to consensus and social harmony.

Willis' (1977) analysis of school counter-culture is particularly revealing in exposing the oppositional and collective properties of joking. He highlights how 'piss-taking' and intimidatory joking at school are creative elements in the oppositional group logic of the 'lads'. Their informal resistance provides an alternative definition of what it means to be successful to that offered by the dominant values of the education system. Willis (1977) shows how the 'false promise' of upward mobility through educational success is scorned by the lads, who pursue more immediate forms of gratification, excitement, and the establishment of male identity. The ability to produce a laugh is a defining characteristic of group membership. This working class joking culture establishes a non-conformist, highly masculine, sense of identity for its members, which celebrates practical manual work, and ridicules passive, unmanly mental work, both in school and employment.

Willis' (1979) analysis is particularly illuminating in its linkage of working class group culture, masculinity, joking and resistance. Nevertheless, it contains a tendency to *romanticize* the lads' joking culture. This is revealed in a failure to explore fully, the contradictions of both the joking culture itself and the search to secure a masculine identity that is mediated through shop-floor humour. Admittedly, he highlights the paradoxical consequence of the lads' resistance, which, in celebrating working class life as a form of freedom, encourages them to seek out precisely those manual jobs, through which their subordination is guaranteed. Yet the internal divisions of the group culture

Reprinted from *Organization Studies* 1988, 9/2: 181–199 © 1988 EGOS.

and the destructive and self-defeating consequences of the search to realise this masculine identity are left under-explored.

In failing to question the lads' proud boastings and often apocryphal accounts of their culture, Willis (1977) neglects to examine the deep-seated social and psychological insecurities which reflect and reinforce their concern to establish and embellish gender and group identity. In one-sidedly treating identify constructions as expressions of resistance, 'the darker side' of shop-floor humour tends to be neglected in Willis' (1977) analysis. As the following case study will demonstrate, the preoccupation with defending and protecting self through humour is a powerful logic, that not only defines the boundaries of, but can also generate divisions within, the group.

The data emerged out of research conducted between 1979 and 1983 in a lorry-making factory in the North West of England (Collinson, 1981). The research, which was approved by the management, concentrated in the components division of the plant. This consisted of the departments of fabrication; axle assembly; toolroom; loading bay; paint spray; stores and two machine shops. The division employed an exclusively male workforce of 250, the vast majority of whom were classified as skilled engineers. Interviews with over sixty of these workers were conducted by the writer on a regular basis and were supplemented by non-participant observation. The primary focus of the research was management/shop-floor industrial relations. Yet, as the research progressed, a recognition of the significance of humour, in this all-male, shop-floor context, simultaneously emerged. The humour of the components division was a crucial mechanism through which shop-floor relations and practices were mediated. It reflected and reinforced the central values and practices of these male manual workers and contained elements of resistance and control, creativity and destructiveness. These contrasting elements of the joking culture will now be elaborated in turn.

HUMOUR AS RESISTANCE

Shop-floor humour was in part a form of resistance both to the tightly controlled repetitous work tasks and to the social organization of production within the company. The spontaneous and cutting creativity of shop-floor banter was indeed conditioned by a desire to make the best of the situation and to enjoy the company of others. Many of the workers themselves saw the humorous reparte as a way of dealing with the monotonous work itself, as one told me,

> 'Some days it feels like a fortnight. A few years ago I got into a rut. I had to stop myself getting bored so I increased the number of pranks at work.'

'Having a laff' allowed these men to resist their mundane circumstances, providing the illusion of separation from an otherwise alienating situation. In addition, this frivolity and absurdity reflected and reinforced a shared sense of self and group identity and differentiation. This was illustrated by the following comment,

> 'He's writing a book about this place, it'll be a best seller, bigger than Peyton Place with all the characters in here!'

The men were concerned to show that they were 'big enough' to laugh at themselves. Joking reflected the nature of the person. This collective self identity as a community of comedians was strengthened by the reputations of its members. These were often preserved in nicknames that were based on exaggerated and stereotypes personal characteristics. Their daily use in shop-floor discourse helped to create a mythical and imaginary world that sustained a distance from boredom and routine.

'Fat Rat', 'Bastard Jack', 'Big Lemon' and 'The Snake' were names conjured up daily in the components division. 'Electric Lips' was unable to keep secrets. 'Pot Harry' was so nicknamed because, as a teaboy, thirty years before, he had dropped and broken all the drinking 'pots'. 'Tom Pepper' was reputed to have never spoken the truth in his life. Another man was known as 'Yoyo' because of his habit of walking away and then returning during a conversation and even in mid-sentence. His 'Yoyo' record had been calculated as fifteen returns in one conversation. Although exaggerated, these culture identities contributed to shop-floor cohesion by developing a shared sense of masculinity. For only 'real men' would be able to laugh at themselves by accepting highly insulting nicknames.

The joking culture also facilitated manual workers' self-differentiation from, and antagonism to, white collar staff and managers. This defensive stance was partly the result of the conditions of shop-floor experience, which threatened the workers' sense of dignity. Of all company employees, those on the shop-floor worked the longest hours in the most insecure and tightly controlled jobs, enjoyed the worst canteen and car park facilities and the poorest holiday, pension and sickness provision. These conditions confirmed to shop-floor workers that they were the least valued and most easily disposable of employees.

'Dirty Bar' displayed how manual workers typically dealt with this degrading experience. He emphasized how manual work was the very essence of masculinity,

> 'Fellas on the shop-floor are genuine. They're the salt of the earth, but they're all twats and nancy boys in th'offices.'

Like 'the lads', the fellas on the shop-floor perceived their own joking culture to be a symbol of freedom and autonomy, which contrasted with the more reserved work conditions and character of the office staff. The uncompromising banter of the shop-floor, which was permeated by uninhibited swearing, mutual ridicule, displays of sexuality and 'pranks', was contrasted, exaggerated and elevated above the middle class politeness, cleanliness and more restrained demeanour of the offices. Ironically, when compared with others, the subordinated world of the shop-floor came to be seen as a free space in which the 'true self' could be expressed, as another worker put it,

> 'You can have a load of fun on the shop-floor, but in the offices, they're not the type to have a laff and a joke. You can't say 'you fucking twat!" in the offices.'

In a similar way, the joking culture reflected and reinforced the sense of 'us and them' in relations with the management. The perceived conformism of managers and their reputed inability to make decisions led to them being nicknamed 'the yes men', and to being ridiculed as effeminate. On one occasion, as a result of a workforce 'go-slow', a significant shortfall occurred on management's projected production levels. This stimulated the axle shop steward to joke,

>'(The production manager) will have a baby when he sees these figures.'

Shop-floor humour directed at managers was usually concerned to negate and distance them, as Figure 1 illustrates.

The irony that three foremen had not been informed of a course in communication skills, to which they had been assigned, was not lost on many shop-floor workers. In general, however, shop-floor humour tended to remain within the confines of the group culture.

By contrast, management repeatedly sought to engage shop stewards in humorous interaction. Yet, the stewards were aware that managerial humour was intended to obscure conflict behind personalized relations, which tried to deny the hierarchical structure of status and power. Hence they avoided participating, for as the AUEW convenor explained,

>'You've always got to retain a difference from management because they try to draw you in.'

Six years earlier the company had been taken over by an American multinational. The personal approach of the new regime had been rejected by the stewards,

>'At first they tried to come on a bit, but we didn't think much of their jokes.'

As part of the American's campaign to win the trust of the workforce, a company in-house magazine was introduced. The paper was dismissed widely as a 'Let's be pals act' and nicknamed by the convenor as 'Goebbel's Gazette.' This criticism stimulated a 'jokey' response in the paper by the editors,

>'Did you know that 'X' is being called Goebbel's Gazette in some quarters?'

When the body was first made all parts wanted to be SUPERVISORS.
The Brain insisted. 'Since I control everything and do all the thinking, I should be Supervisor.'
The Feet said, 'Since we carry man where he wants to go, we should be Supervisors.' The Hands said, 'Since we do all the work and earn all the money to keep the rest of you going, we should be Supervisors.' The Eyes too staked their claim, 'Since we must watch out for all of you, we should be Supervisors.'
An so it went on: the Heart; the Ears and finally . . . the BUM! How all the other parts laughed to think the Bum should be Supervisor!!!
Thus the Bum became mad and refused to function. The Brain became feverish: the Eyes crossed and ached: the Legs got wobbly and the Stomach went sick.
ALL pleaded with the Brain to relent and let the Bum be Supervisor. And so it came to be. That all the other parts did their work and the Bum simply Supervised and passed a load of CRAP.

* * *

MORAL: You don't have to be a Brain to be a Supervisor—only a Bum.

Figure 1. Joke Found on the Trade Union Noticeboard.

'No I didn't, but thank you for bringing it to my Achtung'

'Don't get me wrong, but it is propaganda isn't it?'

'If propaganda is informing everyone on topics which previously were known to only a handful of people, the answer is "Yes". We do concentrate on the plus points of the company but so what? Our performance compares favourably with the company's plants anywhere in the world, so why present any other picture?'

The intention of managerial humour, to reduce conflict and emphasize organizational harmony, had the opposite effect of merely reinforcing the polarization between management and shop-floor.

HUMOUR AS CONFORMITY

The joking culture was based as much on the internal demands of group conformity as on collective resistance. These demands were enbedded in specific rules that simulated the 'laws' of natural selection. Social 'survival of the fittest' was the underlying principle behind the pressure to be able to give and take a joke, to laugh at oneself and expect others to respond likewise to cutting remarks. The men in the components division were concerned to be how others expected them to be. Defensively engaged in the mock battles of male sparring, bluff and bravado, it was expected that these workers would be aggressive, critical and disrespectful, so as to create embarrassment in others. For this was the symbolic scalp of the successful 'piss-take', as one engineer explained,

> 'You've got to give it or go under. It's a form of survival, you insult first before they get one back. The more you get embarrassed, the more they do it, so you have to fight back. It can hurt deep down, although you don't show it.'

and his workmate interjected 'you'll learn fuck all there!' to which he responded 'You see what I mean, you've got to get the knife in the back first.' Behind this image of toughness, masculinity and an apparent ability to withstand ridicule from others was an acknowledgement that the jibes could, and did sometimes, hurt, as one man privately conceded,

> 'I detest being embarrassed, so I take the piss out of the others.'

Nevertheless, in adhering to the rules of social survival, workers prided themselves on their predatory ability to 'pounce' on the weaknesses of their colleagues, so as to 'wind them up', as Jack exemplified,

> 'I can get Fred going easy. Friday, I pointed to the foreman's cabin and said, "I can remember when you said, That was going to be mine!" Then he was at it all afternoon.'

Some were 'bullet makers' and some were 'firers' of the joking attacks, which were considered to be skilled penetrations of other's weaknesses. Practical jokes in particular 'sounded out' their victims, who had to show that they could 'stand' being the object of humour. For example, an amateur weightlifter was assured that he would not be able to lift Allan, because the latter could increase his weight at will. The weightlifter failed. This was because

Allan had nailed his shoes to the duckboard and therefore the man was trying to lift Allan, the board, and himself. The element of surprise was also exploited to maximum effect in practical jokes, like the 'plastic spider trick', as Allan again outlined,

> 'It was fucking essence with Brown and the spider. It was his first day back from illness and he was reading so we lowered it over his shoulder. He finished up fighting with it.'

Newcomers to the shop-floor, in particular, were quickly informed of the requirements for group acceptance. Apprentices, for example, had to negotiate a series of degrading and humiliating initiation ceremonies. Such ceremonies were viewed by their perpetrators as worthwhile experience, and as real learning about taking a joke and being a man. Being able to take a joke was a sign that the lessons of the shop-floor had been learnt.

Exposure to the joking culture, not only instructed new members on how to act and react, but also constituted a test of the willingness of initiates to be part of the male group and to accept its rules. For example, one apprentice had to sing Christmas carols to the rest of the workforce as part of his initiation in 'bringing me out of meself',

> 'There were three of us. It was embarrassing but everybody does it, so you accept it, you've got to "laff back", it's the only way. I used to get embarrassed easy, but not now here.'

Similarly, pancake Tuesday was celebrated by 'greasing the bollocks' of the apprentices with emulsion and then 'locking them in the shithouse, bollock naked.' The lads had to 'take it', in order to survive on the shop-floor. Having graduated through these degradation ceremonies, they would be recognized as mature men worthy of participating fully in the shop-floor culture and banter. That is, if they could also 'take' the daily practical jokes, for which their lack of knowledge made them ideal victims, as one engineer exemplified,

> 'I like shocking the apprentices. A classic is sending one of the lads for a "a long stand". They go over and say, "Bob sent me for a long stand". The other bloke'll say "O.K.' and then after a while he'll say, "Is that long enough?" "Fucking hell" the apprentice will think.'

But some failed the test as the same engineer complained,

> 'The new apprentice is religious and looks away from women. I'm really pissed off with him because you can't have a caper with him.'

Those who were perceived to be 'different' were either kept at a distance, or had to accept incorporation into the joking culture on its own terms. For example, the story of one lad, who entered the company with 'diplomas galore', was often recited,

> 'They had a French letter on his back by ten o'clock. They had him singing and dancing in the loo with the pretext of practicing for a pantomime . . . we soon brought him round to our way of thinking.'

These practical jokes enabled manual workers to alleviate any feelings of inferiority by undermining the sense of superiority assumed to be harboured by this lad.

I too had to be trained to 'think correctly', and was rechristened by members of the culture, who were attempting to transcend the uncertainty and 'strangeness' of my presence and observation of their world. Surprised that anyone could be paid 'just for going around talking to people', I was seen as 'something to do with psychiatry', which my new shop-floor nicknames reflected. Different areas of the factory created different names for me, such as 'Dr. Bob', 'the Headshrinker', 'Rand and Rave', (rhymes with Dave) 'The Absent-minded Professor' and 'The Lardee-da University Lad'. When these comments became open criticisms, it seemed to represent a humorous sign of partial acceptance, at least on their terms, into the cultural fabric. Yet, the motive was not merely the production of humour. Behind such comments as 'Keep your business out of our fucking nose' and 'He'll have you talking all day will this sod!' was a real warning that I was 'sniffing' in places that ought to remain private. It also reflected the suspicion about my motives for research. For example, my visits were half jokingly interpreted as 'fact-finding missions' to 'get the mood of the shop-floor' for management, 'Why else would they let you in?' I was asked. The comments that followed my initiation tended to be directed at the issues which seemed to differentiate them from me, often concentrating on undermining what was assumed to be important to me,

> 'This cunt thinks that a manual labourer is a Spanish bullfighter! Your tutor must have some trouble with you! . . . He went to Dublin University this lazy cunt! . . . This twat's a spy for E.R.F. . . . Fancy talking to this fucker outside, it's alright when you're paid to do it, but there'd be no way outside! . . . Are you going to call this book, "How I Wasted Twelve Months"?'

The jokes maintained a very conscious sense of difference and ideological support for their own world. Hence when washing my hands in the toilet I was asked, with great concern, 'Have you fallen over?' The implication being that, as a 'mental worker', this could be the only possible way of getting my hands dirty. It is important to recognize that despite the overtly humorous exterior of these comments, another more serious meaning lurked beneath the surface. Workers retained a masculine pride in their manual, productive skills and practical experience, remaining suspicious of purely theoretical ideas that were seen as inferior to 'commonsense.' Like the apprentices, initiation was also facilitated, by practical jokes. On more than one occasion, I spent much of the day unknown to myself carrying flowers made from paper cups on my back. The news that I had been enrolled into the distinguished order, below, seemed to be final confirmation that I was not as clever as they thought, I thought, I was. One worker asked me for tenpence on the pretext of buying a cup of coffee. In receipt, I was given the following card,

> You were just conned out of 10p and you are now a member of the
> ### DUMB FUCKERS CLUB
> In order to resign from this honourable and distinguished organisation, you must pass the Membership Card on to another Cunt like yourself and your fee will be refunded.
> Should you fail to get a refund, you will automatically become president and bestowed the honour of being the
> ### DUMBEST FUCKER IN TOWN

Such ridicule facilitated the display of tough masculinity and the testing of these same qualities in others. The rules of the joking culture reflected the content of much shop-floor discourse, which centred on a preoccupation with male sexuality and the differentiation of working class men from women.

Within the all-male environment of the components division, masculine sexual prowess was a pervasive topic. Mediated through bravado and joking relations, a sterotypical image of self, which was assertive, independent, powerful and sexually insatiable was constructed and protected. By contrast, women were dismissed as passive, dependent and only interested in catching a man. These images contributed to male unity on the shop-floor and consti-tuted a powerful pressure, to which shop-floor workers were required to conform.

Photos of female nudes could be found on most shop-floor walls in the division. Many of these had been supplied by the 'Porn King' who maintained a 'sex library' of magazines for shop-floor edification. In addition, proud boasts and comments such as the following were part of the daily fabric of shop-floor interaction:

> 'I've had many a jump at the local train station.'
> 'Men come from the womb and spend the rest of their lives trying to get back in'.
> 'You'll never win with women because they're sitting on a goldmine. They'll always have the power.'
> 'At school I was very shy. I went red if the girls talked to me. If they talk to me now, I'll shag them!'

Such statements confirmed to manual workers and their colleagues who, and what, they were, i.e. tough, autonomous and invulnerable men who simply expressed their predatory nature in joking about sexual matters.

Two primary and typical forms of male sexuality, related to the conven-tional male life-cycle, permeated shop-floor discourse. Younger men tended to display a fetishization of sexuality and a reduction of women to sexual objects. This was exemplified by the 'sexploitative' mentality of twenty-three-year-old 'Boris'. Much of his shop-floor contact was spent embellishing his infamous reputation as a self-defined 'superstud'. He maintained a 'sex diary' which listed all his past 'conquests'. Concerned to 'trap' females, Boris graded out of ten the 'performance' of his twenty 'victims'. A 'scientific analysis' revealed that the older the woman (especially if she was married), the higher she was graded. Boris proudly boasted of his escapades and the 'carpet burns on my knees.' But his exaggerated accounts of sexual exploits were received with disbelief and ridicule. A recurrent comment by Ernie was,

> 'He's a Don Juan is Boris . . . When he's had Juan he's Don!'

Alternatively, older manual workers often prioritized their domestic power as the family breadwinner. Accordingly, they treated work primarily as a means of securing an income. This role of the provider, invariably constituted a crucial element of masculine self-respect, as 'Dirty Bar' indicated,

> 'I think you should be useful with your life. I love family responsibility.

I would have ten kids, if I could afford them. It's easy to have kids, but it takes a man to bring them up.'

The older men's joking reflected their concern with the preservation of male authority in the home and with economic instrumentalism at work. For example, a majority of those interviewed claimed that they did not reveal the size of their wage packet to their wives. The few who admitted that they did, were attacked unmercifully. Fred, a general labourer, was ridiculed by Jack, the axle shop steward, for 'tipping' his wage packet. The former's henpecked home-life was always an amusing theme on which to draw, as Jack outlined,

> 'She was Fred chasing his own tail at home. See what an effect it has on him, he's in a daze, he's had a sheltered life. He'd prefer to read a book than have sex!

This contrasts with Jack, who had kept his wages secret from his wife throughout their eleven married years,

> 'I don't think a woman should see your wage packet. It's a matter of understanding in our house. She understands I am in command.'

The emphasis of the joking culture therefore shifted from 'trapping' to 'tipping', from sexuality to domestic power. As one older worker explained,

> 'At eighteen I thought they were good for screwing. Now I realise they've other uses.'

One male self-identity, as sexually rampant, was superceded by another, that of the responsible family breadwinner. In both cases, however, shop-floor workers were expected to subscribe to the masculine assumptions of the joking culture. Yet these demands to conform inevitably generated a form of reluctant compliance from some workers which rendered shop-floor unity at best precarious and fragile. The oppositional values of personal freedom, masculine independence and autonomy, enshrined in the breadwinner role, contributed to these divisions, in particular, by compounding the separation between the 'public' sphere of work and the 'private' world of home. The collective experience of shared masculinity at work often contradicted the individualistic orientation to life outside.

For example, the profuse swearing of the men on the shop-floor contrasted sharply with their behaviour outside, as other research has discovered (e.g. Pitt 1979; Cockburn 1983). In the presence of women, it was often considered a 'mark of respect' to refrain from swearing. One axle assembler, infamous for his 'foul-mouthed grumpiness', exemplified this contrast between the collectivity of work and the private individualism of home,

> 'I'm noted for swearing in here, but I'd never swear in the house. At work we're all lads together. It's natural isn't it? But I can easily stop it. You can't swear at home, so you let it out at work.'

Similar assumptions were revealed in the following shop-floor banter,

> 'There's two parts to me. I'm free and easy here. At work I swear and sing my head off, and in the games room, but if women are present I won't, it's respect. I don't like to hear a woman swear.'

Bert, who was divorced, interjected, 'I used to tell mine to fuck off.' Steve, who was married, replied 'Aye, that's why he's separated.' Bert, 'Yea, but he has to put his hand up to speak to his missus'. Although he was a major participant in the piss-taking, Bert also revealed privately, the extent to which relations between the men remained superficial and distant, despite their collective appearance,

> 'Yea, they take the piss out of you here, but it would not bother me if they were a load of strangers.'

Moreover some respondents conceded that their involvement in macho joking was merely a performance designed to comply with the demands of the culture,

> 'It's accepted to swear here. You want to feel accepted but it's a false picture. They think it's soft to stir tea with a spoon. You've got to use your ruler, so you don't look effeminate . . . But the real me is the one at home where I don't swear.'

Similarly, workers sometimes objected to the use of shop-floor nicknames in their 'private' leisure time, as 'Dirty Bar' complained,

> 'In a pub recently the landlord said, 'Ah Dirty Bar, and this must be Mrs. Dirty Bar!' Now that is too personal. I don't mind being called "Dirty Bar" in work . . . well there's nothing I can do about it. If I don't like it, they'll call it me behind my back. But I won't accept it outside.'

The whole masculine style of shop-floor joking was aimed at testing and displaying the individual's inner strength to withstand teasing and ridicule. Yet, paradoxically, many of the men who subscribed to the culture and articulated its demands could not, in fact, handle them. The pressing and pervasive desire to secure male dignity in the eyes of others was repeatedly found to be incompatible with a concern to display impregnability and a disregard for the crit/witicisms of others. The sensitivity of working-class male identity meant that joking was often misinterpreted, when used as a pretence of hostility, and construed correctly when employed to 'make a point'. Invariably, the result was that its victim would 'snap'. Snapping was the cultural term of a successful breaking down of another's defences. 'Billy Snap' was so named because he very quickly failed to see the joke. Colleagues sometimes had to be 'wiped up off the floor' after making Billy the butt of their jokes. 'Losing your rag' was almost as commonplace as 'having a joke' in these shop-floor relations.

   Workers themselves differentiated between 'taking the piss' on the one hand, and 'one-upmanship' and 'malicious piss-taking', on the other. The result of the latter was division, as one scapegoated worker in the paint-spray shop illustrated,

> 'I've never known a more awkward lot than in the other room. Fellas there like to laff at your own failure. They enjoy taking the piss in a different way. It's serious not funny. We've not spoken to them for weeks and weeks.'

In the case of 'Deaf Dave', the joking resulted in his total emotional breakdown. In conforming to the 'macho' verbal violence that denied any concern for its victim, Dave had his 'leg pulled' and took 'the pain' 'like a man'. But his disability made him an easy target for the practical joke and one day the men went too far. His locker was removed and hidden on three separate occasions, but then replaced each time before Dave returned with the foreman. On the third occasion, Dave broke down. After the incident, although he continued to claim 'it's a good job I can take it', receiving only unsympathetic replies such as 'you fucking have to mate!' the men tended to turn their attention elsewhere for a scapegoat.

The concern to differentiate self on the criteria of being able to laff and take a joke was not confined to those employees outside the shop-floor, as one axle fitter illustrated,

> 'Them in the bottom shop, they're only after the money. They're a bunch of miserable fuckers, but we're a breed on our own in here. "Lostock" (another section of the plant) are even worse. They're very vindictive.'

This statement reveals a tension between the informal culture of 'having a laff' and the formal collective bonus system which encouraged workers to pursue high wages. It is a tension that reflects a conflict between two different forms of resistance and two separate manifestations of masculinity. First, there was the *collective* group culture of piss-taking, which was united in a shared masculinity and in the avoidance, or at least restriction, of work output. Second, there was the individual economic instrumentalism which distanced self, while maximizing wages, in order to provide for dependents in the home. It is along these conflicting axes that the most serious shop-floor conflicts occurred. The pressure of the bonus scheme and the preoccupation with male identity combined to generate disputes between specific workers in all seven departments where research took place.

HUMOUR AS CONTROL

Conflict in the Components Division was often the result of veiled insults, mediated through ambiguous piss-takes, which implied that other men were either miserable or lazy. In such cases, the pressure to conform to routine shop-floor values and practices was thereby transformed into worker strategies of mutual control and discipline. In the bottom machine shop, for example, several men had not spoken to each other for a number of years. One man had threatened to go to the foreman because another continually criticized him for being a 'lazy bastard'. In the axle department an apprentice was constantly attacked because he was a 'lazy cunt'. One older worker was particularly sarcastic, as he asked me,

> 'Has he told you about his dreams, 'cos that's all he does here!'

This was just one example of a steady stream of cutting remarks designed to act as a social control over 'deviants'. The precariousness and fragility of shop-floor identity repeatedly led to the collapse of work relationships, as the 'bullets' hit their target and workers began to 'snap'. For example, Jimmy 'Silver Sleeve' (he did not use a handkerchief) and Tony were school chums, drinking partners and workmates. Yet conflict broke out between them,

'Tony likes to give it, but snaps sometimes when I do it back. Once he really snapped. "That's enough" he said "or I'll drop you!", I said, "Right, let's get out on the croft". He didn't speak to me for three days, then he was alright again.'

The dispute centred on Jimmy's accusation about Tony's laziness, as the former continued,

'They're a motley crew in the stores. Some there I wouldn't pay in marbles! They just go to work to clown about half the time!'

In the top machine shop two distinct groups of antagonistic workers emerged. A younger section comprised 'Dirty Bar', Boris, Allan, 'Silent Night' and Brian, while an older group, close to retirement, included 'Eyebrow' and 'Ronnie Barker'. The former faction were heavily embroiled in piss-taking, but the latter were more serious and reserved. The relationship between 'Ronnie Barker' and 'Silent Night' had deteriorated after the latter had sent the rate-fixer to re-time 'Ronnie's job' with the implication that he was lazy. Ronnie complained,

'It's childish, they're like little kids. I don't speak to Brian. He started it, but then he couldn't take it. People in glass houses shouldn't throw stones. When I started back, he said, "You're a cunt, getting personal". But you've got to go one better.'

Concerned to protect himself from such piss-taking, Ronnie was unable to acknowledge the extent to which he also lived in a 'glass house.'

Similarly, a dispute between 'Dirty Bar' and 'Eyebrow' degenerated into a 'slanging match' in the foreman's office. They had been 'good mates' and 'Eyebrow' had originally helped 'Dirty Bar' with his work. Then 'Dirty Bar' started to call 'Eyebrow' a 'miserable cunt', who 'thinks he does all the work', while the latter responded,

'You always get this aggro creeping in. Dirty Bar was a piss-taker, that's alright, but if he gets a bollocking back, he didn't like it.'

The following practical joke by 'Dirty Bar' had exacerbated this rift,

'Eyebrow was off for a week. So we stuffed his overalls, put a face on it, pen and paper open on the crossword page, fag in his mouth and glasses. When he came back, he didn't speak to a few for a week or so.'

With both accusing each other of laziness, the relationship collapsed completely as 'Eyebrow' shut a door in the face of 'Dirty Bar', who was carrying steel sheets and the latter responded by supplying the former with 'bent, dirty, wrong length bars and the worst quality I can find' (hence his nickname).

Another breakdown in work relationships was also mediated through a clash of the two shop-floor practices of 'having a laff' and of 'maximizing wages'. Len in the top machine shop was particularly proud of his reputation as a 'character'. He sought to reconfirm his self image as 'the works idiot' within the everyday joking banter of the shop-floor. Being the butt of the majority of jokes confirmed to Len his popularity and prestige, as he explained,

'I'm one of the characters in here. A lot are just another brick in the wall, but I stand out . . . There's been at least three punch-ups in here. I've been involved in action . . . mainly running away!'

He recounted the following story with pride,

'Tony followed me into the loo and shouted my name. When he heard me voice, over came a bucket of water!'

Did that upset you?

'No, that was a bit of fun. He was me mate. And I'd asked for it. I'd said his wife was like a pig . . . but she is a bit!'

During interviews with Len, numerous people would come up to 'rib' him, and criticize him for skiving,

'Your just like your Dad, I used to pull him off the ceiling twice a day! You won't get any sense out of him! It's a wonder they make a profit with him working here! Get some work done!'

Len's usual defence was to attack others for their laziness. He had nicknamed one worker on an adjacent lathe as 'No Bonus Stanley'.

'You're not as clever as you think you are. Stan is much more intelligent because he earns a hundred quid a week for doing nothing, but you get nowt!'

Once again, what began as the pretence of hostility collapsed as the serious messages underlying this piss-taking surfaced. Tom was Len's main assailant. In response, Len had nicknamed him 'Council Flat Tommy', whom he described, in the following pejorative statement,

'He's very simple. He lives in a council house and dips his bread in his fucking beer. "Tom Hops" they call him. I never let anyone call me simple because I'm a property owner. They say they wouldn't like the responsibility, but it would worry me having a council house. That (pointing to Tom) is an example of what this place does to you after twelve years.'

Involving myself in what I understood to be a strongly developed form of joking disrespect, I asked Tom, 'What do you think of Len?' He replied, 'I don't.'

Soon after this altercation neither person was prepared to talk to the other. Len's defence had been to criticize Tommy for failing in his role of male provider. For several respondents, house ownership was an important source of independence and male dignity as the family breadwinner. When Tom reported Len for skiving, the latter responded,

'This fella is a malicious liar. He's just thick. I'm not dealing with such rubbish. My critics are all council house half-wits!'

As a result of these shop-floor battles for dignity, which emerge in jokes but collapse into mutual disdain, hierarchical control becomes unnecessary, as Len pointed out,

'The men are the gaffers now. They watch each other like hawks. The nature of the blokes is such that they turn on each other. Human nature plays against itself. You're more worried about what the men think than the gaffers . . . I'm just as bad if there's someone not working.'

For a while, the group sanctioning led by Tommy coerced Len to work harder and to resign from the joking game. Old habits die hard, however, and the inevitable sarcasm returned. One morning, two months later I was confronted by a raging Len, who shouted at me, 'I may be a silly cunt but at least I own my own house.' It was explained to me later that Tommy had 'set Len up' by informing him that I had said, 'I see that silly cunt is still here!' The banter had stopped only temporarily.

CONCLUSION

This article has highlighted three specific aspects of the joking culture. First, humour was shown to operate as one medium through which collective solidarity to *resist* boredom, the organizational status system and managerial control emerged. Second, shop-floor joking was found to embody considerable social pressure to *conform* to its central preoccupation with working-class masculinity. Manual workers were required to display a willingness, for example, to give and take a joke, to swear, to be dismissive of women, and to retain their domestic authority. Third, the research discovered that shop-floor humour became a means by which workers sought to *control* those perceived to be not 'pulling their weight'. Accordingly, a romanticized account of the culture had to be avoided since deepseated and longstanding shop-floor conflicts emerged out of joking relationships that went 'too far'. Clearly the bonus scheme, which was calculated on a collective basis (see Collinson 1981), reinforced some workers' concern to control and discipline colleagues. However, the preoccupation with masculine working-class identity, expressed in 'having a laff' at work, or in maximizing wages to provide for domestic dependents, was an equally crucial factor which compounded shop-floor divisions. The collective bonus scheme merely exposed the precariousness of masculine identity on the shop-floor and revealed the fragility of shop-floor collectivity.

The privatized male identity as family breadwinner also contributed to a weakening of shop-floor solidarity. Indeed these additional domestic responsibilities constituted an important difference between the working class 'lads' of the school counter-culture highlighted by Willis (1977) and the 'fellas' on the shop-floor. For the latter, the pressures to conform were greater because of the threat of job loss and the probable need to 'provide for a family'. Hence it was more difficult for the fellas to engage in similar oppositional practices to those of the 'lads', who could see no material vested interests in remaining at school. The danger of romanticizing working-class shop-floor culture is therefore all the more important to avoid. The material realities of shop-floor life, combined with the symbolic preoccupation with working-class masculinity resulted in relationships between the men that were largely defensive and superficial. This was no basis to establish the mutual closeness, commitment and respect from which effective, collective shop-floor resistance could emerge. The evidence presented highlights the importance of theorizing the social construction of gender identity as a means of analyzing much of both the creativity and the 'dark side' of organizational humour.

Ultimately, in this company, the pervasive concern to differentiate a highly masculine sense of self from the organization through joking and other working-class cultural relations contradicted the reality or organizational power and managerial control. This was illustrated most sharply in 1983 when closure of the components plant was announced with the loss of 153 jobs. Rather than reinforcing the male solidarity of the shop-floor, to fight at the minimum for improved redundancy payments, this decision merely exacerbated the fragementation of the workforce. Despite, or perhaps indeed because of, the central values of the joking culture, which emphasized personal virility, privatized freedom and masculine independence, workers voted to accept the lump-sum package without a fight. Ironically, their resistance had finally been exposed as little more than a joke.

NOTE

The author would like to thank Jeff Hearn and David Morgan for their comments on a earlier draft of this paper.

REFERENCES

Burawoy, Michael
1979 *Manufacturing consent*. Chicago: Chicago University Press.
Cockburn, Cynthia
1983 *Brothers: Male dominance and technological change*. London: Pluto Press.
Collinson, David L.
1981 'Managing the shop-floor'. Unpublished Msc, Department of Management Sciences, UMIST, Manchester.
Linstead, Steve
1985 'Jokers wild: the importance of humour in the maintenance of organizatonal culture'. *The Sociological Review* 33/4 (November): 741–767.
Pitt, Malcolm
1979 *The world on our backs*. London: Lawrence and Wishart.
Roy, Donald F.
1958 'Banana time: job satisfaction and informal interaction'. *Human Organisation* 18: 158–168.
Willis, Paul
1977 *Learning to labour*. London: Saxon House.
Willis, Paul
1979 'Shop-floor culture, masculinity and the wage form' in *Working class culture*. J. Clarke, C. Critcher, and R. Johnson (eds.), 185–198. London: Hutchinson.

Ben Fong-Torres

WHY ARE THERE NO MALE ASIAN ANCHOR*MEN* ON TV?

Connie Chung, the best-known Asian TV newswoman in the country, is a co-anchor of *1986*, a primetime show on NBC. Ken Kashiwahara, the best-known Asian TV newsman, has been chief of ABC's San Francisco bureau for seven years; his reports pop up here and there on ABC's newcasts and other newsrelated programs.

Wendy Tokuda, the best-known Asian TV newswoman in the Bay Area, is a co-anchor of KPIX's evening news. David Louie, the most established Asian TV newsman, is a field reporter, covering the Peninsula for KGO.

And that's the way it is: among Asian American broadcasters, the glamor positions—the anchor chairs, whose occupants earn more than $500,000 a year in the major markets—go to the women; the men are left outside, in the field, getting by on reporters wages that top out at about $80,000.

The four Bay Area television stations that present regular newscasts (Channels 2, 4, 5 and 7) employ more than 40 anchors. Only two are Asian Americans: Tokuda and Emerald Yeh, a KRON co-anchor on weekends. There is no Asian male in an anchor position, and there has never been one. (Other Asian women who have anchored locally are Linda Yu [KGO] and Kaity Tong [KPIX], now prime-time anchors in Chicago and New York.)

None of the two dozen broadcasters this reporter spoke to could name a male Asian news anchor working anywhere in the United States.

Don Fitzpatrick, a TV talent headhunter whose job it has been for four years to help television stations find anchors and reporters, maintains a video library in his San Francisco office of 9000 people on the air in the top 150 markets.

There are, in fact, several reasons proposed by broadcasters, station executives, talent agents and others.

- Asian men have been connected for generations with negative stereotypes. Asian women have also been saddled with false images, but, according to Tokuda, "In this profession, they work for women and against men."
- Asian women are perceived as attractive partners for the typical news anchor: a white male. "TV stations," says Henry Der, director of Chinese for Affirmative Action, "have discovered that having an Asian female with a white male is an attractive combination." And, adds Sam Chu Lin, a former reporter for both KRON and KPIX, "they like the winning formula. If an Asian woman works in one market, then another market duplicates it. So why test for an Asian male?"
- Asian women allow television stations to fulfill two equal-opportunity slots with one hiring. As Mario Machado, a Los Angeles-based reporter and producer puts it, "They get two minorities in one play of the cards. *They* hit the jackpot."
- Asian males are typically encouraged by parents toward careers in the sciences and away from communications.

This article is a revised version of an article that appeared in the "Datebook" section of the *San Francisco Chronicle* July 13, and is printed with their permission.

- Because there are few Asian men on the air, younger Asian males have no racial peers as role models. With few men getting into the profession, news directors have a minuscule talent pool from which to hire.

And, according to Sumi Haru, a producer at KTLA in Los Angeles, the situation is worsening as stations are being purchased and taken over by large corporations. At KTTV, the ABC affiliate, "The affirmative action department was the first to go." At her own station, the public affairs department is being trimmed. "We're concerned with what little Asian representation we have on the air," said Haru, an officer of the Association of Asian-Pacific American Artists.

HONORS THESIS

Helen Chang, a communications major at UC Berkeley now working in Washington, DC, made the missing Asian anchorman the subject of her honors thesis. Chang spoke with Asian anchorwomen in Los Angeles, Chicago and New York as well as locally. "To capsulize the thesis,"she says, "it is an executive decision based on a perception of an Asian image. On an executive decision level, the image of the Asian woman is acceptable."

"It's such a white bread medium; it's the survival of the blandest," says a male Asian reporter who asked to remain anonymous. A native San Franciscan, this reporter once had ambitions to be an anchor, but after several static years at his station, "I've decided to face reality. I have a white man's credentials but it doesn't mean a thing. I'm not white. How can it not be racism?"

"Racism is a strong word that scares people," says Tokuda.

"But whatever's going on here is some ugly animal. It's not like segregation in the south. What it is is very subtle . . . bias."

To Mario Machado, it's not that subtle. Machado, who is half Chinese and half Portuguese, is a former daytime news anchor in Los Angeles who's had the most national television exposure after Kashiwahara. Being half-Chinese, he says, has given him no advantage in getting work. "It's had no bearing at all. There's a move on against Asians, period, whether part-Asian or full Asian."

TV executives, he charges, "don't really want minority males to be totally successful. They don't want minority men perceived as strong, bright, and articulate. We can be cute second bananas, like Robert Ito on *Quincy*. But having an Asian woman—that's always been the feeling from World War II, I guess. You bring back an Asian bride, and she's cute and delicate. But a strong minority man with authority and conviction—I don't think people are ready for that."

WAR IMAGE

Bruno Cohen, news director at KPIX, agrees that "for a lot of people, the World War II image of Japanese, unfortunately, is the operative image about what Asian males are all about."

That image, says Serena Chen, producer and host of *Asians Now!* on KTVU, was one of danger. "They may be small, but they're strong. So watch out, white women!"

The Vietnam war and recent movies like *Rambo*, Machado says, add to the historic negativity. "You never went to war against Asian women," he says. "You always went to war against Asian men."

Today, says Tokuda, Asian men are saddled with a twin set of stereotypes. "They're either wimpy—they have real thick glasses and they're small and they have an accent and they're carrying a lot of cameras—or they're a murderous gangster." "Or," says Les Kumagai, a former KPIX intern now working for a Reno TV station, "they're businessmen who are going to steal your jobs."

"The Asian woman is viewed as property, and the Asian male has been denied sexuality," says Chen. "Eldridge Cleaver created a theory of the black male being superglorified in the physical and superdecreased in the mental. It's very difficult for people to see a successful black male unless he's an athlete or a performer. If he's in a corporate situation, everyone says, 'Wow, he's the product of affirmative action.' That theory holds that in this society, people who have potential to have power have to be male, and have both mental and physical [strength] to be the superior male. In this society, they took away the black male's mental and gave him his physical. The Asian male has been denied the physical and given the mental."

Veteran KRON reporter Vic Lee listens to a tally of stereotypes and images associated with Asian men. "All those reasons limit where an Asian American can work. I've always said to my wife, if I'm fired here, there're only a couple of cities I can go to and get a job based on how well I do my work, not how I look or what color my skin is. There are cities with Asian American populations, and you can count them on one hand: Seattle, Los Angeles, New York, Boston, and possibly Washington.

"The rest of the country? You might as well forget Detroit. They *killed* a [Chinese] guy just 'cause he looked Japanese." Lee is referring to Vincent Chin, who was beaten to death by two white auto workers who mistook him for a Japanese and blamed him for their unemployment.

"EXOTIC" FEMALES

In contrast to the threatening Asian male, says Les Kumagai, "Females are 'exotic.' They're not threatening to non-Asian females and they're attractive to non-Asian males. You're looking to draw the 18-to-45-year-old female demographic for advertising. You just won't get the draw from an Asian male."

To Tokuda, the Asian woman's persisting stereotype is more insidious than exotic. "It's the Singapore girl: not only deferential but submissive. It's right next to the geisha girl."

At KGO, says one newsroom employee, "somebody in management was talking about [recently hired reporter] Janet Yee and blurted out, 'Oh, she's so cute.' They don't care about her journalistic credentials. . . . That type of thinking still persists."

AGGRESSIVE

Janet Yee says she can take the comment as a compliment, but agrees that it is "a little dehumanizing." Yee, who is half Chinese and half Irish-Swedish, says she doesn't get the feeling, at KGO, that she was hired for her looks. Stereotypes "are the things I've fought all my life," she says, adding that she isn't at all submissive and deferential. "I'm assertive and outgoing, and I think that's what got me the job."

Emerald Yeh, who worked in Portland and at CNN (Cable News Network) in Atlanta before joining KRON, says she's asked constantly about the part being an Asian woman played in her landing a job. "The truth is that it's a factor, but at the same time, there is absolutely no way I can keep my job virtually by being Asian."

Despite the tough competition for jobs in television, Yeh, like Tokuda and several peers in Los Angeles, is vocal about the need to open doors to Asian men. "People think Asians have done so well," she says, "but how can you say that if one entire gender group is hardly visible?"

George Lum, a director at KTVU who got into television work some 30 years ago at Channel 5, has a theory of his own. "The Asian male is not as aggressive as the Asian female. In this business you have to be more of an extrovert. Men are a little more passive."

Headhunter Don Fitzpatrick agrees. "Watching my tapes, women in general are much more aggressive than men. . . . My theory on that is that—say a boy and girl both want to get into television, and they have identical SATs and grade point average. Speakers tell them, you'll go to Chico or Medford and start out making $17,000 to $18,000 a year. A guy will say, 'This is bull. If I stay in school and get into accounting or law . . .' And they have a career change. A woman will go to Chico or Medford and will get into LA or New York."

"In Helen Chang's paper," recalls Tokuda, "she mentions the way Asian parents have channeled boys with a narrow kind of guidance."

"With Japanese kids," says Tokuda, "right after the war, there was a lot of pressure on kids to get into society, on being quiet and working our way back in." In Seattle, she says, "I grew up with a whole group of Asian American men who from the time they were in junior high knew they were going to be doctors—or at least that they were gonna be successful. There was research that showed that they were very good in math and sciences and not good in verbal skills. With girls there's much less pressure to go into the hard sciences."

Most of the men who do make it in broadcasting describe serendipitous routes into the field, and all of them express contentment with being reporters. "Maybe I'm covering my butt by denying that I want to anchor," says Kumagai, "but I do get a bigger charge being out in the field."

Still, most Asian male reporters do think about the fame and fortune of an anchor slot. Those thoughts quickly meet up against reality.

David Louie realizes he has little chance of becoming the 6 o'clock anchor. "I don't have the matinee idol look that would be the most ideal image on TV. Being on the portly side and not having a full head of hair, I would be the antithesis of what an anchorman is supposed to look like."

Kind of like KPIX's Dave McElhatton? Louie laughs. "But he's white," he says, quickly adding that McElhatton also has 25 years of experience broadcasting in the Bay Area.

At least Louie is on the air. In Sacramento, Lonnie Wong was a reporter at KTXL (Channel 40), and Jan Minagawa reported and did part-time anchoring at KXTV (Channel 10). Both have been promoted into newsroom editing and production jobs. And neither is thrilled to be off the air.

Wong, who says he was made an assignment editor because, among reporters, he had "the most contacts in the community," says his new job is "good management experience. But I did have a reservation. I was the only minority on the air at the station; and I know that's valuable for a station."

Minagawa's station, KXTV, does have an Asian on the air: a Vietnamese woman reporter named Mai Pham. "That made the decision easier," says Minagawa, who had been a reporter and fill-in anchor for seven years. A new news director, he says, "had a different idea of what should be on the air" and asked him to become a producer. "I didn't like it, but there was nothing I could do."

Mitch Farris rejects any notion of a conspiracy by news directors against Asian American men. In fact, he says, they are "desperate" for Asian male applicants. "Just about any news director would strive to get an Asian on the air and wouldn't mind a man."

To which Machado shouts, "We're here! We're here! We're looking for work."

Martin P. Levine

THE STATUS OF GAY MEN
IN THE WORKPLACE

Work poses manifold meanings in modern American life (Julian and Kornblum, 1983:489–492). On one hand, it denotes the quality of our economic well being. For most of us, our job determines how much money we make, and this in turn affects how well we live. Work also signifies our social status. What we do for a living strongly influences how other people evaluate and rank us. And finally, work affects how we think about ourselves. What we do often determines how we feel about who we are.

Jobs hold additional meanings for men. For them, work demonstrates manliness (Pleck, 1982; Doyle, 1983). To prove their masculinity, men attempt to be breadwinners. This test applies most strongly for men, typically blue collar workers, who adhere to the traditional male role (Le Masters, 1975). These men demonstrate their manliness by earning enough to support a wife and family. Men who follow the modern male role, usually white collar workers or "yuppies," emphasize professional success (Ehrenreich, 1983; Gould, 1974). These men prove their masculinity by achieving corporate power, professional recognition, and high earnings.

Gay men experience great difficulty in meeting this manly test. The deep-seated cultural antipathy towards men who love men, called homophobia, prevents homosexuals from obtaining good jobs. Homophobia drives gay men into nonprestigious, low paying, white collar or service jobs, which are commonly regarded as unsuitable for men (Harry, 1982:181–183; Harry and

DeVall, 1978:159–160). This, in turn, reinforces the popular impression of homosexuals as effeminate.

This article explores the status of homosexuals in the work force. After examining the prevailing stereotypes of gay men, I will consider the effect of these stereotypes on attitudes towards the hiring of homosexuals, and then examine how these attitudes provoke employment discrimination against gay men.

STEREOTYPES OF HOMOSEXUALS

Americans view homosexuals as "failed men."[1] Most of us equate masculinity with heterosexuality and believe that "real men" love women. We accordingly associate homosexuality with a spoiled masculinity—with a lack of the physical, emotional, or social characteristics of real men.[2]

The stereotypes of homosexuals incorporate these assumptions and include several interrelated images of gay men: (1) the swishy pansy, (2) the cultivated fop, (3) the diseased pervert, and (4) the immoral degenerate. The first two stereotypes link homosexuality with unmasculine behaviors and interests. As swishy pansies, gay men prance with mincing gaits, shriek in lisping voices, and dress in womanly garb. Their physiques, moreover, are puny and thin.[3] As cultivated fops, gays revel in haute cuisine, couture, and culture. They adore trendy food and nightspots, decorate and dress in the latest styles, and flock to the ballet, opera, and theater.[4] The last two stereotypes link homosexuality with unmanly illnesses and vices. As diseased perverts, gay men suffer from twisted erotic desires and illnesses. Their deranged upbringing fosters unnatural sexual interests, compulsive promiscuity, and susceptibility to AIDS.[5] As immoral degenerates, gay men are sex crazed, substance abusing, molesters of children. Their twisted emotions provoke uncontrollable urges for sex, liquor, and drugs, which prompts them to drink, snort cocaine, and molest young boys.[6]

ATTITUDES TOWARDS THE EMPLOYMENT OF HOMOSEXUALS

These stereotypes account for our conflicting attitudes towards the employment of gay men. On one hand, we endorse the principle of equal job opportunities for homosexuals (Schneider and Lewis, 1984:18). Americans have recently accepted the doctrine of equal opportunity in the work place, which by extension fosters support for equal job opportunities for racial, religious, and sexual minorities (Schneider and Lewis, 1984:18). A recent poll, for instance, found that nearly two-thirds of the public favored equal rights in the labor force for homosexuals (Gallup, 1982). On the other hand, we also favor banning gay men from particular lines of work. Americans oppose employing homosexuals for either jobs typically done by men, or jobs involving maternal duties (Schneider and Lewis, 1984:18).

Homophobic stereotypes account for these attitudes. Americans perceive homosexuals as swishy pansies and cultivated fops, and therefore consider gay men as unfit for the jobs traditionally assigned to men (Harry, 1982:181–183). "Men's work" expresses, stereotypically masculine traits like rationality, toughness, and aggressiveness, which tend to be concentrated in high status, better paying, blue or white collar fields (Davidson and Gordon, 1979:72–75). Public opinion polls record extensive opposition to homosexuals doing men's work. By large pluralities, we disapprove of gay men working as judges, doctors, policemen, and government officials (Levitt and Klassen, 1974; Scheider and Lewis, 1984:18).

The stereotypes foster the belief that homosexuals *are* suitable for tradition- ally feminine jobs, "women's work" (Davidson and Gordon, 1979:72–75). These jobs embody traditionally feminine attributes like domesticity, com- passion, and dependency. All of these jobs tend to be in low status, poorly paying, white collar or service fields (Benokratis and Feagin, 1985:52–53). Polls indicate widespread support for gay men doing nutrient, decorative, or expressive forms of women's work. By overwhelming majorities, we approve of homosexuals working as artists, beauticians, musicians, florists, and retail clerks (Schneider and Lewis, 1984:18; Levitt and Klassen, 1974). These jobs can be classified as "sissy work."

We do not, however, regard gay men as fit for all kinds of women's work. Americans also believe that homosexuals are diseased perverts and immoral degenerates, which evokes strong opposition to gay men doing jobs involving such maternal responsibilities as intimate contact, moral training, and the care of children. We believe that homosexuals are too "sick" for these jobs—their perverted nature will lead them to corrupt or molest young people. By huge pluralities, we disapprove of homosexuals working as clergy, teachers, prin- cipals, and camp counselors (Schneider and Lewis, 1984:18; Gallup, 1987).

EMPLOYMENT DISCRIMINATION AGAINST GAY MEN

Homophobic stereotypes provoke discriminatory practices against gay men in the work place (National Gay Task Force, 1981). Work associates share the cultural stereotypes of gay men, which cause them to hold extremely negative perceptions of homosexual workers. For example, employers and co-workers view gay men as swishy pansies and debauched lechers and they therefore believe that homosexual workers would dress like women and sexually harass people on the job (Maddocks, 1969:101–102). Employers also regard gay men as diseased perverts and they consequently believe that homosexual workers would be emotionally unstable, which would result in high rates of absentee- ism and low rates of productivity (Weinberg and Williams, 1974:223–228; Bellard Weinberg, 1978:141–142).

These images affect the attitudes of workplace associates towards the em- ployment of gay men in particular jobs. Employers and co-workers hold similar attitudes towards this issue as the general public, believing gay men to be unsuitable for traditionally masculine or maternal lines of work but fit for "sissy" jobs.

AIDS fosters additional negative perceptions of gay employees. Miscon- ceptions about the nature of this disease appear to be fairly widespread. Despite all the evidence that AIDS cannot be spread by casual contact, many Americans believe that AIDS can be spread through such casual means as handshakes, bathroom facilities or shared work spaces (Institute of Medicine, 1988:67; Jennings, 1988:66).

This misconception influences the attitudes of workplace associates toward homosexual workers. Employers and co-workers view gay men as diseased perverts who are infected with the AIDS virus and consequently fear that homosexual employees will give them AIDS. In addition, employers worry about the high medical costs and lost productivity incurred by people afflicted with this disease (Leonard, 1975; Smothers, 1988; Hamilton et al., 1987).

These attitudes prompt job discrimination against gay men. This victimization can be either direct or indirect (Harry and De Vall, 1978:159). In direct job discrimination, workplace associates either harass gay men or discriminate against them in hiring, retention, and advancement. In indirect job discrimination, fear of victimization drives homosexuals into stereotypically "sissy" lines of work.

Direct Job Discrimination   This form of employment discrimination occurs primarily in jobs considered unsuitable for gay men. Many employers, in typically male or maternal fields, consider homosexuality grounds for not hiring, promoting, or retaining otherwise qualified individuals (Maddock, 1969). They consequently refuse to employ, advance, or retain gay men.

The practice of direct job discrimination varies according to openness about sexual orientation. Homosexuals differ in their ability to hide their sexual preference from work associates (Bell and Weinberg, 1978). Sociologists use the terms "discredited" and "discreditable" to describe these differences (Goffman, 1963:4). Discredited gay men are unable to hide their sexual orientation from work associates. The reasons for this are twofold: First, discredited men may be labeled homosexual in the official records of the courts, armed forces, and medical facilities. Employers regularly check these records, and consequently discover the homosexuality of discredited men (Levine, 1979). These men are involuntarily discredited.[7] Second, feelings of pride, self-affirmation or intimacy may compel discredited men to reveal their sexual preference to work associates (Troiden, 1988). These men are voluntarily discredited. Discreditable gay men are able to hide their sexual orientation from work associates. Employers and coworkers consequently are unaware of their sexual preference. Discredited and discreditable gay men are victimized differently during hiring procedures and after employment.

Hiring Procedures   Employers do not want to hire homosexuals. They therefore routinely ask questions during the hiring process that expose the homosexuality of discredited and discreditable men. These questions appear on standard application and interview forms. Nearly all forms ask prospective employees about their personal interests and background. More specifically, they inquire about prior criminal, military, medical, marital, and residential experiences. They also ask about hobbies and community service.

These questions place involuntarily discredited men in a classic double bind. If they answer the questions truthfully, they will disclose their sexual orientation and lose the job:

> I applied for a job at G.E. and told them about my discharge. He said he could have hired me if I had served my time in prison for murder but not with that discharge. The department stores told me, we're sorry but we don't employ homosexuals (Williams and Weinberg, 1971:116).

If they lie and hide their homosexuality, they will be terminated once the records are checked.

The questions concerning personal interests threaten the hiring of voluntarily discredited men. These men typically reveal their sexual preference while discussing pastimes or community service. To illustrate, they may state that they volunteer for a local gay charity. The effects of voluntary disclosure are documented in two recent studies. Adam (1982) investigated the hiring practices of law firms in Ontario, Canada. He sent each firm an application form and resume for an entry level position known as articling, which is open to recent law school graduates. The applications and resumes were identical except for the sex and sexual preference of the applicant. Sexual orientation was indicated by listing "active in local Gay People's Alliance" under the Personal Background section of the resume. The findings reveal that homosexual applicants were the least likely to obtain interviews; heterosexual men received 1.6 times more interview offers than gay men. The American Sociological Association's Task Group on Homosexuality investigated the employment practices of American sociology departments (Huber, 1982). The Task Group asked the heads of these departments about their ability to hire sociologists who were self-proclaimed gay or lesbian rights activists. More than half of the chairs reported that employing such activists would cause serious problems or that it just could not be done.

The questions about marital status, living arrangements, medical histories, and personal interests jeopardize the employment of discreditable gay men. Employers regard particular answers to these questions as evidence of homosexuality. They assume that men who state that they have never married, live with a male roommate, or dwell in a gay neighborhood are homosexual, as are men who report frequent exposures to sexually transmitted diseases or interest in the arts. These statements typically cost men the position.

Job interviews also endanger the hiring of discreditable gay men. Employers commonly check the applicant's demeanor and appearance for signs of homosexuality during the interview. They presume that men who are effeminate, well dressed, or slightly built are gay, and consequently refuse to employ them.

Placement agencies further threaten employment (Brown, 1976:163; Zoglin, 1974). These agencies regularly scrutinize prospective employees' application forms and interviews for evidence of homosexuality. Men evincing these signs are thought to be gay, and their forms are coded with a letter or number signifying homosexuality. Most agencies will not refer suspected homosexuals to potential employers because they believe that such referrals would damage business with these employers.

After Employment   Workplace associates, moreover, do not want to retain or promote gay men. They consequently ask questions after hiring that reveal the homosexuality of discredited and discreditable gay men. These questions appear in either standard personnel investigations or on-the-job conversations. Almost all employers conduct periodic investigations into the background of their staff, usually for purposes of promotion or retention. These investigations commonly inquire about arrest records, sexual orientation, and personal life.

The arrest questions expose the homosexuality of involuntarily discredited men. Many of these men have been arrested after hiring for such homosexual offenses as sodomy, solicitation for illegal sexual conduct, or loitering for purposes of engaging in deviant sexual intercourse (Boggan, et al., 1983).[8]

Employers discover these arrests while checking police records, and therefore detect the men's homosexuality, which may cost them the job or promotion.

The questions about sexual preference jeopardizes the employment of discreditable men. Many employers require these men to answer direct questions about their sexual orientation during polygraph (lie-detector) tests that disclose false replies to the questions. Employers frequently fire or deny promotions to men whose test results indicate that they lied about being gay.

Polygraph tests put discreditable gay men in a "no-win" situation. If they take the test, they will disclose their homosexuality and lose their job or promotion. If they refuse to be tested, they will also be fired or denied promotion:

> I had to turn down a job offer which was conditional on my agreement to take a lie-detector test, because I was afraid they would ask The Question (Jay and Young, 1979:706).

The questions about personal lives further threaten the jobs of discreditable men. Employers typically question these men about their living arrangements, recreational interests, and friendship circles. They perceive certain kinds of answers to these questions as evidence of homosexuality. They presume that men who report living with other men, attending cultural events, or associating with gay people, organizations or gathering places are homosexual. These answers cost men the job or promotion.

Industrial intelligence agencies are often used to verify the answers concerning personal lives (Levine, 1979). These agencies frequently utilize investigative procedures that encroach upon constitutional rights to privacy. Some of these procedures include secretly monitoring daily activities and interrogating family, friends, and neighbors:

> Lloyd, at age fifty-three, had worked his way up from a door-to-door salesman for a large insurance company to the point where in 1973, he was about to be promoted to a vice-presidency. . . . Lloyd was a homosexual who had been living for twelve years with a man he told neighbors and visitors was his cousin. In 1968 Lloyd's lover was crippled in an automobile accident and confined for the rest of his life to a wheelchair. Lloyd made him the beneficiary of his own life insurance policy, explaining to the company that he had an obligation to provide for a relative who was no longer able to work.
>
> As part of a final check on the man they were about to promote, the senior officers sent an investigator to speak with Lloyd's neighbors and to interview people in his "cousin's" hometown. The investigator used the standard ploy—the young man was about to become the beneficiary of an $80,000 insurance policy. His former neighbors talked freely, and the investigator soon learned that the man was in fact not related to Lloyd. Back in Lloyd's town, he learned that the two men had been living together for years. With the investigator's report in hand, the company officials called Lloyd in and demanded his immediate resignation. The word homosexual was not mentioned; they were too polite for that (Brown, 1976:151–152).

The media also informs employers about discreditable men's homosexuality. In many localities, news editors regard arrests for homosexual offenses and gay rights demonstrations as major news features. They consequently spotlight these arrests and demonstrations as front page or lead stories. These stories, moreover, usually include the names, addresses, occupations, and occasionally pictures of the offenders and demonstrators. Employers see these stories, discover an employee's homosexuality, and fire or deny this man a promotion:

> I was fired from my job I held for thirteen years (engineering management) because I am homosexual. They discovered this when a letter I wrote decrying oppression was published in the local newspaper (Jay and Young, 1979:705).

Co-workers also endanger the employment of discreditable men. Work associates are often the first to recognize that a colleague is gay (Harry and De Vall, 1978:161–162). Their suspicions arise from the disclosures men make about their private lives during on-the-job conversations.[9] For example, the men may show little interest in sports, dating or sex talk, or they may receive frequent telephone calls from male friends or roommates. Co-workers discriminate against men they presume to be gay. They either harass them into quitting or pressure employers into firing them:

> On the job I was ridiculed and made the butt of jokes until I retaliated by losing my head and temper over something minor, resulting in my dismissal (Jay and Young, 1979:705).

> The other people used to abuse me because of it. Finally I got tired of pussyfooting around and complained about it and they told me I was through (Bell and Weinberg, 1978:144).

In addition, they may use this knowledge to advance their career at the expense of the man thought to be gay:

> The guy was after my job. He suspected I was gay and started to spread it through the office, making all sorts of wisecracks, trying to damage my reputation. Eventually, the atmosphere in the office grew very hostile (Interview with author).

Homosexuals are further victimized in terms of job responsibilities. Many gay men find their work assignments curtailed after employers discover their homosexuality. They may be demoted to a less responsible position or transferred to a job beneath their qualifications (Zoglin, 1974):

> The owner of a Portland-based international firm recruited a 44-year-old man for a position as director of marketing. The owner found out that this man was homosexual and wanted to fire him immediately, but because the company was in financial difficulty he was kept on. After a year his responsibilities were gradually taken from him until he resigned (Task Force on Sexual Preference, 1978:47).

Special Cases of Direct Job Discrimination: Occupational Licenses and Security Clearances   A wide range of jobs, in both private industry and the civil service, demand occupational licenses or security clearances. According to one count (Boggan, et al., 1983:25), over 350 different fields require occupational licenses, including such diverse trades as doctor, teacher, and barber—and about 7 million people work in licensed jobs. In addition, many positions within the Defense and State Department demand security clearances, as do thousands of jobs in security-related research and manufacturing industries. Approximately 2.2 million people work in these industries (Boggan, et al., 1983:53).

The agencies authorized to grant occupational licenses routinely discriminate against gay men. Virtually every jurisdiction has created special boards for administering occupational licensing. These boards issue licenses, which are certificates stating that an individual is authorized to engage in a particular occupation, on the basis of legally proscribed professional and moral standards. The professional standards specify certain skill levels, age requirements, work experiences, and educational backgrounds. The moral standards prohibit licensing people who either lack "good moral character" or have committed criminal offenses or unprofessional conduct. The boards construe homosexuality as evidence of "moral failure" and consequently revoke or refuse to grant licenses to gay men, which prevents them from working in their field:

> My chief of service, a well-meaning but misguided man who had used me as a resident for four years, had a delayed guilt reaction for having "harbored" a homosexual. He decided that he must tell the truth for the good of all concerned. So he informed the ACS (American College of Surgeons) and my specialty board that I was a homosexual. To their credit, the ACS approved my membership, making me an FACS (Fellow of the American College of Surgeons). The specialty board, however, turned down my request to take the exam on the grounds of "poor moral character . . . This lack of formal certification meant I might not be reappointed to my hospital and raised questions about my competency. It delayed my career as a neurosurgeon (Brown, 1976:154).

> My arrest record [for a homosexual offense] caused my California teacher's license to be rescinded. I'm not allowed to teach in the public schools because of it (Bell and Weinberg, 1978:144).

Homosexuals are also regularly victimized in the awarding of security clearances. A handful of government agencies (such as the federal Defense Industrial Security Office and the Civil Service Commission) grant such clearances, which are documents permitting the holder access to classified information about matters pertaining to the national security. These agencies perceive homosexuality as a threat to the national security. First, they believe that gay men are too emotionally unstable to keep classified information secret. Second, they believe that gay men can be easily blackmailed into divulging official secrets through threats of exposing their homosexuality (Walters, 1986). The agencies thus revoke or refuse to issue security clearances to gay men, which prevents them from working in their field:

> I lost my security clearance and am unable to get one. My field was industrial health, radioactive stuff. It requires a security clearance. Anyone that could use me has defense contracts and because they have defense contracts they can't use me. I applied for three or four jobs and they asked for my discharge [Undesirable discharge for homosexuality] and said, "Sorry, we can't use you" (Williams and Weinberg, 1971:118).

The rationale for such discriminatory actions is seriously flawed. There is no evidence that gay men are more emotionally disturbed than straight males. Studies of matched samples of homosexual and heterosexual men show equal rates of psychopathology in both groups (Bell and Weinberg, 1978). Furthermore, gay men are not uniformly vulnerable to blackmail. Voluntarily discredited men cannot be blackmailed about something that is evident. In addition, discreditable men are susceptible only because disclosure of their homosexuality would cost their job. Employment discrimination not homosexuality makes them vulnerable to blackmail.

Coping Strategies   Sociologists classify the tactics homosexuals use to cope with direct job discrimination as techniques for avoiding stigmatization (Goffman, 1963; Humphreys, 1972; ch 8). These strategies enable gay men to evade or lessen victimization. The most widely used tactics include passing, covering, and minstrelization.

Passing as heterosexual is probably the most commonly utilized technique, and is favored mainly by discreditable men (Troiden, 1988:52; Humphreys, 1972:28). In passing, homosexuals conceal their sexual orientation from work associates, which leads employers and co-workers to think that they are heterosexual. Gay men hide their sexual preference through subterfuge, suppression, and nondisclosure. Subterfuge involves overt pretenses of heterosexuality. To convince work associates that they are straight, homosexuals actively pretend to be heterosexual. For example, they may comment about the physical attractiveness of female associates, participate in the traditional lunch-time pastime of "girl-watching," or bring female dates to job-related social events:

> I will often be eating lunch with one of the vice presidents or the controller or somebody, and the talk will get to sex—as it always does. I will play along. For example, when we comment on girls, they all know what my type is (Zoglin, 1974:27).

Dates, moreover, usually pose as girl-friends, fiancees, and even wives:

> I work in an extremely homophobic organization. To protect myself, I married a woman. She was an illegal alien and married me to stay in the country. I married her for a cover. Everyone at work thinks I am straight because I am married (Interview with author).

Suppression entails concealment of evidence of homosexuality. To keep their sexual orientation secret, gay men consciously hide features of their private lives that are considered signs of homosexuality. For example, they purposefully avoid telling work associates that they have male roommates, vacation in gay resorts, or attend the opera. Finally, nondisclosure involves covertness about erotic preference. In this strategy, gay men stop either pretending to be straight or concealing signs of their homosexuality. They instead behave as naturally as they can without revealing their sexual orientation.

Covering constitutes the second most widely used tactic for evading discrimination. In covering, homosexuals convince work associates that they are "normal" by dressing and acting like conventionally masculine men. This strategy enables discredited men to show employers and co-workers that they are not like stereotypical homosexuals, which hopefully thwarts victimization. It also allows discreditable men to deflect any suspicions about their sexual orientation:

> My image at work is decidedly conservative. I always wear dark Brooks Brothers suits, with cuffed pants, button-down shirts, and tortoise shell glasses. I always talk about sports. My act is so straight that no one would think that I am gay (Interview with author).

Passing and covering entail significant psychological and occupational costs. Both techniques involve careful, even tortuous, monitoring of behavior and talk, which generates tremendous feelings of strain and inauthenticity. Anxiety over the possibility of exposing one's homosexuality and then being discriminated against further heightens the anguish (Weinberg and Williams, 1974:226–228). In addition, these techniques require social distance from employers and coworkers, which impedes advancement because promotion often depends on socializing or being friendly with work associates.

Discredited men also avoid victimization through minstrelization. In this strategy, gay men either seek jobs or form businesses (typically small retail establishments) in culturally approved fields dubbed sissy work (Whitam and Marthy, 1986:84–86). These occupations embody traditionally feminine behaviors and are considered suitable for homosexuals (Table I):

> Women usually expect a hairdresser to be homosexual. They aren't threatened by it (Bell and Weinberg, 1978:145).

> There are a number of gays in interior decorating, and it makes things easier in terms of the rest of society. They kind of expect it (Bell and Weinberg, 1978:145).

Furthermore, being gay is generally an asset in these fields because homosexuals actively hire and advance one another (Harry and De Vall, 1978:156):

> Most people in display are queer. It's been easier at times to get ahead because I am homosexual (Bell and Weinberg, 1978:145).

TABLE 1 SISSY WORK

Feminine Field	Occupations
Nurturient Jobs	
Helping professions	Nurse, librarian, secretary
Domestic work	Cook, counterman, airline steward, bellhop, bartender, waiter, orderly
Decorative Jobs	
Home-related	Interior decorator, florist
Grooming	Fashion designer, hairdresser, model
Commercial arts	Graphic designer, window display
Expressive Jobs	
Arts	Dancer, musician, artist
Entertainment	Actor, singer

Note. The listed occupations are illustrative not exhaustive.

Indirect Job Discrimination   Minstrelization constitutes a form of indirect job discrimination and negatively affects the occupational position of gay men. To shield themselves from possible discrimination, some homosexuals avoid jobs in which they anticipate victimization, and instead choose fields in which they are tolerated:

> My whole goals are affected. I have to choose a job where I won't be discriminated against (Bell and Weinberg, 1978:144).

They accordingly shun higher-status, better-paying lines of men's work for lower-status, poorly-paying forms of sissy work:

> Homosexuality forced me out of the service and caused me to become a hairdresser because here only I could be myself (Saghir and Robins, 1973:174).

Moreover, these jobs tend to be below their educational qualifications (Harry and De Vall, 1978:157–160):

> There are plenty of gay Ph.D's waiting tables in San Francisco (Interview with author).

The unusual occupational distribution of gay men flows from indirect discrimination (Levine, 1979). Researchers consistently report high levels of educational attainment among gay men (Harry and De Vall, 1978:155). For example, more than two thirds of Harry and De Vall's (1978:155) homosexual respondents—and about three quarters of Bell and Weinberg's (1978:277) had at least some college education. Yet gay men are often unable to convert their educational qualifications into high income and status jobs. Indirect discrimination forces them to cluster in marginal white collar or service jobs (Harry and De Vall, 1978:156–157).

Extent of Discrimination   No one knows exactly how often gay men are victimized in the workplace. Our inability to do representative sampling in the homosexual community prevents us from obtaining precise measures of this problem (Levine, 1979). Representative sampling requires knowing the size and location of the population under investigation. These parameters are unknown for the gay community. (No exhaustive listings of the homosexual population are presently available.)

There are, however, some empirical studies of homosexual behavior that provide limited data on the magnitude of this problem. (These studies are listed in Table 2.) All of these studies used questionnaires to investigate the social and psychological adjustment of gay men. The questionnaires, moreover, included a few items about employment discrimination. For example, four of the 145 questionnaire items in Weinberg and William's (1974) research—and three out of the 528 items in Bell and Weinberg's (1978) study pertain to job discrimination.

The picture that emerges from these data shows that gay men anticipate and encounter significant victimization in the workplace. More than three quarters of the homosexuals interviewed in Weinberg and William's (1974:106) research feared that there would be problems at work if it became known that they were gay. The men worried primarily about punitive reactions from work associates. Almost half felt that their employers would be intolerant or rejecting; about two fifths expected co-workers to behave similarly.

The studies that uncovered actual instances of discrimination demonstrated that such fears are not groundless. In Williams and Weinberg's (1971:98) work, 16 percent of the respondents lost or were refused jobs because of their homosexuality. Similar figures appear in other studies. Saghir and Saghir (1973:174) discovered that 16 percent of their sample was fired or asked to resign after detection of their sexual orientation. In a later study, Weinberg and Williams (1974:109) found that 16 percent of their respondents lost a job after their homosexuality became known. Finally, Bell and Weinberg (1978:362) reported somewhat lower figures—7 percent of their sample lost or almost lost a job due to erotic preference, and 6 percent were denied better work assignments.

The studies also showed that a considerable percentage of homosexuals believed that their sexual orientation has adversely affected their careers by making them vulnerable to discrimination. Nearly one third of Weinberg and Williams' (1974:108) sample felt that their homosexuality caused them problems on the job. This proportion holds in two other studies. Approximately one third of Saghir and Robin's (1973:172) sample believed that their sexual preference limited their choice of work or their career advancement. In addition, almost a third of William's and Weinbergs' (1971:98) respondents felt that their sexual orientation negatively influenced their economic lives. Likewise, one quarter of Bell and Weinberg's (1978:361) sample believed that their homosexuality adversely affected their careers.

Two of the studies collected data on coping strategies among homosexual workers. Most gay men passed for heterosexual on the job. Nearly three quarters of Weinberg and Williams' (1974:106) respondents—and more than half of Bell and Weinberg's (1978:96) concealed their sexual orientation from employers. Passing appears to be less common with co-workers. Only two fifths of Weinberg and Williams' (1974:106) sample—and one third of Bell and Weinberg's (1978:296) hid their homosexuality from all of their co-workers.

When taken together, these studies afforded a somewhat muddled picture of the scope of employment discrimination. We can, however, obtain a clearer image through a secondary analysis of the data presented in all four studies. We can reanalyze this data to compute approximate measures of victimization because all of the studies posed similar questions about job discrimination and looked at similar samples. (All of the researchers used large but nonrepresentative samples recruited from gay organizations and gathering places, and all of the samples came from urban areas.)

In determining the overall extent of the victimization, we defined perceived adverse consequences on the belief that homosexuality negatively affected careers, and actual discrimination, as firing, nonhiring, or nonpromotion. We calculated the percentages of gay men who perceived adverse consequences or experienced discrimination by dividing the number of respondents in all of the studies which asked questions about these factors by the number who answered these questions affirmatively (Tables 2 and 3).

Nearly one third of the homosexuals surveyed felt that their sexual preference had negatively affected their careers, and almost one sixth of the men had actually experienced job discrimination. The only comparable estimates for lesbians are quite similar, with 31 percent of the lesbians surveyed

TABLE 2 EXTENT OF PERCEIVED
ADVERSE CAREER CONSEQUENCES OF
HOMOSEXUALITY AMONG GAY MEN

Studies	Gay Men Perceiving Adverse Career Consequences (%)
Williams and Weinberg (N = 63)	29
Saghir and Robins (N = 89)	32
Weinberg and Williams (N = 1057)	30
Bell and Weinberg (N = 665)	25
All four studies (N = 1874)	30

anticipating victimization in the workplace and 13 percent actually encountering discrimination (Levine and Leonard, 1984).

Although certainly imposing, these figures offer only an imprecise measure of the extent to which gay men are victimized in employment, and most likely represent a low estimate. There are three reasons for making this claim. First, all the data come from self-report studies in which gay men are queried about their experiences with job discrimination. Yet homosexuals are often unaware of being discriminated against on the job (Harry and De Vall, 1978:161). Employers may be too frightened of adverse public reaction or may be too

TABLE 3 EXTENT OF ACTUAL
EMPLOYMENT DISCRIMINATION AMONG
GAY MEN

Studies	Gay Men Experiencing Discrimination (%)
Williams and Weinberg (N = 63)	16
Saghir and Robins (N = 89)	16
Weinberg and Williams (N = 1057)	16
Bell and Weinberg (N = 665)	7
All four studies (N = 1874)	13

embarrassed to acknowledge that sexual orientation is the reason for not hiring, promoting, or retaining a gay man. They therefore conceal the real motive for taking discriminatory actions by stating that, for example, the position has already been filled or that the homosexual employee was incompetent or unqualified. Second, the gay men participating in these studies lived in cities where, according to various polls, residents are far more accepting of homosexuality than nonurban dwellers (Schneider and Lewis, 1984; Gallup, 1987). In fact, all of these studies included men who lived in San Francisco or New York, cities well known for their acceptance of homosexuality.

CONCLUSION

Whatever the precise statistic may be, homosexuals are clearly victimized in the workplace. Homophobic stereotypes cause employers and co-workers to routinely discriminate against gay men in traditionally masculine lines of work. To cope with this victimization, homosexuals use psychologically taxing or professionally damaging tactics. Moreover, fear of discrimination drives many gay men away from men's work and into sissy jobs, which functions to reinforce prevailing images of gay men as effeminate.

Not only does this discrimination waste promising talents, it also seriously reduces life chances of homosexuals. Many talented and qualified gay men are working at positions far beneath their capabilities because of job discrimination, which robs our society of their potential contributions. In addition, discrimination erodes the ability of homosexuals to earn a living which adversely affects their life-style and self-esteem.

Anti-discrimination laws and policies are needed to curtail the victimization of gay men. A handful of localities have passed laws—and a number of companies have formulated personal policies barring employment discrimination on the basis of sexual orientation. It is time that these laws and policies become commonplace.

NOTES

[1] I am indebted to Michael S. Kimmel for the concept of homosexuals as failed men.

[2] Many Americans believe that homosexuals lack the genetic, hormonal, or familial makeup of real men, which is why they become gay. Familial explanations are perhaps the most popular of these perceptions. It is commonly believed that gay men grow up in households in which parents fail to follow traditional roles. Their mothers are overbearing and dominating; and their fathers, weak and passive, which causes homosexuals to hate women, love men and turn gay. Bell, et al. (1981) found no relationship between this kind of upbringing and adult homosexuality. Approximately equal number of homosexuals and heterosexuals grew up in such family settings.

[3] Research indicates that most gay men are appropriately masculine in demeanor and appearance. Saghir and Robins (1973:106–8) evaluated the effeminacy of their homosexuals respondents, and found that only one sixth of their sample manifested womenly attributes.

[4] The extent to which gay men display these interests is presently unknown. As best we can tell, such interests are not typical of all gay men. Saghir and Robins (1973:175) found that about two thirds of their respondents were interested in individual sports (e.g., swimming, tennis). About half were interested in the arts; a quarter in constructional hobbies like carpentry, and one tenth, in domestic pursuits (e.g., cooking, sewing).

◆ ◆ ◆

Men and Health: Body and Mind

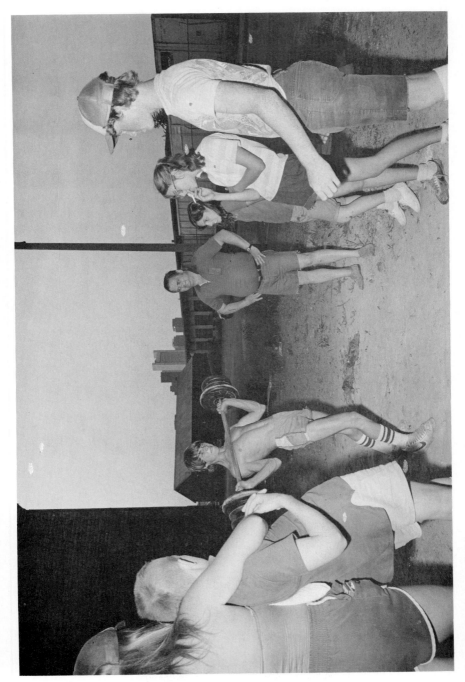

268

Why did the gap between male and female life expectancy increase from two years in 1900 to nearly eight years today? Why do men suffer heart attacks and ulcers at such a consistently higher rate than women do? Why are auto insurance rates so much higher for young males than for females of the same age? Are mentally and emotionally "healthy" males those who conform more closely to traditional cultural prescriptions for masculinity, or is it the other way around?

The articles in this section, though focusing on different specific topics, tend to follow and develop the argument of the men's liberation movement of the mid-1970s: Men do enjoy privileges in patriarchal society, but they often pay a heavy price. Narrow, emotionally inexpressive cultural prescriptions for masculinity are not only "stressful," they are in fact "lethal" for men. Harrison, Chin, and Ficarrotto explore the specific causes of men's lower life expectancy—higher rates of heart disease, cancer, and death by accident or suicide. Three-quarters of the reasons for men's earlier deaths, they argue, have to do with "the male sex role": men rarely ask for help at early signs of physical or emotional troubles; men may deal with stresses by internalizing them and/or by turning to alcohol, tobacco, or other drugs; men take more unnecessary risks driving cars, in their work and in recreation; and men are more successful in their attempts at suicide than are women. Gloria Steinem's humorous meditation on menstruation and masculinity underscores the seriousness of the ways in which men ignore their own health and cast women's bodies as the "other."

In the next article, Barry Glassner demonstrates how dominant conceptions of masculinity are encoded in and symbolized by the development of muscular male bodies. Alongside these dominant cultural conceptions of masculinity, there have always been masculinities that have been marginalized and subordinated. Martin Duberman, in a moving personal account of being gay in the 1950s, shows how his own personal and relational problems—and, by extension, those of hundreds of thousands of closeted gay men—were directly linked to the system of compulsory heterosexuality in which they lived. Only a social movement such as that which flourished in the 1970s could redefine gay sexuality as "healthy," and thus provide a context in which gay individuals, connected with one another rather than isolated, could begin to feel better about themselves and their relationships.

Interestingly as gay men were countering the social disease of homophobia in the 1970s, another disease was making inroads in their communities. The AIDS epidemic, according to Kimmel and Levine, has brought homophobes back out of their closets. Yet they argue that AIDS should *not* be viewed as a "gay disease," rather we should analyze the relationship between AIDS and masculinity. Echoing the more general discussions of men and health that preceded them, Kimmel and Levine conclude that "until we change what it means to be a real man, every man will die a little bit every day."

James Harrison, James Chin, and Thomas Ficarrotto

WARNING: MASCULINITY MAY BE DANGEROUS TO YOUR HEALTH

In 1900, life expectancy in the United States was 48.3 years for women and 46.3 years for men. In 1984, it was 78.2 years for women and 71.2 years for men (U. S. Department of Health and Human Services, 1987). During this 84-year period life expectancy for both men and women increased by more than 24 years, whereas the difference increased from 2 years in 1900 to 7 years in 1984, consistently favoring women.

This difference grew consistently larger during the course of this century, reaching a peak difference between sexes of 7.8 years in 1975 and 1979. (Recent data suggest, however, that women's advantage is decreasing.)

The gains in life expectancy for both men and women can be attributed to better nutrition and improved health care. But how can the difference between men's and women's life expectancies and the consistent increase in the size of this difference during this century be explained?

Two general perspectives—a biogenetic and a psychosocial—can be distinguished. The former attributes men's greater mortality to genetic factors (Montagu, 1953). The latter attributes men's greater mortality in large part to lethal aspects of the male role (Jourard, 1971). This article will evaluate these two perspectives, and assess what can most reliably be said about the consequence of male role behavior for life expectancy.

In comparison to women, there is for men a higher perinatal and early childhood death rate, a higher rate of congenital birth defects, a greater vulnerability to recessive sex-linked disorders, a higher accident rate during childhood and all subsequent ages, a higher incidence of behavioral and learning disorders, a higher suicide rate, and a higher metabolism rate, which may result in greater energy expenditure and a consequent failure to conserve physical resources. In the biogenetic perspective, this broad range of reported physical, psychological, and social sex differences is interpreted as a direct or mediated consequence of genetic differences. These differences are understood to be causally and cumulatively related, and to result in a higher mortality rate for men. There is a quality of inevitability in this perspective—biology is seen as destiny with a vengeance—but in this case males are understood to be in the less favored position. Taken all together, and without consideration of other factors, this perspective constitutes a plausible explanatory system for an array of apparently correct data.

In contrast, the alternative psychosocial perspective hypothesizes that the greater mortality rate of men is at least partially a consequence of the demands of the male role and emphasizes the ways in which male role expectations have a deleterious effect on men's lives, and possibly contribute to men's higher mortality rate. One of the complexities of this sociocultural hypothesis is the problem of specifying what is meant by "male role expectations." This is no simple task.

DEFINING THE MALE ROLE

Brannon (1976) has provided the most detailed and systematic attempt to delineate the various components of the male role. Although noting its elusive quality and the apparent contradictions within it, he abstracts four themes or dimensions that seem to be valid across all specific manifestations of stereotyped male role behavior. He characterizes these components in four short phrases:

1. No Sissy Stuff: the need to be different from women.
2. The Big Wheel: the need to be superior to others.
3. The Sturdy Oak: the need to be independent and self-reliant.
4. Give 'Em Hell: the need to be more powerful than others, through violence if necessary.

Clearly men express more positive and socially valued characteristics than described by these four themes. The attempt to define a normative role specific for only one sex necessarily results in a distorted model of human potential. The fiction that men and women are opposites is perpetuated. The recognition that men and women are essentially similar in what constitutes their humanity although manifesting a range of individual differences both within and between each sex is ignored. It is consequently possible to understand why the attempt to conform to male role expectations has negative consequences for men.

Jourard (1971) assumed that men's basic psychological needs are essentially the same as women's: all persons need to be known and to know, to be depended upon and to depend, to be loved and to love, and to find purpose and meaning in life. The socially prescribed male role, however, requires men to be noncommunicative, competitive and nongiving, and inexpressive, and to evaluate life success in terms of external achievements rather than personal and interpersonal fulfillment. All men are caught in a double bind. If a man fulfills the prescribed role requirements, his basic human needs go unmet; if these needs are met, he may be considered, or consider himself, unmanly. Jourard contended that if these needs are not met, persons risk emotional disorder, they may ignore somatic signals with a resultant failure to seek health care, possibly develop greater vulnerability to illness, and even lose the will to live.

Going beyond Jourard's general assessment, Rosenfeld (1972) has argued that the growing-up process by which boys become men has been made into an achievement or a task rather than a natural unfolding of human potentiality. By what criteria can a boy ever know that he has fulfilled the requirements of the male role? Adults are of little help in clarifying expectations for children, because they too are confused by apparent uncertainties about and inconsistency within male role expectations. Hartley (1959) long since observed that unclear sex-role expectations for children are a major source of anxiety. If severe enough and persistent, such anxiety may lead to serious emotional difficulty that may cause, or contribute to, behavioral and learning disorders.

One way children cope with anxiety derived from sex-role expectations is the development of compensatory masculinity (Tiller, 1967). Compensatory masculine behaviors range from the innocent to the insidious. Boys naturally imitate the male models available to them and can be observed overemphasizing male gait and verbal patterns. But if the motive is a need to prove the right to male status, more destructive behavioral patterns may result, and persist into adulthood. Boys are often compelled to take risks that result in accidents; older youth often begin smoking and drinking as a symbol of adult male status (Farrell, 1974); automobiles are often utilized as an extension of male power; and some men find confirmation of themselves in violence toward those whom they do not consider in conformity to the male role (Churchill, 1967). A convincing case has been made by both Fasteau (1974) and Komisar (1976) that readiness to settle international conflict by war rather than diplomacy is a function of prevalent male role expectations.

In addition, the requirements of the male work role have also been implicated as a cause of men's greater mortality. It has been suggested that stress and the competition to get ahead may result in greater vulnerability for men (Slobogin, 1977).

DATA RELEVANT TO THE BIOGENETIC AND PSYCHOSOCIAL HYPOTHESIS[1]

Madigan's early study (1957) remains influential in defense of the biogenetic perspective because its claimed empirical basis gave it evidential status that the psychosocial hypothesis has only recently begun to amass. The current debate is rightly focused on data about rates of conception, birth, and death that can be attributed to genetic causes, on the one hand, and data about rates of death that can be correlated with sex-role-related behavior.

Rates of Conception and Prenatal Mortality In spite of the theoretically equal opportunity for parity in male and female conceptions (the primary sex ratio), the known ratio of male to female births (the secondary sex ratio) consistently favors males. This ratio is reported variously as between 103 : 100 and 106 : 100 (Tricomi, Serr, & Solish, 1960; Parkes, 1967; Stoll, 1974). The preponderance of evidence suggests that the sex ratio at conception favors

---

[1] Several methodological considerations should be noted: First, the psychosocial hypothesis utilizes a conception of causality involving the complex interaction of biological, psychological, and social factors. When assessing the claims of the psychosocial hypothesis, it is difficult to determine the degree to which illness is a consequence of any one factor, or an interaction among a combination of factors. Second, age must be taken into consideration when accounting for sex differences in mortality. For example, in middle life the incidence of death attributable to heart disease is greater for men than women. In old age the cause of death is frequently heart failure for both sexes. When data for all ages are taken together, the large sex differences at different ages are obscured. Third, sex differences in morbidity may be subject to observational and reporting errors, as well as response bias. In addition, mental illness contributes to physical illness, suicide, and death by accidental cause. Although women are assumed to suffer from mental illness more than men, this notion has been seriously challenged by health professionals (see Harrison, 1975). Finally there are limitations on the use of mortality data. Methods and criteria for collection have changed over time, and adequate data are still unavailable for many nonindustrial societies. Therefore comparisons over time and across cultures are made difficult.

males to an even greater degree, but due to greater loss of males during pregnancy the amount of excess males at birth is reduced. Most studies show a higher ratio of males to females in induced abortions, which indicates a higher conception rate for males, and an even higher ratio of males to females in spontaneous abortions, which suggests that the male fetus is less viable. Accordingly the ratio of male to female conceptions is estimated to be between 108 : 100 and 120 : 100. It is therefore assumed that the male fetus is more vulnerable *in utero*.

Greater male mortality continues during early childhood: utilizing 1982 data, the ratio of male to female deaths due to certain causes in infancy is 140 : 100; and the ratio of male to female deaths at all ages, but attributable to congenital abnormalities, is 118 : 100. Due to an excess of male over female deaths from all causes, parity is achieved in the sexes ratio during the 25–34 year decade (Parkes, 1967). The excess of male over female deaths continues (see Table 1), resulting in an increasing ratio of females to males alive as age advances.

In sum, the genetic evidence suggests that the male fetus and the male neonate are more vulnerable prior to the time when sociocultural factors could exert an influence sufficient to account for a significant amount of the variance. These innate factors, however, are not sufficient to reduce the sex ratio to parity, since parity is not reached until early adulthood, the time of expected procreation. Subsequent to childhood the excess of the male over the female death rate cannot be attributed solely to biological differences between the sexes.

The greater *in utero* and perinatal mortality of males, along with the slightly higher mortality of males at later ages due to congenital anomalies, suggests the operation of a biological factor that may contribute to the overall higher mortality rate of men. In the absence of evidence to demonstrate the operation of social factors, a biologically reductionist explanation appears plausible. For this reason it is essential to examine the available data in which the possible effect of social factors can be discerned.

TABLE 1 RATIO OF MALE TO FEMALE DEATHS (1982 DATA)[a]

Age in Years	Male:Female
Under 1	125:100
1–4	123:100
5–14	153:100
15–24	289:100
25–34	257:100
35–44	189:100
45–54	185:100
55–64	190:100
65–74	164:100
75–84	164:100
85 +	123:100

[a] Recalculated from data in *Vital Statistics of the United States*, 1982 (USDHHS, 1986).

Current Adult Mortality   Mortality data, examined in terms of sex differences in specific causes of death, provide the best evidence for the psychosocial hypothesis. In his early study, Madigan (1957) attempted to determine why men had not benefited from technological advances in health care to the same extent as women. He compared the mortality rates in a sample of cloistered members of religious orders with population rates and he hypothesized that the life expectancy of the male "religious" would approach that of the female "religious" and exceed that of men in the general population, if differential mortality rates were due to male role-induced stress. He found no large departure of his subjects from population norms, and concluded that role strain makes only a small contribution to the differences and that biological factors are the chief source of variance.

Madigan recognized that the men and women subjects did not live under identical conditions—that cloistered men were more likely to drink and to smoke than women, for example. He overlooked completely, however, the consequences of the male subject's socialization into male role patterns prior to entering the religious orders, and the further possibility that a cloistered existence may have contributed to rather than reduced the strain that they experienced.

Enterline (1961) argued that a reductionist biological view could not be sustained when variations over time in specific causes of death in different age groups were examined. He identified several trends in the differential death rate between 1929 and 1958 that could not be simply attributed to biological causes: an increase in deaths due to lung cancer and coronary heart disease among 45- to 64-year-old males. Though he was not able to provide an explanatory hypothesis for these differences, in the absence of a satisfactory biological explanation Enterline concluded that environmental determinants were a more likely explanation.

Conrad (1962) extended the analysis of the determinants of differential mortality rates by specifically considering sociological factors. He identified a variety of means by which male role behaviors may contribute to the higher mortality rates of men: the higher accidental death rate at all ages, the greater physical and emotional strain of the male economic role, and the greater exposure to industrial hazards and contaminants.

Waldron and Johnson (Waldron, 1976, 1983a, 1983b; Waldron & Johnson, 1976) have focused attention on sex differences in causes of death by ranking all causes accounting for more than 1% of all deaths in descending order according to the ratio of male to female deaths. In their presentation the first seven categories and the ratio of male to female deaths in each were as follows:

1. Malignant neoplasm of the respiratory system (5.9 : 1).
2. Other bronchopulmonic disease (4.9 : 1).
3. Motor vehicle accidents (2.8 : 1).
4. Suicide (2.7 : 1).
5. Other accidents (2.4 : 1).
6. Cirrhosis of the liver (2.0 : 1).
7. Arteriosclerotic heart disease, including coronary disease (2.0 : 1).

All seven categories have sex-role behavior correlates, for example, the greater incidence and frequency of smoking, drinking, and propensity toward risk-taking and violence among men.

The present discussion utilizes Waldron's interpretive framework, but is based on more recent data (Tables 2 and 3). The criteria for inclusion of categories of cause of death in Tables 2 and 3 were (1) the 15 major headings defined in the *Vital Statistics* as leading causes of death, (2) following Waldron, all subcategories that account for more than 1% of deaths, and (3) subcategories that have high sex ratios.

There are several significant points of contrast with Waldron's presen-

TABLE 2 CAUSES OF DEATH (1972 DATA)[a]

	Male/Female Ratio[b]	Male/Female Ratio	Percentage of Deaths
Diseases of the heart	418.5 : 310.3	1.35	38.5
Acute myocardial infarction	221.5 : 124.7	1.78	18.2
Chronic ischemic heart disease	157.9 : 151.4	1.04	16.3
Other	21.2 : 15.6	1.36	1.9
Malignant neoplasms	185.7 : 147.2	1.26	17.6
Bucal cavity and pharynx	5.3 : 2.0	2.65	0.4
Digestive organs	50.3 : 41.9	1.20	4.9
Respiratory system	60.3 : 14.8	4.07	3.9
Breasts	0.3 : 29.2	0.01	1.6
Genital organs	18.9 : 21.7	0.87	2.2
Urinary organs	10.5 : 4.8	2.19	0.8
Other	21.6 : 18.5	1.17	2.1
Lymphatic and hematopoic-tic tissue	10.5 : 8.4	1.25	1.0
Cerebrovascular diseases	94.0 : 110.5	0.85	10.9
Cerebral hemorrhage	17.1 : 18.2	0.94	1.9
Cerebral thrombosis	24.9 : 30.2	0.82	2.9
Other	51.6 : 61.6	0.84	6.1
Accidents	78.6 : 33.4	2.35	5.9
Motor vehicle	39.6 : 15.1	2.62	2.9
Other	39.0 : 18.4	2.12	3.0
Influenza and pneumonia	34.2 : 26.1	1.31	3.2
Diabetes mellitus	15.6 : 21.4	0.73	2.0
Certain causes in infancy	19.5 : 13.2	1.48	1.7
Cirrhosis of the liver	21.1 : 10.4	2.03	1.7
Arteriosclerosis	13.5 : 17.6	0.77	1.7
Bronchitis, emphysema, asthma	23.3 : 6.7	3.48	1.6
Suicide	17.5 : 6.8	2.57	1.3
Homicide	15.4 : 3.7	4.16	1.0
Congenital abnormalities	7.7 : 6.4	1.20	0.8
Nephritis and nephrosis	4.6 : 3.6	1.27	0.4
Peptic ulcer	5.1 : 2.5	2.04	0.4
All other	61.1 : 45.6	1.34	11.6

[a] Calculated from data in USDHEW (1976).
[b] Rate per 100,000 population.

TABLE 3 CAUSES OF DEATH (1982 DATA)[a]

	Male/Female Rate[b]	Male/Female Ratio	Percentage of Deaths
Diseases of the heart	353.9 : 299.6	1.18	38.3
Acute myocardial infarction	151.3 : 101.3	1.49	14.7
Old myocardial infarction and other chronic ischemic heart disease	113.2 : 108.7	1.04	13.0
Other forms heart disease	72.4 : 69.3	1.04	8.3
Hypertensive heart disease	7.9 : 10.0	0.79	1.1
Malignant neoplasms[a]	207.6 : 167.8	1.23	22.0
Bucal cavity and pharynx[c]	5.2 : 2.2	2.50	0.4
Digestive organs[c]	52.3 : 45.0	1.15	5.7
Respiratory system[c]	73.7 : 28.0	2.63	5.9
Breasts[c]	0.2 : 31.4	0.01	1.9
Genital organs[c]	21.9 : 19.2	1.14	2.4
Urinary organs[c]	10.7 : 5.3	2.01	0.9
Other[c]	24.8 : 21.2	1.17	2.7
Lymphatic and hematopoietic tissue[c]	10.5 : 9.2	1.14	1.2
Cerebrovascular diseases[c]	56.7 : 78.8	0.72	8.0
Cerebral hemorrhage[c]	8.1 : 9.1	0.89	1.0
Cerebral thrombosis[c]	10.0 : 14.3	0.69	1.4
Other[c]	38.6 : 55.4	0.69	5.5
Accidents[c]	58.4 : 23.8	2.45	4.8
Motor vehicle[c]	29.5 : 10.6	2.78	2.3
Other[c]	28.9 : 13.2	2.18	2.4
Chronic obstructive pulmonary disease and allied conditions	35.2 : 16.9	2.08	3.0
Bronchitis, emphysema, and asthma[c]	11.1 : 5.8	1.91	1.0
Pneumonia and influenza[c]	22.5 : 19.8	1.13	2.5
Diabetes mellitus[c]	12.6 : 17.1	0.73	1.4
Suicide[c]	19.2 : 5.6	3.42	1.4
Chronic liver disease and cirrhosis[c]	15.9 : 8.2	1.93	1.4
Arteriosclerosis[c]	9.4 : 13.6	0.69	1.4
Homicide and legal intervention[c]	15.4 : 4.2	3.66	1.1
Certain conditions originating in perinatal period	10.5 : 7.5	1.40	1.1
Nephritis, nephrotic syndrome, and nephrosis	8.1 : 7.5	1.08	0.9
Congenital abnormalities[c]	6.4 : 5.4	1.18	0.7
Septicemia	4.9 : 5.1	0.96	0.6
All other			11.2

[a] Calculated from data in USDHHS (1986).
[b] Rate per 100,000 population.
[c] Comparable to Table 2 (1972 data) categories.

tation. The data in Tables 2 and 3 are ranked by percentage of deaths attributed to each cause, rather than by rank of the sex ratio, and it is not possible to know how all Waldron's categories compare with those here. In addition, Waldron omitted entirely the cerebrovascular category that accounts for 10.9% of all deaths in our 1972 data and 8.0% of all deaths in our 1982 data, and which in all subcategories account for more female than male deaths. The male to female ratio for homicides accounted for more than 1% of all deaths in 1972 and 1982 with a male to female ratio of 4.16 : 1 and 3.66 : 1, respectively, which would have qualified this cause of death for second place had the data been ranked as in Waldron's presentation.

It is also noteworthy that the *Vital Statistics* for the years 1972 through 1982 were analyzed for each of the 1972 major causes of death and it was determined that the 1982 statistics were within the limits of a linear trend model. This analysis was complicated by changes in categorization of major causes of death that began in the 1979 *Vital Statistics* with the implementation of the use of the Ninth Revision of the International Classification of Diseases, 1975. Only those causes of death indicated by footnote *c* in Table 3 are directly comparable to similar categories in Table 2. Given these caveats, it was concluded that the statistics for the major causes of death in 1982 that also appeared within the 15 major causes of death in 1972 were not artifactual but consistent with trends through these years.

Examination of the differential mortality rates alone reveals nothing about the antecedents of specific causes of death. The importance of Waldron's analysis is her discussion of these antecedents in relationship to sex-role-related behaviors. Fulfilling the requirements of the male role is characterized as an achievement, not simply the consequences of natural growth and development; it is often bought at the cost of risk and stress. Anxiety about failure to achieve may result in compensatory behaviors designed to show outward conformity to the role. Compensatory behaviors involve risk-taking of various kinds that may lead to accidents, exhibition of violence, excessive consumption of alcohol, and smoking. Reciprocally, anxiety about failure to achieve male role requisites may result in denial of dimensions of human experience more stereotypical[ly] associated with women's role. This denial may result in the suppression of gentleness and emotion. These specific male behaviors seem to be significant antecedents to all the major causes of death in which male death rates exceed those of women by a ratio of 2 : 1, a convention established by Waldron as a criterion of a large sex difference.

Diseases of the Heart   In contrast to Waldron's 1967 data, the ratio of male to female deaths does not exceed that 2 : 1 ratio in the 1972 or 1982 data when considering all ages combined. The higher coronary heart disease (CHD) death rates among the elderly, however, obscure large sex differences in mortality ratios for the younger age groups. For instance, for individuals between the ages of 20–44 years old in 1982, the sex-morality ratio exceeds 4 : 1 for acute myocardial infarction and for old myocardial infarction; in the same year, it exceeds 2 : 1 for hypertensive heart disease.

A biogenetic explanation posits that the female advantage in CHD mortality can be attributed to the protective effects of endogenous sex hormones. This argument is based on several investigations that have found that postmenopausal and oophorectomized women (women who have had their ovaries removed) are at an increased risk for CHD (Waldron, 1976, 1983a). Research supporting a biogenetic explanation, however, has been criticized on the basis of methodological flaws and inconsistent findings.

Evidence that links men's greater vulnerability to CHD to sex differences in smoking patterns, as well as to sex differences in aggressive, "hard-driving," behavior, appears to be a stronger argument explaining the sex differential in CHD mortality.

Of the three major risk factors for CHD, cigarette smoking is far more prevalent in the American population than either hypertension or elevated serum cholesterol (U. S. Surgeon General, 1983). Generally, in the past a greater percentage of men have smoked cigarettes compared to women. The proportion of smokers, however, has declined steadily between 1960 and 1980 in both men and women. This decline was steeper among men than among women. In 1970, male smokers smoked 4.1 more cigarettes per day than female smokers, but in 1980 men smoked only 2.0 more cigarettes per day than did women. Although a greater percentage of men still smoked cigarettes in 1980, and continued to smoke a greater average number of cigarettes per day, the differences between the sexes in 1980 was less than that observed a decade earlier (U. S. Surgeon General, 1983). Thus, as the smoking patterns of women become more similar to that of men, we might expect differences between men's and women's death rates as a consequence of smoking-related causes to diminish.

Behavioral patterns are also related to differential risks for heart disease. The Coronary Prone Behavior Pattern, Type A behavior (Friedman & Rosenman, 1974) is characterized by competitive achievement, striving, time urgency, and a potential for hostility. Type A behavior has been associated with an increased risk of CHD mortality in both men and women (Cooper, Detre, & Weiss, 1981; Booth-Kewley & Friedman, 1987).

Considering the major components of Type A behavior, such as excessive aggressiveness and competitiveness, one might suggest that Type A behaviors are associated with traditional masculine sex-role characteristics. At least six investigations have found positive correlations between Type A behavior and self-rated masculine sex-role characteristics in both male and female students (Blascovitch, Major, & Katkin, 1981; DeGregorio & Carver, 1980; Grimm & Yarnold, 1985; Nix & Lohr, 1981; Stevens, Pfost, & Ackerman, 1984; Zeldow, Clark, & Daugherty, 1985).

Although Type A behavior has been cited as being more prevalent among men than women (see Chesney, 1983), women are by no means exempt from the development of Type A behavior. Sex differences in Type A behavior are apparently reduced once a comparison is made between men and women engaged in similar vocational activities (Ficarrotto & Weidner, 1987). In addition, employment outside the home appears to be a crucial factor in the expression of Type A behavior in women, and higher status occupations among women appear to be associated with higher Type A scores (Morell & Katkin, 1982). Thus, it appears that "sex differences" in Type A behavior might have less to do with gender and more to do with whether a person's putative societal role can be defined as traditional male.

It should be noted that several prospective studies have failed to find a link between Type A behavior and CHD mortality (see Chesney, Hecker, & Black, 1987). In fact, Ragland and Brand (1988) found that among men who had already suffered a heart attack, Type A behavior was not associated with subsequent CHD mortality. It appears that certain components of the Type A pattern, such as hostility, might be more directly related to CHD mortality than overall Type A scores (Wright, 1988). Interestingly, men display more hostility than do women (Maccoby & Jacklin, 1974; Pleck, 1981; Waldron, 1976; Weidner, Friend, Ficarrotto, & Polowczyk, 1988). This raises the question of whether sex differences in hostility may contribute to men's higher CHD risk.

Malignant Neoplasms   Taking all types of cancer together, men are slightly more vulnerable than women. Utilizing Waldron's criterion, sex differences greater than 2 : 1 emerge in only four subcategories of malignant neoplasms. Of these, breast cancer is the only category in which women's risk is greater than men's, which seems largely a consequence of endocrine differences. The incidence of all other loci for cancer is greater for men.

Most relevant for this discussion, however, is the male to female ratio for cancer of the mouth and pharynx, 2.65 in 1972 and 2.50 in 1982, and of the respiratory system, 4.07 in 1972 and 2.63 in 1982. Both types of cancer are related to smoking, for which a higher rate is documented for men. Studies of the prevalence of smoking just prior to the1982 data show that the amount of daily smoking among women was approaching that of men and that the age of onset for smoking was getting earlier for both sexes (Schuman, 1977).

The ratio of cancer of the urinary organs was 2.19 in 1972 and 2.01 in 1982. There is evidence that a high level of smoking increases the risk of cancer of the ureter, and is related to cancer of the bladder at all levels of smoking (USDHEW, 1973, 1974, 1975).

It is also important to note that due to different work roles men are also exposed more often and at a higher level to industrial carcinogens.

Other Respiratory Diseases   In 1982, men still smoked more than women, according to all the parameters by which smoking could be measured. The relevance of this difference is seen again in the 3.48 ratio (1972) and 1.91 ratio (1982) of male to female deaths attributable to bronchitis, emphysema, and asthma. Research findings are consistent across national and ethnic groups. Smokers have higher death rates from chronic bronchitis and emphysema proportionately to the number of cigarettes smoked. Smokers are also more frequently subject to other respiratory infections than nonsmokers and require a longer convalescence (USDHEW, 1973, 1974, 1975). In addition, exposure to air pollution and/or industrial pollutants potentiates the effect of smoking.

Cirrhosis of the Liver   More men than women drink alcohol and more men than women drink to excess by an approximate ratio of 4 : 1 (Cahalan, 1970; McClelland et al., 1972). Alcohol serves both as a symbolic manifestation of compensatory masculinity and as an escape mechanism from the pressure to achieve. It is not surprising that males should die from causes of death associated with excessive drinking to a greater degree than women; the ratio of cirrhosis of the liver is 2.03 (1972) and 1.93 (1982).

Deaths due to External Causes   Men die more frequently than women from four external causes of death: motor vehicle accidents, 2.62 in 1972 and 2.78 in

1982; other accidents, 2.12 in 1972 and 2.18 in 1982; suicide, 2.57 in 1972 and 3.42 in 1982; and homicide, 4.16 in 1972 and 3.66 in 1982. Abuse of alcohol is clearly implicated in many automobile fatalities, and is very likely a factor in other deaths due to external causes. The consistent excess of male to female deaths due to accidents of other kinds has led some interpreters to presume an innate accident-prone tendency among males. This interpretation, however, is inconsistent with the emphasis on greater skill development among males in this culture. Consequently the greater accident rate can be accounted for more readily by the different socialization of males to perform high-risk activities, the popular assumption that male children are tougher than females, and the subsequent development of compensatory masculine behavior among men as a means of validating their status as males (Cicone & Ruble, 1978).

The greater vulnerability of males to death by suicide and homicide can be understood as a consequence of the greater socialization of men to aggressive and violent behavior. This is especially notable in contrast to the greater rate of suicide attempts by women, which appear to be requests for help rather than a determination to end life. Women more frequently utilize less violent and less effective means of attempting suicide. In sum, differences in the sex ratio of all external causes of death, which account for more than 1% of all deaths, are plausibly related to sex-role socialization.

CONCLUSIONS

A critical reading of presently available evidence confirms that male role socialization contributes to the higher mortality rate of men. Recognizing the multiplicity of variables within the chain of causality, Waldron (1976) estimates that three-fourths of the difference in life expectancy can be accounted for by sex-role-related behaviors that contribute to the greater mortality of men. She estimates that one-third of the differences can be accounted for by smoking, another one-sixth by coronary prone behavior, and the remainder by a variety of other causes. Using more precise statistical techniques to analyze differences in male/female mortality rates in terms of antecedents to specific causes of death, Retherford (1972) attributes half of the differences to smoking alone.

Waldron's estimate that three-fourths of the current 7.0 year difference in life expectancy is attributable to socialization is plausible and concordant with the difference in life expectancy at the turn of the century of approximately 2 years. The evidence we have reviewed suggests that this portion of the variance may be attributable to biogenetic determinants (1983a). However, any biogenetic factor is exacerbated by male role socialization. Parents assume that male children are tougher, when in fact they may be to some degree more vulnerable than female children. Male children are also more likely to develop a variety of behavioral difficulties such as hyperactivity, stuttering, dyslexia, and learning disorders of various kinds. Maccoby and Jacklin's (1974) review of research on childhood sex differences lends little support to the view that these observed sex differences are genetically determined. Insofar as they may be biogenetically predisposed, certainly the development of more functional behavioral patterns should be the goal of the socialization process. Male socialization into aggressive behavioral patterns seems clearly related to the higher death rate from external causes. Male anxiety about the achievement of masculine status seems to result in a variety of behaviors that can be understood as compensatory.

During the period in which the ratio between men's and women's life expectancy has worsened, social policy in the United States, especially in preparation for war and national defense, has been overwhelmingly directed toward reinforcement and support of the stereotyped male role (Fasteau, 1974; Filene, 1974). Recognition of the lethal aspects of the male role has had to await the emergence of a critical theory of sex-role socialization free of the ideological commitment to the status quo. This has been inspired by a critique of traditional psychological research inspired by the feminist movement (Harrison, 1975) and has been focally articulated for men's roles by Pleck (1976, 1981).

In the psychosocial perspective, sex differences, apart from those specifically associated with reproductive function, are understood to be smaller, less biologically based, and less socially significant. This is demonstrated by the greater range of difference within each sex than the average differences between the sexes. Differences in learned personality traits are understood not to be a necessary function of the development of sexual identity, but rather a consequence of social expectation. Finally, learning only stereotypical sex-typed traits is understood to be a handicap rather than an asset.

Traditional sex-role ideology serves as a rationale for the inevitability of psychological sex differences and the traditional division of family, work, and social responsibilities. The newer role liberation perspective provides not only the basis of reassessment of psychological characteristics and social arrangements, but also a basis for the reinterpretation of many previously observed sex differences (Pleck, 1976, 1981; Miller, 1976). Research suggests that it is not so much biological gender that is potentially hazardous to men's health but rather specific behaviors that are traditionally associated with the male sex role that can be taken on by either gender (Weidner et al., 1988; Wright, 1988). Recent data indicating a slight trend of convergence between sexes in mortality due to specific causes correlated with the convergence of smoking habits between the sexes are supportive of the psychosocial hypothesis. As plausible as this conclusion is, it is nevertheless tentative given the multivariate nature of public health data that need to be thoroughly researched along with prospective health and gender studies (Stillion, 1985).

Contemporary research has failed to demonstrate the existence of important intrinsic psychological differences between men and women. However, research on sex-role stereotypes demonstrates the persistence of the belief in such differences in personality traits (Rosencrantz, Vogel, Bee, Brovermann, & Brovermann, 1968). This continuing belief brings to mind W. I. Thomas's famous dictum: "If men [people] define situations as real, they are real in their consequences" (1928, p. 572). It is time that men especially begin to comprehend that the price paid for belief in the male role is shorter life expectancy. The male sex-role will become less hazardous to our health only insofar as it ceases to be defined as opposite to the female role, and comes to be defined as one genuinely human way to live.

Ironically, Madigan, whose work (1957) continues to have an undeserved credibility in discussions of this issue, supported the best possibility of extending male life expectancy. For him, as for many in our society, a technological solution was more probable than the "profound cultural revolution" that he recognized the psychosocial thesis required. But it is precisely that profound cultural revolution that is our need. The best hope for both men and women is overcoming a view of development that turns maturation into a polarized sex-typed achievement.

REFERENCES

Blascovitch, J., Major, B., & Katkin, E. Sex role orientation and Type-A behavior. *Personality and Social Psychology Bulletin*, 1981, *7*, 600–604.

Booth-Kewley, S., & Friedman, H. Psychological predictors of heart disease: A qualitative review. *Psychological Bulletin*, 1987, *10*, 343–362.

Brannon, R. C. No "sissy stuff": The stigma of anything vaguely feminine. In D. David & R. Brannon (Eds.), *The Forty-Nine Percent Majority*. Reading, MA: Addison-Wesley, 1976.

Broverman, I., Broverman, D., Clarkson, F., Rosenkrantz, P., & Vogel, S. 1970. "Sex Role Stereotypes and Clinical Judgments of Mental Health." *Journal of Consulting Psychology 34:* 1–7.

Cahalan, D. *Problem Drinkers*. San Francisco: Jossey-Bass, 1970.

Chesney, M. Occupational setting and coronary prone behavior in men and women. In T. Dembroski, G. Schmidt, & G. Blumchen (Eds.), *Biobehavioral Bases of Coronary Heart Disease*, pp. 79–90. New York: Karger, 1983.

Chesney, M. A., Hecker, M. H., Black, G. W. 1987. "Coronary-Prone Components of Type-A Behavior in the W.C.G.S.: A New Methodology." In B. K. Houston & C. R. Snyder (eds.) *Type-A Behavior Pattern: Current Trends and Future Directions*. New York: John Wiley, pp. 1–31.

Churchill, W. *Homosexuality in a Cross Cultural Perspective*. Englewood Cliffs, NJ: Prentice-Hall, 1967.

Cicone, M., & Ruble, D. Beliefs about males. *The Journal of Social Issues*, 1978, *34*, 5–16.

Conrad, F. Sex roles as a factor in longevity. *Sociology and Social Research*, 1962, *46*, 195–202.

Cooper, T., Detre, T., & Weiss, S. Coronary prone behavior and coronary heart disease: A critical review. *Circulation*, 1981, *63*, 1199–1215.

DeGregorio, E., & Carver, C. Type A behavior, sex role orientation, and psychological adjustment. *Journal of Personality and Social Psychology*, 1980, *39*, 286–293.

Enterline, P. Causes of death responsible for recent increases in sex mortality differentials in the United States. *Milbank Memorial Fund Quarterly*, 1961, *39*, 312–328.

Farrell, W. *The Liberated Man*. New York: Random House, 1974.

Fasteau, M. *The Male Machine*. New York: McGraw-Hill, 1974.

Ficarrotto, T., & Weidner, G. Sex differences in coronary heart disease mortality: A psychosocial perspective. Unpublished manuscript, 1987.

Filene, P. *Him/Her/Self: Sex Roles in Modern America*. New York: Harcourt, Brace, Jovanovich, 1974.

Friedman, M., & Rosenman, R. *Type A behavior and your heart*. Greenwich, CT: Fawcett Publications, 1974.

Grimm, L., & Yarnold, P. Sex typing and the coronary prone behavior pattern. *Sex Roles*, 1985, *12*, 171–177.

Harrison, J. A critical evaluation of research on "masculinity/femininity." Doctoral dissertation, New York University, 1975. *Dissertation Abstracts International*, 1975, *36*, 1903B. (University Microfilms No. 75-22890.)

Hartley, R. Sex role pressures in the socialization of the male child. *Psychological Reports*, 1959, *5*, 457–468.

Jourard, S. *The Transparent Self*. New York: Van Nostrand, 1971.

Komisar, L. Violence and the masculine mystique. In D. David and R. Brannon (Eds.), *The Forty-Nine Percent Majority*. Reading, MA: Addison-Wesley, 1976.

Maccoby, E., & Jacklin, C. *The Psychology of Sex Differences*. Stanford, CA: Stanford University Press, 1974.

Madigan, F. Are sex mortality differentials biologically caused? *Millbank Memorial Fund Quarterly*, 1957, *35*, 202–223.

McClelland, D., et al. *The Drinking Man*. Riverside, NJ: Free Press, 1972.

Miller, J. *Towards a New Psychology of Women*. Boston, MA: Beacon Press, 1976.

Montagu, A. *The Natural Superiority of Women*. New York: Macmillan, 1953.

Morell, M., & Katkin, E. Jenkins activity survey scores among women of different occupations. *Journal of Consulting and Clinical Psychology*, 1982, *50*, 588–589.

Nathanson, C. Illness and the feminine role: A theoretical review. *Social Science and Medicine*, 1975, *9*, 57–62.

Nix, J., & Lohr, J. Relationship between sex, sex role characteristics, and coronary prone behavior in college students. *Psychological Reports*, 1981, *48*, 739–744.

Parkes, A. The sex-ratio in man. In A. Allison (Ed.), *The Biology of Sex*. Baltimore, MD: Penguin Books, 1967.

Pleck, J. The male sex role: Definitions, problems, and sources of change. *Journal of Social Issues*, 1976, *32*(3), 155–163.

Pleck, J. *The Myth of Masculinity*. Cambridge, MA: The MIT Press, 1981.

Ragland, D., & Brand, R. Type A behavior and mortality from coronary heart disease. *New England Journal of Medicine*, 1988, *318*, 65–69.

Retherford, R. Tobacco smoking and the sex mortality differential. *Demography*, 1972, *9*, 203–216.

Rosenfield, A. Why men die younger. *Readers Digest*, 1972, 121–124.

Rosenkrantz, P., Vogel, S., Bee, H., Brovermann, I., & Brovermann, D. Sex-role stereotypes and self-concepts in college students. *Journal of Consulting and Clinical Psychology*, 1968. *32*, 287–295.

Schuman, L. Patterns of smoking behavior. In Jarvik, M., Cullen, J., Gritz, E., Vogt, T., & West, L. (Eds.), *Research on Smoking Behavior*. NIDA Research Monograph 17. Washington, DC: U. S. Government Printing Office, 1977.

Slobogin, K. Stress. *The New York Times Magazine*. November 20, 1977, 48–50, 96, 98, 100, 102, 104, 106.

Stevens, M., Pfost, K., & Ackerman, M. The relationship between sex role orientation and the Type A behavior pattern: A test of the main effect hypothesis. *Journal of Clinical Psychology*, 1984, *40*, 1338–1341.

Stillion, J. *Death and the Sexes*. Washington, D.C. Hemisphere Publishing Corp., 1985.

Stoll, C. *Female and Male*. Dubuque, IA: Wm. C. Brown, 1974.

Thomas, W. *The Child in America*. New York: Alfred A. Knopf, 1928.

Tiller, P. Parental role division and the child's personality. In E. Dahlstrom (Ed.), *The Changing Roles of Men and Women*. Boston, MA: Beacon, 1967.

Tricomi, V., Serr, O., & Solish, C. The ratio of male to female embryos as determined by the sex chromatin. *American Journal of Obstetrics and Gynecology*, 1960, *79*, 504–509.

U. S. Department of Health and Human Services. The Health Consequences of Smoking: Chronic Obstructive Lung Disease: A Report of the U.S. Surgeon General, 1984. Rockville, MD: Public Health Service, Office on Smoking and Health; Washington, D.C., 1984. (D.H.H.S. [PHS] 84-50205)

United States Department of Health Education and Welfare. *The Health Consequences of Smoking*. Washington, DC: The U. S. Government Printing Office, 1973, 1974, 1975.

United States Department of Health Education and Welfare. *Vital Statistics of the United States*. 1972 (Vol. 2). Washington, DC: U. S. Government Printing Office, 1976.

United States Department of Health and Human Services. *Vital Statistics of the United States*, 1982 (Vol. 2). Washington, DC: U. S. Government Printing Office, 1987.

United States Department of Health and Human Services. *Vital Statistics of the United States*, 1984 (Pre-Publication Monograph). Washington, DC: U. S. Government Printing Office, 1987.

Verbrugge, L. M. 1980. "Recent Trends in Sex Mortality Differentials in the United States." *Women and Health 5:* 17–37.

Waldron, I. Why do women live longer than men? *Journal of Human Stress*, 1976, *2*, 1–13.

Waldron, I. Sex differences in human mortality: The role of genetic factors. *Social Science and Medicine*, 1983a, *17*, 321–333.

Waldron, I. Sex differences in illness incidence, prognosis and mortality: Issues and evidence. *Social Science and Medicine*, 1983b, *17*, 1107–1123.

Waldron, I., & Johnson, S. Why do women live longer than men? *Journal of Human Stress*, 1976, *2*, 19–29.

Weidner, G., Friend, R., Ficarrotto, T., Mendell, N. R. Hostility and cardiovascular reactivity to stress in women and men. *Psychosomatic Medicine*.

Wright, L. The Type A behavior pattern and coronary artery disease: Quest for the active ingredients and the elusive mechanisms. *American Psychologist*, 1988, *43*, 2–14.

Zeldow, P., Clark, D., & Daugherty, S. Masculinity, femininity, Type A behavior and psychosocial adjustment in medical students. *Journal of Personality and Social Psychology*, 1985, *45*, 481–492.

Gloria Steinem

IF MEN COULD MENSTRUATE—

A white minority of the word has spent centuries conning us into thinking that a white skin makes people superior—even though the only thing it really does is make them more subject to ultraviolet rays and to wrinkles. Male human beings have built whole cultures around the idea that penis-envy is "natural" to women—though having such an unprotected organ might be said to make men vulnerable, and the power to give birth makes womb-envy at least as logical.

In short, the characteristics of the powerful, whatever they may be, are thought to be better than the characteristics of the powerless—and logic has nothing to do with it.

What would happen, for instance, if suddenly, magically, men could menstruate and women could not?

The answer is clear—menstruation would become an enviable, boast-worthy, masculine event:

Men would brag about how long and how much.

Boys would mark the onset of menses, that longed-for proof of manhood, with religious ritual and stag parties.

Congress would fund a National Institute of Dysmenorrhea to help stamp out monthly discomforts.

Sanitary supplies would be federally funded and free. (Of course, some men would still pay for the prestige of commercial brands such as John Wayne Tampons, Muhammad Ali's Rope-a-dope Pads, Joe Namath Jock Shields— "For Those Light Bachelor Days," and Robert "Baretta" Blake Maxi-Pads.)

Military men, right-wing politicians, and religious fundamentalists would cite menstruation ("*men*-struation") as proof that only men could serve in the

Army ("you have to give blood to take blood"), occupy political office ("can women be aggressive without that steadfast cycle governed by the planet Mars?"), be priests and ministers ("how could a woman give her blood for our sins?"), or rabbis ("without the monthly loss of impurities, women remain unclean").

Male radicals, left-wing politicians, and mystics, however, would insist that women are equal, just different; and that any woman could enter their ranks if only she were willing to self-inflict a major wound every month ("you *must* give blood for the revolution"), recognize the preeminence of menstrual issues, or subordinate her selfness to all men in their Cycle of Enlightenment.

Street guys would brag ("I'm a three-pad man") or answer praise from a buddy ("Man, you lookin' *good!*") by giving fives and saying, "Yeah, man, I'm on the rag!"

TV shows would treat the subject at length. ("Happy Days": Richie and Potsie try to convince Fonzie that he is still "The Fonz," though he has missed two periods in a row.) So would newspapers. (SHARK SCARE THREATENS MENSTRUATING MEN. JUDGES CITES MONTHLY STRESS IN PARDONING RAPIST.) And movies. (Newman and Redford in "Blood Brothers"!)

Men would convince women that intercourse was *more* pleasurable at "that time of the month." Lesbians would be said to fear blood and therefore life itself—though probably only because they needed a good menstruating man.

Of course, male intellectuals would offer the most moral and logical arguments. How could a woman master any discipline that demanded a sense of time, space, mathemathics, or measurement, for instance, without that in-built gift for measuring the cycles of the moon and planets—and thus for measuring anything at all? In the rarefied fields of philosophy and religion, could women compensate for missing the rhythm of the universe? Or for their lack of symbolic death-and-resurrection every month?

Liberal males in every field would try to be kind: the fact that "these people" have no gift for measuring life or connecting to the universe, the liberals would explain, should be punishment enough.

And how would women be trained to react? One can imagine traditional women agreeing to all these arguments with a staunch and smiling masochism. ("The ERA would force housewives to wound themselves every month": Phyllis Schlafly. "Your husband's blood is as sacred as that of Jesus—and so sexy, too!": Marabel Morgan.) Reformers and Queen Bees would try to imitate men, and *pretend* to have a monthly cycle. All feminists would explain endlessly that men, too, needed to be liberated from the false idea of Martian aggressiveness, just as women needed to escape the bonds of menses-envy. Radical feminists would add that the oppression of the nonmenstrual was the pattern for all other oppressions. ("Vampires were our first freedom fighters!") Cultural feminists would develop a bloodless imagery in art and literature. Socialist feminists would insist that only under capitalism would men be able to monopolize menstrual blood. . . .

In fact, if men could menstruate, the power justifications could probably go on forever.

If we let them.

Barry Glassner
MEN AND MUSCLES

America was built of male muscle, at least according to our popular lore. The standard version of our early years speaks of rugged pioneers fighting the forces of nature and mastering savages with their bare hands. American industry likewise is understood to have been the product of male brawn. The captains of industry in the late nineteenth and early twentieth centuries were portrayed as almost animalistic in their physical power and drive. Aspiring young men were urged to display their own commitment to the same values. A 1920s manual for salesmen, like some of its counterparts in the 1980s, recommended exercises each morning, because muscular strength "imparts a feeling of enthusiasm, physical vigor and power of decision that no other faculty can give."

Bernarr Macfadden, creator of the physical culture movement early in this century, exhorted men to realize that "it lies with you, whether you shall be a strong virile animal . . . or a miserable little crawling worm."

During the world wars, male strength was equated—in political speeches and posters—with patriotism. And men who grew up just after the World War II remember vividly the Charles Atlas ads in comic books of the period. "I manufacture weaklings into MEN," read the headline on the back page of a 1952 issue of *The Fighting Leathernecks* (ten cents a copy). Beside a huge picture of Atlas, "the world's most perfectly developed man," appeared the famous story of how he used to be a ninety-seven-pound weakling. The choice every man had to face is made explicit in these ads: he could either keep his "skinny, pepless, second-rate body" or turn it over to Atlas (or the high school coach or the trainer at the local gym), who would "cram it so full of handsome, healthy, bulging new muscle that your friends will grow bug eyed."

Generations of boys have received the message loud and clear. Sociologist James Coleman asked high school boys in the early sixties how they would like to be remembered. Nearly half chose "athletic star," far more than opted for "brilliant student" or even "most popular." Neither hippies nor drugs nor the women's movement has changed things very much since. When the same question was asked of high schoolers in the seventies and again in the eighties, the same results were obtained: close to half answered "athletic star." What's more, in contemporary studies of college students, muscular men have been shown to be better liked by others and happier with themselves than their less well-developed classmates.

Boys suffer if they can't or won't accept the obligation to develop manly physiques. Every one of 256 nonmuscular adolescent boys examined in one study suffered mood or behavior problems connected to feelings of physical inadequacy. *Sissy* is, after all, a much more negative term than *tomboy*. While a girl is expected to outgrow her tomboyism, a boy who doesn't act boyish may well be sent to a psychiatrist for help. So a boy must prove decisively his commitment to masculinity, and the primary way to do it is through athletics and muscularity.

Reprinted from *Bodies: Why We Look the Way We Do (And How We Feel About It)*. New York: Putnam, 1988. Copyright © by Barry Glassner.

Muscles are *the* sign of masculinity. Author Nancy Huston has pointed out that women are distinguished from men by their ability to give birth, but men have no parallel "mark" of their gender. To fill in for this lack of a distinctive male trait, Huston says, many cultures have granted physical strength to boys and men as a characteristic uniquely their own. Over the years, innumerable scientific and superstitious explanations have been advanced purporting to prove it was God or Nature that made males stronger than females.

Because of the great meaning attached to muscles, nonathletic boys often grow into insecure men. In an "About Men" column in *The New York Times Magazine*, Mark Goodson, the television producer, wrote humorously about the drawbacks of disliking sports. Soon after arriving in New York in the 1940s, "hungry, anxious, in need of work," he was offered a job hosting a sports quiz. "I felt the blood leave my face," he recalls, but he accepted the assignment. Every Monday night for twenty-six weeks he feigned an interest in the subject, well enough that the radio station offered him a job announcing a baseball game. Never having been to a baseball game, he rushed out to buy a book on the rules of the game. "As I got to the tenth page, I collapsed," he reports. "Much as I needed the money, I knew there was no way that I could manage this bluff."

Goodson built a TV production empire despite such setbacks, and he jokes about them now. But he also recognizes that to be male and nonathletic is serious business. "I approach this subject with a light touch, but in truth," he writes, "it has been a problem that has plagued me for most of my life." From early childhood until late adulthood, he hid his disinterest and inability for fear of seeming homosexual. Yet "even after three marriages, three children, and some in between love affairs, plus the sure knowledge that I adore women, I still feel, from time to time, that, somehow, I must be lacking in the right male genes."

One irony, of course, is that for many years now it has not been much easier for a man to be nonathletic if he's gay than if he's straight. The ideal man within the gay world, as in the heterosexual, is powerfully built. "What a shock I had when I came out," said Jim, a twenty-nine-year-old real estate agent I interviewed at the San Francisco apartment he shares with his lover.

Jim had waited until his junior year in college to become involved in the gay community. One aspect of coming out that he'd eagerly anticipated was the opportunity to dress the way he wanted. As far back as he could remember he'd been careful not to wear flamboyant clothes and to camouflage his thin arms and concave chest with a sports coat or sweater.

"I was basically a sissy as a kid," he told me, "and I had a lot of defenses about it. I would get stomachaches from having to play baseball. The whole idea of having to play games at recess or gym class was too much for me. I made a big distinction between intellect and athletics. I always felt that I was a head person and not a body person. Most of the boys in the little Wisconsin town where I grew up were very jock-y. Since I wasn't that, I kept to myself and read a lot and drew pictures. Fortunately, my family never gave me problems about who I was."

Still, Jim was anxious and unhappy during childhood. He remembers crying in the school bathroom in third grade because some boys had mocked him. After that, he practiced a tougher swagger and spiced up his speech with words like "shit" and "pussy."

Things changed in junior high. For starters, there was no more "recess," so he wasn't forced to play ball games; and for another, he found a new role for himself. The boys and girls started mixing with one another, awkwardly, and Jim served as a go-between. He was handsome, but he didn't go after girls sexually, and thus the girls considered him both appealing and trustworthy. For their part, the boys appreciated having a guy around who was neither a nerd nor a competitor.

Still, the idea that he might appear effeminate was abhorrent to him. Once the other kids starting dating, he made sure he always had a girlfriend—Catholic girls who, all the boys knew, would never let anyone past first base.

So it was with great anticipation of ending his long years of inauthenticity that he went public with his homosexuality midway through college. He'd had one affair with a man prior to that time but had kept his feelings secret.

"I'd been active in the ecology movement on campus, so I decided that a good way to come out would be through politics. I joined a gay rights group, and of course those were guys who were immersed in gay culture. Most of them at that time were very hard types, and I didn't know what I was getting into. They told me that it would just be a matter of time before I would become a sophisticated S-and-M'er. In a couple of months I would understand why it was correct to be tough and wear leather all the time."

"I tried to make it happen," he laughed, "but there was no way. It took me a few years and a set of barbells to accept that that wasn't me. It's taken even longer to accept the fact that gay men expect one another to dress in tight shirts and tight pants that emphasize their asses and their chests and their dicks. I mean, I've gotten comfortable dressing like that to be camp at a party, but I wouldn't dress that way to walk around Castro Street or go to work."

Instead, Jim dresses unusually "straight," even preppy. For our meeting he wore a cotton V-neck sweater and loose-fitting slacks, neither of which threw into relief any part of his body. On the other hand, Jim hasn't exactly stayed undeveloped. Partly as a result of the AIDS epidemic, the strong-and-healthy look is very much the order of the day where Jim lives. In addition to the barbells he bought in college, he owns a small trampoline and a sit-up board, and while he doesn't relish the thirty minutes every morning he spends exercising, he admitted it's made him happier with himself and has kept his partner interested.

BICEPS MAKE THE MAN

Gay men are by no means the only ones to have experienced conflicts over a lack of muscles. A national survey of 62,000 readers of *Psychology Today* found that a man's self-esteem correlates directly with having a muscular upper body. And in experiments in which male college students are given weight training, as the men grow stronger they become more outgoing and their degree of satisfaction with themselves increases.

Yet there is great variation in how men cope with the physical ideals placed upon them. Some men devote most of their lives to building up their bodies, while others scarcely exercise at all. Generally, a man's choice of one of these options or the other, or something in between, depends on what other people made of his body earlier in his life.

Those who suffer as adults are men who somehow never got into athletics while growing up but always felt parental and community pressure to do so. "I make a great pretense of being happy with these arms," said Larry, the thirty-six-year-old owner of an advertising agency in Atlanta, as he demonstrated how thin his left arm is by cupping the thumb and middle finger of his right hand almost completely around his upper arm. "I kid my friends who work out. I tell them, 'Biceps are just ugly bulges.' But the truth is, I'm not happy with my body.

"There's an event that sticks in my mind," he continued. "Nineteen seventy-two. We'd just graduated from Oberlin, and about a dozen of us took over the summer house of somebody's parents on a private lake in upstate New York for a week. One afternoon they all decided to go skinny-dipping. I begged off at first. I don't take off my clothes even in front of people I'm totally comfortable with. I make love in the dark when I have a choice in the matter. But those were the days of free sex and do-your-own-thing, and it wasn't considered cool to be hung up about nudity. They hassled me until I finally stripped and jumped in the water.

"It was about the worst experience of my life. First off, the other guys all had better bodies than I did. My stomach stuck out, even then, and I had no shoulders or chest, and of course, no biceps." Larry laughed nervously.

"The thing that really did me in was when an ex-girlfriend of mine swam by with the man she was living with at the time and made a comment about how I won the funniest-shape-of-the-day award. It was as if someone had run me over with a Mack truck. I felt embarrassed and betrayed."

Fifteen years later, and Larry still has a puny body he's ashamed about. Now not only doesn't he go skinny-dipping, he doesn't even go swimming. But he's not unattractive. In fact, he has a pleasant face and a full head of wavy black hair. One could easily imagine that if he stood up straight and added an inch or two of muscle in strategic spots, he's look great in the stylish clothes he wears.

Why doesn't Larry simply work out a few hours a week so that he can feel decent about himself physically? He was unable to answer that question directly. The answer came out, nonetheless, at another point in our discussion, when he described his parents and the nature of his relationship with them as a child. His mother used to criticize him for not being the son she'd imagined having, but anytime he showed some independence or virility, she was unsatisfied with his performance.

As he described it: "Either you played ball with the other kids or you weren't a Real Man. My mother's brother Don was a Real Man. He's been a guard for the basketball team. He's very tall and very fast. He ran a marathon this summer to celebrate his sixtieth birthday. My mother was very pretty in high school, very 'popular,' and she wanted me to be the same. If I'd had a sister, or even if there'd been another boy for her to lay it on, maybe I wouldn't have felt so pressured. I think I wimped out of sports just to spite her constant chirping about how I ought to be more like my Uncle Don."

At the same time, Larry's father, a man who was already distant, became even more so on the few occasions when Larry shelved his stamp collection and put on a baseball mitt. And at an early age Larry noticed that his mother was affectionate with his father only when his father was sick, a handy trick Larry came to deploy himself.

It's clear that in the crevices of Larry's adult mind there lives the belief that he cannot be fit without losing the attention of those he depends on. In his experience, to be fit was to yield to the wishes of an overpowering mother, whereas to be weak was to gain attention from the most important man in his world. This is just the opposite of many boys, who seduce Mom and buddy up to Dad by playing sports.

Larry survived high school thanks to an extracurricular activity that allowed him to relate to his father and to other males. He took up photography, a longstanding hobby of his father's. Working for the school yearbook, he was assigned to photograph football and basketball games. He became friends with other staffers, and in his senior year he was appointed editor. "The yearbook room was my safe zone, the camera was my weapon," he said.

At artsy Oberlin College in the late sixties, his camera attracted the attention of desirable women. It wasn't until that episode at the lake that he started to pay a price again for his physique.

He was safe in high school and college in part because the culture had changed. Some decades are better than others for men like Larry; fashions in brawn wax and wane. During certain periods, American body trends reward less muscular men. Historians have documented several such periods, including the years just after the Civil War, and the 1960s. At other times, including the early years of this century and the seventies and eighties, American men have been required to be overtly strong in order to be received as attractive and healthy

Physical fashions for men reflect national political trends. During the Vietnam War, men's bodies took on special significance. In fact, the war was *over* bodies. Each side claimed victory less on the basis of territory taken than on "body counts." Those who opposed the war actively deployed their bodies in the service of opposition. Some were beaten up in protests in Chicago, and many more recast their bodies into symbols of defiance—wearing long hair, beards, and odd clothes that distinguished them from Marines. Suddenly, men who'd enjoyed athletics in high school were viewed as no sexier than their comrades who'd earlier been teased for throwing a ball like a girl. Muscles didn't necessarily contribute much to an antiwar image.

After the war, the oppositional look largely disappeared. The current ideal American male body stands as a symbol of reunification. *We have the same basis values*, the post-Vietnam body proclaims, and these are manifest in the trim, strong figure we admire in our men (and, to a limited degree, in our women). *Our goals are identical*, the post-Vietnam body reassures: liberal or conservative, black or white, we just want to be secure and prosperous and in charge of our own destiny. The American body politic, once torn asunder, is mended.

"Muscles have come to *mean* something again: an obsession with the beauty of health and a growing impatience with having sand kicked in our face have combined to give back to muscles a national symbolic credibility," Charles Gaines observed in *Esquire*.

But let's return to Larry, who hasn't fared at all well during the age of brawn. Just after college he married a graphic artist, who helped him set up his ad agency until she grew bored and status-hungry and went back to school for an MBA. A few years ago, she left Larry for someone she met at the health club where she has a corporate membership.

According to Larry, it's hard to have much success on the singles scene when you're out of shape. An analysis I conducted of "personals" ads in ten newspapers and magazines from across the U.S. and from London bears him out. Words like "athletic" and "well-built" appear in a majority of the men's descriptions of themselves and women's descriptions of their desired mates.

Women who advertise in these publications are primarily upper-middle-class, well educated, and looking for men of the same stripe. Since they've broken out of traditional roles themselves to some extent, they might be expected to be more receptive to less traditionally masculine men. In fact, they often prefer to have rather macho men around, perhaps to offset their fears that they may not be sufficiently feminine. Christine, for instance, the corporate vice-president, made it very clear she has no interest in "pale hairless guys who make great pasta," whom she calls "newts." She dates tall, well-built, handsome fellows. "I don't need to be taken care of," she said, "and I can forge my own way and make a lot of money. I'd sort of like the feminine side of me reinforced by being with a man who is more male than I am. Dealing with a man who has a real female side is unsettling."

Politically left-leaning women can also be suspicious of men with sunken chests. One woman I interviewed, who has refused to wear makeup her entire adult life on the grounds that the cosmetics industry is a capitalist plot to enslave women, said sternly about men: "The obligation to be beautiful is oppressive, the obligation to be strong is empowering. A woman who refuses to 'fix her face' is simply rejecting patriachal oppression, but a man who refuses to build up his body isn't making any kind of statement at all, except that he's lazy."

FEAR MAKES THE BICEPS

Given their poor reception in the outside world, men who are physically weak understandably experience low self-confidence. What's surprising is that their mirror opposites—the hunks and superjocks—often suffer from the same problem.

Perhaps the single greatest force that keeps men working out is insecurity. This is evident in those who exercise chiefly because they're afraid of heart disease. But almost all avid male exercisers are engaged in a passionate battle with their own sense of vulnerability. Herein lies an important distinction between men and women. For both, the key motivation to exercise is improved self-esteem, but the genders differ on what they believe produces these benefits. When surveyed as to why they exercise, women talk about accomplishment, beauty, affiliation with others; men say they're motivated by the chance to pit themselves against nature or other men and to confront physical danger. In other words, men seek to prove to themselves and others that they can survive, that they're winners.

The harder a man exercises, the more he may be trying to overcome his feelings of inadequacy or helplessness. Most bodybuilders in a study conducted in southern California were found to have been stutterers, dyslexics, thin, fat, short, nearsighted, or otherwise unacceptable to their parents when they were children. The author of the study, sociologist Alan Klein, proposes that body-building serves as a kind of "therapeutic narcissism." Through it, those who feel deeply insecure are offered a way to devote their full attention to making themselves big, strong, and commanding of attention.

I developed a vivid appreciation for the sweat-for-salvation aspect of male fitness when I visited a place where a high concentration of America's best-developed men live—a maximum security prison. There I met a man named Nathan, who is famous in several California prisons as an advocate for strengthening and perfecting the body while in jail.

Attractive and well-groomed, Nathan wore a short-sleeved yellow Lacoste shirt along with his starched gray prison pants and gave off a scent of expensive cologne. His closely cropped beard was cut precisely to complement his square features and his short curly black hair, which had obviously been styled by a talented barber. (He had an arrangement, he explained, with an inmate who had worked in a Hollywood hair salon prior to his conviction on drug charges.) Nathan's huge arms, covered with blue tattoos of eagles and naked women, offered a strange counterpoint to his fastidious grooming.

In a small room off the main visiting area, I asked Nathan to describe the different types of men who build up their bodies in jail.

"You got the superheavyweights, over six feet and massively built," he began, over the constant hum of prisoners yelling from the cell blocks in the adjoining buildings. "Then you got the real short guys. The tall ones are usually pretty smart—they don't have a college education, but they have common sense. They don't want to be overly aggressive, they just want to keep people away and do their time. The short ones usually are abrasive. They're looking for trouble. They've got that Napoleon complex. Then you've got the guys that want to box. They go through a very rigorous boxing discipline. They run, they practice all the boxing techniques, jump rope, hit the heavy bag."

Nathan estimated that two-thirds of the inmates at the prisons he's been in are seriously involved in exercise of some type. "When you come to jail you have a lot of time on your hands," he said at first. But as he talked on about prison life, and his own biography, a more complex picture emerged.

"When you're in the streets," he said, "you have a lot of time, but it's not structured into roll calls and meals, so it seems to go very fast. In here you're really conscious of time, and one of the pastimes that you can see some results from is lifting weights. You see people around you and you say, 'Wow, that looks nice, that guy has a nice build.' The way he carries himself, the way he walks, the way people respect him. And when you get big it gives you an artificial sense of security."

In what way is it artificial? I asked, feeling oddly comfortable after only ten or fifteen minutes with this Herculean man whom I knew to have been convicted of murder.

"It's artificial because you have to defeat the fear within your heart," he answered. "How big or small you are doesn't have anything to do with it. I had nineteen-and-a-half-inch arms at one point, but I couldn't pacify the fear in my heart, and people could see that."

His personal fear, he went on to explain, is that he'll spend his entire life in jail. He was first locked up, in a mental hospital, when he was five and a half years old. On that occasion he'd been playing with matches; he set fire to a sheet and his family's apartment went up in flames. His father, who was confined to bed for a back injury, died in the blaze. "My mother wanted to love me," he said with practiced dispassion, having relayed the story many times, "but she couldn't because she blamed me for the death of my father."

Nathan was cast out by his mother and didn't fare much better in his neighborhood. His light-brown skin and his ethnic background marked him for trouble from the time he was a young child. His father had come from the Cape Verde Islands and his mother from Brazil. In the barrio where Nathan grew up, "people had names like Carlos and José, and here I was Nathan. Kids used to think I was white because I'm so light, and there I was being acculturated into the Chicano culture, yet I couldn't identify with them physically. Everywhere I went it was understood I wasn't one of them."

Most of his formative years were spent in juvenile detention facilities. He was angry and confused, and he struck out with acts of violence ranging from schoolyard fights to armed robbery.

During one of his longer stays on the outside, at age twelve, Nathan shot heroin. He continued off and on until he hit forty, when he took up yoga and physical fitness in prison. The inmate who taught the yoga course espoused the view that drugs are poison and drug users pathetic creatures.

After his release on parole, Nathan became a community crusader against drugs, combing the streets for strung-out kids he could Pied Piper into his martial arts classes, which he conducted free at a recreation center in Watts. The more respect Nathan got in the neighborhood from his physical abilities, the more grandiose he grew, and within a few months he was preaching about "eradicating drugs from the face of the earth."

One afternoon, when an adolescent follower arrived with the news that another was in a coma from an overdose, Nathan went looking for the drug dealer who had sold him the stuff. He beat the man up badly and left him bleeding in an alley. The man died a few hours later, and Nathan was sentenced to twenty-five years to life for murder.

"Once I was back in the joint," Nathan remembered, "I borrowed some law books. I knew I'd spend the rest of my life in the joint unless I could find a way to get around this sentence. But it was hard to concentrate because I was on an open block. You have TVs and radios on full-blast and people yelling twenty-four hours a day, seven days a week. I had to be able to pull myself inward and digest this material, to think of an approach to use at my defense."

Nathan initiated a daily regimen of physical development and purification which he still continues. He says it gave him the willpower to study the law and to argue successfully before the parole board in 1985 that his sentence should be reduced to six to twelve years.

Today, Nathan's routine goes something like this. He rises at 5:00 A.M., when the cell block is still reasonably quiet. Without making enough noise to wake anyone, he repeats twelve times each a series of special exercises that combine calisthenics and yoga. In describing these to me, he left his chair and demonstrated. Assuming a squatting position, he took a very deep breath that expanded his chest muscles to their fullest; he held this for a few seconds, then gracefully raised himself upward to a full standing position, from which he bent forward while slowly exhaling, until his palms touched the floor.

On his way back up, Nathan caught a glimpse of the concerned expression on the face of the guard outside our cubicle and sat down again. He continued his description: "As you see, I don't look anything like yogis. If you see them in a book, they look like they're malnourished, whereas my body is well-developed everywhere. Yet I can put my elbows on the ground from a standing position with my knees locked. I'm superflexible. In America you want to have a good, healthy, rich image, not malnourished. My concept is that you can maintain that look and at the same time have flexibility."

After his predawn exercises, which take an hour, Nathan eats breakfast in his cell. He refuses to eat in the mess hall he said, because the food isn't healthy. Instead, with money or cigarettes earned from advising other inmates on legal matters, he orders health foods through the prison commissary. Friends who work in the mess hall also bring him milk, fish, and vegetables a few times a week.

After lineup, he attends a class offered in the prison by a local university. At the juvenile detention faciles where Nathan grew up, schooling was provided only a few hours a day; the rest of the time Nathan hauled coal and cut grass. His formal education was poor at best, and so it's no minor accomplishment that at the time I met him, he was about to graduate from college as valedictorian of his prison class of twenty-eight.

He credited his educational achievement to his bodily discipline. "It really opened my mind and gave me a sense of direction and a focus for my energies," he said. Classes in the prison are offered in the mornings and early evenings. In between, nonstop from 1:00 until 5:00 P.M., Nathan can be found in the jailyard working out with a group of inmates who have taken up his fitness system. They run a few laps to limber up, then move into the same sorts of exercises Nathan performs alone in his cell.

Life in a hot, violent, noisy prison is hell for anyone. Still, Nathan has a busy and secure life behind bars. "This has become like a womb for me, where I can function and be successful," he let drop at one point in the interview. Each time he's been released, he's come unhinged within a few months. As an adolescent, "just having been in prison was a status symbol. When I went home they had a party and everybody said, 'There goes a sure-enough bad dude.' I felt great. Then, two days later, I had to prove myself all over, and I'd get into trouble again." As an adult who has spent so much time behind bars, he says he can't maintain routines when he's on the outside. "I overindulge. I stay out every night dancing and having sex, trying to make up for lost time. I become totally fatigued, and then I feel bad because I'm not keeping my mind and body as sharp as I know I'm supposed to. I get paranoid and confused on the street."

It may be ironic, and it's surely unfortunate, but Nathan feels more at home in jail than he does on the outside. Behind bars he can maintain some measure of self-respect and control, thanks to his fitness regimen. His exercise program has given his life order and predictability and is a source of personal pride.

CALMING THE STORM

Among the law-abiding men I interviewed who exercise obsessively for periods of weeks or months, the same basic motivations apply. They discipline themselves through fitness in order to stave off the impending chaos they confront in their daily lives.

A case in point is Roger, a forty-two-year-old Chicago lawyer. While growing up, he played softball in the neighborhood; in college he did nothing beyond a morning wakeup routine of push-ups and sit-ups; and in law school he "hardly had time to eat." Although Roger was in the top quarter of his University of Chicago Law School class, he was terrified he'd fail the bar exam, as his older brother had. He countered his fears by bingeing on exercise. "I've played racquetball exactly twenty-two times in my life, and they were all within the space of the last three weeks before my bar exam," he reported. "Racquetball made me feel better. When I couldn't study, it loosened me up. I didn't play particularly *well*, but nobody played *harder*. I broke several racquets and messed up my arm pretty badly a couple of times."

That was the first of three times in the past fifteen years that Roger has gone on and off the exercise wagon. From the day he received notification that he'd passed the bar, about the only exercise Roger got was lifting heavy law books in the back offices of a large firm—until, that is, his second exercise blitz, which began a couple of years out of law school when he found himself unable to sleep the nights before he was to do battle with another lawyer in court. He'd awaken at four in the morning, his jaws clenched and his stomach knotted. In the middle of an argument in the courtroom the next day, his mouth would go dry and he'd lose his train of thought. Once a judge asked him to approach the bench and in a peevish voice advised Roger to request that his firm send him to a public speaking course.

Instead, Roger took up running. On his way back from court, he bought an expensive pair of Etonics, and each morning thereafter he ran three or four miles around Grant Park before going to his office in the Loop. "My father had had a heart attack at a young age," he said. "With all the reports coming out at that time about the benefits of running, I decided to join in." Before long he was doing eight miles a day, then ten and twelve. Some days he didn't feel like running but would run anyway: "A mile into the run I would get that feeling of relaxation, of going on forever, a real kind of power." And he was able to sleep at night and to present a strong case in court.

By the end of his third year out of law school Roger was, in his own words, "a damned good trial attorney." Within a year, his confidence firmly in place, the running fell off to a few miles every other day, then diminished to nothing. He blames the long hours at work required to make partner.

Except for a taste of golf, which he found boring, Roger again went without exercise until a year before our interview. The event that precipitated this, his third exercise spree, was sudden rejection by a long-term girlfriend. As an antidote to the pain and vulnerability he felt, Roger hired a private exercise trainer known in Chicago executive circles to be unsparing, even sadistic, in his drive to get his clients back in shape. For ten months prior to our meeting, the trainer had greeted Roger every Monday, Wednesday, and Thursday at 6:00 p.m. upon Roger's arrival home from work, and Saturdays at 4:00 P.M. For a grueling hour he orchestrated Roger's workout in the gym they set up in the spare bedroom of Roger's Lake Shore apartment. "I never would have thought it possible that I could be in such great physical condition," Roger claimed. "I feel great and I look great."

Nevertheless, when I met him he was already showing signs that the end of this current exercise cycle was in sight. He told me of plans to decrease the number of training sessions each week; and although he "swore off women" after his disappointment the year before, a few weeks prior to our interview he began sleeping regularly with a thirty-two-year-old physician.

Men who exercise for purposes of deliverance (like Roger and Nathan), as well as those who abstain from exercise (like Larry), differ in an important regard from men who are at neither of those extremes. Exercise is not a highly charged activity for those who pursue it in a more moderate way. They don't attach magical significance to lifting heavy objects or hitting balls.

A hallmark of a sane exercise program is that it is integrated into a person's daily life. It's just something a man does, like eating lunch or getting a haircut. He goes to the Y or health club regularly to play basketball or handball or pump a little iron with his buddies. And although his sports activities may take up a fair amount of leisure time, he foregoes them if a family or business emergency takes precedence.

At times—when he's angry with someone at work, for instance—he may play rough and injure himself, but the displacement of frustration is not what his athleticism is about. The role of athletics in his life is much more basic than that. Typically he has been involved with sports since childhood. He loves to reminisce about a particular game from his youth, or the day his dad installed a hoop on the garage at the end of the driveway when he was five or six. He has a vivid memory of his father placing the massive basketball in his arms and lifting him up so he could sink it through the basket. In the twenty or thirty or forty years since, there's never been a period when he hasn't played some kind of sport; in high school he may even have made it onto a team. And he devotedly follows college and pro teams on TV.

Lifelong jocks are living evidence for a current view of human development called, appropriately enough, "continuity theory." It holds that our interests during adulthood are usually extensions of what we enjoyed as children. Continuity theory disputes the myth perpetrated by sports magazines and health clubs—that a devoted couch potato can, with a bit of willpower, transform himself at age forty into a championship marathon runner or ball player. Men who try athletics for the first time during adulthood seldom succeed; like Roger, they don't stick with any activity very long.

Several studies show that men who engage in exercise on a regular basis as adults also did so during their childhood or adolescence. One of the best predictors of whether a man will be athletic in midlife (and later) is whether his father participated in sports and brought him up to do so as well.

Men who've grown up athletic are the great beneficiaries of the American male role. When social scientists track down high school athletes ten or more years after graduation, they find them holding better-paying, higher-status jobs than their classmates from similar socioeconomic backgrounds. Their body image and self-esteem are greater too.

Who can say whether these positive outcomes are the result of their athleticism or are coincidental with it? Whichever it may be, other men envy these men their comfort with their masculinity and their physiques, and women wish it were as easy for them to stay pretty as it is for these men to stay handsome. How unfair, I've heard women complain, that such men need merely continue to play the games of their youth, while to maintain their beauty women must spend hours in beauty salons having perms, facials, manicures, and pedicures; must starve themselves on diets; must wear uncomfortable shoes . . . and on top of all that, exercise whether they enjoy it or not.

Although some men do fit that picture, they're a small minority. Most men, even if they've kept themselves reasonably fit, are privately insecure about their looks and more vain than others imagine them to be.

Martin Duberman

GAY IN THE FIFTIES

My first sexual experience with a man? About age 20. Well, a few earlier ones. At summer camp in the forties we did something we called "fussing." We had a mattress at the bottom of the closet in our bunk. (The closet no less!) We were pretty well organized. Don't know how old I was—about 12, I think. The code question we'd ask each other was, "You feel like 'fussing'?" If "yes," we'd go into the closet two at a time. Body-rubbing, essentially. There was a definite hierarchy, too. You know: who got to into the closet with whom—who did the choosing. Just like a gay bar.

On one level, I knew early on I was gay. At seventeen, for instance, I went on a bike trip—old fashioned "bike"—across the country. Camped out every night, went through the Rockies: all that. At one point we stopped in Calgary, Canada for the big rodeo. I remember going to see a fortune teller. She told me to write on a piece of paper "the question closest to my heart" and to put it under the (literal) crystal ball sitting on the table between us. "Put it under the crystal, close your eyes, concentrate very hard and I will then be able to answer your question". What I wrote on the piece of paper was, "Will I always be homosexual?"

Fortunately—being rebellious by nature—I didn't follow her instructions to the letter. I peeked. I saw her take the piece of paper out through some opening in the bottom of the table, read it, then put it back. "Open your eyes now," she said. "You're a very troubled young man. I'm getting that very strongly. But your particular trouble can be cured. What you must do is leave your old life and join our gypsy caravan." Even the gypsies were into "cures."!

I was tempted—though I'd seen her trick with the piece of paper. A measure, I guess, of my desperation. "Maybe she can *cure you," I thought, "maybe you should go with her." I felt terribly torn up, couldn't decide. In the end, I did not show up at dawn with all my worldly goods.*

The "sickness" model of homosexuality had been drummed into me. That's why I waited so long before I had sex. It wasn't until my first year in graduate school at Harvard in 1953 that I finally got up the courage to go into my first gay bar. Soon after, I met a man—I'll call him "Larry"—and was with him for five years. Our relationship wasn't entirely monogamous, but nearly so for the first few years. I was very close to him. He was different from me in many ways—I'm usually attracted to opposites; not always, but usually. Larry was 19 or 20 when we met (I was 22) working class Irish Catholic, from a small town near Boston. Very attractive phys-ically—to me anyway. He was my romantic ideal, I was his intellectual one. That's one way to put it, I suppose. I was living in the graduate dorm and later, from 1954–57 in

From "Interview: Martin Duberman," *Gay Sunshine*, Spring 1977. Reprinted from *Salmagundi*, Fall 1982–Winter 1983.

*Adams House as a resident tutor, Larry lived with his family, but he'd often stay with
me. There was no way we could afford to live together on a regular basis. Neither of us
had any money. He had a lousy job in a department store, I was trying to get by on my
tutor's salary . . .*

*You know, sometimes when I think about the Fifties, I think everything has changed
—the culture, me, the community. Other times I think very little has changed. A
student of mine from when I taught at Princeton (1962–1971) recently came to see me
(1977). He's 26 now, but has been "out" only a year. His big breakthrough to date has
been meeting a guy in one of the johns at the porno movies he frequents who "actually
talked to me!" This is a bright, politically sophisticated guy—active in SDS as an
undergraduate. Yet here he is at age 26 not knowing where to go to meet other gay men,
except for bathrooms. It made me think things are no easier for gay people now than they
ever were. In other moods I know—or hope—that's wrong. But I'm not sure.*

*Like take my relationship with Larry. We had a damn good thing. And a support
group, a circle of friends. There were bars, too. The life was circumscribed and secretive,
of course. And our self-image wasn't so hot. I remember long talks with my gay friends
at Harvard about whether we could achieve any sort of satisfying life, "stunted" as we
were. We accepted as given that as homosexuals we could never reach "full adult
maturity"—whatever the fuck that means. Then it meant what everybody said it did:
marrying, settling down, having a family. We knew we'd never qualify, and despised
ourselves for it. But it's too simple to reduce "growing up gay in the Fifties" to a
one-dimensional horror story . . .*

EXCERPTS FROM MY DIARY OF 1956-7—PLUS MY FEELINGS ON RE-READING THEM IN 1981

August 28, 1956   Told Weintraupt today [*the therapist I'd been seeing for about a
year*] that I was going to quit. By the time the hour was up, I had, as usual,
changed my mind. Mostly because I got him to qualify the ban on homosexual
contacts. He now says it's *Larry* I must stay away from [*following Weintraupt's
dictate, I'd broken off with Larry a month previously*], not necessarily all contacts—though the greater the abstemiousness, the better. All I needed was an
opening: I spent three hours touring the bars, river, common, etc. . . .

August 29   Is any genuine commitment between homosexuals possible?
God knows I miss Larry. How I wish he were here tonight waiting for me in
bed, sweet, affectionate . . . and yet I can't really settle down with him. I
have no confidence in our building any sort of life . . .

September 2   . . . went to the bars. I was in one of my exuberantly vain
moods.

Got quite drunk and came home with a youngish guy who I thought would
be a good fuck. But he was lousy in bed—inexperienced physically, inane in
every other way.

After two hours of non-erect activity, we finally managed an orgasm. I was
afterwards completely repulsed by what I'd done; this absurd compulsive

intimacy with an anonymous body—and a disappointing one at that (which is perhaps why I'm so righteously repulsed).

He left early this morning. I've been moping around ever since. Came very close to rushing off to see Larry on the Cape. It's extraordinary how "right" seeing him would make everything. But I've yielded to this too many times before, and always without lasting satisfaction. It's been a full month now since we've seen each other— I've *got* to hold off—I *cannot* form any lasting relationship with him—why. I'm not sure—but this I do know, that it won't work, and I must give him a chance to free himself.

September 3   The great drought is over—with the usual awful results. Last night Larry called. I was so glad to hear from him, and under almost no pressure, agreed to meet him . . . eventually I was talking drunkenly— meaning it all—about giving up on the analysis, about missing him terribly, etc. And finally, sex. As miraculous as ever, and followed as ever, by panic over what I had done and remorse over what I had said.

Will it ever be resolved? When I seem him I'm lost; and I can't seem to stop myself from seeing him. Yet it's never enough. Could I really give up the analysis and accept my life as it now stands? Also impossible . . .

September 4   Nervous about having to tell Weintraupt what happened last night. Half hoping, like a renegade schoolboy, to be "dismissed." But I was unable to goad either him or myself into it.

The confessional did me good. And now, I suppose, the usual drifting till the next crisis. What of all the promises I made to Larry last night? Today I consummate the immorality by not even calling him. What else can I do? If I call, I merely re-establish a lifeline that consists of half-promises that always remain unfulfilled, and yet always remain. If only I could know that after my physical and neurotic needs are spent, there's still something left for us to live on. I sometimes think there is—but Weintraupt has thrown so many of my feelings into doubt and confusion, I can't even be sure of "sometimes." And so I'll continue to drift; trying not to call—hoping he'll call me, continuing to go to Weintraupt—planning imminently to quit.

(1981): Weintraupt was not my first therapist. I had previously gone (been sent, *by my parents) at age 15 to find out why I was so monosyllabic and moody. It was enlightened in 1945 to send your kid for therapy. It would have been more so if everyone in the family had gone: I wouldn't have felt that tensions at home were exclusively of my making. The therapist helped further to convince me that they were. I saw him for several months, at the end of which time he announced his "solution": I should embrace my mother and tell her how much I loved her. Yup—swear to God! I paced my bedroom for hours trying to get up the courage; I had trouble talking to my mother, let alone touching her. "Do it!" I yelled at myself, "Do it!!" I went downstairs, grabbed the startled woman, hugged her like a robot out of R.U.R., and said a loud, metallic, "I love you!"—and was promptly showed with tears of joy. "I knew it was going to be all right," she kept repeating, "I knew it would be." Idiot therapist! The thaw at home lasted a couple of days or weeks. Then* status quo ante pace.

I never told that therapist about my homosexual feelings—though I was already aware of them. I think I came closest when relating a dream. I was in a glass house masturbating (or was it having sex with a man?), terrified that people were watching from every adjacent apartment house. "What were you terrified of," asked Sigmund Pangloss. "Dunno," I mumbled.

September 7. 1:30 a.m. Just back from the bars. Larry was there and we mooned around each other—with intermittent snarls—all night. Curse Weintraupt and my bloody fine powers of resistance! I'm so sick of considering consequences, "looking ahead"—to what? To a question mark, to the bare possibility that I may someday be able to marry and have children.

September 8. 2:00 a.m. I'm like a stupid child who can't profit from experience. Larry returned the car during the afternoon and I invited him up, although I was playing cards. He slept while we played and then when the others left, I woke him, crawled into bed, caressed him—and that was that. I simply made no effort to resist. Why invite him up in the first place? Why not wake him hurriedly?—"late for dinner"; "let's catch the early show," etc. No, none of those sensible things. Attraction, tenderness, wonderfully passionate sex—and then the usual regret over the destructiveness of my lust, both to Larry and to my analysis.

September 10. I quit the analysis this morning. After months of indecision, the final action was almost unexpected. I told Weintraupt about Saturday night with Larry—and about a dream in which my "auditing" a course evolved into a symbolic reenactment of my attitude towards the analysis—i.e., an onlooker, an auditor, rather than a participator. From there it was only a step to being told my attitude made the analysis circular and endless; and since in honesty I couldn't swear that I would be able to change it, it was mutually agreed that it would be best to stop. Yet having made the decision, I can't accept it. Accepting it means accepting my life, being satisfied with it. And I can't . . . What to do? I need more time to think. My first impulse is to resume analysis—but this time making the greatest possible effort to resist all homosexual contact. Have I ever *really* tried before? Or have I assumed incapability and infirmity and comforted myself with the thought that although I continued to act out, I was nevertheless "improving" simply by sticking to the mechanics of treatment. If I go back this time, I must *truly* commit myself to it . . .

September 11. 1:30 a.m. Didn't call Weintraupt. I think I've passed beyond the initial stage of feeling lost and helpless. I'm going to try it this way for a while . . . saw Larry for dinner. We had sex later—how great not to follow it with panic and guilt: I told him I'd quit the analysis but that I wouldn't be able to commit myself to a monogamous relationship, that I remain incapable (don't all homosexuals?) of finding satisfaction permanently with one person. He didn't press for further explanation or commitment, since he sensed I wasn't ready or willing. He's extraordinarily perceptive in gauging my moods. And extraordinarily tolerant of them.

(1981): To spell out the obvious: I'd wholly internalized the then standard view of the "homosexual condition"—namely, to be homosexual was to be incapable of commitment to another human being. I'd internalized, too, the sex negativism of the culture: not to be monogamous, to enjoy sex with more than one person was to be "irresponsible." Homosexuality equalled promiscuity, and promiscuity equalled irresponsibility. Put another way, "health" could be recognized by the absence of desire—or at least the need to act on the desire—for more than one person.

Though I now take issue with the perjorative label "promiscuous" being automatically applied to all non-monogamous sexual activity, I do still feel (a residue from the earlier years of psychoanalytic indoctrination?) that some distinction exists and needs to be maintained between compulsive promiscuity and enjoying a variety of sexual experiences. The degree of compulsiveness involved—the driven quality—may be central to that distinction; it's the difference between being open to the pleasures of variety and obsessively needing a multiplicity of sexual experiences (to reinforce a sense of self-worth, or whatever).

As for Larry and men, after being together for three years, I had discovered—as do most people—that after obsession eases, resistance lessens, mutuality increases, the rest of the world comes back into focus—and some of it in shapely form. Again like most people (in the Fifties) I took this deviation from the monogamous ideal as a symptom of incapacity—for commitment, intimacy—even though I deviated more in the realm of fantasy than action.

September 13. New York   1:00 a.m. Drove down from Boston today for the rehearsal for Don's [*a boyhood friend*] wedding . . . so *much* contentment . . . wives beaming, husbands beaming . . . perhaps I mistake it—and am merely romanticizing . . .

September 15. New York   . . . dinner with Kenny [*an old friend; in 1975 he was murdered in New York City by a hustler*] at "East 55." Good meal, but expensive. and my! so elegant. The place filled with babbling queens who, because they can afford to spend $5 on a dinner, feel they are also entitled to talk at the top of their lungs. Oh why criticize—I suppose the sick should stick together!

(1981): Since my homophobia's already well established, the only real surprise in this entry is $5 for dinner being thought "expensive."

September 18   Adams House—and Cambridge—full of sound again. It's exciting watching everyone return and bustle about. And being busy. I love squeezing in my research [*I was working on my doctoral thesis in history*] between appointments, meetings, errands, etc. It exhilarates me to have a crowded daily schedule. Am I afraid of too much free time—empty, unplanned, threatening of the unexpected? Oh in part, yes—but surely not *all* my responses are sick! Being on the threshold of new experiences—buying new books, thinking of a new teaching schedule, directing a new play in the House—it's *fun*, damn it, and I refuse to reduce all my experiences and motives to psychological (neurotic) explanations . . .

(1981): In these years I was rarely in touch with my anger at being categorized as "sick"—after all, I believed it—and still less often did I let it surface (as in the above entry). Yet a subterranean defiance, however suppressed and deprecated, helped (I now see in retrospect) to sustain and, ultimately to extricate me from reductive psychosocial "explanations" of my being. Yet the rebellion against self-castigation which therapy (society) instilled in me would take a long, long time to consolidate and assert itself with any consistency. Before that could happen, I needed to recognize the importance of culture—of the role social moralizing about same gender love and lust plays in producing disabling self-recrimination. I also needed to understand (and this awaited the gay liberation movement of the late sixties/early seventies) that it isn't individual variations on the norm that require "amelioration" (through "treatment," punishment, guilt) but rather a cultural climate that equates variance with "disturbance."

September 21   Peculiarly depressed today. No apparent reason. I think I begin to regret leaving the analysis. Every *thing* is in order: all goes well—I am "free," busy, have enough money again, etc. No overt problems—nothing, in other words, on which to focus my anxiety. Nothing is wrong. And yet nothing is right.

September 22   Big scene with Larry. I told him the plain truth—I don't want to lose him but can't be completely faithful. What a goddamn mess I am. Simply not capable of love. Can anything be worse than a life of promiscuity, of objects not people? That's what I'm faced with and have to accept. Larry put a ban on our having sex. "We've got to try to form a new kind of relationship—friends, since lovers hasn't worked; and occasional sex with each other is merely postponing the adjustment." Sensible, logical. But the unfortunate fact remains that we *want* to continue going to bed with each other. If exclusive, Larry would consider it ideal; if occasional, I would. But the thought of *never*, frightens me more than Larry. *I* want everything.

(1981): Part of the trouble, probably most of it, was the going social definition of what constituted being a "mess." Homosexuality was sign enough, as the current consensus saw it, but to want to sleep with more than one man during a lifetime was considered the equivalent of unable to "love." The One-Person-Now-And-Forever model of "health" was applied in the Fifties almost as rigorously to heterosexuals. That is, officially. As Kinsey had already shown in his books, a large percentage of married men paid greater fealty to the ideal of monogamy in their rhetoric than in their behavior. Like most American women, I had been trained to believe that interest in anyone other than the Beloved was all at once a definition of emotional immaturity and the equivalent of emotional treachery.

October 4   Spend the evening with Frank D. He's just failed his Generals [*Ph.D. Orals*] and is badly affected . . . a horrible blow to those as self-centered as most homosexuals are. With their intellectual self-respect destroyed, there's nothing much to fall back on, since the "academic queens" at least have been long using it as a compensation—a mask—for what they consider to be their other defects and inadequacies. With the "binder" gone, Frank has quite literally fallen apart.

(1981): Apparently I'd never seen a straight person "fall apart" after failing Generals. Which means I either couldn't see or had a remarkably limited circle of friends.

October 14   Went to a most enjoyable party at Margaret R's—charmed by a cameo-like Radcliffe girl named Ann. But promptly at 10:00—fearing I would turn into a man!—I deserted the party on some pretext and rushed to the bars for a little more self-torture. And I got it. Larry was there, faithfully watching and waiting—compounding thereby my unhappiness. Out of default I left with him and talked "straight"—I hate tormenting him and yet I am incapable now of changing my insane pace of promiscuity. [*As I look back over the diary, I had had sex once in two weeks.*] I said I am useless to both of us. We agreed not to see each other any more.

October 15   Spent a pleasant evening at Ray's [*my closest friend, also a graduate student*] . . . lots of drink, talk. Nice people—like them all . . . especially David E., who I haven't known before . . . warm, sensitive . . . not at all an intrusive, "look-at-me" personality. Rare anywhere, but especially in a homosexual. I must stop this business of judging homosexuals as a separate breed (but aren't they?) and being so persistently amazed at the occasional nice ones—there are few enough anywhere and should be admired as such apart from categories—

October 18   . . . Larry called unexpectedly . . . The usual happened—talk leading to desire leading to sex . . . The desire returns, but not sufficiently to make me want to give up my roaming.

October 19   3:00 a.m. . . . told Larry he could stay over at my place—since he has to go to work in the morning. But passing the river [*Harvard's chief cruising ground*] on our way home, he saw that it was crowded and decided to stop off. That was an hour ago and he hasn't appeared. Obviously he's met someone, and . . . I'm upset. But when I dropped him at the river I was actually *relieved.* I didn't want to have sex with him and rushed home to get to "sleep" before he returned . . . He just arrived. Has only been talking to someone he previously met. He's all affection. What an imbecile I am—I disgust myself at times . . .

October 20 . . . Stayed in tonight . . . I feel so much better when I do . . . Really a bourgeois at heart—early to bed, etc. Feel cleaner and more satisfied with myself.

(1981): Maybe Descartes is where it all went wrong—all the splits and separations, the moralistic dichotomies (staying at home versus the "neurotic" drive to look for sex/ companionship, etc.) The hideous overlay of metaphysical categories on garden variety shifts in moods and needs!

October 23 Larry was here tonight and we had sex . . . we simply wanted to and we did. I sometimes think all our "scenes"—eternal farewells, etc.—are indulged in part for pleasure: the stimulation of love forsaken and found again; of playing on the subtler threads of the relationship to test how far we can or cannot drive the other and then how easily we can or cannot recapture him. If we were legally tied to each other—as in marriage—it might soon degenerate into mutual disinterest.

November 19 I feel towards this delinquent Diary the way I used to towards Weintraupt—guilt at not keeping it up! . . . My routine, in truth is so busily monotonous, that I'm lulled into a dull sort of contentment . . . I feel repugnance at merely recording the trivial and the obvious, partly because the thesis writing is proving some sort of catharsis for my energies.

But, we'll try again—

November 20 One of my tutees, Alex S., a sophomore, came to see me today—appealingly confused, boyishly upset at his sudden lack of interest in history . . . He wants to "justify" his work, to find value beyond mere enjoyment (he doesn't seem to realize how rare *that* is among the "professionals") . . . I tried to keep my own disillusionment out of it, so as not to confuse him still further . . . I think I did well by him and this pleased me; helped him to see his *own* problems and aims without (miracolo!) obtruding mine. Of course, his extraordinary attractiveness accounted for my special effort . . . we are not indistrimate in our attentions—no one treats all the world alike . . .

(1981): I do still feel that eroticism is often a component of good teaching. I can be attracted to (care about) qualities of character or mind enough to make a special effort. But if I care about a body too, that much more of myself goes into the contact. And if the body is spectacular enough, the effort will match it—even without qualities of character or mind. I want to matter (become part of?) my somatic ideal. I think the Greeks understood this—even to sanctioning physical contact between older men (teachers, guides) and younger. In our society, the mere recognition that an erotic element is present in teaching—and of course not only male/male—would constitute an enormous advance. Finding a way to acknowledge that element would constitute utopia.

November 26   . . . Isabel [*she and I had met at Ogunquit the previous summer*] was here for a weekend—mainly because Don, Joan, *et al* were due from New York for the Yale-Harvard festivities and I felt compelled to produce a date. Isabel means more to me than a convenience . . . yet I was relieved to see her leave early Sunday . . .

(1981): I'm almost sure it was on this visit that Isabel came into my bed one morning (she was sleeping on the sofa bed, in the living room). Sweetly, warmly, she cuddled with me. Tensely, mechanically, I cuddled back, frightened that she wanted to have sex. Either she didn't or she got my message; we never did more than cuddle. And I felt guilty and wretched over my "inadequacy."

All of which reminds me of my debate at Fordham in April, 1973 with Dr. Irving Bieber. Three out of four male homosexuals he's studied show "fear of female genitalia." Pathology, he says. And the source? A detached, minimizing father. But has anyone studied the degree of fear in male hetero-sexuals? I suspect it might match or exceed that of homosexuals—especially if the sample studied was as skewed (102 patients in treatment) as Bieber's. Besides, Bieber ignores the contribution of social pressure in producing "fear" (whether in gay or straight men). If society didn't insist that the definition of male adultness was omnipresent desire to fuck females, there wouldn't be the built-in sense of inadequacy when that desire isn't present, nor the avoidance of closeness with women as a device for avoiding the feeling of inadequacy . . . I wonder what it might have been like for Isabel and me if I hadn't gotten into that bed with a destructive set of expectations in my head. I would have enjoyed the cuddle. And maybe more.

. . . Jim came over . . . a new contact [*we met the previous week*], someone I was attracted to and eager to impress. We spent about four hours drinking—and five in bed—which has left me feeling empty and disgusted . . . I was interested in Jim—beyond the physical . . . the sex partly cooled my ardor (for what? conquest?) and the conversation completed the job. There was something hard about him which came out only by degrees, occasionally blatant egoism, sometimes just (just indeed!) a lack of concern, of tenderness for his partner—in conversation or sex. I suppose I'll see him again, but the disappointment adds to this morning's depression. I keep telling myself I'm looking for something permanent—someone to grow with, to do things for, to bring meaning into routine. Yet when I go to the bars, I consistently look for the most physically appealing person. These pick-up bars don't allow for any other form of contact. Sex is the basis of meeting, and sex is the first, rather than the final expression of the relationship. I tell myself how meaningless this anonymous cycle of body and body is, but I continue to repeat it; partly, no doubt, because of the necessity to keep proving myself, but also because the means of forming a healthier, more complete relationship are slight. With Jim, I thought there was some hope; I really don't now. But my disappointment is real, which makes me hope that my desire for permanence is also real.

(1981): The standard social values and therapeutic vocabulary of the day: sexual pleasure can only be justified in the context of a "meaningful" (i.e., "caring," "permanent") relationship; disconnected lust leads to emptiness and disgust. The self-

recriminations that followed my failing to measure up to sterotypic norms were more than a strategy of atonement, expiation fo having experienced pleasure not officially sanctioned. They affected the experience itself, diluting and distorting it. As the entry makes clear, what one expects in advance from an encounter is usually what one ends up taking away from it.

February 16, 1957   For some reason I feel like writing an entry today—the first in many weeks. Some impressions I want to get down after a surfeit night of drink and sex. I successfully maneuvered Thom II, one of my heros—at a distance—to bed. Good sex. Though my fantasy of 6′3″ of rock-like masculinity progressively flattened as the usual nice, ineffectual mama's boy came out. But still, good, if not ideal. And yet today my guilt, or at least revulsion, is working overtime. All sorts of resolutions, too. Eager for work—never going to waste time barhopping again, etc. No satisfaction there anyway. All set for a return to analysis; must have a wife and family, only possible things that matter, etc. These illuminations, of course, are easy to produce after the appetite has been depressed by booze and sex.

(1981): I can't help but smile as I type the above. At the unerring self-dramatization. At the sorrowings of young Werther. At the conviction that everyone else (but especially all heterosexuals) were and would be happier than I. At the effort—age 26—to strike a world-weary elegaic note. And—the smile disappears here—at the air-tight formulas into which I kept squeezing my experience; formulas which accurately parroted social norms of the day, but almost entirely failed to help me understand what in fact I was living through.

I wish to change . . . but parallel with this desire runs the stronger current of neurotic drive and compulsion, thwarting most of my efforts to change. I can neither give up my homosexual activities, nor devote myself guiltlessly to them. Paralyzed on the one side by desire and on the other by knowledge. Is this merely the neurotic or the human condition?

If I could only maintain the strong sense of disgust and reunuciation which I felt all day—perhaps than I could make the necessary effort to change the pattern of my life. But I can already feel the resolution draining out of me, and the old empty compulsion taking its place—

(1981): I should have read more anthropology. A Siwan version of the above: When Arab offered me his son last night for anal intercourse—as any thoughtful host would— my pleasure in the boy was compromised by my neurotic equation of sexual satisfaction with heterosexuality. As a result, intercourse seemed little more than mutual masturbation. If I could maintain the strong sense of disgust that I felt all day, perhaps then I could make the necessary effort to change the pattern of my life.

I've sought advice from the Elders. They feel I hold on to my deviance out of defiance—a stubborn refusal to let nature take its bisexual course. Their words make entire sense to me. Yet I can already feel the resolution draining away, and the empty compulsion to sleep only with women taking its place.

September 16   Now that I'm settled in at Yale [*my first full-time teaching job*] I thought I'd try keeping the Diary again . . .

I just got back last night from a quick run up to Boston. Classes begin on Wednesday and after that the chances of me getting away will be less. Spent most of the time alone with Larry . . . Why is it that only on the point of severance do I become most keenly aware of the deep affection . . . as if I allow myself the full emotion only when I safely know that it can be indulged in only infrequently.

September 20   Dr. Igen [*therapist*] accepted me as a patient today—3 times a week at $20 per hour—I don't really want to start the pain and upset of analysis all over again. But I must, if I'm ever to have an identity . . .

(1981): Meaning, its perhaps redundant to add, an "acceptable" identity, some placation of my passionate craving to fit in, to "belong."

September 21   Much depressed—woke up feeling this way. Stomach kicking up, which both helped cause the "pits" and was the result of them. Spent the day reading and doing odds and ends around the apartment [*I was living off campus*] . . . evening went to gay bars, which I had sworn pre-arrival at New Haven; that I would stay out of. Once having started, I'll probably continue; I can't really stay away from it. So I risk my job—but I'm sufficiently depressed not to care. If I could stand still and *understand* the depression (something about teaching and the insecurities it arouses, plus being unsettled and lonesome—but this doesn't get below the surface), I'd no doubt be better off. But homosexuality has been a channel—*the* channel—for so long—that it's easier to keep running.

(1981): Poor bastard. You wanted some companionship and sex, but had "learned" to cover over those human enough needs with a shit-load of self-castigation.

September 24   Had a good session with Dr. Igen today, but my stomach trouble and depression continue apace. Called Larry this evening for a little long-distance solace. Can't wait till he arrives on Friday. Despite the wild fluctuations in my feeling for him over the last few years, my genuine attachment to him has never been more apparent.

September 29   Larry just left. We had an awfully good weekend together—didn't really do very much—saw the Yale-Conn. football game yesterday (boring as always) and had dinner at Mory's. Except for that—none of it exactly new and exciting for me—we stayed near the apartment, ran errands, took rides, etc. It all want too fast. If I don't love him, why did I cry so painfully when it came time for him to leave? If I do love him, why has our relationship fluctuated so wildly the last few years. A riddle I long since gave up on. Anyway, it's awful being alone again . . .

(1981): The riddle's a little less dense these days: it's hard to sustain intimacy if you can't sustain a sense of self-worth. And to have grown up gay in America in the Fifties was to view oneself as emotionally shallow, stunted.

October 2   Went to the Taft, George and Harry's and Pierelli's [*New Haven's semi-gay bars—that is, bars where gay men were known to appear*] tonight—the works? Nothing happened, but aside from that, I've all but given up the idea of restricting my activity to outside N. Haven. The hell with it—N.Y. and Boston are too far away and I'm too horny. Anyway I now tell myself that nothing really dire could happen . . . if a student reports me to a Dean or some such, what can he really say except that he saw me in a homosexual bar. It's unlikely the Administration would take action on what is only a suspicion.

(1981): My concern was realistic, not paranoid. These were the years when a half dozen male faculty members were hounded from their jobs at Smith when discovered to be in possession of "pornographic" (gay) materials. As I was soon to discover, attitudes at Yale were comparable. In 1958 ('59?) a faculty member and friend of mine—I'll call him "Eli"—was fired, though under somewhat different circumstances than having been seen in a compromising bar. At a drunken student/faculty party, Eli followed up on a student's verbal pass—groped him in a corner? whispered sweet scatalogical nothings in his ear? I don't know. Whatever, the student freaked, ran shouting (literally) into the night—and ultimately into the Dean's office. The Administration (humanely, some might argue, given the fierce homophobia of the day) hinted that if Eli would deny the incident, it would be overlooked. Eli wouldn't. The Administration then asked for his resignation, offering to help him find work in an administrative capacity (not as a teacher) in some other school. Eli refused that, too.

October 13   Saturday night, bar-hopping in New York. Met a Bill N, in the Annex [*a gay bar*]. Despite my attraction, shouldn't have gone with him mainly because (a) he had a lover—no future and (b) he was of limited interest to me as a person—also no future. Yet my six weeks in New Haven made me feel as if I "had" to have sex, so off we went and on the whole, it came off rather better than most of my experiences of this nature do. He was sufficiently attractive physically, and technically proficient, to make bearable, even to a degree unnecessary, the lack of emotional attachment.

October 14   Feeling lonely most of the day, though a full evening's work has helped dissipate it. The prospect of spending my life alone has become more alive and painful—living off campus and inaccessible to casual "droppers-in" and having to cook and eat by myself. The prospects of a lasting homosexual relationship are too slim for me to get much comfort from the possibility; and a satisfying heterosexual relationship is still so remote that I can barely even wish for it. But perhaps either luck in the first area or Dr. Igen in the latter will make one or the other come true. In the meantime, I remain skeptical and unhappy.

October 21   The weekend in Boston started badly, with Larry failing to meet me according to arrangement, or waiting for dinner as I'd asked him to—all the result, though he won't admit it, of my having gone to New York last weekend instead of to Boston. Understandable enough; since we have no "official ties, his resentment has to come out indirectly. On my side, I was more angered at his studied disinterest that I had a "legal" right to be, clinging as I do to the double standard of my freedom and his devotion . . . By Saturday, we had more or less patched things up . . . I think.

October 29   Staying busy, which I need to avoid the real anguish of loneliness I've been feeling. I've never been so fully conscious of being quite literally "apart," "unconnected." My impulse at times like this is to run—to give up teaching, friends, the future—and devote myself to find *the* one—that never-never "right" person who'll make everything sweet and meaningful. Yet when I do search, I invariably end up in frantic pursuit not of a person but of a mere physical fantasy.

Dr. I. feels that at this point I would be foolish to try to resolve basic difficulties by any rash decisions—e.g., giving up teaching, moving to New York, etc. I have to sit tight and try to work the problems out slowly and deliberately through the analysis. So sit we will.

(1981): I still think it makes sense to take time with important decisions—and to try to avoid making them under the pressure of momentary panic or impulse. But impulses should be attended to, not dismissed out of hand; a valuable insight can come swiftly— and prolonged brooding can dissipate rather than clarify its force. Besides, some complaints deserve to be taken at face value; they aren't always a cover, a technique of avoidance. A worker in an automobile factory who complains about the boredom of the assembly line isn't necessarily displacing his "status anxiety." The "surface" problems I brought to therapy—aobut loneliness, teaching, the life of scholarship, living in New Haven—deserved more serious consideration as valid issues in themselves; I was never encouraged to regard them as other than a "blind."

November 5   To New York. Ended up going to Everard's two nights in a row.

(1981): Everard's was a gay bathhouse. It still is, though it closed briefly a few years back after a disastrous fire—caused by the criminal negligence of the management in failing, as specified by law, to install a proper sprinkling system—killed and maimed a dozen men.

Everard's was one of the places I frequented during the late Fifties/early Sixties on my weekend trips to New York. My usual pattern at the baths was to meet one man and go to a room with him. I avoided orgiastic scenes, especially the steamroom. If I was going to be gay, I was going to be gay in a way that was "seemly." In a way that approximated how straight people—sensible, adult, healthy straight people—behaved. You find one person and stick with him (her). My sexual repertoire was comparably limited in those days. With Larry I played the stereotypical male (dominant) role; out of bed, made the decisions, in bed did the fucking.

Much reasonably enjoyable sex with moderately attractive people—sufficient to black out any upsetting hesitations and doubts. But lack of sleep (I spent the weekend on Henry's [*a New York friend*] living room floor) soon produced the ripe conditions for reaction. Driving back up here last night filled with thoughts of renunciation, of an acute sense of the "disarray" such wantonness produces in my life. But resolution, like the guilt which prompts it, soon disappears. I can hardly lose sight of the fact that such behavior is destructive, but the compulsion to such activity (the bars being only a lesser version) remains even stronger . . .

November 7   Beginning to pick up the pieces after the upset of my weekend "frolic" in New York; though the degree of upset varies with the type of experience. I'm less prone than in the past to lay my sense of frustration or dissatisfaction at the door of "inadequate" sex (i.e. not the "right" person). . . I begin to see that it's the homosexual act itself which disturbs me—despite the physical pleasure and neurotic gain involved.

(1981): The new therapist—a decent, likeable man—had been helping me to this "clarification." Dr. Igen was less given to ideology than most psychiatrists of the day. Still, he had no doubt that homosexuality was symptomatic of a character disorder. But he never scrutinized—apparently never dreamed there might be a need to scrutinize— any of the assumptions that underlay his diagnoses and prescriptions. He merely accepted (as did most people in the Fifties, therapists and otherwise) the dictum that homosexuality by its nature was destructive in individual growth; biological law—unspecified, unexamined—not oppressive social norms, produced the disturbing bi-products of same gender love or lust.

November 10   Went to New York last night to meet Tom F., who was in from Texas . . . We spent the night together at Henry's (who was away for the weekend). If we could have stopped short of actual sex, the evening would have been far pleasanter. The preliminaries were deeply satisfying—I felt close and complete—but proceeding beyond, we seemed to draw further apart. I wanted his affection, not his body; being pushed into contact with his body, I gradually lost whatever affection I had felt. Ended up feeling distant and antagonistic and said good bye this morning with feelings of real relief . . .

Dr. Igen left today for his eye operation. Surprised myself by the depth of my upset— surprised and yet pleased at such a sign of significant involvement. He won't be back for at least a month. Rather than "hold the fort," I'll more likely destroy it. Don't see how I can curtail my activity without at least the security and profit of my visits to him. At any rate, a comfortable excuse for future promiscuity.

(1981): Igen, like Dr. Weintraupt before him, had recently made it clear that if I hoped to make further progress in analysis, I had to make a greater effort to control my

impulses and show more willingness to face rather than run from my anxiety. I can still hear his litany: "Homosexuality is the channel through which you act out your anxieties. We must close the escape hatch. Only in that way can the anxieties surface, be analyzed and treated." I had explained (implored) that I'd tried that before, with Dr. Weintraupt, and the strain had proved intolerable. He persuaded me that I'd changed since then, that I was now older and wiser, better able to understand the neurotic pressure to "act out." Besides, as he put it, "the injunction from above now coincides more exactly with what you feel within." Flattered, encouraged, I once more swore to take the veil.

November 22   Picked the wrong weekend to stay in New Haven. Everything is crawling with Yalies and their dates—the big Yale/Harvard weekend. Stayed here to catch up on work and especially to prepare my next two lectures. Hoped to take in the New Haven bars in the process, but quick reconnaissance tonight convinced me of the folly of that—too many students wandering into too many strange places. Just not worth the chance. Yet I wish so much that someone was here with me tonight.

(1981): For a moment I thought this might have been the football weekend of my drunken tangle in the small park that fronted fraternity row. But now I remember that was much earlier—when I was an undergraduate at Yale (in 1951 or '52): I followed some stocky, equally drunk 20 year old out-of-towner into the park and (I think he encouraged me), groped him. He reacted in a rage, swung at me drunkenly, got hold of the collar of my jacket and ripped it down my back as I struggled out of reach and raced down the street. I told my roommates I'd gotten into a fight with "some townie." With my torn jacket as proof, I was treated as a hero. I trembled inside for days.

This was, if my sense of chronology holds, my very first homosexual "contact"—give or take those rubbing sessions as a boy in summer camp; plus one experiment in mutual fellatio with a high school friend (not to orgasm).

But soon after my fraternity row fracas Don, an undergraduate friend, casually mentioned that I should stay away at night from the "Green" (the large park in front of the Old Campus)—it's a hangout for fairies." I was shocked—and overjoyed; at last a place to meet someone (I was 20 years old). That same night I got drunk, reeled down to the Green and sat on a bench opposite the only other person I could see in the area—a very fat, middle-aged black man. He whistled tantalizingly in my direction. I got up, reeled over and stood boldly in front of him. He started playing with my cock, then took it out of my pants. Wildly excited, I started to fondle him.

"Do you have any place we can go?" I whispered.

"Nope. No place."

Suddenly I heard laughter and noise coming in our direction. I was sure it was some undergraduates—and equally sure we'd been seen. Zipping up my fly, I ran out of the park—ran without stopping, panicked, hysterical, ran for my life back to my dorm room. I stayed in the shower for hours, cleaning, cleaning. I actually washed my mouth out with soap, though I hadn't used my mouth—other than to make a prayerful pact with the Divinity that if He let me off this time, I'd never, never go near the Green again. The panic lasted for days. By the end of the week I was back on the Green, drunk again. I met a dancer. We had sex in his car—that is, I let him blow me.

I can remember only one other experience while an undergraduate: being picked up by an older man cruising the area in his car. I got in, then changed my mind. He begged me to stay, said he'd "do anything I wanted to do." I got out, not unmindful (I now suspect) of the special pleasure fellow victims can derive from tormenting each other. Those are the only undergraduate encounters I can recall, the sum of my "sex life" until age 21. With men, I mean.

I had been through most of the heterosexual rituals. At age 15 (16?), staying with two high school friends at one of their parent's homes in Palm Beach, we went to a whore house one night. (A version of this, with some—and I don't know for certain which— details re-imagined, is my one-act play. "The Recorder"). I hadn't been able to get an erection. The prostitute kindly put some ointment in the urethral opening of my cock, wrapped in in gauze and snapped on a rubberband. (Can this really have been standard preventive treatment for v.d. in the Forties?). With the outward credentials of having fucked, I could brag about "how great it had been" to my friends (one of whom had no gauze bandage; suspicion deflected to him). I remember the prostitute's effort to comfort me with off-handed remarks: "married men often come into the house and can't get it up either—it's nothing to worry about kid." I made her promise not to tell my friends that I'd "failed." She agreed; I remember her warm, sympathetic smile.

Still more vivid is the night of the senior prom in high school. I was 17 and had been dating a "wild" girl, Rachel for a long time. We had promised ourselves—and announced to our friends—that we would "consummate our love" that night. (Some of this is also in "The Recorder"). After the prom our crowd went to Al's family apartment: very fancy, fit setting for the Big Event. Everyone lay around on the living room floor drinking and making out—and waiting for the moment when Rachel and I would go into the back bedroom; the whole group was vicariously losing its virginity through us. In the bedroom, Rachel and I got undressed and lay together on the huge bed. Again, I was impotent—but this time desperate, crazed:

"The doctor warned me that I've been making out too much. He said this would happen if I didn't cut down."

Rachel neither questioned nor accused. "I love you. I love you even if you can't get it up."

Again I lied to my friends. This time the excuse (agreed to by Rachel—I was lucky in my choice of women) was that we hadn't been able to do it because she was having a period. I was celibate till age 20, when I had those few furtive experiences on the New Haven Green.

During my first year of graduate school at Harvard (1952–3), I made my first timid foray into a gay bar, the Napoleon. I met Ray. We went home that same night and had sex in my dormitory room. For weeks afterwards I avoided him, rushing in the opposite direction whenever I caught sight of him on campus. He finally cornered me one day: "Look—can't we be friends at least?" Caught somewhere between hysteria and relief, I managed to mumble "yes."

It was the beginning of a friendship that's lasted to the present day. The beginning, too, of allowing myself to know other gay people socially, of gradually developing a circle of friends and entering a subculture that brought me from individual isolation to collective secrecy—a considerable advance, if one can understand (in a day when all furtiveness is decried) the quantum jump in happiness from private to shared anguish.

Soon after, I had my first affair—with "Rob" (at the time, as with most affairs, it seemed a good deal more profound; but then I was measuring it against the few desperate, anonymous forays of my undergraduate years, not against the intensity of the relationship with Larry that was soon to begin). I met Rob on one of my first visits to the Napoleon. He had been a classmate at Yale, but we had barely known each other there. Rob had long been "out" sexually, adored and pursued me, glamorized me with his family estates and connections. He came from a rich WASP family, long on lineage, proud of its service in the diplomatic corps.

One evening Rob took me to meet his grandmother; something of a formal presentation. She received us in the library of her Manhattan triplex (not, I presume, as the prospective in-law her grandson had in mind—but one can never be sure about the sophisticated insights of the upper class in these matters). The butler ushered us into the presence of a seemingly ancient and unquestionably formidable woman. Sitting unmoving in an armchair, dressed in a full length black gown, a mass of snow-white hair framing a still beautiful face, she allowed the exchange of a few rigorous pleasantries. Dazed and intimated, I neither heard them fully then nor can recall any part of them now. But I do remember it was that same night, as Rob and I changed clothes in an upstairs bedroom, that I told him I probably loved him. For the first time. Tit for tat, he let me fuck him. I resisted his badgering insistence that I pronounce it the "best fuck" I had ever had, though I had had precious few. It may have been my father's peasant stubbornness asserting itself, bristling at the hint of droit de seigneur.

Though we called ourselves "lovers," our lovemaking was sharply circumscribed. Most of the time I was "trade" for Rob—I would let him blow me. The boundaries suited us both; they assuaged my guilt, fed his preferred image as guide to the uninitiated. Within a few months, our affair ended traumatically. I had to drop out of graduate school for a series of operations on my back, and while recuperating at home, wrote a "compromising" letter that my mother intercepted. She demanded an explanation, tapped a ready reservoir of self-loathing. I explained that Rob was queer, but I, of course, was not; I had let him blow me now and then because "my back problem prevented me from seeking the usual sexual outlets": he had been a convenience. My mother "accepted" the explanation. In gratitude, I broke off with Rob. I've never seen him since. My memories of him are ungenerous, ironic. Even now—my head ostensibly transformed—resentment against the man who tried to take me a step beyond furtive anonymity in sex, lies like a stone in my gut, an immutable pleistocene fossil.

December 1   Disappointing holiday in Boston. Larry and I got along only sporadically. My feelings toward him, as always, fluctuated between deep affection and sudden antagonism. I don't excuse him completely. He did two or three overtly nasty things (suggesting, for example, that we go to the Turkish baths together Saturday night). The weekend ended in a burst of mutual recrimination and sullenness . . . Time, I suppose, finally to put an end to the whole torturous business . . . But I still feel so tied to him—in some deeply neurotic way—that I can't seriously envision cutting off all contact.

(1981): Why "neurotic"? Because of the fluctuations in feelings? But that's true of all deep attachments. Maybe our arc swung wider and more often than most, but I automatically ascribed that to personal deficiencies, never to the self-distrust engendered in us by a culture insistent that it was wrong ("sinful," "neurotic"—depending on whether the rhetoric was based on the religious or psychiatric model) for two men to be physical lovers, to care "too" much about each other.

December 5   A lengthy, elegant meal at Jack's [*a gay faculty member I'd recently come to know*] for a group of bachelor fellows. Superb food, beautifully prepared and served; all very "upper-class homosexual." Mozart on the victrola, white Wedgewood plates, much clever banter. Pleasant enough people, I don't deny, but my points of meaningful contact with them are limited and I don't wish to join with an artificial band of "solidarity" what genuine interest and affection cannot cement.

I intend to try to stay put this weekend—not so much because of my workload, but more for the analysis. "Sitting still and suffering for science." (No—I must keep remembering it's for *me*).

December 17   Getting lax with this . . . nothing vivid enough to make me want to record it. Stayed in New Haven again over the weekend and went to a gay party . . . had a long chat with my first two real live "dikes" [*sic*]—both very feminine and talkative. Hope to seem them in New York; a safe way of enjoying female company.

(1981): I cringe at this, but have resisted—barely—the temptation to delete it. With the possible exception of the last clause, it could have been written by John Wayne. Which is why I've included it: it serves as a measure of the gulf between gay men and lesbian women (now as well as then, though less so now—I think), as well as graphically demonstrating the usually unacknowledged bond between gay men and straight men. In their behavior and values, gay men are often males first and gays second. The priority has recently begun to shift—at least within limited circles. But many gay men continue to patronize lesbians, dismissing them with the same stereotypic contempt employed by the society at large. And this is the chief (though not the only) reason gay men and lesbians have had so much trouble working together harmoniously in the "movement." On the other hand, I don't think sexism is as strong among gay men as among straight; some gay men—and in increasing number, I believe—are more than rhetorically committed to feminism. But many feminists would dispute that, and others would go no further than wary optimism.

December 20   Ever since the bad time with Larry three weeks ago, I've been rushing around filling the void with the usual pointless activities. The last two weekends I've had bad experiences. First with a set of lovers from Jersey— almost panic-stricken with regret after going home with them.

(1981): I remember it well. They picked me up in a bar in New York City, then drove me out to their place in the country. The older of the two was tall and angular— marginally attractive. The younger was devastating: a short, powerfully-built farm boy from Maine, with an enormous cock. We started out to have a threesome, but the older man soon withdrew and went upstairs to bed. I was surprised and confused. Did he find me unattractive (as I did him), or had it been prearranged between them—had I been picked up to keep the younger one happy? I remember how lonesome I felt, after sex, when Maine withdrew upstairs to sleep with his lover, not inviting me to join them. I dozed for a few hours on the living room couch, then woke them early morning and asked to be taken to the bus. Why the panic? That model in my head again. The contrast

between my aloneness, my "inability to make it with someone on a sustained basis," and their togetherness.

The other bad experience was last weekend in New York . . . met a guy named Lou in the Big Dollar [*a gay bar*] and went home with him. Rugged Italian type . . . one track mind sexually—wanted deliriously, to fuck me. His persistence excited me. It brought out all my passive desires—to be used, possessed, overpowered; which only occasionally come to the surface and which I act on rarely. I was tempted to give in this time, but controlled the impulse by telling myself what I knew was true—that the fantasy of being "taken" was more exciting than the actuality, and that the subsequent psychological upset, plus the worry over disease, would far overbalance the slight pleasure. I wonder what lies behind the fantasy in the first place. I present an exterior of manliness, and in much of my actual sex life, play the dominant role, but there is a parallel and conflicting desire in me—sometimes very strong—to be passive sexually. In some complicated way I think all my homosexual activity is an attempt (among other things) to identify with a masculinity I was never sure I had. Being entered by a man is perhaps the most direct way of incorporating and absorbing that masculinity. And yet when I do allow myself to be "browned" [*the going genteel gay euphemism for "fucked"*] I almost never receive physical pleasure from it; that comes instead from assuming the opposite role—from browning others. But the fantasy remains strong: to be possessed by—and thereby to possess—a real man and his qualities.

(1981): A "real man" penetrated, dominated, fucked. This kind of sexual stereotyping —still so prevalent—was an integral aspect of the medical model of sexuality with which I identified. It managed all at once to be homophobic and patriarchal: a "real man" was heterosexual and unyieldingly dominant. All sexual acts intrinsically denoted "active" or "passive" attributes. There seemed to be no understanding—certainly none that was transmitted to patients wavering "dangerously" in their proclivities— that the muscular contractions of the anus, say, or the vagina, could, by several definitions, be considered an "active" agent in producing any cohabitation worthy of the name. The strict division of all sexual behavior into active or passive categories did serve as a convenient guide for those terrified of being confused (especially in their own minds) about the proper role to assume, which acts to perform (or not) in order to win certification as Male.

Though I now get angry at these one-dimensional models—being "entered" connotes "passivity," connotes "femininity"—that did so much to shape and constrict my understanding. I have to resist the urge to be just as categorical in rejecting them, for the latest theories and vocabularies have no conclusive validation either and will themselves doubltless by subjected in time to yet further reformulations.

Besides, the derision with which I view my former values, the contempt with which I regard my former self, may be designed in part to keep me from owning (which is harder than owning up to) the person I was. Yes, I was often callow, fatuous (especially in my tenacious "self-scrutiny"), grandiose. Yet not taking possession of the earlier me, amounts to not accepting myself now; for despite my efforts at disassociation, the two are one, the past is present, has left some mark; denying it raises the suspicion that the mark may be more pronounced than I like to admit. Memory is one powerful ingredient in forming identity. If I cut off my own legs, that leaves me floating in space. A neat trick, but not one in my non-Eastern bag. It's important to stop talking about "him" and "me"—to accept the totality. "He" may have been simplistic and self-pitying, but so would any mocking disavowal of him be (tempted though I am to indulge it). Not to forgive my earlier self is not to do several things that need doing: to implicate society for the self-sabotage it generated in gay people: to refuse myself an anterior history which, however, painful, is an integral part of my being: to deny that I had a place from which I needed to grow . . .

January 5, 1958   Back from spending vacation in New York with Larry. Looks like the final split between us. Larry announced it was time to recognize that what was left of our relationship is only a "bad joke," that he felt unwelcome, that I should please not write or contact him at all from now on. I agreed with little reluctance—though I've since had occasional pangs. The simple and absurd truth is that we're basically incompatible and nothing either of us can do will ever change that. Unfortunately, incompatibility is no guarantee against strong attraction and real feeling . . . I'm fired up again with determination to resist all homosexual contact, to change . . .

(1981): I wish, at this juncture of my life, I'd been encouraged to ask a different set of questions about what did indeed prove to be the final break-up with Larry. They might have produced a different attitude about myself and a different set of expectations for the future. I wish I'd looked more closely at what our "incompatibility" consisted of. I only know our obvious differences—in background, education, temperament. I doubt if these constituted a significant, let alone sufficient explanation for the problems we had. Our differences often made for some of our happiest times—we knew about different things and saw some things in different ways, and by that much added to each other's lives.

More basic to the split, in retrospect, was our shared assumption (much stronger on my part, though Larry's Catholic upbringing induced guilt enough) that two men could never make it together, that to be homosexual was, by definition, to be incapable of sustained commitment to another human being. Plus the conviction, bred into us by the culture (into heterosexuals, too) that sexual fidelity and an unwavering level of caring were the two crucial indices for evaluating the "success" of a relationship. Any erosion of erotic zest for one's partner was suspect, suggestive of incompatibility as well as immaturity. But the reigning standard of sexual fidelity was applied more stringently to gay men than to straight ones, "adventuring" automatically seen in them as a symptom of character disorder.

Such formulas squeezed my experience into dry moulds that caricatured it. What I needed were terms—ways of thinking—that would have helped me to question those formulas. That's precisely where psychiatry failed me.

I wish I'd been encouraged to ask why I wanted a lifetime companion, and then—if convinced I did—to recognize that if my choice was to settle down into "matehood," I had better stop thinking of the relationship in the adolescent/romantic terms of perfect accord, unconditional caring, eternal bliss.

Beyond my relationship with Larry, the standard psychoanalytic formulas (the moral norms of the country, or my corner of it) on which I was weaned in the Fifties, kept me from myself—encouraged me to distrust my feelings, to malign "mere" sexual pleasure, to avoid risk, to associate legitimate social discontent with private neurosis, to do bt my capacity for closeness and to misread and denigrate any evidence to the contrary.

I wish I had spent my time analyzing the tyrannical formulas then current for recognizing a "real" relationship, instead of repetitively exploring the presumed neuroses which I was told (and believed) would forever obstruct its realization. But I learned what was taught. I learned to regard any hope of a loving relationship with another man as the essence of fantasy and to set the goal of monogamous heterosexuality as the essence of reality. What I needed to change during my years with Larry—and for many years thereafter—was my self-centered, perfectionist view of what relationships are— not who they're with.

EPILOGUE

I remained in therapy—with brief time out for bad behavior—for nearly a dozen years, becoming still more intensively involved after I moved to New York City in 1964. At that point I added group therapy to my individual sessions. During those many years I continued to hear the familiar litany about my "sickness," about the need to renounce my ways and devote myself to "getting well." Spasmodically I tried to follow instructions, the effort alternating with intervals of furious rebellion—a cycle already gruesomely familiar from the Fifties. In retrospect, I'm astonished at the tenacity with which I continued to buy into imposed, arbitrary definitions of "normalcy" and self-worth— into a state of self-abdication. Suffice it to say that no one will ever have to explain to me the "mystery" of Jonestown.

By the late Sixties, my entangled cocoon did finally begin to unravel, a process greatly aided by the advent of the the modern homophile movement, with its liberating new perspectives and options.

Dispiriting residues remain, sometimes propelling back into my head with those once-favorite lines from Matthew Arnold:

"Wandering between two worlds, one dead,
the other powerless to be born . . ."

Sometimes: but less and less and less.

Michael S. Kimmel and Martin P. Levine

MEN AND AIDS

Over 93% of all adult Americans with AIDS are men (as of December 1987), and 73% of all adult AIDS cases occur among gay men (and all cases among homosexuals are male). Eight out of every 10 cases linked to intravenous drug use are men (AIDS Surveillance Report, Center for Disease Control, December 1987). In New York City, AIDS is the leading cause of death among men aged 30 to 44.[1] Most instances of the other AIDS-related disease are also among men. These conditions mark earlier stages of infection with the virus causing AIDS, the Human Immune Deficiency virus (HIV). They include AIDS-related complex (ARC) and AIDS virus antibody positivity (HIV

Note: This essay is dedicated to the memory of José A. Vigo, 1950–1988.

seropositivity). Although the prevalence of these conditions is presently un-known, they appear to be concentrated among male intravenous drug users and homosexual men (Institute of Medicine, 1986).

And yet no one talks about AIDS as a men's disease. No one talks about why men are so overwhelmingly at greater risk for AIDS, ARC, and HIV seropositivity. No one talks about the relationship between AIDS and mascu-linity. In fact, the rhetoric is more often about AIDS as a moral disease. Christian Voice leader Bob Grant says that people with AIDS are simply "reaping the results" of their "unsafe and immoral behavior" (Knopp, 1987). Evangelist Jerry Falwell calls AIDS "the wrath of God among homosexuals" (cited in Altman, 1986: 67).[2] These pronouncements enjoy some popular acceptance. Almost one-third of the respondents in one survey believed that "AIDS is a punishment that God has given homosexuals for the way they live." (Although, echoing Falwell, these respondents seem to be unaware that lesbians who are not intravenous drug users are virtually risk free.) And one-fourth of those same respondents believed that AIDS victims are "getting what they deserve" (*Los Angeles Times*, 12 December 1985). "The poor homo-sexuals," explained Patrick Buchanan, a conservative columnist and aide to President Reagan, sarcastically, "they have declared war upon Nature, and now Nature is exacting an awful retribution" (*The New York Post*, 24 May 1983). And almost two-fifths of the respondents (37%) to another survey said that AIDS had made them less favorably disposed toward homosexuals than they had been before (*The New York Times*, 15 December 1985).

Such beliefs confuse the cause of the disease with transmission. Sin does not cause AIDS, a virus does. Homosexual intercourse and sharing intra-venous needles are but two of the ways in which this virus is transmitted. Other forms include heterosexual relations, blood transfusions, and exchange of blood during pregnancy. In fact, in Africa, most people infected are heterosexual nonintravenous drug users (Quinn, Mann, Curran, and Prot, 1986).

But in the United States, AIDS is a disease of men. The seriousness of the disease demands that we pose the question: what is it about masculinity that puts men at greater risk for AIDS-related illness? To answer that question, we will explore the links between manliness and practices associated with risks for HIV infection; that is, we will examine the relationship between masculin-ity and risk-taking. To do this, we will first outline the norms of masculinity, the defining features of what it means to be a "real" man in our society. Then we will look at how these norms predispose men to engage in behaviors that place them at greater risk for AIDS. And finally, we will discuss how this perspective may shed new light on strategies of AIDS prevention.

MASCULINITY AS SOCIAL CONSTRUCTION

What does it mean to be a man in contemporary American society? Most experts believe that the answer to this question lies in the prevailing cultural construction of masculinigy.[3] This perspective maintains that our under-standing of masculinity and femininity derives less from biological impera-tives or psychological predispositions than from the social definitions of what is appropriate behavior for each gender. Men acquire the scripts that define gender-appropriate behavior through socialization; the family, educational and religious institutions, and the media all contribute to this cultural definition. Such a perspective insists that the cultural definitions of masculinity and femininity are not universal, but culturally and historically specific; what it means to be a man or a woman varies from culture to culture, within any one culture over time, and over the course of one's life.[4]

What, then, are the expectations of gender behavior that men in the United States learn? What are the norms of manliness? Social scientists Deborah David and Robert Brannon (Brannon, 1976) group these rules into four basic themes: (1) *No Sissy Stuff:* anything that even remotely hints of femininity is prohibited. A real man must avoid any behavior or characteristic associated with women; (2) *Be a Big Wheel:* masculinity is measured by success, power, and the admiration of others. One must possess wealth, fame, and status to be considered manly; (3) *Be a Sturdy Oak:* manliness requires rationality, toughness, and self-reliance. A man must remain calm in any situation, show no emotion, and admit no weakness; (4) *Give'em Hell:* men must exude an aura of daring and aggression, and must be willing to take risks, to "go for it" even when reason and fear suggest otherwise.

This cultural construction of masculinity indicates that men organize their conceptions of themselves as masculine by their willingness to take risks, their ability to experience pain or discomfort and not submit to it, their drive to accumulate constantly (money, power, sex partners, experiences), and their resolute avoidance of any behavior that might be construed as feminine. The pressures accompanying these efforts cause higher rates of stress-related illnesses (heart disease, ulcers) and venereal diseases among men. The norms encouraging risk-taking behaviors lead men to smoke, drink too much, and drive recklessly, resulting in disproportionate incidences of respiratory illness, alcoholism, and vehicular accidents and fatalities. And the rules urging aggressiveness induce higher rates of violence-related injury and death among men. Over a century ago, Dr. Peter Bryce, director of a mental institution in Alabama, underscored the relationship between masculinity and mental health. "The causes of general paresis," Dr. Bryce wrote (cited in Hughes, 1988: 15):

> are found to prevail most among men, and at the most active time of life, from 35 to 40, in the majority of cases. Habitual intemperance, sexual excesses, overstrain in business, in fact, all those habits which tend to keep up too rapid cerebral action, are supposed to induce this form of disease. It is especially a disease of *fast life,* and fast business in large cities.

"Warning," writes one modern psychologist, "the male sex role may be dangerous to your health!" (Harrison, 1978).

MASCULINITY AND MALE SEXUALITY

These norms also shape male sexuality, organizing the scripts that men follow in their sexual behaviors. Men are taught to be rational, successful, and daring in sex: Real men divorce emotions from sexual expression, have sex without love and are concerned solely with gratification. Real men "score" by having lots of sex with many partners, and they are adventurous and take risks.

The norms defining masculinity also significantly increase men's vulnerability to AIDS. The virus causing AIDS is spread through bodily fluids such as blood, semen, and vaginal secretions. To become infected with this virus, men (and women) must engage in practices that allow these fluids to enter the bloodstream. Such practices are known as "risk behaviors" (see Frumkin and Leonard, 1987: Ch. 4).

The most common risk behaviors among adults are unprotected sexual intercourse, oral sex, and sharing needles. Heterosexual or homosexual intercourse can cause tiny breaks in the surface linings of these organs, through which infected bodily fluids can enter the bloodstream directly. In oral sex, the fluids enter through breaks in the lining of the mouth.[5] Sharing needles allows these infected fluids to enter the bloodstream directly on needles containing contaminated blood.

Fortunately, there are ways one can avoid contact with the AIDS virus. Authorities recommend avoiding risk behaviors. This can be accomplished in several ways: (1) abstinence: the avoidance of sexual contacts and use of intravenous drugs; (2) safer sex: the avoidance of all sexual behaviors in which semen or blood are passed between partners (usually accomplished by the use of condoms); and (3) safer drug use: avoidance of all unsterilized needles. Safer drug use means not sharing needles if possible; if needles must be shared, they must be cleaned (with bleach or rubbing alcohol) before each use.

Unfortunately, these types of risk-reduction behavior are in direct contradiction with the norms of masculinity. The norms of masculinity propel men to take risks, score, and focus sexual pleasure on the penis. Real men ignore precautions for AIDS risk reduction, seek many sexual partners, and reject depleasuring the penis. Abstinence, safer sex, and safer drug use compromise manhood. The behaviors required for the confirmation of masculinity and those required to reduce risk are antithetical.

STRATEGIES OF AIDS PREVENTION

Given this perspective, how might we evaluate the various strategies that have been developed to combat the AIDS epidemic? To what extent do they reproduce or encourage precisely the behaviors that they are designed to discourage? The procedures developed to combat the AIDS epidemic ignore the links between masculinity and risk behaviors. The battle against AIDS relies heavily upon the public health strategies of testing and education (Gostin, in Dalton and Burris, 1987). But each of these is limited by the traditional norms of masculinity, as well as other factors.

Testing Testing involves the use of the HIV antibody test to screen the blood for antibodies to the AIDS virus, and posttest counseling. People who test positive for the HIV antibodies are regarded as infected, that is, as carrying the virus and capable of transmitting it to others. These individuals are counseled to avoid risk behaviors.

AIDS antibody testing, however, even when coupled with counseling, is not a sufficient methods to deal with the AIDS epidemic. The rationale for testing has been that it will encourage safer-sex behavior among those already infected but not yet ill, and thus curtail the epidemic. Yet this rationale remains unproven. Although this procedure may have been successful in the past with other infectious diseases, Dr. William Curran of the Harvard School of Public Health argues that it does not apply to AIDS (Curran, 1986). One study found that a positive result on the AIDS antibody test does not necessarily promote safe-sex behaviors. "It is not the test that promotes safe sex," the authors write, "but education and social support for safe sex" (Beeson, Zones, and Nye, 1986: 14).

AIDS antibody testing also has negative side effects, such as psychological distress, the possibility of social sanctions such as losing one's job, loss of medical care or life insurance, or the possibility of forced quarantine, if specific public policy recommendations are adopted by voters. Thus, antibody testing is opposed by nearly all medical and epidemiological experts. The Institute of Medicine of the National Academy of Sciences recently summarized their findings that testing was

> impossible to justify now either on ethical or practical grounds . . . [raising] serious problems of ethics and feasibility. People whose private behavior is illegal are not likely to comply with a mandatory screening program, even one backed by assurances of confidentiality. Mandatory screening based on sexual orientation would appear to discriminate against or to coerce entire groups without justification. (Institute of Medicine, 1986: 14)

From our perspective, as well, we must examine the ways in which the norms of masculinity impede the effectiveness of AIDS antibody testing. These rules compel men to shun stereotypical "feminine" concerns about health. "Real" men do not worry about the dangers associated with smoking, drinking, and stress—why should they worry about the risks associated with intravenous drug use and sex? Manly nonchalance will keep men from getting tested. Early reports from New York City indicate that more women than men are being tested for AIDS (Sullivan, 1987).

These norms of masculinity also impede the effectiveness of counseling. During counseling, men are warned against spreading the virus. Such warnings, however, contradict the dictates of manliness. "Real" men score, and their sexuality is organized phallocentrically, so counseling, which would encourage men to deemphasize the penis and emphasize sexual responsibility, may fall on deaf ears. To demonstrate manliness, seropositive men may actually give the virus to someone else.

Public Health Education   Public health authorities have also utilized education as an AIDS prevention strategy. The Institute of Medicine of the National Academy of Sciences recommends "a major educational campaign to reduce the spread of HIV" and that "substantially increased educational and public awareness activities be supported not only by the government, but also by the information media, and by other private sector organizations that can effectively campaign for health." For intravenous drug users, the Institute recommends "trials to provide easier access to sterile, disposable needles and syringes" (Institute of Medicine, 1986: 10, 12, 13).

Educational efforts have been developed by both public sector agencies, such as federal, state, and local health departments, and private organizations, such as local AIDS groups, and groups of mental health practitioners. These public and private efforts are each faced with a different set of problems, and each confronts different components of the norms of masculinity.

Public health education campaigns, funded by taxpayer dollars, have utilized mass transit advertisements, billboards, brochures, and hotlines to explain the medical facts about AIDS, its causes, how it affects the body, how it is transmitted, and who is at risk. Such campaigns deemphasize information about safe sex behaviors, because such information might be seen as condoning or even encouraging behaviors that are morally or legally proscribed. As Dr. James Mason, undersecretary for health in the Department of Health and Human Services said, "[w]e don't think that citizens care to be funding material that encourages gay lifestyles" (cited in Anderson, 1985). Editor and writer Normal Podhoretz criticized any efforts to stop AIDS because to do so would encourage homosexuality so that "in the name of compassion they are giving social sanction to what can only be described as brutish degradation" (cited in *New York Times*, 18 March 1986). And North Carolina Senator Jesse Helms, one of the nation's most vocal critics of education programs, sponsored an amendment that stipulated that no federal funds be used to promote or encourage homosexual activity, and emphasized that AIDS education emphasize abstinence outside a sexually monogamous marriage as the only preventive behaviors that the government would fund. The choice that Helms offers, he claims, is "Reject sodomy and practice morality. If they are unwilling to do that, they should understand the consequences" (Helms, 1987).

The content of these educational campaigns reflects the political ideology embedded within them. The pamphlet issued by the U.S. Public Health Service's Center for Disease Control, "What You Should Know About AIDS," counsels that the "safest way to avoid being infected by the AIDS virus is to avoid promiscuous sex and illegal drugs." Teenagers, especially, "should be encouraged to say 'no' to sex and illegal drugs" (Center for Disease Control, 1987).

The effectiveness of such strategies is extremely limited by the myopic moralizing that is embedded within them. "It is too late to be prudish in discussing the crisis with youngsters," warns an editorial in *The Washington Post*, urging explicit safe-sex education in the schools ("AIDS Education," 1987). But more than this, they are limited because they violate the traditional norms of masculinity. Just saying "no" contradicts the norms that inform men that "real" men score in sex, by having many sexual partners and by taking risks, or, more accurately, by ignoring potential risks in their pursuit of sex. Because of the norms of masculinity, which are especially salient for teenagers and younger men, the burden of just saying "no" will undoubtedly fall upon the shoulders of women. Efforts to halt the spread of a sexually transmitted disease by encouraging men to abstain have never been successful in American history, although such strategies have been attempted before, during the syphillis epidemic following World War I (see Brandt, 1986).

Private-Agency Educational Campaigns   Educational campaigns sponsored by privately funded agencies have developed various mechanisms that are far less negative about sexuality, and may, therefore, have far greater chances of reaching male populations. These campaigns vary in tone and effect. Some organizations that have emerged from within the gay community in major cities across the nation have given explicit information about safer sex practices. "Plain Talk about Safe Sex and AIDS" (published by Baltimore Health Education Resource Organization and also distributed in Boston) uses scare tactics:

> You must be aware that AIDS will almost certainly kill you if you get it. No fooling. It's that deadly. And at this moment it's incurable. This is no wishy washy Public Health "warning" from the Surgeon General, determining that cigarette smoking is dangerous to your health. The medical breakthrough hasn't happened yet. In other words, if you contract AIDS, the chances are that you'll be dead within a year, probably. Got it? Let's put it in plain language. If you develop AIDS, kiss your ass goodbye.

The San Francisco AIDS Foundation condemns past practices among gay men, such as anonymous sex, bathhouses, backrooms, bookstores, and parks, while giving this advice:

> We do know that the long standing health problems caused by sexually transmitted disease in the gay community could be reduced if everyone were to heed the suggestions outlined here. If, as many believe, repeated infections also weaken the immune system, these suggestions can help you lead a healthier and safer life. If our comments sound rather judgmental or directive, understand that we, too, have and are experiencing these diseases and are trying to follow our own recommendations. . . . [W]e believe that intimacy, both sexual and emotional, is necessary as we move toward a more healthy regard for our own bodies and those we love.

Other educational efforts attempt to remain sex-positive, such as Houston's "AIDS Play Safe" campaign, whose slogan is "Adapt, Enjoy, Survive." Their pamphlet states:

> You don't have to give up good times, being social, having fun, going out, or even having sex, but you can change to safe sex, accept the experience and enjoy it. The results are lower risk of AIDS, less fear and anxiety, your health, and possibly your life. Come on, let's party. Don't be left behind, don't sit at home fretting. You can still have a good time, you can still enjoy your sexuality, you can still enjoy your lifestyle, you can still party, dance, play, have sex, and get the most out of life. You don't have to deny it to yourself. Adapt, enjoy and survive. And we'll see you around next year.

This position is echoed in the "Healthy Sex Is Great Sex" pamphlet published by the Gay Men's Health Crisis in New York City. Other efforts to educate gay men about safe sex practices include safe sex videos, house parties where information and free condoms are distributed on a model of Tupperware parties, and workshops run by professionals on eroticizing safe sex encounters.

In general, these campaigns developed by local gay organizations have had remarkable success. By a variety of measures—impressionistic, comparative and surveys—unsafe sex practices have declined sharply among those groups who have access to explicit information about safe sex behaviors. Impressionistic journalistic reports indicate that gay baths and bars are less crowded and monogamous coupling is on the rise. The rates of other venereal disease, a certain marker of promiscuity and unsafe sex practices, have plummeted among gay men across the country.

The results of survey data reveal a significant decrease in unsafe sex practices among gay men. The San Francisco AIDS Foundation found in 1984 that almost all respondents were aware that certain erotic behavior could result in AIDS, and two-thirds had stopped engaging in high risk behavior (*Advocate*, 428, 3 September 1985). Another San Francisco survey found widespread awareness about safe sex guidelines, and a continued decline in high risk behaviors among subjects between 1984 and 1985 (Research and Decisions Corporation, 1985).

Some Lingering Problems   But we are concerned not with the significant numbers of men who have altered their behavior in the face of serious health risk, but with the residual numbers who have not changed. How can we explain that one-third of those men surveyed in 1984 and one-fifth of the men surveyed in 1985 continued to engage in unsafe sex? How do we explain the conclusion of the 1985 study, which reported that the "men in these groups were uniformly well informed for AIDS risk reduction. Despite their knowledge of health directives, the men in this sample displayed discrepancies between what they believed about AIDS and their sexual behavior" (McKusik, et al. 1985:495). It appears that a significant number of men continue to engage in high risk behavior, even though they know better.

Such continued high risk behavior cannot be attributed to homphobia, since the information provided is by local gay groups. And it is not attributable to sex-negativism, since much of the material is also sexually explicit about safe sex practices and gay-affirmative in tone. We believe that the cultural norms of masculinity compose one of the hidden impediments to safe sex education. That men's sexuality is organized around scoring, associates danger with sexual excitement, and is phallocentric limits the effectiveness of safer sex educational campaigns. In one study, 35% of the gay men who agreed that reducing the number of sexual partners would reduce risks had sex with more than five different men during the previous month (McKusik, et al. 1985). Over four-fifths of the men who agreed with the statement "I use hot anonymous sex to relieve tension" had three or more sexual partners the previous month. And almost 70% of the men having three or more sexual partners the previous month agreed with the statement "It's hard to change my sexual behavior because being gay means doing what I want sexually."

CHALLENGING TRADITIONAL MASCULINITY AS RISK REDUCTION

Here we see the question in its boldest form: gay male sex is, above all, male sex, and male sex, above all, is risky business. Here, we believe, the social scientist can inform public health campaigns and epidemiological research. We need to recapitulate our understanding of how masculinity informs sexual behavior, and how masculinity might serve as an impediment to safer sex behaviors among men. Since there is no anticipatory socialization for homosexuality, boys in our culture all learn norms for heterosexual masculinity. This means that gay or straight, men in our culture are cognitively oriented to think and behave sexually through the prism of gender. Gay male sexuality and straight male sexuality are both enactments of scripts appropriate to gender; both have, in their cognitive orientations, "male" sex.

What this means concretely includes the meanings that become attached to our sexual scripts in early adolescence. Through masturbation and early sexual experiences, boys learn that sex is privatized, that emotions and sexuality are detached, that the penis is the center of the sexual universe, that fantasy allows heightened sexual experience, that pleasure and guilt are intimately linked, and that what brings sexual pleasure is also something that needs to be hidden from one's family. Masculinity is enacted in sexual scripts by the emphasis on scoring, by its recreational dimension (the ability to have sex without love), and by the pursuit of sexual gratification for its own sake, and by the association of danger and excitement (enacted through the link of pleasure and guilt). The male sexual script makes it normative to take risks, to engage in anonymous sex, and to have difficulty sustaining emotional intimacy, and it validates promiscuous sexual behavior.

In such a script, "safe sex" is an oxymoron. How can sex be safe? How can safety be sexy? Sex is about danger, excitement, risk; safety is about comfort, security, softness. And if safe sex isn't sexy, many men, enacting gender scripts about masculinity, will continue to practice unsafe sex. Or they may decide not to engage in sex at all. "I find so-called safe sex comparable to putting my nose up against a window in a candy store when I'm on a diet. I'd rather not go near the window at all, because seeing the candy makes me want to eat at least three or four pieces," said one man explaining his two-year voluntary celibacy as a response to AIDS ("Sex in the Age of AIDS," 1986). To educate men about safe sex, then, means to confront the issues of masculinity.

In spite of the efforts of some policy makers, whose misplaced moralism is likely to cost thousands of lives, we know that "health education is the only tool that can stem this epidemic," as the executive director of the Gay Men's Health Crisis put it. "AIDS education should have started the moment it was realized that this disease is sexually transmitted," wrote one medical correspondent (cited in Watney, 1987: 135). It would appear that a public health policy that was truly interested in reducing the spread of AIDS (instead of punishing those who are already stigmatized and at risk) would need to add two more considerations to the impressive educational efforts already underway. First, we will need to make safer sex sexy. Second, we will need to enlarge the male sexual script to include a wider variety of behaviors, to allow men a wide range of sexual and sensual pleasures.

Safer sex can be sexy sex. Many organizations are developing a safer sex pornography. GMHC in New York City offers safe sex videos as a form of "pornographic healing." In his important new book, *Policing Desire: Pornography, AIDS, and the Media,* English author Simon Watney argues that gay men "need to organize huge regular Safe Sex parties in our clubs and gay centers . . . with workshops and expert counseling available. We need to produce, hot, sexy visual materials to take home, telephone sex-talk facilities, and safe sex porno cinemas" (Watney, 1987: 133).

And while we make safer sex into sexy sex, we also need to transform the meaning of masculinity, to enlarge our definition of what it means to be a man, so that sexuality will embrace a wider range of behaviors and experiences. As Watney argues, we "need to develop a culture which will support the transition to safer sex by establishing the model of an erotics of protection, succour and support within the framework of our pre-AIDS sex lives" (Watney, 1987: 132).

CONCLUSION

The process of transforming masculinity is long and difficult, and AIDS can spread so easily and rapidly. Sometimes it feels as if there isn't enough time. And there isn't. While we are eroticizing safer sex practices and enlarging the range of erotic behaviors available to men, we must also, as a concerned public, increase our compassion and support for AIDS patients. We must stand with them because they are our brothers. We are linked to them not through sexual orientation (although we may be) or by drug-related behavior (although we may be), but by gender, by our masculinity. They are not "perverts" or "deviants" who have strayed from the norms of masculinity, and therefore brought this terrible retribution upon themselves. They are, if anything, overconformists to destructive norms of male behavior. They are men who, like all real men, have taken risks. And risk taking has always implied danger. Men have always known this and have always chosen to take risks. Until daring has been eliminated from the rhetoric of masculinity, men will die as a result of their risk taking. In war. In sex. In driving fast and drunk. In shooting drugs and sharing needles. Men with AIDS are real men, and when one dies, a bit of all men dies as well. Until we change what it means to be a real man, every man will die a little bit every day.

NOTES

1. New York City Department of Health, personal communication, January 11, 1988.
2. For an overview of moralistic interpretations of AIDS, see Fitzpatrick (1988).
3. Our work here draws upon the "social constructionist" model of gender and sexuality. The pioneering work of John Gagnon and William Simon, *Sexual Conduct* (1973), has been followed up by our recent work. See, for example, Michael Kimmel and Jeffrey Fracher (1987), "Hard Issues and Soft Spots: Counseling Men About Sexuality," John Gagnon and Michael Kimmel (1988), *Gender and Desire*, and Martin P. Levine (1986), *Gay Macho: The Ethnography of the Homosexual Clone.*
4. Gender norms also vary within any culture by class, race, ethnicity, and region. Although there are many masculinities or feminities in the contemporary United States, however, we will elaborate the standard for white middle-class men in major metropolitan areas, because this is the model that is the hegemonic form that is defined as generalizable and normative. It is essential to understand its universality as a power relation and not as a moral ideal (see Connell, 1987).
5. The evidence for oral sex as a mode of transmission is only speculative. To date, there are no reported instances of transmission in this way (Green 1987).

REFERENCES

"AIDS Education." Editorial in *Washington Post*, 28 February 1987.

"AIDS: The Public Reacts." *Public Opinion*, 8, December 1986.

Altman, Dennis. 1986. *AIDS in the Mind of America*. New York: Doubleday.

Anderson, Jack, 1985. "Fear consigns AIDS material to the shelf." *Newark Star Ledger*, 11 November 1985.

Beeson, Diane R., Jane S. Zones and John Nye, 1986. "The social consequences of AIDS antibody testing: Coping with stigma." Paper presented at annual meetings of the Society for the Study of Social Problems, New York.

Brandt, Alan. 1986. *No Magic Bullet*. New York: Oxford University Press.

Brannon, Robert. 1976. "Introduction." In Robert Brannon and Deborah David, eds. *The Forty-Nine Percent Majority*. Reading, MA: Addison-Wesley.

Center for Disease Control. "AIDS Surveillance Report," December 1987.

Curran, William. 1986. AIDS. Cambridge: Harvard School of Public Health.

Dalton, Harlon and Scott Burris, eds. 1987. *AIDS and the Law: A Guide for the Public*. New Haven: Yale University Press.

Fitzpatrick, James K. "AIDS is a Moral Issue" in Lynn Hall and Thomas Mode, (eds.). *AIDS Opposing Viewpoints*. St. Paul: Greenhaven Press, pp. 32–37.

Frumkin, Lyn and John Leonard, 1987. *Questions and Answers on AIDS*. New York: Avon.

Gagnon, John and William Simon. 1973. *Sexual Conduct*. Chicago: Aldine.

Gagnon, John and Michael Kimmel. 1989. *Gender and Desire*. New York: Basic Books, in progress.

Gostin, Larry. 1987. "Traditional public health strategies." In Harlon Dalton and Scott Burris, eds. *AIDS and the Law: A Guide for the Public*. New Haven: Yale University Press.

Green, Richard. 1987. "The transmission of AIDS." In Harlon Dalton and Scott Burris, eds. *AIDS and the Law: A Guide for the Public*. New Haven: Yale University Press.

Hall, Lynn and Thomas Modl, eds. 1988. *AIDS: Opposing Viewpoints*. St. Paul: Greenhaven Press.

Harrison, James. 1978. "Caution: Masculinity may be hazardous to your health." *Journal of Social Issues*, 34(1), pp. 65–86.

Helms, Jesse. 1987. "Only morality will effectively prevent AIDS from spreading." Letter to *The New York Times*, November 12, 1987.

Hughes, John. 1988. "The madness of separate spheres: Insanity and masculinity in late 19th century Alabama." Paper presented at Conference on Masculinity in Victorian America. Barnard College, 9 January 1988.

Institute for Advanced Study of Human Sexuality. 1986. *Safe Sex in the Age of AIDS*. Secaucus, NJ: Citadel Press.

Institute of Medicine, National Academy of Sciences. 1986. *Confronting AIDS: Directions for Public Health, Health Care and Research*. Washington, D.C.: National Academy Press.

Kimmel, Michael and Jeffrey Fracher. 1987. "Hard issues and soft spots: Counseling men about sexuality." In Murray Scher et al., eds. *Handbook of Counseling and Psychotherapy with Men*. Newbury Park, CA: Sage Publications.

Kropp, Arthur. 1987. "Religious right cashing in on AIDS epidemic." *Houston Texas Post*, July 20, 1987.

Levine, Martin P. *Gay Macho: The Ethnography of the Homosexual Clone*. Ph.D. dissertation, New York University, 1986.

Los Angeles Times, 12 December 1985.

McKusik, Leon, William Hortsman and Thomas J. Coates. 1985. "AIDS and sexual behavior reported by gay men in San Francisco." *American Journal of Public Health*, 75(5). May.

New York Post, 24 May 1983.

The New York Times, 15 December 1985.

The New York Times, 18 March 1986.

Quinn, Thomas C., Jonathan M. Mann, James W. Curran and Peter Prot. 1986. "AIDS in Africa: An epidemiological paradigm." *Science*, 234, November 21.

"Sex in the Age of AIDS," a symposium. 1986. *The Advocate*, July 8.

Sullivan, Ronald. 1987. "More women are seeking test for AIDS." *The New York Times*, 23 May 1987.

Watney, Simon. 1987. *Policing Desire: Pornography, AIDS and the Media.* Minneapolis: University of Minnesota Press.

◆ ◆ ◆

PART SIX

Men with Women: Intimacy and Power

Why do many men have problems establishing and maintaining intimate relationships with women? What different forms do male–female relational problems take within different socioeconomic groups? How do men's problems with intimacy and emotional expressivity relate to power inequities between the sexes? Are rape and domestic violence best conceptualized as isolated deviant acts by "sick" individuals, or are they the illogical consequences of male socialization? This complex web of male–female relationships, intimacy, and power is the topic of this section.

Lillian Rubin begins this section with a psychoanalytic interpretation of male–female relational problems. Early-developmental differences, rooted in the social organization of the nuclear family (especially the fact that it is women who care for infants), have set up fundamental emotional and sexual differences between men and women that create problems and conflicts for heterosexual couples. Clyde W. Franklin, in examining conflicts between black males and females, focuses more on how the larger socioeconomic structure of society places strains on black family life, and especially on black males' work and family roles. Whereas Rubin's and Franklin's articles tend to portray both males and females as being victimized by socially structured gender differences and problems with intimacy and communiction, Jack W. Sattel asks some different questions. Male emotional and verbal inexpressivity, rather than being a "tragedy," might better be conceptualized as situational strategy that males utilize to retain control in their relationships with women. Intimacy and power are closely intertwined.

Men's anger and insecurities toward women surface in other ways. Wayne Ewing's examination of the dynamics of domestic violence, Jane Hood's exploration of adolescent gang rape, and Tim Beneke's dissection of the ideology of rape show that violence against women is the illogical consequence of insecurity, anger, the need for control, the need to assert and demonstrate manliness—all within a social context that condones sexual violence. As sociologist Diana Russell has written:

> Rape is not so much a deviant act as an over-conforming act. Rape may be understood as an extreme acting-out of qualities that are regarded as super masculine in this and many other societies: aggression, force, power, strength, toughness, dominance, competitiveness. To win, to be superior, to be successful, to conquer—all demonstrate masculinity to those who subscribe to common cultural notions of masculinity, i.e., the *masculine mystique*. And it would be surprising if these notions of masculinity did not find expression in men's sexual behavior. Indeed, sex may be the arena where these notions of masculinity are most intensely played out, particularly by men who feel powerless in the rest of their

lives, and hence, whose masculinity is threatened by this sense of powerlessness. (P. 1)

(Diana Russell, "Rape and the Masculine Mystique," paper presented to the American Sociological Association, New York, 1973.)

What links all the articles in this section is *not* a sense that males are inherently incapable of authentic emotional connections with women, or that men are "naturally" batterers or rapists. The problems that men and women have relating to each other are rooted in the socially structured system of gender difference and inequality. As feminists have long argued, the humanization of men is directly linked to the social empowerment of women. As long as men feel a need to control and subordinate women, either overtly or subtly, their relationships with women will be impoverished.

Lillian B. Rubin

THE APPROACH–AVOIDANCE DANCE:
MEN, WOMEN, AND INTIMACY

For one human being to love another, that is perhaps the most difficult of all our tasks, the ultimate, the last test and proof, the work for which all other work is but preparation.

—Rainer Maria Rilke

Intimacy. We hunger for it, but we also fear it. We come close to a loved one, then we back off. A teacher I had once described this as the "go away a little closer" message. I call it the approach–avoidance dance.

The conventional wisdom says that women want intimacy, men resist it. And I have plenty of material that would *seem* to support that view. Whether in my research interviews, in my clinical hours, or in the ordinary course of my life, I hear the same story told repeatedly. "He doesn't talk to me," says a woman. "I don't know what she wants me to talk about," says a man. "I want to know what he's feeling," she tells me. "I'm not feeling anything," he insists. "Who can feel nothing?" she cries. "I can," he shouts. As the heat rises, so does the wall between them. Defensive and angry, they retreat—stalemated by their inability to understand each other.

Women complain to each other all the time about not being able to talk to their men about the things that matter most to them—about what they themselves are thinking and feeling, about what goes on in the hearts and minds of the men they're relating to. And men, less able to expose themselves and their conflicts—those within themselves or those with the women in their lives—either turn silent or take cover by holding women up to derision. It's one of the norms of male camaraderie to poke fun at women, to complain laughingly about the mystery of their minds, wonderingly about their ways. Even Freud did it when, in exasperation, he asked mockingly, "What do women want? Dear God, what do they want?"

But it's not a joke—not for the women, not for the men who like to pretend it is.

> The whole goddamn business of what you're calling intimacy bugs the hell out of me. I never know what you women mean when you talk about it. Karen complains that I don't talk to her, but it's not talk she wants, it's some other damn thing, only I don't know what the hell it is. Feelings, she keeps asking for. So what am I supposed to do if I don't have any to give her or to talk about just because she decides it's time to talk about feelings? Tell me, will you: maybe we can get some peace around here.

The expression of such conflicts would seem to validate the common understandings that suggest that women want and need intimacy more than men do—that the issue belongs to women alone; that, if left to themselves, men would not suffer it. But things are not always what they seem. And I wonder: "If men would renounce intimacy, what is their stake in relationships with women?"

Some would say that men need women to tend to their daily needs—to prepare their meals, clean their houses, wash their clothes, rear their children—so that they can be free to attend to life's larger problems. And, given the traditional structure of roles in the family, it has certainly worked that way most of the time. But, if that were all men seek, why is it that, even when they're not relating to women, so much of their lives is spent in search of a relationship with another, so much agony experienced when it's not available?

These are difficult issues to talk about—even to think about—because the subject of intimacy isn't just complicated, it's slippery as well. Ask yourself: What is intimacy? What words come to mind, what thoughts?

It's an idea that excites our imagination, a word that seems larger than life to most of us. It lures us, beckoning us with a power we're unable to resist. And, just because it's so seductive, it frightens us as well—seeming sometimes to be some mysterious force from outside ourselves that, if we let it, could sweep us away.

But what is it we fear?

Asked what intimacy is, most of us—men and women—struggle to say something sensible, something that we can connect with the real experience of our lives. "Intimacy is knowing there's someone who cares about the children as much as you do." "Intimacy is a history of shared experience." "It's sitting there having a cup of coffee together and watching the eleven o'clock news." "It's knowing you care about the same things." "It's knowing she'll always understand." "It's him sitting in the hospital for hours at a time when I was sick." "It's knowing he cares when I'm hurting." "It's standing by me when I was out of work." "It's seeing each other at our worst." "It's sitting across the breakfast table." "It's talking when you're in the bathroom." "It's knowing we'll begin and end each day together."

These seem the obvious things—the things we expect when we commit our lives to one another in a marriage, when we decide to have children together. And they're not to be dismissed as inconsequential. They make up the daily experience of our lives together, setting the tone for a relationship in important and powerful ways. It's sharing such commonplace, everyday events that determines the temper and the texture of life, that keeps us living together even when other aspects of the relationship seem less than perfect. Knowing someone is there, is constant, and can be counted on in just the ways these thoughts express provides the background of emotional security and stability we look for when we enter a marriage. Certainly a marriage and the people in it will be tested and judged quite differently in an unusual situation or in a crisis. But how often does life present us with circumstances and events that are so out of the range of ordinary experience?

These ways in which a relationship feels intimate on a daily basis are only one part of what we mean by intimacy, however—the part that's most obvious, the part that doesn't awaken our fears. At a lecture where I spoke of these issues recently, one man commented also, "Intimacy is putting aside the masks we wear in the rest of our lives." A murmur of assent ran through the audience of a hundred or so. Intuitively we say, "yes." Yet this is the very issue that also complicates our intimate relationships.

On the one hand, it's reassuring to be able to put away the public persona—to believe we can be loved for who we *really* are, that we can show our shadow side without fear, that our vulnerabilities will not be counted against us. "The most important thing is to feel I'm accepted just the way I am," people will say.

But there's another side. For, when we show ourselves thus without the masks, we also become anxious and fearful. "Is it possible that someone could love the *real* me?" we're likely to ask. Not the most promising question for the further development of intimacy, since it suggests that, whatever else another might do or feel, it's we who have trouble loving ourselves. Unfortunately, such misgivings are not usually experienced consciously. We're aware only that our discomfort has risen, that we feel a need to get away. For the person who has seen the "real me" is also the one who reflects back to us an image that's usually not wholly to our liking. We get angry at that, first at ourselves for not living up to our own expectations, then at the other, who becomes for us the mirror of our self-doubts—a displacement of hostility that serves intimacy poorly.

There's yet another level—one that's further below the surface of consciousness, therefore, one that's much more difficult for us to grasp, let alone to talk about. I'm referring to the differences in the ways in which women and men deal with their inner emotional lives—differences that create barriers between us that can be high indeed. It's here that we see how those early childhood experiences of separation and individuation—the psychological tasks that were required of us in order to separate from mother, to distinguish ourselves as autonomous persons, to internalize a firm sense of gender identity—take their toll on our intimate relationships.

Stop a woman in mid-sentence with the question, "What are you feeling right now?" and you might have to wait a bit while she reruns the mental tape to capture the moment just passed. But, more than likely, she'll be able to do it successfully. More than likely, she'll think for a while and come up with an answer.

The same is not true of a man. For him, a similar question usually will bring a sense of wonderment that one would even ask it, followed quickly by an uncomprehending and puzzled response. "What do you mean?" he'll ask. "I was just talking," he'll say.

I've seen it most clearly in the clinical setting where the task is to get to the feeling level—or, as one of my male patients said when he came into therapy, to "hook up the head and the gut." Repeatedly when therapy begins, I find myself having to teach a man how to monitor his internal states—how to attend to his thoughts and feelings, how to bring them into consciousness. In the early stages of our work, it's a common experience to say to a man, "How does that feel?," and to see a blank look come over his face. Over and over, I find myself listening as a man speaks with calm reason about a situation which I know must be fraught with pain. "How do you feel about that?" I'll ask. "I've just been telling you," he's likely to reply. "No," I'll say, "you've told me what happened, not how you *feel* about it." Frustrated, he might well respond, "You sound just like my wife."

It would be easy to write off such dialogues as the problems of men in therapy, of those who happen to be having some particular emotional difficulties. But it's not so, as any woman who has lived with a man will attest. Time and again women complain: "I can't get him to verbalize his feelings."

"He talks, but it's always intellectualizing." "He's so closed off from what he's feeling, I don't know how he lives that way." "If there's one thing that will eventually ruin this marriage, it's the fact that he can't talk about what's going on inside him." "I have to work like hell to get anything out of him that resembles a feeling that's something besides anger. That I get plenty of—me and the kids, we all get his anger. Anything else is damn hard to come by with him." One woman talked eloquently about her husband's anguish over his inability to get problems in his work life resolved. When I asked how she knew about his pain, she answered:

> I pull for it, I pull hard, and sometimes I can get something from him. But it'll be late at night in the dark—you know, when we're in bed and I can't look at him while he's talking and he doesn't have to look at me. Otherwise, he's just defensive and puts on what I call his bear act, where he makes his warning, go-away faces, and he can't be reached or pene-trated at all.

To a woman, the world men live in seems a lonely one—a world in which their fears of exposing their sadness and pain, their anxiety about allowing their vulnerability to show, even to a woman they love, is so deeply rooted inside them that, most often, they can only allow it to happen "late at night in the dark."

Yet, if we listen to what men say, we will hear their insistence that they *do* speak of what's inside them, *do* share their thoughts and feelings with the women they love. "I tell her, but she's never satisfied," they complain. "No matter how much I say, it's never enough," they grumble.

From both sides, the complaints have merit. The problem lies not in what men don't say, however, but in what's not there—in what, quite simply, happens so far out of consciousness that it's not within their reach. For men have integrated all too well the lessons of their childhood—the experiences that taught them to repress and deny their inner thoughts, wishes, needs, and fears; indeed, not even to notice them. It's real, therefore, that the kind of inner thoughts and feelings that are readily accessible to a woman generally are unavailable to a man. When he says, "I don't know what I'm feeling," he isn't necessarily being intransigent and withholding. More than likely, he speaks the truth.

Partly that's a result of the ways in which boys are trained to camouflage their feelings under cover of an exterior of calm, strength, and rationality. Fears are not manly. Fantasies are not rational. Emotions, above all, are not for the strong, the sane, the adult. Women suffer them, not men—women, who are more like children with what seems like their never-ending preoc-cupation with their emotional life. But the training takes so well because of their early childhood experience when, as very young boys, they had to shift their identification from mother to father and sever themselves from their earliest emotional connection. Put the two together and it does seem like suffering to men to have to experience that emotional side of themselves, to have to give it voice.

This is the single most dispiriting dilemma of relations between women and men. He complains, "She's so emotional, there's no point in talking to her." She protests, "It's him you can't talk to, he's always so darned rational." He says, "Even when I tell her nothing's the matter, she won't quit." She says,

"How can I believe him when I can see with my own eyes that something's wrong?" He says, "Okay, so something's wrong! What good will it do to tell her?" She cries, "What are we married for? What do you need me for, just to wash your socks?"

These differences in the psychology of women and men are born of a complex interaction between society and the individual. At the broadest social level is the rending of thought and feeling that is such a fundamental part of Western thought. Thought, defined as the ultimate good, has been assigned to men; feeling, considered at best a problem, has fallen to women.

So firmly fixed have these ideas been that, until recently, few thought to question them. For they were built into the structure of psychological thought as if they spoke to an eternal, natural, and scientific truth. Thus, even such a great and innovative thinker as Carl Jung wrote, "The woman is increasingly aware that love alone can give her her full stature, just as the man begins to discern that spirit alone can endow his life with its highest meaning. Fundamentally, therefore, both seek a psychic relation one to the other, because love needs the spirit, and the spirit love, for their fulfillment."*

For a woman, "love"; for a man, "spirit"—each expected to complete the other by bringing to the relationship the missing half. In German, the word that is translated here as spirit is *Geist*. But *The New Cassell's German Dictionary* shows that another primary meaning of *Geist* is "mind, intellect, intelligence, wit, imagination, sense of reason." And, given the context of these words, it seems reasonable that *Geist* for Jung referred to a man's highest essence—his mind. There's no ambiguity about a woman's calling, however. It's love.

Intuitively, women try to heal the split that these definitions of male and female have foisted upon us.

> I can't stand that he's so damned unemotional and expects me to be the same. He lives in his head all the time, and he acts like anything that's emotional isn't worth dealing with.

Cognitively, even women often share the belief that the rational side, which seems to come so naturally to men, is the more mature, the more desirable.

> I know I'm too emotional, and it causes problems between us. He can't stand it when I get emotional like that. It turns him right off.

Her husband agrees that she's "too emotional" and complains:

> Sometimes she's like a child who's out to test her parents. I have to be careful when she's like that not to let her rile me up because otherwise all hell would break loose. You just can't reason with her when she gets like that.

It's the rational-man-hysterical-woman script, played out again and again by two people whose emotional repertoire is so limited that they have few real options. As the interaction between them continues, she reaches for the strongest tools she has, the mode she's most comfortable and familiar with: She becomes progressively more emotional and expressive. He falls back on his best weapons: He becomes more rational, more determinedly reasonable.

* Carl Gustav Jung, *Contributions to Analytical Psychology* (New York: Harcourt, Brace & Co., 1928), p. 185.

She cries for him to attend to her feelings, whatever they may be. He tells her coolly, with a kind of clenched-teeth reasonableness, that it's silly for her to feel that way, that she's just being emotional. And of course she is. But that dismissive word "just" is the last straw. She gets so upset that she does, in fact, seem hysterical. He gets so bewildered by the whole interaction that his only recourse is to build the wall of reason even higher. All of which makes things measurably worse for both of them.

> The more I try to be cool and calm her the worse it gets. I swear, I can't figure her out. I'll keep trying to tell her not to get so excited, but there's nothing I can do. Anything I say just makes it worse. So then I try to keep quiet, but . . . wow, the explosion is like crazy, just nuts.

And by then it *is* a wild exchange that any outsider would agree was "just nuts." But it's not just her response that's off, it's his as well—their conflict resting in the fact that we equate the emotional with the nonrational.

This notion, shared by both women and men, is a product of the fact that they were born and reared in this culture. But there's also a difference between them in their capacity to apprehend the *logic* of emotions—a difference born in their early childhood experiences in the family, when boys had to repress so much of their emotional side and girls could permit theirs to flower.

. . . It should be understood: Commitment itself is not a problem for a man; he's good at that. He can spend a lifetime living in the same family, working at the same job—even one he hates. And he's not without an inner emotional life. But when a relationship requires the sustained verbal expression of that inner life and the full range of feelings that accompany it, then it becomes burdensome for him. He can act out anger and frustration inside the family, it's true. But ask him to express his sadness, his fear, his dependency—all those feelings that would expose his vulnerability to himself or to another—and he's likely to close down as if under some compulsion to protect himself.

All requests for such intimacy are difficult for a man, but they become especially complex and troublesome in relations with women. It's another of those paradoxes. For, to the degree that it's possible for him to be emotionally open with anyone, it is with a woman—a tribute to the power of the childhood experience with mother. Yet it's that same early experience and his need to repress it that raises his ambivalence and generates his resistance.

He moves close, wanting to share some part of himself with her, trying to do so, perhaps even yearning to experience again the bliss of the infant's connection with a woman. She responds, woman style—wanting to touch him just a little more deeply, to know what he's thinking, feeling, fearing, wanting. And the fear closes in—the fear of finding himself again in the grip of a powerful woman, of allowing her admittance only to be betrayed and abandoned once again, of being overwhelmed by denied desires.

So he withdraws.

It's not in consciousness that all this goes on. He knows, of course, that he's distinctly uncomfortable when pressed by a woman for more intimacy in the relationship, but he doesn't know why. And, very often, his behavior doesn't please him any more than it pleases her. But he can't seem to help it.

Clyde W. Franklin II

BLACK MALE–BLACK FEMALE CONFLICT:
INDIVIDUALLY CAUSED AND CULTURALLY NURTURED

Who is to blame? Currently, there is no dearth of attention directed to Black male–Black female relationships. Books, magazine articles, academic journal articles, public forums, radio programs, television shows, and everyday conversations have been devoted to Black male–Black female relationships for several years. Despite the fact that the topic has been discussed over the past several decades by some authors (e.g., Frazier, 1939; Drake and Cayton, 1945; Grier and Cobb, 1968), Wallace's *Black Macho and the Myth of the Superwoman* has been the point of departure for many contemporary discussions of the topic since its publication in 1979.

Actually, Wallace's analysis was not so different in content from other analyses of Black male–Black female relationships (e.g., Drake and Cayton's analysis of "lower-class life" in *Black Metropolis*). But Wallace's analysis was "timely." Coming so soon on the heels of the Black movement in the late 1960s and early 1970s, and, at a time when many Black male-inspired gains for Blacks were disappearing rapidly, the book was explosive. Its theme, too, was provocative. Instead of repeating the rhetoric of the late 1960s and early 1970s that blamed conflictual relationships between Black men and Black women on White society, Wallace implied that the blame lay with Black males. In other words, the blame lay with those Black warriors who only recently had been perceived as the "saviors" of Black people in America. Wallace's lamenting theme is captured in a quote from her book: "While she stood by silently as he became a man, she assumed that he would finally glorify and dignify Black womanhood just as the White man has done for White women." Wallace goes on to say that this has not happened for Black women.

Wallace updates her attack on Black men in a later article entitled "A Black Feminist's Search for Sisterhood (1982:9). Her theme, as before, is that Black men are just as oppressive of Black women as White men. She states:

> Whenever I raised the question of a Black woman's humanity in conversations with a Black man, I got a similar reaction. Black men, at least the ones I knew, seemed totally confounded when it came to treating Black women like people. . . . I discovered my voice and when brothers talked to me, I talked back. This had its hazards. Almost got my eye blackened several times. My social life was like guerilla warfare. Here was the logic behind our grandmother's old saying, "A nigga man ain't shit."

Wallace, however, is not alone in placing the blame on Black men for deteriorating relations between Black men and Black women. Allen (1983:62), in a recent edition of *Essence* magazine, states:

> Black women have a tendency to be male-defined, subjugating their own needs for the good of that fragile male ego. . . . The major contra-

From *Journal of Black Studies* 15 (2, December 1984): 139–154. © 1984 Sage Publications, Inc. Reprinted by permission of Sage Publications, Inc.

diction is that we Black women, in our hearts, have a tendency to believe Black men need more support and understanding than we do. We bought the Black Revolutionary line that a woman's place was three paces behind the man. We didn't stomp Stokeley when he made the statement that the only position for a woman in the movement was prone.

Such attacks on Black men have been met with equally ferocious counterattacks by some Black authors (both Black men and Black women). A few months following the publication of Wallace's book, an entire issue of the *Black Scholar* was devoted to Black male–Black female relationships. Of the responses to Wallace by such scholars as Jones (1979), Karenga (1979), Staples (1979), and numerous others, Karenga's response is perhaps the most controversial and maybe the most volatile. Karenga launches a personal attack on Wallace suggesting that she is misguided and perhaps responding from personal hurt. Recognizing the complexity of Black male–Black female relationships, Karenga contends that much of it is due not to Black men but to the White power structure. Along similar lines, Moore (1980) has exhorted Black women to stop criticizing Black men and blame themselves for disintegrating bonds between Black men and Black women.

Staples, in his response to Wallace and others who would place the blame on Black men for disruptive relationships between Black men and Black women, points out that while sexism within the Black culture may be an emerging problem, most Black men do not have the institutionalized power to oppress Black women. He believes that the Black male's "condition" in society is what bothers Black males. Staples devotes much atention to the institutional decimation of Black men and suggests that this is the reason for Black male–Black female conflict. Noting the high mortality and suicide rates of Black men, the fact that a half a million Black men are in prison, one-third of urban Black men are saddled with drug problems and that 25% to 30% do not have steady employment, Staples implied that Black male–Black female conflict may be related to *choice*. This means that a shortage of Black men may limit the choices that Black women have in selecting partners. As Braithwaite (1981) puts it, the insufficient supply of Black men places Black women at a disadvantage by giving Black men the upper hand. In a specific relationship, for example, if a Black woman fails to comply with the Black man's wishes, the Black man has numerous other options, including not only other Black women but also women of other races.

In a more recent discussion of Black male–Black female relationships, Alvin Poussaint (1982:40) suggests that Black women "adopt a patient and creative approach in exploring and creating new dimensions of the Black male–Black female bond." Others, like Ronald Braithwaite, imply in their analyses of relationships between Black men and Black women that Black women's aggressiveness, thought to be a carryover from slavery, may be partly responsible for Black male–Black female conflict.

Succinctly, by and large, most Black male and Black female authors writing on the subject seem to agree that many Black male–Black female relationships today are destructive and potentially explosive. What they do not agree on, however, are the causes of the problems existing between Black men and Black women. As we have seen, some believe that Black men are the cause.

Others contend that Black women contribute disproportionately to Black male–Black female conflict. Still others blame White racism solely, using basic assumptions that may be logically inadequate (see Franklin, 1980). Many specific reasons for the conflict often postulated include the notions that Black men are abusive toward Black women, that Black men are irresistibly attracted to White women (despite the fact that only approximately 120,000 Black men were married to White women in 1980), that too many Black men are homosexual, that Black women are too aggressive, that Black women don't support Black men—the list goes on. Few of these reasons, however, really explore the underlying cause of the conflict. Instead, they are descriptions of the conflict-behaviors that are indicators of the tension between Black men and Black women. But what is the cause of the behavior—the cause of the tension that so often disrupts harmony in Black male–Black female relationships?

Given the various approaches many Black authors have taken in analyzing Black male–Black female relationships, it is submitted that two major sources of Black male–Black female conflict can be identified: (1) the noncomplementarity of sex-role definitions internalized by Black males and Black females; and (2) structural barriers in the environments of Black males and Black females. Each source is explored separately below.

SOURCES OF CONFLICT BETWEEN BLACK MEN AND BLACK WOMEN

Sex-Role Noncomplementarity among Black Males and Black Females   Much Black male–Black female conflict stems directly from incompatible role enactments by Black males and Black females. Incompatible role enactments by Black men and Black women occur because they internalize sex-role definitions that are noncomplementary. For example, a Black woman in a particular conflictual relationship with a Black male may feel that her Black man is supposed to assume a dominant role, but she also may be inclined to exhibit behaviors that are opposed to his dominance and her subordinance. In the same relationship, the Black man may pay lip service to assuming a dominant role but may behave "passively" with respect to some aspects of masculinity and in a dominant manner with respect to other aspects.

One reason for role conflict between Black men and Black women is that many contemporary Black women internalize two conflicting definitions of femininity, whereas many contemporary Black men internalize only a portion of the traditional definition of masculinity. Put simply, numerous Black women hold attitudes that are both highly masculine and highly feminine. On the other hand, their male counterparts develop traits that are highly consistent with certain aspects of society's definition of masculinity, but that are basically unrelated to other aspects of the definition. Thus, in a given relationship, one may find a Black woman who feels and behaves in ways that are both assertive and passive, dominant and subordinant, decisive and indecisive, and so on. Within that same relationship, a Black man may exhibit highly masculine behaviors, such as physical aggressiveness, sexual dominance, and even violence, but behave indifferently with respect to the masculine work ethic—

assuming responsibility for family-related activities external to the home, being aggressive in the work place and the like.

The reason these incongruent attitudes and behaviors exist among Black men and Black women is that they have received contradictory messages during early socialization. It is common for Black women to have received two messages. One message states, "Because you will be a Black woman, it is imperative that you learn to take care of yourself because it is hard to find a Black man who will take care of you." A second message frequently received by young Black females that conflicts with the first message is "your ultimate achievement will occur when you have snared a Black man who will take care of you." In discussing early socialization experiences with countless young Black women in recent years, I have found that most of them agree that these two messages were given them by socialization agents and agencies such as child caretakers, relatives, peer group members, the Black church, and the media.

When internalized, these two messages often produce a Black woman who seems to reject aspects of the traditional female sex role in America such as passivity, emotional and economic dependence, and female subordinance while accepting other aspects of the role such as expressiveness, warmth, and nurturance. This is precisely why Black women seem to be more androgynous than White women. Black women's androgyny, though, may be more a function of necessity than anything else. It may be related to the scarcity of Black men who assume tradtional masculine roles in male–female relationships.

Whatever the reason for Black women's androgynous orientations, because of such orientations Black women often find themselves in conflictual relationships with Black men or in no stable relationships at all. The scenario generally can be described as follows. Many Black women in early adulthood usually begin a search for a Black Prince Charming. However, because of the dearth of Black men who can be or are willing to be Prince Charmings for Black women, Black women frequently soon give up the search for such a Black man. They give up the search, settle for less, and "like" what they settle for even less. This statement is important because many Black women's eventual choices are destined to become constant reminders that the "female independence" message received during the early socialization process is the correct message. But, because Black women also have to deal with the second socialization message, many come to feel that they have failed in their roles as women. In an effort to correct their mistakes, Black women often choose to enact the aspect of their androgynous role that is decidedly aggressive and/or independent. They may decide either to "go it alone" or to prod their Black men into becoming Prince Charmings. The first alternative for Black women often results in self-doubt, lowered self-esteem, and, generally, unhappiness and dissatisfaction. After all, society nurtures the "find a man" message far beyond early socialization. The second message, unfortunately, produces little more than the first message because Black women in such situations usually end up in conflictual relationships with Black men, who also have undergone a rather complicated socialization process. Let us explore briefly the conflicting messages numerous Black men receive during early socialization.

One can find generally that Black men, too, have received two conflicting messages during early socialization. One message received by young Black males is "to become a man means that you must become dominant, aggressive, decisive, responsible, and in some instances, violent in social encounters with others." A second message received by young Black males that conflicts with the first is, "You are Black and you must not be too aggressive, too dominant, and so on, because the *man* will cut you down." Internalization of these two messages by some Black men (a substantial number) produces Black men who enact a portion of the traditional definition of masculinity but remain inactive with respect to other parts of traditional masculinity. Usually those aspects of traditional masculinity that can be enacted within the Black culture are the ones exhibited by these Black men. Other aspects of the sex role that require enactment external to the Black culture (e.g., aggressiveness in the work place) may be related to impassively by Black men. Unfortunately, these are aspects of the male sex role that must be enacted if a male is to be "productive" in American society.

Too many Black men fail to enact the more "productive" aspects of the male sex role. Instead, "being a man," for many Black males who internalize the mixed messages, becomes simply enacting sexual aggression, violence, sexism, and the like—all of which promote Black male–Black female conflict. In addition, contributing to the low visibility and low salience of "productive" masculine traits among Black men is the second socialization message, which provides a rationale for nonenactment of the role traits. Moreover, the "man will get you" message serves to attenuate Black men's motivations to enact more "positive" aspects of the traditional male sex role. We must keep in mind, however, that not all of the sources of Black male–Black female conflict are social-psychological. Some of the sources are structural, and in the next section these sources are discussed.

Structural Barriers Contributing to Black Male–Black Female Conflict   It is easy to place the blame for Black male–Black female conflict on "White society." Several Black authors have used this explanatory approach in recent years (e.g., Anderson and Mealy, 1979). They have suggested that Black male–Black female conflict is a function of America's capitalistic orientation and White society's long-time subjugation of Black people. Certainly historical conditions are important to understand when discussing the status of Black people today. Often, however, too much emphasis is placed on the historical subjugation of Black people as the source of Black male–Black female conflict today. Implicit in such an emphasis is the notion that independent variables existing at some point in the distant past cause a multiplicity of negative behaviors between Black males and Black females that can be capsulized as Black male–Black female conflict. A careful analysis of the contemporary environments of Black men and women today will show, instead, that factors responsible, in part, for Black male–Black female conflict are inextricably interwoven in those environments. In other words, an approach to the analysis of conflict between Black men and Black women today must be ahistorical. Past conditions influence Black male–Black female relationships only in the sense that vestiges of these conditions exist currently and are identifiable.

Our society today undoubtedly remains structured in such a manner that the vast majority of Black men encounter insurmountable barriers to the attainment of a "masculine" status as defined by most Americans (Black and

White Americans). Black men still largely are locked within the Black culture (which has relatively limited resources), unable to compete successfully for societal rewards—the attainment of which defines American males as "men." Unquestionably, Black men's powerlessness in society's basic institutions such as the government and the economy contributes greatly to the pathological states of many Black men. The high mortality and suicide rates of young Black men, the high incarceration rates of Black men, the high incidence of drug addiction among Black men, and the high unemployment rate of Black men are all functions of societal barriers to Black male upward mobility. These barriers render millions of Black males socially impotent and/or socially dysfunctional. Moreover, as Staples has pointed out, such barriers also result in a scarcity of functional Black men, thereby limiting Black women's alternatives for mates.

While some may be tempted to argue for a psychological explanation of Black male social impotence, it is suggested here that any such argument is misguided unless accompanied by a recognition of the role of cultural nurturance factors. Cultural nurturance factors such as the rigid castelike social stratum of Blacks in America foster and maintain Black men's social impotence. The result is powerless Black men primed for conflictual relationships with Black women. If Black men in our society were not "American," perhaps cultural nurturance of Black people's status in our society could not be translated into cultural nurturance of Black male–Black female conflict. That Black men are Americanized, however, is seen in the outcome of the Black movement of the last decade.

The Black movement of the late 1960s and early 1970s produced little structural change in America. To be sure, a few Black men (and even fewer Black women) achieved a measure of upward mobility; however, the vast majority did not reap gains from the Black movement. What did happen, though, was that Black people did get a glimpse of the rewards that can be achieved in America through violence and/or aggression. White society did bend when confronted by the Black movement, but it did not break. In addition, the few upward mobility doors that were ajar during the height of the movement were quickly slammed shut when the movement began to wane in the middle and late 1970s. Black men today find themselves in a position similar to the one Black men were in prior to the movement. The only difference this time around is that Black men are equipped with the psychological armor of aggression and violence as well as with a distorted perception of a target—Black women, the ones who "stood silently by."

Wallace's statement that Black women "stood silently by" must not be taken lightly. Black women did this; in addition, they further internalized American definitions of masculinity and femininity. Previously, Black women held modified definitions of masculinity and femininity because the society's definition did not fit their everyday experiences. During the Black movement they were exhorted by Black men to assume a sex role that was more in line with the traditional "feminine" role White women assumed in male–female relationships. Although this may have been a noble (verbal) effort on the part of Black men to place Black women on pedestals, it was shortsighted and doomed to fail. Failure was imminent because even during the peak of the Black movement, societal resistance to structural changes that would benefit Black people was strong. The strength of this resistance dictated that change in Black people's status in America could come about only through the united efforts of both Black men and Black women.

Unfortunately, the seeds of division between Black men and Black women were sown during the Black movement. Black men bought the Moynihan report (1965) that indirectly blamed Black women for Black people's under-class status in America. In doing so, Black men convinced themselves that they could be "men" only if they adopted the White male's sex role. An examination of this role reveals that it is characterized by numerous contra-dictions. The traditional White masculine role requires men to assume protec-tive, condescending, and generally patriarchal stances with respect to women. It also requires, ironically, that men display dominant, aggressive, and often violent behaviors toward women. Just as important, though, is that White masculine role enactment can occur only, when there is full participation in masculinist American culture. Because Black men continue to face barriers to full participation in American society, the latter requirement for White male sex-role assumption continues to be met by only a few Black men. The result has been that many Black men have adopted only a part of the culture's definition of masculinity because they are thwarted in their efforts to partici-pate fully in society. Structural barriers to Black male sex-role adoption, then, have produced a Black male who is primed for a conflictual relationship with Black women. In the next section, an exploration is presented of some possible solutions to Black male–Black female conflict that arise from the interactive relationship between the noncomplementarity of sex-role internalization by Black men and Black women and structural barriers to Black men's ad-vancement in American society.

TOWARD SOLVING BLACK MALE–BLACK FEMALE CONFLICT

Given that societal conditions are extremely resistant to rapid changes, the key to attenuating conflict between Black men and Black women lies in altering three social psychological phenomena: (1) Black male and Black female socialization experiences; (2) Black male and Black female role-playing strategies; and (3) Black male and Black female personal communication mechanisms. I first propose some alterations in Black male and Black female socialization experiences. . . .

Black female socialization must undergo change if Black men and Black women are to enjoy harmonious relationships. Those agents and agencies responsible for socializing young Black females must return to emphasizing a monolithic message in young Black female socialization. This message can stress warmth, caring, and nurturance, but it must stress simultaneously self-sufficiency, assertiveness, and responsibility. The latter portion of this message requires that young Black females must be cautioned against sexual freedom at relatively early ages—not necessarily for moral reasons, but be-cause sexual freedom for Black women seems to operate against Black wom-en's self-sufficiency, assertiveness, and responsibility. It is important to point out here, however, that this type of socialization message must be imparted without the accompanying castigation of Black men. To say "a nigger man ain't shit" informs any young Black female that at least one-half of herself "ain't shit." Without a doubt this strategy teaches self-hate and sets the stage for future Black male–Black female conflict.

Young Black males, on the other hand, must be instructed in self-sufficiency, assertiveness, and responsibility without the accompanying warning opposed to these traits in Black males. Such warnings serve only to provide rationales for future failures. To be sure, Black men do (and will) encounter barriers to upward mobility because they are Black. But, as many Black men have shown, such barriers do not have to be unsurmountable. Of course it is recognized that innumerable Black men have been victims of American racist policies, but some, too, have been victims because they perceived only that external factors hindered their upward mobility and did not focus on some internal barriers that may have thwarted their mobility. The former factors are emphasized much too often in the contradictory socialization messages received by most young Black males.

Along with the above messages, young Black males must learn that the strong bonds that they establish with their mothers can be extended to their relationships with other Black women. If Black men perceive their mothers to be symbols of strength and perseverance, they must also be taught that most other Black women acquire these same qualities and have done so for generations. It must become just as "cool," in places like urban Black barbershops, to speak of Black women's strength and dignity as it is now to hear of Black women's thighs, breasts, and hips.

On an issue closely related to the above, few persons reading this article can deny that Black men's attempts to enact the White male sex role in America are laughable. Black men are relatively powerless in this country, and their attempts at domination, aggression, and the like, while sacrificing humanity, are ludicrous. This becomes apparent when it is understood that usually the only people being dominated and aggressed against by Black men are Black women (and other Black men). Moreover, unlike White males, Black males receive no societal rewards for their efforts; instead, the result is Black male–Black female disharmony. Black men must avoid the tendency to emulate the nauseatingly traditional male sex role because their experiences clearly show that such a role is counterproductive for Black people. Because the Black man's experiences are different, his role-playing strategies must be different and made to be more complementary with Black females' altered role-playing strategies. The Black females' role-playing strategies, as we have seen, are androgynous, emphasizing neither the inferiority nor the superiority of male or female sex roles.

On a final note, it is important for Black people in our society to alter their personal communication mechanisms. Black men and Black women interact with each other in diverse ways and in diverse situations, ranging from intimate to impersonal. Perhaps the most important element of this diverse communication pattern is empathy. For Black people in recent years, this is precisely the element that has undergone unnecessary transformation. As Blacks in America have accepted increasingly White society's definition of male–female relationships, Black men and Black women have begun to interact with each other less in terms of empathy. While Black women have retained empathy in their male–female relationships to a greater degree than Black men have, Black men have become increasingly nonexpressive and nonempathic in their male–female relationships. Nearly 60% of Black women (approximately 25,000) in a recent *Essence* survey cited nonexpressiveness as a problem in male–female relationships; 56% also pointed out that Black male nonempathy was a problem (Edwards, 1982). It seems, then, that as Black males have attempted to become "men" in America they have shed some of the important qualities of humanity. Some Black women, too, who have embraced the feminist perspective also have discarded altruism. The result of both phenomena, for Black people as a whole, has been to divide Black men and Black women further. Further movement away from empathic understanding in Black male–Black female relationships by both Black men and Black women undoubtedly will be disastrous for Black people in America.

REFERENCES

Allen B. 1983 "The Price for Giving It Up." *Essence* (February):60–62, 118.

Anderson, S. E., and R. Mealy 1979 "Who Originated the Crisis: A Historical Perspective." *Black Scholar* (May/June):40–44.

Braithwaite, R. L., 1981 "Interpersonal Relations between Black Males and Black Females." In *Black Men*, L. E. Gary, ed., pp 83–97. Beverly Hills, Calif.: Sage.

Drake, S. C., and H. R. Cayton 1945 *Black Metropolis*. New York: Harcourt.

Edwards, A. 1982 "Survey Results: How You're Feeling." *Essence* (December):73–76.

Franklin, C. W., II 1980 "White Racism As a Cause of Black Male–Black Female Conflict: A Critique." *Western Journal of Black Studies* 4 (1):42–49.

Frazier, E. F. 1939 *The Negro Family in the United States*. Chicago: University of Chicago Press.

Grier, W. II., and P. M. Cobb 1968 *Black Rage*. New York: Basic Books.

Jones, T. 1979 "The Need to Go beyond Stereotypes." *Black Scholar* (May/June):48–49.

Karenga, M. R. 1979 "On Wallace's Myth: Wading through Troubled Waters." *Black Scholar* (May/June):36–39.

Moore, W. F. 1980 "Black Women, Stop Criticizing Black Men—Blame Yourselves." *Ebony* (December):128–130.

Moynihan, D. P. 1965 *The Negro Family: The Case for National Action*. Washington, D.C.: U.S. Department of Labor, Office of Planning and Research.

Poussaint, A. F. 1982 "What Every Black Woman Should Know about Black Men." *Ebony* (August):36–40.

Staples, R. 1979 "The Myth of Black Macho: A Response to Angry Black Feminists." *Black Scholar* (March/April):24–32.

Wallace, M. 1979 *Black Macho and the Myth of the Superwoman*. New York: Dial.

1982 "A Black Feminist's Search for Sisterhood." In *All the Blacks Are Men, All the Women Are White, but Some of Us Are Brave*, G. T. Hull et al., eds. pp. 5–8. Old Westbury, N.Y.: Feminist Press.

Jack W. Sattel

THE INEXPRESSIVE MALE:
TRAGEDY OR SEXUAL POLITICS?

In this brief essay, I am concerned with the phenomenon of "male inexpressiveness" as it has been conceptualized by Balswick and Peek (1971). In their conceptualization, male inexpressiveness is seen as a culturally produced temperament trait which is learned by boys as the major characteristic of their forthcoming adult masculinity. Such inexpressiveness is evidenced in two ways. First, adult male behavior which does not indicate affection, tenderness, or emotion is inexpressive behavior. Second, and somewhat differently, behavior which is not supportive of the affective expectations of one's wife is inexpressive behavior. It is the latter variety of inexpressiveness which occupies the major concern of Balswick and Peek. They suggest that the inability of the American male to unlearn inexpressiveness in order to relate effectively to a woman is highly dysfunctional to the emerging standards of the companionate, intimate American marriage. Ironically, Balswick and Peek see inexpressiveness in contexts outside the marriage relationship as functional insofar as in nonmarital situations the inexpressiveness of the male to females other than one's spouse works to prevent threats to the primacy of the marital bond, that is, it presumably functions to ward off infidelity. The authors further suggest two styles of adult inexpressiveness: the "cowboy—John Wayne" style of almost total inarticulateness and the more cool, detached style of the "playboy," who communicates only to exploit women sexually.

The article has proved to be an important one in forcing sociologists to rethink old conceptual stereotypes of masculinity and femininity. In part, it has helped to contribute to efforts to rescue for both sexes qualities and potentials that previously were thought to belong to only one sex. On the other hand, it would be unfortunate if Balswick and Peek's conceptualization would enter the sociological literature as the last word on the dilemma of male inexpressiveness–unfortunate because, despite their real insight, I think they fundamentally misconstrue both the origin and the playing out of male inexpressiveness in our society.

In the note which follows, I would like to reconsider the phenomenon of male inexpressiveness, drawing upon my own and other men's experiences in consciousness-raising groups (especially as recounted in *Unbecoming Men: A Men's Consciousness-Raising Group Writes on Oppression and Themselves* (Bradley et al., 1971), as well as some of the literature which has appeared since Balswick and Peek first published their article.

BECOMING INEXPRESSIVE: SOCIALIZATION

The process of becoming inexpressive is cast by Balswick and Peek in the traditional vocabulary of the literature of socialization:

> Children, from the time they are born both explicitly and implicitly are
> taught how to be a man or how to be a woman. While the girl is taught to

act "feminine," . . . the boy is taught to be a man. In learning to be a man, the boy in American society comes to value expressions of masculinity . . . [such as] physical courage, toughness, competitiveness, and aggressiveness. (1971: 363–364)

Balswick and Peek's discussion of this socialization process is marred in two ways. Theoretically, their discussion ignores the critique of the socialization literature initially suggested by Wrong (1961) in his analysis of sociology's "oversocialized concept of man [sic]." Wrong, using a largely Freudian vocabulary, argued that it is incorrect to see the individual as something "hollowed out" into which norms are simply poured. Rather, "conformity" and "internalization" should always be conceptualized as problematic. For example, if we consider inexpressiveness to be a character trait, as do Balswick and Peek, we should also be aware that the normative control of that trait is never complete—being threatened constantly by both the presumably more expressive demands of the id and the excessive ("perfectionist") demands of the "internalized norms" of the superego. Wrong's point is well taken. While the norms of our society may well call for all little boys to grow up to be inexpressive, the inexpressiveness of the adult male should never be regarded as complete or total, as Balswick and Peek would have it.

For them to have ignored this point is particularly crucial given their concern to rescue some capacity of authentic expressiveness for the male. Their suggestion that men simply "unlearn" their inexpressiveness through contact with a woman (spouse) is unsatisfactory for two reasons. First, it forfeits the possibility that men can rescue themselves through enhanced self-knowledge or contact with other men. Second, *it would seem to make the task of rescuing men just one more task of women.* That is, the wife is expected to restore to her husband that which was initially taken from him in socialization.

A second problem with Balswick and Peek's discussion of socialization and inexpressiveness is that they ignore the peculiarly asymmetrical patterns of socialization in our society which make it much more dangerous for a boy to be incompletely socialized than a girl. For example, much of the literature suggests that parents and other adults exert greater social control to insure that boys "grow up male" than that girls "grow up female" (Parsons, 1951)—as can be seen in the fact that greater stigma is attached to the boy who is labeled a sissy than to the girl who is known as a tomboy. Failure to even consider this asymmetry reveals, I think, the major weakness of Balswick and Peek's conceptualization of male inexpressiveness. They have no explanation of *why* male inexpressiveness exists or *how* it came into being and is maintained other than to say that "our culture demands it." Thus, while we can agree that male inexpressiveness is a tragedy, their analysis does not help us to change the social conditions which produce that tragedy.

INEXPRESSIVENESS AND POWER

To break this chain of reasoning, I would like to postulate that, in itself, male inexpressiveness is of no particular value in our culture. Rather, it is an instrumental requisite for assuming adult male roles of power.

Consider the following. To effectively wield power, one must be able both to convince others of the rightness of the decisions one makes and to guard against one's own emotional involvement in the consequences of that decision; that is, one has to show that decisions are reached rationally and efficiently. One must also be able to close one's eyes to the potential pain one's decisions have for others and for onself. The general who sends troops into battle must show that his decision is calculated and certain; to effectively implement that decision—hence, to maintain his position of power to make future decisions —the general must put on a face of impassive conviction.

I would argue, in a similar vein, that a little boy must become inexpressive not simply because our culture expects boys to be inexpressive *but because our culture expects little boys to grow up to become decision makers and wielders of power*.

From this example, I am suggesting that inexpressiveness is not just learned as an end in itself. Rather, it is learned as a means to be implemented later in men assuming and maintaining positions of power. More generally:

(A) INEXPRESSIVENESS in a role is determined by the corresponding *power* (actual or potential) of that role.

In light of this generalization, we might consider why so many sociologists tend to merge the universalistic–particularistic (rational) and the affective neutrality–affectivity (expressive) distinction in any discussion of real social behavior. In the case of the general, it would seem that the ability to give an inexpressive—that is, an affectively neutral—coloring to his decisions or positions contributes to the apparent rationality of those decisions or po- sitions. Inexpressiveness validates the rightness of one's position. In fact, the social positions of highest power—not incidentally always occupied by men—demand veneers of both universalism and inexpressiveness of their incumbents, suggesting that at these levels *both* characteristics merge into a style of control. (Consider both Kennedy in the missle crisis and Nixon at Watergate. While otherwise quite dissimilar, in a crisis and challenge to their position, both men felt that "stonewalling" was the solution to the situation.)

From the above, it also follows logically the inexpressiveness might be more a characteristic of upper-class, powerful males than of men in the working classes. Many people—sociologists included—would probably object to such a deduction, saying the evidence is in the other direction, pointing at the Stanley Kowalski or Marty of literary fiction. I am not so sure. To continue with examples from fiction for a moment, the early autobiographical novels of, say, James Baldwin and Paul Goodman, dealing with lower- and working- class youth, consistently depicted "making it" as a not unusual tradeoff for one's sensitivity and expressiveness. More empirically, the recent work of Sennett and Cobb in their study of working-class life, *The Hidden Injuries of Class* (1972), suggests that upward mobility by working-class men was seen by them as entailing a certain phoniness or inauthentic relationship with one's *male* peers as well as a sacrifice of a meaningful expressive relationship with children and wife. The result of this for the men interviewed by Sennett and Cobb was often a choice to forego upward mobility and power because it involved becoming something one was not. It involved learning to dissemble inauthentic display of expressiveness toward higher-ups as well as involving the sacrifice of already close relationships with one's friends and family.

INEXPRESSIVENESS AND POWER AS
SITUATIONAL VARIABLES

In their article, Balswick and Peek include a notion of inexpressiveness not just as a socially acquired temperament trait but also as a situational variable. Thus while they argue that all males are socialized into inexpressiveness, they also argue that "for many males . . . through progressively more serious involvements with women (such as going steady, being pinned, engagement, and the honeymoon period of marriage), [these males] begin to make some exceptions. That is, they may learn to be *situationally rather than totally inexpressive*" (1971, 365–366). As noted above, this is seen by Balswick and Peek as functional for men and for the marriage relation in two ways. It meets the wife's expectation of affective support for herself while usually being accompanied by continued inexpression toward women who are not one's spouse. Thus, in this sense, the situational unlearning of inexpressiveness enhances the marital relationship while guarding against extramarital relationships which would threaten the basic pairing of husband-wife.

There is, on the surface, a certain descriptive validity to Balswick and Peek's depiction, although, interestingly, they do not consider a latent function of such unlearning. To the extent that an ability to be expressive *in situ* with a woman leads to satisfactory and gratifying consequences in one case, it probably doesn't take long for the male to learn to be expressive with *any* woman—not just his spouse—as a mode of approaching that woman. Some men, for example, admit to this in my consciousness-raising group. This, in fact, is a way of "coming on" with a woman—a relaxation of the usual standards of inexpressiveness as a calculated move to establish a sexual relationship. Skill at dissembling in this situation may have less to do with handing a woman a "line" than with showing one's weaknesses and frailties as clues intended to be read by her as signs of authentic male interest. In many Latin cultures, which might be considered to epitomize traditional male supremist modes, the style of *machismo*, in fact, calls for the male to be dependent, nominally open, and very expressive to whichever woman he is currently trying to "make." The point of both these examples is to suggest that the *situational unlearning* of inexpressiveness need not lead to strengthening the marriage bond and, in fact, may be detrimental to it, since what works in one situation will probably be tried in others.

Following the argument developed in the previous section concerning the interplay between power and inexpressiveness, I would suggest a different conceptualization of the situational relevance of inexpressiveness:

(B) EXPRESSIVENESS in a sexist culture empirically emerges as an effort on the part of the male to *control* a situation (once again, on his terms) and to maintain his position.

What I am suggesting is that in a society such as ours, which so permeates all social relationships with notions of power and exchange, even what may appear on the surface to be authentic can be an extension rather than a negation of (sexual) politics.

This is even more true of male inexpressive behavior in intimate male–female relationships. The following dialogue is drawn from Erica Jong's novel of upper-middle-class sexual etiquette, *Fear of Flying*. Consider the political use of male inexpressiveness:

SHE: "Why do you always have to do this to me? You make me feel so lonely."

HE: "That comes from you."

"What do you mean it comes from me? Tonight I wanted to be happy. It's Christmas Eve. Why do you turn on me? What did I do?"

Silence

"What did I do?"

He looks at her as if her not knowing were another injury. "Look, let's just go to sleep now. Let's just forget it."

"Forget what?"

He says nothing.

"Forget the fact that you turned on me? Forget the fact that you're punishing me for nothing? Forget the fact that I'm lonely and cold, that it's Christmas Eve and again you've ruined it for me? Is that what you want me to forget?"

"I won't discuss it."

"Discuss what?" "What won't you discuss?"

"Shut up! I won't have you screaming in the hotel."

"I don't give a fuck what you won't have me do. I'd like to be treated civilly. I'd like you to at least do me the courtesy of telling me why you're in such a funk. And don't look at me that way . . ."

"What way?"

"As if my not being able to read your mind were my greatest sin. I *can't* read your mind. I *don't* know why you're so mad. I can't intuit your wish. If that's what you want in a wife you don't have it in me."

"I certainly don't."

"Then what is it? Please tell me."

"I shouldn't have to."

"Good God! Do you mean to tell me I'm expected to be a mind reader?"

"Is that the kind of mothering you want?"

"If you had any empathy for me . . ."

"But I *do*. My God, you just don't give me a chance."

"You tune out. You don't listen."

"It was something in the movie wasn't it?"

"What in the movie?"

"The quiz again. Do you have to quiz me like some kind of criminal. Do you have to cross-examine me? . . . It was the funeral scene . . . The little boy looking at his dead mother. Something got you there. That was when you got depressed."

Silence

"Oh come on, Bennett, you're making me *furious*. Please tell me. Please."

(He gives the words singly like little gifts. Like hard little turds.) "What was it about the scene that got me?"

"Don't quiz me. Tell me!" (She puts her arms around him. He pulls away.

She falls to the floor holding onto his pajama leg. It looks less like an embrace than a rescue scene, she sinking, he reluctantly allowing her to cling to his leg for support.)
"Get up!"
(Crying) "Only if you tell me."
(He jerks his leg away.) "I'm going to bed." (Jong, 1973: 108–109)

One wonders if this is what Balswick and Peek mean by a man "unlearning" his inexpressiveness. Less facetiously, this is clearly an example which indicates that inexpression on the part of the male is not just a matter of inarticulateness or even a deeply socialized inability to respond to the needs of others. The male here is *using* inexpression to guard his own position. To *not* say anything in this situation is to say something very important indeed: that the battle we are engaged in is to be fought by my rules and when I choose to fight. In general:

(C) Male INEXPRESSIVENESS empirically emerges as an intentional manipulation of a situation when threats to the male position occur.

INEXPRESSIVENESS AND MALE CULTURE

Balswick and Peek see inexpressiveness as a major quality of male–female interaction. I have tried to indicate about where they might be right in making such an attribution as well as some of the inadequacies of their conceptualization of the origins of that inexpressiveness. A clear gap in their conceptualization, however, is their lack of any consideration of the inexpressive male in interaction with other men. In fact, their conceptualization leads to two contradictory deductions. First, given the depth and thoroughness of socialization, we might deduce that the male is inexpressive with other men, as well as with women. Second, the male, who is only situationally inexpressive, can interact and express himself truly in situations with other men. This latter position finds support in the notions of male bonding developed by Lionel Tiger (1969). The former position is validated by some of the contributors to Pleck and Sawyer's recent reader on *Men and Masculinity* (1974; esp. Candell, Jourard, and Fasteau). In this section, I would like to raise some of the questions that bear on the problem of male-to-male inexpressiveness. (1) Is there a male subculture? Subcultural differences are usually identified as having ethnic, religious, occupational, etc., boundaries; gender is not usually considered to define subcultural differences. This is so even though gender repeatedly proves to be among the most statistically significant variables in most empirical research. Yet, if we think of a subculture as consisting of unique patterns of belief, value, technique, and language use, there would be a *prima facie* case for considering "male" and "female" definitive of true subcultures in almost all societies. (2) What is the origin of male and female subcultures? This question is probably the most inclusive of all the questions one can ask about gender and sex-role differences. It thrusts us into the very murky swamp of the origin of the family, patriarchy, sexism, etc. Sidestepping questions of the ultimate origin of male and female cultural differences, I would only suggest that a good case might be made for considering the persistence—if not the origin—of male and female subcultural differences as due to male efforts to maintain privilege and position *vis-à-vis* women. This is the point anthropologists have been quick to make about primitive societies. The ritual and magic of the males is a secret to be guarded against the women's eyes. Such magic is privy only to the men, and access to it in rites of passage finally determines who is man and who is only *other*. Similar processes are at work in our own society. Chodorow's distinction between "being" and "doing" (1971) is a way of talking about male and female subcultural differences that makes it clear that what men "do" defines not only their own activity but the activity ("being") of women as well. Benston's (1969) distinction between male production of exchange-value in the public sphere and female creation of use-value in the private sphere captures the same fundamental differential of power underlying what appears to be merely cultural. (3) Is male culture necessarily inexpressive? Many observers would say it is flatly wrong to assert that men are inexpressive when interacting with other men. Tiger (1969), for example, talks of the games (sport) men share as moments of intense and authentic communication and expression. In fact, for Tiger, sport derives from the even more intense solidarity of the prehistoric hunt—a solidarity that seems, in his scheme to be almost genetic in origin. I think Tiger, and others who would call our attention to this capacity for male expressiveness, are saying something important but partial. Perhaps the following example drawn from adult reminiscences of one's fourteenth year can make this clearer:

> I take off at full speed not knowing whether I would reach it but knowing very clearly that this is *my* chance. My cap flies off my head . . . and a second later I one-hand it as cool as can be. . . . I hear the applause. . . . I hear voices congratulating my mother for having such a good athlete for a son. . . . Everybody on the team pounds my back as they come in from the field, letting me know that I've *made* it. (Candell in Pleck and Sawyer, 1974: 16)

This is a good picture of boys being drawn together in sport, of sharing almost total experience.

But is it? The same person continues in the next paragraph:

> But I know enough not to blow my cool so all I do is mumble thanks under a slightly trembling upper lip which is fighting the rest of my face, the rest of being, from exploding with laughter and tears of joy. (Candell in Pleck and Sawyer, 1974: 19)

Why this silence? Again, I don't think it is just because our culture demands inexpression. I think here, as above, silence and inexpression are the ways men learn to *consolidate* power, to make the effort appear as effortless, to guard against showing the real limits of one' potential and power by making it *all* appear easy. Even among males alone, one maintains control over a situation by revealing only strategic proportions of oneself.

Further, in Marc Fasteau's very perceptive article "Why Men Aren't Talking" (Pleck and Sawyer, 1974), the observation is made that when men do talk, they talk of "large" problems—war, politics, art—but never of anything really personal. Even when men have equal credentials in achieved success, they tend not to make themselves vulnerable to each other, for to do so may be interpreted as a sign of weakness and an opportunity for the other to secure advantage. As Fasteau puts it, men talk, but they always do so for a *reason*— getting together for its own sake would be too frightening—and that reason often amounts to just another effort at establishing who *really* is best, stronger, smarter, or ultimately, more powerful.

INEXPRESSIVENESS AND THE SOCIOLOGY OF SEX ROLES

In the preceding sections, I have tried to change the grounds of an explanation of male inexpressiveness from one which holds that it is simply a cultural variable to one which sees it as a consequence of the political (power) position of the sexes in our society. I have not tried to deny that male inexpressiveness exists but only that it does so in different forms and for different reasons than Balswick and Peek suggest. I am making no claims for the analytic completeness of the ideas presented here.

A direct result of the feminist movement has been the effort on the part of sociologists concerned with family and sex-role-related behavior to discard or recast old concepts in the face of the feminist critique. One tendency of this "new sociology" has been an attempt to rescue attributes of positive human potential from the exclusive domain of one sex and, thus, to validate those potentials for all people. Although they do not say this explicitly, some such concern certainly underlies Balswick and Peek's effort. I think that this is social science at its best.

On the other hand, I am not convinced, as Balswick and Peek seem to be, that significant change in the male sex role will be made if we conceptualize the problem as one that involves individual males gradually unlearning their inexpressiveness with individual females. Balswick (1974) wrote an article based on the analysis developed with Peek entitled "Why Husbands Can't Say 'I Love You'" and printed it in a mass distribution women's magazine. Predictably, the article suggests *to the wife* some techniques she might develop for drawing her husband out of his inexpressive shell. I think that kind of article—at this point in the struggle of women to define themselves—is facile and wrongheaded. Such advice burdens the wife with additional "emotional work" while simultaneously creating a new arena in which she can—and most likely will—fail.

Similarly, articles that speak to men about their need to become more expressive also miss the point if we are concerned about fundamental social change. Such arguments come fairly cheap. Witness the essentially honest but fatally narrow and class-bound analyses of Korda (1973) and Farrell (1974). Their arguments develop little more than strategies capable of salvaging a limited number of upper-class male heterosexual egos. The need I see and feel at this point is for arguments and strategies capable of moving the majority of men who are not privileged in that fashion. What such arguments would say—much less to whom they would be addressed—is a question I cannot now answer. But I know where my work lies. For if my argument is correct— and I believe it is—that male inexpressiveness is instrumental in maintaining positions of power and privilege for men, then male sociologists might well begin to search through their own experiences and the accumulated knowledge of the sociological literature for sensitizing models which might indicate how, and if, it would be possible to relinquish the power which has historically been ours.

REFERENCES

Balswick, Jack. 1974. "Why husbands can't say 'I love you.' " *Woman's Day.* April.

Balswick, Jack and Charles Peek. 1971. "The inexpressive male: a tragedy of American society." *The Family Coordinator*, 20:363–368.

Benston, Margaret. 1969. "The political economy of women's liberation." *Monthly Review*, 21:13–27.

Bradley, Mike. 1971. *Unbecoming Men: A Men's Consciousness-Raising Group Writes on Oppression and Themselves.* New York: Times Change Press.

Chodorow, Nancy. 1971. "Being and doing: a cross-cultural examination of the socialization of males and females." Pp. 259–291 in Gornick and Moran (ed.), *Women in Sexist Society.* New York: New American Library.

Farrell, Warren. 1974. *The Liberated Man.* New York: Random House.

Jong, Erica. 1973. *Fear of Flying.* New York: New American Library.

Korda, Michael. 1973. *Male Chauvinism: How It Works.* New York: Random House.

Parsons, Talcott. 1951. *The Social System* (Chapter VI and VII). Glencoe, Illinois: Free Press.

Pleck, Joseph and Jack Sawyer. 1974. *Men and Masculinity.* Englewood Cliffs, New Jersey: Prentice-Hall.

Sennett, Richard and Jonathan Cobb. 1973. *The Hidden Injuries of Class.* New York: Random House.

Tiger, Lionel. 1971. *Men in Groups.* London: Granada Publishing.

Wrong, Dennis. 1961. "The oversocialized conception of man in modern sociology." *American Sociological Review*, 26:183–193.

Wayne Ewing
THE CIVIC ADVOCACY OF VIOLENCE

The ruling paradigm for male supremacy remains, to this hour, physical violence. This paradigm remains unchecked and untouched by change. Critically, the permissive environment for male violence against women is supported by a civic advocacy of violence as socially acceptable, appropriate and necessary. Physically abusive men, particularly men who batter their spouses, continue for the most part to be a protected population. And the sources which provide us with what we know of the batterer—largely clinical

Reprinted from *M.*, Spring 1982.

Adapted from a paper delivered in the Women's Studies Division of the Western Social Science Association annual meeting, 1981, and part of a book-length manuscript in progress, *Violence Works/Stop Violence.*

and treatment models—have themselves remained too isolated from sexual politics and from a social analysis of male cultures. Until the code of male violence is read, translated and undone, male batterers will not be largely affected by what we are coming to know about them.

PROFILING THE MALE BATTERER

I sometimes think that none of the literature will ever move our knowledge dramatically further than Erin Pizzey's observation that all batterers are either alcoholics or psychotics or psychopaths or just plain bullies. That is good common sense applied to the all too ordinary affair of men beating up women. I also think that the following observation, more often than not made rhetorically and politically, has a measure of significance that we can draw on. When the question is raised, "Who is the male batterer?" the answer is sometimes given, "Every man!" Without pushing too quickly let me simply point out here that this observation is accurate. It is not simply an attention-getter. Attempts to profile the male batterer always wind up with a significant body of information which points to . . . every man.

I believe the most striking example of this is found in those studies which support the—in my estimation, accurate—view of male violence as a learned behavior. Depending on the study, 81% to 63% of the population of batterers researched have either experienced abuse as victims in the home of their childhood or have witnessed their fathers beat their mothers. While that is significant enough to support our forming knowledge that socialization into violence in the home perpetuates violence, and that individual men can be conditioned to domestic violence as normal, I do not believe we have spent enough time looking at the chilling fact that remains: from 19% to 37% of these populations have literally invented violence in an intimate relationship. It is clear that the experience as victim or observer of physical violence is not necessary to "produce" a violent, abusive man.

And so it is with any of the many categories of inquiry applied to populations of male batterers. I will tick some of these off here, and in each case refer to the batterers with whom I work in Denver. *Ethnic backgrounds*, for example, will closely parallel the ethnic makeup of the community in which the study is made. In intake interviews of men either volunteering or ordered by the Courts into the men's groups of our project in Denver, the statistics generated on ethnicity are the statistics available about our community in general. *Age* is not a major factor. While most physically abusive men are in their 20s or early 30s, batterers are also under 20 and over 50. The fact that slightly more than half the men we deal with in Denver are in their 20s is attributable to so many other possibilities, that the fact itself recedes in significance. *Education* is not a major determinant. While a majority of batterers may have a high school education, the ones we know are equally balanced on either side by men with undergraduate, graduate and professional degrees and men with less than a high school education. *Income* studies do not support the popular idea that battering men are low income earners. Over a third of the men studied in Denver have incomes of $15,000 and above; and regular employment is as much a feature of the batterer as is infrequent employment. The *onset and frequency of violence* within a relationship are not consistent indicators of the behavior profile of the male batterer. The only conclusion safely drawn from these inquiries is that the probability of maiming and permanently crippling injury for the victim rises with the increase of frequency, and that the period of contrition on the part of the batterer becomes briefer between episodes as frequency increases. *Substance abuse* may as easily accompany battering episodes as not. In Denver, it is involved in a little over a third, while in other populations studied, substance abuse may figure in as much as 80% of battering episodes. And of course the self-reported *"causes"* of violence from both victims and abusers runs from sex to in-laws to money to housework to children to employment and around and around and around. There is no real clue to the profile of the abusive male in these reported occasions for battering episodes. With respect to the *psychological makeup* of the abusive male, there is considerable consensus that these men evidence low self-esteem, dependency needs, unfamiliarity with their emotions, fear of intimacy, poor communication skills and performance orientation. But what is intriguing about these observations is that they span all of these other indicators.

And so I end this brief review where I started. The abusive male—that is, the violent man of low self-esteem, high dependency need, slow on affect, fearful of intimacy, poor in communicating emotions, and oriented to performance—the abusive male is every man.

THE CYCLE OF VIOLENCE

How is it we know so little, then, about the male batterer? In part this is due to the fact that the movement begun by the female victims of male violence has not spawned a fervent desire to look at the abuser. The simple fact is that as massive as male domestic violence is, we know more about the victims than we do about the abusers. There are some very obvious realities at work here. If we are to serve, counsel, protect, renurture and heal victims, we must come to know them, to understand the cycle of violence in which they are terrorized and victimized. We need to elicit from them the motivation to break the cycle of violence. But if we are to intervene in the cycle of violence in society at large—which is after all, the sustainer of violence from men toward women—the batterer must be known as well. For every female victim who is freed from the cycle of violence without intervening in the actual behavior of the male abuser, we still have a battering male-at-large.

We do know that a particular characteristic of the cycle of male violence—the period of contrition—is critical to how the cycle repeats itself in relationships: the building up of tension and conflict; the episode of battering; the time of remorse; the idyllic time of reconciliation. And then the cycle begins again. What is going on in the time of remorse? How is it that this apparent recognition of violent behavior is insufficient to provoke change and to begin a cycle of nonviolent behaviors? It seems to me that remorse is a time-honored device, within male-dominant, sexist cultures, for "making things right" again. I refer of course to the Judeo-Christian model of "making things right"—as it was always stated until very recently in the texts of theology and of devotion—between "God and man." This whole pattern of remorse, guilt, repentance, newly invigorated belief, and forgiveness has had one of the most profound symbolic impacts on Western male consciousness.

When a man physically abuses a woman, it is a matter of course for him to fall back on this model. Things can be "made right," not by actual change, but by feeling awful, by confessing it, and by *believing* that the renewal of the relationship is then effected. That this is more hocus-pocus than authentically religious hardly matters. A crippling consequence of this major model for renewal and change—remorse followed by forgiveness-taken-for-granted—is an almost guaranteed start up of the previous behavior once again. The *non* resolution which we violent men rehearse by remorse and "resolve" is vacuous. It is the exercise of a mere accompaniment to violence. And particularly where our dependency on the female victim of our abuse is so strong, the simple telling of the "resolve" not to be violent again is seen as establishing how good we are in fact.

Actually, the interweaving of the violence and the remorse is so tight that the expression of remorse to the victim establishes how good we have been, and how good we are. The remorse is not even a future-oriented "resolve"; it is more an internalized benediction we give to the immediately preceding episode of battery. There is no shock of recognition here in the cycle of violence. It is not a matter of "Oh my god, did I do that?" It is a matter of *stating* "Oh my god, I couldn't have done that," implying that *I in fact did not do it*. The confession of remorse then only reinforces the self-perception that I did not do it. Remorse, in this model of "making things right" again, literally wipes the slate clean. Over and over again we violent men are puzzled as to how it is our victims come to a place where they will not tolerate our violence and so report us or walk out on us. Can't they see that the violence no longer counts as real, because I said I was sorry?

Whatever clinical research reveals to us about the population of batterers, the fact of denial built into the cycle of violence itself veils from both us and the batterer the reality of the violence. Over and over again, abusive men will ask what the fuss is all about. They hold as a right and privilege the behavior of assault and battery against "their" women. Our groups in Denver are filled with men from all walks and circumstances of life to whom it has never occurred that battering is wrong. In other words, one reason we know so little about male batterers is that they only reluctantly come to *speak* of battering at all.

Another factor further veils this population from us. Male batterers continue to be deliberately protected in the careful construction of familial silence; in the denial of neighbors, friends, clergy, teachers and the like that battering can be "true" for John and Mary; in the failure of law enforcement to "preserve and protect" the victims of domestic violence; in the unwillingness of local and state governments to provide shelter for victims; or in the editorializing of the Eagle Forum that the safe house movement is an anti-male, lesbian conspiracy. Male violence has become the ordinary, the expected, the usual.

THE CIVIC ADVOCACY OF VIOLENCE

What remains is for us to deal with what very few of us want to confront: American life remains sexist and male supremacist in spite of the strides of the second wave of American feminism. Whether it be snide—"You've come a long way, baby"—or whether it be sophisticated—George Gilder's *Sexual Suicide*—the put down of women's quest for equality, dignity and freedom from male oppression is damn near total in the America of the 1980s. I contend that the ultimate put down is the continuing advocacy of violence against women, and that until we confront that advocacy with integrity and resolve, the revolution in men's consciousness and behavior cannot get underway.

I used to think that we simply tolerated and permitted male abusiveness in our society. I have now come to understand rather, that we *advocate* physical violence. Violence is presented as effective. Violence is taught as the normal, appropriate and necessary behavior of power and control.

We apparently have no meaningful response to violence. I am convinced that until the voices that say "No!" to male violence are more numerous than those that say "Yes?," we will not see change. Nor will we men who want to change our violent behaviors find the support necessary to change. And silence in the face of violence is heard as "Yes!"

Under the governing paradigm of violence as effective and normal, every man can find a place. The individual male who has not beaten a woman is still surrounded by a civic environment which claims that it *would* and *could* be appropriate for him to beat a woman. He is immersed in a civic advocacy of violence which therefore contends that should he have committed battery, it is normal; and should he have not committed battery, it is only that he has not *yet* committed battery, given the ordinary course of affairs. In sexual political terms, we men can simply be divided into pre-battery and post-battery phases of life.

The teaching of violence is so pervasive, so totally a part of male experience, that I think it best to acknowledge this teaching as a *civic*, rather than as a cultural or as a social phenomenon. Certainly there are social institutions which form pieces of the total advocacy of violence: marriage and family; ecclesiastical institutions; schools; economic and corporate institutions; government and political institutions. And there are cultural and sub-cultural variations on the theme and reality of violence, of course. I believe, however, that if we are to crack the code of violent male behavior, we must begin where the environment of advocacy is total. Total civic advocacy is the setting for all the varieties of cultural adaptations from which violent men come.

For this total, pervasive advocacy of violence, I can find no better word than *civic*. The word has a noble ring to it, and calls up the manner in which the people of a nation, a society, a culture are schooled in basic citizenship. That's precisely what I want to call up. Civic responsibilities and civil affairs are what we come to expect as normal, proper and necessary. Violence, in male experience, *is* just such an expectation. Violence is *learned* within the environment of civic advocacy.

Demonstrating this is perhaps belaboring the obvious. But when we fail to belabor the obvious, the obvious continues to escape us and becomes even in its pervasiveness, part of an apparently innocent environment or backdrop. "Oh, say can you see. . . ." Our National Anthem can perhaps be thought of as simply romanticizing war, mayhem, bloodshed and violence. But more than that, reflection on the content of the song shows that we pride ourselves, civically, on the fortress mentality of siege, endurance and battle. The headier virtues of civic responsibility—freedom and justice—are come to only in the context of violence. "The rockets' red glare, the bombs bursting in air," are as ordinary to us as the school event, the sporting event, the civic sanction in which we conjure up hailing America "o'er the ramparts."

"I pledge allegiance. . . ." The flag of violence becomes the object of fidelity and devotion for American children even before they know the meaning of "allegiance." Yet feudal-like obeisance—the hand over the heart and devotional hush to the recitation—to the liege lords of violence is sanctioned as appropriate behavior quite calmly with this ritual.

We might assume of course that because this is ritual no one takes it seriously. That's precisely my point. We don't take it seriously at all. We just take it, live it, breathe it, feel awkward when we don't participate in the ritual, feel condemnatory when others around us don't participate in the ritual, and so on. The environment of civic advocacy of violence *is* ordinary, and not extraordinary.

THE EVERYDAY LANGUAGE OF VIOLENCE

Language is not innocent of meaning, intent and passion. Otherwise, there would be no communication between us at all. Yet words fall from our mouths—even in the civil illustrations above—as if there were no meaning, intent and passion involved. What I make of this is that the advocacy of violence is so pervasive, that the human spirit somehow, someway, mercifully inures itself to the environment. We are numbed and paralyzed by violence, and so continue to speak the language of violence as automatons.

I am not referring to the overt, up front renditions of violence we men use in describing battery and battering. "Giving it to the old woman" and "kicking the shit out of her" however, are phenomenologically on the same level of meaning, intention and passion as: assaulting a problem; conquering fear, nature, a woman; shooting down opinions; striking out at injustices; beating you to the punch; beating an idea to death; striking a blow for free enterprise, democracy; whomping up a meal; pounding home an idea; being under the gun to perform; "It strikes me that. . . ." You can make your own list of violent language. Listen to yourself. Listen to those around you. The meaning, intent and passion of violence are everywhere to be found in the ordinary language of ordinary experience.

Analyses which interweave the advocacy of male violence with "Super-Bowl Culture" have never been refuted. It is too obvious. Civic expectations—translated into professionalism, financial commitments, city planning for recreational space, the raising of male children for competitive sport, the corporate ethics of business ownership of athletic teams, profiteering on entertainment—all result in the monument of the National Football League, symbol and reality at once of the advocacy of violence. How piously the network television cameras turn away from out-and-out riots on the fields and in the stands. But how expertly the technologies of the television medium replay, stop action, and replay and replay and replay "a clean hit." Like the feelies of George Orwell's 1984, giant screens in bar and home can go over and over the bone-crunching tackle, the quarterback sack, the mid-air hit—compared in slow motion to dance and ballet, sophisticating violence in aesthetic terms. We love it. We want it. We pay for it. And I don't mean the black market price of a Bronco season ticket or the inflated prices of the beer, automobile accessories and tires, shaving equipment and the like which put the violence on the screen. I mean the human toll, the broken women and children of our land, and we frightened men who beat them. And even if I were to claim that neither you nor I is affected by the civic advocacy of violence in commercialism and free enterprise, we would still have to note that the powers and scions of industry *believe*—to the tune of billions of dollars a year—that we are so affected.

Pornography is no more a needed release for prurient sexual energies than would be the continuation of temple prostitutes. But it is sanctioned, and the civic advocacy of violence through pornography is real. It is not on the decrease. Soft porn is no longer *Charlie's Angels* or the double entendres of a Johnny Carson-starlet interview; that's simply a matter of course. Soft porn is now *Playboy*, *Penthouse*, and *Oui*, where every month, right next to the chewing gum and razor blades at the corner grocery, air-sprayed photographs play into male masturbatory fantasies. Hard porn itself is becoming more "ordinary" every day; child porn and snuff films lead the race in capturing the male market for sex and violence. We love it. We want it. And we pay for it. Violence works.

Insofar as violence works, the male batterer is finally, and somewhat definitively, hidden from us. I would not denigrate or halt for a moment our struggle to know the male batterer through clinical research models. But I would call all who are interested in knowing him and in intervening in and ending the cycle of the violence of men against women, to the larger context of the civic advocacy of violence. There, I believe, is the complement of the analysis generated by profiling the male batterer.

Until the code of male violence is undone, male dominance and sexism will prevail. Until the commerce in violence against women ceases, and we finally create an environment in which violence is no longer acceptable or conceivable, male supremacy will remain a fact of life for all of us.

Jane Hood

"LET'S GET A GIRL":
MALE BONDING RITUALS IN AMERICA

PROLOGUE

Wednesday, April 19, 1989: 10:05 P.M. "A 28 year old investment banker, jogging through Central Park, was attacked by a group of teenagers. They kicked and beat her, smashed her in the head with a pipe and raped her. The teenagers who were from East Harlem, were quickly arrested" (Terry 1989, p. 28).

Wednesday, March 1, 1989: c. 6:00 P.M. In Glen Ridge, New Jersey, five high school football players sexually assaulted a 17-year-old mentally handicapped girl in a basement while eight other teenagers looked on (Foderado 1989). "No sexual intercourse took place, investigators said, but the girl was believed to have been forced to perform sexual acts with the boys and she was raped with several objects including a broomstick and a miniature baseball bat" . . . "The arrests were announced on May 24 by Essex County Prosecutor, Herbert H. Tate, Jr whose office took over the case last month when the son of Lieut. Richard Corcoran, a Glen Ridge officer, was identified as being present when the assault took place" (*New York Times* 1989).

For weeks following the April 19 assault of the Central Park jogger, newspapers around the nation carried stories about the backgrounds of the youths who had attacked her. Newspapers reported that the assailants had been rampaging through the park attacking victims at will, a practice that some people called "wilding." Talk show participants debated whether the attack was racially motivated, and both black and white community leaders worried about how the publicity following the attack would affect race relations in the city. While sociologists discussed the socioeconomic roots of urban violence and clinicians described the psychic terror experienced by youths growing up in East Harlem, incumbent politicians urged "get tough" policies to "stamp out" "terrorism in the streets." Over a month after the attack, local New York City newspapers still carried headlines on the jogger's condition such as "Jogger Kisses Cardinal."

With the exception of some excellent articles in the *Village Voice* (1989) and op-ed articles by Susan Chace (1989) and Elizabeth Holtzman (1989), hardly any of this "media orgy" dealt with gender or the phenomenon of gang rape. However, by the time news of the Glen Ridge assault surfaced on May 24, at least part of the media spotlight had shifted to rape. On May 29, *New York Times* readers finally learned that 28 other rapes had been reported to New York City police during the week of April 16 and that nearly all of these were of black and Hispanic women (Terry 1989). Of all these assaults, only the rape of an upper-middle class white jogger by a group of black youths had made the news.

This essay is a revised and expanded version of the full text of an article originally published in the *New York Times* under the title, "Why Our Society is Rape Prone" (Hood 1989). This version includes examples cut from the original text as well as references to the Glen Ridge case.

GANG RAPE AS A MALE BONDING RITUAL

Why did eight teenagers beat and rape a jogger in Central Park? Mostly missing from the analyses of "wilding," and lost among the suggestions for preventing similar tragedies, is one crucial issue: gender.

With the exception of prison assaults, gang rape is a crime committed almost exclusively by males against females. Yet few commentators have focused on gender and what it means to be raised male in America. Like the proverbial fish who cannot describe water, we Americans see everything *but* gender at work in the April 19 assault.

Given over 30 years of research on patterns of forcible rape, our myopia is hard to explain. In his classic 1959 study of 646 Philadelphia rapes, Menachem Amir (1971) described the prototype for the Central Park assault. Of 646 cases, 43% were pair or group rapes. Like the boys from Schomberg Plaza, the offenders were disproportionately very young (10 to 19). Amir also found that group rapes were much more likely than single-offender rapes to involve violence far beyond what would be necessary to restrain the victim. In an attempt to make sense of this pattern, several researchers (Amir 1971; Brownmiller 1975; Groth 1979; Sanday 1981; Herman 1984) reached a similar conclusion: In a society that equates masculinity with dominance and sex with violence, gang rape becomes one way for adolescents to prove their masculinity both to themselves and to each other.

Although other studies of sexual assault patterns do not find as high an incidence of pair and group rape as did Amir (Groth 1979, p. 110; Ageton 1983), when group rape does occur, the attack has a dual focus. Interaction among the assailants may take center stage as the men compete with each other in punishing, dominating, and humiliating the victim (Groth 1979, p. 118; Scully and Marolla 1985). In addition to being an outlet for rage and the need to dominate, gang rapes can also be a form of group recreation. The Schomburg Plaza boys said that they were "just having fun," and gang rapists interviewed by Scully and Marolla (1985, p. 260) described cruising an area "looking for girls" that they could pick up, drive to a deserted area, and then rape. Although not as well practiced in the art of gang rape as Scully and Marolla's informants, the teenagers rampaging through Central Park reportedly said, "Let's get a girl" shortly before they attacked the jogger (Chace 1989).

The attack on the investment banker was particularly brutal, but both it and the Glen Ridge assault have something in common with gang rapes of the sort portrayed in the film, "Saturday Night Fever." There, one boy lures a girl into the back seat of a car so that a whole group can have sex with her. An event that started as "sex" becomes rape as the boys begin to compete with each other, disregarding the girl's welfare or feelings. Similarly, in Glen Ridge, the girl appears to have gone willingly to the house with the boys before she was subjected to an hour of degradation at the hands of four boys while another urged them on and eight others watched (Foderaro 1989). Because victims may be reluctant to report this kind of assault to police or interviewers, Scully and Marolla (1985) think that these "date gang rapes" may be much more common than either police reports or the Uniform Crime Surveys indicate.

Both the Central Park and the Glen Ridge incidents also share some characteristics of "gang bangs" in fraternity houses and random violence against women on college campuses. These apparently diverse phenomena are connected, not by the severity of the crime and not by the characteristics of the victim, but rather by the common context of an adolescent male-bonding ritual in a rape-prone society.

In her research on gang rapes at the University of Pennsylvania, anthropologist Peggy Sanday has compiled vivid descriptions of gang rapes, which she suspects are a common practice on college campuses all over the United States (Sanday 1986, p. 99; 1988). They are, as are most gang rapes, planned in advance. The intended victim is plied with alcohol and/or pills until she can be dragged into a bedroom where she is then systematically raped by one boy after the other while the others look on. Afterward, the boys use the excuse that the girl was drunk and did not know what she was doing.

In comparing the fraternity members to the street gangs that Amir studied in the 1950s, Sanday argues that the two groups are similar in that both are peripheral to society. Whereas members of Amir's lower class Philadelphia street gangs may never escape their peripheral social and economic status, college males are temporarily peripheral "while they are learning skills they will eventually use to usurp their fathers' places in the corporate world" (Sanday 1986, p. 99).

Gang rape may be the most shocking male bonding ritual on college campuses, but it is not the only one that depends on objectifying women.

In an excellent article on the use of sexist jokes among fraternity men Peter Lyman (1987) describes an incident that took place at a sorority house. There a group of 45 fraternity men shoved their way into the dining room, encircled the women residents, and forced them to watch for 10 minutes while one "pledge" stroked a rubber phallus and another recited a speech on penis envy. After a resident advisor told the men to leave, the pranksters were surprised. After all (like the boys in Central Park), they were "just having fun," and the penis envy joke was a tradition. The women, however, argued that the raid had rape overtones and asked, "Why do you men always think about women in terms of violating them, in sexual imagery?" Why indeed?

RAPE-FREE VS. RAPE-PRONE SOCIETIES

The answer, I think, lies in understanding the difference between what University of Pennsylvania anthropologist Peggy Sanday calls "rape-prone" societies and those that are "rape-free." In a study of 95 band and tribal societies, Sanday (1981) found a high incidence of rape to be associated with militarism, interpersonal violence in general, an ideology of male toughness, and distant father–child relationships. Rape-free societies, on the other hand, encourage female participation in the economy and political system and male involvement in child-rearing.

In rape-free societies men speak of women with respect. For example, a Minangakabau man in West Sumatra told Peggy Sanday:

> Women are given more privileges because people think that women determine the continuation of the generations. Whether the next generation is good or bad depends upon women . . . Women have more human feeling and they are more humanitarian. They think more about people's feelings and because of this they should be given rights to speak. (Sanday 1986, pp. 96–97)

In nonindustrial rape-free societies, women and men may have different roles, but the roles that women play are highly valued and help to shape the culture as a whole.

Despite recent moves toward gender equality, our society is still very much "rape-prone." In fact, the United States has the distinction of being among the most rape-prone of all modern societies (Scully and Marolla 1985). In surveys of U.S. and Canadian college students, for example, psychologist Neil Malamuth finds that one of three college men say that if they could get away with it, they would be at least "somewhat likely" to rape a woman (Malamuth 1981). Similarly, several recent surveys of high school students find 40 to 50% of both boys and girls agreeing with such statements as, "If a girl goes to a guy's apartment after a date, it's OK for him to force her to have sex" (Hall, Howard, & Boezio 1986; Kikuchi 1989). Even jurors in rape trials studied by LaFree and Reskin (LaFree 1989, p. 219) found it hard to believe that an attractive man would rape a woman if he could have just as easily seduced her. As many authors point out, in rape-prone societies, rape is easily confused with "normal" sex.

In our own society, sex is so inextricably linked to violence that attempts to uncouple the two can fail in ways some of us may find hard to imagine. For example, after the release of *The Accused* (a film dramatizing the New Bedford pool hall gang rape), some middle-class male viewers were observed cheering at the harrowing gang rape scene (*The Nation*, 5-29-1989). Like the Schomburg Plaza boys, these movie goers had learned that masculinity means domination over others through sex and violence.

PREVENTION STRATEGIES

In a letter to the *New York Times*, John Gutfreund (1989), the jogger's employer, called for "an all-out national emergency effort to solve the problem of violence on urban streets." Others urged prosecuting the teenagers as adults and advocated long prison terms. Ridiculing the earlier version of this article, the *Richmond Times-Dispatch* called for "A little more jail time and a little less blame-society-first rationalizing."

Unfortunately, more lights in Central Park, more police on the streets, and more time in jail for convicted rapists will not do much to lower the overall incidence of rape. A man caught robbing a jewelry store is unlikely to use the defense that "it wasn't really a robbery." For rapists, however, the defense that "it wasn't really a rape" is commonplace (LaFree 1989; Scully and Marolla 1985). In spite of the creation of special Sexual Offense units in police departments and in spite of the adoption of "rape shield" laws that disallow questions concerning the victim's moral character, most rapes are never reported to the police and of those that are reported only a small proportion result in any jail time for offenders. Thus, in a study of 881 rapes reported to Indianapolis police in 1970, 1973, and 1975. LaFree found that only 12% resulted in convictions (LaFree 1989, p. 60). Because both male and female jurors believe that only certain kinds of men can rape and only certain kinds of women can be raped, rapes that do not fit the public's stereotype of "a real rape" are less likely to yield convictions.

As long as rapes of wives, girlfriends, hitchhikers, women in bars, and girls at fraternity parties are dismissed as "not really rape," doubling the jail time for the few men that are convicted will do little to reduce American women's one-out-of-three lifetime probability (Johnson 1980) of sexual assault. If our society is to become less rape-prone, we must instead find ways of redefining gender relationships so that women become men's peers and boys can become men without controlling, dominating, and objectifying girls and women.

Therefore, if corporate leaders want to mount an effective national campaign to prevent assaults on women by bands of young men, they should target, not "criminals," but

- advertisements portraying women as sex objects
- sexual harassment in the work place

- resistance to paternity leave policies
- Rambo dolls and other violent games and toys
- gender inequality in the workplace.

For their part, community groups can do the following:

- Bring more fathers into daycare and kindergarten classrooms to show that "real men" are nurturing people.
- Support sex education programs that teach that rape is not sex but violence and that good sex takes place in the context of love and respect.
- Encourage co-ed sports at the elementary and middle school levels so that boys can learn that girls are not "the other," to be made fun of and put down.
- Learn the common "rape myths" ("You can tell a rapist by the way he looks." "Women enjoy being raped." "Good girls don't get raped.") and teach against them on all fronts.
- Protest the production and showing of "slasher" films that eroticize violence.

In his otherwise excellent May 2 column, Tom Wicker (*New York Times* 1989) described the Central Park rape as "a chance event that could have happened to anyone." In a way it was. On the other hand, when was the last time anyone has heard of a gang of teenage girls raping and beating a man in Central Park? To get to the roots of this particular brand of violence, we need to look beyond race and class to gender relations in America.

REFERENCES

Ageton, S. 1983. *Sexual Assault among Adolescents*. Lexington, MA: D.C. Heath.

Amir, M. 1971. *Patterns of Forcible Rape*. Chicago: University of Chicago Press.

Brownmiller, S. 1975. *Against Our Will: Men, Women and Rape*. New York: Simon and Schuster.

Chace, S. 1989. "Safety in the Park: In Women's Hands." *New York Times*, April 27.

Foderaro, L. 1989. "After a Sex Assault, a Town Worries Its Athletes Were too Often Forgiven." *New York Times*, June 12.

Groth, A. N. 1979. *Men Who Rape: The Psychology of the Offender*. New York: Plenum Press.

Gutfreund, J. 1989. "Letters to the Editor." *New York Times*, April 27.

Hall, E., J. Howard, and S. Boezio 1986. "Tolerance of Rape: A Sexist or Anti-Social Attitude?" *Psychology of Women Quarterly* 10:101–118.

Herman, D. 1984. "The Rape Culture." Pp. 20–38 in *Women: A Feminist Perspective*, edited by J. Freeman. Palo Alto, CA: Mayfield.

Holtzman, E. 1989. "Rape: The Silence is Criminal." *New York Times*, May 5.

Hood, J. 1989. "Why Our Society is Rape-Prone." *New York Times*, May 16.

Johnson, A. G. 1980. "On the Prevalence of Rape in the United States." *Signs: Journal of Women in Culture and Society* 6:136–146.

Kikuchi, J. 1989. Presentation on Rhode Island rape attitudes study at meetings of Association of Women in Psychology, Providence, R.I., March.

LaFree, G. 1989. *Rape and Criminal Justice: The Social Construction of Sexual Assault*. Belmont, CA: Wadsworth.

Lyman, P. 1987. "The Fraternal Bond as a Joking Relationship." Pp. 148–164 in *Changing Men*, edited by M. Kimmel. Newbury Park, CA: Sage.

Malamuth, N. 1981. "Rape Proclivity among Males." *Journal of Social Issues* 37:138–157.

New York Times 1989. "5 New Jersey Youths Held in Sexual Assault on Impaired Girl, 17." May 25.

Richmond Times-Dispatch 1989. "Blame Society First." May 19.

Sanday, P. R. 1981. "The Socio-Cultural Context of Rape: A Cross Cultural Study." *Journal of Social Issues* 37:5–27.

———. 1986. "Rape and the Silencing of the Feminine." Pp. 84–101 in *Rape*, edited by S. Tomaselli and R. Porter. Oxford: Basil Blackwell.

———. 1988. Excerpts from Sanday's unpublished manuscript on sexual expression among college students read as part of discussant's comments at the Annual Meetings of the American Anthropological Association, Phoenix, AZ, November 19.

Scully, D., and J. Marolla 1985. "Riding the Bull at Gilley's": Convicted Rapists Describe the Rewards of Rape." *Social Problems* 32:251–263.

Terry, D. 1989. "In Week of an Infamous Rape, 28 Other Victims Suffer." *New York Times*, May 29.

Village Voice 1989. "The Voices Not Heard: Black and Women Writers on the Central Park Rape." May 9.

Tim Beneke

MEN ON RAPE

Rape may be America's fastest growing violent crime; no one can be certain because it is not clear whether more rapes are being committed or reported. It *is* clear that violence against women is widespread and fundamentally alters the meaning of life for women; that sexual violence is encouraged in a variety of ways in American culture; and that women are often blamed for rape.

Consider some statistics:

- In a random sample of 930 women, sociologist Diana Russell found that 44 percent had survived either rape or attempted rape. Rape was defined as sexual intercourse physically forced upon the woman, or coerced by threat of bodily harm, or forced upon the woman when she was helpless (asleep, for example). The survey included rape and attempted rape in marriage in its calculations. (Personal communication)
- In a September 1980 survey conducted by *Cosmopolitan* magazine to which over 106,000 women anonymously responded, 24 percent had been raped at least once. Of these, 51 percent had been raped by friends, 37 percent by strangers, 18 percent by relatives, and 3 percent by husbands. 10 percent of the women in the survey had been victims of incest. 75 percent of the women had been "bullied into making love." Writer Linda Wolfe, who reported on the survey, wrote in reference to such bullying: "Though such harassment stops short of rape, readers reported that it was nearly as distressing."
- An estimated 2–3 percent of all men who rape outside of marriage go to prison for their crimes.[1]
- The F.B.I. estimates that if current trends continue, one woman in four will be sexually assaulted in her lifetime.[2]
- An estimated 1.8 million women are battered by their spouses each year.[3] In extensive interviews with 430 battered women, clinical psychologist Lenore Walker,

Reprinted from *Men on Rape* by Tim Beneke. New York: St. Martin's Press, 1982.

author of *The Battered Woman*, found that 59.9 percent had also been raped (defined as above) by their spouses. Given the difficulties many women had in admitting they had been raped, Walker estimates the figure may well be as high as 80 or 85 percent. (Personal communication.) If 59.9 percent of the 1.8 million women battered each year are also raped, then a million women may be raped in marriage each year. And a significant number are raped in marriage without being battered.

- Between one in two and one in ten of all rapes are reported to the police.[4]
- Between 300,000 and 500,000 women are raped each year outside of marriage.[5]

What is often missed when people contemplate statistics on rape is the effect of the *threat* of sexual violence on women. I have asked women repeatedly, "How would your life be different if rape were suddenly to end?" (Men may learn a lot by asking this question of women to whom they are close.) The threat of rape is an assault upon the meaning of the world; it alters the feel of the human condition. Surely any attempt to comprehend the lives of women that fails to take issues of violence against women into account is misguided.

Through talking to women, I learned: *The threat of rape alters the meaning and feel of the night*. Observe how your body feels, how the night feels, when you're in fear. The constriction in your chest, the vigilance in your eyes, the rubber in your legs. What do the stars look like? How does the moon present itself? What is the difference between walking late at night in the dangerous part of a city and walking late at night in the country, or safe suburbs? When I try to imagine what the threat of rape must do to the night, I think of the stalked, adrenalated feeling I get walking late at night in parts of certain American cities. Only, I remind myself, it is a fear different from any I have known, a fear of being raped.

It is night half the time. If the threat of rape alters the meaning of the night, it must alter the meaning and pace of the day, one's relation to the passing and organization of time itself. For some women, the threat of rape at night turns their cars into armored tanks, their solitude into isolation. And what must the space inside a car or an apartment feel like if the space outside is menacing?

I was running late one night with a close woman friend through a path in the woods on the outskirts of a small university town. We had run several miles and were feeling a warm, energized serenity.

"How would you feel if you were alone?" I asked.

"Terrified!" she said instantly.

"Terrified that there might be a man out there?" I asked, pointing to the surrounding moonlit forest, which had suddenly been transformed into a source of terror.

"Yes."

Another woman said, "I know what I can't do and I've completely internalized what I can't do. I've built a viable life that basically involves never leaving my apartment at night unless I'm directly going some place to meet somebody. It's unconsciously built into what it occurs to women to do." When one is raised without freedom, one may not recognize its absence.

The threat of rape alters the meaning and feel of nature. Everyone has felt the psychic nurturance of nature. Many women are being deprived of that nurturance, especially in wooded areas near cities. They are deprived either because they cannot experience nature in solitude because of threat, or because, when they do choose solitude in nature, they must cope with a certain subtle but nettlesome fear.

Women need more money because of rape and the threat of rape makes it harder for women to earn money. It's simple: if you don't feel safe walking at night, or riding public transportation, you need a car. And it is less practicable to live in cheaper, less secure, and thus more dangerous neighborhoods if the ordinary threat of violence that men experience, being mugged, say, is compounded by the threat of rape. By limiting mobility at night, the threat of rape limits where and when one is able to work, thus making it more difficult to earn money. An obvious bind: women need more money because of rape, and have fewer job opportunities because of it.

The threat of rape makes women more dependent on men (or other women). One woman said: "If there were no rape I wouldn't have to play games with men for their protection." The threat of rape falsifies, mystifies, and confuses relations between men and women. If there were no rape, women would simply not need men as much, wouldn't need them to go places with at night, to feel safe in their homes, for protection in nature.

The threat of rape makes solitude less possible for women. Solitude, drawing strength from being alone, is difficult if being alone means being afraid. To be afraid is to be in need, to experience a lack; the threat of rape creates a lack. Solitude requires relaxation; if you're afraid, you can't relax.

The threat of rape inhibits a woman's expressiveness. "If there were no rape," said one woman, "I could dress the way I wanted and walk the way I wanted and not feel self-conscious about the responses of men. I could be friendly to people. I wouldn't have to wish I was ugly. I wouldn't have to make myself small when I got on the bus. I wouldn't have to respond to verbal abuse from men by remaining silent. I could respond in kind."

If a woman's basic expressiveness is inhibited, her sexuality, creativity, and delight in life must surely be diminished.

The threat of rape inhibits the freedom of the eye. I know a married couple who live in Manhattan. They are both artists, both acutely sensitive and responsive to the visual world. When they walk separately in the city, he has more freedom to look than she soes. She most control her eye movements lest they inadvertently meet the glare of some importunate man. What, who, and how she sees are restricted by the threat of rape.

The following exercise is recommended for men.

> Walk down a city street. Pay a lot of attention to your clothing; make sure your pants are zipped, shirt tucked in, buttons done. Look straight ahead. Every time a man walks past you, avert your eyes and make your face expressionless. Most women learn to go through this act each time we leave our houses. It's a way to avoid at least some of the encounters we've all had with strange men who decided we looked available.[6]

To relate aesthetically to the visual world involves a certain playfulness, spirit of spontaneous exploration. The tense vigilance that accompanies fear inhibits that spontaneity. The world is no longer yours to look at when you're afraid.

I am aware that all culture is, in part, restriction, that there are places in America where hardly anyone is safe (though men are safer than women virtually everywhere), that there are many ways to enjoy life, that some women may not be so restricted, that there exist havens, whether psychic, geographical, economic, or class. But they are *havens*, and as such, defined by threat.

Above all, I trust my experience: no woman could have lived the life I've lived the last few years. If suddenly I were restricted by the threat of rape, I would feel a deep, inexorable depression. And it's not just rape; it's harassment, battery, Peeping Toms, anonymous phone calls, exhibitionism, intrusive stares, fondlings—all contributing to an atmosphere of intimidation in women's lives. And I have only scratched the surface; it would take many carefully crafted short stories to begin to express what I have only hinted at in the last few pages. I have not even touched upon what it might mean for a woman to be sexually assaulted. Only women can speak to that. Nor have I suggested how the threat of rape affects marriage.

Rape and the threat of rape pervade the lives of women, as reflected in some popular images of our culture.

"SHE ASKED FOR IT"—BLAMING THE VICTIM[7]

Many things may be happening when a man blames a woman for rape.

First, in all cases where a woman is said to have asked for it, her appearance and behavior are taken as a form of speech. "Actions speak louder than words" is a widely held belief; the woman's actions—her appearance may be taken as action—are given greater emphasis than her words; an interpretation alien to the woman's intentions is given to her actions. A logical extension of "she asked for it" is the idea that she wanted what happened to happen; if she wanted it to happen, she *deserved* for it to happen. Therefore, the man is not to be blamed. "She asked for it" can mean either that she was consenting to have sex and was not really raped, or that she was in fact raped but somehow she really deserved it. "If you ask for it, you deserve it," is a widely held notion. If I ask you to beat me up and you beat me up, I still don't deserve to be beaten up. So even if the notion that women asked to be raped had some basis in reality, which it doesn't, on its own terms it makes no sense.

Second, a mentality exists that says: a woman who assumes freedoms normally restricted to a man (like going out alone at night) and is raped is doing the same thing as a woman who goes out in the rain without an umbrella and catches a cold. Both are considered responsible for what happens to them. That men will rape is taken to be a legitimized given, part of nature, like rain or snow. The view reflects a massive abdication of responsibility for rape on the part of men. It is so much easier to think of rape as natural than to acknowledge one's part in it. So long as rape is regarded as natural, women will be blamed for rape.

A third point. The view that it is natural for men to rape is closely connected to the view of women as commodities. If a woman's body is regarded as a valued commodity by men, then of course, if you leave a valued commodity where it can be taken, it's just human nature for men to take it. If you left your stereo out on the sidewalk, you'd be asking for it to get stolen. Someone will just take it. (And how often men speak of rape as "going out and *taking* it.") If a woman walks the streets at night, she's leaving a valued commodity, her body, where it can be taken. So long as women are regarded as commodities, they will be blamed for rape.

Which brings us to a fourth point. "She asked for it" is inseparable from a more general "psychology of the dupe." If I use bad judgment and fail to read the small print in a contract and later get taken advantage of "screwed" (or "fucked over") then I deserve what I get; bad judgment makes me liable. Analogously, if a woman trusts a man and goes to his apartment, or accepts a ride hitchhiking, or goes out on a date and is raped, she's a dupe and deserves what she gets. "He didn't *really* rape her" goes the mentality—"he merely took advantage of her." And in America it's okay for people to take advantage of each other, even expected and praised. In fact, you're considered dumb and foolish if you don't take advantage of other people's bad judgment. And so, again, by treating them as dupes, rape will be blamed on women.

Fifth, if a woman who is raped is judged attractive by men, and particularly if she dresses to look attractive, then the mentality exists that she attacked him with her weapon so, of course, he counter-attacked with his. The preview to a popular movies states: "She was the victim of her own *provocative beauty*." Provocation: "There is a line which, if crossed, will *set me off* and I will lose control and no longer be responsible for my behavior. If you punch me in the nose then, of course, I will not be responsible for what happens: you will have provoked a fight. If you dress, talk, move, or act a certain way, you will have provoked me to rape. If your appearance *stuns* me, *strikes* me, *ravishes* me, *knocks me out*, etc., then I will not be held responsible for what happens; you will have asked for it." The notion that sexual feeling makes one helpless is part of a cultural abdication of responsibility for sexuality. So long as a woman's appearance is viewed as a weapon and sexual feeling is believed to make one helpless, women will be blamed for rape.

Sixth, I have suggested that men sometimes become obsessed with images of women, that images become a substitute for sexual feeling, that sexual feeling becomes externalized and out of control and is given an undifferentiated identity in the appearance of women's bodies. It is a process of projection in which one blurs one's own desire with her imagined, projected desire. If a woman's attractiveness is taken to signify one's own lust and a woman's lust, then when an "attractive" woman is raped, some men may think she wanted sex. Since they perceive their own lust in part projected onto the woman, they disbelieve women who've been raped. So long as men project their own sexual desires onto women, they will blame women for rape.

And seventh, what are we to make of the contention that women in dating situations say "no" initially to sexual overtures from men as a kind of pose, only to give in later, thus revealing their true intentions? And that men are thus confused and incredulous when women are raped because in their sexual experience women can't be believed? I doubt that this has much to do with men's perceptions of rape. I don't know to what extent women actually "say no and mean yes"; certainly it is a common theme in male folklore. I have spoken to a couple of women who went through periods when they wanted to be sexual but were afraid to be, and often rebuffed initial sexual advances only to give in later. One point is clear: the ambivalence women may feel about having sex is closely tied to the inability of men to fully accept them as sexual beings. Women have been traditionally punished for being openly and freely sexual; men are praised for it. And if many men think of sex as achievement of possession of a valued commodity, or aggressive degradation, then women have every reason to feel and act ambivalent.

These themes are illustrated in an interview I conducted with a 23 year old man who grew up in Pittsburgh and works as a file clerk in the financial district of San Francisco. Here's what he said:

"Where I work it's probably no different from any other major city in the U.S. The women dress up in high heels, and they wear a lot of makeup, and they just look really *hot* and really sexy, and how can somebody who has a healthy sex drive not feel lust for them when you see them? I feel lust for them, but I don't think I could find it in me to overpower someone and rape them. But I definitely get the feeling that I'd like to rape a girl. I don't know if the actual act of rape would be satisfying, but the *feeling* is satisfying.

"These women look so good, and they kiss ass of the men in the three-piece suits who are *big* in the corporation, and most of them relate to me like "Who are *you?* Who are *you* to even *look* at?" They're snobby and they condescend to me, and I resent it. It would take me a lot longer to get to first base than it would somebody with a three-piece suit who had money. And to me a lot of the men they go out with are superficial assholes who have no real feelings or substance, and are just trying to get ahead and make a lot of money. Another things that makes me resent these women is thinking, "How could she want to hang out with somebody like that? What does that make her?"

"I'm a file clerk, which makes me feel like a nebbish, a nurd, like I'm not making it, I'm a failure. But I don't really believe I'm a failure becuase I know it's just a phase, and I'm just doing it for the money, just to make it through this phase. I catch myself feeling like a failure, but I realize that's ridiculous."

What exactly do you go through when you see these sexy, unavailable women?

"Let's say I see a woman and she looks really pretty and really clean and sexy, and she's giving off very feminine, sexy vibes. I think, 'Wow, I would love to make love to her,' but I know she's not really interested. It's a tease. A lot of times a woman knows that she's looking really good and she'll use that and flaunt it, and it makes me feel like she's laughing at me and I feel *degraded*.

"I also feel dehumanized, because when I'm being teased I just turn off, I cease to be human. Because if I go with my human emotions I'm going to want to put my arms around her and kiss her, and to do that would be unacceptable. I don't like the feeling that I'm supposed to stand there and take it, and not be able to hug her or kiss her; so I just turn off my emotions. It's a feeling of humiliation, because the woman has forced me to turn off my feelings and react in a way that I really don't want to.

"If I were actually desperate enough to rape somebody, it would be from wanting the person, but it would be a very spiteful thing, just being able to say, 'I have power over you and I can do anything I want with you,' because really I feel that *they* have power over *me* just by their presence. Just the fact that they can come up to me and just melt me and make me feel like a dummy makes me want revenge. They have power over me so I want power over them. . . .

"Society says that you have to have a lot of sex with a lot of different women to be a real man. Well, what happens if you don't? Then what are you? Are you half a man? Are you still a boy? It's ridiculous. You see a whiskey ad with a guy and two women on his arm. The implication is that real men don't have any trouble getting women."

How does it make you feel toward women to see all these sexy women in media and advertising using their looks to try to get you to buy something?

"It makes me hate them. As a man you're taught that men are more powerful than women, and that men always have the upper hand, and that it's a man's society; but then you see all these women and it makes you think, 'Jesus Christ, if we have all the power how come all the beautiful women are telling us what to buy?' And to be honest, it just makes me hate beautiful women because they're using their power over me. I realize they're being used themselves, and they're doing it for money. In *Playboy* you see all these beautiful women who look so sexy and they'll be giving you all these looks like they want to have sex so bad; but then in reality you know that except for a few nymphomaniacs, they're doing it for the money; so I hate them for being used and for using their bodies in that way.

"In this society, if you ever sit down and realize how manipulated you really are it makes you pissed off—it makes you want to take control. And you've been manipulated by women, and they're a very easy target because they're out walking along the streets, so you can just grab one and say, 'Listen, you're going to do what I want you to do,' and it's an act of revenge against the way you've been manipulated.

"I know a girl who was walking down the street by her house, when this guy jumped her and beat her up and raped her, and she was black and blue and had to go to the hospital. That's beyond me. I can't understand how somebody could do that. If I were going to rape a girl, I wouldn't hurt her. I might *restrain* her, but I wouldn't *hurt* her. . . .

"The whole dating game between men and women also makes me feel degraded. I hate being put in the position of having to initiate a relationship. I've been taught that if you're not aggressive with a woman, then you've blown it. She's not going to jump on *you*, so *you've* got to jump on *her*. I've heard all kinds of stories where the woman says, 'No! No! No!' and they end up making great love. I get confused as hell if a woman pushes me away. Does it mean she's trying to be a nice girl and wants to put up a good appearance, or does it mean she doesn't want anything to do with you? You don't know. Probably a lot of men think that women don't feel like real women unless a man tries to force himself on her, unless she brings out the 'real man,' so to speak, and probably too much of it goes on. It goes on in my head that you're complimenting a woman by actually staring at her or by trying to get into her pants. Lately, I'm realizing that when I stare at women lustfully, they often feel more threatened than flattered."

NOTES

[1] Such estimates recur in the rape literature. See *Sexual Assault* by Nancy Gager and Cathleen Schurr, Grosset & Dunlap, 1976, or *The Price of Coercive Sexuality* by Clark and Lewis, The Women's Press, 1977.

[2] *Uniform Crime Reports*, 1980

[3] See *Behind Closed Doors* by Murray J. Strauss and Richard Gelles, Doubleday, 1979.

[4] See Gager and Schurr (above) or virtually any book on the subject.

[5] Again, see Gager and Schurr, or Carol V. Horos, *Rape*, Banbury Books, 1981.

[6] From "Willamette Bridge" in *Body Politics* by Nancy Henley, Prentice-Hall, 1977, p. 144.

[7] I would like to thank George Lakoff for this insight.

◆ ◆ ◆

PART SEVEN

Men with Men: Friendships and Fears

(Photo by Ebet Roberts.)

What is the nature of men's relationships with other men? Do most men have close, initimate male friends, or do they simply bond together around shared activities and interests? How do competition, homophobia, and violence enter into men's relationships with each other?

Traditionally, in literature and in popular mythology, the Truly Great Friendships are those among men. In the late 1960s and early 1970s, the concept of civilization being a "fraternity of men" was criticized by feminists, who saw women as isolated and excluded from public life. In the mid-1970s, though, the men's liberation literature began to focus on the *quality* of men's relationships, and found them wanting. Men, we discovered, have "acquaintances," "activities buddies," but rarely true friends with whom they can intimately share their inner lives. Lillian Rubin and others argued that it is not that men do not want or need closeness with other men, it is just that they are so very threatened by the actuality of intimacy. Thus, when men organize their time together around work, watching a game, or playing cards, the structure of the activity mediates their time together, thus maintaining a "safe" level of emotional distance.

But why do men need emotional distance from each other? And what are the costs of maintaining emotionally shallow relationships with other men? What kinds of pressure does this place on women to be the primary "emotion workers" in men's lives? In this section, Perry Garfinkel points out that most men, when asked who their best friend is, will name a woman, often their wife. (Few women, by the way, will name their husband—most will name another woman.) Men, he points out, rarely feel comfortable with intimate self-disclosure with other men. Certainly an overemphasis on competition among males, from a very early age, is one factor that places a damper on intimate self-disclosure among men. Why would a man give away information that would make him vulnerable among his competitors in games, education, or the workplace? Another important barrier to male–male intimacy, as the article by Gregory Lehne points out, is homphobia. The fear of homosexuality–or of being thought to be homosexual by others—places severe limitations on the emotional, verbal, and physical interactions among men. Next, Peter M. Nardi discusses the contemporary political importance of friendship among gay men. Finally, Martin Simmons illustrates the ways that confronting racism together becomes a central element in cementing black men's friendships.

If men's power over women and other men (sexism and homophobia) is one of the central elements of the construction of masculinities then we must address the negative consequences of male–male intimacy. Kathryn Ann Farr's discussion of the Good Old Boys Sociability Group illustrates that men's friendships may be about both intimacy among men and the maintenance of masculine privilege. She thus offers a caution against the uncritical embrace of a romanticized view of men's friendships in a context of the reproduction of men's privilege. And Susan Brownmiller describes male rape in prison as an act usually performed by otherwise "straight" men as a means of solidifying positions of power and control in the intermale dominance hierarchy. Here, competition among men, homophobia, and the devaluation of the "feminine" all come together. The same distorted need for power and control that leads men to rape women, we learn, forms the basis for male rape of other men.

Gregory K. Lehne

HOMOPHOBIA AMONG MEN:
SUPPORTING AND DEFINING THE MALE ROLE

Homophobia is the irrational fear or intolerance of homosexuality. Although both men and women can be homophobic, homophobia is most often associated with the fear of male homosexuality. Homophobia is not currently classified as a "mental illness" (neither is homosexuality), although psychiatrists such as Dr. George Weinberg (1972) have stated, "I would never consider a patient healthy unless he had overcome his prejudice aginst homosexuality." Homophobia is the threat implicit in *"What are you, a fag?"* If male homosexuality were no more threatening than being left-handed, for example, homophobia would not exist. In many ways, and in all but extreme cases, homophobia is a socially determined prejudice much like sexism or racism, rather than a medically recognized phobia.

Homophobia, as I will show, does not exist in most cases as an isolated trait or prejudice; it is characteristic of individuals who are generally rigid and sexist. Homophobia, with its associated dynamic of fear of being labeled a homosexual, is an underlying *motivation* in maintaining the male sex role. I believe that it must be eliminated for fundamental changes to occur in male and female roles. To support this thesis, I will discuss first whether homophobia reflects an accurate perception and understanding of homosexuality or whether it is an irrational fear. Then I will examine the social aspects of homophobia and personal characteristics of people who are highly homophobic. Finally, I will explore the social functions of homophobia in maintaining the male sex role, and its effects on society and the individual.

IS HOMOPHOBIA IRRATIONAL?

Homophobia is irrational because it generally embodies misconceptions and false stereotypes of male homosexuality. These belief systems, or prejudices, are rationalizations supporting homophobia, not causes of homophobia. Levitt and Klassen's 1973 Kinsey Institute study of 3,000 American adults found the following beliefs about homosexuality to be widespread: homosexuals are afraid of the opposite sex (56% of the sample believed this), homosexuals act like the opposite sex (69%), only certain occupations are appropriate for homosexuals, homosexuals molest children (71%), and homosexuality was unnatural.

First, let us consider the mistaken belief that homosexual med no not like women. Since relations with women (especially sexual) are considered one of the proving grounds of masculinity, homosexual men who do not treat women as sex objects are regarded as suspect and unmanly in our male-oriented culture. Research does not support the belief, however, that homosexual males are afraid of women. About 20% of men who consider themselves homosexuals have been married, or currently are married; about half of these gay men are fathers (Bell and Weinberg, 1978). Around 75% of homosexual males have engaged in heterosexual kissing and necking, and about 50% have participated in heterosexual intercourse in their youth, with a frequency and success rate highly similar to that of heterosexual males (Saghir and Robins, 1973). About 50% of the homosexual men in this comprehensive study reported to have at some time established a relationship with a woman, lasting more than one year and including sexual relations.

Although homosexual males were not adequately satisfied with their heterosexual experiences, they generally did not have negative reactions toward women or heterosexual activities. In studies measuring the change in the penis to various stimuli, it was found that homosexual men gave neutral (not negative) responses to pictures of female nudes (McConaghy, 1967; Freund, Langevin, Gibiri, and Zajac, 1973), pictures of mature vulva or breasts (Freund, Langevin, and Zajac, 1974), or auditory or written descriptions of heterosexual intercourse (Freund, Langevin, Chamberlayne, Deosoran, and Zajac, 1974). Heterosexual men, in comparison, were turned on by the pictures of female nudes, but revealed their homophobia through decreased penile volume in response to pictures of male nudes, or male homosexual activities (McConaghy, 1967; Turnbull and Brown, 1977). Thus, the evidence shows that homosexual males have no particular aversion to women or heterosexual intercourse, although heterosexual males often do have aversions to male nudes and homosexual activity.

Another popular stereotype is that homosexual men are similar to women, in appearance and/or psychological functioning. For example, Tavris (1977) reports that 70% of the *Psychology Today* readership believes that "homosexual men are not fully masculine." Studies reported by Freedman (1971) as well as Saghir and Robins (1973) suggest that only about 15% of male homosexuals appear effeminate. Effeminancy itself is highly stigmatized in the homosexual subculture. Weinberg and Williams (1974) estimate that not more than 20% of male homosexuals are suspected of being gay by the people they come in contact with, although Levitt and Klassen (1973) report that 37% of the American public believes that "it is easy to tell homosexuals by how they look."

Appearances aside, some studies indicate that homosexual men are psychologically sex typed similar to heterosexual men (e.g., Heilbrun and Thompson, 1977), whereas others find they are more androgynous or sex-role undifferentiated than heterosexuals (Spence and Helmreich, 1978). Homosexual men have not been found to be similar to women in their psychological functioning. Androgynous sex-role behavior, expressing a wider variety of interests and sensitivity than stereotypic male or female roles, is believed by many to represent a better level of psychological adjustment than more rigid sex-role-defined personalities (for example, see Kaplan and Bean, 1976). Several studies report that the psychological adjustment of homosexuals who have accepted their sexual orientation is superior in many cases to most heterosexual males in terms of openness and self-disclosure, self-actualization, lack of neurotic tendencies, and happiness or exuberance (Bell and Weinberg, 1978; Freedman, 1975; Weinberg and Williams, 1974).

Levitt and Klassen (1973) found that many people (the percentages given in parentheses below) stereotyped some professions as appropriate for homosexuals and others as inappropriate. For example, the "unmasculine" careers of artist (83%), beautician (70%), florist (86%), and musician (84%) were believed appropriate for homosexual men. But the "masculine" careers of medical doctors (66%), government officials (66%), judges (76%), teachers (76%), and ministers (75%) were considered inappropriate for homosexuals.

Gallup in 1977 found a decrease since 1970 in public opinion seeking to deny homosexuals the right to be doctors (44%), teachers (65%), or ministers (54%). Notice that the professions that people would close to homosexuals are those characteristic bastions of either male power or social influence. In the real world of work, however, there is no evidence that homosexual men tend to avoid characteristically "masculine" or professional occupations. Ironically it may be true that heterosexual men avoid certain stereotyped "homosexual" occupations, resulting in a higher proportion of homosexuals in those fields.

Many studies of homosexual males have found that they tend to be disproportionately concentrated in higher status occupations, especially those requiring professional training (Saghir and Robins, 1973; Weinberg and Williams, 1974). A study in Germany suggests that homosexual males tend to be more upwardly mobile than comparable heterosexuals (Dannecker and Reiche, 1974). This carefully conducted study of a large group of homosexuals found that the social class of the families of homosexual men was representative of the general population, whereas the social status of the homosexual men themselves was higher than would be predicted from their family backgrounds, even when the mobility trends of the entire population were taken into account. This suggests that in spite of the prejudice that homosexuals encounter in work, they are still highly successful in fields outside the low-status occupations that the general public seems to feel are appropriate for homosexuals.

Although the belief that homosexuals often molest children is widespread, I have been unable to locate any scientific research supporting it. A pedophile, an adult who seeks sex with young children, generally does not have sexual relationships with other adults and thus could not appropriately be considered either heterosexual or homosexual. Many of these individuals have sex with children of either gender. Pedophilia is a rare disturbance. Heterosexual rape, involving adolescents or adults, is much more common than homosexual rape, according to court records and sexual experience surveys. The fear that homosexuals molest chilren (or rape adolescents) is grossly exaggerated, and ultimately is based on the confusion of pedophilia with homosexuality.

There is evidence supporting the effectiveness of gay people in positively dealing with children. Gay parents tend to provide a psychologically healthy environment for their own children, who are actually no more predisposed than the children of heterosexuals to become homosexuals themselves, or to exhibit signs of psychological disturbance (Bell, 1973; Kirkpatrick, Roy, and Smith, 1976). Dorothy Riddle (1978) has done a sensitive analysis of the positive ways in which gay people relate to children, and their effectiveness as role models fostering healthy psychological development in children. Public fears of the negative effects of gay people on children tend to be totally unfounded.

A final misconception relevant to homophobia is the idea that homosexuality is "unnatural." Evidence reviewed by Ford and Beach (1951) indicates that homosexual activities occur in the majority of species of animals. Some porpoises form lifelong, monogamous, homosexual relationships. Homosexual relations are common, and are important in establishing dominance, among monkeys and various canines. Lorenz (1974) has discussed homosexual coupling among geese and other birds, concluding that it is often very adaptive.

Homosexual activities are as common or "natural" in human society as in the animal world. In 49 of the 77 societies for which we have adequate anthropological data, homosexual activities are socially sanctioned; in some situations they are virtually compulsory (Churchill, 1967). In most of Europe and many other parts of the world, homosexual relations are legal. The "unnatural" rationalization supporting homophobia receives further disconfirmation from the experiences of the 37% of the American male population who Kinsey, Pomeroy, and Martin (1948) reported had homosexual experiences to orgasm after adolescence.

Robert Brannon characterizes contemporary scientific thinking about the "naturalness" of homosexuality in this way:

> Every human society in the world today, from vast industrial nations to the smallest and simplest tribes in remote parts of the world, has some degree of homosexuality. Every society in the history of the Earth for which we have records, going back to the beginnings of recorded history, had some degree of homosexuality.
>
> Some of these societies accepted homosexuality readily while others severely condemned it, but *all* human societies have been aware of it because homosexuality has always existed wherever human beings have existed.
>
> The closest scientific analogy to homosexuality is probably the phenomenon of left-handedness, the origins and causes of which also remain unknown to science. Like homosexuality, left-handedness exists for a minority of people in every human society on record. There is no more objective reason to consider homosexuality unnatural than there is to consider left-handedness unnatural.

These facts about homosexuality suggest an interesting dilemma. Even if the stereotypes about homosexuality were accurate (I have tried to show that they are not), then why should homosexuality be threatening to males who presumably do not fit these stereotypes? If these stereotypes are not valid, then how and why are the rationalizations of homophobia maintained?

Since sexual orientation, unlike race or sex, is rarely known for certain in everyday interactions, it is relatively easy to maintain false stereotypes of the invisible minority of homosexuals. Men who appear to exhibit parts of the stereotypes are labeled homosexual, and the rest are presumed to be heterosexual. Thus, as long as most homosexuals conceal their sexual preference, homophobia is easily maintained, because heterosexuals are rarely aware of homosexuals who do not reflect their stereotypes of homosexuality.

Since stereotypes of homosexuals are not characteristic of most homosexuals, it is clear that these stereotypes are not learned from direct experiences with homosexuals. Homophobia is socially learned and transmitted. It precedes and encourages the development of stereotypes of homosexuals, in a world in which most homosexuals are not known. The presence of homophobia even among some homosexuals, whose experiences disconfirm stereotypes of homosexuality, suggests that homophobia must be derived from other sources. For homophobia to exist as a threat, it is necessary that the associated stereotypes of homosexuality be false; otherwise the taunt, *"What are you, a fag?,"* would be so patently untrue that it would not be threatening.

HOMOPHOBIA AND SOCIAL BELIEFS

Although there is no rational basis for the negative stereotypes of homosexuals, and thus homophobia, nevertheless homophobia is widespread. It is characteristic of entire societies as well as individuals. The bases for homophobic social attitudes are generally related to (1) religious beliefs that homosexuality is morally wrong, (2) scientific theories of homosexuality as an illness or deviance, and (3) social beliefs that homosexuality is damaging to society.

Religious prohibitions have sometimes been considered to be the source of homophobia (Symonds, 1896; Churchill, 1967; Weinberg, 1972; Weinberg and Williams, 1974). The United States, as a result of its puritan heritage, is generally considered one of the most homophobic (and erotophobic) cultures in the world. Although some researchers (such as Irwin and Thompson, 1977) have shown a strong relationship between church attendance, religious beliefs, and antihomosexual attitudes, religion seems unlikely to be a causal factor in homophobia for most Americans.

Science seems to have replaced religion as a source of justification of homophobia for many people. However, there is no scientific evidence that homosexuality is a mental illness. In 1973 the American Psychiatric Association removed the classification of homosexuality from its official list of mental illnesses. The belief among many psychiatrists that homosexuality is a mental illness, in spite of the lack of scientific evidence, is probably a result of their uncritical acceptance of common stereotypes of homosexuals (see Fort, Steiner, and Conrad, 1971; Davidson and Wilson, 1973), and the important fact that they frequently overgeneralize from homosexuals who were possibly mentally ill, and sought treatment, to the entire homosexual population. Nevertheless, the psychologically untenable conceptualization of homosexuality per se as a mental illness, which can be "cured," is still believed by 62% of the American adult population, according to Levitt and Klassen (1973).

Certain psychological theories, such as Freud's, posit that although homosexuality is not an illness, it is nevertheless also not "normal." Freud viewed it as a form of arrested psychosexual development, related to aspects of the parent/child relationship. Psychoanalysts such as Bieber (Bieber *et al.*, 1962) have selectively analyzed cases of homosexuals from their clinical practice that they interpret as supporting Freud's theory. Bieber's conclusions have not been supported in other studies sampling a cross section of homosexuals (Saghir and Robins, 1973).

Freud further believed that homophobia, and also paranoia, is related to "latent homosexuality," which he thought to be present in nearly everyone, since he conceived of people being born ambisexual and later developing heterosexuality. Freud's belief in latent homosexuality has received general acceptance in our culture, both among heterosexuals and homosexuals. Latency, by definition, implies the existence of no behavioral evidence. Therefore if it is possible for anyone to be a latent homosexual, in spite of the absence of sexual activity, it becomes extremely difficult for a person to prove beyond a doubt that he is not a homosexual. Thus, the concept of latent homosexuality contributes in a major way to homophobia, for it allows the possibility that anyone might be a secret homosexual even though the person does not exhibit any of the stereotypes, or behaviors, or homosexuals.

Sociological studies of homosexuality provide another popular scientific justification of homophobia, as they tend to label homosexuality as deviant since it is practiced by only a small proportion of society. However, the term deviant has taken on moral connotations not in keeping with its scientific meaning of "not majority." (See Scarpitti and McFarlane, 1975, for further discussion of this point.) When Simmons (1965) asked a cross section of Americans to list the people who they considered deviant, the most common response was homosexuals (49%). The equation of deviance with bad or immoral, although it may be indicative of popular thinking, is not inherent in sound sociological research.

Another possible source of homophobia is the belief that homosexuality is damaging to society. An Opinion Research Center poll in 1966 showed that more than 67% of the people contracted viewed homosexuality as "detrimental to society." The Harris Survey has been asking large cross sections of American households whether they feel homosexuals (and other groups) do more harm than good for the country. In 1965 homosexuals were placed third (behind Communists and atheists), with 82% of the males and 58% of the females thinking they were primarily a danger to the country. In 1973 about 50% of the respondents still felt that homosexuals did more harm than good. Levitt and Klassen (1973) similarly found that 49% of their sample agreed that "homosexuality is a social corruption which can cause the downfall of a civilization." These studies do not make it clear, however, why homosexuality is perceived as a social menace, especially by men. Legislatures in 24 states have decriminalized sexual activities commonly engaged in by consenting homosexual adults, as recommended in the model penal code of the American Bar Association. Homosexuality is also legal in most other countries, including Canada, England, Germany, and France. Thus, there is not general official support or evidence, either here or abroad, for the misconception that homosexuality is damaging to society.

Two arguments have been frequently advanced against legalization of homosexuality, in states considering legal reform. Groups such as firemen and policemen have argued that if homosexuality is legalized, homosexuals will "sexually corrupt" their fellow workers. (This is also a belief of 38% of Americans, according to Levitt and Klassen, 1973.) In reality, homosexual men have little interst in sexual relationships with unwilling heterosexual colleagues.

The most influential argument advanced against decriminalizing homosexuality is that it would allow homosexuals to "convert" or to molest children. We have discussed the distinction between pedophiles and homosexuals and the mistaken stereotype that homosexuals molest children. The children's issue is a red herring because in no state has legalization of sex acts between adults and children ever been proposed. Homosexuals are not seduced or converted into homosexuality. In a study by Lehne (1978) only 4% of the male homosexuals reported that they were somewhat seduced into their first homosexual act, and in not one case was force involved. By comparison, Sorensen

(1973) reports that the first sexual experience of 6% of adolescent girls was heterosexual rape. Lehne's study also found that most of the homosexual men reported that they were aware of their sexual orientation (because of their sexual fantasies) about four to five years before their first homosexual experience. The notion that homosexuals, legally or illegally, will seduce, rape, or convert others into homosexuality is not supported by any substantial data. There seems to be no reason to believe that homosexuals act any less morally than most Americans of different sexual orientations, or that they in fact pose a threat to socity.

HOMOPHOBIA AND THE INDIVIDUAL

Although homophobia is still widespread in American society, it is increasingly a fear of only a minority of people. Studies of homophobia in individuals suggest that it is not an isolated prejudice or fear; it is consistently related to traditional attitudes about sex roles and other social phenomena. This supports the conceptualization that homophobia functions as a motivation or threat in defining and maintaining the male role.

In an early study of homophobic attitudes, Smith (1971) found that college students who held negative attitudes toward homosexuals were significantly more status conscious, more authoritarian, and more sexually inflexible than individuals scoring low on homophobia. Later research refined Smith's methodology and analysis to show that homophobia is most closely related to traditional sex-role beliefs, and to general lack of support for equality between the sexes (see Morin and Garfinkle, 1978).

MacDonald (MacDonald, 1974, 1976; MacDonald, Huggins, Young, and Swanson, 1973; MacDonald and Games, 1974) developed effective scales of Attitudes toward Homosexuality and a Sex Role Survey. In research with several different adult populations, he demonstrated clear relationships between negative attitudes toward homosexuality and support for the double standard in sex-role behavior and conservative standards of sexual morality. Through the analysis of the semantic differential, he showed that homosexual males are devalued and viewed as less powerful due to their association with femininity, whereas lesbians are seen to be more powerful than heterosexual women because they are believed to be more masculine. Similar analyses were also reported by Storms (1978) and Shively, Rudolph, and DeCecco (1978). The public confusion between sexual orientation and sex role contributes to the devaluation of homosexuals, since they are believed to violate sex-role norms.

MacDonald's findings have been confirmed by numerous other researchers. Weinberger and Millham (1979) concluded that "homophobia is associated with valuing traditional gender distinctions," whereas Minnigerode (1976) found that nonfeminist and conservative sex attitudes were closely related to homophobia. These and other researchers found that people reacted more negatively to same-sex homosexuals, and in particular men were more negative toward male homosexuals than they were toward lesbians, and men overall were more negative in their homophobic attitudes than were women (Nutt and Sedlacek, 1974; Steffensmeier and Steffensmeier, 1974; Turnbull and Brown, 1977). Some researchers, including MacDonald, did not find such clear sex differences; Morin and Garfinkle (1978) have reviewed these studies and related the lack of findings of sex differences to the different methodologies that were used.

A constellation of traditional or sex-negative beliefs was found to be characteristic of homophobic individuals in several other studies. Morin and Wallace (1975, 1976) found that belief in a traditional family ideology was a slightly better predictor of homophobia than traditional beliefs about women; traditional religious beliefs and general sexual rigidity were also related. Negative beliefs about premarital and extramarital affairs were closely associated with homophobia in Nyberg and Alston's (1976–77) analysis of a representative sample of the American population. With a similar sample, Irwin and Thompson (1977) found traditional sex-role standards to be closely related to homophobia. Individuals with nontraditional sex-role behavior were less likely to hold negative attitudes toward homosexuality (Montgomery and Burgoon, 1977), whereas personal anxiety and guilt about sexual impulses were also characteristic of homophobic individuals (Berry and Marks, 1969; Millham, San Miguel, and Kellogg, 1976).

The general picture that emerges from this research is that individuals who are not comfortable with changes in sex roles and sexual behavior are most likely to be homophobic. Cross-cultural research has confirmed the relationship between high levels of sex-role stereotyping and antihomosexual attitudes among West Indians, Brazilians, and Canadians (Dunbar, Brown, and Amoroso, 1973a; Dunbar, Brown, and Vourinen, 1973b; Brown and Amoroso, 1975). Research with homosexuals has also shown that although they are not generally as homophobic as heterosexuals, those holding negative attitudes toward homosexuality are also likely to have traditional beliefs of sex-role stereotyping. Those homosexuals with positive attitudes and self-concepts are more likely to support equality between the sexes and have positive views on feminism (May, 1974; Lumby, 1976; McDonald and Moore, 1978; Glenn, 1978). Thus, homophobia seems to be a dynamic in maintaining traditional sex-role distrinctions, rather than an isolated belief or attitude.

The negative influence of homophobic attitudes on social behavior has been demonstrated in several clever research studies. Morin, Taylor, and Kielman (1975) showed that in an interview situation, men and women sit further away from an interviewer wearing a "Gay and Proud" button than they do from the same nonidentified interviewer; this effect is strongest for men, who sit three times as far away from a male homosexual than a lesbian. On a task arranging stick figures, Wolfgang and Wolfgang (1971) found that homosexuals were placed further away than were marijuana users, drug addicts, and the obese, and past homosexuals were viewed as even less desirable and less trustworthy than present homosexuals. Subjects, particularly men, in another experiment were found to be significantly less willing to personally interact with homosexuals than heterosexuals (Millham and Weinberger, 1977). San Miguel and Millham (1976) found that people with homophobic attitudes were significantly more aggressive toward homosexuals than heterosexuals, even when they lost money in a cooperation experiment as a result of their aggression. They were highly aggressive regardless of whether their interaction with the individual prior to labeling as a homosexual was positive, and they were most aggressive toward homosexuals perceived as otherwise similar to themselves. Clearly homophobia is not only reflected in attitudes, but influences social behavior, and thus can have a potent influence in maintaining conformity to conventional sex-role behavior.

The process of homosexual labeling also has strong influences on behavior. Men labeled as homosexuals were perceived as more feminine, emotional, submissive, unconventional, and weaker than when the same men were not labeled (Weissbach and Zagon, 1975). Karr (1978) found also that the male who identified another man as a homosexual was perceived as more masculine, sociable, and desirable, and that highly homophobic individuals would sit further away from the labeled homosexual. Karr effectively demonstrates that one's status as a man can be improved in social situations merely by the act of labeling someone else as gay. Another study found that men who were (incorrectly) labeled as a homosexual became increasingly more stereotypically masculine in their behavior (Farina, 1972); thus, the stigmitization of homosexuals can be a powerful molder of social behavior and conformity to traditional sex roles.

This growing body of research clearly supports the conceptualization that homophobia among individuals is closely related to traditional beliefs about sex roles, rather than individual prejudices against homosexuals. Furthermore, it demonstrates that these homophobic attitudes devalue in thought and action anyone who deviates from traditional sex-role stereotypes, and that this devaluation is reflected in social behavior. Homophobia reduces the willingness of others to interact with a suspected or labeled homosexual, and it may support direct aggression against the labeled deviant. Clearly homophobia is a powerful motivation for maintaining traditional sex-role behavior. MacDonald's assertions (1974, 1976) that sex-role issues are crucial for gay liberation, and that people seeking changes in traditional sex roles must be prepared to also challenge homophobia, are strongly supported by these data.

HOMOPHOBIA AND THE MALE ROLE

The male role is predominantly maintained by men themselves. Men devalue homosexuality, then use this norm of homophobia to control other men in their male roles. Since any male could potentially (latently) be a homosexual, and since there are certain social sanctions that can be directed against homosexuals, the fear of being labeled a homosexual can be used to ensure that males maintain appropriate male behavior. Homophobia is only incidentally directed against actual homosexuals—its more common use is against the heterosexual male. This explains why homophobia is closely related to beliefs about sex-role rigidity, but not to personal experience with homosexuals or to any realistic assessment of homosexuality itself. Homophobia is a threat used by societies and individuals to enforce social conformity in the male role, and maintain social control. The taunt *"What are you, a fag?"* is used in many ways to encourage certain types of male behavior and to define the limits of "acceptable" masculinity.

Since homosexuals in general constitute an invisible minority that is indistinguishable from the 49% male majority in most ways except for sexual preference, any male can be accused of being a homosexual, or "latent" homosexual. Homosexuality, therefore, can be "the crime of those to whom no crime could be imputed." There is ample historical evidence for this use of homophobia from Roman times to the present. For example, even homosexual fantasies were make illegal in Germany in 1935, and Hitler sent more than 220,000 "homosexuals" to concentration camps (Lauritsen and Thorstad, 1974). It is probable that many of these men actually were not homosexuals. But since there was no satisfactory way for individuals to prove that they were not homosexuals (and for this offense in Germany, accusation was equivalent to conviction), imputed homosexuality was the easiest way to deal with undesirable individuals. Homosexuality was likewise an accusation during the American McCarthy hearings in the 1950s when evidence of Communism was lacking. The strong association of homophobia with authoritarianism means that the potential for this exploitation of homophobia is very real during times of stress and strong-arm governments. This is no accident, but is in fact an explanation for the maintenance of homophobia. When homosexuality is stigmatized, homophobia exists as a device of social control, directed specifically against men to maintain male behavior appropriate to the social situation.

Homophobia may also be used to enforce social stereotypes of appropriate sex-role behavior for women. In general men define and enforce women's roles, and men who do not participate in this process may be suspected of being homosexuals. The direct use of homophobia to maintain female roles is necessary only in extreme cases, since male power is pervasive. But it is sometimes alleged that women who do not defer to men, or who do not marry, or who advocate changes in women's roles, are lesbians. There are, of course, other factors besides homophobia that maintain sex roles in society. I am arguing not that the elimination of homophobia will bring about a change in sex roles, but that homophobia must be eliminated before a change in sex roles can be brought about.

THE PERSONAL PAIN OF HOMOPHOBIA

The pain that *heterosexual* males bear as a consequence of homophobia is so chronic and pervasive that they probably do not notice that they are in pain, or the possible source of their discomfort. Homophobia is especially damaging to their personal relationships. Homophobia encourages men to compete. Since competition is not a drive easily turned on and off at will, there is probably a tendency for homophobic men to compete with others in their personal lives as well as at work. Only certain types of relationships are possible between competitors. Love and close friendship are difficult to maintain in a competitive environment because to expose your weaknesses and admit your problems is to be less than a man, and gives your competitor an advantage.

When men realize the intensity of their bonds with other men, homosexuality can be very threatening, and might lead to a limiting of otherwise fulfilling relationships. On the basis of a suggestion from Lester Kirkendall, I've asked men to describe their relationships with their best male friends. Many offer descriptions that are so filled with positive emotion and satisfaction that you might think they were talking about their spouses (and some will admit that they value their close male friendships more than their relationship with their wife, "although they're really different, not the same at all"). However, if I suggest that it sounds as if they are describing a person whom they love, these men become flustered. They hem and haw, and finally say, "Well, I don't think I would like to call it love, we're just best friends. I can relate to him in ways I can't with anyone else. But, I mean, we're not homosexuals or anything like that." Homosexual love, like heterosexual love, does not imply participation in sex, although many people associate love with sex. The social stigma of homosexual love denies these close relationships the validity of love in our society. This potential loss of love is a pain of homophobia that many men suffer because it delimits their relationships with other men.

Because men are unwilling to admit the presence of love in their male friendships, these relationships may be limited or kept in careful check. If male love is recognized, these men may be threatened because they may mistakenly believe this indicates they are homosexuals. Male friendships offer an excellent opportunity to explore ways in which individuals can relate as equals, the type of relationship that is increasingly demanded by liberated women. Most men have learned to relate to some other men as equals, but because they deny themselves the validity of these relationships they respond to equality with women out of fear, or frustration that they don't know how to deal with this "new" type of relationship. Loving male relationships are part of the experiences of many men that are rarely thought about or discussed because of homophobia. As a consequence, many men are unable to transfer what they have learned in these male relationships to their relationships with women. They may also deny to themselves the real importance of their relationships with other men. Male love is so pervasive that it is virtually invisible.

Homophobia also circumscribes and limits areas of male interest. Homophobic men do not participate in sissy, womanly, "homosexual" activities or interests. Maintenance of the male sex role as a result of homophobia is as limiting for men as female sex roles are for women. An appreciation of many aspects of life, although felt by most men at different times in their lives, cannot be genuinely and openly enjoyed by men who must defend their masculinity through compulsively male-stereotyped pursuits. Fear of being thought a homosexual thus keeps some men from pursuing areas of interest, or occupations, considered more appropriate for women or homosexuals.

The open expression of emotion and affection by men is limited by homophobia. Only athletes and women are allowed to touch and hug each other in our culture; athletes are allowed this only because presumably their masculinity is beyond doubt. But in growing up to become men in our culture, we learned that such contact with men was no longer permissible, that only homosexuals enjoy touching other men, or that touching is only a prelude to sex. In a similar way men learn to curb many of their emotions. They learn not to react emotionally to situations in which, although they may feel the emotion, it would be unmasculine to express it. Once men have learned not to express some of their emotions, they may find it difficult to react any other way, and may even stop feeling these emotions. Men are openly allowed to express anger and hostility, but not sensitivity and sympathy. The expression of more tender emotions among men is thought to be characteristic only of homosexuals.

Is a society without homophobia a fairy tale, or will it become a reality? Only when men begin to make a serious attempt to deal with their prejudice against homosexuality can we look forward to living in a world that is not stratified by rigid sex-role distinctions.

REFERENCES

Alston, J. P. "Attitudes toward extramarital and homosexual relations." *Journal of the Scientific Study of Religion*, 1974, *13*, 479–481.

Bell, A. P. "Homosexualities: Their range and character," In J. K. Cole & R. Dienstbier (Eds.), *Nebraska Symposium on Motivation*, Vol. 21. Lincoln: University of Nebraska Press, 1973.

Bell, A. P., & M. Weinberg. *Homosexualities: A Study of Human Diversity*. New York: Simon & Schuster, 1978.

Berry, D. F., & F. Marks."Antihomosexual prejudice as a function of attitudes toward own sexuality." *Proceedings of the 77th Annual Convention of the American Psychological Association*, 1969, *4*, 573–574.

Bieber, I. *et. al. Homosexuality: A Psychoanalytic Study of Male Homosexuals*. New York: Basic Books, 1962.

Brown, M., & D. Amoroso. "Attitudes toward homosexuality among West Indian male and female college students." *Journal of Social Psychology*, 1975, *97*, 163–168.

Churchill, W. *Homosexual Behavior Among Males: A Cross-Cultural and Cross Species Investigation*. Englewood Cliffs, N.J.: Prentice-Hall, 1967.

Dannecker, M., & R. Reiche. *Ger gewoehnliche Homosexuelle*.Frankfurt am Main, Germany: S. Fischer, 1974.

Davidson, G., & T. Wilson. "Attitudes of behavior therapists toward homosexuality." *Behavior Therapy*. 1973, *4*(5), 686–696.

Dunbar, J., M. Brown, & D. Amoroso, "Some correlates of attitudes toward homosexuality." *Journal of Social Psychology*, 1973, *89*, 271–279. (a)

Dunbar, J., M. Brown, & S. Vourinen. "Attitudes toward homosexuality among Brazilian and Canadian college students." *Journal of Social Psychology*, 1973, *90*, 173–183. (b)

Farina, A. "Stigmas potent behavior molders." *Behavior Today*, 1972, *2*, 25.

Ford, C., & F. Beach. *Patterns of Sexual Behavior*, New York: Harper & Row, 1951.

Fort, J., C. Steiner, & F. Conrad. "Attitudes of mental health professionals toward homosexuality and its treatment." *Psychological Reports*, 1971, *29*, 347–350.

Freedman, M. *Homosexuality and Psychological Functioning*. Belmont, Ca.: Brooks/Cole, 1971.

Freedman, M. "Homosexuals may be healthier than straights." *Psychology Today*, 1975, *1*(10), 28–32.

Freund, K., R. Langevin, R. Chamberlayne, A. Deosoran, & Y. Zajac. "The phobic theory of male homosexuality." *Archives of General Psychiatry*, 1974, *31*, 495–499.

Freund, K., R. Langevin, S. Gibiri, & Y. Zajac. "Heterosexual aversion in homosexual males." *British Journal of Psychiatry*, 1973, *122*, 163–169.

Freund, K., R. Langevin, & Y. Zajac. "Heterosexual aversion in homosexual males: A second experiment." *British Journal of Psychiatry*, 1974, *125*, 177–180.

Gallup, G. "Gallup poll on gay rights: Approval with reservations." *San Francisco Chronicle*, July 18, 1977, 1, 18.

Gallup, G. "Gallop poll on the attitudes homosexuals face today." *San Francisco Chronicle*, July 20, 1977, 4.

Glenn, G. L. "Attitudes toward homosexuality and sex roles among homosexual men." Unpublished M. A. Thesis: Antioch University/Maryland, 1978.

Heilbrun, A. B., & N. L. Thompson. "Sex-role identity and male and female homosexuality." *Sex Roles*, 1977, *3*, 65–79.

Irwin, P., & N. L. Thompson. "Acceptance of the rights of homosexuals: A social profile." *Journal of Homosexuality*, 1977, *3*, 107–121.

Kaplan, A. G., & J. P. Bean (Eds.). *Beyond Sex-Role Stereotypes: Readings toward a Psychology of Androgyny*. Boston: Little, Brown, 1976.

Karr, R. "Homosexual labeling and the male role." *Journal of Social Issues*, 1978, *34*(3), 73–84.

Kinsey, A., W. Pomeroy, & C. Martin. *Sexual Behavior in the Human Male*. Philadelphia: Saunders, 1948.

Kirkpatrick, M., R. Roy, & K. Smith. "A new look at lesbian mothers." *Human Behavior*, August 1976, 60–61.

Langevin, R., A. Stanford, & R. Block. "The effect of relaxation instructions on erotic arousal in homosexual and heterosexual males." *Behavior Therapy*, 1975, *6*, 453–458.

Lauritsen, J., & D. Thorstad. *The Early Homosexual Rights Movement* (1864–1935). New York: Times Change Press, 1974.

Lehne, G. "Gay male fantasies and realities." *Journal of Social Issues*, 1978, *34*(3), 28–37.

Levitt, E., & A. Klassen. "Public attitudes toward sexual behavior: The latest investigation of the Institute for Sex Research." Paper presented at the annual convention of the American Orthopsychiatric Association, 1973.

Levitt, E., & A. Klassen. "Public attitudes toward homosexuality: Part of the 1970 National Survey by the Institute for Sex Research." *Journal of Homosexuality*, 1974, *1*, 29–43.

Lorenz, K. Interviewed by R. Evans in *Psychology Today*, November 1974, 82–93.

Lumby, M. E. "Homophobia: The quest for a valid scale." *Journal of Homosexuality*, 1976, *2*, 39–47.

MacDonald, A. "The importance of sex role to gay liberation." *Homosexual Counselling Journal*, 1974, *1*, 169–180.

MacDonald, A. "Homophobia: Its roots and meanings." *Homosexual Counselling Journal*, 1976, *3*, 23–33.

MacDonald, A., & R. Games. "Some characteristics of those who hold positive and negative attitudes toward homosexuals." *Journal of Homosexuality*, 1974, *1*, 9–27.

MacDonald, A., J. Huggins, S. Young, & R. Swanson. "Attitudes toward homosexuality: Preservation of sex morality or the double standard?" *Journal of Counselling and Clinical Psychology*, 1973, *40*, 161. Extended report available from the author (1972).

May, E. P. "Counselors', psychologists', and homosexuals' philosophies of human nature and attitudes toward homosexual behavior." *Homosexual Counselling Journal*, 1974, *1*, 3–25.

McConaghy, N. "Penile volume changes to moving pictures of male and female nudes in heterosexual and homosexual males." *Behavior Research and Therapy*, 1967, *5*, 43–48.

McDonald, G., & R. Moore. "Sex-role self-concepts of homosexual men and their attitudes toward both women and male homosexuality." *Journal of Homosexuality*, 1978, *4*, 3–14.

Millham, J., C. San Miguel, & R. Kellogg. "A factor analytic conceptualization of attitudes toward male and female homosexuals." *Journal of Homosexuality*, 1976, *2*, 3–10.

Millham, J., & L. Weinberger. "Sexual preference, sex role appropriateness and restriction of social access." *Journal of Homosexuality*, 1972, *2*, 343–357.

Minnigerode, F. "Attitudes toward homosexuality: Feminist attitudes and social conservation." *Sex Roles*, 1976, *2*, 347–352.

Montgomery, C., & M. Burgoon. "An experimental study of the interactive effects of sex and androgyny on attitude change." *Communication Monographs*, 1977, *44*, 130–135.

Morin, S., & E. Garfinkle. "Male homophobia." *Journal of Social Issues*, 1978, *34*, 29–47.

Morin, S., K. Taylor, & S. Kielman. "Gay is beautiful at a distance." Paper presented at the meeting of the American Psychological Association, Chicago, August 1975.

Morin, S., & S. Wallace. "Religiosity, sexism, and attitudes toward homosexuality." Paper presented at the meeting of the California State Psychological Association, March 1975.

Morin, S., & S. Wallace. "Traditional values, sex-role stereotyping, and attitudes toward homosexuality." Paper presented at the meeting of the Western Psychological Association, Los Angeles, April 1976.

Nutt, R., & W. Sedlacek. "Freshman sexual attitudes and behaviors." *Journal of College Student Personnel*, 1974, *15*, 346–351.

Nyberg, K., & J. Alston. "Analysis of public attitudes toward homosexual behavior." *Journal of Homosexuality*, 1976–77, *2*, 99–107.

Riddle, D. "Relating to children: Gays as role models." *Journal of Social Issues*, 1978, *34*, 38–58.

Rooney, E., & D. Gibbons. "Social reactions to crimes without victims." *Social Problems*, 1966, *13*, 400–410.

Saghir, M., & E. Robins. *Male and Female Homosexuality: A Comprehensive Investigation*. Baltimore: Williams & Wilkins, 1973.

San Miguel, C., & J. Millham. "The role of cognitive and situational variables in aggression toward homosexuals." *Journal of Homosexuality*, 1976, *2*, 11–27.

Scarpitti, F., & P. McFarlane (Eds.). *Deviance: Action, Reaction, Interaction.* Reading, Mass.: Addison-Wesley, 1975.

Shively, M., J. Rudolph, & J. DeCecco. "The identification of the social sex-role stereotypes." *Journal of Homosexuality*, 1978, *3*, 225–234.

Simmons, J. "Public stereotypes of deviants." *Social Problems*, 1965, *13*, 223–232.

Smith, K. "Homophobia: A tentative personality profile." *Psychological Reports*, 1971, *29*, 1091–1094.

Sorensen, R. *Adolescent Sexuality in Contemporary America.* New York: World, 1973.

Spence, J., & R. Helmreich. *Masculinity & Feminity.* Austin, Tx.: University of Texas Press, 1978.

Steffensmeier, D., & R. Steffensmeier. "Sex differences in reactions to homosexuals: Research continuities and further developments." *The Journal of Sex Research*, 1974, *10*, 52–67.

Storms, M. "Attitudes toward homosexuality and feminity in men." *Journal of Homosexuality*, 1978, *3*, 257–263.

Symonds, J. *A Problem in Modern Ethics*, London: 1896.

Tavris, C. "Men and women report their views on masculinity." *Psychology Today*, January, 1977, 35.

Turnbull, D., & M. Brown. "Attitudes toward homosexuality and male and female reactions to homosexual slides." *Canadian Journal of Behavioural Science*, 1977, *9*, 68–80.

Weinberg, G. *Society and the Healthy Homosexual.* New York: Doubleday, 1972.

Weinberg, M., & C. Williams. *Male Homosexuals.* New York: Oxford University Press, 1974.

Weinberger, L., & J. Millham. "Attitudinal homophobia and support of traditional sex roles." *Journal of Homosexuality*, 1979, *4*, 237–246.

Weissbach, T., & G. Zagon. "The effect of deviant group membership upon impressions of personality." *Journal of Social Psychology*, 1975, *95*, 263–266.

Wolfgang, A., & J. Wolfgang. "Exploration of attitudes via physical interpersonal distance toward the obese, drug users, homosexuals, police and other marginal figures." *Journal of Clinical Psychology*, 1971, *27*, 510–512.

Peter M. Nardi

THE POLITICS OF GAY MEN'S FRIENDSHIPS

Towards the end of Wendy Wasserstein's Pulitzer Prize play, *The Heidi Chronicles*, a gay character, Peter Patrone, explains to Heidi why he has been so upset over all the funerals he has attended recently: "A person has so many close friends. And in our lives, our friends are our families" (Wasserstein, 1990: 238). In his collection of stories, *Buddies*, Ethan Mordden (1986: 175) observes: "What unites us, all of us, surely, is brotherhood, a sense that our friendships are historic, designed to hold Stonewall together. . . . It is friendship that sustained us, supported out survival." These statements succinctly summarize an important dimension about gay men's friendships: Not

Peter Nardi is Professor of Sociology at Pitzer College, one of the Claremont Colleges, located near Los Angeles. He has edited a book on men's friendships for Sage and has published articles on children of alcoholics, AIDS, hate crime violence, and the world of magic and magicians.

only are friends a form of family for gay men and lesbians, but gay friendships are also a powerful political force.

Mordden's notion of "friends is survival" has a political dimension that becomes all the more salient in contemporary society where the political, legal, religious, economic, and health concerns of gay people are routinely threatened by the social order. In part, gay friendship can be seen as a political statement, since at the core of the concept of friendship is the idea of "being oneself" in a cultural context that may not approve of that self. For many people, the need to belong with others in dissent and out of the mainstream is central to the maintenance of self and identity (Rubin, 1986). The friendships formed by a shared marginal identity, thus, take on powerful political dimensions as they organize around a stigmatized status to confront the dominant culture in solidarity. Jerome (1984: 698) believes that friendships have such economic and political implications, since friendship is best defined as "the cement which binds together people with interests to conserve."

Suttles (1970: 116) argues that

> The very basic assumption friends must make about one another is that each is going beyond a mere presentation of self in compliance with "social dictates." Inevitably, this makes friendship a somewhat deviant relationship because the surest test of personal disclosure is a violation of the rules of public propriety.

Friendship, according to Suttles (1970), has its own internal order, albeit maintained by the cultural images and situational elements that structure the definitions of friendship. In friendship, people can depart from the routine and display a portion of the self not affected by social control. That is, friendships allow people to go beyond the basic structures of their cultural institutions into an involuntary and uncontrollable exposure of self—to deviate from public propriety (Suttles, 1970).

Little (1989) similarly argues that friendship is an escape from the rules and pieties of social life. It's about identity: who one is rather than one's roles and statuses. And the idealism of friendship "lies in its detachment from these [roles and statuses], its creative and spiritual transcendence, its fundamental skepticism as a platform from which to survey the givens of society and culture" (Little, 1989: 145). For gay men, these descriptions illustrate the political meaning friendship can have in their lives and their society.

The political dimension of friendship is summed up best by Little (1989; 154–155):

> the larger formations of social life—kinship, the law, the economy— must be different where there is, in addition to solidarity and dutiful role-performance, a willingness and capacity for friendship's surprising one-to-one relations, and this difference may be enough to transform social and political life. . . . Perhaps, finally, it is true that progress in democracy depends on a new generation that will increasingly locate itself in identity-shaping, social, yet personally liberating, friendships.

The traditional, nuclear family has been the dominant model for political relations and has structured much of the legal and social norms of our culture. People have often been judged by their family ties and history. But as the family becomes transformed into other arrangements, so do the political and social institutions of society. For example, the emerging concept of "domestic partnerships" has affected a variety of organizations, including insurance companies, city governments, private industry, and religious institutions (Task Force on Family Diversity Final Report, 1988).

For many gay people, the "friends as family" model is a political statement, going beyond the practicality of developing a surrogate family in times of needed social support. It is also a way of refocusing the economic and political agenda to include nontraditional family structures composed of both romantic and nonromantic nonkin relationships.

In part, this has happened by framing the discussions in terms of gender roles. The women's movement and the emerging men's movement have highlighted the negative political implications of defining gender roles according to traditional cultural norms or limiting them to biological realities. The gay movement, in turn, has often been one source for redefining traditional gender roles and sexuality. So, for example, when gay men exhibit more disclosing and emotional interactions with other men, it demonstrates the limitations of male gender roles typically enacted among many heterosexual male friends. By calling attention to the impact of homophobia on heterosexual men's lives, gay men's friendships illustrate the potentiality for expressive intimacy among all men.

Thus, the assumptions that biology and/or socialization have inevitably constrained men from having the kinds of relationships and intimacies women often typically have can be called into question. This questioning of the dominant construction of gender roles is in itself a sociopolitical act with major implications on the legal, religious, and economic order.

White (1983: 16) also sees how gay people's lives can lead to new modes of behavior in the society at large:

> In the case of gays, our childlessness, our minimal responsibilities, the fact that our unions are not consecrated, even our very retreat into gay ghettos for protection and freedom: all of these objective conditions have fostered a style in which we may be exploring, even in spite of our conscious intentions, things as they will someday be for the heterosexual majority. In that world (as in the gay world already), love will be built on esteem rather than passion or convention, sex will be more playful or fantastic or artistic than marital—and friendship will be elevated into the supreme consolation for this continuing tragedy, human existence.

If, as White and others have argued, gay culture in the post-Stonewall, sexual liberation years of the 1970s was characterized by a continuous fluidity between what constituted a friend, a sexual partner, and a lover, then we need to acknowledge the AIDS decade of the 1980s as a source for restructuring of gay culture and the reorganization of sexuality and friendship. If indeed gay people (and men in particular) have focused attention on developing monogamous sexual partnerships, what then becomes the role of sexuality in the initiation and development of casual or close friendships? Clearly, gay culture is not a static phenomenon, unaffected by the larger social order. Certainly, as the moral order in the AIDS years encourages the re-establishment of more traditional relationships, the implications for the ways sexuality and friendships are organized similarly change.

Friends become more important as primary sources of social and emotional support when illness strikes; friendship becomes institutionally organized as "brunch buddies" dating services or "AIDS buddies" assistance groups; and self-help groups emerge centering on how to make and keep new friends without having "compulsive sex." While AIDS may have transformed some of the meanings and role of friendships in gay men's lives from the politicalization of sexuality and friendship during the post-Stonewall 1970s, the newer meanings of gay friendships, in turn, may be having some effect on the culture's definitions of friendships.

Interestingly, the mythical images of friendships were historically more male-dominated: bravery, loyalty, duty, and herosim (see Sapadin, 1988). This explained why women were typically assumed incapable of having true friendships. But today, the images of true friendship are often expressed in terms of women's traits: intimacy, trust, caring, and nurturing, thereby excluding the more traditional men from true friendship. However, gay men appear to be at the forefront of establishing the possibility of men overcoming their male socialization stereotypes and restructuring their friendships in terms of the more contemporary (i.e., "female") attributes of emotional intimacy.

To do this at a wider cultural level involves major sociopolitical shifts in how men's roles are structured and organized. Friendships between men in terms of intimacy and emotional support inevitably introduce questions about homosexuality. As Rubin (1985: 103) found in her interviews with men: "The association of friendship with homosexuality is so common among men." For women, there is a much longer history of close connections with other women, so that the separation of the emotional from the erotic is more easily made.

Lehne (1989) has argued that homphobia has limited the discussion of loving male relationships and has led to the denial by men of the real importance of their friendships with other men. In addition, "the open expression of emotion and affection by men is limited by homophobia. . . . The expression of more tender emotions among men is thought to be characteristic only of homosexuals" (Lehne, 1989: 426). So men are raised in a culture with a mixed message: strive for healthy, emotionally intimate friendships, but if you appear to intimate with another man you might be negatively labelled homosexual.

This certainly wasn't always the case. As a good illustration of the social construction of masculinity, friendship, and sexuality, one need only look to the changing definitions and concepts surrounding same-sex friendship during the nineteenth century (see Rotundo, 1989; Smith-Rosenberg, 1975). Romantic friendships could be erotic but not sexual, since sex was linked to reproduction. Because reproduction was not possible between two women or two men, the close relationship was not interpreted as being a sexual one:

> Until the 1880s, most romantic friendships were thought to be devoid of sexual content. Thus a woman or man could write of affectionate desire for a loved one of the same gender without causing an eyebrow to be raised (D'Emilio and Freedman, 988: 121).

However, as same-sex relationships became medicalized and stigmatized in the late 19th century, "the labels 'congenital inversion' and 'perversion' were applied not only to male sexual acts, but to sexual or romantic unions between women, as well as those between men" (D'Emilio and Freedman, 1988: 122). Thus, the twentieth century is an anomaly in its promotion of female equality, the encouragement of male-female friendships, and its suspicion of intense emotional friendships between men (Richards, 1987). Yet, in Ancient Greece and the medieval days of chivalry, comradeship, virtue, patriotism, and heroism were all associated with close male friendship. Manly love, as it was often called, was a central part of the definition of manliness (Richards, 1987).

It is through the contemporary gay, women's, and men's movements that these twentieth century constructions of gender are being questioned. And at the core is the association of close male friendships with negative images of homosexuality. Thus, how gay men structure their emotional lives and friendships can affect the social and emotional lives of all men and women. This is the political power and potential of gay friendships.

REFERENCES

D'Emilio, John and Freedman, Estelle. (1988). *Intimate Matters: A History of Sexuality in America*. New York: Harper & Row.

Jerome, Dorothy. (1984). Good company: The sociological implications of friendship. *Sociological Review*, 32(4), 696–718.

Lehne, Gregory. (1989 [1980]). Homophobia among men: Supporting and defining the male role. In M. Kimmel and M. Messner (Eds.), *Men's Lives* (pp. 416–429). New York: Macmillan.

Little, Graham. (1989). Freud, friendship, and politics. In R. Porter and S. Tomaselli (Eds.), *The Dialectics of Friendship* (pp. 143–158). London: Routledge.

Mordden, Ethan. (1986). *Buddies*. New York: St. Martin's Press.

Richards, Jeffrey. (1987). "Passing the love of women": Manly love and Victorian society. In J. A. Mangan and J. Walvin (Eds.), *Manliness and Morality: Middle-Class Masculinity in Britain and America (1800-1940)* (pp. 92–122). Manchester, England: Manchester University Press.

Rotundo, Anthony. (1989). Romantic friendships: Male intimacy and middle-class youth in the northern United States, 1800–1900. *Journal of Social History*, 23(1), 1–25.

Rubin, Lillian. (1985). *Just Friends: The Role of Friendship in Our Lives*. New York: Harper & Row.

Sapadin, Linda. (1988). Friendship and gender: Perspectives of professional men and women. *Journal of Social and Personal Relationships*, 5(4), 387–403.

Smith-Rosenberg, Carroll. (1975). The female world of love and ritual: Relations between women in nineteenth-century America. *Signs*, 1(1): 1–29.

Suttles, Gerald. (1970). Friendship as a social institution. In G. McCall, M. McCall, N. Denzin, G. Suttles, and S. Kurth, *Social Relationships* (pp. 95–135). Chicago: Aldine.

Task Force on Family Diversity. (1988). *Strengthening Families: A Model for Community Action*. City of Los Angeles.

Wasserstein, Wendy. (1990) *The Heidi Chronicles*. San Diego: Harcourt, Brace, Jovanovich.

White, Edmund. (1983). Paradise found: Gay men have discovered that there is friendship after sex. *Mother Jones*, June, 10–16.

Martin Simmons

THE TRUTH ABOUT MALE FRIENDSHIPS

If a dude buys me a drink, drops the winning two points through the hoop or comes stepping out with a fine woman, I might say, "My man! Slap me five!" Twenty or 30 minutes later, I might lay another "my man" on someone else. It's not that the term "my man" used in these contexts doesn't mean anything. It's just that it doesn't mean anything much. It's transitory, and has more to do with the style and stance that Black men adopt with each other during brief encounters than with the real substance of their relationships.

But when I say "My *main* man," I'm talking about my stone ace boon coon. My running cut buddy. My partner. Number One. Him and me against the world. And that's different. It is not temporary or transitory. It's been long-term, and frankly, I hope it will be forever. Or at least until one of us is dropped into a hole in the ground.

For Black men in this society, the world is a hostile, dangerous place—a jungle. It is uncompromising territory where a man is either the hunter or the hunted; he either seizes the power or loses it; he either rises to the never-ending tests of his manhood or falls a victim. Since Black men's relationship to power and sense of manhood has always been challenged in this land, we must always be on the move, always wary, always careful, always thinking and always on guard. We must walk that fine line between paranoia and prudence. It helps if we have a main man to walk it with. In fact, I think it's critical.

Without that main partner who helps you keep sight of the line, you can easily fall prey to the hunter. Without that main man to walk with, relate to, bounce thoughts off, you can easily lose sight of the real meaning of power and manhood. To walk alone means that it is always necessary to present a "front," an image, a projection of bravado that ensures protection.

Every Black man knows such bravado is sometimes a must. In public he knows he is supposed to be a bad dude. He is expected to brag and strut and lie. To do otherwise is to be considered less than a man. But in his private moments, those honest times when he faces only himself, he is—regardless of his true strength—likely to be haunted by insecurities, fears, doubts and an overwhelming sense of powerlessness. He can lie to the world, but never to the image in the mirror.

Of course, most men travel through life in some sort of partnership with women. It is relatively easy for a man to find a woman to whom he can relate. It seems to me, though, that if he is a thinking man, he knows the areas of his psyche that he can and cannot allow a woman access to. He can rarely let her know that he can or wants to be violent, that he is sometimes so angry with a world that would cheat him of his manhood that he often wants to kill or explode, because he knows that her response would be maternal and protective. She would want him to suppress those feelings lest they being him harm. Furthermore, if they've been to bed a couple of times, he knows that he has a claim on her feelings, and he knows the things that she would be sympathetic to. He can therefore let her see that he is gentle, tender or sometimes even afraid.

But just let him go bopping down to the corner talking about how gentle or tender he is. Or let him try to tell the guys over a beer that he doesn't control his woman, that he doesn't sock it to her because he can't or doesn't want to. He'd be laughed out of the bar, and branded a punk, a chump, a fool—maybe even a faggot. In front of the boys, he'd better have made it with every woman he has ever said he wanted. He'd better be rough, tough, don't take no stuff. Out in the jungle, he'd better be a lion.

It's hard. It ain't funny. The image of the rootin'-tootin', six-shooting' Black man willing to fight and die because someone stepped in front of him in the supermarket line, thereby challenging his manhood, takes a lot of energy to keep up. At some point he *must* relax—totally, completely and absolutely.

So a man is lucky to find another man in whose presence he does not have to brag and strut and lie. Extremely lucky to find a cut buddy, an ace, a main man to fall back on. I've been that lucky. I have a main man.

Any man who has roamed the jungle alone—and I have—knows that the slightest hill can be as steep and slippery as Mt. Everest in January. But I also know that a good friend is another set of hands to help you make the climb. My ace not only has his own pick and climbing boots but has an extra set for me. He's got my back, and if necessary, I can get a lift on his shoulders. If I slip, I know he'll grab me. If I fall, he'll catch me. All he expects is that I do the same for him.

This is not to say that women don't often give such support to men. But I know the truth is that whatever the relationship a man has with a woman, rarely will he tell her everything, or be too weak in her presence, because he knows that she, like everyone else, ultimately expects him to be a lion. Besides, other men expect a man to exercise control over a woman, and to reveal weakness to her means relinquishing a measure of control. Most important, however, a man knows that women do not have to move through the jungle in quite the same way he does. Though as Black people we are up against the same forces, those forces strike men and women in entirely different ways—with entirely different results.

Black men do not become cut buddies unless they have in common a basic and instinctive understanding of each other's psychological and emotional needs, as well as the forces they must confront, and share a willingness to meet those needs and forces. This instinctive understanding is built on shared experiences, which is why so many main-man partnerships go back to grade school or high school or the military. Although my partner and I spent our youths in widely separated places and environments, we are both struggling artists, we both know that it is the loneliest business in the world.

More important, my partner and I know the common forces that we as Black men are up against as we move to forge our definitions of what it means to be men. We know that no one—not friends, not family, not the wife who may want you to get a nine to five and a steady income—no one, except your main man, believes in your worth as a writer until it is demonstated by some commercial standard of success; your name on a book jacket, your byline appearing 40 times.

Try to build a dream or realize a vision and the world won't buy in until the elevator reaches the fifth floor. But your main man buys in at the basement. He believes in you because he knows you. He believes in you because to believe in you is to believe in himself and the power of every Black man to make his dream come true, his own way in the world.

Since meeting seven years ago, my main man and I have faced crises together, fought battles side by side and back to back, cruised the jungle as twin panthers each looking out for predators who would endanger us.

For a Black man in particular, to roam the jungle alone—without the backup of a main man—is to be without perspective or protection. It means being afraid, and feeling that you are the only one who knows fear. It means thinking that no one else thinks like you do, and wondering if you should trust your own thoughts. It means not knowing that other men are sometimes gentle, sometimes weak, sometimes crazy—just as you sometimes are. It means you have no positive way to measure manhood or maleness, so what gets played out in behavior are false and often negative definitions of maleness: brutality, cold-bloodedness, hardheartedness. In short, being a "bad dude," being the kind of man you think you're supposed to be, which, in a very real way, can mean being insane.

But with a main man, an ace, you have not only another set of hands but another set of eyes—eyes that see you and accept you as you are and reflect what he is too. My main man came of age at about the same time I did. We see the same world, which means we can reinforce each other's position in it. We share the same attitude toward life in all important respects. We walk in the same direction and we walk side by side. We understand each other, advise each other and keep each other on track. Together we are more than when we are apart, because our strengths are complementary and our weaknesses compensatory.

I can confide in my ace, share secrets and real feelings and never fear that he'll think I'm a fool, or a clown or a coward—or anything less than a man. As I said before, I know I'm lucky because so much of what being a man is supposed to mean has to do with being a "strong, silent type" who keeps his emotions in check and his feelings locked away. Deep emotional friendships among men are not usually encouraged. I know, too, that truly trusting relationships between any two people are not common because trust, faith and honesty with another person have somehow become equated with weakness.

As for me, I know that having this running buddy has made me stronger. I respect the brother, I trust the brother. I love the brother. He is my other ear, eye and mind. His opinions matter as much to me as my own. They take on equal weight, they get equal consideration. In this jungle of a world, he halves my burdens and doubles my joys.

Unfortunately, there are women who feel threatened by the relationship my partner and I have. Though they may have girlfriends, they somehow don't grasp the need for men to run together or hand together. The fact is, men need the company of each other as much as women need the company of other women or men need the company of women. Men need to shoot the breeze, talk shit, chase women and run the jungle together. More to the point, Black men need to reaffirm their worth in this place that is constantly denying that worth—and such affirmation can only come from other Black men.

When I tell my partner that during a job interview, the white boy sitting behind the desk said that my résumé would threaten most of the white males already in the company and that therefore he wouldn't hire me, I know that my main man understood the insidiousness of that in a way that my woman never could. What Black men ultimately understand with each other is that we "are all in this together." Women provide sympathy. Most men, I think, neither need or want sympathy from other men. What they need and get in good male relationships is *empathy*. Black men's thoughts and conversations are colored by the fact that society treats them always as political entities. Black men who come together, therefore, have a "you and me against the world" attitude. It seems to me that women are more insular and home-centered, and their concerns tend to be for those things they label "security" and "stability." Their attitude when they are with their men is "you and me. I fixed you a hot meal. Don't worry about the world tonight."

A woman who truly loved me and had my interests at heart would understand that her view of the world and the world's view of her are unlike those of the man in her life. She would realize that in many ways there can be no emphathetic understanding between us. She would, therefore, not try to come between me and my main man. She would understand the differences between my relationship with her and with my partner, and recognize that both are equally important and equally necessary. And, if she could be honest with herself, she would know that both are limited: neither she nor he can be my whole world.

My cut buddy, although he will give me a blunt and honest opinion of the woman I'm dealing with, would not attempt to come between her and me because he knows she fulfills needs he can't. He knows that what I seek, what he seeks and what most men seek from women is the fulfillment of relatively mundane, though absolutely critical, needs: sex, physical warmth and touching, love, care for their health, home and children.

I think that men who cannot or have not established deep friendships with other men—men who have no main man or say that their best friends are their wives or their women—are men without strong psychological support, without another worldly male view, without a truly empathetic understanding of the social and political forces at work in the jungle, so they are often too paranoid, prudent or alone to challenge the world.

"Him and me against the world" may sound like a serious phrase for a serious world, but it's not always so heavy. There are times when I'm hanging with my ace and the world is lightweight. We can talk and laugh and joke and run a smooth, sweet double-game on any and everybody. Fortunately, we are as different physically as we are alike spiritually. This physical difference means that women who are attracted or attractive to me are seldom attracted or attractive to him and vice versa. Therefore, we never have to fight over women.

Which is not to say that we don't compete. Like most men, we are both very competitive—and we both play to win. We just confine our competition to the game board or to those situations in which competition will benefit both of us by sharpening and honing our skills, our perspective and our ability to do battle with the world at large.

When we do compete, the winner gloats and crows and laughs in the loser's face. God knows, we're both poor winners. But we aren't poor losers because, win or lose against each other, I know in the final go-down that I can count on him. My main man. My running partner. My ace. Me and him against the world.

Kathryn Ann Farr

DOMINANCE BONDING THROUGH THE GOOD OLD BOYS SOCIABILITY GROUP

> Boyhood is remembered as a golden age of freedom; when time was long, nights were warm, and the world, though infinitely detailed, was manageable. In the challenge to authority, the 'mischief' and the 'trouble,' there was a harmony between personal identity and the collective 'spirit' of the group. (Tolson, 1977, p. 41)

For the youthful insider, boyhood affords marvelous opportunities to establish a sense of masculine superiority through the power of collective alliance. Bolstered by a set of activities organized for them (and later by them) around sport and play, boys gather in exclusionary groups to learn and celebrate the masculinity of camaraderie, competition, aggressiveness, and independence. Within the confines of the male peer group, young boys develop a repertoire of behaviors and attitudes which define masculinity and affirm its superiority. Included in this repertoire is a masculine language, which "prescribes certain topics (sports, machines, competitions) and certain ways of speaking (jokes, banter, and bravado)" (Tolson, 1977, p. 32). This early male experience, David and Brannon further suggest, is celebrated through a "glamorous idealizing of reckless adventure, daring exploits, and bold excesses of all kinds" (1976, p. 30).

Young girls quickly recognize the value placed on, as well as their exclusion from, these boys' activities (see Connor & Serbin, 1978; Fasteau, 1974; Phillips, 1982; Tyron, 1980). According to Comer, "it is always the boys who represents the exciting and the desirable and to experience it, the girl has to identify with the male" (1974, p. 13). Yet while the girl may intermittently join the company of boys, she must remain on the periphery of the boys' group, often simply serving as a source of masculinity validation through her roles as observer and admirer (Franklin, 1984). With its emphasis on heterosexual and athletic prowess, the adolescent male peer group also excludes some males. It serves, then, as a general stratification mechanism by (a) excluding females and nonmasculine males and (b) fostering competition for status among masculine males. The meaning of these early experiences is not lost on adult men who have benefited from them during their childhood and adolescent years. In fact, I would suggest, masculine identity and male privilege are perpetuated in adulthood through group processes that mirror the early experiences of boys in groups.

The focus of the present study was on one such group, organized by and for high-status adult males (and having its origin in their high-school and college friendships) in accordance with principles of masculine sociability. It is my contention that this group form—hereafter referred to as the Good Old Boys Sociability (GOBS) group—functions to perpetuate masculine identity and male privilege through what I have chosen to refer to as *dominance bonding*, i.e.,

Reprinted from *Sex Roles*, Vol. 18, Nos. 5/6, 1988. © Plenum Publishing Corporation.

a process of collective alliance through which the group and its members affirm and reaffirm their superiority.

METHODOLOGY

My exposure to and observations of GOBS began some 25 years ago, when, as a young adult female, I began to strive for inclusion in activities planned and engaged in by my male friends. Unsure of the requirements for inclusion, I opted for imitative strategies, e.g., developing skills in certain games and sports, becoming knowledgeable about topics on which male conversations centered, and conforming to expectations regarding "having a good time." In spite of my efforts to "join in," I realized that I was never more than a peripheral member of the group; there were barriers to full inclusion that I neither understood nor was able to overcome. Indeed, some events were simply off-limits to girlfriends and wives.

As my professional interest in gender phenomena grew, my personal experiences with male groups seemed to present an opportunity for empirical exploration. Using as my sample two groups (with whose members I retained close personal ties), I undertook and completed (after two years of data collection) an ethnographic study of the structure, processes, and functions of what I have since labeled the GOBS group.

I did begin the study with one major assumption, i.e., that the male social groups to which I personally had been exposed reflected and reinforced perceptions of the superiority of masculine play. However, recognizing that my assumption could be in error, I was careful throughout to look for information that might contradict this assumption.

My first task was to identify group members and gather from them information about their personal histories as well as the group's history. Such information was gathered both through informal conversations with individual men and through participation in GOBS group events (as well as the planning and recounting of such events). Over the two-year period, I attended a total of 22 GOBS group events organized and engaged in by members of the two sample groups. Included among these events were regular gathering in taverns or bars, weekend golf games, monthly poker games, and one hunting trip. I also questioned at length members of each group about five special events (at which women were not allowed) that took place during the data collection period. In addition, I was present at numerous mixed-sex gatherings in private homes where future events were planned and prior events recounted. At these gatherings, I was able to observe (and subsequently record) the interplay between the men and "their women" during discussions of future and past GOBS group events.

As the process proceeded, I began to organize my notes into categories drawn from the data. For example, under "events," the data provided me with subcategories of spontaneous, regular, and special (events). Similarly, a category that I initially labeled "member resources" was eventually broken down into four subcategories. Following the early lead of Glaser and Strauss (1964, 1967), I terminated the data collection phase when it became clear that no new categories (nor content for them) were being uncovered. At this time, I was prepared to develop a model of the GOBS group as an ideal type, again using the data for purposes of illustration and analysis.

In the beginning, I attended GOBS group events as a (peripheral) participant and did not inform subjects of my research purpose. Over time, however, I began to discuss with individual members of the groups my research interests and thus my need for further elaboration and clarification of data that I had collected thus far. For the most part, the men were themselves interested and open to probes. In fact, three of the men (two from one sample group and one from the other) read early drafts of my manuscript, offering suggestions and modifications (some of which I accepted and others of which, on the basis of my data, I did not accept). It should be noted that the outcome of this research was the elaboration of an ideal type, and as such, is intended as a model for future research on men's groups. Nevertheless, prior studies do suggest that the model, with some variations, may be useful for examining informal mechanisms for maintaining masculine identity.

MEN IN GROUPS: SOME CONSIDERATIONS

Holding to a sociobiological perspective, Lionel Tiger (1969) has argued that male bonding is a natural phenomenon triggered by an evolutionary need for hunting specialization and breeding advantage. In Tiger's view, males are predisposed to form a collective bond in exclusion from the weaker and yet seductive female (who would disrupt the hunt both by her physical incapacities and by diverting the male's focus from the hunt to competitive sexual strivings). Evidence of the progression of structures and strategies for generating and protecting male alliances is found, according to Tiger, in the proliferation of exclusionary, ritualistic male groups (e.g., clubs, fraternities, secret societies). Modern derivations of the hunting activity (gambling, games, and sports) are seen as essential to the "web of male affiliation." Among contemporary social scientists, Tiger's is clearly a minority point of view. In fact, his theoretical assumption that "humans are predisposed to live in relatively small-scale communities where males control dominance systems" (1969, p. 132) is, according to many feminists, representative of the kind of ideological pandering that legitimates structures of male dominance.

While Tiger's premises can be criticized for lack of empirical data, his descriptions of contemporary games and sports as vehicles for male solidarity are less questionable. Recent works abound with descriptions of the ways in which competitive games and sports facilitate masculine identity (Coleman, 1976; Fasteau, 1974; Moreland, 1980; Pleck, 1974; Sabo & Runfola, 1980). Fasteau suggests that competitive games provide for a display of masculinity and shape the way in which men relate to one another:

> Competition is the principal mode by which men relate to each other—at one level because they don't know how else to make contact, but more basically because it is a way to demonstrate, to themselves and others, the key masculine qualities of unwavering toughness and the ability to dominate and control. (1974, p. 11)

In analyzing an informant's dscription of his weekly rugby game, Tolson relates the "masculinity of the game" to the earlier experiences of boyhood:

> Here, the explicit masculinity of the game itself—a mixture of mock heroism and camaraderie—provides a kind of regression back to the world of 'the boys.' (1977, p. 106)

The camaraderie/competition mix in male group activities is also facilitated by the exclusion as well as the manipulation of women. Fasteau points out that one way in which men maintain psychic distance from women is simply to exclude them physically. In describing his attempt to integrate an all-male eating club at Harvard Law School, Fasteau reports that the men offered numerous rationales for the exclusion of women; however, he states,

> The objection repeated most often . . . and the one most impenetrable to further explanation was: 'The atmosphere will be ruined.' (1974, p. 65)

Franklin (1984) argues that the masculinity-validating function of male groups requires the devaluation of all that is feminine; one result of this requirement is that women are not seen as potential contributors to group goals and thus their exclusion is rationalized as legitimate. However, in certain situations, men attempt to gain masculinity validation by displaying their masculine prowess in front of women; thus, Franklin continues, females may be used as "pawns in these competitive gains" (1984, p. 49).

It is important to note that bonding styles and collective alliances among men may vary in accordance with social position, e.g., age, class, and race. For example, the work of Levinson, Darrow, Klein, Levinson, and McKee (1978) on developmental phases in the life cycle of men provides an age context for the understanding of shifting relationships among men as they move from early adulthood to the "settling down" phase of midlife. Similarly, class-based patterns in male relationships have been identified in several studies. Research on working-class social roles has revealed a pattern of conjugal role segregation in which men and women meet companionship needs through same-sex groupings (Bott, 1971; Komarovsky, 1964; Young & Wilmott, 1957). A classic example of working-class men gathering in neighborhood taverns to share fun, talk, and drink in the company of other men has been described by LeMasters (1975) in his study of blue-collar aristocrats. Hannerz (1970) has identified a similar phenomenon among ghetto males who gather on street corners to exchange stories of past exploits involving drinking, drugs, and women. Tolson (1977) has suggested that exaggerated expressions of masculinity may function to compensate working-class males for occupational and other class failures that have lowered masculine esteem.

On the other hand, in instrumental good old boys networks, upper-class men gather to enhance (rather than compensate for) their class positions (see, for example, Domhoff, 1974). Upper-class members of exclusionary networks in which male privilege is maintained may be politically committed to sexual and other forms of equality. As Fasteau notes,

> Senior partners of prestigious law firms and investment-banking houses, who have served in high positions in liberal Democratic administrations, meet to cultivate business friendships and close deals in men-only luncheon clubs in the financial district. (1974, p. 65)

Whether or not these men recognize such contradictions between the political and the personal is not clear.

In still another example of the effect of position, Franklin (1984) contends that because of their history of subordination, black males share a greater intimacy with one another than do white males. Although black males, according to Franklin, do play out themes of dominance and competition within the black subculture, their exposure to a larger society that is hostile to them leads to the creation of special bonds of "brotherhood."

It seems clear, then, that while definitions of masculinity and dimensions of the male role are understood and to a great extent shared by men across social categories, the ways in which they are played out by men in groups vary in accordance with the experiences and resources of men who are differentially positioned in the stratification system. In the present study, the ways in which one category of "well-positioned" men play out themes of masculinity and male dominance through the sociability group are explored.

AN INTRODUCTION TO THE GOBS GROUP

The men in these sociability groups plan and engage in a variety of activities that feature certain themes and props associated with male fun and pleasure. While there may be numerous male sociability groups that facilitate masculine identity and camaraderie, the group form under study provides a unique forum for dominance bonding in that its membership consists of class- and gender-confident men who share objective and subjective histories that have generated such confidence. In many ways, the members fit the description of the proverbial "good old boys"—they are white, upper- (or upper middle-) class men in their productive adult years with established informal networks through which instrumental favors are exchanged and barriers to inclusion are erected. They are unified through chauvinistic, class, and local traditions that afford them "insider" privileges. However, unlike the good old boy groups described in much of the literature, the group under study is *not* organized around the use of informal networks to achieve instrumental ends, i.e., business, political, or professional gain. Rather, it is a primary group purposively organized to facilitate retreats from the world of work (and family). Although members perceive GOBS group activities as temporary retreats, the GOBS group *experience* nurtures feelings of dominance and superiority that pervade many domains of members' lives. Thus, the GOBS group functions to reinforce members' perceptions of themselves as gender and class elites.

The dominance-bonding phenomenon is facilitated through the GOBS group in several ways. First, that the members possess highly valued resources—class and gender success, geographic entrenchment, flexible time, and a history of successful sociability—gives objective reality and subjective credibility to their superior status. Additionally, dominance bonding is facilitated in that sociability—the operating principle of the group—reaffirms the superiority of masculine play (the superiority of which was first affirmed in the exclusionary play activities of young boys in groups). Finally, certain bonding properties of the group, i.e., collectivity, exclusivity, autonomy, and ritualism, foster solidarity and commitment. These and other features of the GOBS group (outlined in Fig. 1) are elaborated in the following pages.

MEMBERSHIP

The Small GOBS Group   The core membership of the small GOBS group consists of four to seven men who maintain close, intimate ties as well as regular contact with one another (inside and outside GOBS group settings).

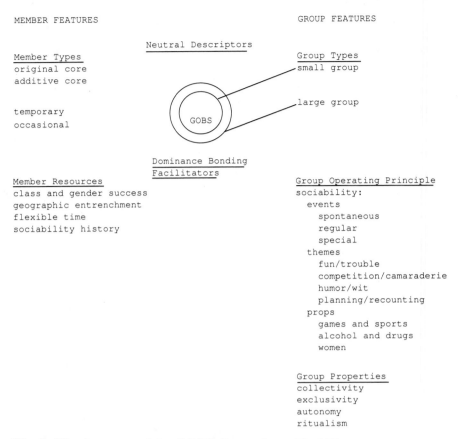

MEMBER FEATURES   GROUP FEATURES

Neutral Descriptors

Member Types   Group Types
original core   small group
additive core

temporary   large group
occasional   GOBS

Dominance Bonding
Facilitators
Member Resources   Group Operating Principle
class and gender success   sociability:
geographic entrenchment   events
flexible time   spontaneous
sociability history   regular
                                                       special
                                                    themes
                                                       fun/trouble
                                                       competition/camaraderie
                                                       humor/wit
                                                       planning/recounting
                                                    props
                                                       games and sports
                                                       alcohol and drugs
                                                       women

                                                   Group Properties
                                                   collectivity
                                                   exclusivity
                                                   autonomy
                                                   ritualism

Fig. 1. The Anatomy of the GOBS Group As an Ideal Type.

The friendships of the original core members typically date back to adolescent or college years, and it was during these years that their GOBS group began to develop. The occasional disaffiliation of an original core member may be prompted by a geographical move or, less frequently, by a failure to live up to the group's expectations. However, the approximate small group size is always maintained as additive core members are incorporated into the group. The core membership is highly stable; rarely is there a loss or addition of more than one member over a period of several years. Not all core members attend all GOBS group events. However, without at least two core members in attendance, the group does not function as a GOBS group.

In addition to core members, the small GOBS group has occasional and temporary members. Occasional members are men who share the traits of and know all core members, but who attend only specific events or any given event sporadically. Temporary members are men who share the traits of and know one or more core members, but whose participation in an event is situationally precipitated (e.g., a man who happens upon an event in process in a public place; a man who is an out-of-town guest of a core member). Unlike core members, occasional and temporary members do not initiate events, are not automatically included in all events, and do not maintain regular contact with all members of the group. As long as their behaviors and attitudes conform to the principle of sociability, however, occasional and temporary members are afforded full membership in the group for the duration of the event in which they are participating.

Core Members of the Sample GOBS Groups   At the time of the study, there were six core members of Group A. Four of the six were original core members and had known one another since high school; however, their GOBS group did not become cemented until they had graduated from college and returned to their hometown. The first additive core member joined the group several years following the postgraduation "reunion" of the original group. The second additive core member (who graduated from the same university as two of the original core members) joined the group more recently. The ages of core members of Group A ranged from 39 to 44 years; all were, at the time of the study, financially and occupationally successful (a doctor, an attorney, a business executive, and three owners or coowners of businesses). Three were married, one was separated, and two were divorced. All but one came from upper and upper middle-class backgrounds. The one exception (the second additive core member) came from a stable small-town, working-class family; prior to his entrance into the group, this man was known (by reputation) to the other core members in that he had been a star football player at the state university.

Group B also consisted, at the time of the study, of six core members (all of whom were original core members). Four of the six had become friends when they attended an all-male Catholic high school; the additional two members (non-Catholics) joined the friendship circle during college (five of the six went to the same university and intermittently lived in off-campus apartments with one another). It was during the college years that GOBS Group B solidified. The ages of core members of Group B ranged from 32 to 35 years. The core members of this group were just beginning to stabilize their careers and achieve financial success. There were among them one attorney, two salespersons, two independent contractors, and one tavern manager. These men, who attended college during the late 1960s (and perhaps were influenced by those times), had put off joining "the establishment" until they were in their late 20s. In fact, two of the members did not appear to put much effort into establishing an upper status career. However, core members of Group B did not view their own occupational and income achievements *to date* as indicators of their social class position.[1] All came from upper- or upper middle-class backgrounds and identified with an upper status lifestyle. In spite of their income limitations (relative to Group A), they self-presented (e.g., choice of clothing, restaurants or bars, conversational style and content) as upper status

[1] Since the data on these men's occupational status were first collected (approximately two years ago), two members of Group B have become quite successful and are currently earning annual job incomes between $60,000 and $70,000. One of the independent contractors has become an insurance salesperson. The tavern manager has moved from a core to an occasional member of the GOBS group, and according to other members of Group B, has perhaps become an additive core member of a working-class sociability group.

persons. Two of the members of Group B had recently married, two co-habited with women, and two were single.

The behavior of members of Group B was less aggressive and less *overtly* masculine than that of members of Group A. For example, Group A events in taverns and bars were generally louder and more raucous than those of Group B. Also, members of Group A were more confrontational with one another than were members of Group B. However, conflict between members of Group A was shortlived and did not appear to negatively affect the good times these men had when together. In spite of the differences between these two sample groups, the "anatomy" of the GOBS groups of which they were members was strikingly similar.

The Large GOBS Group: A Variation   Certain special events serve as vehicles through which large GOBS groups (from 10 to 50 members) are temporarily formed and the male collective is confirmed. Large-group special events may occur only one time (a bachelor party), or every one or more years (an annual golf tournament, a fraternity reunion). Members of large GOBS groups are also long-time friends, and most are core or occasional members of small-group GOBS. At the least, they share with members of small-group GOBS sociodemongraphic traits and commitments to masculine sociability. Collective unity (fostered by the intimacy of the small GOBS group) is enhanced in the large group by an intense shared focus on a particular dimension of sociability, e.g., competition in the game at a tournament, exclusion of good women (wives and girlfriends), and inclusion of bad women (strippers) at a stag party. Relative to small-group events, large-group events are formally organized and highly structured. For example, the annual golf tournament in which members of sample Group A participated involved arranging accommodations at an out-of-town resort, pairing roommates as well as golf teams, printing and sending out invitations, and scheduling minievents. The game itself was elaborately structured, including a variety of betting procedures and activities, multiple categories of winners, and complex schemes for equalizing opportunities for "winning something."[2] Following the scheduled event, large-group GOBS groups disband until called together for another special event. The disbanding process, however, is not as abrupt as it might seem at first glance. Because members of large-group GOBS groups frequently see each other in business as well as social circles, they can engage in the recounting of the event for some time after its occurrence.

MEMBER RESOURCES AS
DOMINANCE-BONDING FACILTATORS

Class and Gender Success   Original core members of GOBS groups come from upper- or upper middle-class socioeconomic backgrounds. They are college educated, and they either have achieved or expect to achieve material wealth. Through their up-bringings, they have been exposed to and take for granted a

---

[2] Winning something, however, required a demonstration of instrumental skill, e.g., scoring below your handicap, hitting the longest drive. The "real winner" was always acknowledged as such in that the top prize went to the man with the lowest golf score regardless of handicap.

lifestyle that includes luxury consumerism and admiration from others less fortunately positioned. While most additive core, occasional, and temporary members also come from upper socioeconomic backgrounds, some may come from working-class (but never poverty-class) backgrounds. Those who do come from working-class backgrounds are clearly upwardly mobile—college educated, career achieved (or career oriented), and knowledgeable about upper status lifestyles. All members have family backgrounds and/or past achievements (e.g., games or sports skills, academic credentials, career-potential demonstrations) through which to demonstrate their worth. In testimonial fashion, GOBS group members typically support one another through verbal exchanges in which the worth of individual members ("You're so smart, skilled, etc.") as well as the membership as a whole ("We're so smart, skilled, etc.") is confirmed. Such exchanges serve as continual reinforcement of self-and group images of superiority in intelligence, cleverness, and potential.

GOBS group members also perceive themselves as gender successful; again, group activities and conversations serve to reinforce the manliness of the group as well as individual members. Members are heterosexual and have enjoyed considerable popularity with women. These men do not view them-selves as sexist, and they do not appear to be viewed by the women *with whom they interact* as sexist. In their choice of wives and girlfriends, the majority of these men seem to value independent and intelligent women. Yet their social-ization into a male-dominated environment and a culture in which male sociability is highly valued causes them to think and act in ways that conflict with their intellectual assessments of the worth of and the value of social relationships with women. They resolve this conflict in part by asserting that their GOBS group involvement allows them time-out behavior, a retreat to a "boys" lifestyle in which they feel particularly comfortable. The comment of one member is illustrative:

> We can't help it; we were just raised to like to do things with the boys. That's what we did in high school and college, and sometimes we just like to go back to those times.

Geographic Entrenchment   Another resource that facilitates dominance bonding is geographic entrenchment. Most of the original core members of the sample GOBS groups were classmates or friends in high school. At the least they grew up in the same city. All went out of town or state to college, but returned to begin their careers in their hometown (which for the groups under study was a West Coast City with a population of approximately 400,000). The men shared a confident knowledge of their community as well as a broad network of well-connected men with whom they exchanged busi-ness or professional favors. Geographic entrenchment provides for GOBS group members a sense of control over their environment; the men are firmly located in and familiar with a "place" in which their social histories are grounded. In fact, the geographic grounding of traditions appears a powerful resource for the maintenance of group bonds. On two observed occasions, men who had lived out of town for some time but had been close high-school and/or college friends of group members attended (during a return visit to the city) a GOBS group event. On both occasions, it would have been difficult for an outsider to distinguish the visiting participant from the core members of the group. Social ties were easily resumed; traditions were observed and carried out on (familiar) cue.

Flexible Time   GOBS group members also have a fair amount of control over time. Men in the observed groups had lifestyles that afforded them flexible time. With the exception of one member of Group B, they were not locked into 9 to 5 jobs from which they could not escape without special permission from a superior. Similarly, family responsibilities did not tie these men down on a regular basis. All with children had wives or ex-wives who had the primary responsibility for child care.[3] Flexible time allowed for participation in spontaneous as well as planned GOBS group events (and, if necessary, time to recuperate from such events).

Sociability History   Finally, GOBS group members share a sociability history. This is, they have engaged in GOBS group events since boyhood; many can and do recount stories of their fathers' involvement in similar activities. The men have the same or similar stories about their own past experiences. All view the possession of a sociability history as a necessary condition for masculine identity.

SOCIABILITY

Events   GOBS group activities include three types of events: spontaneous, regular, and special. Spontaneous events occur when three or more members make contact in person or by telephone, and plan a "get together" for that day or the day after. Examples of spontaneous events are meeting for beer after work, playing golf, or watching a sports event on television. Regular events include any of the above or any other event that takes place routinely (weekly, bimonthly, or monthly), and about which three or more members are informed and attend on a regular basis, e.g., the Saturday golf game, the monthly poker game. Special events are elaborately planned far in advance, and may take place only one time or may be an annual event. Spontaneous and regular events generally involve from three to seven participants. Some regular events, e.g., a monthly poker game, may be attended by as many as ten persons. Special events are either attended by a small number of members (three to five) or are an occasion around which a large-group GOBS is formed.

Themes and Props   Fun and trouble enjoy a symbiotic relationship as sociability themes. Having fun refers to getting together with the guys and engaging in or talking about drinking/taking drugs, flirting, and games and sports. GOBS group fun also calls for constant conversation, in particular conversa-

---

[3] I do not mean to imply that these men were irresponsible in job duties, nor that they failed to participate in family activities. On occasion, job or family activities that had been scheduled in advance did prevent men from attending a GOBS group event. However, flexible time allowed for flexible scheduling in various domains of the men's lives; furthermore, it provided them with the feeling of freedom that comes from the knowledge that the decision to take time off is usually their own.

tion that produces laughter. Furthermore, having fun involves talking about past fun and planning future fun. Trouble refers to activities in which the good old boys behave as bad little boys, e.g., staying out late and not calling home, fooling around with a "bad woman," getting drunk or loaded, losing money gambling. While not all fun is trouble, most trouble is fun. The observed GOBS group members had fun conversing about their involvement in present trouble ("We're in trouble"), in past trouble ("I got in trouble last weekend"), and future trouble ("We're out to get in some trouble"). In fact, many GOBS group activities do cause actual trouble, e.g., making wives or girlfriends angry, having a hangover, losing money. However, due to their superior resources, the negative consequences of trouble are rarely serious or permanent.

Competition and camaraderie are also interdependent themes of sociability. The central activity of many GOBS group events is a game or sport. Games and sports are always competitive—bets are made, winning is valued, and adjustments are made for differential skills that might otherwise make the contest noncompetitive. Competition, however, does not generate antagonism; rather, it nurtures camaraderie. The observed men kidded one another, treated one another as essential contributors to the fun of the game, and praised one another's skills and cleverness.

Whether played or viewed, games and sports are almost always accompanied by drinking. In fact, alcohol (and less frequently other drugs) is used as a prop at virtually all GOBS group events. When engaging in a particularly grueling or dangerous sport (e.g., basketball, hunting), alcohol consumption is delayed until after the game, serving as a reward for the physical effort expended as well as to prolong the GOBS group event.

Being sociable also means being humorous and responding to humor. While in the observed groups, some humor was expressed in crude sex or ethnic jokes, more frequently expressed and more highly valued was witty humor (regardless of the topic). Exchanges of spontaneous, witty comments involve another form of competition/camaraderie; members engage in subtle games of oneupmanship as they try to outdo one another with clever conversation.

Finally, planning and recounting are important sociability themes. One way in which current fun is confirmed is to plan a future similar (or bigger and better) event while the current event is in process. Recounting past events during current events is equally fun enhancing. Additionally, during mixedsex social gatherings at which wives and girlfriends are present, GOBS group events may be recounted with the captive female audience in mind. Women may reinforce the GOBS group by reacting to recounts with laughter, admiration, or good-natured disbelief. Angry or disapproving female reactions may reinforce the GOBS group members' beliefs that women do not know how to be sociable or do not understand sociability. Generally, men do not recount in the presence of their wives or girlfriends their own involvement in trouble. However, other GOBS group members may report to a wife or girlfriend (in the presence of her husband or boyfriend) on the trouble involvement of her mate (e.g., "You should have seen _____ on the dance floor," or "Guess who was the big money loser last night?"). Although these remarks might be followed by a reassurance to the women ("We were actually good boys," or "It was all innocent fun"), they at times are intended to or actually do cause more trouble. This then serves as a topic for future GOBS group conversations—a recount of the recount—in which the man who has had his fun/trouble involvement revealed admonishes (in good humor) the informant, and a conversation on the trouble the recount has caused ensues.

Wives and girlfriends also serve as props in the planning of special GOBS group events. They may participate in the establishment of the trouble theme, expressing concern about what the men are going to do, nagging them about exclusion, or trying to convince them not to go. Such confrontations provide for the men a test of their skills in avoiding real trouble at home, e.g., convincing their women that they will be "good," selling the perception that this is all innocent fun, or pointing out that men need time for male camaraderie. Women may also play the role of server by preparing food for the men to take along or seeing that the men have suitable clothing/equipment—in fact, playing mother to the boys. Such behavior reinforces the traditional domestic role of women as well as the superiority of the male role. Women serve and stay at home; men go out for excitement and fun.

Sociability, then, is organized around events, themes, and props that facilitate dominance bonding among men. The superiority of masculine play is reaffirmed, and the value of male camaraderie is elevated. In addition to its operating principle, the GOBS group has certain properties that function to promote solidarity and thus group bonding. These properties are elaborated here.

BONDING PROPERTIES OF THE GOBS GROUP

The group properties that serve to unify the GOBS group are collectivity, exclusivity, autonomy, and ritualism. Such properties are not unique to GOBS groups; indeed, they have been observed in other studies of group and community mechanisms for maintaining cohesion and solidarity (see, for example, Kanter, 1972). However, such properties are particularly functional when (as in the case of the GOBS group) they are underwritten by group members' possession of objectively superior and highly regarded resources. Under such conditions, the group is (a) less dependent on or restricted by external material and social demands, (b) more likely to be seen by outsiders as desirable and enviable, and (c) more confident of the high esteem in which it holds itself.

Collectivity   The GOBS group functions as an alliance in which the male collective is celebrated. Individual identity is rooted in the collective, and the attitudes and behaviors are given meaning through the collective. The collective is most personal and intimate in the GOBS small group. In addition to sharing the sociability experience, members of small-group GOBS can directly reinforce the worth of the group and the individuals within through supportive verbal exchanges. "Serious talk," in which members counsel or bolster the ego of a member who expresses temporary concern about his class or gender success, punctuates the sociability conversations engaged in most frequently. The male collective, however, is also celebrated when large-group GOBS gather for a special event. Collectivity is facilitated at such large-group gatherings by an intense focus on some dimension of male sociability.

Exclusivity   A highly functional property of the GOBS group is exclusivity. Exclusivity may be enforced directly or indirectly. Some events are directly closed to outsiders and requests for inclusion are denied. Exclusion may also be indirect, e.g., outsiders are not informed of an upcoming event; barriers are erected by nonverbal behaviors. An example of the latter technique was observed in a tavern in which the GOBS group sat at a corner table and faced their chairs away from others sharing the larger public space. Additionally, men who join the group for an event (either invited or uninvited) who do not have at least some of the dominance-bonding resources and who do not understand and enjoy sociability are effectively discouraged from further participation. During two observed spontaneous tavern events, such an "inappropriate" man attempted to join the group. In one case, the lively conversation of the GOBS group members simply stopped; within a short time, the uninvited outsider picked up his beer and moved to another table. In the other case, the conversation continued, but the outsider was totally ignored; he, too, left after a brief time.

The most notable feature of GOBS group exclusivity, however, has to do with women. Women can never be members of GOBS groups, and it is their exclusion that sustains male solidarity and dominance. "Good women" (wives and girlfriends) are never included in special events. However, "bad women" may serve as props at special events (e.g., a stripper who performs at a stag party). Additionally, women who are not wives or girlfriends of members may serve as the "bad women" props at regular or spontaneous events (e.g., women who are flirted with or made fun of at a bar or tavern). On occasion, "good women" attend regular or spontaneous events, e.g., a wife or girlfriend may join the group after work for a few beers or play poker one night with the boys. As long as they do not contradict the norms of the group, one or two "good women" may attend a GOBS group event *upon occasion* without seriously disrupting the functioning of the GOBS group. However, if more than two "good women" are present, or if the number of "good women" is not substantially less than the number of men, the group ceases to function as a GOBS group.

Finally, recounting past sociability events in the presence of wives or girlfriends who were excluded from these events validates for the men male superiority (in sociability skills) and male dominance (in controlling the conversation). The women, who do not share a sociability history with the men, are excluded a second time through the recounting process.

Autonomy   Related to collectivity and exclusivity is the property of autonomy. As a close-knit and exclusive unit, the GOBS group is viewed by its members as separate from and superior to other social units. It has the power to discourage or deprive outsider participation. It can manipulate and control good and bad women, and it has the capacity to engage in fun and trouble without serious consequences. Also, because members possess superior resources, their group does have more objective autonomy. GOBS group conversations about such resources serve to reinforce members' views that they are in control of their life conditions.

A belief in the autonomy and thus power of the group encourages members to take risks and challenge outsiders within the GOBS group setting. It is possible that such attitudes and behaviors carry over into non-GOBS group domains of these men's lives. The men, after all, are secure in the knowledge that they will be regularly reinforced with each retreat into a GOBS group setting.

Ritualism   Ritualism is essential to the maintenance of the GOBS group. Regular and special events are in themselves ritualistic. Events also include certain rituals. For example, Group B regularly ended weekly poker games with a game of "guts," a particularly exciting and risky form of the game. On an annual out-of-town weekend trip to attend a particular football game, members of Group A always started the day with a round of "Bloody Marys." For the observed groups, the most valued special events took place out of town. In anticipation of their annual out-of-town golf tournament, members of Group A organized several planning events (held each time and each year at the same tavern), the first of which took place five months prior to the actual tournament.

The content of ritualistic behaviors engaged in at regular events may be periodically changed. For example, one member of Group B, after reading an earlier draft of my manuscript, informed me that the poker game of "guts" had been used as a closing ritual for several months, but that prior to that time, the men had ended the poker event with breakfast at a nearby all-night cafe. Similarly, regular events may themselves be relatively temporary—eventually dropped and replaced by others. For several months, members of Group B gathered regularly to have lunch, play cards, and watch "Perry Mason" at one member's house. This occurred, according to my informant, because two of the members were working on a contracting job on the same block as the third member's apartment. When the contracting job was completed, the regular event was abandoned. In another example, members of Group A had met regularly at a specific tavern to collectively discuss and individually make football bets (which were then placed with a bookie by one member). With the end of the football season, this regular event was terminated.

It is my contention that the changing and replacing of ritualistic events, behaviors, and places gives the GOBS group vitality and reinforces members' beliefs in their own creativity and cleverness. On the other hand, the perpetuation of specific rituals for a given time period gives the group stability and continuity.

CONCLUDING REMARKS

The GOBS group is but one form of male alliance in which masculinity may be celebrated. However, it is of particular importance as an example of one way in which majority (white, heterosexual, upper-status) men use the male group to affirm to themselves and communicate to outsiders the superiority of their class and gender positions. The components of masculinity that men learn (and, more importantly, learn to value) during boyhood are displayed through the sociability events, themes, and props of the GOBS group. The sharing of successful and entrenched histories fosters dominance bonding in especially powerful ways. The GOBS group members are men who have had their gender and class successes acknowledged since boyhood; they have always been insiders, and they know it. If doubts occur, the GOBS group provides them with renewed confidence.

Yet outside GOBS group settings, the gender expressions of these men suggest something less than total commitment to the traditional male sex role. More in alignment with what Pleck (1981) describes as the modern male role, these men value and engage in expressive intimacies with their girlfriends or wives. In the company of these women, the men rarely express open hostilities toward women, gay men, nonwhites or the working class; in fact, even within GOBS group settings, they often make fun of exaggerated "machismo" and the snobbery of class-conscious elites. Such expressions may foster expectations of inclusion among the "good women" with whom these men interact. Indeed, in my observations, women seemed less cognizant than outsider men of the futility of efforts to weaken or join the GOBS group; at the least, they were more tenacious in their efforts to intervene. Women who hope to become girlfriends or wives may try to become a part of the group in order to win favor with a particular member. Women who are already girlfriends or wives of members typically try to dissuade "their man" from continuing to participate in the GOBS group or try unsuccessfully to join. These reactions suggest that while women may not fully understand or accept their exclusion, they recognize the power of and value placed on the GOBS group.

The extent to which the GOBS group phenomenon is shaped by characteristics or traditions of particular local communities is at this time unclear. However, it does seem clear that the sharing of locally grounded social histories is critical to the sustenance of the group. Whether or not the demise of the GOBS group will occur as members pass through the middle years of the life cycle is a question whose answer is also beyond the scope of the present study. However, the findings from this study do indicate that for men who share dominance-bonding resources and value masculine sociability, the GOBS group is a highly functional unit well into the middle years of adulthood. The bonds between GOBS group members are real—rooted in time, place, and position and sustained through group mechanisms. It is perhaps because of its dual functions—the preservation of status superiority and the provision of companionate pleasure—that the GOBS group thrives and survives.

REFERENCES

Bott, E. *Family and social network: Roles, norms, and external relationships* (2nd ed.). New York: The Free Press, 1971.

Coleman, J. S. Athletics in high school. In D. S. David & R. Brannon (Eds.), *The forty-nine percent majority: The male sex role*. Reading, MA: Addison-Wesley, 1976.

Comer, L. *Wedlocked women*, Leeds: Feminist Press, 1974.

Connor, J. M., & Serbin, L. A. Children's responses to stories with male and female characters. *Sex Roles*, 1978, *4*, 637–645.

David, D. S., & Brannon, R. (Eds.). *The forty-nine percent majority: The male sex role*. Reading, MA: Addison-Wesley, 1976.

Domhoff, G. W. *The Bohemian Grove and other retreats: A study in ruling-class cohesiveness*. New York: Harper & Row, 1974.

Fasteau, M. F. *The male machine*. New York: McGraw Hill, 1974.

Franklin, C. W. *The changing definition of masculinity*. New York: Plenum Press, 1984.

Glaser, B. G., & Strauss, A. *Awareness of dying*. Chicago: Aldine, 1964.

Glaser, B. G., & Strauss, A. *The discovery of grounded theory*. Chicago: Aldine, 1967.

Hannerz, U. What ghetto males are like: Another look. In N. E. Whitten and J. F. Szwed (Eds.), *Afro-American anthropology: Contemporary perspectives*. New York: The Free Press, 1970.

Kanter, R. M. *Commitment and community: Communes and utopias in sociological perspective*. Cambridge, MA: Harvard University Press, 1972.

Komarovsky, M. *Blue collar marriage*. New York: Random House, 1964.

LeMasters, E. E. *Blue collar aristocrats: Life-styles at a working-class tavern*. Madison, WI: University of Wisconsin Press, 1975.

Levinson, D., Darrow, C., Klein, E. B., Levinson, M. H., & McKee, B. *The seasons of a man's life*. New York: Knopf, 1978.

Moreland, J. Age and change in the adult male sex role. *Sex Roles*, 1980, 6, 807–818.

Phillips, B. S. *Sex-role socialization and play behavior on a rural playground*. Unpublished master's thesis, Department of Sociology, Ohio State University, Columbus, OH, 1982.

Pleck, J. H. My male sex role—and ours. *WIN Magazine*, April 11, 1974, 8–12.

Pleck, J. H. *The myth of masculinity*. Cambridge, MA: The MIT Press, 1981.

Sabo, D. F., & Runfola, R. (Eds.). *Jock: Sports and male identity*. Englewood Cliffs, NJ: Prentice Hall, 1980.

Tiger, L. *Men in groups*. New York: Random House, 1969.

Tolson, A. *The limits of masculinity*. London: Tavistock, 1977.

Tyron, B. W. Beliefs about male and female competence held by kindergarten and second graders. *Sex Roles*, 1980, 6, 85–97.

Young, M. D., & Wilmott, P. *Family and kinship in East London*. London: Routledge and Kegan Paul, 1957.

Susan Brownmiller

WHEN MEN ARE THE VICTIMS OF RAPE

It is finally being acknowledged that one of the main problems of prison life is the assault and rape of other inmates by their fellow men. Shrouded in secrecy and misinformation, so-called homosexual "abuse" in prison was formerly thought to be symptomatic of the deranged brutality of a few prison guards or an "infection" spread throughout a cellbock by a certain number of avowed homosexuals within the prison population. More information and a relatively enlightened modern perspective have drastically altered this old-fashioned view. Prison rape is generally seen today for what it is: an acting out of power roles within an all-male, authoritarian environment in which the younger, weaker inmate, usually a first offender, is forced to play the role that in the outside world is assigned to women. . . .

In the summer of 1973 a 28-year-old Quaker pacifist named Robert A. Martin, a former seaman with a background in journalism, held a stunning press conference in Washington, D.C. Arrested during a peace demonstration in front of the White House, Martin had chosen to go to prison rather than post a $10 bond. . . .

During his first evening recreation period . . . the boyish-looking pacifist was invited into a cell on the pretext that some of the men wanted to talk with him. Once inside, he said, "My exit was blocked and my pants were forcibly taken off me, and I was raped. Then I was dragged from cell to cell all evening." Martin was promised protection from further assaults by two of his violators. The next night his "protectors" initiated a second general round of oral and rectal rape. The pair stood outside his cell and collected packs of cigarettes from other prisoners wanting a turn. When his attackers gave him a brief rest period to overcome his gagging and nausea, Martin made his escape and alerted a guard. He was taken to D.C. General Hospital where he underwent VD tests and a rectal examination. The following morning a Quaker friend posted his bond. . . .

Public recognition of rape in prison is increasing. From a pile of newsclips I can pull the following items:

- Nine inmates at Sumter Correctional Institute in Florida are charged with raping other prisoners during a prison riot.
- Two inmates at Florida's Raiford Prison are charged with raping other inmates at knife point.
- A county judge in upstate New York refuses to send a young offender, who is homosexual, to Attica. His stated reason: "I just couldn't see throwing him into that situation. He'd become an object of barter there, completely dehumanized if he wasn't killed. This is a heck of a thing, and the public ought to know about it."
- Two bright young Nixon aides who plead guilty to Watergate offenses and know they face a jail sentence admit they are apprehensive about the possibility of a sexual assault. . . .

A comprehensive study of rape within the Philadelphia prison system was jointly conducted in 1968 by the district attorney's office and the Philadelphia police department after two embarrassing incidents came to light. One was a gang rape by detainees in a sheriff's van upon a youth who was being transported to court for this trial; the second incident concerned a youth who was sexually assaulted "within minutes of his admission" to the Philadelphia Detention Center for a presentencing evaluation. (In both cases the youth's lawyer reported his rape to the court.)

Alan J. Davis, the chief assistant district attorney who was put in charge of the resulting investigation, was forced to conclude that sexual assault in Philadelphia prisons was "epidemic." Meticulously documenting 156 cases of rape during a two-year period through the task-force interviews with more than 3,000 reluctant inmates and guards, the use of lie-detector tests and examination of prison records, Davis believed he had merely touched "the top of the iceberg," and that the true number of rapes during this period was probably closer to 2,000 in a shifting inmate population of 60,000 men. However, a total of only 96 rapes had actually been reported by victimized inmates to prison authorities, and of this number only 64 had been written up in prison records. Prison officials had imposed some form of internal discipline on 40 of the offenders and 26 of the cases had been passed on to the police for legal prosecution.

Davis disclosed that "virtually every slightly built young man committed by the courts is sexually approached within a day or two after his admission to prison. Many of these young men are repeatedly raped by gangs of inmates. . . .

Homosexual rape in the Philadelphia prisons turned out to be a microcosm of the female experience with heterosexual rape. Davis discovered that prison guards put pressure on inmates not to report their rapes by using the argument that the victim wouldn't want his parents and friends to find out about his humiliation. But not telling did not cause the humiliation to "go away": "After a young man has been raped," Davis learned, "he is marked as a victim for the duration of his confinement. This mark follows him from institution to institution. Many of these young men return to their communities ashamed and full of hatred."

Matching the woman's experience with rape in the outside world, Davis found that in a closed society without women, men who raped other men in prison as a group were on the average three years older, one inch taller and fifteen pounds heavier than their prison victims. Also in parallel to the outside world, prison rape appeared to be a function of youthful aggression. Although the average age of an inmate within the Philadelphia prison system was 29, the average prison rapist was found to be 23 years old and the average age of his victim was slightly under 21. Men who raped in prison had usually been put there for crimes of violence: robbery, assault, and heterosexual rape. Men *who were raped* in prison looked young for their years, appeared unathletic and were noticeably better looking than their predators. Their crimes, as might be expected, were usually on the nonassaultive end of the spectrum: auto theft, going AWOL, or violating parole. . . .

Homosexual rape in prison could not be primarily motivated by the need for sexual release, Davis observed, since autoerotic masturbation to orgasm is "much easier and more normal." But conquest and degradation did appear to be a primary goal: "We repeatedly found that aggressors used such language as 'Fight or fuck,' 'We're going to take your manhood,' 'You'll have to give up some face,' and 'We're gonna make a girl out of you.'" Significantly, in the penal institution, economic clout proved as persuasive as physical force: "Typically, an experienced inmate will give cigarettes, candy, sedatives, stainless-steel blades, or extra food pilfered form the kitchen to an inexperienced inmate, and after a few days the veteran will demand sexual repayment." In the fear-charged atmosphere of prison society, the "threat of rape, expressed or implied, would prompt an already fearful young man to submit" for a guarantee of future protection from gang assault or for an easier time of it. "Prison officials," Davis concluded, "were too quick to label such activities 'consensual.'"

In sum, Davis found that prison rape was a product of the violent subculture's definition of masculinity through physical triumph, and those who emerged as "women" were those who were subjugated by real or threatened force.

PART EIGHT

◆ ◆ ◆

Male Sexualities

How do many men learn to desire women? What are men thinking about when they are sexual with women? Are gay men more sexually promiscuous than straight men? Are gay men more obsessed with demonstrating their masculinity than straight men, or are they likely to be more "effeminate?" Recent research indicates that there are no simple answers to these questions. What is increasingly clear though is that men's sexuality, whether homosexual, bisexual, or heterosexual, is experienced as an experience of their gender.

Since there is no anticipatory socialization for homosexuality and bisexuality, future straight and gay men receive the same socialization as boys. As a result, sexuality as a gender enactment is often a similar internal experience for all men. Early socialization teaches us—through masturbation, locker-room conversations, sex-ed classes and conversations with parents, and the tidbits that boys will pick up from various media—that sex is private, pleasurable, guilt provoking, exciting, and phallocentric, and that orgasm is the goal toward which sexual experience is oriented.

The articles in this section explore how male sexualities express issues of masculinity. Alan E. Gross describes the ways in which male heterosexuality is related to masculinity. Robert Staples explains how the norms of masculinity are expressed in somewhat different ways among black heterosexual males. Jeffrey Fracher and Michael Kimmel argue that men discuss their sexual experiences—both their "successes" and their "failures"— in terms of gender, not pleasure. A man experiencing, for instance, premature ejaculation would be more likely to complain that he wasn't "enough of a man" than that he was unable to feel enough pleasure. Leonore Tiefer suggests the ways in which a medical model of male sexual problems helps men to "rescue" a sense of their manhood that they perceive is threatened by the inability to live up to unrealizable ideals of sexual performance.

Articles by Edward Donnerstein and David Linz, and by Chris Clark explore some of the controversial political implications of pornography as a source of both straight and gay men's sexual information. Next, M. Rochlin's questionnaire challenges us to question the normative elements of heterosexuality. In a similar vein, Gary Kinsman argues that we can begin to understand the present lives of gay men only by constructing a "history of heterosexuality." In the past, what we call "homosexual behavior" has always existed, but social definitions and meanings surrounding sexual expression have shifted dramatically—most recently in response to the gay liberation movement.

HOMO vs. HETERO
WHICH IS BETTER?

ADVANTAGES

- ECSTASY
- HAPPINESS
- FULFILLMENT
- SOCIETAL APPROVAL
- SHARE CLOTHING

DISADVANTAGES

- HEARTBREAK
- SHAME
- GUILT
- HERPES
- AIDS
- PERSECUTION
- BREED LIKE RABBITS
- LOOKS RIDICULOUS

Cartoon by Matt Groening. Copyright © 1988. Reprinted by permission.

Alan E. Gross

THE MALE ROLE AND HETEROSEXUAL BEHAVIOR

Whether myth or biological fact, men and women generally believe and act as if sex is more central, enjoyable, and necessary for males. For example, responses to an extensive series of interviews with married couples (Rainwater, 1965) indicate that husbands, especially those in the lower economic classes, are much more likely than their wives to find sex enjoyable. A typical husband in Rainwater's sample asserts, "Sex is the most important thing, say 95% of marriage" (p. 83). In contrast, many wives in the same sample simply tolerate sex: "He thinks sex is very important . . . He couldn't live without it,

Revised version of article from *Journal of Social Issues* 34(1), 1978. © 1988 by Alan Gross. Reprinted by permission of the author.

I guess. . . . Me, I could do without it; our feelings are completely opposite" (p. 113).

Some men have escaped or resisted socialization forces which encourage them to sexualize relationships, but even these men are usually aware that they must meet the general sexual expectations of others to be considered truly manly. A particularly poignant example of a boy attempting to fulfill sexual role expectations was related in a letter to Ann Landers (1976). the 16-year-old letter writer, responding to a previous letter in which a 15-year-old girl lamented that she had to either "put out or sit home," revealed why the boys in his crowd were sexually aggressive with girls: "Most of us try because we think it's expected. But it's a relief when the answer is no. Then we don't have to prove anything."

Men tend to isolate sex from other social aspects of life. A major consequence of early genital focus, reinforced in adolescence by heavy peer pressure to seek sex in order to validate masculinity (Kanin, 1967), is that men tend to experience sex as separate from other social and psychological aspects of living. At the extreme this tendency may manifest itself as an overwhelming or even exclusive emphasis on sexuality in a relationship. It is probably true that in recent years the purely sexual male image has assumed more subtle forms, but these new low-key seduction styles seem more surface adaptations than evidence that men have relinquished the basic belief that it is necessary to be "on the make" to be masculine.

Fasteau (1974) hypothesizes that isolated sex is a defense against male vulnerability. He believes that when men allow themselves to combine sexual attraction and intimacy, they become dependent on their partner, and that this kind of dependency, especially on a woman, is not compatible with the internalized masculine ideal. A more general explanation for the reluctance of some males to establish deep intimate bonds with women is that women are generally viewed unfavorably (Broverman et al., 1972; McKee & Sherriffs, 1957), and that men, especially men concerned about their masculinity, feel hesitant to relate closely to women because the association is potentially stigmatizing (Brannon, 1976).

Certainly a picture of the male as interested only in isolated sex is overdrawn, but there are recent data which indicate that men more than women are likely to view any heterosexual relationship in a sexual-romance framework (Rytting, 1975). College males in Rytting's study less often made distinctions between friendly and sexual relationships, and were more likely to expect sex as part of the relationship. Additional support for the view of men as evaluating heterosexual relationships along a central sexual-romantic dimension comes from Guinsburg's (1973) study of platonic and romantic relationships. Males in this study had difficulty distinguishing the two kinds of relationships.

From the sex differences which emerge in his study, Rytting proposes that definitions of intimacy from masculine and feminine perspectives differ: Men view "sex as being ubiquitous and therefore a focal point for all relationships with woman," while women distinguish sexual from nonsexual intimacy. Drawing on additional data, especially a negative correlation between perceived sexual behavior and verbal intimacy for males, Rytting concludes that the male perspective leads to indiscriminate sexual decision making and, even worse, tends to inhibit intimacy.

Sexual problems between men and women often develop because genital focus and subsequent sexual isolation in the male are out of phase with female development. Gagnon and Henderson (1975) have outlined some of the problems that emerge when boys and girls first meet each other sexually in adolescence:

> The young male, pressed on by his male peers and his prior masculinity training . . . pushes for more sexual activity when dating. Conversely, many young females . . . spend a good deal of time preventing sexual intimacy. Therefore, because of earlier differences in learning how to be sexual, males committed to sexuality but less trained in affection and love, may interact with females who are committed to love but relatively untrained in sexuality. (p. 38)

These difficulties are not limited to youth. Many adult men find it difficult or impossible to integrate heterosexual sex with friendship. In the worst cases, sex becomes so incompatible with emotional closeness that it actually seems to preempt intimacy.

This sex difference is both reflected and maintained by numerous features of Western culture. Purely pornographic materials as well as slick sexually-oriented magazines of the *Playboy* genre are aimed at the male market, while emotional love stories are typically found in women's publications. Even the language used by boys and men to denote sexual intercourse is more explicitly sexual and frequently aggressive, e.g., "screw," "fuck," "bang," as contrasted with favored female phrases for coitus, such as "make love with," "go to bed with," which extend the context and diminish sexual/genital connotations (Sanders, Note 3).

GOALS AND SUCCESS

One of the dominant themes that a boy learns as he approaches manhood is that success in his work is important, and that success is operationalized in terms of specific goals. The American male has been characterized as having his eye so firmly fixed on objectives as he attempts to climb the status ladder that he is unconcerned with the present quality of his life. This achievement theme has some obvious implications when it is transferred from the work place to the sexual arena.

The most direct parallel to goal orientation at work is orgasm orientation in bed. Preoccupation with orgasm as an indicator of sexual accomplishment not only applies to the traditional male's selfish attempts to satisfy himself, but it extends to the modern male-lover's preoccupation with bringing his partner to climax. As Fasteau (1974) puts it, "Since orgasm is thought to be the only real point of making love, physically competent performance, delivering the goods, easily becomes the sole basis for men's sexual self-esteem" (p. 27).

It is not surprising that traditional adult men still count mental notches for each sexual partner or even for each sexual act, while more sophisticated modern men count the number of orgasms they "produce" for their partners. And in some subcultures, this quantitative approach to sexuality expresses itself as a positive association between degree of masculinity and number of children.

While the orgasm itself is a specific goal, many men consider the entire sexual encounter as a goal. Fasteau (1974) observes that "For most men, courting and seduction are nuisances. The focus is almost exclusively on reaching the goal of conquest with all possible speed" (p. 32). Whether the goal is general—"conquest"—or more specific—orgasm—men's concerns with ends often cheat them of process pleasures.

When sex is perceived as goal rather than process, a man may come to value sexual activities not according to his own feelings, but contingent on the feedback he receives from his partner. And women, not insensitive to the frailty of the male sexual ego, often collude by providing the positive responses the man seems to need, ranging from mild verbal praise to passionate histrionics; in one survey (Tavris, 1973) more than two-thirds of women reported faking orgasm.

Perhaps the most deleterious consequence of the male obsession with goals and success is that honest communication is often inhibited between men and their sexual partners. Success or the appearance of success becomes so important to the man that he cannot—and his partner knows he cannot—tolerate critical comments or even friendly suggestions related to his sexual functioning.

CONTROL AND POWER

Not surprisingly, characteristic male behaviors and attitudes associated with maintaining control and power at work and home are commonly found in sexual relationships as well. One means by which a man maintains sexual control is to play the role of initiator.

Carlson concludes that the "initiation of sexual activity is (still) viewed by both spouses as being a husband-oriented activity" (p. 105). A very recent study of college-educated young marrieds yielded data which corroborate Carlson's results that husbands are the primary initiators (Crain and Roth, Note 1). And Peplau et al. (1977) note that virtually all of the men in their sample of college couples exert positive control by playing the role of initiator.

The initiation norm that prescribes that the man must make the first sexual move is usually extended to prescribe male control during the sexual interaction itself.

Safilios-Rothschild (1977) believes that even contemporary women feel uncomfortable taking the sexual lead and that their discomfort may be related to their empathy with the male's fear of losing control: "[Men are] ambivalent in their reactions toward sexually active and skilled women" (p. 112). And some of Komarovsky's (1976) intensive interviews with college males support the notion that men have difficulty accepting sexual invitations from women.

The male role of sexual expert is closely related to a general male caveat against help-seeking. Rugged independence, even when inappropriate or harmful, has become an integral part of traditional masculinity. This is illustrated in a modern fable dealing with the socialization of a young boy (Allen, 1972). The boy is instructed, "You must never ask anyone for help, or even let anyone know that you are confused or frightened. That's part of learning to be a man." In sexual matters, so central to the male ego, admitting ignorance, asking for information, or seeking help are especially difficult. In a recent survey, Skovholt, Nagy, and Epting (Note 4) found that college men were significantly less able than college women to ask sexual questions of a friend.

This male attitude toward admitting ignorance publicly may explain the tremendous burgeoning of sex manuals in the past few years. Although some of these manuals do provide helpful information, many of them tend to promote sex as a purely technical and therefore less human activity. This technical approach to sex has the advantage of allowing private learning, but it permits men to remain in control by appearing to solve difficult human problems within a typical masculine framework which values logic and concrete results (Farrell, 1974).

Like some other aspects of the traditional male role, needs for power and control have important negative effects on heterosexual relationships. When men occupy the role of expert, teacher, initiator, leader, pleasure-giver, etc., women are deprived of experiencing the positive aspects of these roles; moreover men deprive themselves of positively experiencing complementary roles which involve relaxing and receiving pleasure.

AGGRESSION AND VIOLENCE

Probably the most extreme sexual manifestation of male aggression is rape. A number of writers (Brownmiller, 1975; Medea & Thompson, 1974; Russell, 1975) view rape as less an aberrant criminal act than a natural outgrowth of traditional male socialization. Russell, whose analysis is based on accounts of rape by rapists and their victims, suggests:

> [Rape] may be understood as an extreme acting out of the qualities that are regarded as supermasculine in this and many other societies: aggression, force, power, strength, toughness, dominance, competitiveness . . . sex may be the arena where those notions of masculinity are most intensely acted out, particularly by men who feel powerless in the rest of their lives. (p. 260)

Because only a small percentage of men actually commit rape, and even fewer are brought to trial and convicted, there has been a tendency to view sexual aggression as a relatively limited phenomenon applying only to rapists and their victims. A series of interview studies by Eugene Kanin provides a sobering counterpoint to the comforting belief that heterosexual sex offenses are perpetuated only by a small population of deviant criminals. Offenses committed even by males of above average education are so pervasive that in one study (Kanin, 1965) more than 25% of the male undergradute respondents admitted at least one incident of "sex aggression" since entering college. Sex aggression in this study was defined as a self-reported forceful attempt at coitus that resulted in the victim reacting by "crying, fighting, screaming, pleading, etc." (p. 221).

Both Kanin (1957) and Russell (1975) point out that heterosexual aggression may be encouraged by male fantasies that are commonly portrayed in the media. A dangerous prototype of this sort occurs in Peckinpaugh's violent film, *Straw Dogs*, in which a female rape victim valiantly resists for a few moments before acquiescing and ultimately responding ardently to her attacker. Selkin (1975) provides some evidence that these fantasies are some-times translated into violent action. He reports that some convicted rapists insist that their victims enjoy sexual assault. Along these lines, Russell (1975), relates this account of a rape: "Her date finally succeeded in raping her after a two-hour struggle, but he could not understand why she was so upset. . . . he considered himself a lover in the tradition of forceful males and expected to have a continuing relationship with her" (p. 258). In milder form, many women can attest to the sometimes unconscious confusion of sex and aggres-sion that emerges in the many forms of "normal" male heterosexual activity.

Although peers probably reward men more for charming and manipulating women into bed than for coercing sex from female victims, it is likely that the overwhelming pressure on men to prove their masculinity via sexual perfor-mance indirectly leads to aggression and rape. Kanin (1970) reports that college peer groups, especially fraternities, "stress the erotic goal to such a degree that, in the face of sexual failure, there is a resorting to physical aggression" (p. 35).

TRADITIONAL AND MODERN MALE SEX ROLES

In the popular literature there presently exist at least two popularly held but contradictory characterizations of heterosexual man:

1. Man as exploitative sexual animal, an insensitive user of women, constantly on the prowl, grasping at any sexual opportunity, and gratifying himself quickly with little if any real caring or feeling for his partner.
2. Man as technically competent lover who strives to create multiple orgasmic pleasure for his partner; he asks, or better even senses, what she wants and then endeavors to provide it in his undaunting efforts to satisfy her.

The second, apparently more sensitive characterization has gained promi-nence in the past few years. Although the evolution from animal to technician (reflected and influenced by the proliferation of modern sex manuals, and perhaps best chronicled in the *Playboy* Advisor column) may at first appear egalitarian and progressive, it can be argued that this shift is basically a superficial one, and in any event largely restricted to the middle class (Rain-water, 1965; Rubin, 1976; Pleck, 1976).

In making a general distinction between modern and traditional sex roles, Pleck (1976) argues that the modern role has not served as a panacea for heterosexual ills; in fact it has brought with it a host of new problems. Using a sexual example, Pleck discusses the shift from the traditional male goal of numerous sexual acts with many women to the more modern goal of sexually satisfying at least one woman. Both goals are quantitative: number of con-quests in the former case, number of orgasms in the latter.

Rubin (1976) captures the essence of a related modern problem in an interview with one of several wives in her sample who were preoccupied with their own orgasms "primarily because their husbands' sense of manhood rested on it":

> It's really important for him that I reach a climax and I try to every time. He says it just doesn't make him feel good if I don't. But it's hard enough

to do it once! What'll happen if he finds out about those women who have lots of climaxes? (p. 92)

While few contemporary couples retain nostalgia for the days when men could efficiently "exercise marital rights" rather than "make love," it is apparent that the modern male role with its focus on sexual competence has created a whole set of new problems for heterosexual relationships.

NOTES

1. Crain, S., & Roth, S. "Interactional and interpretive processes in sexual initiation in married couples." Paper presented at the meeting of the American Psychological Association, San Francisco, August 1977.

2. Rytting, M. B. "Sex or intimacy: Male and female versions of heterosexual relationships." Paper presented at the meeting of the Midwestern Psychological Association, Chicago, May 1976.

3. Sanders, J. S. *Female and male language in communication with sexual partners.* Paper presented at the meeting of the Association for Women in Psychology, St. Louis, February 1977.

4. Skovholt, T. M., Nagy, F., & Epting, F. "Teaching sexuality to college males." Paper presented at the meeting of the American Psychological Association, Washington, D.C., August 1976.

REFERENCES

Allen, B. Liberating the manchild. *Transactional Analysis Journal*, 1972, *2*, 68–71.

Allen, J. G., & Haccoun, D. M. Sex differences in emotionality: A multidimensional approach. *Human Relations*, 1976, *29*, 711–722.

Balswick, J., & Avertt, C. P. Differences in expressiveness: Gender, interpersonal orientation, and perceived parental expressiveness as contributing factors. *Journal of Marriage and the Family*, February 1977, pp. 121–127.

Balswick, J., & Peek, C. The inexpressive male: A tragedy of American society. *The Family Coordinator*, 1971, *20*, 363–368.

Bardwick, J. M. Psychological conflict and the reproductive system. In J. M. Bardwick, E. Douvan, M. S. Horner, & D. Gutmann (Eds.), *Feminine personality and conflict*. Monterey, CA: Brooks/Cole, 1970.

Bardwick, J. M. *Psychology of women*. New York: Harper & Row, 1971.

Bem, S. L. The measurement of psychological androgyny. *Journal of Consulting and Clinical Psychology*, 1974, *72*, 155–162.

Bengis, I. *Combat in the erogenous zone*. New York: A. A. Knopf, 1972.

Berkowitz, L. *A survey of social psychology*. Hinsdale, IL: Dryden Press, 1975.

Brannon, R. The male sex role: Our culture's blueprint of manhood, and what it's done for us lately. In D. S. David & R. Brannon (Eds.), *The forty-nine percent majority: The male sex role*. Reading, MA: Addison-Wesley, 1976.

Broverman, I. K., Broverman, D. M., Clarkson, F. E., Rosenkrantz, P. S., & Vogel, S. R. Sex-role stereotypes and clinical judgments of mental health. *Journal of Consulting Psychology*, 1972, *34*, 1–7.

Brownmiller, S. *Against our will*. New York: Simon & Schuster, 1975.

Byrne, D. Social psychology and the study of sexual behavior. *Personality and Social Psychology Bulletin*, 1977, *3*, 3–30.

Carlson, J. E. The sexual role. In F. I. Nye (Ed.), *Role structure and analysis of the family*. Beverly Hills, CA: Sage Publications, 1976.

Davies, N. H., & Fisher, A. Liberated sex: The rise and fall of male potency. *Marriage and Divorce*, March/April 1974, pp. 66–69.

Deaux, K. *The behavior of women and men.* Monterey, CA: Brooks/Cole, 1976.

Farrell, W. *The liberated man: Beyond masculinity.* New York: Random House, 1974.

Fasteau, M. F. *The male machine.* New York: McGraw-Hill, 1974.

Freud, S. *Sexuality and the psychology of love.* New York: Macmillan (Collier Books), 1963. (Originally published, 1905.)

Gagnon, J. *Human Sexualities.* Glenview, IL: Scott, Foresman and Company, 1977.

Gagnon, J., & Henderson, B. *Human sexuality: An age of ambiguity.* Boston: Educational Associates, 1975.

Gagnon, J., & Simon, W. *Sexual conduct: The social sources of sexuality.* Chicago: Aldine, 1973.

Gingold, J. One of these days—Pow! Right in the kisser: The truth about battered wives. *Ms.*, August 1976, p. 51.

Ginsberg, G. L., Frosch, W. A., & Shapiro, T. The new impotence. *Archives of General Psychiatry*, 1972, *26*, 218–220.

Griffin, S. Rape: The all-American crime. *Ramparts Magazine*, September 1971, pp. 26–35.

Guinsburg, P. F. An investigation of the components of platonic and romantic heterosexual relationships. (Doctoral dissertation, University of North Dakota, 1973). (University Microfilms No. 73–39, 623)

Hunt, M. Today's man. *Redbook*, October 1976, pp. 112–113; 163–170.

Julty, S. A case of "sexual dysfunction." *Ms.*, November 1972, pp. 18–21.

Kaats, G. R., & Davis, K. E. The social psychology of sexual behavior. In L. S. Wrightsman (Ed.), *Social psychology in the seventies.* Monterey, CA: Brooks/Cole, 1972.

Kanin, E. J. Male aggression in dating-courtship relations. *American Journal of Sociology*, 1957, *63*, 197–204.

Kanin, E. J. Male sex aggression and three psychiatric hypotheses. *Journal of Sex Research*, 1965, *1*, 221–231.

Kanin, E. J. Reference groups and sex conduct norm violations. *The Sociological Quarterly*, 1967, *8*, 495–504.

Kanin, E. J. Selected dyadic aspects of male sex aggression. *Journal of Sex Research*, 1969, 5.

Kanin, E. J. Sex aggression by college men. *Medical Aspects of Human Sexuality*, September 1970, pp. 28–40.

Kinsey, A., Pomeroy, W. B., & Martin, C. E. *Sexual behavior in the human male.* Philadelphia: W. B. Saunders, 1948.

Kirkpatrick, C., & Kanin, E. Male sex aggression on a university campus. *American Sociological Review*, 1957, *22*, 52–58.

Koedt, A. *The myth of the vaginal orgasm.* Somerville, MA: New England Free Press, 1970.

Komarovsky, M. Cultural contradictions and sex roles. *American Journal of Sociology*, 1946, *52*, 182–89.

Korda, M. *Male chauvinism: How it works.* New York: Random House, 1973.

Landers, A. One boy's view of sex. The *St. Louis Post-Dispatch*, May 29, 1976.

Maccoby, E. E., & Jacklin, C. N. *The psychology of sex differences.* Stanford, CA: Stanford University Press, 1974.

Masters, W. H., & Johnson, V. E. *Human sexual response.* Boston: Little, Brown & Company, 1966.

Masters, W. H., & Johnson, V. E. *Human sexual inadequacy.* Boston: Little, Brown & Company, 1970.

McKee, J. P., & Sherriffs, A. C. The differential evaluation of males and females. *Journal of Personality*, 1957, *25*, 356–371.

Medea, A., & Thompson, K. *Against rape.* New York: Farrar, Straus, and Giroux, 1974.

Nichols, J. *Men's liberation: A new definition of masculinity.* New York: Penguin Books, 1975.

Nobile, P. What is the new impotence, and who's got it? *Esquire*, 1972, pp. 95–98.

Peplau, L. A., Rubin, Z., & Hill, C. T. Sexual intimacy in dating relationships. *Journal of Social Issues*, 1977, *33*(2), 86–109.

Pietropinto, A., & Simenauer, J. *Beyond the male myth: What women want to know about men's sexuality*. New York: Times Books, 1977.

Pleck, J. H. The male sex role: Definitions, problems, and sources of change. *Journal of Social Issues*, 1976, *32*(3), 155–164.

Rainwater, L. Sexual and marital relations. In *Family Design*. Chicago: Aldine, 1965.

Reik, T. *Sex in men and women: Its emotional variations*. New York: Noonday Press, 1960.

Rook, K. S., & Hammen, C. L. A cognitive perspective on the experience of sexual arousal. *Journal of Social Issues*, 1977, *33*(2).

Rubin, L. *Worlds of pain: Life in the working class family*. New York: Basic Books, 1976.

Russell, D. E. H. *The politics of rape: The victim's perspective*. New York: Stein & Day, 1975.

Rytting, M. B. *Self-disclosure in the development of a heterosexual relationship*. Unpublished doctoral dissertation, Purdue University, 1975.

Safilos-Rothschild, C. *Love, sex, and sex roles*. Englewood Cliffs, NJ: Prentice-Hall, 1977.

Sawyer, J. On male liberation. *Liberation*, 1970, *15*, 32–33.

Selkin, J. Rape. *Psychology Today*, August 1975, pp. 70–76.

Sheehy, G. *Passages: Predictable crises of adult life*. New York: E. P. Dutton & Co., 1976.

Singer, M. Sexism and male sexuality. *Issues in Radical Therapy*, 1976, *3*, 11–13.

Stein, M. L. *Lovers, friends, slaves*. New York: Berkeley Publishing Company, 1974.

Tavris, C. Woman & man. In C. Tavris (Ed.), *The female experience*. Del Mar, CA: CRM Publishing Company, 1973.

Tavris, C., & Pope, D. Masculinity: What does it mean to be a man? *Psychology Today*, October 1976, pp. 59–63.

Tavris, C. Men and women report their views on masculinity. *Psychology Today*, August 1977, pp. 34–42, 82.

Tharp, R. G. Dimensions of marriage roles. *Marriage and Family Living*, November 1963, pp. 389–404.

Weis, K., & Borges, S. S. Victimology and rape: The case of the legitimate victim. *Issues in Criminology*, 1973, *8*, 71–115.

Robert Staples

STEREOTYPES OF BLACK MALE SEXUALITY:
THE FACTS BEHIND THE MYTHS

It is difficult to think of a more controversial role in American society than that of the black male. He is a visible figure on the American scene, yet the least understood and studied of all sex–race groups in the United States. His cultural image is typically one of several types: the sexual superstud, the athlete, and the rapacious criminal. That is how he is perceived in the public consciousness, interpreted in the media and ultimately how he comes to see and internalize his own role. Rarely are we exposed to his more prosaic role as worker, husband, father and American citizen.

The following essay focuses on the stereotypical roles of black male heterosexuality, not to reinforce them, but to penetrate the superficial images of black men as macho, hypersexual, violent and exploitative. Obviously, there must be some explanation for the dominance of black men in the nations' negative statistics on rape, out-of-wedlock births, and premarital sexual activity. This is an effort to explore the reality behind the image.

BLACK MANHOOD

As a starting point, I see the black male as being in conflict with the normative definition of masculinity. This is a status which few, if any, black males have been able to achieve. Masculinity, as defined in this culture, has always implied a certain autonomy and mastery of one's environment. It can be said that not many white American males have attained this ideal either. Yet, white males did achieve a dominance in the nuclear family. Even that semblance of control was largely to be denied black men. During slavery he could receive the respect and esteem of his wife, children and kinsmen, but he had no formal legal authority over his wife or filial rights from his children. There are numerous and documented instances of the slave-owning class's attempts to undermine his respect and esteem in the eyes of his family.[1]

Beginning with the fact that slave men and women were equally subjugated to the capricious authority of the slaveholder, the African male saw his masculinity challenged by the rape of his woman, sale of his children, the rations issued in the name of the woman and children bearing her name. While those practices may have presaged the beginning of a healthier sexual egalitarianism than was possible for whites, they also provoked contradictions and dilemmas for black men in American society. It led to the black male's self-devaluation as a man and set the stage for internecine conflict within the black community.

A person's sex role identity is crucial to their values, life-style and personality. The black man has always had to confront the contradiction between the normative expectations attached to being male in this society and the proscriptions on his behavior and achievement of goals. He is subjected to societal opprobrium for failing to live up to the standards of manhood on the one hand and for being super macho on the other. It is a classical case of "damned if you do and damned if you don't." In the past there was the assertion that black men were effeminate because they were raised in households with only a female parent or one with a weak father figure. Presently, they are being attacked in literature, in plays, and at conferences as having succumbed to the male chauvinist ideal.

Although the sexual stereotypes apply equally to black men and women, it is the black male who has suffered the worst because of white notions of his hypersexuality. Between 1884 and 1900 more than 2,500 black men were lynched, the majority of whom were accused of sexual interest in white women. Black men, it was said, had a larger penis, a greater sexual capacity and an insatiable sexual appetite. These stereotypes depicted black men as primitive sexual beasts, without the white male's love for home and family.[2] These stereotypes persist in the American consciousness.

It is in the area of black sexual behavior, and black male sexuality in particular, that folk beliefs are abundant but empirical facts few. Yet public policy, sex education and therapeutic programs to deal with the sex-related problems of black people cannot be developed to fit their peculiar needs until we know the nature and dynamics of black sexual behavior. Thus, it is incumbent upon researchers to throw some light on an area enmeshed in undocumented myths and stereotypes.

SEXUALITY OF THE MALE ADOLESCENT

The Kinsey data, cited by Bell,[3] reveal that black males acquire their knowledge about condoms at a later age than white males. The white male learns about sexual intercourse at a later age than black males. Because of poorer nutrition, the black male reaches puberty at a later age than his white male counterpart. A critical distinction between black and white males was the tendency of the more sexually repressed white male to substitute masturbation, fellatio and fantasy for direct sexual intercourse. Masturbation, for instance, was more likely to be the occasion of the first ejaculation for the white male while intercourse was for the black male. A larger percentage of white males reported being sexually aroused by being bitten during sexual activity, seeing a member of the opposite sex in a social situation, seeing themselves nude in the mirror or looking at another man's erect penis, hearing dirty jokes, reading sadomasochistic literature and viewing sexy pictures. Conversely, black males tended to engage in premarital intercourse at earlier ages, to have intercourse and to reach orgasm more frequently. As Bell notes in his analysis of these data, the black male's overabundance of sexuality is a myth. The sexuality of black and white men just tends to take different forms and neither group has any more self-control or moral heroism than the other.

Among young black American males, sexual activity begins at an earlier age, is more frequent and involves more partners. Apparently white males are more likely to confine their associations in the adolescent years with other men. Larson and his associates found that black male adolescents were twice as likely to be romantically involved with women than white males.[4] The kind of rigid gender segregation found in white culture is largely absent from black society. For example, blacks are less likely to be associated with all male clubs, organizations or colleges.

The sexual code of young black males is a permissive one. They do not, for example, divide black women into "good" (suitable for marriage) and "bad" (ineligible for marriage) categories. In the lower income groups, sexual activity is often a measure of masculinity. Thus, there is a greater orientation toward premarital sexual experimentation. In a study of premarital sexual standards among blacks and whites in the 1960s, Ira Reiss found that the sexual permissiveness of white males could be affected by a number of social forces (e.g., religion), but the black male was influenced by none of them.[5] Leanor Johnson and this author found that few black male adolescents were aware of the increased risk of teenage pregnancy, but there was an almost unanimous wish not to impregnate their sexual partner. Another survey of black male high school students reported their group believed that a male respects his partner when he uses a condom.[6]

POVERTY AND THE BLACK FATHER

The period of adolescence, with its social, psychological and physical changes (particularly sex-role identity and sexuality), is the most problematic of the life cycle stages. The prolongation of adolescence in complex technological society and the earlier onset of puberty have served to compound the problem. While adolescents receive various messages to abandon childlike behavior, they are systematically excluded from adult activity such as family planning. This exclusion is justified not only by their incomplete social and emotional maturity, but by their lack of marketable skills which are necessary to command meaningful status-granting jobs. Unskilled adolescents are further disadvantaged if they are members of a minority racial group in a racially stratified society.

Parenthood at this stage of the life cycle is most undesirable. Yet, recent upsurges in teenage pregnancy and parenthood have occurred, specifically among females younger than 14. Approximately 52% of all children born to black women in 1982 were conceived out-of-wedlock. Among black women under age 20, about 75% of all births were out-of-wedlock compared with only 25% of births to young white women.[7] Although the rate of white out-of-wedlock pregnancy is increasing and that of non-whites decreasing, black unwed parenthood remains higher than that of whites.

Because life and family support systems of black males are severely handicapped by the effects of poverty and discrimination, the consequences of becoming a father in adolescence are more serious for the minority parent. Many family planning agencies offer counseling to the unwed mother, while the father is usually involved only superficially or punitively—as when efforts are made to establish legal paternity as a means for assessing financial responsibilty. This omission, however, is not unique to black males. It is, perhaps, the single fact of inadequate economic provision which has resulted in the social agencies' premature conclusion that unwed fathers are unwilling to contribute to the future of their child and the support of the mother. Furthermore, sociological theory purports that slavery broke the black man's sense of family responsibility. Thus, it is assumed that black women do not expect nor demand that black men support them in raising their children.

FAMILY PLANNING

Recent evidence, however, suggests that the matrifocality of present theory and social services is myopic. Studies have demonstrated that most unwed fathers are willing to face their feelings and responsibilities.[8] The findings suggest that unmarried black males do not consider family planning a domain of the female, but rather a joint responsibility to be shared by both parents.[9]

Throughout the world one of the most important variables affecting birth rates is the male attitude toward family planning and the genesis of this attitude. Too often we are accustomed to thinking of reproduction as primarily a female responsibility. Since women are the main bearers and main rearers of children in our society, we tend to believe that they should be primarily concerned with planning the size of a family and developing those techniques of contraception consistent with family's earning power, their own health and happiness and the psychological well-being of their children.

However, in a male-dominated world it is women who are given the burden of having and rasing children, while it is often men who determine what the magnitude of that burden should be. Unfortunately, the male's wishes in regard to the size of his family are not contingent on the effect of childbearing on the female partner, but are often shaped by his own psychological and status concerns.

Within many societies there is an inseparable link between men's self-image and their ability to have sexual relations with women and the subsequent birth of children from those sexual acts. For example, in Spanish-speaking cultures this masculine norm is embedded in the concept of "machismo." "Machismo," derived from the Latin word "masculus," literally means the ability to produce sperm and thus sire—abilities which define the status of a man in society. In male-dominated society other issues involved in reproduction are subordinated to the male's desire to affirm his virility, which in turn confirms his fulfillment of the masculine role. The research literature tells us that the male virility cult is strongest in countries and among groups where the need for family planning is greatest.

Thus, we find that in underdeveloped countries—and among low-income ethnic groups in industrialized societies, including much of the black population in the U.S.—men are resistant to anything but natural controls on the number of children they have. Studies show that males who strongly believe that their masculine status is associated with their virility do not communicate very well with their wives on the subject of family planning. As a result the wives are less effective in limiting their families to the number of children they desire.

SEXUAL AGGRESSION

Sexual attacks against women are pervasive and sharply increasing in this country. The typical rapist is a black male and his victim is most often a black female. However, the most severe penalties for rape are reserved for black males accused of raping white women. Although 50% of those convicted for rape in the South were white males, over 90% of those executed for this crime in that region were black. Most of their alleged victims were white. No white male has ever been executed for raping a black women.[10]

As is probably true of white females, the incidence of rape of black women is underreported. Ladner reported that an eight-year-old girl has a good chance of being exposed to rape and violence if she is a member of the black underclass.[11] While widespread incidents of this kind are rooted in the sexist socialization of all men in society, it is pronounced among black men who have other symbols of traditional masculinity blocked to them. Various explanations have been put forth to explain why black men seem to adopt the attitudes of the majority group toward black women. Poussaint believes that because white men have historically raped black women with impunity, many black males believe they can do the same.[12]

Sexual violence is also rooted in the dynamics of the black dating game. The majority of black rape victims know their attacker—a friend, relative, or neighbor. Many of the rapes occur after a date and are what Amir describes as misfired attempts at seduction.[13] A typical pattern is for the black male to seek sexual compliance from his date, encounter resistance which he thinks is feigned, and proceed to forcibly obtain his sexual gratification from her. Large numbers of black men believe sexual relations to be their "right" after a certain amount of dating.

Rape, however, is not regarded as the act of a sexually starved male but rather as an aggressive act toward females. Students of the subject suggest that it is a long-delayed reaction against authority and powerlessness. In the case of black men, it is asserted that they grow up feeling emasculated and powerless before reaching manhood. They often encounter women as authority figures and teachers or as the head of their household. These men consequently act out their feelings of powerlessness against black women in the form of sexual aggression. Hence, rape by black men should be viewed as both an aggressive and political act because it occurs in the context of racial discrimination which denies most black men a satisfying manhood.

Manhood in American society is closely tied to the acquisition of wealth. Men of wealth are rarely required to rape women because they can gain sexual access through other means. A female employee who submits to the sexual demands of a male employer in order to advance in her job is as much an unwilling partner in this situation as is the rape victim. The rewards for her sexual compliance are normatively sanctioned, whereas the rapist does not often have the resources to induce such sexual compliance. Moreover, the concept of women as sexual property is at the root of rape. This concept is peculiar to capitalistic, western societies rather than African nations (where the incidence of rape is much lower). For black men, rape is often an act of aggression against women because the kinds of status men can acquire through success in a job is not available to them.

RECOMMENDATIONS

To address the salient issues in black male sexuality, I offer the following recommendations:

1. An educational program for black men must be designed to sensitize them to the need for their responsibility for, and participation in, family planning. This program will best be conducted by other men who can convey the fact that virility is not in and of itself the measure of masculinity. Also, it should be emphasized that the use of contraception—or obtaining a vasectomy—does not diminish a male's virility.
2. An over-all sex education program for both sexes should begin as early as kindergarten, before the male peer group can begin to reinforce attitudes of male dominance. Sex education courses should stress more than the physiological aspects in its course content. Males should be taught about the responsibility of men in sex relations and procreation. Forms of male contraception should be taught along with female measures of birth control.
3. The lack of alternative forms of role fulfillment avaiable to many men, especially in industrialized societies, must be addressed. In cases of unemployment and underemployment, the male often resorts to the virility cult because it is the only outlet he has for a positive self-image and prestige within his peer group. Thus, we must provide those conditions whereby men can find meaningful employment.
4. Lines of communication must be opened between men and women. A supplement to the educational program for men should be seminars and workshops involving both men and women. Hopefully, this will lead to the

kind of dialog between men and women that will sensitize each of them to the feelings of the other.

NOTES

[1] Robert Staples, *The Black Family: Essays and Studies*. (Belmont, CA: Wadsworth, 1978.)

[2] Robert Staples, *Black Masculinity*, (San Francisco: The Black Scholar Press, 1982.)

[3] Alan P. Bell, "Black Sexuality: Fact and Fancy" in R. Staples, ed., *The Black Family: Essays and Studies*, pp. 77–80.

[4] David Larson, et al., "Social Factors in the Frequency of Romantic Involvement Among Adolescents." *Adolescence* 11: 7–12, 1976.

[5] Ira Reiss, *The Social Context of Premarital Sexual Permissiveness*. (New York: Holt, Rinehart and Winston, 1968.)

[6] Leanor Johnson and Robert Staples, "Minority Youth and Family Planning: A Pilot Project." *The Family Coordinator* 28: 534–543, 1978.

[7] U.S. Bureau of the Census, *Fertility of American Women*. (Washington, D.C. U.S. Government Printing Office, 1984.)

[8] Lisa Connolly, "Boy Fathers." *Human Behavior* 45: 40–43, 1978.

[9] B. D. Misra, "Correlates of Males' Attitudes Toward Family Planning" in D. Bogue, ed., *Sociological Contributions to Family Planning Research*. (Chicago: Univ. of Chicago Press, 1967), pp. 161–167.

[10] William J. Bowers, *Executions in America*. (Lexington Books, 1974).

[11] Joyce Lander, *Tomorrow's Tomorrow: The Black Woman*. (Garden City, New York: Doubleday, 1971.)

[12] Alvin Poussaint, *Why Blacks Kill Blacks*. (New York: Emerson-Hall, 1972.)

[13] Menachim Amir, "Sociocultural Factors in Forcible Rape" in L. Gross, ed., *Sexual Behavior*. (New York: Spectrum Publications, 1974), pp. 1–12.

Jeffrey Fracher and Michael S. Kimmel[1]

HARD ISSUES AND SOFT SPOTS:
COUNSELING MEN ABOUT SEXUALITY

Nothing shows more clearly the extent to which modern society has atomized itself than the isolation in sexual ignorance which exists among us. . . . Many cultures, the most primitive and the most complex, have entertained sexual fears of an irrational sort, but probably our culture is unique in strictly isolating the individual in the fears that society has devised.

—Lionel Trilling[2]

Reprinted from *Handbook of Counseling and Psychotherapy with Men* (edited by Murray Scher, Mark Stevens, Glenn Good, and Gregg Eichenfield). Newbury Park, CA: Sage Publications, 1987. © 1987 by Sage Publications. Reprinted by permission.

Sam[3] is a 28-year-old white, single factory worker. He lives alone in a two-family home which he owns, and attends night school at a community college. The third of six sons in a blue-collar, Eastern European Catholic family, Sam is a conscientious, hardworking, and responsible man with very traditional values. He describes himself as a sexual late-bloomer, having begun dating only after graduation from an all-male Catholic high school. Although strong and handsome, he has always lacked confidence with women, and describes himself as male peer oriented, actively involved in sports, and spending much of his leisure time with "the boys."

Prior to his first sexual intercourse, two years ago at age 26, Sam had fabricated stories to tell his friends so as not to appear inadequate. He felt a great deal of shame and embarrassment that his public presentation of his sexual exploits had no basis in reality. His limited sexual knowledge caused him great anxiety and difficulty, especially since the woman with whom he was involved had had previous sexual encounters. Upon completion of inter-course, she reported that "he came too fast" (i.e., less than one minute, or after several thrusts), a statement that, he reported, "hit me between the eyes." His second attempt at intercourse was no more successful, inspite of his use of a condom to reduce sensation, and he subsequently broke off this relationship because of the shame and embarrassment about his sexual incompetence, and the fear that word would leak out to his friends. He subsequently developed a secondary pattern of sexual avoidance, and when he first came to treatment, indicating that he was "not a real man because I can't satisfy a woman," he had not had sex for two years, and was reluctant to resume dating until his premature ejaculation was vastly improved.

Joe is a 34-year-old C.P.A. who has been married for three years. The youngest of five children and the only male in a middle class Irish-American family, Joe feels his father had high expectations from him, and exhibited only neutrality or criticism. Joe was without a male role model who conveyed that it was OK to fail. In fact, he portrayed men as strong, competent, without feelings, and without problems or failings, and believes he can never live up to the image his father had for him. Consequently, Joe is terrified that failure to please a woman sexually may result in criticism that will challenge his masculinity; he will not be a "real man." Anticipating this criticism from his wife, his sexual interest is reduced.

When first seen in therapy, Joe evidenced a total lack of sexual interest in his wife, but a high degree of sexual interest involving sexual fantasies, pornography, and masturbation. He said "lust is an obsession with me," indicating a high sex drive when sex is anonymous and though he felt sexually inadequate with his wife, he felt sexually potent with women he devalues, such as prostitues. He could not understand his almost total lack of sexual interest in his wife.

Bill is a 52-year-old engineer, who has been married for 25 years. From a white, middle-class Protestant background, he has one grown child, and initially came to treatment upon referral from a urologist. He had seen numerous physicians after experiencing erectile dysfunction three years ago, and has actively sought a physical explanation for it.

Bill's wife, Ann was quite vocal about her disappointment in his failure to perform sexually. Bill had always been the sexual initiator, and Ann had come to expect that he should be in charge. Both believed that the only "real sex" is intercourse with an erect penis. Ann frequently commented that she felt "emotionally empty" without intercourse, thereby adding to his sense of inadequacy. The loss of his capacity for erection, Bill told the therapist, meant that he had lost his masculinity, and he worried openly about displeasing Ann and her possibly leaving him.

His fear of lost masculinity spilled over into his job performance, and he became depressed and withdrew from social activities. Bill was unaware that as an older man, he required more direct penile stimulation for an erection, since he had never required it in the past, and was unable to ask for it from Ann. He felt that a "real man never has to ask his wife for anything sexually," and should be able to perform without her help. The pattern of erectile dysfunction was part of a broader pattern of inability to tolerate failure, and he had begun to lose self-confidence since his masculinity was almost entirely predicated upon erectile functioning. "Nothing else matters," he confided, if his masculinity (evidenced by a functional erection) was not present. Everything was suddenly on the line—his self-worth, his marriage, and his career—if he proved unable to correct his problem.

Sam, Joe, and Bill manifest the three most common sexual complaints of men seeking therapy. But underlying premature ejaculation, inhibited sexual desire, and erectile dysfunction is a common thread, binding these and other sexual problems together. Each fears that his sexual problem damages his sense of masculinity, making him less of a "real man." In a sense, we might say that all three men "suffer" from masculinity.

This chapter will explore how gender becomes one of the key organizing principles of male sexuality, informing and structuring men's sexual experiences. It will discuss how both gender and sexuality are socially constructed, and how therapeutic strategies to help men deal with sexual problems can raise issues of gender identity. This is especially important, of course, since so many therapeutic interventions rely on a diagnostic model that is simultaneously overly individualistic (in that it locates the source of the problem entirely within the individual) and transhistorical (in that it assumes that all cultures exhibit similar patterns at all times). The chapter combines a comparative and historical understanding of how both gender and sexuality are socially constructed with a psychoanalytic understanding of the transformative possibilities contained within the therapeutic relationship. This combination will lead us to discuss both social and therapeutic interventions that might facilitate healthier sexual expression for men.

THE SOCIAL CONSTRUCTION OF SEXUALITY
AND MASCULINITY

Sexuality is socially constructed, a learned set of both behaviors and cognitive interpretations of those behaviors. Sexuality is less the product of biological drives than of a socialization process, and this socialization process is specific to any culture at any particular time. This means that "social roles are not vehicles for the expression of sexual impluse but that sexuality becomes a vehicle for expressing the needs of social roles" (Gagnon and Simon, 1973: 45). *That* we are sexual is determined by a biological imperative toward reproduction, but *how* we are sexual—where, when, how often, with whom, and why—has to do with cultural learning, with meanings transmitted in a cultural setting. Sexuality varies from culture to culture; it changes in any one culture over time; it changes over the course of each of our lives. Sexual beings are made and not born; we make ourselves into sexual beings within a cultural framework. Although it may appear counterintuitive, this perspective suggests that the elusive quality commonly called "desire" is actually a relatively unimportant part of sexual conduct. As Gagnon and Simon argue (1973: 103), "the availability of sexual partners, their ages, their incomes, their point in the economic process, their time commitments . . . shape their sexual careers far more than the minor influence of sexual desire." Sexuality is learned in roughly the same way as anything else is learned in our culture. As Gagnon writes (1977: 2):

> In any given society, at any given moment, people become sexual in the same way as they become everything else. Without much reflection, they pick up directions from their social environment. They acquire and assemble meanings, skills and values from the people around them. Their critical choices are often made by going along and drifting. People learn when they are quite young a few of the things that they are expected to be, and continue slowly to accumulate a belief in who they are and ought to be through the rest of childhood, adolescence, and adulthood. Sexual conduct is learned in the same ways and through the same processes; it is acquired and assembled in human interaction, judged and performed in specific cultural and historical worlds.

If sexuality is socially constructed, perhaps the most significant element of the construction, the foundation on which we construct our sexuality, is gender. For men, the notion of masculinity, the cultural definition of manhood, serves as the primary building block of sexuality. It is through our understanding of masculinity that we construct a sexuality, and it is through our sexualities that we confirm the successful construction of our gender identity. Gender informs sexuality; sexuality confirms gender. Thus, men have a lot at stake when they confront a sexual problem: they risk their self-image as men.

Like sexuality, gender in general, and masculinity in particular is socially constructed; that is, what we understand to be masculine varies from culture to culture, over historical time within any one culture, and over the course of any one person's life within any culture. What we consider masculine or feminine in our culture is the result of neither some biological imperative nor some religious requirement, but a socially organized mode of behavior. What is masculine is not set in stone, but historically fluid. The pioneering research on gender by anthropologist Margaret Mead (1935) and others has specified how widely the cultural requirements of masculinity—what it takes to be a "real man" in any particular culture—vary. And these gender categories also shift in any one culture over time. Who would suggest, for example, that what was prescribed among upper class Frenchmen in the eighteenth century— rare silk stockings and red patent leather high heels, prolific amounts of perfume and facial powder, powdered wigs and very long hair, and a rather precious preoccupation with love poems, dainty furniture, and roses— resembles our contemporary version of masculinity?

The assertion of the social construction of sexuality and gender leads naturally to two related questions. First, we need to specify precisely the dimensions of masculinity within contemporary American culture. How is masculinity organized as a normative set of behaviors and attitudes? Second, we need to specify precisely the ways in which this socially constructed gender identity informs male sexual development. How is masculinity expressed through sexuality?

Brannon's (Brannon and David, 1976: 12) summary of the normative structure of contemporary American masculinity is relevant here. Masculinity requires the avoidance and repudiation of all behaviors that are even remotely associated with feminity ("no sissy stuff"); this requires a ceaseless patrolling of one's boundaries and an incessant surveillance of one's performances to ensure that one is sufficiently male. Men must be "Big Wheels," since success and status are key determinants of masculinity, and be "Sturdy Oaks," exhuding a manly air of self-confidence, toughness, and self-reliance, as well as reliability. Men must "Give 'em Hell," presenting an aura of aggression and daring, an attitude of constantly "going for it."

The normative organization of masculinity has been verified empirically (cf. Thompson and Pleck, 1986) and has obviously important implications for male sexuality. In a sense, sexuality is the location of the enactment of masculinity; sexuality allows the expression of masculinity. Male sexual socialization informs men that sexuality is the proving ground of adequate gender identity, and provides the script that men will adopt, with individual modification, as the foundation for sexual activity.

In a sense, when we examine the normative sexuality that is constructed from the typical organization of masculinity, it is not so much sexual problems that are of interest, but the problematization of "normal" sexuality, understanding perhaps the pathological elements within normal sexual functioning. This allows us to bridge the chasm between men who experience sexual dysfunction and those who, ostensibly, do not, and explore how men array themselves along a continuum of sexual expressions. Because masculinity provides the basic framework of sexual organization, and because masculinity requires adherence to certain rules that may retard or constrain emotional expression, we might fruitfully explore how even "normal" male sexuality evidences specific pathological symptoms, so that men who present exaggerated versions of these symptoms in therapy may better perceive their problems in a larger, sociological context of gender relations in contemporary society.[4]

The social construction of male sexuality raises a crucial theoretical issue. In the past, both social science research and clinical practice were informed by a model of discrete dichotomies. Categories for analysis implied a dualistic world view in which a phenomenon was classified as either X or Y. Thus, one was either male or female, heterosexual or homosexual, normal or pathological. Since the pioneering studies of Alfred Kinsey and his associates (cf. Kinsey et al., 1948, 1953), however, this traditional model of mutually exclusive dichotomous variables has given way to a model of a continuum of behaviors along which individuals array themselves. The continuum model allows individuals to reposition themselves at different moments in the life course, and it allows the researcher or clinician a point of entry into a relationship with the behaviors being discussed. The people we study and the people we counsel are less some curious "other" and more a variation on a set of behaviors that we, ourselves, embody as well. The articulation of the continuum model also requires that the level of analysis of any behavior include a social analysis of the context for behavior and the social construction of definitions of normality. It thus permits a truly *social* psychology.

THE MALE SEXUAL SCRIPT

Male sexual socialization teaches young men that sex is secret, morally wrong, and pleasurable, The association of sexual pleasure with feelings of guilt and shame is articulated early in the young boy's development, and reinforced throughout the life course by family, school, religion, and media images of sexuality. Young males are instructed, in locker rooms and playgrounds, to detach their emotions from sexual expression. In early masturbatory experience, the logic of detachment accommodates the twin demands of sexual pleasuring and guilt and shame. Later, detachment serves the "healthy" heterosexual male by permitting delay of orgasm in order to please his sexual partner, and serves the "healthy" homosexual male by permitting numerous sexual partners without cluttering up the scene with unpleasant emotional connection. (We will return to an exploration of the similarities between heterosexual and homosexual male sexuality below.)

Detachment requires a self-objectification, a distancing from one's self, and the development of a "secret sexual self" that performs sexual acts according to culturally derived scripts (Gagnon and Simon, 1973: 64). That men use the language of work as metaphors for sexual conduct—"getting the job done," "performing well," "achieving orgasm"—illustrates more than a passing interest in turning everything into a job whose performance can be evaluated; it reinforces detachment so that the body becomes a sexual machine, a performer instead of an authentic actor. The penis is transformed from an organ of sexual pleasure into a "tool," an instrument by which the performance is carried out, a thing, separate from the self. Many men report that they have conversations with their penises, and often cajole, plead with, or demand that they become and remain erect without orgasmic release. The penis can become the man's enemy, ready to engage in the most shameful conspiracy possible: performance failure. Is it any wonder that "performance anxiety" is a normative experience for male sexual behavior?

Men's earliest forays into sexuality, especially masturbation, are the first location of sexual anxiety. Masturbation teaches young men that sexuality is about the detachment of emotions from sex, that sex is important in itself. Second, men learn that sex is something covert, to be hidden; that is, men learn to privatize sexual experience, without skills to share the experience. And masturbation also teaches men that sexuality is phallocentric, that the penis is the center of the sexual universe. Finally, the tools of masturbation, especially sexual fantasy, teach men to objectify the self, to separate the self from the body, to focus on parts of bodies and not whole beings, often to speak of ones self in the third person.

Adolescent sexual socialization reinforces these behavioral demands that govern male sexuality. Passivity is absolutely forbidden, and the young male must attempt to escalate the sexual element at all times. To do otherwise is to avoid "giving 'em hell" and expose potential feminine behaviors. This constant pressure for escalation derives from the phallocentric component to male sexuality—"it only counts if I put it in" a student told one of the authors.

Since normative heterosexuality assigns to men the role of "doer" and to women the role of "gatekeeper," determining the level of sexual experience appropriate to any specific situation, this relentless pressure to escalate prevents either the male or the female from experiencing the sexual pleasure of any point along the continuum. No sooner does he "arrive" at a particular sexual experience—touching her breast, for example, than he begins strategizing the ways in which he can escalate, go further. To do less would expose him as less than manly. The female instantly must determine the limits of the encounter and devise the logistics that will prevent escalation if those limits have been reached. Since both male and female maintain a persistent orientation to the future (how to escalate and how to prevent escalation) neither can experience the pleasure of the points en route to full sexual intercourse. In fact, what men learn is that intercourse is the appropriate end-point of any sexual encounter, and that only intercourse "counts" in the tabulation of sexual encounters.

Since the focus is entirely phallocentric and intercourse is the goal to be achieved in adolescent sexual encounters, the stakes regarding sexual performance are extremely high, and consequently so is the anxiety about performance failure. Big wheels and sturdy oaks do not experience sexual dysfunction.

This continuum of male sexual dysfunction—ranging from what we might call the "normatively operative dysfunctional" to the cases of extreme distress of men who present themselves for therapeutic intervention—is reinforced in adult heterosexual relations as well. How do men maintain the sexual distancing and objectification that they perceive are required for healthy functioning? American comedian Woody Allen described, in his nightclub routines, a rather typical male strategy. After describing himself as "a stud," Allen comments:

> While making love, in an effort [pause] to prolong [pause] the moment of ecstasy, I think of baseball players. All right, now you know. So the two of us are making love violently, and she's digging it, so I figure I better start thinking of baseball players pretty quickly. So I figure it's one out, and the Giants are up. Mays lines a single to right. He takes second on a wild pitch. Now she's digging her nails into my neck. I decide to pinch-hint for McCovey. [pause for laughter] Alou pops out. Haller singles, Mays takes third. Now I've got a first and third situation. Two outs and the Giants are behind by one run. I don't know whether to squeeze or to steal. [pause for laughter] She's been in the shower for ten minutes already. [pause] I can't tell you anymore, this is too personal. [pause] The Giants won.[5]

Readers may be struck by several themes—the imputation of violence, how her pleasure leads to his decision to think of baseball players, the requirement of victory in the baseball game, and the sexual innuendo contained within the baseball language—but the text provides a startlingly honest revelation of male sexual distancing. Here is a device that is so successful at delaying ejaculation that the narrator is rendered utterly unaware of his partner. "She's been in the shower for ten minutes already, " Allen remarks, as if he's just noticed.

Much of peer sexual socialization consists of the conveying of these strategic actions that the male can perform to make himself a more adequate sexual partner. Men are often told to think of sports, work, or some other nonsexual event, or to repeat multiplication tables or mathematical formulas in order to keep themselves from premature ejaculation. It's as if sexual adequacy could be measured by time elapsed between penetration and orgasm, and the sexual experience itself is transformed into an endurance test in which pleasure, if present at all, is almost accidental.

The contemporary male sexual script—the normative construction of sexuality—provides a continuum along which men array themselves for the script's enactment. The script contains dicta for sexual distancing, objectification, phallocentrism, and a pressure to become and remain erect without ejaculation for as long as possible, all of which serve as indicators of masculinity as well as sexual potency. Adequate sexual functioning is seen as the proof of masculinity, so sexual problems will inevitably damage male gender identity. This is what makes treatment of sexual disorders a treatment of gender-identity issues.

Although this chapter has concentrated on sexual disorders for heterosexual men, this is neither for analytic reasons nor from a sense of how these problems might manifest differently for gay men. Quite the contrary, in fact. Since gender identity is the key variable in understanding sexual behaviors, we would argue that heterosexual and homosexual men have more in common in regard to their sexuality than they evidence differences. This is especially true since 1969, when the Stonewall riots in New York, and the subsequent emergence of the Gay Liberation Movement, led to the possibility for gay men to recover and repair their "damaged" sense of masculinity. Earlier gay men had been seen as "failed men," but the emergence of the gay male "clone" particularly has dispelled that notion. In the nation's gay ghettos, gay men often enact a hypermasculine ethic, complete with its attendant sexual scripting of distancing, phallocentrism, objectification, and separation of emotion from physical sensation. Another reason that heterosexual and homosexual men exhibit similar gender-based sexual behaviors is that all boys are subject to an anticipatory socialization toward heterosexuality, regardless of their eventual sexual preference. There is no anticipatory socialization toward homosexuality in this culture, so male gender socialization will be enacted with both male and female sexual partners. Finally, we have not focused on gay men as a specific group because to do so would require the marginalization of gay men as a group separate from the normative script of male sexuality. Both gay and straight men are men first, and both have "male sex."

THERAPEUTIC INTERVENTIONS

Our analysis of the social context of men's sexual problems makes it essential that therapeutic strategies remain aware of a context larger than simple symptom remission. Treatment must also challenge the myths, assumptions, and expectations that create the dysfunctional context for male sexual behavior (cf. Kaplan, 1974, 1983; LoPiccolo and LoPiccolo 1978; Tollison and Adams, 1979).

Men seeking treatment for sexual difficulties will most often present with a symptom such as erectile failure, premature ejaculation, or inhibited desire. However, the *response* to this symptom, such as anxiety, depression, or low self-esteem, is usually what brings the man into treatment, and this response derives from the man's relationship to an ideal vision of masculinity. The construction of this masculine ideal, therefore, needs to be addressed, since it often creates the imperative command—to be in a constant state of potential sexual arousal, to achieve and maintain perfectly potent erections on command, and to delay ejaculation for a long time—which results in the performance anxiety that creates the symptom in the first place.

Sex therapy exercises, such as those developed by Willam Masters and Virginia Johnson and others, are usually effective only when the social context of gender ideals has also been addressed. This is accomplished by exploring and challenging the myths of male sexuality, modeling by the therapist of a different version of masculinity, giving permission to the patient to fail, and self-disclosure by the therapist of the doubts, fears of inadequacy, and other anxieties that all men experience. These will significantly reduce the isolation that the patient may experience, the fear that he is the only man who experiences such sexually linked problems. These methods may be used to reorient men's assumptions about what constitutes masculinity, even though the therapist will be unable to change the entire social edifice that has been constructed on these gender assumptions. Both the cognitive as well as the physical script must be addressed in treating sexual dysfunction; the cognitive script is perhaps the more important.

Recall these specific examples we drew from case materials. Sam's sexual performance was charged with anxiety and shame regarding both female partners and male peers. He was adamant that no one know he was seeking therapy, and went to great lengths to assure that confidentiality be preserved. He revealed significant embarrassment and shame with the therapist in early sessions, which subsided once the condition was normalized by the therapist.

Sam had grown up with exaggerated expectations of male sexual performance—that men must perform sexually on cue and never experience any sexual difficulty—that were consistent with the social milieu in which he was raised. He held women on a pedestal, and he believed that a man must please a woman or risk losing her. The stakes were thus quite high. Sam was also terrified of appearing "unmanly" with women, which resulted in a high degree of performance anxiety, which, in turn, prompted the premature ejaculation. The cycle of anxiety and failure finally brought Sam to treatment. Finally, Sam was detached from his own sexuality, his own body both sexually and emotionally. His objectification of his penis made it impossible for him to monitor impending ejaculation, and he was therefore unable to moderate the intensity of sensation prior to the point of ejaculatory inevitability. This common pattern among men who experience premature ejaculation suggests that such a response comes not from hypersensitivity but rather an atrophied sensitivity, based on objectification of the phallus.

Sam's treatment consisted of permission to experience this problem from another man, and the attempt by the therapist to normalize the situation and reframe it as a problem any man might encounter. The problem was redefined as a sign of virility rather than an indication of its absence; Sam came to understand his sexual drive as quite high, which led to high levels of excitement that he had not yet learned to control. The therapist presented suggestions to control ejaculation that helped him moderate the intensity of arousal in order to better control his ejaculation. The important work, however, challenged the myths and cognitive script that Sam maintained regarding his sexuality. The attention given to his sexual performance, what he demanded of himself and what he believed women demanded of him, helped him reorient his sexuality into a less performance-oriented style.

Joe, the 34-year-old C.P.A. experienced low sexual desire with his wife though he masturbated regularly. Masturbatory fantasies involving images of women wanting him, finding him highly desirable, populated his fantasy world. When his self-esteem was low, as when he lost his job, for example, his sexual fantasies increased markedly. These fantasies of prowess with devalued women restored, he felt, his worth as a man. Interest in pornography included a script in which women were passive and men in control, very unlike the situation he perceives with his wife. He complained that he is caught in a vicious cycle, since without sexual interest in his wife he's not a "real man," and if he's not a "real man" then he has no sexual desire for her. He suggested that if he could only master a masculine challenge that was not sexual, such as finding another job or another competitive situation, he believed his sexual interest in his wife would increase. He felt he needed the mastery of a masculine challenge to confirm his sense of self as a man, which would then find further conformation in the sexual arena. This adds an empirical confirmation of Gagnon and Simon's argument (1973) that genital sexuality contains many nonsexual motives, including the desire for achievement, power, and peer approval. Joe came to therapy with a great deal of shame at having to be there, and was especially ashamed at having to tell another man about his failures as a man. He was greatly relieved by the therapist's understanding, self-disclosure, and nonjudgmental stance, which enhanced the therapist's credibility and Joe's commitment to treatment.

One cognitive script that Joe challenged in counseling was his embrace of the "madonna/whore" ideology. In this formulation, any woman worth having (the madonna—mother or wife) was perceived as both asexual and as sexually rejecting of him, since his failures rendered him less of a real man. A "whore," on the other hand, would be both sexually available and interested in him, so she is consequently devalued and avoided. He could be sexual with her because the stakes are so low. This reinforces the cultural equation between sexual pleasure and cultural guilt and shame, since Joe would want to be sexual only with those who would not want to be sexual with him. This common motif in male sexual socialization frequently emerges in descriptions of "good girls" and "bad girls" in high school.

Joe's therapy included individual short-term counseling with the goal of helping him see the relationship between his self-esteem and his inhibited sexual desire. Traditional masculine definitions of success were the sole basis for Joe's self-esteem, and these were challenged in the context of a supportive therapeutic environment. The failure of childhood male role models was contrasted with new role models that provide permission to fail and helped Joe view sexuality as noncompetitive and nonachievement-oriented activity. Joe began to experience a return of sexual desire for his wife, as he became less phallocentric and more able to see sex as a vehicle for expressing intimacy and caring rather than a performance for an objectified self and other.

Bill, the 52-year-old married engineer presented with erectile failure, which is part of a larger pattern of intolerance of failure in himself. The failure of his penis to function properly symbolized to him the ultimate collapse of his manhood. Not surprisingly, he had searched for physiological etiologies before seeking psychological counseling, having been referred by a urologist. It is estimated that less than 50% of all men who present themselves for penile implant surgery have a physiological basis for their problem; if so, the percentage of all men who experience erectile disorders whose etiology is physiological is less than 5%. Yet the pressure to salvage a sense of masculinity that might be damaged by a psychological problem leads thousands of men to request surgical prosthesis every year (cf. for example, Tiefer, 1986).

Bill and his wife, Ann, confronted in therapy the myths of male sexuality that they embraced, including such dicta as "a real man always wants sex," "the only real sex is intercourse," and "the man must always be in charge of sex." (cf. Zilbergeld, 1978). The therapist gave Bill permission to fail by telling him that all men at some time experience erectile dysfunction. Further, Bill was counseled that the real problem is not the erectile failure, but his reaction to this event. Exercises were assigned in which Bill obtained an erection through manual stimulation and then purposely lost the erection to desensitize himself to his terrible fear of failure. This helped him overcome the "what if" fear of losing the erection. Bill was counseled to "slow down" his sexual activity, and to focus on the sensations rather than the physical response, both of which were designed to further remove the performance aspects from his sexual activity. Finally, the therapist helped Bill and Ann redefine the notion of masculinity by stating that "a real man is strong enough to take risks, eschew stereotypes, to ask for what he needs sexually from a partner, and, most of all, to tolerate failure."

As Bill and Ann's cognitive script changed, his ability to function sexually improved. Though Bill still does not get full erections on a consistent basis, this fact is no loner catastrophic for him. He and Ann now have a broader script both physically and cognitively, which allows them to have other sexual play and the shared intimacy that it provides.

As one can see from these case studies, several themes run consistently through therapeutic strategies in counseling men about sexual problems, and many of these themes also relate directly to issues of social analysis as well as clinical practice. For example, the therapeutic environment must be experienced as supportive, and care must be taken so that the therapist not appear too threatening or too "successful" to the patient. The gender of the therapist with the male patient will raise different issues at this point. A male therapist can empathize with the patient, and greatly reduce his sense of isolation, whereas a female therapist can provide positive experience with a woman that may translate to nontherapeutic situations.

Second, the presenting symptom should be "normalized," that is it should be cast within the wider frame of male socialization to sexuality. It is not so much that the patient is "bad," "wrong," or "abnormal," but that he has experienced some of the contradictory demands of masculinity in ways that have become dysfunctional for his sexual experiences. It is often crucial to help the patient realize that he is not the only man who experiences these problems, and that these problems are only problems seen from within a certain construct of masculinity.

In this way, the therapist can help the patient to dissociate sexuality from his sense of masculinity, to break the facile identification between sexual performance and masculinity. Masculinity can be confirmed by more than erectile capacity, constant sexual interest, and a long duration of intercourse; in fact, as we have argued, normal male sexuality often requires the disso-ciation of emotional intimacy and connectedness for adequate sexual function-ing. Raising the level of analysis from the treatment of individual symptoms to a social construction of gender and sexuality does not mean abandoning the treatment of the presenting symptoms, but rather retaining their embedded-ness in the social context from which they emerge. Counseling men about sexuality involves, along with individualized treatment, the redefinition of what it means to be a man in contemporary American society. Therapeutic treatments pitched at both the social and the individual levels can help men become more expressive lovers and friends and fathers, as well as more "functional" sexual partners. That a man's most important sexual organ is his mind is as true today as ever.

NOTES

1. This paper represents a full collaboration, and our names appear in alphabetical order for convenience. Critical reactions from John Gagnon, Murray Scher, and Mark Stevens have been very helpful.
2. Lionel Trilling, *The Liberal Imagination*. New York: Alfred Knopf, 1954.
3. The names of the individual patients have been changed.
4. To assert a pathological element to what is culturally defined as "normal" is a contentious argument. But such an argument derives logically from assertions about the social construction of gender and sexuality. Perhaps an analogy would prove helpful. One might also argue that given the cultural definition of femininity in our culture, especially the normative prescriptions for how women are supposed to look to be most attractive, *all* women manifest a problematic relationship to food. Even the most "normal" woman, having beeen socialized in a culture stressing unnatural thinness, will experience some pathological symptoms around eating. This assertion will surely shed a very different light on the treatment of women presenting eating disorders, such as bulimia or anorexia nervosa. Instead of treating them in their *difference* from other women, by contex-tualizing their symptoms within the larger frame of the construction of femininity in American culture, they can be seen as *exaggerating* an already culturally prescribed problematic relationship to eating. This position has the additional benefit, as it would in the treatment of male sexual disorders, of resisting the temptation to "blame the victim" for her/his acting out an exaggerated version of a traditional script.
5. Woody Allen, *The Nightclub Years*, United Artists Records, 1971. Permission requested.

REFERENCES

Brannon, Robert and Deborah David (1976). *The Forty-Nine Percent Majority*. Reading, MA: Addison-Wesley.

Gagnon, John (1977). *Human Sexualities*. Chicago: Scott, Foresman.

Gagnon, John and William Simon (1973). *Sexual Conduct*. Chicago: Aldine.

Kaplan, Helen Singer (1974). *The New Sex Therapy*. New York: Brunner-Mazel.

Kaplan, Helen Singer (1983). *The Evaluation of Sexual Disorders*. New York: Brunner-Mazel.

Kimmel, Michael, ed. (1987). *Changing Men; New Directions in Research on Men and Masculinity*. Beverly Hills, CA: Sage Publications.

Kinsey, Alfred C., Wardell Pomeroy, and C. Martin (1948). *Sexual Behavior in the Human Male*. Chicago: Saunders.

Kinsey, Alfred C. and Paul Gebhard (1953). *Sexual Behavior in the Human Female*. Chicago: Saunders.

LoPiccolo, J. and L. LoPiccolo (1978). *Handbood of Sex Therapy.* New York: Plenum Press.

Mead, Margaret (1935). *Sex and Temperament in Three Primitive Societies.* New York: William Morrow.

Thompson, Edward and Joseph Pleck (1986). "The Structure of Male Role Norms." *American Behavioral Scientist* 29(5), May-June.

Tiefer, Leonore (1986). "In Pursuit of the Perfect Penis: the Medicalization of Male Sexuality." *American Behavioral Scientist* 29(5).

Tollison, C. D. and H. Adams (1979). *Sexual Disorders: Treatment, Theory, and Research.* New York: Gardner Press.

Wagner, Gorm and Richard Green (1984). *Impotence: Physiological, Psychological, Surgical Diagnosis and Treatment.* New York: Plenum.

Zilbergeld, Bernard (1978). *Male Sexuality.* New York: Simon and Schuster.

Leonore Tiefer

IN PURSUIT OF THE PERFECT PENIS
THE MEDICALIZATION OF MALE SEXUALITY

SEXUAL VIRILITY—the ability to fufill the conjugal duty, the ability to procreate, sexual power, potency—is everwhere a requirement of the male role, and, thus, "impotence" is everywhere a matter of concern. Although the term has been used for centuries to refer specifically to partial or complete loss of erectile ability, the first definition dictionaries give for impotence never mentions sex but refers to a general loss of vigor, strength, or power. Sex therapists, concerned about these demeaning connotations, have written about the stigmatizing impact of the label "impotent":

> The word *impotent* is used to describe the man who does not get an erection, not just his penis. If a man is told by his doctor that he is impotent, the man turns to his partner and says he is impotent, they are saying a lot more than that the penis cannot become erect. (Kelley, 1981, p. 126)

Yet a recent survey of the psychological literature found that the frequency of articles with the term "impotence" in the title has risen dramatically since 1970, in contrast with the almost total disappearance of the term "frigidity," a term with comparable pejorative connotations and comparable frequency of use from 1940 to 1970 (Elliott, 1985).

In this article I would like to show how the persistence and increased use of the stigmatizing and stress-inducing label of impotence reflects a significant moment in the social construction of male sexuality. The factors that create this moment include the increasing importance of life-long sexual activity in personal life, the insatiability of mass media for appropriate sexual topics, the expansionist needs of specialty medicine and new medical technology,and the highly demanding male sexual script. I will show how these factors interact to produce a medicalization of male sexuality and sexual impotence that limits many men even as it offers new options and hope to others. Let me begin with a discussion of men's sexuality, and then discuss what medicine has recently had to offer it.

MALE SEXUALITY

Sexual competence is part—some would say the *central* part—of contemporary masculinity, whether we are discussing the traditional man, the modern man, or even the "new" man:

> What so stokes male sexuality that clinicians are impressed by the force of it? Not libido, but rather the curious phenomenon by which sexuality consolidates and confirms gender. . . . An impotent man always feels that his masculinity, and not just his sexuality, is threatened. In men, gender appears to "lean" on sexuality . . . the need for sexual performance is so great. . . . In women, gender identity and self-worth can be consolidated by other means. (Person, 1980, pp. 619, 626)

Gagnon and Simon (1973) explained how, during adolescent masturbation, genital sexuality (i.e., erection and orgasm) acquires nonsexual motives such as the desire for power, achievement, and peer approval that have already become important during preadolescent gender role training. "The capacity for erection is an important sign element of masculinity and control" (Gagnon & Simon, 1973, p. 62) without which a man is not a man. Gross (1978) argues that by adulthood few men can accept other successful aspects of masculinity in lieu of adequate sexual performance.

Masculine sexuality assumes the ability for potent function, but the performances that earn acceptance and status often occur far from the bedroom. Tolson (1977) has described how working-class men engage in an endless performance of sexual stories, jokes, and routines:

> As a topic on which most men could support a conversation and as a source of jokes, sexual talk and gesture were inexhaustible. In the machine noise a gesture suggestive of masturbation, intercourse or homosexuality was enough to raise a conventional smile and re-establish a bond over distances too great for talking. (Marsden, quoted in Tolson, 1977, p. 60)

Tolson argues that this type of ritualized sexual exchange validates working men's bond of masculinity in a situation that otherwise emasculates them. This is an example of the enduring homosocial function of heterosexuality that develops from the adolescent experience (Gagnon & Simon, 1973).

Psychologically, then, male sexual performances may have as much or more to do with male gender role confirmation and homosocial status as with pleasure, intimacy, or tension release. This may explain why men express so many rules concerning proper sexual performance: Their agenda relates not merely to personal or couple satisfaction but to acting "like a man" in intercourse in order to qualify for the title elsewhere.

We can draw on the writings of several authorities to compile an outline of the ten sexual beliefs to which many men subscribe (Doyle, 1983; Zilbergeld, 1978; LoPiccolo, 1985): (1) Men's sexual apparatus and needs are simple and straightforward, unlike women's. (2) Most men are ready, willing, and eager for as much sex as they can get. (3) There is suspicion that other men's sexual experiences approximate ecstatic explosiveness more closely and more often than one's own. (4) It is the responsibility of the man to teach and lead his partner to experience pleasure and orgasm(s). (5) Sexual prowess is a serious, task-oriented business, no place for experimentation, unpredictability, or play. (6) Women prefer intercourse to other sexual activities, particularly "hard-driving" intercourse. (7) All really good and normal sex must end in intercourse. (8) Any physical contact other than a light touch is meant as an invitation to foreplay and intercourse. (9) It is the responsibility of the man to satsify both his partner and himself. (10) Sexual prowess is never permanently earned; each time it must be reproven.

Many of these demands directly require—and all of them indirectly require—an erection. Nelson (1985) pointed out that male sexuality is dominated by a genital focus in several ways: Sexuality is isolated from the rest of life as a unique experience with particular technical performance requirements; the subjective meaning for the man arises from genital sensations first practiced and familiar in adolescent masturbation and directly transferred without thought to the interpersonal situation; and the psychological meaning primarily depends on the confirmation of virility that comes from proper erection and ejaculation.

It is no surprise, then, that any difficulty in getting the penis to do what it "ought" can become a source of profound humiliation and despair, both in terms of immediate self-esteem and the destruction of one's masculine reputation, which is assumed will follow.

> Few sexual problems are as devastating to a man as his inability to achieve or sustain an erection long enough for successful sexual intercourse. For many men the idea of not being able to "get it up" is a fate worse than death. (Doyle, 1983, p. 205)

> What's the worst thing that can happen? I asked myself. The worst thing that can happen is that I take one of these hip, beautiful, liberated women to bed and I can't get it up. I can't get it up! You hear me? She tells a few of her friends. Soon around every corner there's someone laughing at my failure. (Parent, 1977, p. 15)

BIOMEDICAL APPROACHES TO MALE SEXUAL PROBLEMS

Within the last decade, both professional and popular discussion about male sexuality has emphasized physical causes and treatments for sexual problems. There is greater awareness and acceptance within the medical profession of clinical and research work on sexuality, and sexually dissatisfied men are increasingly willing to discuss their problems with a physician (Bancroft, 1983). The professional literature on erection problems has focused on methods of differentiating between organic and nonorganic causes (LoPiccolo, 1985). Recent reviews survey endocrine, neurological, medication-related, urological, surgery-related, congenital, and vascular causes and contrast them with psychological and relationship causes (Krane, Siroky, & Goldstein, 1983).

Although the physiological contributions to adequate sexual functioning can be theoretically specified in some detail, as yet few diagnostic tests exist that enable specific indentification of one type of pathophysiological contribution versus another. Moreover, as yet few medical treatments are available for medically caused erectile disorders aside from changing medications (particularly in the case of hypertension) or correcting an underlying disease process. The most widely used medical approach is an extreme one: surgical implantation of a device into the penis that will permit intromission. This is the penile prosthesis.

The history of these devices is relatively short (Melman, 1978). Following unsuccessful attempts with bone and cartilage, the earliest synthetic implant (1948) was of a plastic tube placed in the middle of the penis of a patient who had had his urethra removed for other reasons. Today, several different manufacturers produce slightly different versions of two general types of implant.

One type is the "inflatable" prosthesis. Inflatable silicone cylinders are placed in the *corpora cavernosa* of the penis, the cylindrical bodies of erectile tissue that normally fill with blood during erection. The cylinders are connected to a pump placed in the scrotum that is connected to a small, saline-filled reservoir placed in the abdomen. "When the patient desires a tumescent phallus, the bulb is squeezed five or six times and fluid is forced from the reservoir into the cylinder chambers. When a flaccid penis is wanted, a deflation valve is pressed and the fluid returns to the reservoir" (Melman, 1978, p. 278).

The other type of prosthesis is a pair of semirigid rods, now made of silicone, with either a bendable silver core or a hinge to allow concealment of the erection by bending it down or up against the body when the man is dressed.

Because these devices have been implanted primarily by private practitioners, the only way to estimate the number of implant operations is from manufacturers' sales figures. However, many devices are sold that are not used. A French urologist estimated that 5,000 patients were given penile implants in 1977 alone (Subrini, 1980). It seems reasonable to guess that by the mid-1980s hundreds of thousands of men had received implants.

Needless to say, many articles have been written stressing the need to evaluate men carefully who might be candidates for the procedure. Surgeons are concerned to exclude

> patients at risk of becoming psychotic or suicidal, developing chronic psychogenic pain, or initiating inappropriate malpractice suits. . . . A second important concern has been to rule out patients whose erectile dysfunction is psychogenic and could be cured without surgery . . . although several urologists have reported high patient satisfaction when carefully selected patients with psychogenic dysfunction received penile prostheses. (Schover & von Eschenbach, 1985, p. 58)

Postimplant follow-up studies have typically been conducted by surgeons interested in operative complications and global measures of patient satisfaction (Sotile, 1979). Past reports have encouraged the belief that the devices function mechanically, are adjusted to by the man and his partner without difficulty, and result in satisfactory sexual function and sensation. But recent papers are challenging these conclusions. One review of the postoperative follow-up literature was so critical of methodological weaknesses (brief follow-up periods, rare interviews with patients' sexual partners, few objective data or even cross-validation of subjective questions about sexual functioning, among others) that the authors could not summarize the results in any meaningful way (Collins & Kinder, 1984). Another recent summary criticized the implants' effectiveness:

> First, recent reports indicate that the percentage of surgical and mechanical complications from such prosthetic implants is much higher than might be considered acceptable. Second, despite claims to the contrary by some surgeons, it appears likely that whatever degree of naturally occurring erection a man is capable of will be disrupted, and perhaps eliminated by the surgical procedures and scarring involved in prosthetic implants. Finally, it has been my experience that, although patients are typically rather eager to have a prosthesis implanted and report being very happy with it at short-term surgical follow-up, longer term behavioral assessment indicates poor sexual adjustment in some cases. (LoPiccolo, 1985, p. 222)

Three recent urological papers report high rates of postoperative infection and mechanical failure of the inflatable prosthesis, both necessitating removal of the device (Apte, Gregory, & Purcell, 1984; Joseph, Bruskewitz, & Benson, 1984; Fallon, Rosenberg, & Culp, 1984) In the first paper, 43% of patients required at least one repeat surgery; in the second paper, the device malfunctioned in 47% of 88 cases operated on since 1977; in the third, 48% of 95 patients have had their prosthesis malfunction in one way or another since 1977.

In perhaps the only paper reporting on the effectiveness of penile implants in gay men, a therapist who had worked with three such patients indicated that

> the implants were less successful with homosexuals than with heterosexuals because there tends to be much more direct penile contact in gay sexuality than in heterosexual sexuality. The person with the implant is aware of the difference, not his partner. (Paff, 1985, p. 15)

One of the patients had to have the implant removed because of a mechanical malfunction.

PUBLIC INFORMATION ABOUT PENILE PROSTHESES

Public sexual information is dominated by health and medical science in both language and substance. Newspapers present "new" discoveries. Magazines have "experts" with advanced health degrees outline "new" norms and ways to achieve them. Television and radio talk-show guests, health-degreed "experts," promote their latest book or therapeutic approach as "resources" are flashed on the screen or mentioned by the host. Sexuality is presented as a life problem—like buying a house, having a good relationship, dealing with career choices—the "modern" approach is to be rational, orderly, careful, thorough, up-to-date, and in tune with the latest pronouncements of the experts.

The public accepts the assumption that scientific discoveries improve our ability to manage and control our lives and welcomes new biomedical developments in areas perceived to be dominated by the biomedical developments in areas perceived to be dominated by the physical or by standards of health and illness. Sexual physiology has a tangibility that "love" and "lust" lack, increasing its propriety as a language for public discourse. When biomedicine, health, and physiology are considered the appropriate sexual discourse, scientists and health care providers are the appropriate authorities.

The media have presented information about penile protheses in the same straightforward, rational, scientific, informative way as other "news" about sexuality. One article in *The New York Times* in 1979 presented the findings of a urological paper that had appeared in the *Journal of the American Medical Association* the day before. It gave the address of the prosthesis manufacturer as well as typical financial cost, length of hospital stay, and insurance coverage. A *JAMA* editorial, criticizing the study's inattention to the patients' sexual partners, was mentioned.

An article in *Vogue* exclusively discussed new medical/surgical approaches to impotence under a typically simple and optimistic title, "Curing Impotence: The Prognosis Is Good." The financial cost of the devices is mentioned as well as an in-development "electrostimulatory device to be inserted in the anus before intercourse and controlled by a ring or wristwatch-like switch so that patients can signal appropriate nerves to produce an erection" (Hixson, 1985, p. 406). The style is technical and mechanical and so simple and cheerful that it is hardly amazing to read in a sentence following the anal electrode description, "While psychological impotence problems probably also require psychological treatment, the doctors feel that successful electronic intercourse may provide the confidence needed by some men" (p. 406).

Literature for patients has been developed by the major prosthesis manufacturers and is available at patient education centers, in doctors' waiting rooms, and through self-help groups such as Impotents Anonymous. A typical booklet is seven pages of high-quality glossy paper, with photographs of healthy young couples in a garden, watching a beautiful sunset, sitting by the ocean (Mentor Corporation, 1984). Entitled *Overcoming Impotence*, the text reads

> Impotence is a widespread problem that affects many millions of men. It can occur at any age and at any point in a man's sexual life. The myth of impotence as an "old man's disease" has finally been shattered. Impotence is a problem of men but also affects couples and families. Now, as a result of recent medical advances, impotence need no longer cause frustration, embarrassment and tension. New solutions are now available for an age-old problem.

In the second section, on causes of impotence, the booklet reads as follows:

> The causes can be either physical or psychological. For many years, it was believed that 90 percent of impotent men had a psychological cause for their problem; but as a result of recent medical research, it is now known that at least half of the men suffering from impotence can actually trace its origin to a physical problem.

After a lengthy discussion of the methods used to distinguish between physical and psychological impotence, the booklet continues in its relentlesly upbeat way:

> For the majority of men who are physically impotent and for those who are psychologically impotent and do not respond to counselling, a penile

implant offers the only complete, reliable solution. It offers new hope for a return to satisfactory sexual activity and for the disappearance of the anxieties and frustrations of impotence.

This, of course, seems to be merely a straightforward technological solution to a technical problem. No mention is made of individual differences in adjustment to the prosthesis, or even that adjustment will be necessary at all. The mechanical solution itself will solve the problem; the person becomes irrelevant.

Other patient information booklets are similar: informative about the device and reassuring about the outcome. In addition to lengthy and detailed discussion of specific physical causes of impotence, brief mention is made of psychogenic impotence.

> Another group of patients have some type of mental barrier [sic] or problem. This latter group may account for as high as 50% of the people with impotence, but only a small number of these people are candidates for a penile implant. (Medical Engineering Corp., 1983)

It is any wonder that men who "fail" the physical tests and are diagnosed as having psychogenic impotence cannot understand why they should be deprived of the device?

Urologists have begun in recent years to specialize in the diagnosis and surgical treatment of impotence. A quarterly publication from a prosthesis manufacturer "for surgeons practicing prosthetic urology" devoted a front page recently to the subject "Impotence Clinics: Investments in the Future" (American Medical Systems, 1984). Newspaper advertisements have begun to appear from groups of urologists with such names as Potency Plus in California. Another California group calling itself Potential advertises "Impotence . . . there could be a medical reason and a medical solution." An ad in a New York newspaper is headlined "Potent Solution to Sexual Problem."

Another source of publicity about the physical causes and treatments for erectile difficulties has come from The Impotence Institute of America, an organization founded by a man who describes how his own search ended happily with an implanted penile prosthesis. Although the subhead on the not-for-profit institute's stationery is "Bringing a 'total-care' concept to overcoming impotency," the ten men on the board of directors are all urologists.

In 1982 the institute created two consumer-oriented groups, Impotents Anonymous (IA) and I-Anon, based on the Alcoholics Anonymous models (both the institute's founder and his wife had formerly been members of Al-Anon). Recent correspondence from the institute indicates 70 chapters of IA operating and another 20 planned. A 1984 news article about IA, "Organization Helps Couples with Impotence as Problem," repeated the now familiar information that "until five years ago most physicians believed that up to 95% of all erectile impotence stemmed from psychological problems, [but that] medical experts now agree that about half of all impotence is caused by physical disorders" (*New York Times*, 1984). The IA brochure cites the same numbers.

Let us turn now to a critique of the biomedical approach to male sexuality, beginning with this question of organic and psychogenic etiology.

CRITIQUE OF THE BIOMEDICAL APPROACH

The frequent claim that psychogenic impotence has been oversold and organic causes are far more common than realized has captivated the media and legitimated increased medical involvement in sexuality. An *International Journal of Andrology* editorial summarizes the shift:

> Medical fashions come and go and the treatment of erectile impotence is no exception. In the 20s and 30s, physicians and surgeons looked for physical causes and tried out methods of treatment, most of which now seem absurd. Since that time there has been a widely held view that 90–95% of cases of impotence are psychologically determined. Where this figure came from was never clear [some sources cite Havelock Ellis], but it has entered into medical folklore. In the past five years or so, the pendulum has been swinging back. Physical causes and methods of treatment are receiving increasing attention. (Bancroft, 1982, 353)

In the Center for Male Sexual Dysfunction in the Department of Urology, Beth Israel Medical Center, New York City, over 800 men have been seen since 1981 because of erectile problems. Very few who, on the basis of a simple history and physical, could be unambiguously declared "psychogenic" were immediately referred for sex therapy; the remainder underwent a complete medical and psychological workup. Over 90% of these patients believed that their problem was completely or preponderantly physical in origin; yet we have found that only about 45% of patients have exclusively or predominantly medically caused erectile problems, and 55% have exclusively or predominantly psychologically caused problems. This approximately 50/50 split is, in fact, what is being observed by the mass media. But it is based on a sample of men usually referred by their primary physicians (over 75%) because of their likely medical etiology and their need for a comprehensive workup.

A Chicago group found that 43% of a group of men coming to a urology clinic for impotence evaluation had at least partly an organic basis for their problems, whereas only 11% of men coming to a psychiatry department sex clinic had organic contributing factors (Segraves, Schoenberg, Zarins, Camic, & Knopf, 1981). A review of all patients seen at the Johns Hopkins Sexual Behaviors Consultation Unit between 1972 and 1981 showed 105 men over 50 years old with a primary complaint of erectile dysfunction. Even in this age group, only 30% could be assigned an organic etiology (Wise, Rabins, & Gahnsley, 1984). After listing 66 possible physical causes of secondary impotence, Masters and Johnson (1970, pp. 184–185) reported that only seven of their 213 cases (3%) had an organic etiology.

Obviously, one cannot describe the actual rate of occurrence of any particular problem (e.g., "organic impotence") without describing the population from which the sample comes. The urology departments' findings that approximately half of the patients seen for erectile problems have a medical cause *cannot* be generalized to other groups (e.g., men in general practitioners' waiting rooms reading prosthesis manufacturers' literature, men watching a TV program about impotence) without further normative data collection. It is important to emphasize that even men with diabetes, a known cause of peripheral neural and vascular difficulties that could result in impotence, are as often potent as not (Schiavi, Fisher, Quadland, & Glover, 1984; Fairburn, McCulloch, & Wu, 1982), a result that cannot be predicted from the duration of the diabetes or the presence of other physical complications.

An even more serious criticism of the biomedical trend is the common tendency to contrapose organic and psychogenic causes of impotence as mutually exclusive phenomena.

> Conceptually, most of the research suffers from the flaw of attempting to categorize the patients into discrete, nonoverlapping categories of organic *or* psychogenic erectile failure. Yet, many cases, and perhaps the majority of cases, involve *both* organic and psychogenic erectile factors in the genesis of erectile failure. (LoPiccolo, 1985, p. 221)

Schumacher and Lloyd (1981), in a review of 102 cases seen at two different medical school centers, conclude that "all patients reported psychological distress associated with their impotence [including] inhibitions, shame, avoidance, insecurity, inadequacy, guilt, hostility, fear of intimacy" (p. 46). One prominent urologist reviewed 388 cases and concluded

> There are wholly organic bases and also totally psychological causes for impotency; yet the two generally coexist. It is most probable that in all cases of organic impotency a psychologic overlay develops. (Finkle & Finkle, 1984, p. 25)

It is not so much, I believe, that all cases involve a mixture of factors but that all cases involve psychological factors to some degree. The director of a New York sexuality clinic sums up her impressions similarly:

> We have found in our work . . . that, where organic determinants are diagnosed, inevitably there will also be psychological factors involved, either as co-determinants of the erectile dysfunction or as reactive to it. . . . A man's emotional reactions to his erectile failures may be such that it serves to maintain the erectile problem even when the initial physiological causes are resolved. (Schreiner-Engel, 1981, p. 116)

The consequences of this implication are particularly serious given that, as LoPiccolo (1985) notes, "many physicians currently will perform surgery to implant a penile prosthesis if any organic abnormality is found" (p. 221). The effect of psychological factors is to make the dysfunction look worse than the medical problem alone would warrant. Altering the man's devastated attitudes will improve the picture, whatever else is going on.

Perelman (1984) refers to "the omnipresent psychogenic component existing in any potency problem regardless of the degree of organicity" (p. 181) to describe his successful use of cognitive-behavioral psychotherapy to treat men diagnosed with organic impotence. He reminds us that physical sexual function has a psychosomatic complexity that is not only poorly understood but that may have the "ability to successfully compensate for its own deficits" (p. 181). Thus the search for *the* etiology that characterizes so much of the biomedical approach to male sexual problems seems to have less to do with the nature of sexuality than the nature of the medical enterprise.

THE ALLURE OF MEDICALIZED SEXUALITY

Men are drawn to a technological solution such as the penile prosthesis for a variety of personal reasons that ultimately rest on the inflexible central place of sexual potency in the male sexual script. Those who assume that "normal" men must always be interested in sex and who believe that male sexuality is a simple system wherein interest leads easily and directly to erection (Zilbergeld, 1978) are baffled by any erectile difficulties. Their belief that "their penis is an instrument immune from everyday problems, anxieties and fears" (Doyle, 1983, p. 207) conditions them to deny the contribution of psychological or interpersonal factors to male sexual responsiveness. This denial, in turn, results from fundamental male gender role prescriptions for self-reliance and emotional control (Brannon, 1976).

Medicalized discourse offers an explanation of impotence that removes control, and therefore responsibility and blame, for sexual failure from the man and places it on his physiology. Talcott Parsons (1951) originally argued that an organic diagnosis confers a particular social role, the "sick role," which has three aspects: (1) The individual is not held responsible for his or her condition; (2) illnesses are legitimate bases for exemption from normal social responsibilities; and (3) the exemptions are contingent on the sick person recognizing that sickness is undesirable and seeking appropriate (medical) help. A medical explanation for erectile difficulties relieves men of blame and thus permits them to maintain some masculine self-esteem even in the presence of impotence.

> Understandably, for many years the pattern of the human male has been to blame sexual dysfunction on specific physical distresses. Every sexually inadequate male lunges toward any potential physical excuse for sexual malfunction. From point of ego support, would that it could be true. A cast for a leg or a sling for an arm provides socially acceptable evidence of physical dysfunction of these extremities. Unfortunately, the psychosocial causes of perpetual penile flaccidity cannot be explained or excused by devices for mechanical support. (Masters & Johnson, 1970, pp. 187–188)

Perhaps in 1970 "devices for mechanical support" of the penis were not in widespread access, but we now have available, ironically, precisely the type of medical vindication Masters and Johnson suggested would be the *most* effective deflection of the "blame" men feel for their inability to perform sexually.

Men's willingness to accept a self-protective, self-handicapping (i.e., illness label) attribution for "failure" has been demonstrated in studies of excuse-making (Snyder, Ford, & Hunt, 1985). Reduced personal responsibility is most sought in those situations in which performance is related to self-esteem (Snyder & Smith, 1982). It may be that the frequent use of physical excuses for failure in athletic performance provides a model for men to use in sexuality. Medical treatments not only offer tangible evidence of non-blameworthiness, but they allow men to avoid psychological treatments such as marital or sex therapy, which threaten embarrassing self-disclosure and admissions of weakness men find aversive (Peplau & Gordon, 1985).

The final allure of a technological solution such as the penile prosthesis is its promise of permanent freedom from worry. One of Masters and Johnson's (1970) major insights was their description of the self-conscious self-monitoring that men with erectile difficulties develop in sexual situations. "Performance anxiety" and "spectatoring," their two immediate causes of sexual impotence, generate a self-perpetuating cycle that undermines a man's confidence about the future even as he recovers from individual episodes. Technology seems to offer a simple and permanent solution to the problem of lost or threatened confidence, as doctors from *Vogue* to the *Journal of Urology* have already noted.

THE RISING IMPORTANCE OF SEXUALITY
IN PERSONAL LIFE

Even though we live in a time when the definition of masculinity is moving away from reliance on physical validation (Pleck, 1976), there seems no apparent reduction in the male sexual focus on physical performance. Part of the explanation for this must rest with the increasing importance of sexuality in contemporary relationships. Recent sociocultural analyses have suggested that sexual satisfaction grows in importance to the individual and couple as other sources of personal fulfillment and connection with others wither.

> I would say that with the collapse of other social values (those of religion, patriotism, the family, and so on), sex has been forced to take up the slack, to become our sole mode of transcendence and our only touchstone of authenticity. . . . In our present isolation we have few ways besides sex to feel connected with each other. (White, 1980, p. 282)

> People are being deprived more and more of opportunities to feel they are worth something to others, to experience what they are doing as something of significance, and to know that they are indispensable to the lives of their families or at least a few friends. The experience of power-lessness, dependency, inner emptiness, and one's own meaninglessness becomes radical and merciless; the vacuum left behind sucks in any experiences which make one at least temporarily aware of one's own importance. . . . A particularly important mode of compensation for narcissistic deprivation is the couple relationship or, more precisely, the emotions it can mobilize, such as falling in love and sexual desire and satisfaction. (Schmidt, 1983, pp. 4–5)

The increasing pressure on intimate relationships to provide psychological support and gratification comes at the same time that traditional (i.e., economic and family-raising) reasons for these relationships are declining. Both trends place more pressure on compatibility and companionship to maintain the relationship. Given that men have been raised "not to be emotionally sensitive to others or emotionally expressive or self-revealing" (Pleck, 1981, p. 140), much modern relationship success would seem to depend on sexual fulfillment. Although some contemporary research indicates that marriages and gay relationships can be rated successful despite the presence of sexual problems (Frank, Anderson, & Rubinstein, 1978; Bell & Weinberg, 1978), popular surveys suggest that the public believes sexual satisfaction is essential to relationship success.

The importance of sexuality also increases because of its use by consumption-oriented capitalism (Altman, 1982). The promise of increased sexual attractiveness is used to sell products to people of all ages. Commercial sexual meeting places and playgrounds are popular in both gay and heterosexual culture. A whole system of therapists, books, workshops, and magazines sells advice on improving sexual performance and enjoyment. Restraint and repression are inappropriate in a consumer culture in which the emphasis is on immediate gratification.

The expectation that sexuality will provide ever-increasing rewards and personal meaning has also been a theme of the contemporary women's movement, and women's changing attitudes have affected many men, particularly widowed and divorced men returning to the sexual "market." Within the past decade, sexual advice manuals have completely changed their tone regarding the roles of men and women in sexual relations (Weinberg, Swensson, & Hammersmith, 1983). Women are advised to take more responsibility for their own pleasure, to possess sexual knowledge and self-knowledge, and to expect that improved sexual functioning will pay off in other aspects of life. Removing responsibility from the man for being the sexual teacher and leader reduces the definition of sexual masculinity to having excellent technique and equipment to meet the "new woman" on her "new" level.

Finally, the new importance of sexual performance has no upper age limit.

> The sexual myth most rampant in our culture today is the concept that the aging process *per se* will in time discourage or deny erective security to the older age-group male. As has been described previously, the aging male may be slower to erect and may even reach the plateau phase without full erective return, but the facility and ability to attain erection, presuming general good health and no psychogenic blocking, continues unopposed as a natural sequence well into the 80-year age group. (Masters & Johnson, 1970, p. 326)

Sex is a natural act, Masters and Johnson said over and over again, and there is no "natural" reason for ability to decline or disappear as one ages. Erectile difficulties, then, are "problems" that can be corrected with suitable treatment. Aging provides no escape from the male sexual role.

THE MEDICALIZATION OF IMPOTENCE: PART OF THE PROBLEM OR PART OF THE SOLUTION?

The increased use of the term "impotence" that Elliott (1985) reported can now be seen as part of a process of medicalization of sexuality. Physicians view the medical system as a method for distributing technical expertise in the interest of improved health (Ehrenreich & Ehrenreich, 1978). Their economic interests, spurred by the profit orientation of medical technology manufacturers, lie in expanding the number and type of services they offer to more and more patients. Specialists, in particular, have dramatically increased their incomes and prestige during the postwar era by developing high-reimbursement relationships with hospitals and insurance companies (Starr,

1982). In the sexual sphere, all these goals are served by labelling impotence a biomedical disorder, common in men of all ages, best served by thorough evaluation and appropriate medical treatment when any evidence of organic disorder is identified.

There are many apparent advantages for men in the medicalization of male sexuality. As discussed earlier, men view phsycial explanations for their problems as less stigmatizing and are better able to maintain their sense of masculinity and self-esteem. Accepting medicine as a source of authority and help reassures men who feel under immense pressure from role expectations but are unable to consult with or confide in either other men or women because of pride, competitiveness, or defensiveness. That "inhibited sexual excitement . . . in males, partial or complete failure to attain or maintain erection until completion of the [sic] sexual act" is a genuine disorder (American Psychiatric Association, 1980, p. 279) legitimates an important aspect of life that physicians previously dismissed or made jokes about. And, as I have said, permanent mechanical solutions to sexual performance worries are seen as a gift from heaven in erasing, with one simple operation, a source of anxiety dating from adolescence about failing as a man.

The disadvantages to medicalizing male sexuality, however, are numerous and subtle. (My discussion here is informed by Riessman's 1983 analysis of the medicalization of many female roles and conditions.) First, dependence on medical remedies for impotence has led to the escalating use of treatments whose long-term effects are not known and, in many cases, seem to be harmful. Iatrogenic ("doctor-caused") consequences of new technology and pharmacology are not uncommon and seem most worrisome when medical treatments are offered to men with no demonstrable organic disease. Second, the use of medical language mystifies human experience, increasing dependence on professionals and experts. If sexuality becomes fundamentally a matter of vasocongestion and myotonia (as in Masters & Johnson's famous claim, 1966, p. 7), personal experience requires expert interpretation and explanation. Third, medicalization spreads the moral neutrality of medicine and science over sexuality, and people no longer ask whether men "should" have erections. If the presence of erections is healthy and their absence (in whole or part) is pathological, then healthy behavior is correct behavior and vice versa, again increasing dependence on health authorities to define norms and standards for conduct.

The primary disadvantage of medicalization is that it denies, obscures, and ignores the social causes of whatever problem is under study. Impotence becomes the problem of an individual man. This effect seems particularly pertinent in the case of male sexuality in which the social demands of the male sexual role are so related to the meaning of erectile function and dysfunction. Recall the list of men's beliefs about sexuality, the evaluative criteria of conduct and performance. Being a man depends on sexual adequacy, which depends on potency. A rigid, reliable erection is necessary for full compliance with the script. The medicalization of male sexuality helps a man conform to the script rather than analyzing where the script comes from or challenging it. Research and technology are directed only toward better and better solutions. Yet the demands of the script are so formidable, and the pressures from the sociocultural changes we have outlined so likely to increase, that no technical solution will ever work—certainly not for everyone.

Medicine attracts public resources out of proportion to its capacity for health enhancement, because it often categorizes problems fundamentally social in origin as biological or personal deficits, and in so doing smothers the impulse for social change which could offer the only serious resolution. (Stark & Flitcraft, in Riessman, 1983, p. 4)

PREVENTIVE MEDICINE: CHANGING THE MALE SEXUAL SCRIPT

Men will remain vulnerable to the expansion of the clinical domain so long as masculinity rests heavily on a particular type of physiological function. As more research uncovers subtle physiological correlates of genital functioning, more men will be "at risk" for impotence. Fluctuations of physical and emotional state will become cues for impending impotence in any man with, for example diabetes, hypertension, or a history of prescription medication usage.

One of the less well understood features of sex therapy is that it "treats" erectile dysfunction by changing the individual man's sexual script.

This approach is primarily educational—you are not curing an illness but learning new and more satisfactory ways of getting on with each other. (Greenwood & Bancroft, in Bancroft, 1983, p. 305)

Our thesis is that the rules and concepts we learn [about male sexuality] are destructive and a very inadequate preparation for a satisfying and pleasurable sex life. . . . Having a better sex life is in large measure dependent upon your willingness to examine how the male sexual mythology has trapped you. (Zilbergeld, 1978, p. 9)

Sexuality can be transformed from a rigid standard for masculine adequacy to a way of being, a way of communicating, a hobby, a way of being in one's body—and *being* one's body—that does not impose control but rather affirms pleasure, movement, sensation, cooperation, playfulness, relating. Masculine confidence cannot be purchased, because there can never be perfect potency. Chasing its illusion may line a few pockets, but for most men it will only exchange one set of anxieties and limitations for another.

REFERENCES

Altman, D. (1982). *The homosexualization of America, The Americanization of the homosexual*. New York: St. Martin's Press.

American Psychiatric Association. (1980). *Diagnostic and statistical manual of mental disorders* (3rd ed.). Washington, DC: Author.

Apte, S. M., Gregory, J. G., & Purcell, M. H. (1984). The inflatable penile prosthesis, reoperation and patient satisfaction: A comparison of statistics obtained from patient record review with statistics obtained from intensive followup search. *Journal of Urology, 131*, 894–895.

Bancroft, J. (1983). *Human sexuality and its problems*. Edinburgh: Churchill-Livingstone.

Bancroft, J. (1982). Erectile impotence: Psyche or soma? *International Journal of Andrology, 5*, 353–355.

Bell, A. P., & Weinberg, M. S. (1978). *Homosexualities: A study of diversity among men and women*. New York: Simon & Schuster.

Brannon, R. (1976). The male sex role: Our culture's blueprint of manhood, and what it's done for us lately. In D. David & R. Brannon (Eds.), *The forty-nine percent majority: The male sex role.* Reading, MA: Addison-Wesley.

Collins, G. F., & Kinder, B. N. (1984). Adjustment following surgical implantation of a penile prosthesis: A critical overview. *Journal of Sex and Marital Therapy, 10,* 255–271.

Doyle, J. A. (1983). *The male experience.* Dubuque, IA: William C. Brown.

Ehrenreich, B., & Ehrenreich, J. (1978). Medicine and social control. In J. Ehrenreich (Ed.), *The cultural crisis of modern medicine.* New York: Monthly Review Press.

Elliott, M. L. (1985). The use of "impotence" and "frigidity": Why has "impotence" survived? *Journal of Sex and Marital Therapy, 11,* 51–56.

Fairburn, C. G., McCulloch, D. K., & Wu, F. C. (1982). The effects of diabetes on male sexual function. *Clinics in Endocrinology and Metabolism, 11,* 749–767.

Fallon, B., Rosenberg, S., & Culp, D. A. (1984). Long-term follow-up in patients with an inflatable penile prosthesis. *Journal of Urology, 132,* 270–271.

Finkle, A. L., & Finkle, C. E. (1984). Sexual impotency: Counseling of 388 private patients by urologists from 1954–1982. *Urology, 23,* 25–30.

Frank, E., Anderson, C., & Rubinstein, D., (1978). Frequency of sexual dysfunction in "normal" couples. *New England Journal of Medicine, 299,* 111–115.

Gagnon, J. H., & Simon, W. (1973). *Sexual conduct: The social sources of human sexuality.* Chicago: Aldine.

Gross, A. E. (1978). The male role and heterosexual behavior. *Journal of Social Issues, 34,* 87–107.

Hixson, J. R. (1985, April). Curing impotence: The prognosis is good. *Vogue,* p. 406.

Impotence clinics: Investments in the future. (1984). *Colleagues in Urology Newsletter,* Fourth Quarter, p. 1. Minnetonka, MN: American Medical Systems.

Joseph, D. B., Bruskewitz, R. C., & Benson, R. C. (1984). Long-term evaluation of the inflatable penile prosthesis. *Journal of Urology, 131,* 670–673.

Kelley, S. (1981). Some social and psychological aspects of organic sexual dysfunction in men. *Sexuality and Disability, 4,* 123–128.

Krane, R. J., Siroky, M. B., & Goldstein, I. (1983). *Male sexual dysfunction.* Boston: Little, Brown.

LoPiccolo, J. (1985). Diagnosis and treatment of male sexual dysfunction. *Journal of Sex and Marital Therapy, 11,* 215–232.

Masters, W. H., & Johnson, V. E. (1966). *Human sexual response.* Boston: Little, Brown.

Masters, W. H., & Johnson, V. E. (1970). *Human sexual inadequacy.* Boston: Little, Brown.

Medical Engineering Corporation. (1983). *Patient information booklet discussing the surgical correction of impotency.* Racine, WI: Author.

Melman, A. (1978). Development of contemporary surgical management for erectile impotence. *Sexuality and Disability, 1,* 272–281.

Mentor Corporation. (1984). *Overcoming impotence.* Minneapolis, MN: Author.

Nelson, J. (1985). Male sexuality and masculine spirituality. *Siecus Report, 13,* 1–4.

Organization helps couples with impotence as problem. (1984, June 24). *New York Times,* Section 1, Pt. 2, p. 42.

Paff, B. (1985). Sexual dysfunction in gay men requesting treatment. *Journal of Sex and Marital Therapy, 11,* 3–18.

Parent, G. (1977). *David Meyer is a mother.* New York: Bantam.

Parsons, T. (1951). *The social system.* New York: Free Press.

Peplau, L. A., & Gordon, S. L. (1985). Women and men in love: Gender differences in close heterosexual relationships. In V. E. O'Leary, R. K. Unger, & B. S. Wallston (Eds.), *Women, gender and social psychology.* Hillsdale, NJ: Lawrence Erlbaum.

Perelman, M. (1984). Rehabilitative sex therapy for organic impotence. In R. T. Segraves & E. J. Haeberle (Eds.), *Emerging dimensions of sexology.* New York: Praeger.

Person, E. S. (1980). Sexuality as the mainstay of identity: Psychoanalytic perspectives. *Signs, 5,* 605–630.

Pleck, J. H. (1976). The male sex role: Definitions, problems and sources of change. *Journal of Social Issues*, *32*, 155–164.

Pleck, J. H. (1981). *The myth of masculinity*. Cambridge: MIT Press.

Riessman, C. K. (1983). Women and medicalization: A new perspective. *Social Policy 14*, 3–18.

Schiavi, R. C. Fisher, C., Quadland, M., & Glover, A. (1984). Erectile function in nonimpotent diabetics. In R. T. Segraves & E. J. Haeberle (Eds.), *Emerging dimensions of sexology*. New York: Praeger.

Schmidt, G. (1983). Introduction: Sexuality and relationships. In G. Arentewicz & G. Schmidt, *The treatment of sexual disorders*. New York: Basic Books.

Schover, L. R., & Von Eschenbach, A. C. (1985). Sex therapy and the penile prosthesis: A synthesis. *Journal of Sex and Marital Therapy*, *11*, 57–66.

Schreiner-Engel, P. (1981). Therapy of psychogenic erectile disorders. *Sexuality and Disability*, *4*, 115–122.

Schumacher, S., & Lloyd, C. W. (1981). Physiological and psychological factors in impotence. *Journal of Sex Research*, *17*, 40–53.

Segraves, R. T., Schoenberg, H. W., Zarins, C., Camic, P., & Knopf, J. (1981). Characteristics of erectile dysfunction as a function of medical care system entry point. *Psychosomatic medicine*, *43*, 227-234.

Snyder, C. R., Ford, C. E., & Hunt, H. A. (1985, August). *Excuse-making: A look at sex differences*. Paper presented at American Psychological Association annual meeting, Los Angeles.

Snyder, C. R., & Smith, T. W. (1982). Symptoms as self-handicapping strategies: The virtues of old wine in a new bottle. In G. Weary & H. L. Mirels (Eds.), *Integration of clinical and social psychology*. New York: Oxford University Press.

Sotile, W. M. (1979). The penile prosthesis: A review. *Journal of Sex and Marital Therapy*, *5*, 90–102.

Starr, P. (1982). *The transformation of American medicine*. New York: Basic Books.

Subrini, L. P. (1980). Treatment of impotence using penile implants: Surgical, sexual, and psychological follow-up. In R. Forleo & W. Pasini (Eds.), *Medical sexology*. Littleton, MA: PSG Publishing.

Surgical implants correct impotence. (1979, June 12). *New York Times*, Section C, p. 3.

Tolson, A. (1977). *The limits of masculinity*. New York: Harper & Row.

Weinberg, M. S., Swensson, R. G., & Hammersmith, S. K. (1983). Sexual autonomy and the status of women: Models of female sexuality in U.S. sex manuals from 1950 to 1980. *Social Problems*, *30*, 312–324.

White, E. (1980). *States of desire*. New York: E. P. Dutton.

Wise, T. N., Rabins, P. V., & Gahnsley, J. (1984). The older patient with a sexual dysfunction. *Journal of Sex and Marital Therapy*, *10*, 117–121.

Zilbergeld, B. (1978). *Male sexuality*. Boston: Little, Brown.

Edward Donnerstein and Daniel Linz

MASS MEDIA SEXUAL VIOLENCE AND MALE VIEWERS:
CURRENT THEORY AND RESEARCH

The influence of pornography on male viewers has been a topic of concern for behavioral scientists for many years, as well as a recent volatile political and legal question. Often research on pornography and its effects on behavior or attitudes are concerned with sexual explicitness. But it is not an issue of sexual explicitness; rather, it is an issue of violence against women and the role of women in "pornography" that is of concern to us here. Research over the last decade has demonstrated that sexual images per se do not facilitate aggressive behavior, change rape-related attitudes, or influence other forms of antisocial behaviors or perceptions. It is the violent images in pornography that account for the various research effects. This will become clearer as the research on the effects of sexual violence in the media is discussed. It is for these and other reasons that the terms *aggressive pornography* and *sexually violent mass media images* are preferred. We will occasionally use the term *pornography* in this article for communication and convenience.

In this chapter we will examine both the research on aggressive pornography and the research that examines nonpornographic media images of violence against women—the major focus of recent research and the material that provokes negative reactions. Our final section will examine the research on nonviolent pornography. We will also refer to various ways in which this research has been applied to the current political debate on pornography and offer suggestions to mitigate the negative effects from exposure to certain forms of pornography and sexually violent mass media.

RESEARCH ON THE EFFECTS OF
AGGRESSIVE PORNOGRAPHY

Aggressive pornography, as used here, refers to X-rated images of sexual coercion in which force is used or implied against a woman in order to obtain certain sexual acts, as in scenes of rape and other forms of sexual assault. One unique feature of these images is their reliance upon "positive victim outcomes," in which rape and other sexual assaults are depicted as pleasurable, sexually arousing, and beneficial to the female victim. In contrast to other forms of media violence in which victims suffer, die, and do not enjoy their victimization, aggressive pornography paints a rosy picture of aggression. The myths regarding violence against women are central to the various influences this material has upon the viewer. This does not imply that there are not images of suffering, mutilation, and death—there are. The large

Reprinted from *American Behavioral Scientist*, 29(5), May/June 1986. © 1986 by Sage Publications. Reprinted by permission.

AUTHORS' NOTE: This research was partially funded by National Science Foundation Grant BNS-8216772 to the first author and Steven Penrod.

majority of images, however, show violence against women as justified, positive, and sexually liberating. Even these more "realistic" images, however, can influence certain viewers under specific conditions. We will address this research later.

There is some evidence that these images increased through the 1970s (Malamuth & Spinner, 1980). However, more recent content analysis suggests that the increase has abated in the 1980s (Scott, 1985). The Presidential Commission on Obscenity and Pornography of 1970 did not examine the influence of aggressive pornography, mainly because of its low frequency. This is important to note, as it highlights differences between the commission and the position outlined in this chapter. The major difference is not in the findings but in the type of material being examined. (The Commission on Obscenity and Pornography was interested only in sexually explicit media images.)

In many aggressive pornographic depictions, as noted, the victim is portrayed as secretly desiring the assault and as eventually deriving sexual pleasure from it (Donnerstein & Berkowitz, 1982; Malamuth, Heim, & Feshbach, 1980). From a cognitive perspective, such information may suggest to the viewer that even if a woman seems repelled by a pursuer, eventually she will respond favorably to forceful advances, aggression, and overpowering by a male assailant (Brownmiller, 1975). The victim's pleasure could further heighten the aggressor's. Viewers might then come to think, at least for a short while, that their own sexual aggression would also be profitable, thus reducing restraints or inhibitions against aggression (Bandura, 1977). These views diminish the moral reprehensibility of any witnessed assault on a woman and, indeed, suggest that the sexual attack may have a highly desirable outcome for both victim and aggressor. Men having such beliefs might therefore be more likely to attack a woman after they see a supposedly "pleasurable" rape. Furthermore, as there is a substantial aggressive component in the sexual assault, it could be argued that the favorable outcome lowers the observers' restraints against aggression toward women. Empirical research in the last few years, which is examined below, as well as such cases as the New Bedford rape, in which onlookers are reported to have cheered the rape of a woman by several men, suggests that the above concerns may be warranted.

AGGRESSIVE PORNOGRAPHY AND SEXUAL AROUSAL

Although it was once believed that only rapists show sexual arousal to depictions of rape and other forms of aggression against women (Abel, Barlow, Blanchard, & Guild, 1977), research by Malamuth and his colleagues (Malamuth, 1981b, 1984; Malamuth & Check, 1983; Malamuth & Donnerstein, 1982; Malamuth, Haber, & Feshbach, 1980; Malamuth, Heim, & Feshbach, 1980) indicates that a nonrapist population will show evidence of increased sexual arousal to media-presented images of rape. This increased arousal primarily occurs when the female victim shows signs of pleasure and arousal, the theme most commonly presented in aggressive pornography. In addition, male subjects who indicate that there is some likelihood that they themselves would rape display increased sexual arousal to all forms of rape depictions, similar to the reactions of known rapists (Malamuth, 1981a, 1981b; Malamuth

& Donnerstein, 1982). Researchers have suggested that this sexual arousal measure serves as an objective index of a proclivity to rape. Using this index, an individual whose sexual arousal to rape themes was found to be similar to or greater than his arousal to nonaggressive depictions would be considered to have an inclination to rape (Abel et al., 1977; Malamuth, 1981a; Malamuth & Donnerstein, 1982).

AGGRESSIVE PORNOGRAPHY AND ATTITUDES
TOWARD RAPE

There are now considerable data indicating that exposure to aggressive pornography may alter the observer's perception of rape and the rape victim. For example, exposure to a sexually explicit rape scene in which the victim shows a "positive" reaction tends to produce a lessened sensitivity to rape (Malamuth & Check, 1983), increased acceptance of rape myths and interpersonal violence against women (Malamuth & Check, 1981), and increases in the self-reported possibility of raping (Malamuth, 1981a). This self-reported possibility of committing rape is highly correlated with (a) sexual arousal to rape stimuli, (b) aggressive behavior and a desire to hurt women, and (c) a belief that rape would be a sexually arousing experience for the rapist (see Malamuth, 1981a; Malamuth & Donnerstein, 1982). Exposure to aggressive pornography may also lead to self-generated rape fantasies (Malamuth, 1981b).

AGGRESSIVE PORNOGRAPHY AND AGGRESSION
AGAINST WOMEN

Recent research (Donnerstein, 1980a, 1980b, 1983, 1984; Donnerstein & Berkowitz, 1982) has found that exposure to aggressive pornography increases aggression against women in a laboratory context. The same exposure does not seem to influence aggression against other men. This increased aggression is most pronounced when the aggression is seen as positive for the victim and occurs for both angered and nonangered individuals.

Although this research suggests that aggressive pornography can influence the male viewer, the relative contribution of the sexual and the aggressive components of the material remains unclear. Is it the sexual nature of the material or the messages about violence that are crucial? This is an extremely important question. In many discussions of this research the fact that the material is aggressive is forgotten and it is assumed that the effects occur owing to the sexual nature of the material. As we noted earlier, the sexual nature of the material is not the major issue. Recent empirical studies shed some light on this issue.

THE INFLUENCE OF NONPORNOGRAPHIC DEPICTIONS
OF VIOLENCE AGAINST WOMEN

It has been alleged that images of violence against women have increased not only in pornographic materials but also in more readily accessible mass media materials ("War Against Pornography," 1985). Scenes of rape and violence have appeared in daytime TV soap operas and R-rated movies shown on cable television. These images are sometimes accompanied by the theme, common in aggressive pornography, that women enjoy or benefit from sexual violence. For example, several episodes of the daytime drama *General Hospital* were devoted to a rape of one of the well known female characters by an equally popular male character. At first the victim was humiliated; later the two characters were married. A similar theme was expressed in the popular film, *The Getaway*. In this film, described by Malamuth and Check (1981):

> Violence against women is carried out both by the hero and the antagonist. The hero, played by Steve McQueen, is portrayed in a very "macho" image. At one point, he slaps his wife several times causing her to cry from the pain. The wife, played by Ali McGraw, is portrayed as deserving this beating. As well, the antagonist in the movie kidnaps a woman (Sally Struthers) and her husband. He rapes the woman but the assault is portrayed in a manner such that the woman is depicted as a willing participant. She becomes the antagonist's girlfriend and they both taunt her husband until he commits suicide. The woman then willingly continues with the assailant and at one point frantically searches for him. (p. 439)

In a field experiment, Malmuth and Check (1981a) attempted to determine whether or not the depiction of sexual violence contained in *The Getaway* and in another film with similar content influenced the viewers' perceptions of attitudes toward women. A total of 271 male and female students participated in a study that they were led to believe focused on movie ratings. One group watched, on two different evenings, *The Getaway* and *Swept Away* (which also shows women as victims of aggression within erotic contexts). A group of control subjects watched neutral, feature-length movies. These movies were viewed in campus theaters as part of the Campus Film Program. The results of a "Sexual Attitudes Survey," conducted several days after the screenings, indicated that viewing the sexually aggressive films significantly increased male but not female acceptance of interpersonal violence and tended to increase rape myth acceptance. These effects occurred not with X-rated materials but with more "prime-time" materials.

A recent study by Donnerstein and Berkowitz (1985) sought to examine more systematically the relative contributions of aggressive and sexual components of aggressive pornography. In a series of studies, male subjects were shown one of four different films: (1) the standard aggressive pornography used in studies discussed earlier, (2) an X-rated film that contained no forms of aggression or coercion and was rated by subjects to be as sexual as the first; (3) a film that contained scenes of aggression against a woman but without any sexual content and was considered less sexual and also less arousing (physiologically) than were the previous two films; and (4) a neutral film. Although the aggressive pornographic film led to the highest aggression against women, the aggression-only film produced more aggressive behavior than did the sex-only film. In fact, the sex-only film produced no different results than did the neutral film. Subjects were also examined for their attitudes about rape and their willingness to say they might commit a rape. The most callous attitudes and the highest percentage indicating some likelihood to rape were found in the aggression-only conditions; the X-rated sex-only film was the lowest.

This research suggests that violence against women need not occur in pornographic or sexually explicit context in order for the depictions to have an impact on both attitudes and behavior. Angered individuals became more aggressive toward a female target after exposure to films judged not to be sexually arousing but that depict a woman as a victim of aggression. This supports the claim by Malamuth and Check (1983) that sexual violence against women need not be portrayed in a pornographic fashion for greater acceptance of interpersonal violence and rape myths.

In the Malamuth and Check study the victim's reaction to sexual violence was always, in the end, a positive one. Presumably the individual viewer of nonsexually explicit rape depictions with a positive outcome comes to accept the view that aggression against women is permissible because women enjoy sexual violence. In the studies by Donnerstein and Berkowitz, however, several other processes may have been at work. Exposure to nonpornographic aggression against women resulted in the highest levels of aggressive behavior when subjects were first angered by a female confederate of the experimenter or when the victim of aggression in the film and the female confederate were linked by the same name. Presumably, subjects did not come to perceive violence as acceptable because victims enjoy violence from this material. Instead, the cue value or association of women with the characters in the film (Berkowitz, 1974) and the possibility that the pain cues stimulated aggression in angry individuals might better account for the findings. When the individual is placed in a situation in which cues associated with aggressive responses are salient (for example, a situation involving a female victim) or one in which he is predisposed to aggression because he is angered, he will be more likely to respond aggressively both because of the stimulus-response connection previously built up through exposure to the films and/or because the pain and suffering of the victim reinforce already established aggressive tendencies.

An important element in the effects of exposure to aggressive pornography is violence against women. Because much commercially available media contain such images, researchers have begun to examine the impact of more popular film depictions of violence against women. Of particular interest have been R-rated "slasher" films, which combine graphic and brutal violence against women within a sexual context. These types of materials do not fit the general definition of pornography, but we believe their impact is stronger.

THE EFFECTS OF EXPOSURE TO
R-RATED SEXUALIZED VIOLENCE

In a recent address before the International Conference on Film Classification and Regulation, Lord Harlech of the British Film Board noted the increase in R-rated sexually violent films and their "eroticizing" and "glorification" of rape and other forms of sexual violence. According to Harlech:

> Everyone knows that murder is wrong, but a strange myth has grown up, and been seized on by filmmakers, that rape is really not so bad, that

it may even be a form of liberation for the victim, who may be acting out what she secretly desires—and perhaps needs—with no harm done. . . . Filmmakers in recent years have used rape as an exciting and titillating spectacle in pornographic films, which are always designed to appeal to men.

As depictions of sex and violence become increasingly graphic, especially in feature-length movies shown in theaters, officials at the National Institute of Mental Health are becoming concerned:

Films had to be made more and more powerful in their arousal effects. Initially, strong excitatory reactions [may grow] weak or vanish entirely with repeated exposure to stimuli of a certain kind. This is known as "habituation." The possibility of habituation to sex and violence has significant social consequences. For one, it makes pointless the search for stronger and stronger arousers. But more important is its potential impact on real life behavior. If people become inured to violence from seeing much of it, they may be less likely to respond to real violence.

This loss of sensitivity to real violence after repeated exposure to films with sex and violence, or "the dilemma of the detached bystander in the presence of violence," is currently a concern of our research program. Although initial exposure to a violent rape scene may act to create anxiety and inhibitions about such behavior, researchers have suggested that repeated exposure to such material could counter these effects. The effects of long-term exposure to R-rated sexually violent mass media portrayals are the major focus of our ongoing research program investigating how massive exposure to commercially released violent and sexually violent films influence (1) viewer perceptions of violence, (2) judgments about rape and rape victims, (3) general physiological desensitization to violence, and (4) aggressive behavior.

This research presents a new approach to the study of mass media violence. First, unlike many previous studies in which individuals may have seen only 10-30 minutes of material, the current studies examine 10 hours of exposure. Second, we are able to monitor the process of subject's desensitization over a longer period of time than in previous experiments. Third, we examine perceptual and judgmental changes regarding violence, particularly violence against women.

In the program's first study, Linz, Donnerstein, and Penrod (1984) monitored desensitization of males to filmed violence against women to determine whether this desensitization "spilled over" into other kinds of decision making about victims. Male subjects watched nearly 10 hours (five commercially released feature-length films, one a day for five days) of R-rated or X-rated fare—either R-rated sexually violent films such as *Tool Box Murders, Vice Squad, I Spit on Your Grave, Texas Chainsaw Massacre;* X-rated movies that depicted sexual assault; or X-rated movies that depicted only consensual sex (nonviolent). The R-rated films were much more explicit with regard to violence than they were with regard to sexual content. After each movie the men completed a mood questionnaire and evaluated the films on several dimensions. The films were counterbalanced so that comparisons could be made of the same films being shown on the first and last day of viewing. Before participation in the study subjects were screened for levels of hostility, and only those with low hostility scores were included to help guard against the possibility of an overly hostile individual imitating the filmed violence during the week of the films. This is also theoretically important because it suggests that any effects we found would occur with a normal population. (It has been suggested by critics of media violence research that only those who are already predisposed toward violence are influenced by exposure to media violence. In this study, those individuals have been eliminated.) After the week of viewing the men watched yet another film. This time, however, they saw a videotaped reenactment of an actual rape trial. After the trial they were asked to render judgments about how responsible the victim was for her own rape and how much injury she had suffered.

Most interesting were the results from the men who had watched the R-rated films such as *Texas Chainsaw Massacre or Maniac*. Initially, after the first day of viewing, the men rated themselves significantly above the norm for depression, anxiety, and annoyance on a mood adjective checklist. After each subsequent day of viewing, these scores dropped until, on the fourth day of viewing, the males' levels of anxiety, depression, and annoyance were indistinguishable from baseline norms.

What happened to the viewers as they watched more and more violence? We believe they were becoming desensitized to violence, particularly against women, which entailed more than a simple lowering of arousal to the movie violence. The men actually began to perceive the films differently as time went on. On Day 1, for example, on the average, the men estimated that they had seen four "offensive scenes." By the fifth day, however, subjects reported only half as many offensive scenes (even though exactly the same movies, but in reverse order, were shown). Likewise, their ratings of the violence within the films receded from Day 1 to Day 5. By the last day the men rated the movies less graphic and less gory and estimated fewer violent scenes than they did on the first day of viewing. Most startling, by the last day of viewing graphic violence against women the men were rating the material as significantly less debasing and degrading to women, more humorous, and more enjoyable, and they claimed a greater willingness to see this type of film again. This change in perception due to repeated exposure was particularly evident in comparisons of reactions to two specific films—*I Spit on Your Grave* and *Vice Squad*. Both films contain sexual assault; however, rape is portrayed more graphically in *I Spit on Your Grave* and more ambiguously in *Vice Squad*. Men who were exposed first to *Vice Squad* and then to *I Spit on Your Grave* gave nearly identical ratings of sexual violence. However, subjects who had seen the more graphic movie first saw much less sexual violence (rape) in the more ambiguous film.

The subjects' evaluations of a rape victim after viewing a reenacted rape trial were also affected by the constant exposure to brutality against women. The victim of rape was rated as more worthless and her injury as significantly less severe by those exposed to filmed violence when compared to a control group of men who saw only the rape trial and did not view films. Desensitization to filmed violence on the last day was also significantly correlated with assignment of greater blame to the victim of her own rape. (These types of effects were not observed for subjects who were exposed to sexually explicit but nonviolent films.)

MITIGATING THE EFFECTS OF EXPOSURE TO SEXUAL VIOLENCE

This research strongly suggests a potential harmful effect from exposure to certain forms of aggressive pornography and other forms of sexualized violence. There is now, however, some evidence that these negative changes in attitudes and perceptions regarding rape and violence against women not only can be eliminated but can be positively changed. Malamuth and Check (1983) found that if male subjects who had participated in such an experiment were later administered a carefully constructed debriefing, they actually would be less accepting of certain rape myths than were control subjects exposed to depictions of intercourse (without a debriefing). Donnerstein and Berkowitz (1981) showed that not only are the negative effects of previous exposure eliminated, but even up to four months later, debriefed subjects have more "sensitive" attitudes toward rape than do control subjects. These debriefings consisted of (1) cautioning subjects that the portrayal of the rape they had been exposed to is completely fictitious in nature, (2) educating subjects about the violent nature of rape, (3) pointing out to subjects that rape is illegal and punishable by imprisonment, and (4) dispelling the many rape myths that are perpetrated in the portrayal (e.g., in the majority of rapes, the victim is promiscuous or has a bad reputation, or that many women have an unconscious desire to be raped).

Surveys of the effectiveness of debriefings for male subjects with R-rated sexual violence have yielded similar positive results. Subjects who participated in the week-long film exposure study that was followed by a certain type of debriefing changed their attitudes in a positive direction. The debriefings emphasized the fallacious nature of movie portrayals that suggests that women deserve to be physically violated and emphasized that processes of desensitization may have occurred because of long-term exposure to violence. The results indicated an immediate effect for debriefing, with subjects scoring lower on rape myth acceptance after participation than they scored before participation in the film viewing sessions. These effects remained, for the most part, six weeks later. The effectiveness of the debriefing for the subjects who participated in two later experiments (one involving two weeks of exposure to R-rated violent films) indicated that even after seven months, subjects' attitudes about sexual violence showed significant positive change compared to the preparticipation levels.

This research suggests that if the callous attitudes about rape and violence presented in aggressive pornography and other media representations of violence against women are learned, they can likewise be "unlearned." Furthermore, if effective debriefings eliminate these negative effects, it would seem possible to develop effective "prebriefings" that would also counter the impact of such materials. Such programs could become part of sex education curricula for young males. Given the easy access and availability of many forms of sexual violence to young males today, such programs would go a long way toward countering the impact of such images.

THE IMPACT OF NONAGGRESSIVE PORNOGRAPHY

An examination of early research and reports in the area of nonaggressive pornography would have suggested that effects of exposure to erotica were, if anything, nonharmful. For instance:

> It is concluded that pornography is an innocuous stimulus which leads quickly to satiation and that the public concern over it is misplaced. (Howard, Liptzin, and Reifler, 1973, p. 133)

> Results . . . fail to support the position that viewing erotic films produces harmful social consequences. (Mann, Sidman, & Starr, 197, p. 113)

> If a case is to be made against "pornography" in 1970, it will have to be made on grounds other than demonstrated effects of a damaging personal or social nature. (President's Commission on Obscenity and Pornography, 1970, p. 139)

A number of criticisms of these findings, however (such as Cline, 1974; Dienstbier, 1977; Wills, 1977), led to reexamination of the issue of exposure to pornography and subsequent aggressive behavior. Some—for example, Cline (1974)—saw major methodological and interpretive problems with the Pornography Commission report; others (for example, Liebert & Schwartzberg, 1977) believed that the observations were premature. Certainly the relationship between exposure to pornography and subsequent aggressive behavior was more complex than first believed. For the most part, recent research has shown that exposure to nonaggressive pornography can have one of two effects.

A number of studies in which individuals have been predisposed to aggression and were later exposed to nonaggressive pornography have revealed increases in aggressive behavior (such as Baron & Bell, 1977; Donnerstein, Donnerstein, & Evans, 1975; Malamuth, Feshbach, & Jaffe, 1977; Meyer, 1972; Zillmann, 1971, 1979). Such findings have been interpreted in terms of a general arousal model, which states that under conditions in which aggression is a dominant response, any source of emotional arousal will tend to increase aggressive behavior in disinhibited subjects (for example, Bandura, 1977; Donnerstein, 1983). A second group of studies (Baron, 1977; Baron & Bell, 1973; Donnerstein et al., 1975; Frodi, 1977; Zillmann & Sapolsky, 1977) reports the opposite—that exposure to pornography of a nonaggressive nature can actually reduce subsequent aggressive behavior.

These results appear contradictory, but recent research (Baron, 1977; Donnerstein, 1983; Donnerstein et al., 1975; Zillmann, 1979) has begun to reconcile seeming inconsistencies. It is now believed that as pornographic stimuli become more arousing, they give rise to increases in aggression. At a low level of arousal, however, the stimuli distract individuals, and attention is directed away from previous anger. Acting in an aggressive manner toward a target is incompatible with the pleasant feelings associated with low-level arousal (see Baron, 1977; Donnerstein, 1983). There is also evidence that individuals who find the materials "displeasing" or "pornographic" will also increase their aggression after exposure, whereas those who have more positive reactions to the material will not increase their aggression even to highly arousing materials (Zillmann, 1979).

The research noted above was primarily concerned with same-sex aggression. The influence of nonaggressive pornography on aggression against women tends to produce mixed effects. Donnerstein and Barrett (1978) and Donnestein and Hallam (1978) found that nonaggressive pornography had no effect on subsequent aggression unless constraints against aggressing were reduced. This was accomplished by both angering male subjects by women and giving subjects multiple chances to aggress. Donnerstein (1983) tried to reduce aggressive inhibitions through the use of an aggressive model but found no increase in aggression after exposure to an X-rated nonviolent film. It seems, therefore, that nonaggressive sexual material does not lead to aggression against women except under specific conditions (for example when inhibitions against aggression are lowered deliberately by the experimenter).

Almost without exception, studies reporting the effects of nonviolent pornography have relied on short-term exposure; most subjects have been exposed to only a few minutes of pornographic material. More recently, Zillman and Bryant (1982, 1984) demonstrated that long-term exposure (4 hours and 48 minutes over a six-week period) to pornography that does not contain overt aggressiveness may cause male and female subjects to (1) become more tolerant of bizarre and violent forms of pornography, (2) become less supportive of statements about sexual equality, and (3) become more lenient in assigning punishment to a rapist whose crime is described in a newspaper account. Furthermore, extensive exposure to the nonaggressive pornography significantly increased males' sexual callousness toward women. This latter finding was evidenced by increased acceptance of statements such as "A man should find them, fool them, fuck them, and forget them," "A women doesn't mean 'no' until she slaps you," and "If they are old enough to bleed, they are old enough to butcher." Zillman and others (such as Berkowitz, 1984) have offered several possible explanations for this effect, suggesting that certain viewer attitudes are strengthened through long-term exposure to nonviolent pornographic material.

A common scenario of the material used in the Zillman research is that women are sexually insatiable by nature. Even though the films shown do not feature the infliction of pain or suffering, women are portrayed as extremely permissive and promiscuous, willing to accommodate any male sexual urge. Short-term exposure to this view of women (characteristic of early studies of nonviolent pornography) may not be sufficient to engender changes in viewers' attitudes congruent with these portrayals. However, attitudinal changes might be expected under conditions of long-term exposure. Continued exposure to the idea that women will do practically anything sexually may prime or encourage other thoughts regarding female promiscuity (Berkowitz, 1984). This increase in the availability of thoughts about female promiscuity or the ease with which viewers can imagine instances in which a female has been sexually insatiable may lead viewers to inflate their estimates of how willingly and frequently women engage in sexual behavior. The availability of thoughts about female insatiability may also affect judgments about sexual behavior such as rape, bestiality, and sadomasochistic sex. Further, these ideas may endure. Zillman and Bryant (1982), for example, found that male subjects still had a propensity to trivialize rape three weeks after exposure to nonviolent pornography. It is important to point out, however, that in these studies long-term exposure did not increase aggressive behavior but in fact decreased subsequent aggression.

Unfortunately, the role that images of female promiscuity and insatiability play in fostering callous perceptions of women can only be speculated upon at this point because no research has systematically manipulated film content in an experiment designed to facilitate or inhibit viewer cognitions. One cannot rule out the possibility, for example, that simple exposure to many sexually explicit depictions (regardless of their "insatiability" theme) accounts for the attitudinal changes found in their study. Sexual explicitness and themes of insatiability are experimentally confounded in this work.

Another emerging concern among political activists about pornography is its alleged tendency to degrade women (Dworkin, 1985; MacKinnon, 1985). This concern has been expressed recently in the form of municipal ordinances against pornography originally drafted by Catherine MacKinnon and Andrea Dworkin that have been introduced in a variety of communities, including Minneapolis and Indianapolis. One central feature of these ordinances is that pornography is the graphic "sexually explicit subordination of women" that also includes "women presented in scenarios of degradation, injury, abasement, torture, shown as filthy or inferior, bleeding, bruised, or hurt in a context that makes these conditions sexual" (City County general ordinance No. 35, City of Indianapolis, 1984). These ordinances have engendered a great deal of controversy, as some individuals have maintained that they are a broad form of censorship. A critique of these ordinances can be found in a number of publications (for example, Burstyn, 1985; Russ, 1985).

The framers of the ordinance suggest that after viewing such material, "a general pattern of discriminatory attitudes and behavior, both violent and nonviolent, that has the capacity to stimulate various negative reactions against women will be found" (Defendants' memorandum, U.S. District Court for the Southern District of Indiana, Indianapolis Division, 1984, p. 8). Experimental evidence is clear with respect to the effects of pornography showing injury, torture, bleeding, bruised, or hurt women in sexual contexts. What has not been investigated is the effect of material showing women in scenarios of degradation, as inferior and abased.

No research has separated the effect of sexual explicitness from degradation, as was done with aggressive pornography, to determine whether the two interact to foster negative evaluations of women. Nearly all experiments conducted to date have confounded sexual explicitness with the presentation of women as a subordinate, objectified class. Only one investigation (Donnerstein, 1984) has attempted to disentangle sexual explicitness and violence. The results of this short-term exposure investigation, discussed above, revealed that although the combination of sexual explicitness and violence against a woman (the violent pornographic condition) resulted in the highest levels of subsequent aggression against a female target, the nonexplicit depiction that showed only violence resulted in aggression levels nearly as high and attitudes that were more callous than those that resulted from the combined exposure. The implication of this research is that long-term exposure to material that may not be explicitly sexual but that depicts women in scenes of degradation and subordination may have a negative impact on viewer attitudes. This is one area in which research is still needed.

CONCLUSION

Does pornography influence behaviors and attitudes toward women? The answer is difficult and centers on the definition of pornography. There is no evidence for any "harm"-related effects from sexually explicit materials. But research may support potential harmful effects from aggressive materials. Aggressive images are the issue, not sexual images. The message about violence and the sexualized nature of violence is crucial. Although these messages may be part of some forms of pornography, they are also pervasive media messages in general, from prime-time TV to popular films. Men in our society have callous attitudes about rape. But where do these attitudes come from? Are the media, and in particular pornography, the cause? We would be reluctant to place the blame on the media. If anything, the media act to reinforce already existing attitudes and values regarding women and violence. They do contribute, but are only part of the problem.

As social scientists we have devoted a great deal of time to searching for causes of violence against women. Perhaps it is time to look for ways to reduce this violence. This chapter has noted several studies that report techniques to mitigate the influence of exposure to sexual violence in the media, which involves changing attitudes about violence. The issue of pornography and its relationship to violence will continue for years, perhaps without any definitive answers. We may never know if there is any real causal influence. We do know, however, that rape and other forms of violence against women are pervasive. How we change this situation is of crucial importance, and our efforts need to be directed to this end.

REFERENCES

Abel, G., Barlow, D., Blanchard, E., & Guild, D. (1977). The components of rapists' sexual arousal. *Archives of General Psychiatry, 34*, 395–403, 895–903.

Bandura, A. (1977). *Social learning theory*. Englewood Cliffs, NJ: Prentice-Hall.

Baron, R. A. (1977). *Humn aggression*. New York: Plenum.

Baron, R. A. (1984). The control of human aggression: A strategy based on incompatible responses. In R. Green & E. Donnerstein (Eds.), *Aggression: Theoretical and empirical reviews* (Vol. 2). New York: Academic Press.

Baron, R. A., & Bell, P. A. (1977). Sexual arousal and aggression by males: Effects of type of erotic stimuli and prior provocation. *Journal of Personality and Social Psychology, 35*, 79–87.

Berkowitz, L. (1974). Some determinants of impulsive aggression: Role of mediated associations with reinforcements for aggression. *Psychological Review, 81*, 165–179.

Berkowitz, L. (1984). Some effects of thoughts on anti- and prosocial influences of media events: A cognitive-neoassociation analysis. *Psychological Bulletin, 95*, 410–427.

Brownmiller, S. (1975). *Against our will: Men, women and rape*. New York: Simon & Schuster.

Burstyn, V. (1985). *Women against censorship*. Manchester, NH: Salem House.

Burt, M. R. (1980). Cultural myths and supports for rape. *Journal of Personality and Social Psychology, 38*, 217–230.

Check, J. V. P., & Malamuth, N. (1983). Violent pornography, feminism, and social learning theory. *Aggressive Behavior, 9*, 106–107.

Check, J. V. P., & Malamuth, N. (in press).. Can participation in pornography experiments have positive effects? *Journal of Sex Research.*

Cline, V. B. (Ed.). (1974). *Where do you draw the line?* Salt Lake City: Brigham Young University Press.

Dienstbier, R. A. (1977). Sex and violence: Can research have it both ways? *Journal of Communication, 27*, 176–188.

Donnerstein, E., & Berkowitz, L. (1985). *Role of aggressive and sexual images in violent pornography.* Manuscript submitted for publication.

Donnerstein, E. (1980a). Pornography and violence against women. *Annals of the New York Academy of Sciences, 347*, 277–288.

Donnerstein, E. (1980b). Aggressive-erotica and violence against women. *Journal of Personality and Social Psychology, 39*, 269–277.

Donnerstein, E. (1983). Erotica and human aggression. In R. Geen & E. Donnerstein (Eds.). *Aggression: Theoretical and empirical reviews.* New York: Academic Press.

Donnerstein, E. (1984). Pornography: Its effect on violence against women. In N. Malamuth & E. Donnerstein (Eds.). *Pornography and sexual aggression.* Orlando, FL: Academic Press.

Donnerstein, E., & Barrett, G. (1978). The effects of erotic stimuli on male aggression toward females. *Journal of Personality and Social Psychology, 36*, 180–188.

Donnerstein, E., & Berkowitz, L. (1982). Victim reactions in aggressive-erotic films as a factor in violence against women. *Journal of Personality and Social Psychology, 41*, 710–724.

Donnerstein, E., & Hallam, J. (1978). Facilitating effects of erotica on aggression against women. *Journal of Personality and Social Psychology, 36,*1270–1277.

Donnerstein, E., & Linz, D. (1984, January). Sexual violence in the media, a warning. *Psychology Today*, pp. 14–15.

Donnerstein, E., Donnerstein, M., & Evans, R. (1975). Erotic stimuli and aggression: Facilitation or inhibition. *Journal of Personality and Social Psychology, 32*, 237–244.

Dworkin, A. (1985). Against the male flood: Censorship, pornography, and equality. *Harvard Women's Law Journal, 8.*

Frodi, A. (1977). Sexual arousal, situational restrictiveness, and aggressive behavior. *Journal of Research in Personality, 11*, 48–58.

Howard, J. L., Liptzin, M. B., & Reifler, C. B. (1973). Is pornography a problem? *Journal of Social Issues, 29*, 133–145.

Liebert, R. M. & Schwartzberg, N. S. (1977). Effects of mass media. *Annual Review of Psychology, 28*, 141–173.

Liuz, D., Donnerstein, E., & Penrod, S. (1984). The effects of long-term exposure to filmed violence against women. *Journal of Communication, 34*, 130–147.

MacKinnon, C. A. (1985). Pornography, civil rights, and speech. *Harvard Civil Rights-Civil Liberty Law Review, 20* (1).

Malamuth, N. (1981a). Rape proclivity among males. *Journal of Social Issues, 37*, 138–157.

Malamuth, N. (1981b). Rape fantasies as a function of exposure to violent-sexual stimuli. *Archives of Sexual Behavior, 10*, 33–47.

Malamuth, N. (1984). Aggression against women: Cultural, and individual causes. In N. Malamuth & F. Donnerstein (Eds.) *Pornograpy and sexual aggression.* Orlando, FL: Academic Press.

Malamuth N., Feshbach, S., & Jaffe, Y. (1977). Sexual arousal and aggression: Recent experiments and theoretical issues. *Journal of Social Issues, 33*, 110–133.

Malamuth, N. M., & Spinner, B. (1980). A longitudinal content analysis of sexual violence in the best-selling erotic magazines. *Journal of Sex Research, 16* (3), 116–237.

Malamuth, N., & Check, J. V. P. (1981). The effects of mass media exposure on acceptance of violence against women: A field experiment. *Journal of Research in Personality, 15*, 436–446.

Malamuth, N., & Check, J. V. P. (1983). Sexual arousal to rape depictions: Individual differences. *Journal of Abnormal Psychology, 92,* 55–67.

Malamuth, N., & Donnerstein, E. (1982). The effects of aggressive pornographic mass media stimuli. In L. Berkowitz (Ed.), *Advances in experimental social psychology (vol. 15).* New York: Academic Press.

Malamuth, N., & Donnerstein, E. (Eds.), 1983). *Pornography and sexual aggression.* New York: Academic Press.

Malamuth, N., Haber, S., & Feshbach, S. (1980). The sexual responsiveness of college students to rape depictions: Inhibitory and disinhibitory effects. *Journal of Research in Personality, 14,* 399–408.

Mann, J., Sidman, J., & Starr, S. (1971). Effects of erotic films on sexual behavior of married couples. In *Technical Report of the Commission on Obscenity and Pornography (vol. 8).* Washington, DC: Government Printing Office.

Meyer, T. (1972). The effects of viewing justified and unjustified real film violence on aggressive behavior. *Journal of Personality and Social Psychology, 23,* 21–29.

President's Commission on Obscenity and Pornography (vol. 8). Washington, DC: Government Printing Office.

Russ, J. (1985). *Magic mommas, trembling sisters, puritans and perverts.* New York: Crossing.

Scott, J. (1985). *Sexual violence in* Playboy *magazine: Longitudinal analysis.* Paper presented at the meeting of the American Society of Criminology.

The war against pornography. (1985, March 18). *Newsweek,* pp. 58–62, 65–67.

Wills, G. (1977, November). Measuring the impact of erotica. *Psychology Today,* pp. 30–34.

Zillman, D. (1971). Excitation transfer in communication-mediated aggressive behavior. *Journal of Experimental Social Psychology, 7,* 419–433.

Zillman, D. (1979). *Hostility and aggression.* Hillsdale, NJ: Erlbaum.

Zillman, D. (1984). *Victimization of women through pornography.* Proposal to the National Science Foundation.

Zillman, D., & Bryant, J. (1982). Pornography, sexual callousness, and the trivialization of rape. *Journal of Communication, 32,* 10–21.

Zillman, D., & Bryant, J. (1984). Effects of massive exposure to pornography. In N. Malamuth & E. Donnerstein (Eds.), *Pornography and sexual aggression.* New York: Academic Press.

Zillman, D., & Sapolsky, B. S. (1977). What mediates the effect of mild erotica on annoyance and hostile behavior in males? *Journal of Personality and Social Psychology, 35,* 587–596.

Chris Clark

PORNOGRAPHY WITHOUT POWER?

I like to look at naked men. I admit it. I have for a long time now. I liked it as a child when I'd play "I'll show you mine/You show me yours" with other boys. I liked it growing up seeing older men in locker rooms. I liked it in puberty, discovering my father's collection of *Playboy* and being fascinated with pictures of naked men in the "Sex in Cinema" features; or going to the library and looking through sex books or any book—art, theater, photography—that had a picture of a naked man. I liked it in my late teens, having girlfriends who knew I was gay buy *Playgirl* for us to look at. I like to look at naked men.

Reprinted from *Changing Men,* Fall 1985. Reprinted by permission.

As a product of this desire to see naked men, I discovered pornography, specifically gay male pornography. This brought to light a whole new dimension to my pleasure, seeing naked men together, holding, touching, naked men being sexual together. I think I remember that first picture: two men embracing on a dock, no genitals visible, one man with one eye partially open, looking at the viewer. There were stories and real-life fantasies and occurrences, all for my pleasure. It and my masturbation viewing it, was an *affirmation* of my sexuality.

Yet, my pleasure was private! It had to be hidden. I had to sneak the porn into my house—not only was it pornography, "dirty" in itself, but it was *gay* porn! It became somewhat of an obsession. I would sneak it in with other magazines, with other packages, any way I could. When I widened my freedom by moving out on my own, I also removed the bars on my obsession—I became a collector.

At first, I collected whole magazines, and when that grew too bulky, I started cutting pictures out and putting them in collections—"My Favorite Porn"—then simply collecting the pictures in large plain envelopes. They were "my men," my sexuality.

Not coincidentally, my entrance into "gay culture" was through porn. Growing up in a small city, the only openly advertised public sex venue was a gay male porn movie house—complete with live nude dancers. (Until I went, I was never really sure whether it was for men or women—that's how "openly gay" it was.) Here I saw films of men having sex (doing things I didn't know existed or had only read about), and I saw men dancing naked, again for my pleasure. I felt my sexuality affirmed. How could I now take any position other than *for* that which first affirmed and then later confirmed my deviant sexuality?

> To gay men, the fear of sexuality, especially in the form of internalized self-hatred and self-disgust, is the most pernicious expression of sexism in our society. The first step towards personal communal liberation is unlearning those lessons of socialization which make our cocks and asses dirty. The acceptance of our bodies, the unhindered celebration of our sexuality and the act of loving other men spiritually, romantically and physically is the necessary first step toward liberation. Anything that helps to free our repressed selves—including pornography—has a positive value.

This is a radical statement. (It's from "Gay Porn—a discussion" in *Achilles Heel*, a British anti-sexist men's magazine.) Pornography, like other expressions of sexuality must be put into context, viewed through cultural, social, political and economic filters.

Many in the argument over porn seek to clarify the distinction between pornography and erotica. Though noble in purpose, such distinctions are themselves reflective of sexual preferences and social norms and biases. As Ellen Willis argues, it may simply become: "What turns me on is erotica, what turns you on is pornographic." To maintain a broad perspective, I use Ellen Willis' definition of pornography as "any image or description intended or used to arouse sexual desire," and follow her generalization that

> pornography is the return of the repressed, of feelings and fantasies driven underground by a culture that atomizes sexuality, defining love

as a noble affair of the heart and mind, lust as a base animal urge centered in unmentionable organs. Prurience—the state of mind I associate with pornography—implies a sense of sex as forbidden, secretive pleasure, isolated from any emotional or social context.

It is here that gay male pornography and straight pornography overlap—a union rarely seen or addressed.

We are all affected by the social construction of gender and sexuality. Women, gay men and other sexual "minorities" and sub-cultures are oppressed. Straight men are forced, some with an unwillingness in spite of the many rewards, into the role of oppressor. This polarization of gender identity into female and male is what produces pornography. Three issues converge here: power, violence, and objectification. The three issues together form the basis of the anti-porn argument, and are also why I have some reservations about taking a pro-porn position.

Power is linked to socially defined sexuality in exactly the same way that aggression is linked to "maleness." Pornography as a product of male sexuality is thus a reflection of power issues. Power *can* be sexual and yet sexuality *can* be portrayed without power. Sex without power is often portrayed in gay porn where the relation between two partners has the possibility of gender equality. Sexual power is evident in most straight porn because of the imbalance of power implicit in the relations between men and women. To refute this distinction between gay and straight porn is itself homophobic; since gay men begin as gender-equals, the only way to conflate gay and straight porn is to label one participant as the passive-feminine role.

Power and violence are linked to sexuality in our culture and porn simply reflects this situation. As Gloria Steinem argues,

> It takes violence or the threat of it to maintain the unearned dominance of any group of human beings over another. Moreover, the threat must be the most persuasive wherever men and women come together intimately and are most in danger of recognizing each other's humanity.

However, though violence maintains dominance, and porn often depicts violence, attacking porn is not the answer. This is trying to cure the symptoms—pornography—and leaving the disease—our socialization into strictly dichotomous roles—to express itself elsewhere. Those opposing pornography are venting their rage at sexual oppression and violence on a by-product of the oppression.

My other reservation in taking a proporn position is also common to both straight and gay pornography: objectification. It is an implicit function of any representation of reality, a function of focus. Pornography is a representation of sexuality; it focuses intently on it, and thus objectifies it. I am victimized by this objectification because I want a link between my sexuality and my emotions. Pornography obscured that link even while affirming my sexuality. In my case, objectification manifested itself in promiscuity. Realizing this, I began to examine my objectification of sexual partners. I began to control the objectification and restore the link between sex and emotion. I see now how porn aided the construction of my sexuality; I also see, and can now control, the side-effects.

Arguments over pornography produce, from many positions, many solutions. The most visible, advocated by those against porn, is censorship or restriction of visibility of porn, such as legal ordinances against pornography. But Steinem reminds us that

> . . . any societal definition of pornography in a male-dominated society . . . probably would punish the wrong people. Freely chosen homosexual expression might be considered more "pornographic" than snuff movies, or contraceptive courses for teenagers more "obscene" than bondage. Furthermore, censorship in itself . . . would drive pornography into more underground activity . . .

This moralistic solution, in a patriarchal society would reify the good girl/bad girl split for women, the repression of any "unacceptable" sexuality—i.e., that which is not heterosexual or male defined. Instead, I would suggest, with Deirdre English, that we "need, even more than women against pornography . . . , women pornographers—or eroticists, if that sounds better." The gay porn I've seen has been moving in this direction. Movies are focusing more on coming out and love relationships. Magazines are shifting toward more self-affirming stories and photo images. We need *more* porn addressing our oppression and affirming our sexuality. Let's join forces—those of us who are repressed by current norms—and create a new porn, a pornography without power, that glorifies the freedom to choose our own form of sexual expression.

REFERENCES

"Gay Porn—a Discussion," *Achilles Heel*, 1983.

Gloria Steinem, "Erotica vs. Pornography" in *Outrageous Acts and Everyday Rebellions* (NY: Holt, Rinehart, 1983).

Ellen Willis, "Feminism, Moralism and Pornography," *Village Voice*, 1979.

M. Rochlin

THE HETEROSEXUAL QUESTIONNAIRE

1. What do you think caused your heterosexuality?
2. When and how did you decide you were a heterosexual?
3. Is it possible that your heterosexuality is just a phase you may grow out of?
4. Is it possible that your heterosexuality stems from a neurotic fear of others of the same sex?
5. If you have never slept with a person of the same sex, is it possible that all you need is a good Gay lover?
6. Do your parents know that you are straight? Do your friends and/or roommate(s) know? How did they react?
7. Why do you insist on flaunting your heterosexuality? Can't you just be who you are and keep it quiet?

8. Why do heterosexuals place so much emphasis on sex?
9. Why do heterosexuals feel compelled to seduce others ino their lifestyle?
10. A disporportionate majority of child molesters are heterosexual. Do you consider it safe to expose children to heterosexual teachers?
11. Just what do men and women *do* in bed together? How can they truly know how to please each other, being so anatomically different?
12. With all the societal support marriage receives, the divorce rate is spiraling. Why are there so few stable relationships among heterosexuals?
13. Statistics show that lesbians have the lowest incidence of sexually transmitted diseases. Is it really safe for a woman to maintain a heterosexual lifestyle and run the risk of disease and pregnancy?
14. How can you become a whole person if you limit yourself to compulsive, exclusive heterosexuality?
15. Considering the menace of overpopulation, how could the human race survive if everyone were heterosexual?
16. Could you trust a heterosexual therapist to be objective? Don't you feel s/he might be inclined to influence you in the direction of her/his own leanings?
17. There seem to be very few happy heterosexuals. Techniques have been developed that might enable you to change if you really want to. Have you considered trying aversion therapy?
18. Would you want your child to be heterosexual, knowing the problems that s/he would face?

Gary Kinsman

MEN LOVING MEN:
THE CHALLENGE OF GAY LIBERATION

The limits of "acceptable" masculinity are in part defined by comments like "What are you, a fag?"[1] As boys and men we have heard such expressions and the words "queer," "faggot," and "sissy" all our lives. These words encourage certain types of male behavior and serve to define, regulate, and limit our lives, whether we consider ourselves straight or gay. Depending on who is speaking and who is listening, they incite fear or hatred.

Even among many heterosexual men who have been influenced by feminism, the taboo against loving the same sex remains unchallenged. Lines like "I may be anti-sexist, but I am certainly not gay" can still be heard. These men may be questioning some aspects of male privilege, but in attempting to remake masculinity they have not questioned the institution of heterosexuality.[2] As a result their challenge to male privilege is partial and inadequate.

Gay men have often found much support in the "men's movement" or in groups of men against sexism. At the same time we have also seen our concerns as gay men marginalized and pushed aside and have often felt like

Reprinted from *Beyond Patriarchy: Essays by Men on Pleasure, Power and Change*, Michael Kaufman, ed. Toronto: Oxford University Press, 1987.

outsiders, Joe Interrante expresses some of the reservations of gay men about the "men's movement" and its literature:

> As a gay man . . . I had suspicions about the heterocentrist bias of this work. It told me that my gayness existed "in addition to" my masculinity, whereas I found that it colored my entire experience of manhood. I distrusted a literature which claimed that gay men were just like heterosexual men except for what they did in bed.[3]

The literature of the men's movement has tended to produce an image of men that is white, middle-class, and heterosexual. As Ned Lyttleton has pointed out, "an analysis of masculinity that does not deal with the contradictions of power imbalances that exist between men themselves will be limited and biased, and its limits and biases will be concealed under the blanket of shared male privilege."[4] A series of masculinities becomes subsumed under one form of masculinity that becomes "masculinity." As a result, socially organized power relations among and between men based on sexuality, race, class, or age have been neglected. These power relations are major dividing lines between men that have to be addressed if progressive organizing among men is to encompass the needs and experiences of all men. The men's movement has reached a turning point.[5] It has to choose whether it is simply a movement for men's rights—defending men's rights to be human too—or whether it will deepen the challenge to an interlocked web of oppression: sexism, heterosexism, racism, and class exploitation. We have to choose between a vision of a world in which men are more sensitive and human but are still "real" men at the top of the social order, and a radically new vision that entails the transformation of masculinity and sexuality and the challenging of other forms of domination.

In developing this radical vision—radical in the sense of getting to the roots of the problem—the politics of gay liberation and the politics of lesbian feminism are important. So too are the experiences of those of us who have been made into outsiders, people labelled "faggot," "queer," or "dyke" who have reclaimed these stigmatized labels as ways of naming experiences of the world and as weapons of resistance to heterosexual hegemony. The struggle against the institutionalized social norm of heterosexuality opens up the door to other kinds of social and personal change.

GAY LIBERATION VERSUS HETEROSEXUAL PRIVILEGE

In our society heterosexuality as an institutionalized norm has become an important means of social regulation, enforced by laws, police practices, family and social policies, schools, and the mass media. In its historical development heterosexuality is tied up with the institution of masculinity, which gives social and cultural meaning to biological male anatomy, associating it with masculinity, aggressiveness, and an "active" sexuality. "Real" men are intrinsically heterosexual; gay men, therefore, are not real men.

While gay men share with straight men the privilege of being in a dominant position in relation to women, we are at the same time in a subordinate position in the institution of heterosexuality. As a result, gay men's lives and experiences are not the same as those of heterosexual men. For instance, while we share with straight men the economic benefits of being men in a patriarchal society, we do not participate as regularly in the everyday interpersonal subordination of women in the realms of sexuality and violence. Although, like other men, we have more social opportunities, we are not accepted as open gays in corporate boardrooms or in many jobs, sports, and professions. We can still be labeled "national security risks" and sick, deviant, or abnormal. Consequently, gay men experience a rupture between the presumably universal categories of heterosexual experience and their own particular experience of the world, a rupture that denies many of our experiences; for gay men exist in social situations that allow us to see aspects of life, desire, sexuality, and love that cannot be seen by heterosexual men.[6]

Gay men have had to question the institution of masculinity—which associates masculinity with heterosexuality—in our daily lives. We have experimented with and developed new ways of organizing our sexual lives and our love and support relations, of receiving and giving pleasure. Heterosexual men interested in seriously transforming the fabric of their lives have to stop seeing gay liberation as simply a separate issue for some men that has nothing to say to them. They should begin to ask what the experience of gay men can bring into view for them. As we break the silence and move beyond liberal tolerance toward gays and lesbians, we can begin to see how "queer baiting" and the social taboo against pleasure, sex, and love between men serves to keep all men in line, defining what proper masculinity is for us. Gay liberation suggests that heterosexuality is not the only natural form of sexuality but has instead been socially and culturally made the "normal" sexual practice and identity. As the Kinsey Institute studies suggested, the actual flux of human desire cannot be easily captured in rigid sexual categories. Many men who define themselves as straight have had sexual experiences with other men.[7] This has demonstrated the contradictions that can exist between our actual experiences and desires and the rigid social categories that are used to divide normal from deviant and that imply that any participation in homosexual activity automatically defines one as a homosexual.

Breaking the silence surrounding homosexuality requires challenging heterosexism and heterosexual privilege. Lesbian-feminist Charlotte Bunch once explained to heterosexual women that the best way to find out what heterosexual privilege is all about is to go about for a few days as an open lesbian:

> What makes heterosexuality work is heterosexual privilege—and if you don't have a sense of what privilege is, I suggest that you go home and announce to everybody that you know—a roommate, your family, the people you work with—everywhere that you go—that you're a queer. Try being a queer for a week.[8]

This statement could also be applied to the situation of straight men, and any heterosexual man can easily imagine the discomfort, ridicule, and fear he might experience, how his "coming out" would disrupt "normal" relations at work and with his family. Such experiences are the substance of gay oppression that make our lives different from those of straight men. Gay men in this heterosexist society are labeled with many terms of abuse. Young boys hurl the labels "queer," "fag," or "cocksucker" at each other before they know what the words mean. As we grow up we are denied images of men loving men and any models for our lives outside heterosexuality. In the United

States, the age of consent varies from state to state, usually from sixteen to eighteen, although in some states all homosexual acts remain technically illegal. Under Canadian and British law males under twenty-one are denied the right to have sexual relations with other boys and men. Many members of the medical and psychiatric professions still practice psychological and social terrorism against us by trying to adjust us to fit the norm. We are excluded as open lesbians and gay men from most activities and institutions. When the mass media does cover us they use stereotypes or other means to show us to be sick, immoral, indecent, as some sort of social problem or social menace, or they trivialize us as silly and frivolous.[9] The police continue to raid our bookstores and seize our magazines. In 1983–6, the media fostered fear and hatred against gay men by associating all gay men with AIDS. Such media stories shift and mold public opinion against us. On city streets we are often violently attacked by gangs of "queerbashers." Most countries deny lesbians and gay men the basic civil and human rights, leaving us open to arbitrary firings and evictions.

A variety of sexual laws are used to regulate and control gay men's sexual and community lives. Police in many cities have a policy of systematically entrapping and harassing gays. In recent years hundreds of men across North America have been arrested and often entrapped by the police in washrooms and parks. These campaigns—especially in small towns and cities—and the associated media attention have torn apart the lives of these men, many of whom define themselves as heterosexual and are married with families.

In fact, the society in which we have all grown up is so profoundly heterosexist that even many gays have internalized the social hatred against us in forms of "self-oppression."[10] This fear keeps many of us isolated and silent, hiding our sexuality. One of the first steps in combating this self-oppression is to reject this denial of our love and sexuality by affirming our existence and pride publicly. Assertions that "gay is good" and affirmations of gay pride are the beginning of our resistance to heterosexual hegemony on the individual and social levels.

THE HISTORY OF SEXUALITY

In addressing the matter of gay and lesbian oppression, we have to ask where this oppression has come from. How did heterosexuality come to be the dominant social relation? How did homosexuality come to be seen as a perverse outcast form of sexuality? If we can answer those questions, we can begin to see how we could break down the institution of heterosexuality and its control over our lives.

As a result of numerous cross-cultural and historical studies that have demonstrated that there is no natural or normal sexuality, we can no longer see sex as simply natural or biologically given. Our biological, erotic, and sexual capabilities are only the precondition for the organization of the social and cultural forms of meaning and activity that compose human sexuality. Our biological capabilities are transformed and mediated culturally, producing sexuality as a social need and relation. As Gayle Rubin explained, each social system has its own "sex/gender system" which is the set of arrangements by which a society transforms biological sexuality into products of human activity, and in which these transformed sexual needs are satisfied.[11]

Recent historical studies have challenged the assumed natural categories of heterosexuality and homosexuality themselves.[12] Gay, lesbian, and feminist historians have expanded our understanding of sexual meaning and identity, contesting the dominant ways in which sexuality has been discussed and viewed in our society.[13] The dominant perspective for looking at sexuality is what has been called the "repression hypothesis," which assumes that there is a natural sexuality that is repressed to maintain social and moral order. Many leftists argue that sexuality is repressed by the ruling class—to maintain class society because of capitalism's need for the family and a docile work force. This interpretation was popularized in the writings and activities of Wilhelm Reich,[14] who called for the end of sexual repression through the liberation of natural sexuality, which was for him completely heterosexual. Variations of this repression theory, and its corresponding call for the liberation of natural sexuality, have inspired sexual liberationist politics, including much of the gay liberation movement, which sees homosexuality as a natural sexuality that simply needs to be released from social repression.

The experience by women of the male sexual (i.e., heterosexual) revolution of the sixties and seventies has led much of the feminist movement to a more complex understanding of sexuality than simple theories of sexual repression. Feminism has exposed the contradictions in a sexual revolution that increased women's ability to seek sexual satisfaction but only within male-dominated heterosexual relations. Feminism has also begun to explore how sexuality and social power are bound together and how sexuality has been socially organized in male-dominated forms in this society.[15] This view of sex opens up new possibilities for sexual politics—our sexual lives are no longer seen as divorced from human and social activity but as the results of human praxis (the unity of thought and activity). Sexual relations are therefore changeable and are themselves the site of personal and social struggles. We can then begin to question the natural appearance of such sexual categories as heterosexual and homosexual and to make visible the human activity that is involved in the making of sexuality. This opens up a struggle, not for the liberation of some inherent sexuality that just has to be freed from the bonds of capitalism or repressive laws, but for a much broader challenge to the ways our sexual lives are defined, regulated, and controlled. It opens up questions about the very making and remaking of sex, desire, and pleasure.

Enter the Homosexual   The historical emergence of the "homosexual" required a number of social preconditions, which can be summarized as three interrelated social processes: first, the rise of capitalist social relations, which created the necessary social spaces for the emergence of homosexual cultures;[16] second, the regime of sexuality that categorized and labeled homosexuality and sexual "deviations"; and third, the activities, cultural production, and resistance to the oppression of men in these same-sex desire-based cultures.

The rise of capitalism in Europe between the fifteenth and nineteenth centuries separated the rural household economy from the new industrial economy and undermined the interdependent different-sex household economy. The working class was made, and made itself, in the context of this industrialization, urbanization, and commercialization. This separation of "work" from the household and the development of wage labor meant that it became possible for more men in the cities to live outside the family, earning a wage and living as boarders. Later they would be able to eat at restaurants or taverns and rent their own accommodation. This created the opportunities for some men to start organizing what would become, through a process of development and struggle, the beginnings of a homosexual culture, from the eighteenth century on.[17]

A regime of sexuality has emerged as part of a series of social struggles over the last two centuries. The transition from feudalism to capitalism in the western countries meant a transition in the way kinship and sexual and class relations were organized. The new ruling class was no longer able to understand itself or organize its social life simply through the old feudal ties of blood or lineage.[18] New forms of family and state formation led to new forms of self-understanding, class consciousness, and notions of moral and social order. Sexuality emerged as an autonomous sphere separate from household production. A proper, respectable sexual and gender identity became an essential feature of the class unity of the bourgeoisie. This process is linked to the emergence of the ideology of individual identity. The regime of sexual definitions was first applied to the bodies of the bourgeoisie itself through its educational and medical systems and through the sexological knowledge that was generated by the new professional groups of doctors and psychiatrists and that served to draw a boundary between bourgeois respectability and the "bestial" sexual practices of the outcast poor and "lower orders." These norms of sex and gender definition helped organize the relations of the bourgeois family and its sexual morality.

Later these same norms of sexual identity and morality were used against the urban working class and poor, who were considered a threat to social order by middle-class and state agencies. The working class both resisted this enforcement of social norms and at the same time adopted them as its own. The male-dominated "respectable" sections of the working class developed their own norms of family and sexual life that incorporated the socially dominant norms of masculinity, femininity, and reproductive heterosexuality. The uneven and at times contradictory development of sexual identity in different classes, genders, races, and nationalities is a subject that remains to be more fully explored.

In the big cities sexuality becomes an object to be studied and a terrain for the expanding male-dominated fields of medicine, psychiatry, and sexology. Various forms of sexual behavior were categorized, classified, and ranked, with heterosexuality on the top and homosexuality and lesbianism near the bottom. The norm and the perversions were defined, separating normal and abnormal behavior. In this context sex in the ruling discourses became the truth of our being.[19]

The heterosexual man was no longer simply carrying out the types of activities he had to carry out in the sexual divisions of labor, or the activities that would lead to the reproduction of the species; rather he had become someone with a particular erotic, sexual, and gender identity that linked his masculinity to an exclusively heterosexual way of life. The heterosexual and the homosexual emerged in relation to each other as part of the same historical and social process of struggle and negotiation.

Men who engaged in sexual relations with other men in this emerging regime of sexuality (and who were affected by the ideology of individualism) began to organize their lives around their sexuality and to see themselves as separate and different from other men. They fought against campaigns by religious fundamentalists and the police who wished to curtail their activities.[20] In the last century, the emergence of sexology, increased police regulation of sexual behavior, and the passing of laws against sexual offenses combined with the development of these same-sex desire-based cultures to make the new social experience and social category of homosexuality.

The term homosexual itself was not devised until 1869, when Károly Mária Benkert, a Hungarian, coined the term in an appeal to the government to keep its laws out of peoples lives.[21] The category of homosexuality was originally elaborated by some homosexuals themselves, mostly professional men it seems, in order to name their "difference" and in order to protect themselves from police and legal prohibitions. The word was taken up by the various agencies of social regulation from the medical profession to the police and courts. Homosexuality was defined as an abnormality, a sickness, and a symptom of degeneracy. The efforts of medical and legal experts

> were chiefly concerned with whether the disgusting breed of perverts could be physically identified for courts and whether they should be held legally responsible for their acts.[22]

An early Canadian reference—in 1898—to same-sex "perversion" among men by a Dr. Ezra Stafford (which refers to the work of Krafft-Ebing, one of the grandfathers of sexology) linked sex between men with prostitution in a theory of degeneracy. Stafford wrote that these things "may lead to the tragedy of our species."[23] This connection between homosexuality and prostitution as stigmatized social and sexual practices continued even to England's Wolfenden report of 1957, which linked these topics, and it continues to this day, in, for example, the use by the Canadian police of bawdy-house legislation, originally intended to deal with houses of female prostitutes, against gay men.

Simultaneously the needs of capitalism for a skilled labor force and a continuing supply of wage-laborers led to an emphasis on the heterosexual nuclear family. The rise of modern militarism and the scramble for colonies by the western powers led to demands for a larger and healthier supply of cannon fodder at the beginning of the twentieth century. An intensification of military discipline resulted in stiff prohibitions against homosexuality, which was seen as subversive of discipline and hierarchy in the armed forces. As a result, reproductive heterosexuality was reinforced for men, and motherhood further institutionalized for women.[24]

The category of the male homosexual emerged in sexology as an "invert" and was associated with some form of effeminacy and "gender inversion." A relation between gender dysfunction and abnormal sexuality was established:

> As defined by the ancient civil or canonical codes, sodomy was a category of forbidden acts. . . . The nineteenth century homosexual became a personage, a past, a case history, and a childhood, in addition to

being a type of life, a life form, and a morphology, with an indiscreet anatomy and possibly a mysterious physiology. Nothing that went into his total composition was unaffected by his sexuality. . . . Homosexuality appeared as one of the forms of sexuality when it was transposed from the practice of sodomy onto a kind of interior androgyny, a hermaphrodism of the soul. The sodomite had been a temporary aberration; the homosexual was now a species.[25]

The categorization of "perverse" sexual types also provided a basis for resistance. Sexual categorization, as Foucault puts it,

also made possible the formation of a "reverse" discourse: homosexuality began to speak on its own behalf, to demand that its legitimacy or "naturality" be acknowledged, often in the same vocabulary, using the same categories by which it was radically disqualified.[26]

Homosexuals themselves used this category to name their experiences, to articulate their differences and cultures, moving this category in a more progressive direction. There has been a century-long struggle over the meaning of homosexuality that has involved sexologists, the police, lawyers, psychiatrists, and homosexuals, a struggle that continues today. The regime of sexuality and the specification of different sexual categories in an attempt to buttress the emerging norm of heterosexuality have unwittingly also provided the basis for homosexual experiences, identities, and cultures. Through these experiences a series of new social and sexual needs, human capacities, and pleasures have been created among a group of men. This homosexual experience, along with the slightly later emergence of a distinct lesbian experience,[27] and the feminist movement have created the basis for contemporary challenges to the hegemony of heterosexuality.

Enter Gay Liberation and the Gay Community   Recent social changes in the western capitalist countries have put in question the patriarchal, gender, and sexual relations established during the last century. A prolonged crisis in sexual and gender relations and in the meaning of sexuality has occurred. The feminist and gay liberation movements, for example, have challenged the relegation of sexual relations and particularly "deviant" forms of sexuality to the socially defined private realm, subverting the public/private categories that have been used to regulate our sexual lives. The development of contraceptive and reproductive technologies has made it more and more possible to separate heterosexual pleasure and procreation, although the struggle continues about who will have access to, and control over, this technology. The expansion of consumer markets and advertising in the post-war period has led to an increasing drawing of sexuality and sexual images into the marketplace and the public realm.[28] This increasing public visibility of sexual images and sexual cultures has led to objections from those who would wish to reprivatize sexuality, in particular its "deviant" strains. And feminists have challenged the patriarchal values that are visible in much advertising and heterosexual male pornography.

The social ferment of the sixties—particularly the civil rights, black power, and feminist movements—combined with earlier forms of homosexual activism and the expansion of the gay commercial scene and culture to produce the gay liberation movement, which erupted in 1969 in the Stonewall Riot in New York City.[29] The movement developed a new, positive identity that has served as a basis for our resistance to heterosexual hegemony. The movement's most significant achievements were its contesting of the psychiatric definition of homosexuality as a mental illness and its creation of a culture and community that have transformed the lives of hundreds of thousands of men and women. As usual in a patriarchal society, many more opportunities have opened up for men than for women.

In a challenge to the "universality" of heterosexuality, gays have affirmed that gay is just as good as straight, calling on lesbians and gay men to affirm themselves and their sexualities. This has challenged the gender and social policies of the state, suggesting that sexual activity does not have to be solely for reproduction, but can also be for play, pleasure, love, and support, and questioning the very right of the state to regulate people's sexual lives. We have affirmed our right to sexual self-determination and control over our own bodies and sexuality and have affirmed this right for others as well.

The growth of a visible gay community and the emergence of gay streets and commercial areas in many big cities have led to a reaction from the police, conservative political parties, and the new right. These groups fear the breakdown of "traditional" sexual and family relations, which they associate with social and moral order, and see the challenge that gay liberation presents to heterosexual hegemony as a threat to the ways in which their lives and institutions are organized. They want lesbians and gay men out of public view and back in the closets, threatening our very existence as a public community.

In a sense the gay ghetto is both a playground and a potential concentration camp. While it provides people a place to meet and to explore and develop aspects of their lives and sexuality, it can also separate people from the rest of the population in a much larger closet that can be isolated and contained. The ghetto can tend to obscure the experiences gay men share with other men in their society. Locking people into the new categorization of gays as minority group or community may weaken the critique of sex and gender relations in society as a whole. As Altman explains, the "ethnic homosexual' has emerged, "the widespread recognition of a distinct cultural category which appears to be pressing for the same sort of 'equality,' in Western society as do ethnic minorities."[30] However, lesbians and gay men are not born into a minority group, but like heterosexuals assume a sexual identity through social and psychological processes.[31] Gays and lesbians are not only a minority group but also an oppressed and denied sexuality. The position that gays are simply a new minority group can deflect our challenges to the dominant way of life.

In challenging heterosexuality as the social norm gays have brought into question aspects of the institutions of masculinity and male privilege. Over the last decade images of gay men have shifted from the effeminacy of the "gender invert" to the new macho and clone looks that have dominated the gay men's community. This imagery challenges the previous stereotypes of homosexuals that associated our sexuality with gender nonconfirmity and has asserted that we can be both homosexual and "masculine" at the same time.[32] In defining ourselves as masculine we have had to make use of and transform the existing images of straight masculinity we find around us. These new images challenge heterosexual norms that associate "deviant" gender stereotypes with sexual "deviancy," for instance effeminacy with male homosexuality, but at the same time also tend to create new standards and stereotypes of what gay men are supposed to be like. These images and styles themselves continue to be imprisoned within the polarities of gender dichotomy. While gay men often believe we have freed ourselves from the social organization of gender, what we have actually done is exchange "gender inversion" for a situation where homosexuality can be organized through "normal" gender identification. This assertion of masculinized imagery can to some extent lead us away from the critique of the institution of masculinity and its effects in our lives and persuade us that gender is no longer a problem for gay men.

It is ironic that some forms of resistance to past ways in which we were stigmatized can serve to accommodate us to aspects of the existing order of things. It is in this context that some of the challenges to masculinity and gender norms by straight men fighting against sexism will also be valuable to gay men. To be successful, gay liberation must challenge not only the institutionalization of heterosexuality as a social norm but also the institution of masculinity.

GAY LIBERATION AND THE RULING REGIME OF SEX

Gay liberation has emerged from the contradictions within the ruling system of sexual regulation and definition. It is fundamentally a struggle to transform the norms and definitions of sexual regulation. Gay liberation strives for the recognition of homosexuality as socially equal to the dominant social institution of heterosexuality. Yet as Weeks suggests,

> the strategic aim of the gay liberation movement must be not simply the validation of the rights of a minority within a heterosexual majority but the challenge to all the rigid categorizations of sexuality. . . . The struggle for sexual self-determination is a struggle in the end for control over our bodies. To establish this control we must escape from those ideologies and categorizations which imprison us within the existing order.[33]

The struggle to transform our sexual norms and to end the control of the institution of heterosexuality over our lives holds out the possibility of beginning to disengage us from the ruling regime of sex and gender. As Foucault suggested, movements that have been called sexual liberation movements, including gay liberation, are

> movements that start with sexuality, with the apparatus of sexuality in the midst of which they are caught and which make it function to the limit; but, at the same time, they are in motion relative to it, disengaging themselves and surmounting them.[34]

The struggle for gay liberation can be seen as a process of transformation. The assertion that gay is just as good as straight—which lies at the heart of gay liberation—is formally within the present regime of sexual categorization, for it still separates gay from straight as rigid categories and assigns value to sexuality, thus mirroring the limitations of the current sexual regime. However, the gay liberation movement operates both within *and* against this regime of sexual regulation. In asserting equal value for homosexuality and lesbianism, it begins to turn the ruling practices of sexual hierarchy on their head. Resistance begins within the present regime of sexual definitions, but it begins to shift the sexual boundaries that they have defined, opening up the possibility of transcending their limitations. By naming our specific experiences of the world, gay liberation provides the basis for a social and political struggle that can transform, defy, cut across, and break down the ruling regime of sex and gender.

The gay and lesbian communities, like other oppressed social groups, oscillate between resistance and accommodation to oppression. This is a struggle on two closely interrelated fronts. First, the gay community itself needs to strengthen cultures of resistance by building on sexual and cultural traditions that question gender norms and the relegation of erotic life to the state-defined private sphere. This will involve challenging the internalization and reproduction of sexism, racism, agesim, and class divisions within the gay community, as well as building alliances with other social groups fighting these forms of domination. Secondly, it requires a struggle outside the gay and lesbian communities for the defense of a community under attack by the police, government, and media. A key part of this strategy would be campaigning for new social policies that uproot heterosexuality as *the* social norm.

OPENING UP EROTIC CHOICES FOR EVERYONE

In developing a radical perspective we need to draw on the insights of lesbian feminism about the social power of heterosexuality and also on the historical perspectives provided by the new critical gay history, which reveals the social and historical process of the organization of heterosexual hegemony and the present system of sexual regulation more generally. These understandings create the basis for alliances between feminists, lesbians, gay liberationists, anti-sexist men, and other groups against the institution of heterosexuality, which lies at the root of the social oppression of women, lesbians, and gays. This alliance would contest the hegemony of heterosexuality in the legal system, state policies, in forms of family organization, and in the churches, unions, and other social bodies. The struggle would be for women, gays, and others to gain control over our bodies and sexuality and to begin to define our own eroticism and sexuality. A fundamental aspect of such an approach would be the elaboration and exploration of the experiences and visions of those of us living outside institutionalized heterosexuality.

Proposals for new and different ways of living (including collective and nonsexist ways of rearing children) are particularly vital since the new right and moral conservative in their various incarnations are taking advantage of people's fears about changes in family organization and sexual mores to campaign in support of patriarchal and heterosexist social norms. The defense of a maledominated heterosexuality is not only central to the policies of the new right and moral conservatives regarding feminism and gay liberation, but is a central theme of their racial and class politics as well.[35] The progressive movement's failure to deal with people's real fears, concerns, and hopes regarding sexual and gender politics is an important reason why right-wing groups are able to gain support. Feminism, gay liberation, and all progressive movements will have to articulate a vision that will allow us to move forward beyond the confines of institutionalized heterosexuality.

Gay liberation enables heterosexual men who question heterosexism to contribute to this new social vision. The issues raised by gay liberation must be addressed by all men interested in fundamental change because heterosexism limits and restricts the lives of all men. This challenge will only be effective, however, if heterosexual privilege is challenged in daily life and in social institutions. This could help begin the long struggle to disentangle heterosexual desire from the confines of institutionalized masculinity and heterosexuality. Together we could begin to redefine and remake masculinity and sexuality. If sexuality is socially produced, then heterosexuality itself can be transformed and redefined and its pleasures and desires separated from the social relations of power and domination. Gay liberation can allow all men to challenge gender and sexual norms and redefine gender and sex for ourselves in alliance with feminism; it can allow all men to explore and create different forms of sexual pleasures in our lives. This redefining of masculinity and sexuality will also help destroy the anxieties and insecurities of many straight men who try so hard to be "real men." But the success of this undertaking depends on the ability to develop alternative visions and experiences that will help all people understand how their lives could be organized without heterosexuality as the institutionalized social norm. Such a goal is a radically transformed society in which everyone will be able to gain control of his or her own body, desires, and life.

ACKNOWLEDGMENTS

Special thanks to Ned Lyttleton, Brian Conway, and Bob Gardner for comments on this paper. For more general comments on matters that pertain to topics addressed in this paper I am indebted to Varda Burstyn, Philip Corrigan, Bert Hansen, Michael Kaufman, Ian Lumsden, Dorothy E. Smith, George Smith, Mariana Valverde, and Lorna Weir.

NOTES

[1] See G. K. Lehne, "Homophobia Among Men," in Deborah David and Robert Brannon, *The Forty-Nine Percent Majority* (Reading, Mass.: Addison-Wesley, 1976), 78.

[2] On the notion of institutionalized heterosexuality see Charlotte Bunch, "Not For Lesbians Only," Quest 11, no. 2 (Fall 1975). also see Adrienne Rich, "Compulsory Heterosexuality And Lesbian Existence," in Snitow, Stansell and Thompson, eds., *Powers of Desire: The Politics of Sexuality* (New York: Monthly Review Press, 1983): 177–205.

[3] Joe Interrante, "Dancing Along the Precipice: The Men's Movement in the '80s," *Radical America* 15, no. 5 (September–October 1981): 54.

[4] Ned Lyttleton, "Men's Liberation, Men Against Sexism and Major Dividing Lines," *Resources for Feminist Research* 12, no. 4 (December/January 1983/1984): 33. Several discussions with Ned Lyttleton were very useful in clarifying my ideas in this section and throughout this paper.

[5] Interrante, *op. cit.*, 54.

[6] For further elaboration see my *The Regulation of Desire* (Montreal: Black Rose, 1986).

[7] See Kinsey, Pomeroy, and Martin, *Sexual Behavior in the Human Male* (Philadelphia: W.B. Saunders, 1948) and Mary McIntosh, "The Homosexual Role," in Plummer, ed., *The Making Of The Modern Homosexual* (London: Hutchinson, 1981), 38–43.

[8] Bunch, "Not For Lesbians Only."

[9] See Frank Pearce, "How to be Immoral and Ill, Pathetic and Dangerous all at the same time: Mass Media and the Homosexual," in Cohen and Young, eds., *The Manufacture of News: Deviance, Social Problems and the Mass Media* (London: Constable, 1973), 284–301.

[10] See Andrew Hodges and David Hutter. *With Downcast Gays, Aspects of Homosexual Self-Oppression* (Toronto: Pink Triangle Press, 1977).

[11] Gayle Rubin, "The Traffic In Women: Notes on the Political Economy of Sex," in Reiter, eds., *Towards An Anthropology Of Women* (New York: Monthly Review Press, 1975), 159. I prefer the use of sex and gender relations to sex/gender system since the notion of system tends to conflate questions of sexuality and gender and suggests that sex/gender relations are a separate system from other social relations rather than an integral aspect of them.

[12] See Joe Interrante, "From Homosexual to Gay to?: Recent Work in Gay History," in *Radical America* 15, no. 6 (November–December 1981): Martha Vicinus, "Sexuality and Power: A Review of Current Work in the History of Sexuality," *Feminist Studies* 8, no. 1 (Spring 1982): 133–56; and Robert A. Padgug, "Sexual Matters: On Conceptualizing Sexual In History," *Radical History Review*, "Sexuality in History" Issue, no. 20 (Spring/Summer 1979): 3–23.

[13] See for instance Michel Foucault, *The History Of Sexuality* (New York: Vintage, 1980), vol. 1, *An Introduction;* Jeffrey Weeks, *Sex, Politics and Society: The Regulation of Sexuality since 1800* (London: Hutchinson, 1981); and Jonathan Ned Katz, *Gay/Lesbian Almanac* (New York: Harper and Row, 1983). For recent feminist explorations of sexuality see Snitow. Stansell and Thompson, *Powers of Desire* (New York: Monthly Review, 1983); Carol Vance, ed., *Pleasure and Danger, Exploring Female Sexuality* (Boston: Routledge and Kegan Paul, 1984); Rosalind Coward, *Female Desire, Women's Sexuality Today* (London: Routledge and Kegan Paul, 1984); and Mariana Valverde, *Sex, Power and Pleasure* (Toronto: Women's Press, 1985).

[14] See Wilhelm Reich, *The Sexual Revolution* (New York: Straus and Giroux, 1974) and Baxandall, ed., *Sex-Pol. Essays, 1929–1934, Wilhelm Reich* (New York: Vintage, 1972).

[15] Unfortunately, over the last few years some anti-pornography feminists have suggested that sexuality is only a realm of danger for women, obscuring how it can also be a realm of pleasure. Some anti-porn feminists have been used by state agencies in attempts to clamp down on sexually explicit material including sexual material for gay men and lesbians. See Vance, *Pleasure and Danger;* Varda Burstyn, ed., *Women Against Censorship* (Vancouver and Toronto: Douglas and McIntyre, 1985); and Varda Burystyn, "Anatomy of a Moral Panic" and Gary Kinsman, "The Porn Debate," *Fuse 3*, no. 1 (Summer 1984).

[16] On this see the work of John D'Emilio, for instances his "Capitalism and Gay Identity," in Snitow, Stansell and Thompson, eds., *Powers of Desire*, 100–13, and his *Sexual Politics, Sexual Communities* (Chicago: University of Chicago Press, 1983).

[17] See Randolph Trumbach, "London's Sodomites: Homosexual Behaviour and Western Culture in the 18th Century," *Journal of Social History*, Fall 1977, 1–33; Mary McIntosh, "The Homosexual Role," in Plummer, ed., *The Making of The Modern Homosexual;* Alan Bray, *Homosexuality in Renaissance England* (London: Gay Men's Press, 1982); and Jeffrey Weeks, *Sex, Politics and Society.*

[18] See Foucault, *The History of Sexuality*, vol. 1 and Kinsman, *The Regulation of Desire.*

[19] This idea comes from the work of Foucault.

[20] See Bray, *Homosexuality in Renaissance England* for the activities of the Society for the Reformation of Morals, which campaigned against same-sex desire-based networks in the early eighteenth century.

[21] John Lauritsen and David Thorstad, *The Early Homosexual Rights Movement* (New York: Times Change Press, 1974), 6.

[22] Arno Karlen, *Sexuality and Homosexuality* (New York: W. W. Norton, 1971), 185.

[23] Ezra Hurlburt Stafford, "Perversion," the *Canadian Journal of Medicine and Surgery* 3, no. 4 (April 1898).

[24] On this see Anna Davin, "Imperialism and Motherhood," *History Workshop*, no. 5 (Spring 1978).

[25] Foucault, *op. cit.*, 43.

[26] *Ibid.*, 101.

[27] See Lillian Faderman, *Surpassing The Love Of Men* (New York: William Morrow, 1981); Chris-

tina Simmons, "Companionate Marriage and the Lesbian Threat," in Frontiers 4, no. 3 (Fall 1979); Martha Vicinus, "Sexuality and Power"; and Ann Ferguson, "Patriarchy, Sexual Identity, and the Sexual Revolution," *Signs* 7, no. 1 (Fall 1981): 158–72.

[28] See Gary Kinsman, "Porn/Censor Wars And The Battlefields of Sex," in *Issues of Censorship* (Toronto: A Space, 1985), 31–9.

[29] See John D'Emilio, *Sexual Politics, Sexual Communities.*

[30] Dennis Altman, "What Changed in the Seventies?," in Gay Left Collective, eds., *Homosexuality, Power and Politics* (London: Allison and Busby, 1980), 61.

[31] One prejudice that is embodied in sexual legislation and social policies is the myth that lesbians and gay men are a special threat to young people and that gay men are "child molesters." Most studies show, on the contrary, that more than 90 percent of sexual assaults on young people are committed by heterosexual men and often within the family or home. Breines and Gordon state that, "approximately 92 percent of the victims are female and 97 percent of the assailants are males." See Wini Breines and Linda Gordon, "The New Scholarship on Family Violence," *Signs* 8, no. 3 (Spring 1983); 522. Also see Elizabeth Wilson, *What Is To Be Done About Violence Against Women* (London: Penguin, 1983), particularly 117–34. We have to eliminate special age restrictions on the right to participate in consensual lesbian and gay sex so that lesbian and gay young people can express their desires and instead challenge the principal source of violence against children and young people—the patriarchal family and straight-identified men. We have to propose changes in family relations and schooling and alternative social policies that would allow young people to take more control over their own lives, to get support in fighting unwanted sexual attention *and* to be able to participate in consensual sexual activity.

[32] See John Marshall, "Pansies, Perverts and Macho Men: Changing Conceptions of Male Homosexuality" and Greg Blachford, "Male Dominance In The Gay World," in Plummer, ed., *The Making of The Modern Homosexual;* and also Seymour Kleinberg's article elsewhere in this volume for a different approach.

[33] Jeffrey Weeks, "Capitalism and the Organization of Sex," Gay Left Collective, eds., *Homosexuality, Power and Politics* 19–20.

[34] Michel Foucault, "Power and Sex," *Telos*, no. 32 (Summer 1977): 152–61.

[35] See Allen Hunter, "In the Wings, New Right Ideology and Organization," *Radical America* 15, no. 1–2 (Spring 1981): 127–38.

PART NINE

◆ ◆ ◆

Men in Families

Are men still taking their responsibilities as family breadwinners seriously? Are today's men sharing more of the family housework and childcare than those in previous generations? The answers to these questions are complex, and often depend on which men we are talking about and what we mean when we say "family."

Many male workers long ago won a "family wage," and with it made an unwritten pact to share that wage with a wife and children. But today, as Barbara Ehrenreich argued in her influential book, *The Hearts of Men*, increasing numbers of men are revolting against this traditional responsibility to share their wages, thus contributing to the rapidly growing impoverishment of women and children. Ehrenreich may be correct, at least with respect to the specific category of men who were labeled "yuppies" in the 1980s. But as Ruth Sidel points out in her article, if we are looking at the growing improverishment of women and children among poor, working class, and minority families, the causes have more to do with dramatic shifts in the structure of the economy—including skyrocketing unemployment among young black males—than they do with male irresponsibility. Increasing numbers of men, she argues, have no wage to share with a family.

But how about the New Dual-Career Family? Can we look to this emerging family type as a model of egalitarianism? Hochschild's research indicates that the growth of the two-career family has not significantly altered the division of labor in the household. Women still, she argues, work a "second shift" when they return home from their paid-work job. On another note, Patricia Horn details some of the issues for gay and lesbian couples in coping with constituting themselves as a family.

One of the most significant issues of the 1990s will be fatherhood. Are men becoming more nurturing and caring fathers, developing skills, like the men in Hollywood films such as *Three Men and a Baby*, or is fatherhood more an unrealizable dream than a reality? Ralph LaRossa challenges commonsense assumptions about changes in fatherhood by suggesting that men have not changed all that drastically in their parenting behaviors. Barbara Katz-Rothman examines the ways that the discussion about fatherhood needs to be embedded in the larger context of male–female relationships, and Brian Miller discusses the lives of gay fathers, illustrating the need to expand the definition of what we think of as "the family."

Ruth Sidel

BUT WHERE ARE THE MEN?

somebody almost run off wit alla my stuff/& I was standin there/lookin
at myself/the whole time & it waznt a spirit took my stuff/waz a man
whose ego walked round like Rodan's shadow/was a man faster in my
innocence/waz a lover/i made too much room for/almost run off wit alla
my stuff/& I didnt know i'd give it up so quik/& the one running wit
it/dont know he got it/& i'm shoutin this is mine/& he dont know he got
it/my stuff is the anonymous ripped off treasure of the year.[1]

—*Ntozake Shange*

Over and over as I interviewed women in different parts of the country I heard
stories of men walking out on women. Sometimes the couple was young and
had been together a short time, other times they were middle-aged and had
been together for many years; but almost always, the man was the one who
walked out—often with little or no warning—and the woman and children
were left to cope as best they could. From the women of Maine to the Native
American families of New Mexico, I met mothers and children trying to make
it on their own and trying to deal with their pain and anger.

Men are not always the ones who walk out, of course, Sometimes the
women leave; sometimes the split is mutual; and sometimes the man was never
really there. But whether because of divorce, separation, or not marrying at
all, the grouping that remains is mothers with their children, children with
their mothers. And where are the men? Some have simply vanished, gone on
to other things. Others have started new families. Some feel that they cannot
live up to their roles as fathers because they cannot live up to their roles as
breadwinners.

Barbara Ehrenreich, in her recent book *The Hearts of Men*, claims that over
the past thirty years American men have been fleeing from commitment to the
family. She points out that in the 1950s "adult masculinity was indistinguishable from the breadwinner role. . . ."[2] Gradually, according to Ehrenreich,
the prodding of cultural forces such as *Playboy*—which encouraged, as one
sociologist has described it, the "fun morality"—and the health profession's
warning that the stress that came from the role as breadwinner could well lead
to coronary heart disease encouraged men to drift more and more toward a
commitment to self, toward "doing one's own thing," and away from the
confines and conflicts of wife, children, mortgage, and the pressures of new
shoes for the first day of school. As Ehrenreich states, "The result of divorce,
in an overwhelming number of cases, is that men become singles and women
become single mothers."[3]

While there is little doubt that much of Ehrenreich's analysis is valid, it is
not the whole story. In the first place, her analysis is valid not just for men but
for much of American society as a whole. The shift toward concern with self,
with individual needs and desires, with personal growth, toward narcissism,

has been widespread and is a result, I believe, of fundamental societal developments over the course of the twentieth century—urbanization, the changing nature of work, and the development of a consumer society.

Urbanization has, as is well known, been a major factor in the fragmentation of primary groups. The pressures, variety, and opportunities of the city, together with the anonymity it provides, have made it increasingly possible for individuals to shake off their obligations to others, to walk away without fear of censure from the "group," for there is hardly any group left. If family members are scattered, if there is no defined community, if there are no elders to censure, why not simply walk away from upsetting and restrictive commitments?

While urbanization was disrupting networks of community and kin, specialization was becoming the primary mode of work in twentieth-century America. As French sociologist Emile Durkheim pointed out nearly a hundred years ago, when societies are small and everyone does much the same kind of work, a "collective consciousness" develops based on similar socialization and shared experiences and values. When, however, each person does just one small piece of an overall task, and this task has little relationship to what others are doing, individualism is fostered. Durkheim predicted that such a division of labor and the resulting growth of individualism would lead to a breakdown in commitment to social norms, the situation Ehrenreich seems to be describing.[4] Add to urbanization and an extreme division of labor the pressures of a consumer society—in which we are systematically taught to believe that we are what we wear, what we own, what we buy; an unrelenting pressure to acquire new goods in order to redefine ourselves continually—and a social milieu develops in which individualism and self-gratification are rewarded, and commitment to others is devalued. That commitment is particularly constraining if it seems to diminish one's own options, one's own pleasures, one's own "personal growth."

And, of course, men are not the only ones who have been affected by these profound changes in American society. Women, and specifically those in the women's movement, have been affected by the emphasis on individualism, by the increasing legitimacy of individual needs and aspirations, of individual happiness. If "We Shall Overcome" was the anthem of the 1960s, perhaps Madonna sings the anthem of the 1980s in her song "Material Girl."[5]

It is striking, however, that while many women are concerned with the quality of their lives, with their own development and careers, with their "material world," they remain, as Ehrenreich correctly points out, the primary caregivers for their children. While many men have abdicated their parental responsibilities, women for the most part have not.

Part of the explanation of women's special relationship to their children lies, clearly, in the special nature of the mothering role, with the bonding that takes place in utero and then during the first few weeks and months of an infant's life, and the ongoing intimate relationship women continue to have with children. But another part of the explanation of the male ability to avoid the responsibilities of fatherhood may well lie in the nature of the fathering role in our society. Is the role of father such that it produces a lack of genuine involvement with children, a lack of real connectedness? Are the majority of fathers simply expected to bring home a paycheck and occasionally to throw a baseball around—and is this kind of relationship just too tenuous to bind men to their children? With the increasing erosion of the patriarchal role, we must develop an equally meaningful way for men to relate to their children.

Profound class differences exist in the ways men relate to their families today. The models written up on the women's pages of leading newspapers—of men trying to take paternity leave, of "househusbands," of a recent bestseller in which a father lyrically describes the first year of his daughter's life—are those of relatively few, usually highly educated, upper-middle-class men. While a fair number of men near Columbia University or in Harvard Square or in Berkeley may lovingly carry their babies in Snugglies, it is hardly a common sight at the entrance to auto plants, in accounting firms, or among men who hang out on the streetcorners of urban ghettos. Clearly behavior that is encouraged and rewarded in one segment of the upper middle class is considered unacceptable in much of the rest of the country; until the perceptions of values and norms of the larger society change, we cannot rationally expect individual behavior to alter significantly.

The bottom line of the male flight from commitment, of many fathers' lack of involvement with their children and, above all, of economic factors usually beyond the individual's control, is that the majority of men who are not living with their wives and children are also not supporting them. The issue of child support has received considerable attention over the past few years because of the unprecedented increase in the number of female-headed families during the 1970s. The importance of child support to the economic well-being of mothers and children is underscored by women's low earning ability. According to a Working Paper published by the Wellesley College Center for Research on Women, women "with the sole custody of children experience the most severe decline in family income."[6] A spring 1982 Census Bureau survey found that over 8 million women are raising at least one child whose father is absent from the home. Of these 8 million women, only 5 million had been awarded child support by the courts. Of the women who were supposed to be receiving payments in 1981, 47 percent received the full amount, 37 percent received less than half of what they were supposed to receive, and 28 percent received no payments at all.[7] Ironically, the women most likely to receive court-ordered child support are "educated, employed, divorced women" rather than separated, never married, minority women.[8] The average annual child-support payment in 1981 was $2,180 for white women, $2,070 for Hispanic women, and $1,640 for black women.[9]

Why don't men pay child support more regularly? Some men withhold payment in reaction to the bitterness of a divorce, some as a way of protesting what they feel is an unfair financial settlement, and some because they want to use their money to recapture the sense of being single, of being free.

Betty Levinson, a New York lawyer who devotes approximately one-third of her practice to matrimonial law, feels that in most divorce cases she sees there is simply not enough money to support two households. These families, mostly middle and upper middle class, are "premised on plastic." Often these couples cannot afford to separate; both husbands and wives must learn to "trim their expectations in planning for their lives after divorce."

On the issue of nonsupport Levinson feels that many men would rather pay for a lawyer than support their children. She suggests that one scenario is: "Now that it's over I can't deal with you anymore. You represent a failure for me and therefore I don't want to deal with the kids either because I associate the kids with the failed marriage and with you." Another scenario is that the man has remarried and is supporting his new wife and her children, who, in turn, are not being supported by their father. Part of the message such a man gives to his former wife is, "When you took custody you took responsibility." The fathers who say this, according to Levinson, are frequently men who do not see their kids very often, because they live in another state or for some other reason.

The third scenario involves the father who sees his kids, but mainly for Sunday visits. According to Betty Levinson, "It's incredible the kind of money these fathers will spend on these weekly visits—theater, ski trips, and so forth—but they resist giving more in the way of child support. Often the father's feeling is, 'Yes, I understand that the child needs this now, but I have to think of my future.' The ultimate responsibility for the children," she states flatly, "is with the mother. No matter what happens, the mother takes care of the children."

Researchers and activists, both those who work for more stringent child-support legislation and spokespersons on behalf of men's groups, agree that the payment of child support is often tied to the altered parent-child relationship. Researchers have found that after divorce fathers often experience a loss of identity, a loss of status within the family, and a "particularly poignant sense of loss associated with the altered father-child relationship. The divorced father is no longer part of the day-to-day life of the child, but is abruptly relegated to a visitor status. . . . Many fathers cope by distancing themselves from the parent-child relationship."[10] What better way to do this than by withholding financial support?

James A. Cook, president of the National Congress for Men, a four-year-old coordinating group of 125 men's rights organizations with ten thousand members, also ties the problem of economic support to fathers' lack of access to their children. He asks, "Can we levy responsibility on these fathers without an equivalent right, the right of access to the child?"[11] John A. Rossler of the Equal Rights for Fathers of New York State agrees: "Many men have had to beg for access to their children. The system of divorce in America often results in the removing of all fathering functions save for one, the monetary obligation. A man is more than a wallet to his kids."[12] Rossler and other representatives of men's groups, strongly endorse custody reform: "Whether you call it joint custody, shared custody, liberal visitation or co-parenting, we are talking about actively involving the noncustodial parent in all areas of his child's upbringing."[13]

Betty Levinson, on the other hand, feels that joint custody is a very "trendy" issue; it is thought to be "the thing to do." She claims that men are made to feel that if they do not demand joint custody that they are not the fathers they should be. But it is, she points out, a very difficult arrangement. The husband and wife must cooperate extremely well for it to work. She goes on to state emphatically:

> Joint custody becomes an economic bludgeon on the wife by the husband. Asking for joint custody or trying to take custody away from the mother is a surefire way to freak out the mother. And after they have freaked her out, the father and his lawyer will often say, "Okay, you take 75 percent of our financial agreement instead of 100 percent and I'll give you full custody." It has become a way of negotiating the money.

On August 16, 1984, a comprehensive bill to enforce payment of child support became federal law. Approved by unanimous roll call votes in both houses of Congress, the new law requires child-support orders issued or modified after October 1, 1985, to permit the withholding of wages if a parent becomes delinquent in payments and enables states to "require that an absent parent give security, post a bond, or give some other guarantee" to ensure final payment of child support in cases where there has been a pattern of delinquency.[14] This law is a significant victory for those groups that have been advocating more stringent regulations and collection methods to improve the rate of payment of child support.

But voluntary nonpayment of child support is clearly only one facet of the problem of the absent father. Many fathers provide little or no support—either in economic or emotional terms—to their children and to the children's mothers because they are unable to play the traditional fathering role, that of breadwinner. In January 1983 approximately 12 million people, over 10 percent of the American work force, were actively looking for jobs and were the officially designated unemployed. While that number has since fallen to 7.2 percent, this stark figure, the highest rate since the Great Depression, has stimulated additional studies on the physiological, psychological, and sociological aspects of unemployment.

First, it must be pointed out that federal unemployment statistics significantly minimize the problem of unemployment. Figures released by the Bureau of Labor Statistics do not include those who reluctantly move from full-time to part-time employment; those who take jobs well below their skill level; those who must move from one temporary, low-paying job to the next; and those who become "permanently discouraged" and stop looking for work altogether. Nor do the statistics, as one researcher has movingly written, "reflect the anxiety, depression, deprivation, lost opportunities, violence, insecurity, and anger people feel when their source of livelihood is severed and they lose control of a significant aspect of their environment."[15] As Paula Rayman, sociologist and director of the New England Unemployment Project, has written, "When an adult has work taken away, the focus of life's daily pattern is removed. Time and space, the sense of self, are radically altered, and what is left is a sense of impotency."[16]

The work of Johns Hopkins sociologist and epidemiologist Harvey Brenner demonstrates the dramatic effect unemployment has on the entire family's health and well-being. Brenner has found, for example, that admissions to psychiatric hospitals, deaths from cardiovascular and alcohol-related illnesses, homicide and suicide rates increase significantly during periods of economic decline.[17] Other researchers have found that male unemployment is associated with high blood pressure, alcoholism, increased smoking, insomnia, anxiety, and higher levels of psychiatric symptoms among men. In addition, "The wives in unemployed families were significantly more depressed, anxious, phobic, and sensitive about their interpersonal relationships" than spouses in families in which there is no unemployment.[18] The longer the period of unemployment, the greater the stress on the family and on family cohesion. In a study of the unemployed in Hartford, Rayman and Ramsey Liem found three times as much marital separation among the unemployed group as among the control group.[19]

Clinical observations of unemployed people who go to social agencies for counseling indicate that they are coping with feelings of loss, anger, and guilt—a "sense of losing a part of the self." Observers have likened these feelings to feelings of bereavement. Studies find that people anticipating or experiencing unemployment "suffer loss of self-esteem, loss of personal identity, worry and uncertainty about the future, loss of a sense of purpose, and depression."[20] With these reactions to unemployment, is it any wonder that family stability is being undermined?

While there has been a limited economic recovery since the height of the 1982–1983 recession, many workers' incomes have declined sharply since the late 1970s. For example, the average income of workers laid off by the United States Steel Corporation's South Works in Chicago has fallen in the last five years by 50 percent. Over two thousand workers were laid off from 1979 to 1981, and another thirty-three hundred were laid off from 1981 to 1983. Many of these workers have had long periods of unemployment; 46 percent remained unemployed as of October 1984. The laid-off workers, whose annual household income averaged $22,000 in 1979, had a median household income in 1983 of approximately $12,500. According to one worker. "To go from earning $20,000 plus to being at an employer's mercy for $3.35 an hour is devastating."[21] Moreover, unskilled workers and black and Hispanic male workers have extemely limited opportunities for work and suffer from the highest unemployment rates. In a 1983 study of the New York City job market, it was found that the decline in manufacturing and the expansion of the service sector have led to a decrease in job opportunities in the city for workers with few skills and limited education. Of all adults, black and Hispanic men twenty-five to thirty-four years old "generally do the worst in the job market": They experience extended periods of unemployment, withdraw from the labor force because they become "discouraged," and have a high rate of involuntary part-time work. Moreover, among blacks and Hispanics, the length of unemployment for men is twice what it is for women: for black men, twenty-seven weeks; for black women, twelve weeks; for Hispanic men, twenty-two weeks; for Hispanic women, nine weeks.[22]

Nationally, unemployment among blacks is officially twice the rate for whites, but the statistics tell only part of the story. Researchers at the Center for the Study of Social Policy claim that the true figure is that 4 million out of 9 million working-age black men—46 percent—are jobless. For white men the comparable figure is 22 percent.[23] Unemployment of this magnitude must have a dramatic impact on family stability and therefore be a major cause of the feminization of poverty. In 1960, according to this method of calculation, approximately three-quarters of all black men were employed; today only 54 percent are employed. Since 1960 the number of black families headed by women has more than tripled.[24] There is little question that the unemployment of black men has had a direct impact on the rise of black female-headed families.

Furthermore, unemployment is only one of many severe problems black men must face. The National Urban League recently released a report stating that black men must deal with a "singular series of pressures from birth through adulthood." The report stated, "The gauntlet that black men run takes its toll at every age." In addition to the problems of educational and employment discrimination, Dr. James McGhee, the league's research director, cited higher mortality rates, greater likelihood of being arrested, and the rising incidence of self-destructive behavior such as drug and alcohol abuse. Black men have the highest death rates from accidents and violence of all groups, and their suicide rate has risen far more sharply in recent years than that of white men.[25] In addition, homicide is the leading cause of death for black males ages fifteen to forty-four. Black men represent only 5 percent of the U.S. population but represent 44 percent of its homicide victims.[26] Many studies suggest that there is a direct correlation between feelings of frustration, powerlessness, and hopelessness and high rates of violence. According to sociologist and researcher on black families Andrew Billingsley, because of racial discrimination, many black men are distant from "any meaningful engagement with the economy, education and social system."[27]

Elliot Liebow, in what has become a classic study of streetcorner black men in Washington, DC, points out the close connection between a man's work and his relationships with family and friends: "The way in which the man makes a living and the kind of living he makes have important consequences for how the man sees himself and is seen by others; and these, in turn, importantly shape his relationships with family members, lovers, friends and neighbors."[28] Liebow points out that the unskilled black man has little chance of obtaining a permanent job that would pay enough to support a family. He eventually becomes resigned to being unable to play the traditional father role, and rather than being faced with his own failure day after day, year after year, he often walks away.

Ironically, the children with whom these men are closest are not those they have fathered and therefore have an obligation to support; but rather the children of the women they are currently seeing, who have been fathered by someone else. With someone else's children, whatever the men can give in the way of financial or emotional support is more than they need to give, and it therefore represents a positive gesture rather than yet another failure.[29]

What is saddest about these dismal facts is how American ideology, which is apparently accepted by the majority of Americans and has been legitimized by the Reagan administration, blames the poor, rather than racism and the economic system, for their plight. While some of these issues were briefly addressed during the 1960s, the War on Poverty was woefully inadequate to reverse the damage done, particularly to blacks, in our society; and no sooner did it get started than Vietnam, inflation, and the Nixon administration had begun to subvert it. As Michael Harrington has so aptly stated, "The savior that never was became the scapegoat that is."[30]

American policymakers have an uncanny ability to obfuscate and compartmentalize social problems—to recognize on the one hand that the United States has an unacceptably high level of unemployment, particularly among specific groups, and to recognize that we also have an incredibly high number of female-headed families, particularly within the same groups; but to avoid the cause-and-effect relationship between the two phenomena. This unwillingness to recognize the obvious correlation between the lack of economic opportunities for millions of American men—a lack of opportunity that will consign them, in all likelihood, for their entire lifetimes to the bottom of the class structure—and their lack of commitment to and steady participation in family life, is a shocking denial of the obvious impact of social and economic factors on the well-being of the family group.

As Eleanor Holmes Norton, former chairperson of the Equal Employment

Opportunity Commission and currently a professor at the Georgetown University Law Center, has stated:

> This permanent, generational joblessness is at the core of the meaning of the American ghetto. The resulting, powerful aberration transforms life in poor black communities and forces everything else to adapt to it. The female-headed household is only one consequence. The underground economy, the drug culture, epidemic crimes and even a highly unusual disparity between the actual number of men and women—all owe their existence to the cumulative effect of chronic joblessness among men.[31]

This avoidance has several advantages for those who seek to maintain the status quo in the United States: It discourages those at the bottom from developing a viable political and economic analysis of the American system, instead promoting a blame-the-victim mentality; a false consciousness of individual unworthiness, of self-blame; a belief that if only the individual worked harder, tried harder, he would "make it" and be the success every American thinks he should be. Not only does the unemployed male blame himself for not getting and keeping a decent job, thereby being unable to provide for his family in the way he would like, but the woman may also blame him. As one woman in *Tally's Corner* says with a bitter smile, "I used to lean on Richard. Like when I was having the baby, I leaned on him but he wasn't there and I fell down. . . . Now, I don't lean on him anymore. I pretend I lean, but "I'm not leaning."[32] Or the woman blames herself for not choosing her man more wisely, for not holding the family together despite the odds, for being either too assertive or not assertive enough. And yet virtually no one blames an economic system that deprives millions of workers of jobs and then somehow indicates it is their fault.

Sandra Wittaker, a black woman from California who is raising her two children alone puts it this way:

> Black men are able to cope far less than black women. They are feared more by society and therefore have far fewer opportunities. All the men I have known, my brothers, my father, my male friends, my husband, have not made it in society. Many of them take to drinking and dope— some kind of escape. Black males are suffering far more than females.
>
> My son has had three role models and none of them were any good. He has not had a mature man to model himself on. . . . He has nightmares. He's afraid of being a failure and he's already opted out. By the time he was four, my son did not even want to be black. It is terrible to watch your child and know that he is going to be hurt constantly.

If there is a group that has been hit even harder than blacks, it is Native Americans. Unemployment among the 1 million American Indians is said to range between 45 and 55 percent, but it reaches 80 percent in some areas and in some seasons.[33]

Among the Pueblo Indians who live approximately sixty miles southwest of Albuquerque, New Mexico, for example, the unemployment rate is 70 percent. After the nearby uranium mines were closed in 1981–1982, there were no other jobs available. According to Jean Eller, a young physician who worked at the Acoma Canoncita Laguna Indian Health Hospital in Acoma,

New Mexico, people now just "hang around." There is nothing for them to do. And the young people are torn between their desire to find a job in a nearby town or city and pressure from their elders to return to the reservation. The elders are afraid the young people will lose touch with their culture if they move off the reservation, but there are few opportunities there, either.

Tied to the unemployment rate, Dr. Eller believes, is an enormous problem with alcohol and suicide rate that is the highest of any ethnic group in the country. Alcohol is mainly a male problem; some of the younger women drink, but the older women usually do not. According to Dr. Eller, there are three bars, run by non-Indians, near the reservation. One bar half a mile from the reservation serves "all the beer you can drink" free on Monday nights. These bars serve thirteen-year-olds, fourteen-year-olds and never check their ID's. "Many people hate these places and would like to blow them up!" Dr. Eller states quietly but angrily. She feels the significant amount of wife abuse that exists on these reservations is directly related to the amount of drinking, particularly on the weekends.

According to other medical personnel who work in the area, women are the backbone of the Indian family. Many feel that men have fallen apart more than women and are in a "cycle of destruction." The rates of alcoholism, wife abuse, child neglect, homicide, and suicide are at least three to four times the national rate.

There is also a high rate of teenage pregnancy, particularly among girls fifteen and under. The men rarely support their children, and some women move up and out of the reservation; many are, in fact, ostracized by their communities for doing so. The infant is then often cared for by the grand-mother and brought up with the grandmother's own children as siblings. Indian women are clearly not first-class citizens even within Indian culture but they have very little recourse since the tribal councils are largely run by men.

The reservation in Acoma is in the middle of incredibly beautiful terrain. As you approach Acoma, the earth varies from beige to darker shades of brown, sometimes flat, sometimes hilly, with stark red clay rock formations that look almost like amphitheaters. Acoma is famous for handsome pottery, much of it black, white, and clay-reddish brown; several of the potters from this reservation sell to private collectors, some to museums. Mt. Taylor, snowcapped even in late spring, can be seen in the distance. Amid this truly splendid scenery, the reservation seems unbearably barren and depressed. During the day there is hardly a man to be seen. There are only women, children, and dogs—scrawny, hungry-looking dogs who roam near the houses.

Lena Ross is a heavyset woman with a weathered face and dark hair pulled back at the nape of her neck. She has moved within the past few days to a modern adobe-colored house in a settlement of new homes, most of which are still empty. The house has several bedrooms furnished with beds and colorful quilts and blankets, a kitchen with the latest in modern appliances, and a large, empty living room.

Ten of Lena Ross's thirteen children and her two grandchildren live with her. She has no husband. "I take care of the children myself," she tells me. She receives AFDC for the children who are still in school, and social security for the grandchildren. While we talk, her one-and-a-half-year-old grandson sits on his grandmother's lap. He is a lively boy with long, dark hair and beautiful dark eyes. He is wearing a good-looking blue-and-white-striped shirt and is playing with a small car. Through the living room window is a picture-postcard view of Mt. Taylor.

While some of these families' material needs are being met, there is an overriding sense of hopelessness, of being caught in a net not of their own making, and from which they cannot get free. For they know, as a CBS news report stated succinctly, "Their destiny is in the hands of strangers."[34] The juxtaposition of the new, modern house and this immovable hopelessness is profoundly disturbing.

Mary Sanchez is a thirty-six-year-old mother of five. Her oldest child is seventeen, her youngest ten. Her seventeen-year-old sister is also living with her; she finished only the eighth grade and has two children, one four and one ten months old. In addition, Mary's oldest daughter has a ten-month-old who also lives there, and one of her brothers lives with her as well. In all, eleven people live in a small wooden house off of a small dirt road; Mary's parents live next door.

Mary and most of the children are on welfare and receive food stamps. The two youngest, the ten-month-old babies, are not on welfare because the welfare worker said she wanted to force the fathers to pay for their upkeep. Mary told the worker to forget it.

Both of the men who fathered her children are dead. The first died of natural causes, but the second, the father of four of her children, died while hitchhiking with another man and two women. "They all must have been drunk," she says simply, "and weaving down the street. A gas truck was coming along and swerved to avoid hitting them. The truck turned over and exploded and all four were burned to death. When relatives went to claim the body, they couldn't tell who it was."

The entire time we talked, a soap opera was on in the background, an intricate melodrama of well-dressed upper-middle-class Anglos lulling these women and their children through the day. The women do not seem despairing but rather fatalistic. When I asked if it was hard for them to manage, they said they managed. When I asked what could be done to make things better, they couldn't think of a thing. It feels as though it takes everything they've got just to get from day to day.

NOTES

1. Ntozake Shange, *For Colored Girls Who Have Considered Suicide When the Rainbow Is Enuf* (New York: Bantam, 1980), 53–54.

2. Barbara Ehrenreich, *The Hearts of Men: American Dreams and the Flight from Commitment* (Garden City, N.Y.: Anchor Press, 1983), 20.

3. Ibid., 121.

4. Emile Durkheim, *The Division of Labor in Society* (Glencoe, Ill.: Free Press, 1964; originally published in 1893).

5. Peter Brown and Robert Rans, "Material Girl," on Madonna, *Like a Virgin.* Sire Records, 1984.

6. Joyce Everett, "Patterns and Implications of Child Support and Enforcement Practices for Children's Well-being." Working Paper No. 128 (Wellesley, Mass.: Wellesley College Center for Research on Women, 1984).

7. Ibid.

8. Ibid.

9. "Child Support Frequently Not Paid," *New York Times* (8 July 1983).

10. Everett, "Patterns and Implications of Child Support."

11. Glenn Collins, "Why Fathers Don't Pay Child Support," *New York Times* (1 September 1983).

12. Ibid.

13. Ibid.

14. Robert Pear, "Reagan Signs Bill Forcing Payments for Child Support," *New York Times* (17 August 1984).

15. Thomas Keefe. "The Stresses of Unemployment," *Social Work* 29 (May–June 1984): 264–268.

16. Paula M. Rayman, "The Private Tragedy Behind the Unemployment Statistics," *Brandeis Quarterly* 2 (July 1982): 2–4.

17. M. Harvey Brenner, "Estimating the Effects of Economic Change on National Health and Social Well-Being," study prepared for the use of the Subcommittee on Economic Goals and Intergovernmental Policy of the Joint Economic Committee (Washington, D.C.: U.S. Government Printing Office, 1984): 3.

18. Ramsay Liem and Paula Rayman, "Health and Social Costs of Unemployment," *American Psychologist* 37 (October 1982): 1116–1123.

19. Ibid.

20. Keefe, "The Stresses of Unemployment."

21. Steven Greenhouse, "Former Steelworkers' Income Falls by Half," *New York Times* (31 October 1984).

22. Damon Stetson, "City Survey Finds Unskilled in Bind," *New York Times* (4 September 1983).

23. Tom Joe and Peter Yu, "Black Men, Welfare and Jobs," *New York Times* (11 May 1984).

24. Ibid.

25. James Barron, "Urban League Cites Pressures on Black Men," *New York Times* (1 August 1984).

26. "Curbing the High Rate of Black Homicide," NASW (National Association of Social Workers) *NEWS* (September 1984): 3–4.

27. Ronald Smothers, "Concern for the Black Family: Attention Now Turns to Men," *New York Times* (31 December 1983).

28. Elliot Liebow, *Tally's Corner: A Study of Negro Streetcorner Men* (Boston: Little, Brown, 1967), 210.

29. Ibid., 84.

30. Michael Harrington, *The New American Poverty* (New York: Holt, Rinehart & Winston: 1984), 20.

31. Eleanor Holmes Norton, "Restoring the Traditional Black Family," *New York Times Magazine* (2 June 1985): 43, 79, 93, 96, 98.

32. Liebow, *Tally's Corner*, 132.

33. Ian Robertson, *Sociology* (New York: Worth, 1981), 304.

34. Segment on CBS Sunday morning news, February 10, 1985.

Arlie Hochschild

THE SECOND SHIFT:
EMPLOYED WOMEN ARE PUTTING IN ANOTHER DAY OF WORK AT HOME

Every American household bears the footprints of economic and cultural trends that originate far outside its walls. A rise in inflation eroding the earning power of the male wage, an expanding service sector opening up jobs for women, and the inroads made by women into many professions—all these changes do not simply go on around the American family. They occur *within* a marriage or living-together arrangement and transform it. Problems between couples, problems that seem "unique" or "marital," are often the individual ripples of powerful economic and cultural shock waves. Quarrels between husbands and wives in households across the nation result mainly from a friction between faster-changing women and slower-chaning men.

The exodus of women from the home to the workplace has not been accompanied by a new view of marriage and work that would make this transition smooth. Most workplaces have remained inflexible in the face of the changing needs of workers with families, and most men have yet to really adapt to the changes in women. I call the strain caused by the disparity between the change in women and the absence of change elsewhere the "stalled revolution."

If women begin to do less at home because they have less time, if men do little more, and if the work of raising children and tending a home requires roughly the same effort, then the questions of who does what at home and of what "needs doing" become a source of deep tension in a marriage.

Over the past 30 years in the United States, more and more women have begun to work outside the home, and more have divorced. While some commentators conclude that women's work *causes* divorce, my research into changes in the American family suggests something else. Since all the wives in the families I studied (over an eight-year period) worked outside the home, the fact that they worked did not account for why some marriages were happy and others were not. What *did* contribute to happiness was the husband's willingness to do the work at home. Whether they were traditional or more egalitarian in their relationship, couples were happier when the men did a sizable share of housework and child care.

In one study of 600 couples filing for divorce, researcher George Levinger found that the second most common reason women cited for wanting to divorce—after "mental cruelty"—was their husbands' "neglect of home or children." Women mentioned this reason more often than financial problems, physical abuse, drinking, or infidelity.

A happy marriage is supported by a couple's being economically secure, by their enjoying a supportive community, and by their having compatible needs and values. But these days it may also depend on a shared appreciation of the work it takes to nurture others. As the role of the homemaker is being abandoned by many women, the homemaker's work has been continually devalued and passed on to low-paid housekeepers, babysitters, or day-care workers. Long devalued by men, the contribution of cooking, cleaning, and care-giving is now being devalued as mere drudgery by many women, too.

In the era of the stalled revolution, one way to make housework and child care more valued is for men to share in that work. Many working mothers are already doing all they can at home. Now it's time for men to make the move.

If more mothers of young children are working at full-time jobs outside the home, and if most couples can't afford household help, who's doing the work at home? Adding together the time it takes to do a paid job and to do housework and child care and using estimates from major studies on time use done in the 1960s and 1970s, I found that women worked roughly 15 more hours each week than men. Over a year, they worked an extra month of 24-hour days. Over a dozen years, it was an extra year of 24-hour days. Most women without children spend much more time than men on housework. Women with children devote more time to both housework and child care. Just as there is a wage gap between men and women in the workplace, there is a "leisure gap" between them at home. Most women work one shift at the office or factory and a "second shift" at home.

In my research, I interviewed and observed 52 couples over an eight-year period as they cooked dinner, shopped, bathed their children, and in general struggled to find enough time to make their complex lives work. The women I interviewed seemed to be far more deeply torn between the demands of work and family than were their husbands. They talked more about the abiding conflict between work and family. They felt the second shift was *their* issue, and most of their husbands agreed. When I telephoned one husband to arrange an interview with him, explaining that I wanted to ask him how he managed work and family life, he replied genially, "Oh, this will *really* interest my *wife*."

Men who shared the load at home seemed just as pressed for time as their wives, and as torn between the demands of career and small children. But of the men I surveyed, the majority did not share the load at home. Some refused outright. Others refused more passively, often offering a loving shoulder to lean on, or an understanding ear, as their working wife faced the conflict they both saw as hers. At first it seemed to me that the problem of the second shift *was* hers. But I came to realize that those husbands who helped very little at home were often just as deeply affected as their wives—through the resentment their wives felt toward them and through their own need to steel themselves against that resentment.

A clear example of this phenomenon is Evan Holt, a warehouse furniture salesman who did very little housework and played with his four-year-old son, Joey, only at his convenience. His wife, Nancy, did the second shift, but she resented it keenly and half-consciously expressed her frustration and rage by losing interest in sex and becoming overly absorbed in Joey.

Even when husbands happily shared the work, their wives *felt* more responsible for home and children. More women than men kept track of doctor's appointments and arranged for kids' playmates to come over. More mothers than fathers worried about a child's Halloween costume or a birthday present for a school friend. They were more likely to think about their children while at work and to check in by phone with the babysitter.

Partly because of this, more women felt torn between two kinds of urgency, between the need to soothe a child's fear of being left at day-care and the need to show the boss she's "serious" at work. Twenty percent of the men in my study shared housework equally. Seventy percent did a substantial abount (less than half of it, but more than a third), and 10 percent did less than a third. But even when couples more equitably share the work at home, women do two thirds of the daily jobs at home, such as cooking and cleaning—jobs that fix them into a rigid routine. Most women cook dinner, for instance, while men change the oil in the family car. But, as one mother pointed out, dinner needs to be prepared every evening around six o'clock, whereas the car oil needs to be changed every six months, with no particular deadline. Women do more child care than men, and men repair more household applainces. A child needs to be tended to daily, whereas the repair of household appliances can often wait, said the men, "until I have time." Men thus have more control over when they make their contributions than women do. They may be very busy with family chores, but, like the executive who tells his secretary to "hold my calls," the man has more control over his time.

Another reason why women may feel under more strain than men is that women more often do two things at once—for example, write checks and return phone calls, vacuum and keep an eye on a three-year-old, fold laundry and think out the shopping list. Men more often will either cook dinner *or* watch the kids. Women more often do both at the same time.

Beyond doing more at home, women also devote proportionately more of their time at home to housework than men and proportionately less of it to child care. Of all the time men spend working at home, a growing amount of it goes to child care. Since most parents prefer to tend to their children than to clean house, men do more of what they'd rather do. More men than women take their children on "fun" outings to the park, the zoo, the movies. Women spend more time on maintenance, such as feeding and bathing children—enjoyable activities, to be sure, but often less leisurely or "special" than going to the zoo. Men also do fewer of the most undesirable household chores, such as scrubbing the toilet.

As a result, women tend to talk more intensely about being overtired, sick, and emotionally drained. Many women interviewed were fixated on the topic of sleep. They talked about how much they could "get by on": six and a half, seven, seven and a half, less, more. They talked about who they knew who needed more or less. Some apologized for how much sleep they needed—"I'm afraid I need eight hours of sleep"—as if eight was "too much." They talked about how to avoid fully waking up when a child called them at night, and how to get back to sleep. These women talked about sleep the way a hungry person talks about food.

If, all in all, the two-job family is suffering from a speedup of work and family life, working mothers are its primary victims. It is ironic, then, that often it falls to women to be the time-and-motion experts of family life. As I observed families inside their homes, I noticed it was often the mother who rushed children, saying, "Hurry up! It's time to go," "Finish your cereal now," "You can do that later," or "Let's go!" When a bath needed to be crammed into a slot between 7:45 and 8:00, it was often the mother who called out, "Let's see who can take their bath the quickest!" Often a younger child would rush out, scurrying to be first in bed, while the older and wiser one stalled, resistant, sometimes resentful: "Mother is always rushing us." Sadly, women are more often the lightning rods for family tensions aroused by this speedup of work and family life. They are the villains in a process in which they are also the primary victims. More than the longer hours and the lack of sleep, this is the saddest cost to women of their extra month of work each year.

Raising children in a nuclear family is still the overwhelming preference of most people. Yet in the face of new problems for this family model we have not created an adequate support system so that the nuclear family can do its job well in the era of the two-career couple. Corporations have done little to accommodate the needs of working parents, and the government has done little to prod them.

The Reagan and Bush administrations say they are "pro-family" but confuse being pro-family with being against women's work outside the home. During a time when more than 70 percent of wives and mothers work outside the home (the rate is still climbing), the Reagan administration's Panel on the Family offered as its pro-family policy only a package of measures against crime, drugs, and welfare. In the name of protecting the family, the Republicans proposed to legitimize school prayer and eliminate family-planning services. They did nothing to help parents integrate work and family life. We have to ask, when marriages continue to end becaue of the strains of this life, is it pro-family or anti-family to make life in two-job families so very hard? As working parents beome an interest group, a voting block, and a swing vote in elections, the issue of policies to ease life in two-job families is likely to become a serious political issue in years ahead.

We really need, as sociologist Frank Furstenberg has suggested, a Marshall Plan for the family. After World War II we saw that it was in our best interests to aid the war-torn nations of Europe. Now—it seems obvious in an era of growing concern over drugs, crime, and family instability—it is in our best interests to aid the overworked two-job families right here at home. We should look to other nations for a model of what could be done. In Sweden, for example, upon the birth of a child every working couple is entitled to 12 months of paid parental leave—nine months at 90 percent of the worker's salary, plus an additional three months at about three hundred dollars a month. The mother and father are free to divide this year off between them as they wish. Working parents of a child under eight have the opportunity to work no more than six hours a day, at six hours' pay. Parental insurance offers parents money for work time lost while visiting a child's school or caring for a sick child. That's a true pro-family policy.

A pro-family policy in the United States could give tax breaks to companies that encourage job sharing, part-time work, flex time, and family leave for new parents. By implementing comparable worth policies we could increase pay scales for "women's" jobs. Another key element of a pro-family policy would be instituting fewer-hour, more flexible options—called "family phases"—for all regular jobs filled by parents of young children.

Day-care centers could be made more warm and creative through generous public and private funding. If the best form of day-care comes from the attention of elderly neighbors, students, or grandparents, these people could be paid to care for children through social programs.

In these ways, the American government would create a safer environment for the two-job family. If the government encouraged corporations to consider the long-range interests of workers and their families, they would save on long-range costs caued by absenteeism, turnover, juvenile delinquency, mental illness, and welfare support for single mothers.

These are real pro-family reforms. If they seem utopian today, we should remember that in the past the eight-hour day, the abolition of child labor, and the vote for women seemed utopian, too. Among top-rated employers listed in *The 100 Best Companies to Work for in America* are many offering country-club memberships, first-class air travel, and million-dollar fitness centers. But only a handful offer job sharing, flex time, or part-time work. Not one provides on-site day-care, and only three offer child-care deductions: Control Data, Polaroid, and Honeywell. In his book *Megatrends*, John Naisbitt reports that 83 percent of corporate executives believed that more men feel the need to share the responsibilities of parenting; yet only 9 percent of corporations offer paternity leave.

Public strategies are linked to private ones. Economic and cultural trends bear on family relations in ways it would be useful for all of us to understand. The happiest two-job marriages I saw during my research were ones in which men and women shared the housework and parenting. What couples called good communication often meant that they were good at saying thanks to one another for small aspects of taking care of the family. Making it to the school play, helping a child read, cooking dinner in good spirit, remembering the grocery list, taking responsibility for cleaning up the bedrooms—these were the silver and gold of the marital exchange. Until now, couples committed to an equal sharing of housework and child care have been rare. But, if we as a culture come to see the urgent need of meeting the new problems posed by the second shift, and if society and government begin to shape new policies that allow working parents more flexibility, then we will be making some progress toward happier times at home and work. And as the young learn by example, many more women and men will be able to enjoy the pleasure that arises when family life is family life, and not a second shift.

Patricia Horn

TO LOVE AND TO CHERISH:
GAYS AND LESBIANS LEAD THE WAY IN REDEFINING THE FAMILY

Tom Brougham and Barry Warren share a home in Berkeley, California. They consider themselves life partners—a family. When the city of Berkeley passed a law allowing unmarried partners to register as domestic partners, they were one of the first couples to register.

For the two men, registering was a sweet moment. Ten years ago, Brougham and Warren were pioneers in the domestic partners movement. Like many other committed couples who lived together, they could not receive

Reprinted from *Dollars & Sense* magazine (June, 1990), pp. 9–11, 21–22.

family health benefits at their jobs. Each worked beside married employees whose partners were automatically covered, even if their relationships had not endured as long as Brougham and Warren's had. Fed up with what they considered discrimination, each asked his employer to extend the benefits enjoyed by married employees and their families to domestic partner families.

Warren's employer, the University of California, refused, citing the difficulty of verifying these relationships and the high cost of extending health benefits to unmarried couples. Brougham's employer, the city of Berkelely, asked for time to study the proposal.

The two men continued to develop their ideas on the rights of domestic partners and shared them with others. One person they spoke with was gay San Francisco Supervisor Harry Britt, whom they urged to push for the rights of gay families in San Francisco. In 1982, with the support of many gay rights organizations, Britt introduced a city ordinance that would allow unmarried city employees to include their partners on the city's health-care plan.

Britt's initiative created controversy in San Francisco and throughout the country. The media labeled it the "live-in lover law." Politicians, gay rights groups, and some churches focused on the law as a gay and lesbian issue only, inflaming the nation's fear of homosexuals. Thought the legislation passed the Board of Supervisors by a vote of six to two, Mayor Diane Feinstein vetoed it.

Brougham, Warren, and Britt's initiatives inspired a national movement that is questioning conventional definitions of family. The domestic partner movement encompasses issues relevant not only to gays and lesbians but also to unmarried heterosexual couples and persons in other non-traditional families. Marriage should not be the only factor that qualifies people for the legal rights and economic benefits that families enjoy, assert organizers. That criterion discriminates against many of the nation's self-declared families.

"Most of us aren't living in traditional American families any more," said Los Angeles City Attorney James K. Hahn last October, when he announced the creation of the Consumer Task Force on Marital Status Discrimination. "The rights and privileges extended to a few should be extended to everyone."

The Los Angeles task force, which has done an extensive study of such discrimination, found that "many unmarried people are the victims of widespread . . . discrimination in such areas as rental housing, health-care services, survivors' rights, membership discounts, and insurance."

BEYOND MARRIAGE

Thirty years ago, families of a husband and wife with natural or adopted children were still the norm. Since then, times have changed. Today there are step families, foster families, straight two-parent families, gay and lesbian families, single-parent families, extended families. The domestic partner movement challenges us to begin broadening the accepted national definition of family. As Judge Vito Titone of the Court of Appeals in New York state wrote, legal protection "should not rest on fictitious legal distinctions or genetic history, but instead should find its foundation in the reality of family life."

But when is a group of people living together a family? How does an employer or business determine who is a domestic partner? And how do employees prove the identity of family members to employers and insurance companies worried about costs, fraud, and administrative inconvenience? With a marriage certificate there is no in between: a person either is or is not a spouse.

A California court ruling defined family as people living together who have achieved a certain level of emotional intimacy and economic interdependence—qualities that roommates living together do not have. Cities that have passed domestic partner ordinances have defined such relationships as two people, regardless of gender, who share the common necessities of life, are responsible for each other's common welfare, and are each other's sole domestic partner. They have measured this by asking partners to prove that they are living together, financially interdependent, and have had a relationship of a minimum length of time, demonstrating that the partners are not only seeking the rights of family but also accepting its obligations.

At stake for non-traditional families is the wealth of economic benefits couples now receive only at the altar. Up to 40% of an average worker's total annual compensation is paid out in benefits, including family health and dental plans, parental leave, leave to care for a sick family member, pension benefits, day care, moving expenses, and bereavement leave. Married couples get a larger share of these than single adults and unmarried couples. In effect, two pay scales exist—one for those married and one for those not. In addition, some married couples can reduce their tax liabilities by filing jointly. They are entitled to special government benefits, such as those given surviving spouses and dependents through social security. They can inherit from each other when one partner dies without a will. They cannot be subpoenaed to testify against each other in court. They can visit each other in hospitals and prisons. Reduced travel expenses, health club family plans, access to married student housing, and consumer discounts all go hand-in-hand with marriage.

PARTNERSHIP SHOULD HAVE ITS PRIVILEGES

At the vanguard of the domestic partner movement are gay and lesbian organizations. While straight unmarried couples face the same legal and economic discrimination as gays, they can choose to marry if they need the benefits. Gay and lesbian couples, however, do not have the option of marrying. They are legally cut off from ever receiving those benefits and rights.

In the last 10 years two developments have made the economic and legal discrimination against gay and lesbian families hit home, mobilizing the community to political and legal action. The first is AIDS. In the last decade tens of thousands of gay men have died of AIDS. As their partners and friends died, homosexuals grew more aware of their lack of family rights. They could not get their partners included on their companies' health plans, and without a will they had no claims on their lovers' property, nor even the right to go to the funeral.

At the same time, an increasing number of gay and lesbian couples had children or adopted them. In the San Francisco area alone, at least 1,000 children have been born to or adopted by gay or lesbian couples in the last five years. In addition, an estimated three million to five million lesbian and gay parents have children from former heterosexual relationships. As more gays and lesbians formed families with children, they wanted to protect them in the same ways straight parents did—with good health care, child care, and a secure household.

As gays and lesbians became more politically organized around these issues, they took the domestic partner movement into courts, legislatures, unions, and work places. Eight cities now provide health benefits, sick leave, and/or bereavement leave for domestic partners: Berkeley, West Hollywood, Santa Cruz, and Los Angeles, California; Madison, Wisconsin; Takoma Park, Maryland; Seattle, Washington; and New York City. Domestic partner legislation is being discussed in other cities, including Washington, D.C. and Philadelphia, and in the states of Illinois and New York.

Gay activists have expanded their political clout in other areas as well. They have pushed the passage of laws barring discrimination on the basis of sexual orientation in Massachusetts, Wisconsin, and several cities. They have urged gay politicians to run openly for office. At least 50 elected officials are openly gay today, compared to fewer than six in 1980. The Human Rights Campaign Fund, a gay lobbying group, was the ninth largest independent political action committee in the last presidential election, and 25th on the Federal Election Commission's list of fundraisers.

In the courtrooms, legal-rights organizations are pursuing and winning more sexual orientation and marital status discrimination cases as well. Last year, the American Civil Liberties Union, with the support of the national gay and lesbian legal rights organization Lambda Legal Defense and Education Fund, won a precedent-setting case in the Court of Appeals in New York state. The court granted a gay man whose partner had died the right to stay in a rent-controlled apartment that was leased in his partner's name.

THE LONG AND WINDING ROAD

But these changes are baby steps on a long road to acceptance of family diversity. Domestic partner ordinances are more symbolic than lucrative, and usually directly affect only city employees. Five cities offer sick or bereavement leaves to city employees whose partners become ill or die; these benefits are meaningful but of minimal economic worth. Only three cities—Berkeley, Santa Cruz, and West Hollywood—grant health benefits to their employees' unmarried partners. Seattle will soon follow suit.

Occasionally, domestic partner ordinances have some impact outside city hall. For example, any couple that meets West Hollywood's requirements can register as domestic partners and receive official recognition of their relationship. Benefits include guaranteed visitation rights in city jails and at participating hospitals.

In the private sector, lawsuits, media attention, and organizing have had an impact on some businesses. At least five insurance companies now underwrite plans for domestic partners. Lawsuits prodded Trans World Airlines and most other major airlines to change their frequent-flyer programs to allow any companion instead of only a spouse or relative to receive a frequent flyer's companion ticket. Some stores, like Garfinckel's in Washington, D.C., have changed their spouse discounts to partner discounts. And major health clubs such as Holiday have begun to offer partner discounts in addition to family discounts.

Progressive employers such as the American Friends Service Committee and the National Organization for Women have already instituted health benefits for partners of unmarried employees. Some mainstream companies are also beginning to consider domestic partner benefits. Raymond Kann, managing partner of Hewitt Associates, a benefits and compensations consulting firm, told the *Wall Street Journal* that none of Hewitt's West Coast clients was studying partner benefits in 1984. In 1989, 10% to 20% were studying instituting those benefits.

These signs of change are noteworthy in part because they are rare. Discrimination on the basis of marital status is pervasive in the business world. For example, it is not uncommon for landlords to refuse to rent to unmarried couples or single persons, or for credit unions to refuse to issue joint loans to members and their partners, even fiancées.

The Los Angeles Task Force found discrimination based on sexual orientation and marital status in automobile, renters, homeowners, health, and life insurance. Discrimination can take the form of denial of coverage, limitations in naming of beneficiaries, and rate discrimination. As one example, the task force points to the refusal to allow a life insurance applicant to name a non-spousal life mate as beneficiary. Most companies refuse to offer a family discount on automobile insurance to unmarried couples who live together and share cars, although discounts are offered to blood relatives and married couples. And some companies will not issue a joint homeowner's policy to gay or lesbian couples, although joint policies are given to married couples.

Of the various forms of discrimination, the practice of charging higher rates to insure unmarried individuals than those charged married persons is among the most costly, because the average family spends about 13% of its disposable income on insurance. According to the Insurance Consumers Action Network, that makes insurance the third biggest family expenditure—after shelter and food, but before taxes.

Even when employers want to offer domestic partner benefits, finding an insurance company willing to accommodate them can be difficult. After West Hollywood's 1985 decision to offer health insurance to domestic partners of city employees, 16 companies turned down the city's request to underwrite the plan. After three years of trying to find an insurer, West Hollywood chose to self-insure its health coverage by creating its own insurance company.

"One could surmise the companies were afraid of increased risk associated with AIDS, or maybe they just didn't want to appear to be condoning a lifestyle," West Hollywood's personnel director, Jan Murphy, told the *Los Angeles Times*. "They haven't bothered to explain. They just said no."

In the three years since Berkeley added medical benefits to its domestic partner plan, "there has been no evidence of people with AIDS placing a strain on the health plan," reports Lambda. Insurance companies are also concerned that domestic partner plans will open up the floodgates by prompting people to sign up any acquaintance who needs insurance. This concern is addressed by the establishment of clear eligibility requirements.

The fiercest foes of efforts to win domestic partner rights and stop marital status discrimination are Christian fundamentalists, orthodox Jewish organizations, and the Roman Catholic Church hierarchy. These organizations have crowned themselves the protectors of the traditional institution of marriage. Church groups were the principal opponents of the first domestic partner law in San Francisco. In Madison, they helped thwart the city's attempt to extend health benefits to domestic partners.

Traditional values rule in the courts as well. For this reason, many activists anticipate that most progress will be made not in the courtroom but in work places, unions, businesses, and legislatures. "In many ways society has moved ahead of the government," explains Evan Wolfson, staff attorney at Lambda. "The judiciary is especially a problem. It will be dominated by anti-gay, anti-equality, and anti-minority appointments for years to come."

SAVVY POLITICKING

Because gay and lesbian organizations have led the fight for domestic partner rights, the issue has become a gay issue rather than one embraced by a broader range of non-traditional families. Homophobia has prevented straight unmarried people from joining the movement and inhibited cities, courts, and businesses from changing rulings and policies.

"When I give presentations about domestic partner rights, I downplay the gay issue and talk more about straight folk," says Ginny Cutting, the convener of the Gay and Lesbian Concerns Committee for Local 509 of the Service Employees International Union in Massachusetts. "At times this is difficult, but I'm savvy enough to know if I don't sell it this way I am sinking myself before I even get started."

When San Francisco first passed a domestic partner policy in the early 1980s, the public perceived it mainly as a gay rights issue. Mayor Diane Feinstein vetoed it. In July 1989 San Francisco's Board of Supervisors unanimously approved domestic partner legislation. This time the mayor, Art Agnos, approved it. But opponents gathered enough signatures to place it on the November ballot, where it was defeated 50.5% to 49.5% in an off-year election.

San Francisco may still get domestic partner legislation. In 1989 the city created a task force on family policy. That task force will soon recommend that the city include domestic partner benefits in its benefit package for city employees. In addition, supporters of the original domestic partner ordinance hope to bring it to the voters again this November.

"When I saw what happened in San Francisco in the early 1980s, I decided that the model focusing on gay rights specifically may not be the model for cities who wanted to win domestic partner rights," concluded Thomas Coleman, chairperson of the Los Angeles Task Force on Marital Status Discrimination. "This was reconfirmed for me when I saw what happened to the domestic partner referendum in San Francisco last November."

Coleman believes that in order to win domestic partner rights activists must build a coalition of all types of families. Los Angeles has done just that. The city first formed the Task Force on Family Diversity. From that emerged the Task Force on Marital Status Discrimination. Through this process gay and lesbian organizations have built ties to other groups.

"We found that people who are activists for the rights of elders, disabled people, step families, and foster families are in support of domestic partners because we work on each others' issues," Coleman says.

Nevertheless, change will happen slowly, and building coalitions will be difficult. "Unmarried heterosexual couples and single individuals have never viewed themselves as a political constituency," he says. "There aren't political organizations on rights for single people and unmarried people outside of the gay movement."

Cutting, who is fighing for domestic partner provisions in her union's labor contract, says her present task is to educate people. "Education is what it is all about right now," she comments. "We are bringing the issue to the forefront." The issue may fall by the wayside, but "in a few years we'll do it all over again. This isn't a one shot deal."

Ralph LaRossa

FATHERHOOD AND SOCIAL CHANGE

The consensus of opinion in American society is that something has happened to American fathers. Long considered minor players in the affairs of their children, today's fathers often are depicted as major parental figures, people who are expected to—people who presumably want to—*be there* when their kids need them. "Unlike their own fathers or grandfathers," many are prone to say.

But, despite all the attention that the so-called "new fathers" have been receiving lately, only a few scholars have systematically conceptualized the changing father hypothesis, and no one to date has marshalled the historical evidence needed to adequately test the hypothesis (Demos, 1982; Hanson & Bozett, 1985; Hanson & Bozett, 1987; Lamb, 1987; Lewis, 1986; Lewis & O'Brien, 1987; McKee & O'Brien, 1982; Pleck, 1987; Rotundo, 1985).

Given that there is not much evidence to support the hypothesis, (a) how do we account for the fact that many, if not most, adults in America believe that fatherhood has changed, and (b) what are the consequences—for men, for women, for families—resulting from the apparent disparity between beliefs and actuality? The purpose of this article is to answer these two questions.

THE ASYNCHRONY BETWEEN THE CULTURE AND CONDUCT OF FATHERHOOD

The institution of fatherhood includes two related but still distinct elements. There is the *culture of fatherhood* (specifically the shared norms, values, and beliefs surrounding men's parenting), and there is the *conduct of fatherhood* (what fathers do, their paternal behaviors). The distinction between culture and conduct is worth noting because although it is often assumed that the culture and conduct of a society are in sync, the fact is that many times the two are not synchronized at all. Some people make a habit of deliberately operat-

Reprinted from *Family Relations*, 1988. Copyright © 1988 by the National Council on Family Relations.

ing outside the rules, and others do wrong because they do not know any better (e.g., my 4-year-old son). And in a rapidly changing society like ours, countervailing forces can result in changes in culture but not in conduct, and vice-versa.

The distinction betwen culture and conduct is especially relevant when trying to assess whether fatherhood has changed because the available evidence on the history of fatherhood suggests that the *culture of fatherhood has changed more rapidly than the conduct.* For example, E. Anthony Rotundo (1985) argues that since 1970 a new style of American fatherhood has emerged, namely "Androgynous Fatherhood." In the androgynous scheme,

> A good father is an active participant in the details of day-to-day child care. He involves himself in a more expressive and intimate way with his children, and he plays a larger part in the socialization process that his male forebears had long since abandoned to their wives. (p. 17)

Rotundo (1985) is describing not what fathers lately have been doing but what some people would *like* fathers to *begin* doing. Later on he says that the new style is primarily a middle-class phenomenon and that "even within the upper-middle class . . . there are probably far more men who still practice the traditional style of fathering than the new style." He also surmises that "there are more *women* who *advocate* 'Androgynous Fatherhood' than there are *men* who *practice* it" (p. 20). Similarly, Joseph Pleck (1987) writes about the history of fatherhood in the United States and contends that there have been three phases through which modern fatherhood has passed. From the early 19th to mid-20th centuries there was the father as distant breadwinner. Then, from 1940 to 1965 there was the father as sex role model. Finally, since around 1966 there has emerged the father as nurturer. Pleck's "new[est] father," like Rotundo's "androgynous father" is an involved father. He is also, however, more imagined than real. As Pleck acknowledges from the beginning, his analysis is a history of the "dominant *images* [italics added] of fatherhood" (p. 84).

Rotundo and Pleck are clear about the fact that they are focusing on the culture of fatherhood, and they are careful about drawing inferences about the conduct of fatherhood from their data. Others, however, have not been as careful. John Mogey, for example, back in 1957, appears to have mistaken cultural for behavioral changes when, in talking about the emerging role of men in the family, he asserts that the "newer" father's "behavior is best described as participation, the reintegration of fathers into the conspicuous consumption as well as the child rearing styles of family life" (Mogey, as cited in Lewis, 1986, p. 6). Ten years later, Margaret Mead (1967), too, extolled the arrival of the new father:

> We are evolving a new style of fatherhood, in which young fathers share very fully with mothers in the care of babies and little children. In this respect American men differ very much from their own grandfathers and are coming to resemble much more closely men in primitive societies. (p. 36)

And recently there appeared in my Sunday newspaper the comment that "[Modern men] know more about the importance of parenting. They're aware of the role and of how they are doing it. Fifty years ago, fathers didn't think much about what kind of job they were doing" (Harte, 1987, p. 4G).

Neither Mogey nor Mead nor the newspaper presented any evidence to support their views. One can only guess that they were reporting what they assumed—perhaps hoped—was true generally (i.e., true not only for small "pockets" of fathers here and there), for, as was mentioned before, no one to date has carried out the kind of historical study needed to test the changing father hypothesis. If, however, the professional and lay public took seriously the thesis that fathers have changed and if others writing for professional and popular publications have echoed a similar theme, then one can easily understand how the notion that today's fathers are "new" could become implanted in people's minds. Indeed, there is a good chance that this is exactly what has happened. That is to say, Rotundo (1985) and Pleck (1987) probably are correct: there has been a shift in the culture of fatherhood—the way fathers and mothers think and feel about men as parents. But what separates a lot of fathers and mothers from Rotundo and Pleck is that, on some level of consciousness, the fathers and mothers also believe (incorrectly) that there has been a proportionate shift in the conduct of fatherhood.

I say on "some" level of consciousness because, on "another" level of consciousness, today's fathers and mothers *do* know that the conduct of fatherhood has not kept pace with the culture. And I include the word "proportionate" because, while some researchers have argued that there have been changes in paternal behavior since the turn of the century, no scholar has argued that these changes have occurred at the same rate as the ideological shifts that apparently have taken place. These two points are crucial to understanding the consequences of the asynchrony between culture and conduct, and they will soon be discussed in more detail. But first another question: If the behavior of fathers did not alter the ideology of fatherhood, then what did?

The answer is that the culture of fatherhood changed primarily in response to the shifts in the conduct of motherhood. In the wake of declines in the birth rate and increases in the percentage of mothers in the labor force, the culture of motherhood changed, such that it is now more socially acceptable for women to combine motherhood with employment outside the home (Margolis, 1984). The more it became apparent that today's mothers were less involved with their children, on a day-to-day basis, than were their own mothers or grandmothers, the more important it became to ask the question: Who's minding the kids? Not appreciating the extent to which substitute parents (day-care centers, etc.) have picked up the slack for mothers, many people (scholars as well as the lay public) assumed that fathers must be doing a whole lot more than before and changed their beliefs to conform to this assumption. In other words, mother-child interaction was erroneously used as a "template" to measure father-child interaction (Day & Mackey, 1986).

Generally speaking, culture follows conduct rather than vice-versa (Stokes & Hewitt, 1976). Thus, the fact that the culture of fatherhood has changed more rapidly than the conduct of fatherhood would seem to represent an exception to the rule. However, it may not be an exception at all. What may be happening is that culture *is* following conduct, but not in a way we normally think it does. Given the importance that American society places on mothers as parents, it is conceivable that the conduct of motherhood has had a "cross-fertilizing" effect on the culture of fatherhood. There is also the possibility that the conduct of fatherhood is affecting the culture of fatherhood, but as a stabilizer rather than a destabilizer. As noted, research suggests that androgynous fatherhood as an ideal has failed to become widespread. One reason for this may be that the conduct of fatherhood is arresting whatever "modernizing" effect the conduct of motherhood is having. Put differently, the conduct of fatherhood and the conduct of motherhood may, on a societal level, be exerting contradictory influences on the culture of fatherhood.

THE CONDUCT OF FATHERHOOD VERSUS THE CONDUCT OF MOTHERHOOD

Contending that the conduct of fatherhood has changed very little over the course of the 20th century flies in the face of what many of us see every day: dads pushing strollers, changing diapers, playing in the park with their kids. Also, what about the men who publicly proclaim that they have made a conscientious effort to be more involved with their children than their own fathers were with them?

What cannot be forgotten is that appearances and proclamations (both to others and ourselves) can be deceiving; everything hinges on how we conceptualize and measure parental conduct. Michael Lamb (1987) notes that scholars generally have been ambiguous about what they mean by parental "involvement," with the result that it is difficult to compare one study with the next, and he maintains that if we ever hope to determine whether or not fathers have changed, we must arrive at a definition that is both conceptually clear and comprehensive. The definition which he thinks should be used is one that separates parental involvement into three components: engagement, accessibility, and responsibility. *Engagement* is time spent in one-on-one interaction with a child (whether feeding, helping with homework, or playing catch in the backyard). *Accessibility* is a less intense degree of interaction and is the kind of involvement whereby the parent is doing one thing (cooking, watching television) but is ready or available to do another (respond to the child, if the need arises). *Responsibility* has to do with who is accountable for the child's welfare and care. Responsibility includes things like making sure that the child has clothes to wear and keeping track of when the child has to go to the pediatrician.

Reviewing studies that allow comparisons to be made between contemporary fathers' involvement with children and contemporary mothers' involvement with children, Lamb (1987) estimates that in two-parent families in which mothers are unemployed, fathers spend about one fifth to one quarter as much time as mothers do in an engagement status and about a third as much time as mothers do just being accessible to their children. In two-parent families with employed mothers, fathers spend about 33% as much time as mothers do in an engagement status and 65% as much time being accessible. As far as responsibility is concerned, mothers appear to carry over 90% of the load, regardless of whether they are employed or not. Lamb also notes that observational and survey data indicate that the behavioral styles of fathers and mothers differ. Mother–child interaction is dominated by caretaking whereas father–child interaction is dominated by play.

Mothers actually play with their children more than fathers do but, as a proportion of the total amount of child–parent interaction, play is a much more prominent component of father–child interaction, whereas caretaking is more salient with mothers. (p. 10)

In looking for trends, Lamb relies on one of the few studies which allows historical comparisons to be made—a 1975 national survey that was repeated in 1981 (Juster, 1985). No data apparently were collected on parents' accessibility or responsibility levels, but between 1975 and 1981, among men and women aged 18 to 44, there was a 26% increase in fathers' engagement levels and a 7% increase in mothers'. Despite these shifts, paternal engagement was only about one third that of mothers, increasing from 29% in 1975 to 34% in 1981 (Lamb, 1987).

While there is nothing intrinsically wrong with talking about percentage changes, one should be careful about relying on them and them alone. If, for example, one examines the tables from which Lamb drew his conclusions (Juster, 1985), one finds that the number of hours per week that the fathers spent in child care was 2.29 hours in 1975, compared to 2.88 hours in 1981, which is an increase of about 35 minutes per week or 5 minutes per day. The mothers in the sample, on the other hand, spent 7.96 hours per week in child care in 1975, compared to 8.54 hours per week in child care in 1981, which also is an increase of about 35 minutes per week or 5 minutes per day. Thus, in absolute terms, fathers and mothers increased their child care by the same amount.

Bear in mind also that we are still talking about only *one* component of parental involvement, namely engagement. The two national surveys provide little, if any, information about changes in the accessibility and responsibility levels of fathers and mothers. Perhaps I am being overly cautious, but I cannot help but feel that until we gather historical data which would allow us to compare all three components of fatherhood, we should temper our excitement about surveys which suggest changes in the conduct of fatherhood over time. (For a tightly reasoned alternative viewpoint, see Pleck, 1985.)

Comparisons over time are difficult to make not only because so few scholars have chosen to study the history of fatherhood, but also because the studies carried out over the years to measure family trends provide scant information about fatherhood, per se. For instance, during a recent visit to the Library of Congress, I examined the Robert and Helen Lynd archival collection which I had hoped would include copies of the interview schedules from their two Middletown studies. It had occurred to me that if I could review the raw data from the studies, then I could perhaps plot paternal involvement trends from 1924 to 1935 to 1978, the times of the first, second, and third data collections in the Middletown series (Lynd & Lynd, 1929, 1937; Caplow, Bahr, Chadwick, Hill, & Williamson, 1982). Unfortunately, only four sample interviews from the earlier studies were in the archive. The rest apparently were destroyed. It is a shame that the Middletown data were not saved because the most recent book in the series presents a table which shows an increase in the weekly hours that fathers spent with their children between 1924 and 1987 (Caplow et al., 1982). There is no indication whether this represents an increase in engagement or accessibility or both. Had I been able to look at the interviews themselves, however, I might have been able to discern subtle variations.

What about the dads who are seen interacting with their kids in public (see Mackey & Day, 1979)? A thoughtful answer to this question also must address how we conceptualize and measure paternal involvement. Does the paternal engagement level of fathers in public square with the paternal engagement level of fathers in private, or are we getting an inflated view of fatherhood from public displays? If we took the time to scrutinize the behavior of fathers and mothers in public would we find that, upon closer examination, the division of child care is still fairly traditional. When a family with small children goes out to eat, for example, who in the family—mom or dad—is more accessible to the children; that is to say, whose dinner is more likely to be interrupted by the constant demands to "put ketchup on my hamburger, pour my soda, cut my meat?" And how can one look at a family in public and measure who is responsible for the children? How do we know, for instance, who decides whether the kids need clothes; indeed, how do we know who is familiar with the kids' sizes, color preferences, and tolerance levels for trying on clothes? The same applies to studies of paternal involvement in laboratory settings (see Parke, 1981). What can a study of father–child interaction in, say, a hospital nursery tell us about father–child interaction in general? The fact that fathers are making their presence known in maternity wards certainly is not sufficient to suggest that the overall conduct of fathers has changed in any significant way. Finally, the fact that fathers can be seen in public with their children may not be as important as the question, How much time do fathers spend *alone* with their children? One recent study found that mothers of young children spent an average of 44.45 hours per week in total child-interaction time (which goes beyond engagement), while fathers spent an average of 29.48 hours per week, a 1.5 to 1 difference. If one looked, however, at time spent alone with children, one discovered that 19.56 hours of mothers' child-interaction time, compared with 5.48 hours of fathers' child-interaction, was solo time, a 3.6 to 1 difference. Moreover, while fathers' total interaction time was positively affected by the number of hours their wives worked, fathers' solo time was not affected at all (Barnett & Baruch, 1987).

As for the public proclamations, almost all the books and articles which tout the arrival of "new" fatherhood are written not by a cross-section of the population but by upper-middle class professionals. Kort and Friedland's (1986) edited book, for instance, has 57 men writing about their pregnancy, birth, and child-rearing experiences. But who are these men? For the most part, they are novelists, educators, sculptors, real estate investors, radio commentators, newspaper editors, publishers, physicians, performers, psychologists, social workers, and attorneys. Not exactly a representative sample. As Rotundo (1985) notes, androgynous fatherhood as an ideal has caught the attention of the upper-middle class more than any other group, but that even in this group, words seem to speak louder than actions.

While the perception of fathers in public and the Kort and Friedland (1986) book may not accurately represent what fathers in general are *doing*, they can most certainly have an effect of what people *think* fathers are doing and should be doing. Which brings us back to the question, What are the consequences that have resulted from the apparent disparity between beliefs and actuality?

THE CONSEQUENCES OF ASYNCHRONOUS
SOCIAL CHANGE

Thirty years ago, E. E. LeMasters (1957) made the point that parenthood (and not marriage, as many believe) is the real "romantic complex" in our society, and that even middle-class couples, who do more than most to plan for children, are caught unprepared for the responsibilities of parenthood. Later on, he and John DeFrain (1983) traced America's tendency to romanticize parenthood to a number of popular folk beliefs or myths, some of which are: raising children is always fun, children are forever sweet and cute, children will invariably turn out well if they have "good" parents, and having children will never disrupt but in fact will always improve marital communication and adjustment. Needless to say, anyone who is a parent probably remembers only too vividly the point at which these folk beliefs began to crumble in her/his mind.

The idea that fathers have radically changed—that they now are intimately involved in raising their children—qualifies also as a folk belief, and it too is having an impact on our lives and that of our children. On the positive side, people are saying that at least we have made a start. Sure, men are not as involved with their children as some of us would like them to be, but, so the argument goes, the fact that we are talking about change represents a step in the right direction. (Folk beliefs, in other words, are not necessarily negative. The myth that children are always fun, for example, does have the positive effect of making children more valued than they would be if we believed the opposite: that they are always a nuisance.) But what about the negative side of the myth of the changing father? Is there a negative side? My objective is to focus here on this question because up to now scholars and the media have tended to overlook the often unintentional but still very real negative consequences that have accompanied asynchronous change in the social institution of fatherhood.

I am not saying that professionals have been oblivious to the potentially negative consequences of "androgynization" on men's lives, for one could point to several articles and chapters which have addressed this issue (e.g., Benokraitis, 1985; Berger, 1979; Lamb, Pleck, & Levine, 1987; Lutwin & Siperstein, 1985; Pleck, 1979; Scanzoni, 1979). Rather, the point being made is that scholars and the media, for the most part, have overlooked the difficulties associated with a *specific* social change, namely the asynchronous change in the social institution of fatherhood.

The Technically Present but Functionally Absent Father   The distinction between engagement and accessibility outlined by Lamb (1987) is similar to the distinction between *primary time* and *secondary time* in our study of the transition to parenthood (LaRossa & LaRossa, 1981). The social organization of a family with children, especially young children, parallels the social organization of a hospital in that both are *continuous coverage social systems* (Zerubavel, 1979). Both are set up to provide direct care to someone (be it children or patients) on a round-the-clock or continuous basis. And both the family and the hospital, in order to give caregivers a break every now and then, will operate according to some formal or informal schedule such that some person or persons will be "primarily" involved with the children or patients (on duty) while others will be "secondarily" involved (on call or accessible).

Like Lamb, we also found that the fathers' levels of engagement, accessibility, and responsibility were only a fraction of the mothers', and that fathers tended to spend a greater part of their caregiving time playing with their children. Moreover, we found that the kinds of play that fathers were likely to be involved in were the kinds of activities that could be carried out at a secondary (semi-involved) level of attention, which is to say that it was not unusual for fathers to be primarily involved in watching television or doing household chores while only secondarily playing with their children.

When asked why they wanted to be with their children, the fathers often would answer along the lines that a father has to "put in some time with his kids" (LaRossa, 1983, p. 585). Like prisoners who "do time" in prison many fathers see themselves as "doing time" with their children. If, on some level of consciousness, fathers have internalized the idea that they should be more involved with their children, but on another level of consciousness they do not find the idea all that attractive, one would expect the emergence of a hybrid style: the technically present but functionally absent father (cf. Feldman & Feldman, 1975, cited in Pleck, 1983).

The technically present but functionally absent father manifests himself in a variety of ways. One father in our study prided himself on the fact that he and his wife cared for their new baby on an alternating basis, with him "covering" the mornings and his wife "covering" the afternoons. "We could change roles in a night," he said; "it wouldn't affect us." But when this father was asked to describe a typical morning spent alone with his infant son, he gave the distinct impression that he saw fatherhood as a *job* and that while he was "there" in body, he was someplace else in spirit.

> I have the baby to be in charge of, [which has] really been no problem for me at all. But that's because we worked out a schedule where he sleeps a pretty good amount of that time. . . . I generally sort of have to be with him in the sense of paying attention to his crying or dirty diapers or something like that for anywhere between 30 to 45 minutes, sometimes an hour, depending. But usually I can have two hours of my own to count on each morning to do my own work, so it's no problem. That's just the breaks that go with it.

Another example: Recently, there appeared an advertisement for one of those minitelevisions, the kind you can carry around in your pocket. Besides promoting the television as an electronic marvel, the man who was doing the selling also lauded how his mini-TV had changed his life: "Now when I go to my son's track meets, I can keep up with other ball games" (Kaplan, 1987, p. 32a). The question is: Is this father going to the track meets to see his son race, or is he going simply to get "credit" from his son for being in the stands? One more example: A newspaper story about a father jogging around Golden State Park in San Francisco who is so immersed in his running that he fails to notice his 3-year-old daughter—whom he apparently had brought with him—crying "Daddy, Daddy" along the side of the running track. When he finally notices her, he stops only long enough to tell his daughter that it is not his job to watch her, but her job to watch for him (Gustatis, 1982).

What will be the impact of the mixed messages that these children—and perhaps countless others—are getting from their fathers? Research capable of measuring and assessing the complexity of these encounters is needed to adequately answer this question (Pleck, 1983).

Marital Conflict in Childbearing and Child-Rearing Families   Because our study was longitudinal, we were able to trace changes over time; and we found that from the third, to the sixth, to the ninth month postpartum, couples became more traditional, with fathers doing proportionately less child care (LaRossa & LaRossa, 1981). It was this traditionalization process that provided us with a close-up view of what happens when the bubble bursts; that is, what happens when the romanticized vision of dad's involvement starts to break down.

One father, first interviewed around the third month after his daughter's birth, wanted to communicate that he was not going to be an absentee father like some of his friends were:

> I've got a good friend of mine, he's the ultimate male chauvinist pig. He will not change a diaper. . . . [But] I share in changing the diapers, and rocking the baby, and in doing those kinds of things. . . . I love babies.

During the sixth month interview, however, it was revealed that he indeed had become very much the absentee father. In fact, almost every evening since the first interview he had left the house after dinner to play basketball, or participate in an amateur theater group, or sing in the local choir.

Since what he was doing contradicted what he said he would do, he was asked by his wife to "account" for his behavior. *Accounts* are demanded of social actors whose behavior is thought to be out of line. By submitting an account, which in common parlance generally takes the form of an excuse or justification, and having it honored or accepted by the offended party, a person who stands accused can manage to create or salvage a favorable impression (Scott & Lyman, 1968). Because the wife did not honor the accounts that her husband offered, the father was put in the position of either admitting he was wrong (i.e., apologizing) or coming up with more accounts. He chose the latter, and in due course offered no fewer than 20 different explanations for his conduct, to include "I help out more than most husbands do" and "I'm not good at taking care of the baby." At one dramatic point during the second interview, the husband and wife got into a verbal argument over how much of the husband's contribution to child care was "fact" and how much was "fancy." (He, with his head: "I *know* I was [around a lot]." She with her heart: "[To me] it just doesn't *feel* like he was.")

This couple illustrates what may be happening in many homes as a result of the asynchrony between the culture and conduct of fatherhood. In the past, when (as best we can tell) both the culture and conduct of fatherhood were more or less traditional, fathers may not have been asked to account for their low paternal involvement. If the culture said that fathers should not be involved with their children and if fathers were not involved with their children, then fathers were perceived as doing what they should be doing. No need for an explanation. Today, however, the culture and conduct of fatherhood appear to be out of sync. The culture has moved toward (not to) androgyny much more rapidly than the conduct. On some level of consciousness, fathers and mothers believe that the behavior of fathers will measure up to the myth. Usually, this is early in the parental game, before or just after the birth of the first child. In time, however, reality sets in, and on another level of consciousness it becomes apparent that mom is doing more than planned because dad is doing less than planned. The wife challenges the legitimacy of the (more unequal than she had foreseen) division of child care, demanding an explanation from her husband, which may or may not be offered, and if offered may or may not be honored, and so on.

In short, one would expect more conflict in marriage today centered around the legitmacy of the division of child care than, say, 40 years ago because of the shift in the culture of fatherhood that has occurred during this time. Some may say, "Great, with more conflict there will be needed change." And their point is valid. But what must be kept in mind is that conflict also can escalate and destroy. Given that at least one recent study has reported that the most likely conflict to lead a couple to blows is conflict over children (Straus, Gelles, & Steinmetz, 1980), family researchers and practitioners would be well advised to pay attention to the possibility that violence during the transition to parenthood may be one negative consequence of asynchronous social change.

Fathers and Guilt   Several years ago, Garry Trudeau (1985), who writes *Doonesbury*, captured to a tee the asynchrony between the culture and conduct of fatherhood when he depicted a journalist-father sitting at his home computer and working on an autobiographical column on "The New Fatherhood" for the Sunday section of the newspaper. "My editor feels there's a lot of interest in the current, more involved generation of fathers," the journalist tells his wife who has just come in the room. "He asked me to keep an account of my experiences." Trudeau's punch line is that when Super Dad is asked by his wife to watch his son because she has to go to a meeting, he says no because if he did, he would not meet his deadline. In the next day's *Doonesbury*, Trudeau fired another volley at the new breed of fathers. Now the son is standing behind his computer-bound father and ostensibly is asking for his father's attention. But again Super Dad is too busy pecking away at his fatherhood diary to even look up: "Not now, son. Daddy's busy" (March 24 & 25).

Trudeau's cartoons, copies of which sit on my wall in both my office and my den, are a reminder to me not to be so caught up in writing about what it means to be a father (thus contributing to the culture of fatherhood) that I fail to *be* a father. The fact, however, that I took the time to cut the cartoons out of the newspaper (and make not one but two copies) and the fact that Trudeau, who is himself a father, penned the cartoons in the first place is indicative of a feeling that many men today experience, namely ambivalence over their performance as fathers.

To feel "ambivalent" about something is to feel alternately good and bad about it. The plethora of autobiographical books and articles written by fathers in the past few years conveys the impression that men do feel and, perhaps most importantly, should feel good about their performance as fathers. A lot of men do seem to be proud of their performance, what with all the references to "new" fatherhood and the like. At the same time, however, men are being almost constantly told—and can see for themselves, if they look close enough—that their behavior does not square with the ideal, which means that they are being reminded on a regular basis that they are *failing* as fathers. Failing not when compared with their own fathers or grandfathers perhaps, but failing when compared with the image of fatherhood which has become part of our culture and which they, on some level of consciousness, believe in.

This is not to suggest that in the past men were totally at ease with their performance as fathers, that they had no doubts about whether they were acting "correctly." For one thing, such an assertion would belie the fact that role playing is, to a large degree, improvisational, that in everyday life (vs. the theater) scripts almost always are ill defined and open to a variety of interpretations (Blumer, 1969). Perhaps more importantly, asserting that men in the past were totally at ease with their performance as fathers would ignore the fact that, contrary to what many think, some of our fathers and grandfathers were ambivalent about the kind of job they were doing. In a study just begun on the history of fatherhood in America, I have come across several cases of men in the early 1900s expressing concern over the quality of their paternal involvement. In 1925, for example, one father wrote to a psychologist to ask whether he was *too involved* with his 2-year-old son. Apparently, he had taught the boy both the alphabet and how to count, and he now wondered whether he had forced his son to learn too much too soon (LaRossa, 1988).

So, what *is* the difference between then and now? I would say it is a difference in degree, not kind. I would hypothesize that, given the asynchrony between the culture and conduct of fatherhood, the number of fathers who feel ambivalent and, to a certain extent, guilty about their performance as fathers has increased over the past three generations. I would also hypothesize that, given it is the middle class which has been primarily responsible for the changes in the culture of fatherhood, it is the middle class fathers who are likely to feel the most ambivalent and suffer from the most guilt.

There is a certain amount of irony in the proposition that middle-class men are the ones who are the most likely to experience ambivalence and guilt, in that middle-class men are also the ones who seem to be trying the hardest to act according to the emerging ideal. As noted, the testimonials from the so-called androgynous fathers almost invariably are written by middle-class professionals. But it is precisely because these middle-class professionals are trying to conform to the higher standards that one would expect that they would experience the most ambivalence and guilt. Like athletes training for the Olympics, androgynous-striving fathers often are consumed with how they are doing as fathers and how they can do better. For example:

> Should I play golf today, or should I spend more time playing with Scott and Julie? Should I stay late in the office to catch up or should I leave early to go home and have dinner with the children? There is an endless supply of these dilemmas each day. (Belsky, 1986, p. 64)

Some may argue that the parental anxiety that men are beginning to experience is all for the better, that they now may start feeling bad enough about their performance to really change. This argument does have merit. Yes, one positive outcome of asynchronous social change is that ultimately men may become not only more involved with their children but also more sensitive to what it is like to be a mother. After all, for a long time women have worried about *their* performance as parents. It should not be forgotten, however, that the guilt which many women experience as mothers (and which has been the subject of numerous novels, plays, and films) has not always been healthy for mothers—or families. In sum, when it comes to parenthood, today it would appear that both men and women can be victims as well as beneficiaries of society's ideals.

CONCLUSION

Fatherhood is different today than it was in prior times but, for the most part, the changes that have occurred are centered in the culture rather than in the conduct of fatherhood. Whatever changes have taken place in the behavior of fathers, on the basis of what we know now, seem to be minimal at best. Also, the behavioral changes have largely occurred within a single group—the middle class.

The consequences of the asynchrony between the (comparatively speaking) "modern" culture of fatherhood and the "less modern" or "traditional" conduct of fatherhood are (a) the emergence of the technically present but functionally absent father, (b) an increase in marital conflict in childbearing and child-rearing families, and (c) a greater number of fathers, especially in the middle class, who feel ambivalent and guilty about their performance as fathers.

A number of recommendations seem to be in order. First, more people need to be made aware of the fact that the division of child care in America has not significantly changed, that—despite the beliefs that fathers are a lot more involved with their children—mothers remain, far and away, the primary child caregivers. The reason for publicizing this fact is that if our beliefs represent what we want (i.e., more involved fathers) and we mistakenly assume that what we want is what we have, our complacency will only serve to perpetuate the culture-conduct disjunction. Thus, scholars and representatives of the media must commit themselves to presenting a balanced picture of "new fatherhood."

Second, and in line with the above, men must be held responsible for their actions. In our study of the transition ot parenthood, we found that the language that couples use to account for men's lack of involvement in infant care does not simply reflect the division of infant care, it constructs that division of infant care. In other words, the accounts employed by new parents to excuse and justify men's paternal role distance serves as a social lubricant in the traditionalization process (LaRossa & LaRossa, 1981). Thus, when men say things like "I'm not good at taking care of the baby" or "I can't be with Junior now, I have to go to the office, go to the store, go to sleep, mow the lawn, pay the bills, and so forth" the question must be raised, are these reasons genuine (i.e., involving insurmountable role conflicts) or are they nothing more than rationalizations used by men to do one thing (not be with their children) but believe another ("I like to be with my children")? If they are rationalizations, then they should not be honored. Not honoring rationalizations "de-legitimates" actions and, in the process, puts the burden of responsibility for the actions squarely on the person who is carrying out the actions. Only when men are forced to seriously examine their commitment to fatherhood (vs. their commitment to their jobs and avocations) can we hope to bring about the kinds of changes that will be required to alter the division of child care in this country (LaRossa, 1983).

What kinds of changes are we talking about? Technically present but functionally absent fathers are products of the society in which we live. So also, the traditionalization process during the transition to parenthood and the conflict and guilt it apparently engenders cannot be divorced from the socio-historical reality surrounding us and of which we are a part. All of which means that if we hope to alter the way men relate to their children, we cannot be satisfied with individualistic solutions which see "the problem" as a private therapeutic matter best solved through consciousness raising groups and the like. Rather, we must approach it as a public issue and be prepared to alter the institutional fabric of American society (cf. Mills, 1959). For example, the man-as-breadwinner model of fatherhood, a model which emerged in the 19th and early 20th centuries and which portrays fathers primarily as breadwinners whose wages make family consumption and security possible, remains dominant today (Pleck, 1987). This model creates structural barriers to men's involvement with their children, in that it legitimates inflexible and highly demanding job schedules which, in turn, increase the conflict between market work and family work (Pleck, 1985). More flex-time jobs would help to relieve this conflict. So would greater tolerance, on the part of employers, of extended paternity leaves (Levine, 1976). I am not suggesting that the only reason that men are not as involved with their children is that their jobs keep them from getting involved. The fact that many women also contend with inflexible and highly demanding job schedules and still are relatively involved with their children would counter such an assertion. Rather, the point is that the level of achievement is market work expected of men in America generally is higher than the level of achievement in market work expected of women and that this socio-historical reality must be entered into any equation which attempts to explain why fathers are not more involved.

When we will begin to see significant changes in the conduct of fatherhood is hard to say. The past generally provides the data to help predict the future. But, as the historian John Demos (1982) once noted, "Fatherhood has a very long history, but virtually no historians" (p. 425). Hence, our ability to make informed predictions about the future of fatherhood is severely limited. Hopefully, as more empirical research—historical and otherwise—on fatherhood is carried out, we will be in a better position to not only see what is coming but to deal with what is at hand.

REFERENCES

Barnett, R. C., & Baruch, G. K. (1987). Determinants of fathers' participation in family work. *Journal of Marriage and the Family, 49*, 29–40.

Belsky, M. R. (1986). Scott's and Julie's Daddy. In C. Kort & R. Friedland (Eds.), *The father's book: Shared experiences* (pp. 63–65). Boston: G. K. Hall.

Benokraitis, N. (1985). Fathers in the dual-earner family. In S. M. H. Hanson & F. W. Bozett (Eds.), *Dimensions of fatherhood* (pp. 243–268). Beverly Hills, CA: Sage Publications.

Berger, M. (1979). Men's new family roles—Some implications for therapists. *Family Coordinator, 28*, 636–646.

Blumer, H. (1969). *Symbolic interactionism: Perspective and method.* Englewood Cliffs, NJ: Prentice Hall.

Caplow, T. with Bahr, H. M., Chadwick, B. A., Hill, R., & Williamson, M. H. (1982). *Middletown families: Fifty years of change and continuity.* Minneapolis: University of Minnesota Press.

Day, R. D., & Mackey, W. C. (1986). The role image of the American father: An examination of a media myth. *Journal of Comparative Family Studies, 17,* 371–388.

Demos, J. (1982). The changing faces of fatherhood: A new exploration in American family history. In S. H. Cath, A. R. Gurwitt, & J. M. Ross (Eds.), *Father and child: Developmental and clinical perspectives* (pp. 425–445). Boston: Little, Brown.

Gustatis, R. (1982, August 15). Children sit idle while parents pursue leisure. *Atlanta Journal and Constitution,* pp. 1D, 4D.

Hanson, S. M. H., & Bozett, F. W. (1985). *Dimensions of fatherhood.* Beverly Hills, CA: Sage Publications.

Hanson, S. M. H., & Bozett, F. W. (1987). Fatherhood: A review and resources. *Family Relations, 36,* 333–340.

Harte, S. (1987, June 21). Fathers and sons. Narrowing the generation gap: Atlanta dads reflect a more personal style of parenting. *Atlanta Journal and Constitution,* pp. 4G, 6G.

Juster, F. T. (1985). A note on recent changes in time use. In F. T. Juster & F. P. Stafford (Eds.), *Time, goods, and well-being* (pp. 313–332). Ann Arbor, MI: Institute for Social Research.

Kaplan, D. (1987, Early Summer). The great $39.00 2" TV catch. *DAK Industries Inc.,* p. 32A.

Kort C., & Friedland, R. (Eds.). (1986). *The father's book: Shared experiences.* Boston: G. K. Hall.

Lamb, M. E. (1987). Introduction: The emergent American father. In M. E. Lamb (Ed.), *The father's role: Cross-cultural perspectives* (pp. 3–25). Hillsdale, NJ: Lawrence Erlbaum.

Lamb, M. E., Pleck, J. H., & Levine, J. A. (1987). Effects of increased paternal involvement on fathers and mothers. In C. Lewis & M. O'Brien (Eds.), *Reassessing fatherhood: New observations on fathers and the modern family* (pp. 109–125). Beverly Hills, CA: Sage Publications.

LaRossa, R. (1983). The transition to parenthood and the social reality of time. *Journal of Marriage and the Family, 45,* 579–589.

LaRossa, R. (1986, November). *Toward a social history of fatherhood in America.* Paper presented at the Theory Construction and Research Methodology Workshop, Annual Meeting of National Council of Family Relations, Philadelphia, PA.

LaRossa, R., & LaRossa, M. M. (1981). *Transition to parenthood: How infants change families.* Beverly Hills, CA: Sage Publications.

LeMasters, E. E. (1957). Parenthood as crisis. *Marriage and Family Living, 19,* 352–355.

LeMasters, E. E., & DeFrain, J. (1983). *Parents in contemporary America: A sympathetic view* (4th ed.) Homewood, IL: Dorsey.

Levine, J. A. (1976). *Who will raise the children?* New York: Bantam.

Lewis, C. (1986). *Becoming a father.* Milton Keynes, England: Open University Press.

Lewis, C., & O'Brien, M. (1987). *Reassessing fatherhood: New observations on fathers and the modern family.* Beverly Hills, CA: Sage Publications.

Lutwin, D. R., & Siperstein, G. N. (1985). Househusband fathers. In S. M. H. Hanson & F. W. Bozett (Eds.), *Dimensions of fatherhood* (pp. 269–287). Beverly Hills, CA: Sage Publications.

Lynd, R. S., & Lynd, H. M. (1927). *Middletown: A study in American culture.* New York: Harcourt & Brace.

Lynd, R. S., & Lynd, H. M. (1937). *Middletown in transition: A study of cultural conflicts.* New York: Harcourt & Brace.

Mackey W. C., & Day, R. D. (1979). Some indicators of fathering behaviors in the United States: A crosscultural examination of adult male-child interaction. *Journal of Marriage and the Family, 41,* 287–297.

Margolis, M. L. (1984). *Mothers and such: Views of American women and why they changed.* Berkeley: University of California Press.

McKee, L., & O'Brien, M. (Eds.). (1982). *The father figure.* London: Tavistock.

Mead, M. (1967). Margaret Mead answers: How do middle-class American men compare with men in other cultures you have studied? *Redbook, 129,* 36.

Mills, C. W. (1959). *The sociological imagination.* New York: Oxford University Press.

Parke, R. D. 91981). *Fathers.* Cambridge, MA: Harvard University Press.

Pleck, J. H. (1979). Men's family work: Three perspectives and some data. *Family Coordinator, 28*, 481–488.

Pleck, J. H. (1983). Husbands' paid work and family roles: Current research issues. In H. Z. Lopata & J. H. Pleck (Eds.), *Research in the interweave of social roles. Vol 3. Families and jobs* (pp. 251–333). Greenwich, CT: JAI Press.

Pleck, J. H. (1985). *Working wives/Working husbands.* Beverly Hills, CA: Sage Publications.

Pleck, J. H. (1987). American fathering in historical perspective. In M. S. Kimmel (Ed.), *Changing men: New directions in research on men and masculinity* (pp. 83–97). Beverly Hills, CA: Sage Publications.

Rotundo, E. A. (1985). American fatherhood: A historical perspective. *American Behavioral Scientist, 29*, 7–25.

Scanzoni, J. (1979). Strategies for changing male family roles: Research and practice implications. *Family Coordinator, 28*, 435–442.

Scott, M. B., & Lyman, S. M. (1968). Accounts. *American Sociological Review, 33*, 46–62.

Stokes, R., & Hewitt, J. P. (1976). Aligning actions. *American Sociological Review, 41*, 838–849.

Straus, M., Gelles, R. J., & Steinmetz, S. K. (1980). *Behind closed doors: Violence in the American family.* New York: Anchor/Doubleday.

Trudeau, G. B. (1985, March 24 & March 25). *Doonesbury.* United Press Syndicate.

Zerubavel, E. (1979). *Patterns of time in hospital life: A sociological perspective.* Chicago: University of Chicago Press.

Barbara Katz-Rothman

FATHERING AS A RELATIONSHIP

A personal introduction: My early understanding of what the women's movement was about was that we were going to remove gender as a category where it was not relevant. Which is to say, almost everywhere. In homes, offices, playing fields, laboratories, hospitals, wherever we went, we would not be constrained by gender. There would be no more "men's work" and "women's work," but just work, which men and women would do, according to need, interest, ability, temperament—according to anything but gender.

With some enthusiasm my husband and I tackled the problem at home, in our new marriage. Did I make the dinner parties and he do the electrical work? I'd learn wiring, he'd stuff a goose for ten. We constantly questioned the gender basis of our relationship: were we doing things because we wanted to, because it suited us as individuals, or because we had learned that gender arrangement? And didn't the one flow right into the other, gender shaping our interests? We would circumvent our training by applying the rules of childhood: we would take turns, divide jobs, share.

We were married five years in 1974, and decided to have a child. We figured the same rules would apply. And they did. We shared, divided, took turns. We didn't use "mommy" and "daddy" language—we didn't want to *become* Mommy and Daddy, entrenched in gender-based parenting roles. For a long time the only sure point of communication between us was the diaper box: if we had something urgent to tell each other, that was the place to leave the note. Sometimes it seemed we only saw each other at what we came to call the "changing of the guard," passing the baby back and forth as we ran off to work.

I thought all of this would give my son double the security of mommy-reared children. I learned it also gave him double the vulnerability. Just like any child, he would sometimes cry when I left him. But I also found that I could not always comfort him when Hesch, his father, left. I offered the comfort and security of the breast. And Hesch offered the comfort and security of his shoulder—holding the child's head on his shoulder as month by month, year by year, the legs came to dangle down longer and longer. I've seen my very young children, both the boy and the girl, offer a doll the breast, and I've seen them both hold a doll on their shoulder, walking back and forth in sharp imitation of Hesch.

I know nurturing care, the mothering acts, can be separated from gender.

*   *   *

There are powerful reasons why men should mother, and it is not to save the children from their mothers.

Men should mother, should provide intimate, daily, ongoing nurturing care to children, in the interests not only of the children, but of mothers, of the men themselves, and of achieving economic justice and a better world. As in the general issue of child care, children are not the only ones involved, not the only ones affected by how we organize their care. How the children "turn out" is not the only question to be asked.

How the mothers are doing is also a fair question. Women may not need fathers to share the mothering with, but we certainly need someone. We cannot do it all ourselves. The problem of the double day for women, the unending circuit of paid work and then work in the household, not enough sleep, and back to work, takes its toll. We need help. But why the *father?*

It is not because of his sperm. Like mothering, fathering should not be thought of as a genetic connection, but a social relationship. A fair percentage of us, it turns out, are not genetically related to the men we grew up with as fathers anyway. Some physicians doing tissue typing for organ donations estimate that maybe 20 percent of people are not genetically related to the men who claim fatherhood; others say it is less, perhaps as low as 5 percent. In either case, the social relationship is the essential one: unless one is doing organ transplants, it doesn't much matter. Some children look just like their parents, and some do not. On any inheritable characteristic a child may, or may not, resemble the parent. They are not clones.

The social relationship of parenting, of nurturing and of caring, needs a social base, not a genetic one. Through their pregnancies, women begin to establish that base. Through their relationships with women, and then with children, men too can establish that base. Pregnancy is one of the ways that we begin a social relationship with a child, but obviously not the only one. Remember the fathers' descriptions of eye contact with their babies: the child pulled them in.

If women are not to drop from exhaustion and lose all pleasure in life, someone is gong to have to help with the kids. If women are sharing their lives, and sharing their children, with someone, then that is the obvious person to share the work of child care. For some women that is a lesbian partner, for some the woman's own mother, but for many of us that is our husband. It is not by virtue of their paternity, their genetic ties to children, that men have an obligation to rear and to nurture them, but by virtue of their social relationship. If someone, man or woman, is going to be the life partner, the mate, of a woman who mothers, then that person must share the child care. And in turn it is by sharing the care and rearing of the children that the partner comes to have a place in the life of the child. We have to move beyond a paternity standard to a standard of nurturance.

Mothers also need men who can mother because we *ourselves* need that mothering—women are tired of mothering the whole world. Mothering, like everything else in life, is best learned by doing. I think that the mothering women have done has taught many of us the skills of listening to what is said and to what is not said. I think in mothering we hone our empathic abilities, learn to understand the vulnerability in others without profiting from it. I think that the experience of mothering teaches people how to be more emotionally and intellectually nurturant, how to take care of each other. It is not the only way we learn that lesson, but it is hard to mother and not learn it.

I *know* that mothering teaches us physical nurturance. Having nurtured the literally unselfconscious child, we are more competent, more confident providing other kinds of intimate, physical care. I remember my own awkwardness providing "nursing" care to my mother during an illness of hers in my adolescence. I compare that with the competence with which I can now provide such care. And I particularly remember my husband's awkwardness providing such care to me before our first child, and the skill and ease with which he does it now. Nursing me through my first labor, he was infinitely well meaning. Nursing me through my second, he knew what he was doing. He had been nurturing for seven years, years of nursing earaches, bellyaches, changing diapers, calming night terrors, holding pans for vomit, taking out splinters, washing bloody wounds. He had grown accustomed to the sheer physicality of the body, the sights and sounds and smells. More essentially, what I showed him in my pain and my fear was not foreign—he saw the baby, the child in me, not the one I was birthing, but the one I myself am, and he nursed it. Now *that* is a man to enter old age with.

If men are not providing this kind of care, learning these skills, with their children, they're not going to be much help with their elderly fathers, or with their own sick wives. When women do all the mothering, it's not just the child care the men are being excused from—it's all of the intimate care women end up providing for children, for men, and for each other.

And finally, men should join women in mothering because it is the only way to avoid recreating the gender and class system and still live together.

We can pool our resources, join together in infinite varieties of social arrangements to rear our children, but we must not recreate endlessly the separate worlds of power and of care. We must not do this in any of its guises: not as separate public and private worlds, not as separate worlds of men and of women. It is morally wrong to have children raised by one group for another group, whether it is Mrs. John Smith raising John Smith Jr. in her husband's image, slave nurses raising their masters, or hired caregivers raising the children of dual-career couples.

Caring people can and do raise whole and healthy children, and they do it across lines of gender, class, and race. It is not that the children are "sub-human," but that we ask them to turn away from humanity, away from care, and toward power. We do that whenever we separate the world into the kinds of people who take care of children and the kinds of people who rule the world.

In this I share a vision with Sara Ruddick. With her, I look forward to a day when

> there will be no more "fathers," no more people of either sex who have power over their children's lives and moral authority in their children's world, though they do not do the work of attentive love. There will be mothers of both sexes who live out a transformed maternal thought in communities that share parental care—practically, emotionally, economically and socially. Such communities will have learned from their mothers how to value children's lives.

And in so doing we will learn to value all of our lives—and that is still what I think the women's movement is about.

Brian Miller

LIFE-STYLES OF GAY HUSBANDS AND FATHERS

The words "gay husband" and "gay father" are often regarded as contradictions in terms. This notion is hinted at in Anita Bryant's widely quoted non sequitur, "Homosexuals recruit because they cannot reproduce." Researchers estimate, however, that in America there are six million gay husbands and fathers (Bozett, 1987; Schulenberg, 1985). Why do these men marry and have children? How do they organize their lives? What are their difficulties and joys as a consequence of their behavior?

To address these questions, 50 gay husbands and fathers were contacted in 1976 by means of multiple-source chain-referral samples. At first interview, 24 of the men were living with their wives; three years later at the second interview, only three had intact marriages. Approximately two-thirds of the respondents have been followed to the present and all of them are now separated (Humphreys and Miller, 1980a). To show the modal developments in gay husbands' and fathers' life-styles, the data are organized along a four-point continuum: Covert Behavior, Marginal Involvement, Transformed Participation, and Open Endorsement.

Revised and updated from an article in *Gay Men: The Sociology of Male Homosexuality* by Martin P. Levine. New York: Harper & Row, 1979.

COVERT BEHAVIOR

Early in adult life, gay husbands and fathers tend to regard their homosexual feelings as nothing more than genital urges. They are reluctant to refer to either themselves or their behavior as gay: "I hate labels" is a common response to questions about sexual orientation. These men have unstable self-concepts—one day thinking they are homosexual and another day thinking they are not. Their reluctance to label their same-sex activity as homosexual is not because they hate labels per se; indeed they strive to present themselves to others under a heterosexual label. Rather, they dislike a label that calls attention to behaviors they would prefer to forget.

Premarital homosexual experiences are often explained away with "It's only a phase" or "God, was I drunk last night!" These men report such activities prior to marriage as arranging heterosexual double-date situations in which they would perform coitus in the back seat of the car, for example, while fantasizing about the male in the front seat. Others report collaborating with a buddy to share a female prostitute. These ostensibly heterosexual acts allowed the men to buttress their sense of heterosexuality while gratifying homosexual urges. During the premarital period, respondents discounted gay life-styles and romanticized heterosexual family living as the only way to achieve the stable home life, loyal companionship, and fatherhood they desired.

These men married in good faith, thinking they could overcome their gay desires; they did not believe they were deceiving their spouses. In fact, most men broached the issue of their homosexual feelings to their wives before marriage, but the information was usually conveyed in an oblique manner and downplayed as inconsequential. This kept their future wives from thinking that they might be marrying homosexuals. Wives' denials of their husbands' homosexuality were further facilitated by the fact that half the women, at their nuptials, were pregnant by the men they were marrying.

In the early years of marriage, high libido provided husbands with easy erections for coitus. Respondents report, however, that this situation tended to deteriorate shortly after the birth of the first child. Increasingly, they found themselves fantasizing about gay erotica during coitus.

Marriage engulfs the men in a heterosexual role, making them marginal to the gay world. Their social isolation from others who share their sexual interests burdens them with "I'm-the-only-one-in-the-world" feelings. These men, realizing their behavior is inconsistent with their heterosexual reputation, try to reduce their anxiety and guilt by compartmentalizing gay and nongay worlds. One respondent said: "I never walk in the door without an airtight excuse of where I've been." Some men avoid the strain of remembering stories by intimidating the wife into silence: "She knows better than to question my whereabouts. I tell her, 'I get home when I get home; no questions asked.'" In these respects, respondents have parallels to their adulterous heterosexual counterparts (Libby and Whitehurst, 1977).

Extramarital sex for respondents usually consists of clandestine, impersonal encounters in parks, tearooms, or highway rest stops, with hitchhikers or male hustlers. (Regarding this, single gays sometimes comment, "Married gays give the rest of us a bad name.") Occasionally, furtiveness itself becomes eroticized, making the men sexually dysfunctional in calmer contexts. Recreational gay scenes such as dances, parties, and gay organizations are not used by respondents, primarily because they dread discovery and subsequent marital dissolution. Many are further limited by fears that their jobs would be threatened, by lack of geographical access to gay institutions, or by religious scruples. In fact, these men are largely unaware of gay social events in their communities and have little idea of how to participate in them. They tend to be ideologically ambivalent about the gay world, sometimes thinking of it as exotic, and other times condemning it as "superficial, unstable, full of black-mail and violence." Given their exposure to only the impersonal homosexual underground, and not to loving gay relationships, their negative perception is somewhat justified. As long as they remain marginal to the gay world, the likelihood of their participation in safe, fulfilling gay relationships remains minimal (Miller and Humphreys, 1980).

Some men regard their homosexual desires not as an orientation, but as a compulsion: "I don't want to do these things, but I'm driven to do them." Other accounts that explain away their homosexual behavior, emphasize its nonseriousness, and minimize its consequences include (1) "I might be okay if my wife learned to give good blow jobs." (2) "I only go out for it when I'm drunk or depressed." (3) "I go to the truckstop and meet someone. We're just a couple of horny married guys relieving ourselves. That's not sex. [It] doesn't threaten my marriage like adultery would." (4) "Sex with men is a minor aspect of my life that I refuse to let outweigh more important things."

The respondent who gave this last account also presented conflicting evidence. He spent time, effort, and anxiety in rearranging his schedule to accomodate sex, spending money on his car and fuel to search for willing men, constructing intricate stories to fool work associates and family, and buying his wife penance gifts. He also experienced near misses with police and gay bashers. Still, he viewed all this as only a "minor aspect" of his life.

Another rationalization is "I'm not really homosexual since I don't care if it's a man, woman or dog that's licking my cock. All I want is a hole." Further questioning, however, made clear that this respondent was not looking for just any available orifice. He stated that it was equally important that he persuade the most attractive man available to fellate him.

Another account is the "Eichmann dodge." Men may claim, like Eichmann, that they are the victims of other men's desire, inadvertently caught up and swept along by the events, thereby absolving themselves of responsibility. Men stating this rationalization, however, are often skilled at seducing others into making the first move. Some gay husbands and fathers claim that they limit themselves to one special "friendship" and that no one else of their sex could excite them. If they think of homosexuality at all, they conceive it as promiscuous behavior done by degenerates, not by people like themselves who are loyal and who look conventional.

These accounts help respondents deny homosexuality while practicing it. They find it difficult to simultaneously see themselves as worthwhile persons and as homosexuals, and to reconcile their masculine self-image with the popular image of gays as effeminate. The most they can acknowledge is that they get together with other men to ejaculate and that they fantasize about men during sex with their wives. In spite of their rationalizations, however, these men report considerable anxiety and guilt about maintaining their compartmentalized double lives.

Respondents are reluctant to rate their marriages as "happy," typically referring to them as "duties." The ambivalence is expressed by one who said: "My wife is a good person, but it's funny, I can't live with this marriage and I can't live without it." Respondents report conflict with wives who object to the disproportionate time these men spend away from home, neglecting parental responsibilities. The men view alternatives to marriage as limited, not seeing life in the gay world as a viable option. They find it difficult to talk about their children and express guilt that their work and sex schedules do not allow them to spend as much time with their children as they would like. Nevertheless, most of the men report that their children are the main reason for remaining married: "In this horrible marriage, [the children] are the consolation prize."

MARGINAL INVOLVEMENT

Respondents at this point on the continuum engage in homosexual behavior and have a gay self-identity. However, these men are marginal to the gay community since they have heterosexual public identities, and are often living with their wives. Still, they are much more comfortable with their homoerotic desires than are those in the Covert Behavior group and are more disclosing about their sexual orientation to other gays.

Compared with men in the previous group, Marginally Involved respondents have an expanded repertoire of sexual outlets. They sometimes compile telephone-number lists of sex partners and have limited involvement with small networks of gay friends. The men maintain secrecy by using post office boxes or separate office phones for gay-related business. Fake identities and names may be constructed to prevent identification by sexual partners. Employing male "masseurs" or maintaining a separate apartment for gay sex provide other relatively safe outlets. Consequently, these men are less likely to encounter police entrapment or gay bashers. Gay bars are somewhat inaccessible since they often start too late, and the men cannot regularly find excuses for extended absences from home. Some men resort to lunch-hour or pre-supper "quickies" at the baths.

In spite of these measures, respondents report many facade-shattering incidents with heterosexuals. Such difficulties include being caught on the street with a gay friend whose presence cannot be explained, blurting out praise about an event, then remembering it was attended with a gay friend, not one's wife, and transferring body lice or a veneral disease from a hustler to the wife, an especially dangerous occurrence in this time of AIDS (Pearson, 1986). Many respondents, however, continue to deny wives' knowledge about their homosexuality: "I don't think my wife really knows. She's only mentioned it a couple of times, and only when she was too drunk to know what she was saying."

Men who travel as part of their business or who have loosely structured working hours enjoy relative freedom. For them, absences and sexual incidents may be more easily covered. A minority of men, specifically those in artistic and academic fields, are able to mix their heterosexual and homosexual worlds. Their circle is that of the relatively wealthy and tolerant in which the epithet "perversion" is replaced by the more neutral "eccentricity," and variant behavior is accepted as long as the man is discreet and does not "rub the wife's nose in it." Several respondents socialize openly with similarly situated men or with gay sex partners whom wives and others ostensibly know as merely work assistants or friends of the family.

Because Marginally Involved respondents are "out" to some audiences and not to others, they sometimes resemble, as one man said, " a crazy quilt of contradictions." This is emphasized by playing word games with questioners or with those who try to penetrate their defenses. Playing the role of the eccentric and giving mixed messages provide a smokescreen for their emotional whereabouts from both gays and nongays.

This adjustment, however, is tenuous and respondents are often ambivalent about maintaining their marriages. They fantasize about life as a gay single, and entertain ideas of divorce. The guilt these respondents experience is sometimes reflected in what might be called Santa Claus behavior. They shower their children—and sometimes their wives—with expensive gifts to counteract feelings that they have done a terrible thing to their family by being homosexual: "It's the least I can do for having ruined their chance to grow up in a normal home." Using credit cards to manage guilt has many of these men in serious debt and laboring as workaholics.

Like men in the first category, these men regret that performing their breadwinner, husband, and homosexual roles leaves little time for the father role. Nevertheless, they are reluctant to leave their marriages, fearing permanent separation from their children. They also fear community stigma, ambivalently regard the gay world, and are unwilling to endure the decreased standard of living necessitated by divorce.

Over time, it becomes increasingly difficult for these men to reconcile their discordant identities as husband and as homosexual. Although some are able to routinize compartmentalization, others find sustaining the necessary maneuvers for secrecy to be not worth it. Conspiracies of silence and denial within the families become strained, if not transparent. Respondents tend to seek closure by communicating, directly and indirectly, their orientational needs to wives and by becoming more explicit in their methods of making gay contacts. Others are exposed by vice arrests or by being victimized by men they solicit. Most wives are surprised by the direct confrontation. Respondents are surprised that their wives are surprised since respondents may have thought their wives already knew, and tacitly accepted it. Initially wives often react with disbelief, revulsion, and anger: "I feel betrayed." This frequently gives way to a feeling of couple solidarity, that "we can conquer the problem together." When this is the adaptation, respondents do not come out of the closet so much as take their wives into the closet with them.

Couples try a variety of techniques to shore up the marriages. Respondents may seek therapy to "cure" their homosexuality. Some men generously offer wives the freedom to experience extramarital affairs too, although it appears this is done mostly to relieve respondents' guilt since they know that wives are unlikely to take them up on the offer. When wives do not put the offer to the test, respondents further console their guilt by interpreting this as evidence that the wives are "frigid" or low in "sex drive," although data from the wives dispute this characterization (Hays and Samuels, 1988).

Some couples try instituting new sexual arrangements: a *menage á trois*, or the husband is allowed out one night a week with gay friends. In the former interaction, wives tend to report feeling "used" and, in the latter, men tend to report feeling they are on a "leash."

Sexual conflicts spill into other domestic areas. Tardiness or missed appointments lead to wives' suspicions and accusations and general marital discord. One man calls this compromise period "white-knuckle heterosexuality." By negotiating groundrules that reinstate partial denial and by intellectualizing the situation, some couples maintain for years the compromise period. This uneasy truce ends if groundrules are repeatedly violated and when the wife realizes (1) that her husband finds men sexier than herself, (2) that he is unalterably gay, (3) that her primary place as object of permanent affection is challenged, and (4) that she has alternatives and can cope without the marriage. Wives gradually come to resent romanceless marriages with men who would rather make love to another man, and the homosexual husbands come to resent, as one man said, being "stifled in a nuptial closet."

Couples who remain married after disclosure tend not to have rejected divorce, but rather have an indefinite postponement of it: "After the children leave home." "After the finances are in order." Other considerations that keep the couples together include religious beliefs, family pressure, wives' dependence, and the perceived nonviability of the gay world.

In most cases, the immediate impetus for ending the marriage is the husband's establishment of a love relationship with another man. As such relationships intensify, men begin to reconstruct the gay world as favorable for effecting companionship and social stability. It is usually wives, however, who take action to terminate the marriages. Painful as this experience is, it somewhat eases the men's guilt for causing marital dissolution.

TRANSFORMED PARTICIPATION

Respondents who reach this point on the continuum engage in homosexual behavior and have self-identities—and to a limited extent, public identities—that reflect acceptance of their behavior. These men generally have come out as gay and left their wives.

Acculturation into the gay world involves three areas of concern for respondents: (1) disadvantage of advanced age and late arrival on the scene, (2) the necessity of learning new gay social definitions and skills, and (3) the need to reconcile prior fantasies to the realities of the gay world. Once respondents no longer live with wives and children, they begin to increase their contacts with the gay world and their marginality to it decreases. They may now subscribe to gay publications, join gay religious congregations, and go to gay social and political clubs and private gay parties. They experience a rapid expansion of gay consciousness and skills and take steps to form close friendships with others of their sexual orientation.

Moving out of the closet, these men report a stabilization of self-concept and a greater sense of psychological well-being. Their attitudes toward homoerotic behavior become more relaxed and better integrated into their everyday lives. Most experience a change in body image, exemplified by improved physical fitness and increased care with their appearance. Many report the elimination of nervous and psychosomatic disorders such as ulcers, excessive fatigue, and back aches, as well as substance abuse.

These respondents' sexual orientation tends to be known by significant others with two exceptions: their employers and children. Secrecy sometimes exists with employers since respondents believe the legal system does not protect their interests should they be dismissed for being gay (Levine, 1981).

Relatively little openness about homosexuality also exists with these respondents' children. Typically, only older children (if any) are told, and it is not considered a topic for general discussion. There is fear that, if the man's gayness becomes known in the community, his employer might find out or his ex-wife might become irked and deny him child visits. Successful legal appeal for gay people in such matters is difficult, a situation these men perceive as legally sanctioned blackmail.

In line with this, most respondents, rather than living with their children, have visiting schedules with them. They do not have the financial resources either to persuade their ex-wives to relinquish the children or to hire care for them while devoting time to their own careers.

Men who are able to terminate marriages without their spouse's discovering their homosexuality avoid this problem. However, fear of subsequent exposure and loss of children through a new court order remains and prompts some men to stay partially closeted even after marital dissolution. In spite of these fears, the degree of passing and compartmentalization of gay and nongay worlds is much less for men at this point on the continuum than for those who are Covert and Marginal.

OPEN ENDORSEMENT

Respondents who reach this point on the continuum not only engage in homosexual behavior and have a self-identity reflective of the behavior but also openly champion the gay community. Although they come from the full range of economic backgrounds, they tend to have high social and occupational resources. Some have tolerant employers; some are full-time gay activists; others are self-employed, often in businesses with largely gay clienteles.

Proud of their newfound identity, these men organize their world, to a great extent, around gay cultures. Much of their leisure, if not occupation, is spent in gay-related pursuits. They have experienced unhappy marriages and divorce, the struggle of achieving a gay identity, and now feel they have arrived at a satisfactory adjustment. These men, consequently, distinguish themselves in ideology from respondents in other categories. For example, what the others refer to as "discretion," men in this category call "duplicity" and "sneaking around." Moreover, what closeted men see as "flaunting," openly gay respondents call "being forthright" and "upfront."

Respondents' efforts in constructing this new life are helped not only by having a gay love relationship, but by the Gay Liberation Movement (Humphreys and Miller, 1980b). Parallel processes are at work whereby the building of a personal gay identity is facilitated by the larger cultural context of increasing gay pride and diversification of gay institutions and heritage (Adam, 1987; Harry and DeVall, 1978; Murray, 1979). Still, coming out is not easy or automatic. This is partly due to the fact that there is no necessary conjunction among sexual behavior fantasy, self-identity, and object of affectional attachment. Although there is a strain toward consistency for most people among these components of sexuality, this is not invariably so. The ways these components change over time and the combinations in which they link with each other are multiple (Miller 1983; Simon and Gagnon, 1969).

Men who reach the Open Endorsement point often have fears that their father and ex-husband statuses could distance them from single gays. Sometimes respondents fear that single gays, similar to nongays, regard them with confusion, curiosity, or pity. Integrating gay and father roles requires patience, since it is often difficult for respondents to find a lover who accepts him and his children as a "package deal," and the gay father may feel he has not enough time and energy to attend to both children and a lover. Selecting a lover who is also a gay father is a common solution to this situation.

Most respondents who have custody of their children did not experience court custody battles but gained custody because the mother did not want the children or because the children, being allowed to choose, chose to live with their fathers. Respondents who live with their children are more likely to have a close circle of gay friends as their main social outlet, rather than participating primarily in gay commercial establishments (McWhirter and Mattison, 1984).

Men at this point on the continuum have told their children about their homosexuality. They report children's reaction to be more positive than expected and, when there is a negative reaction, it generally dissipates over time (Miller, 1979). Children's negative reactions centered more on the parent's divorce and subsequent household changes than on the father's homosexuality per se. Daughters tend to be more accepting of their father's homosexuality than sons, although most children feel their father's honesty brings them closer together. Children report few instances of neighborhood homophobia directed against them, possibly because the children try to disclose only to people they know will react favorably. There is no indication that the children of gay fathers are disproportionately homosexual themselves although, of the children who turned out to be gay, there were more lesbian daughters than gay sons. Wives and relatives sometimes worry that gay men's children will be molested by him or his gay friends. Evidence from this study supports earlier research findings that indicate such fears are unwarranted (Bozett, 1987).

DISCUSSION

The general tendency is for the Covert Behavior respondents to move toward Open Endorsement. There are several caveats, however, about this movement. For example, the continuum should not be construed as reifying transient states into types. Additionally, movement out of marriage into an openly gay identity is not unilateral. There are many negotiations back and forth, in and out of the closet. There is not a finite number of stages; not everyone becomes publicly gay and not everyone passes through every step. Few respondents move easily or accidentally through the process. Rather, each level is achieved by a painful search, negotiating with both oneself and the larger world.

The event most responsible for initiating movement along the continuum and reconstructing gay fathers' perceptions of the gay community is the experience of falling in love with another man. By contrast, factors hindering movement along the continuum include inability to perceive the gay world as a viable alternative as well as perceived lack of support from other gays, economic difficulty, family pressure, poor health, wives' dependence, homophobia in respondents or community, and moral/religious scruples.

This study has several findings. Gayness and traditional marital relationships are perceived by the respondents as discordant compared to relationships established when they move into the gay world. Although respondents perceive gayness as incompatible with traditional marriage, they perceive gayness as compatible with fathering. Highly compartmentalized life-styles and deceit sometimes repress open marital conflict, but unresolved tension characterizes respondents' marriages. In contrast, men who leave their spouses and enter the gay world report gay relationships to be more harmonious than marital relationships. They also report fathering to be more salient once having left their marriages. Men who come out perceive less discrimination from family, friends, and co-workers than those who are closeted anticipate. Wives tend to be upset by their husbands' revalations, but respondents are typically surprised by the positive reactions of their children and their parents.

Future prospects for gay fathers hinge largely on the success of the gay liberation movement. If these men can politicize their status, if they can see their difficulties stemming from social injustice and society's homophobic conditioning rather than personal inadequacy, and if they can redefine themselves, not as deviants, but as an oppressed minority, self-acceptance is improved. This helps lift their depression and externalize anger—anger about prejudice and about wasting their precious early years in the closet. Further, it minimizes their guilt and eases adjustment into the gay community (Miller, 1987).

As the gay liberation movement makes alternatives for fathering available within the gay community, fewer gays are likely to become involved in heterosexual marriages and divorce. Adoption, surrogate parenting, and alternative fertilization are some of the new ways single gays can now experience fatherhood (Miller, 1988). If current trends continue, there will be a proliferation of family life-styles so that parenthood becomes available to all regardless of sexual orientation.

REFERENCES

Adam, B. (1987). *The rise of a gay and lesbian movement.* Boston: Hall.

Bozett, F. W. (1987). *Gay and lesbian parents.* New York: Praeger.

Harry, J. & DeVall, W. (1978). *The social organization of gay males.* New York: Praeger.

Hays, D. & Samuels, A. (1988). Heterosexual women's perceptions of their marriages to bisexual or homosexual men. In F. W. Bozett (Ed.), *Homosexuality in the family.* New York: Haworth.

Humphreys, L. & Miller, B. (1980a). Keeping in touch: Maintaining contact with stigmatized respondents. In W. Shaffir, R. Stebbins & A. Turowetz (Eds.), *Field work ecperience: Qualitative approaches in social research.* New York: St. Martin's.

Humphreys, L. & Miller, B. (1980b). Identities in the emerging gay culture. In J. Marmor (Ed.), *Homosexual behavior: A modern reappraisal.* New York: Basic.

Levine, M. (1981). Employment discrimination against gay men. In P. Stein (Ed.), *Single life*. New York: St. Martin's.

Libby, R. & Whitehurst, R. (1977). *Marriage and alternatives*. Glenview, IL: Scott, Foresman.

McWhirter, D. & Mattison, A. (1984). *The male couple*. Englewood Cliffs, NJ: Prentice-Hall.

Miller, B. (1979). Gay fathers and their children. *Family Coordinator* 28: 544–552.

Miller, B. (1983). Foreword. In M. W. Ross (Ed.), *The married homosexual man*. London: Routledge & Kegan Paul.

Miller, B. (1987). Counseling gay husbands and fathers. In F. W. Bozett (Ed.), *Gay and lesbian parents*. New York: Praeger.

Miller, B. (1988). Preface. In F. W. Bozett (Ed.), *Homosexuality in the family*. New York: haworth.

Miller, B. & Humphreys, L. (1980). Lifestyles and violence: Homosexual victims of assault and murder. *Qualitative Sociology*. 3:169–185.

Murray, S. (1979). The institutional elaboration of a quasi-ethnic community. *International Review of Modern Sociology*. 9:165–177.

Pearson, C. (1986). *Good-by, I love you*. New York: Random House.

Schulenberg, J. (1985). *Gay parenting*. New York: Doubleday.

Simon, W. & Gagnon, J. (1969). On psychosexual development. In D. Goslin (Ed.), *Handbook of socialization theory and research*. New York: Rand McNally.

◆ ◆ ◆

PART TEN

Men and the Future

Reprinted with permission by Matt Groening © 1988. Acme Features Syndicate.

Q: Why did you decide to record again?

A: Because *this* housewife would like to have a career for a bit! On October 9, I'll be 40, and Sean will be 5 and I can afford to say "Daddy does something else as well." He's not accustomed to it—in five years I hardly picked up a guitar. Last Christmas our neighbors showed him "Yellow Submarine" and he came running in, saying, "Daddy, you were singing . . . Were you a Beatle?" I said, "Well—yes, right."

—John Lennon, interview *Newsweek*, 1980

Are men changing? If so, in what directions? Can men change even more? In what ways should men be different? We posed many of these questions at the beginning of our exploration of men's lives, and we return to them here, in the book's last section, to examine the directions men have taken to enlarge their roles, to expand the meaning of masculinity, to change the rules.

Several of the articles in this section address the possibility of expanding the definitions of masculinity open to men, so that men may become more responsive to women and to other men. The "Statement of Principles" of the National Organization for Men Against Sexism (NOMAS) provides a political program, and the essay by Harry Brod provides its underlying rationale. The final articles by two noted feminist writers, Bell Hooks and Betty Friedan, conclude the book with hopes for alliance between women and men as we enter the last decade of this century and together will face the next century.

We began this book with a description of men's confusion. Men's confusion often makes men anxious, and some have said that men are experiencing a "crisis of masculinity." This confusion or "crisis" is beautifully captured by the Chinese character for the word "crisis," which is a combination of the characters for the words "danger" and "opportunity." If masculinity is in crisis, if men are confused, it is both dangerous and an exciting opportunity.

The danger is a danger of retreat. Confusion is often a frightening experience; one feels unsettled, problems are unresolved, and identity is off-center. Some people, when they are confused, will retreat to older, familiar ideas—ideas that may have once been appropriate but now are only safe anachronisms that will offer temporary solace from the confusion. Some men are therefore seeking a resolution to their confusion by the vigorous reassertion of traditional masculinity.

But many of us can recognize the opportunity that is presented by confusion. Feeling unsettled, restless, and anxious, confusion pushes us to wrestle with difficult issues, confront contradictory feelings and ideas, and challenge the ways in which our experiences do not fit with

551

the traditional rules and expectations we have inherited from the past. Confusion opens the opportunity to change, to push beyond the traditional norms of masculinity. And with change comes the possibility to become more loving and caring fathers, more emotionally responsive lovers, and more reliable and compassionate friends, and to live longer and healthier lives. It is toward these changes that we hope this work has contributed.

The National Organization for Men Against Sexism

STATEMENT OF PRINCIPLES

The National Organization For Men Against Sexism is an activist organization of men and women supporting positive changes for men. NOMAS advocates a prespective that is pro-feminist, gay-affirmative, and committed to justice on a broad range of social issues including race, class, age, religion, and physical abilities. We affirm that working to make this nation's ideals of equality substantive is the finest expression of what it means to be men.

We believe that the new opportunities becoming available to women and men will be beneficial to both. Men can live as happier and more fulfilled human beings by challenging the old-fashioned rules of masculinity that embody the assumption of male superiority.

Traditional masculinity includes many positive characteristics in which we take pride and find strength, but it also contains qualities that have limited and harmed us. *We are deeply supportive of men who are struggling with the issues of traditional masculinity. As an organization for changing men, we care about men and are especially concerned with men's problems, as well as the difficult issues in most men's lives.*

As an organization for changing men, we strongly support the continuing struggle of women for full equality. We applaud and support the insights and positive social changes that feminism has stimulated for both women and men. We oppose such injustices to women as economic and legal discrimination, rape, domestic violence, sexual harassment, and many others. Women and men can and do work together as allies to change the injustices that have so often made them see one another as enemies.

One of the strongest and deepest anxieties of most American men is their fear of homosexuality. This homophobia contributes directly to the many injustices experienced by gay, lesbian, and bisexual persons, and is a debilitating restriction for heterosexual men. We call for an end to all forms of discrimination based on sexual-affectional orientation, and for the creation of a gay-affirmative society.

We also acknowledge that many people are oppressed today because of their race, class, age, religion, and phsycial condition. We believe that such injustices are vitally connected to sexism, with its fundamental premise of unequal distribution of power.

Our goal is to change not just ourselves and other men, but also the institutions that create inequality. We welcome any person who agrees in substance with these principles to membership in the National Organization For Men Against Sexism.

Harry Brod
FRATERNITY, EQUALITY, LIBERTY

"Fraternity, Equality, Liberty." Those familiar with European history will recognize this as an inversion of the slogan of the French Revolution: "Liberty, Equality, Fraternity." The ordering of these principles by the ideologists of the revolution was not coincidental, but rather reflected a certain conceptual scheme. To their minds, the first order of business was to secure liberty, by which they meant freedom from restrictions imposed upon them by others. Having won this liberty, they would then proceed to establish a society of equality. Subsequently, once men were living in this new society, feelings of fraternity for the brotherhood of man would emerge among all men. From our contemporary vantage point, we recognize that this fraternity excluded women in principle, and in practice excluded or limited the participation of a great number of men who were not of the prescribed class, race, national origin, etc.

What would happen if we were to reverse this progression? Specifically, what would happen if we were to proceed by focusing first on real fraternity, that is, real commonality of interest *as men?* Could such an approach possibly lead to equality between and among men and women, and to real liberty for all?

At first glance this approach would seem to have little hope for success. Would not any identifiable interests men have *as men* be precisely those interests which separate them from and pit them against women? How then could furthering these interests lead to any kind of universal equality and liberty? I believe, however, that these objections pose a false dichotomy. The interests men have in banding together in a fraternal way are interests in overcoming the limitations of the male sex role. And it is precisely this same male sex role which sets women and men at odds. I believe men's interests *as men* lie in overcoming sexism. I believe men have needs for separate strategies and tactics against sexism because we are coming to the project of eliminating sexism with different backgrounds, issues, and perspectives than women, but not ultimately different goals.

If one believes that men have common fraternal interests in ending sexism—a sexism that offers very real material rewards to men, but at too high a personal cost—then one has a *positive* basis upon which to work with other men. I, for example, do not regard men as "the enemy," nor do I believe I am opposing another man or violating his individual rights in moving against his sexism. When I intervene against a man's sexism I am doing him—and myself—a favor, because trapped inside destructive and self-destructive behavior is an individual who would be relieved to be rid of this mode of being if he had a free choice. If one shares my starting assumption that nurturing, intimacy, and support are real human needs, then it follows that it is essential that men establish *real* friendships with each other. Not the implicit, contract of traditional male camaraderie, in which we mutually agree to keep our

An earlier version of this paper was presented at The First Annual Northwest Conference on Men and Masculinity, University of Oregon, Eugene, Oregon, January 18–20, 1985.

defenses up but not to mind it, and to keep our prejudices intact while validating each other's masculinity; rather, a shared intimacy in which feelings, including fears and joys, flow freely. Otherwise, men will continue to turn to women to fulfill these needs. And while women's abilities to nurture are clearly admirable, the necessity that they do so is equally clearly oppressive. Furthermore, such friendships with men are essential for supporting men in making and sustaining the needed longterm changes.

I would like to take the idea of finding a positive approach to working with men against sexism a significant step further. I suggest that we stop looking for the "original sin" on the basis of which men can be said to have erected partiarchy. Many aspects of male psychology are put forth as candidates for "original sin" status. We are said to have innate aggressive instincts, to have dominating sex drives, to have obessive desires for immortality so that we force women to have our children, to have a need to create a despised "Other" in order to establish our own identities, to have a need to compensate for our "womb envy" of women's creative and regenerative powers, to either love or fear each other so much, depending on the theory, that we have institutionalized oppressive heterosexuality, and so on.[1] I propose that we stop looking for the fatal flaw in male psychology which is responsible for sexism. Instead, I will make the seemingly preposterous suggestion that sexist attidues can be understood as stemming from inherently positive aspects of male psychology, aspects which are, however, distorted by an oppressive social order.

Let me explain how I reached this position, and then go on to specify exactly what I have in mind.[2] As a general rule of social analysis, I try to give people, men specifically included, credibility for integrity and insight. Thus, when I observe a group of people acting in what seem to me irrational ways, the question I pose is not "What's wrong with them?" but rather "What are the distorted and distorting features of their situation which make these actions appear rational to them?" Until I have satisfied myself that, if I were in their shoes, their seemingly outrageous or inexplicable actions would also appear as legitimate options to me, I consider myself not to have succeeded in understanding or explaining anything. Applying this methodology to male sexist attitudes, I have obtained the following results. I believe that as we are growing up, in our early childhood years of attitude formation, we are socialized with a crucially important belief, namely the belief that in our society people get what they deserve. While this belief, in its usual interpretations, as applied to material success or social prestige, for example, is blatantly false and can be seen to be so upon reflection, it is nonetheless a principle of justice deeply inculcated in children as they are being raised. Children are also very observant. Specifically, they will observe and note that women are universally treated as less than fully human, in contrast to men. The conjunction of this principle and this observation can be expressed as a logical syllogism:

People get what they deserve.
Women are treated inhumanly.
Women are less than fully human.

I offer the above not as a historical account of the genesis of sexist attitudes and beliefs, but rather as a phenomenological description of the development of sexist beliefs and attitudes in contemporary consciousness. In this light, sexist beliefs and attitudes can be seen to result from an attempt to preserve a belief that the world is justly ordered in the face of observing the existence of gross inequality. Children are faced with a choice: either women really are less deserving than men in some fundamental way, or a basic structuring principle of their world is false, and their world loses coherence and credibility. Everything around them, as well as their own insecurities, impel children to affirm the former, sexist beliefs.

But precisely therein, I would argue, lies the hope for change. If my proposed reconstruction of the genesis of sexist consciousness is correct, then, paradoxically enough, sexist attitudes may be said to be rooted in the child's sense of justice. But as adults, we can now take the bad news that the world is indeed unjust and not reasonably ordered. That same sense of justice, the belief that people should be treated as they deserve, coupled with the belief that people really should have equal rights and freedoms regardless of such factors as the shape or color of their skin, can now be called upon to mobilize men to rectify sexist injustices.

Listen to sexist men defend their attitudes today, listen with a comprehending ear, and you will hear the pleas of someone trying to make sense of a world they never made: "There *must* be *some* reason why the world is this way." "That's just how it is." "It's always been like this, hasn't it." "You just can't change some things." This is the voice of confusion and fear, not a dominating will to power. I propose, then, that we not focus our attention on the search for an ultimate cause for sexism in the nature of the male psyche or body, but rather that we work with men in the here and now to undo the damage sexism does to all of us. While there is some need for a general explanatory theory of patriarchy so that we can properly direct our efforts for change and not pursue the wrong targets, I believe the search for such a theory is, for most of us, a misplaced emphasis.

I think we need to emphasize moving on from here, and worry less about how we got here. This is not simply a pragmatic retreat made because we happen not to have a fully satisfactory theory about the origins of patriarchy or what a future non-patriarchal utopia would look like. The search for such a blueprint for the future is misguided, an all too typically masculine attempt to impose a rigidly constructed plan upon the world. Rather, let us do the more intimately involved work of nurturing that new world to growth with our given materials. If it is true that fundamental change must be positively self-motivated and not merely reactive, then the priority must be to seek positive approaches which will enable men to make revolutionary feminist changes. The direction of these changes, as they emerge, will clearly enough show us what our new society is to look like. This is how I envisage fraternity developing. It is not simply a means to some pre-fabricated goal. To adopt a slogan from the peace movement: there is no way to fraternity, fraternity is the way.

Which brings me to the next of the three guiding concepts, equality. I believe all men are equal. Let me make that more directly relevant by making a statement that I expect some will find terribly false, and others will find trivially true. I hope to show that it is very significantly true. The statement is this: no group of men in our society is any more or less sexist than any other group of men. Gay or straight, black or white, rich or poor, we are all equal in this regard.

Let me proceed by articulating the point of view I take myself to be arguing against. It is fashionable in some circles to characterize our society as one dominated by white males. Fashionable, but inadequate, as many feminists are aware. Socialist feminists, for example, would insist that we are plagued not only by sexism and racism, but also by capitalism.[3] So the description of the dominating group has to be widened to ruling class white males. But why stop there? Our society also systematically discriminates against the old and the young, so one would need to specify the age bracket of the ruling group, and so on. By the time one was finished, one would have constructed a description which fits at most a relative handful of men, who, according to this theory, are somehow oppressing all the rest of us, usually in multiple ways. I regard such a result as untenable for a coherent social theory and practice. It is a mistake, and a serious one, to attempt to reduce the multiple systems of oppression which characterize our society into one matrix.

Let me give a personal example. Some people have attempted to commiserate with my wife, who is Greek, about how sexist Greek or Mediterranean men are. They thought they were practicing international feminist solidarity. What they were really practicing was Anglo-Saxon cultural imperialism. Mediterranean patriarchy is qualitatively different from Anglo-Saxon patriarchy. Each has distinctive features, which are more or less taken for granted within each culture and look more or less objectionable to others. To try to assess these qualitative differences on the same quantitative scale is, as the old saying has it, like trying to mix apples and oranges.[4]

It makes more sense to say that we live in a patriarchy, and under patriarchy men oppress women. Period. We also live under captialism. Under capitalism, the ruling class, men and women, oppresses the working class. Period. And so on with regard to racism, etc. I am aware that the situation is in reality more complex than this. Patriarchy also orders men into hierarchies and capitalism divides the genders. However, the fundamental point I wish to make is that just as, for example, ruling class women's gender does not excuse them from accountability for their class privileges, so too their lack of class privileges does not excuse working class men from accountability for the exercise of their male privileges. These, and all other forms of oppression, are overlapping and interrelated but distinct systems. While it is true that, because they suffer from other forms of oppression, men from oppressed groups do not reap the material rewards of patriarchy to as great an extent as men from dominant groups, one should not therefore conclude that men from oppressed groups are to be held less accountable for their sexism.

I propose therefore that we abandon all discussions and debate about whether gay men, or working class men, or Hispanic men, or any other group of men, are more or less sexist or patriarchal than any other group. I propose instead that we realize that all sexism is simply wrong and unsupportable, and that to attempt to establish some sort of graduated scale is at best meaningless and at worst oppressive in some other form. And I propose further that men go back to their respective communities and get on with the task of instituting the specific and specifically different kinds of fraternities within each community which will enable us to move towards equality and liberty for all people.

Which brings me to the concept of liberty, the last of the triumvirate. Liberty is the most expressly political of the three concepts. I believe it is essential for men to retain a perspective which is self-consciously political, and not merely personal or psychological, regarding the tasks of overcoming male role restrictions. Correspondingly, we must also expressly link our efforts to the feminist movement. Personal freedom, of whatever kind, requires the securing of political liberty.

Let me give one example, drawn specifically from an aspect of the male role many are struggling with. Many men are trying to undo the damage done them by male role restrictions against showing their emotions. In these struggles, they are often joined and offered assistance by women, partly out of sympathy and partly—and this is the point I wish to stress—because women suffer from this aspect of the male role, not merely sympathetically, but in their own right as well. Our male dominated society confers real power on those who are skilled at withholding their emotions in many ways. Again, let us look not to flawed individual psyches but to broader social realities to understand male sexist behaviors and attitudes. Patriarchy draws to itself those who will seek its powers. No matter how much we raise men's consciousness about the value of expressing emotion, as long as patriarchy remains intact it impels men to adopt those emotional masks which give them power. Men's and women's roles cannot be simply conceptualized as complementary and equally restrictive roles, as some men's rights advocates would have us believe. Men's roles do carry real power with them. Any attempt to give up male role restrictions on an individual or apolitical basis is doomed to failure because existing power structures simply reproduce these roles, and exert enormous pressure on individuals to re-assume them. The male sex role maintains itself not becuase men are either evil or stupid, but because it confers benefits and maintains men's distance from those who bear the brunt of the system: women. That is to say, men who are competing to be less emotional are competing to be less womanlike. I believe the same sort of analysis applies not only to emotional expressiveness but to all the other aspects of the male sex role. Male problems are the other side of the coin and are inseparable from male privileges. Hence men aware of the personal drawbacks of the male role should also be drawn to a feminist political identity for themselves.

I think it is important that men claim title to be considered feminist for several reasons. I say this knowing that many men and women whom I would count among my allies on the relevant political questions would disagree. Many men and women sincerely committed to the fight against sexism insist that the label "feminist" can only be applied to women.[5] To refer to feminism as a movement consisting exclusively of women is, I believe, not a sign of radicalism but of misplaced liberalism. It relegates men to a position of sincere support, but from a distance, of women "doing their thing." One of the obstacles all liberation movements have faced is the liberal spirit of abstract tolerance from afar—e.g., it's good that women or blacks are now moving on and I wish them well, but of course this doesn't directly involve me. All too often the ideology of support by granting "autonomy" ends up being a kind of "benign neglect" where real critical thinking and support are withheld for fear of treading where one does not belong. Men should by no means dominate in women's activities of a political or personal nature, but too often a "hands off" kind of support, whose intent may be to create unity and support, may end up creating fragmentation and feelings of abandonment.

I respect the autonomy of the women's movement, but I take this stand as a feminist. My support for women's autonomy is based on a feminist political analysis which demonstrates that this autonomy is neccessary, rather than basing it on a desire for a lesser degree of involvement with the movement. Perhaps an analogy from Marxist theory will be helpful here. One can be a Marxist without being a member of the proletariat, despite the fact that Marxism assigns the key role in revolutionary struggles to the proletariat. For example, being a Marxist and a member of the middle class would simply mean that I have a theory and practice of social change in which I recognize that the struggles of my own group will not play the determining role in bringing about the new society. It means that when organizing within my own group—an important task despite force in revolutionary activity—I orient some of my efforts towards support for more key sectors. As a Marxist, I would also see the necessity for there being a working class party in which members of my class should not hold leadership positions. What I want to stress here is that I would be taking these positions *as a Marxist*—my politics is determined by how I act in my social position, not simply by seeing what class I belong to. The latter view is an example of the most crudely reductionist, determinist sort of analysis.

The relevance of this analogy to the question of men as feminists should be clear. As a male feminist, I see that my activities as a man will not be the determining ones in the struggle for a nonsexist society, and I see the need for an autonomous women's movement of which I would not be a part. But I take these positions *as a feminist*.

Why is this important? In the first place, it affirms the character of the feminist movement as essential for a qualitatively better society, and not just as the concern of a particular interest group (women) within this society. Secondly, it helps to keep in mind the difference between one's life-style and one's politics. All of us are deeply indebted to the women's movement for bringing to popular consciousness the idea that "the personal is political," but the radical importance of this slogan is trivialized and lost if it is taken to mean that everything I do in my life *is* in politics. Politics must be more than life-style, it must involve public, organized political action, and insistence that one need not be a woman to be a feminist restores this dimension to the movement. While I cannot live a woman's life or feelings, being a man, I can however live her politics.

Perhaps most importantly, any stand other than the insistence that men can be feminists betrays the most radical potential of the movement. Under the slogan "Biology is not Destiny," the feminist movement challenged the regressive idea that one's biological make-up should have a role in determining one's social/political/economic role. The stance that men cannot be feminists is a regression back to a standpoint which feminism has surpassed.

Furthermore, part of the oppressive ideology of society is the myth that the divisions between groups have been total and absolute, that there has been allout warfare between women and men, blacks and whites, Jews and Gentiles, etc. While acknowledging the overwhelming reality of oppression, it must nonetheless be said that this is a falsification of our history and a denial of our strengths. The support which the early feminists received from their husbands and male friends *is* part of the history of feminism. The fact that approximately one third of the signatories to the 1848 Seneca Falls Declaration of the Rights of Women were men is as important a part of the history of feminism as the exploits of John Brown are part of the history of Abolitionism in the same century.

I have no doubt that the process of building male–female feminist alliances will be difficult. At times, men will more or less unconsciously continue to play out old patterns of domination and step on the toes of the women they are attempting to assist. When this occurs, I hope and trust it will be corrected. But how many opportunities to support feminist growth will be lost if we do not make efforts to establish such alliances?

I believe a male feminist theory and practice which can have any hope of success in mobilizing men in a politically effective way behind the clear moral imperatives supporting feminism must always remain simultaneously focused on both aspects of the personal/political dialectic. Men as a group benefit from the social powers which correlate with the male sex role. They reap the material rewards the society has to offer. But men individually pay too high a price for these benefits, and it is in their real personal interest to overthrow the system which creates and grants these privileges.[6] The male sex role is both unsatisfying and dangerous. The combination of breadwinner pressures, which make us neurotic, isolated competitors, and the restrictions on male emotional release for these pressures which are also part of the male role is a prescription for the earlier deaths and higher rates of tension-related health problems—heart attacks, ulcers, high blood pressure, suicides—we daily see men suffering from. Though not all men are aware of the source of their difficulties, I believe all men suffer from sexism. These are the disadvantages of the advantages men receive from a sexist system.

In these ways, the call for "Fraternity, Equality, and Liberty" presents us with the beginnings of a positive political analysis of and for changing men. I hope this becomes part of ongoing discussions of how to further feminist brotherhood.

NOTES

1. These hypotheses are among many popular in feminist theory, and one finds them in such frequently used women's studies texts as *Feminist Frameworks*, ed. Alison M. Jaggar and Paula S. Rothenberg (2nd edition McGraw-Hill, 1984) and *The Longest War*, by Carol Tavris and Carole Wade (2nd edition, Harcourt Brace Jovanovich, 1984). See also the articles by Azizah at-Hibri, Eva Feder Kittay, Iris Marion Young, Pauline Bart, and Ann Ferguson in *Mothering: Essays in Feminist Theory*, ed. Joyce Trebilcot (Rowman & Allanheld, 1984).

2. Though he might well reject the analysis in this section, it is inspired by Albert Memmi's analysis of racism. See, for example, the section on "Racism and Oppression" in *Dominated Man*, Beacon, 1968.

3. See *Capitalist Partriarchy and the Case for Socialist Feminism*, ed. Zillah R. Eisenstein (Monthly Review Press, 1979).

4. I am indebted to Maria Papacostaki for clarifying discussions on this topic.

5. See Jon Snodgrass, *For Men Against Sexism: A Book of Readings*, Times Change Press, 1977, p. 9.

6. These points are developed in two brief articles of mine: "Feminism for Men: Beyond Liberalism," *Brother: The Newsletter of the National Oragnization for Changing Men* 3: 3, 1985, and a review of Leo Kanowitz's *Equal Rights: The Male Stake* and William and Laurie Wishard's *Men's Rights* in *M.: Gentle Men for Gender Justice* 12, Spring 1984.

Bell Hooks

MEN:
COMRADES IN STRUGGLE

Feminism defined as a movement to end sexist oppression enables women and men, girls and boys, to participate equally in revolutionary struggle. So far, contemporary feminist movement has been primarily generated by the efforts of women—men have rarely participated. This lack of participation is not solely a consequence of anti-feminism. By making women's liberation synonymous with women gaining social equality with men, liberal feminists effectively created a situation in which they, not men, designated feminist movement "women's work." Even as they were attacking sex role divisions of labor, the institutionalized sexism which assigns unpaid, devalued, "dirty" work to women, they were assigning to women yet another sex role task: making feminist revolution. Women's liberationists called upon all women to join feminist movement but they did not continually stress that men should assume responsibility for actively struggling to end sexist oppression. Men, they argued, were all-powerful, misogynist oppressor—the enemy. Women were the oppressed—the victims. Such rhetoric reinforced sexist ideology by positing in an inverted form the notion of a basic conflict between the sexes, the implication being that the empowerment of women would necessarily be at the expense of men.

As with other issues, the insistence on a "woman only" feminist movement and a virulent anti-male stance reflected the race and class background of participants. Bourgeois white women, especially radical feminists, were envious and angry at privileged white men for denying them an equal share in class privilege. In part, feminism provided them with a public forum for the expression of their anger as well as a political platform they could use to call attention to issues of social equality, demand change, and promote specific reforms. They were not eager to call attention to the fact that men do not share a common social status; that patriarchy does not negate the existence of class and race privilege or exploitation; that all men do not benefit equally from sexism. They did not want to acknowledge that bourgeois white women, though often victimized by sexism, have more power and privilege, are less likely to be exploited or oppressed, than poor, uneducated, nonwhite males. At the time, many white women's liberationists did not care about the fate of oppressed groups of men. In keeping with the exercise of race and/or class privilege, they deemed the life experiences of these men unworthy of their attention, dismissed them, and simultaneously deflected attention away from their support of continued exploitation and oppression. Assertions like "all men are the enemy," "all men hate women" lumped all groups of men in one category, thereby suggesting that they share equally in all forms of male privilege. One of the first written statements which endeavored to make an anti-male stance a central feminist position was "The Redstocking Manifesto." Clause III of the manifesto reads:

> We identify the agents of our oppression as men. Male supremacy is the oldest, most basic form of domination. All other forms of exploitation and oppression (racism, capitalism, imperialism, etc.) are extensions of male supremacy: men dominate women, a few men dominate the rest. All power situations throughout history have been male-dominated and male-oriented. Men have controlled all political, economic, and cultural institutions and backed up this control with physical force. They have used their power to keep women in an inferior position. All men receive economic, sexual, and psychological benefits from male supremacy. All men have oppressed women. (1970, p. 109)

Anti-male sentiments alienated many poor and working class women, particularly non-white women, from feminist movement. Their life experiences had shown them that they have more in common with men of their race and/or class group than bourgeois white women. They know the sufferings and hardships women face in their communities; they also know the sufferings and hardships men face and they have compassion for them. They have had the experience of struggling with them for a better life. This has been especially true for black women. Throughout our history in the United States, black women have shared equal responsibility in all struggles to resist racist oppression. Despite sexism, black women have continually contributed equally to anti-racist struggle, and frequently, before contemporary black liberation effort, black men recognized this contribution. There is a special tie binding people together who struggle collectively for liberation. Black women and men have been united by such ties. They have known the experience of political solidarity. It is the experience of shared resistance struggle that led black women to reject the anti-male stance of some feminist activists. This does not mean that black women were not willing to acknowledge the reality of black male sexism. It does mean that many of us do not believe we will combat sexism or woman-hating by attacking black men or responding to them in kind.

Bourgeois white women cannot conceptualize the bonds that develop between women and men in liberation struggle and have not had as many positive experiences working with men politically. Patriarchal white male rule has usually devalued female political input. Despite the prevalence of sexism in black communities, the role black women play in social institutions, whether primary or secondary, is recognized by everyone as significant and valuable. In an interview with Claudia Tate (1983), black woman writer Maya Angelou explains her sense of the different role black and white women play in their communities:

> Black women and white women are in strange positions in our separate communities. In the social gatherings of black people, black women have always been predominant. That is to say, in the church it's always Sister Hudson, Sister Thomas, and Sister Wetheringay who keep the church alive. In lay gatherings it's always Lottie who cooks, and Mary who's going to Bonita's where there is a good party going on. Also, black women are the nurturers of children in our community. White women

are in a different position in their social institutions. White men, who are in effect their fathers, husbands, brothers, their sons, nephews, and uncles say to white women or imply in any case: "I don't really need you to run my institutions. I need you in certain places and in those places you must be kept—in the bedroom, in the kitchen, in the nursery, and on the pedestal." Black women have never been told this. . . .

Without the material input of black women, as participants and leaders, many male-dominated institutions in black communities would cease to exist; this is not the case in all white communities.

Many black women refused participation in feminist movement because they felt an anti-male stance was not a sound basis for action. They were convinced that virulent expressions of these sentiments intensify sexism by adding to the antagonism which already exists between women and men. For years black women (and some black men) had been struggling to overcome the tensions and antagonisms between black females and males that is generated by internalized racism (i.e., when the white patriarchy suggests one group has caused the oppression of the other). Black women were saying to black men, "we are not one another's enemy," "we must resist the socialization that teaches us to hate ourselves and one another." This affirmation of bonding between black women and men was part of anti-racist struggle. It could have been a part of feminist struggle had white women's liberationists stressed the need for women and men to resist the sexist socialization that teaches us to hate and fear one another. They chose instead to emphasize hate, especially male woman-hating, suggesting that it could not be changed. Therefore no viable political solidarity could exist between women and men. Women of color, from various ethnic backgrounds, as well as women who were active in the gay movement, not only experienced the development of solidarity between women and men in resistance struggle, but recognized its value. They were not willing to devalue this bonding by allying themselves with anti-male bourgeois white women. Encouraging political bonding between women and men to radically resist sexist oppression would have called attention to the transformative potential of feminism. The anti-male stance was a reactionary perspective that made feminism appear to be a movement that would enable white women to usurp white male power, replacing white male supremacist rule with white female supremacist rule.

Within feminist organizations, the issue of female separatism was intially separated from the anti-male stance; it was only as the movement progressed that the two perspectives merged. Many all-female sex-segregated groups were formed because women recognized that separatist organizing could hasten female consciousness-raising, lay the groundwork for the development of solidarity between women, and generally advance the movement. It was believed that mixed groups would get bogged down by male power trips. Separatist groups were seen as a necessary strategy, not as a way to attack men. Ultimately, the purpose of such groups was integration with equality. The positive implications of separatist organizing were diminished when radical feminists, like Ti Grace Atkinson, proposed sexual separatism as an ultimate goal of feminist movement. Reactionary separatism is rooted in the conviction that male supremacy is an absolute aspect of our culture, that women have only two alternatives: accepting it or withdrawing from it to create subcultures. This position eliminates any need for revolutionary struggle and it is in no way a threat to the status quo. In the essay "Separate to Integrate," Barbara Leon (1975) stresses that male supremacists would rather feminist movement remain "separate and unequal." She gives the example of orchestra conductor Antonia Brico's efforts to shift from an all-women orchestra to a mixed orchestra, only to find she could not get support for the latter:

> Antonia Brico's efforts were acceptable as long as she confined herself to proving that women were qualified musicians. She had no trouble finding 100 women who could play in an orchestra or getting financial backing for them to do so. But finding the backing for men and women to play together in a truly integrated orchestra proved to be impossible. Fighting for integration proved to be more a threat to male supremacy and, therefore, harder to achieve.
>
> The women's movement is at the same point now. We can take the easier way of accepting segregation, but that would mean losing the very goals for which the movement was formed. Reactionary separatism has been a way of halting the push of feminism. . . .

During the course of contemporary feminist movement, reactionary separatism has led many women to abandon feminist struggle, yet it remains an accepted pattern for feminist organizing, e.g. autonomous women's groups within the peace movement. As a policy, it has helped to marginalize feminist struggle, to make it seem more a personal solution to individual problems, especially problems with men, than a political movement which aims to transform society as a whole. To return to an emphasis on feminism as revolutionary struggle, women can no longer allow feminism to be another arena for the continued expression of antagonism between the sexes. The time has come for women active in feminist movement to develop new strategies for including men in the struggle against sexism.

All men support and perpetuate sexism and sexist oppression in one form or another. It is crucial that feminist activists not get bogged down in intensifying our awareness of this fact to the extent that we do not stress the more unemphasized point which is that men can lead life affirming, meaningful lives without exploiting and oppressing women. Like women, men have been socialized to passively accept sexist ideology. While they need not blame themselves for accepting sexism, they must assume responsibility for eliminating it. It angers women activists who push separatism as a goal of feminist movement to hear emphasis placed on men being victimized by sexism; they cling to the "all men are the enemy" version of reality. Men are not exploited or oppressed by sexism, but there are ways in which they suffer as a result of it. This suffering should not be ignored. While it in no way diminishes the seriousness of male abuse and oppression of women, or negates male responsibility for exploitative actions, the pain men experience can serve as a catalyst calling attention to the need for change. Recognition of the painful consequences of sexism in their lives led some men to establish consciousness-raising groups to examine this. Paul Hornacek (1977) explains the purpose of these gatherings in his essay "Anti-Sexist Consciousness-Raising Groups for Men":

> Men have reported a variety of different reasons for deciding to seek a C-R group, all of which have an underlying link to the feminist move-

ment. Most are experiencing emotional pain as a result of their male sex role and are dissatisfied with it. Some have had confrontations with radical feminists in public or private encounters and have been repeatedly criticized for being sexist. Some come as a result of their commitment to social change and their recognition that sexism and patriarchy are elements of an intolerable social system that needs to be altered . . .

Men in the consciousness-raising groups Hornacek describes acknowledge that they benefit from patriarchy and yet are also hurt by it. Men's groups, like women's support groups, run the risk of overemphasizing personal change at the expense of political analysis and struggle.

Separatist ideology encourages women to ignore the negative impact of sexism on male personhood. It stresses polarization between the sexes. According to Joy Justice, separatists believe that there are "two basic perspectives" on the issue of naming the victims of sexism: "There is the perspective that men oppress women. And there is the perspective that people are people, and we are all hurt by rigid sex roles." Many separatists feel that the latter perspective is a sign of co-optation, representing women's refusal to confront the fact that men are the enemy—they insist on the primacy of the first perspective. Both perspectives accurately describe our predicament. Men *do* oppress women. People *are* hurt by rigid sex role patterns. These two realities co-exist. Male oppression of women cannot be excused by the recognition that there are ways men are hurt by rigid sex roles. Feminist activists should acknowledge that hurt—it exists. It does not erase or lessen male responsibility for supporting and perpetuating their power under patriarchy to exploit and oppress women in a manner far more grievous than the psychological stress or emotional pain caused by male conformity to rigid sex role patterns.

Women active in feminist movement have not wanted to focus in any way on male pain so as not to deflect attention away from the focus on male privilege. Separatist feminist rhetoric suggested that all men shared equally in male privilege, that all men reap positive benefits from sexism. Yet the poor or working class man has been socialized via sexist ideology to believe that there are privileges and powers he should possess solely because he is male often finds that few if any of these benefits are automatically bestowed him in life. More than any other male group in the United States, he is constantly concerned about the contradiction between the notion of masculinity he was taught and his inability to live up to that notion. He is usually "hurt," emotionally scarred because he does not have the privilege or power society has taught him "real men" should possess. Alienated, frustrated, pissed off, he may attack, abuse, and oppress an individual woman or women, but he is not reaping positive benefits from his support and perpetuation of sexist ideology. When he beats or rapes women, he is not exercising privilege or reaping positive rewards; he may feel satisfied in exercising the only form of domination allowed him. The ruling class male power structure that promotes his sexist abuse of women reaps the real material benefits and privileges from his actions. As long as he is attacking women and not sexism or capitalism, he helps to maintain a system that allows him few, if any, benefits or privileges. He is an oppressor. He is an enemy to women. He is also an enemy to himself. He is also oppressed. His abuse of women is not justifiable. Even though he has been socialized to act as he does, there are existing social movements that would enable him to struggle for self-recovery and liberation. By ignoring these movements, he chooses to remain both oppressor and oppressed. If feminist movement ignores his predicament, dismisses his hurt, or writes him off as just another male enemy, then we are passively condoning his actions.

The process by which men act as oppressors and are oppressed is particularly visible in black communities, where men are working class and poor. In her essay "Notes For Yet Another Paper on Black Feminism, or Will The Real Enemy Please Stand Up?," (1979) black feminist activist Barbara Smith suggests that black women are unwilling to confront the problem of sexist oppression in black communities:

> By naming sexist oppression as a problem it would appear that we would have to identify as threatening a group we have heretofore assumed to be our allies—Black men. This seems to be one of the major stumbling blocks to beginning to analyze the sexual relationships/sexual politics of our lives. The phrase "men are not the enemy" dismisses feminism and the reality of patriarchy in one breath and also overlooks some major realities. If we cannot entertain the idea that some men are the enemy, especially white men and in a different sense Black men too, then we will never be able to figure out all the reasons why, for example, we are beaten up every day, why we are sterilized against our wills, why we are being raped by our neighbors, why we are pregnant at age twelve, and why we are at home on welfare with more children than we can support or care for. Acknowledging the sexism of Black men does not mean that we become "manhaters" or necessarily eliminate them from our lives. What it does mean is that we must struggle for a different basis of interaction with them.

Women in black communities have been reluctant to publicly discuss sexist oppression, but they have always known it exists. We too have been socialized to accept sexist ideology and many black women feel that black male abuse of women is a reflection of frustrated masculinity—such thoughts lead them to see that abuse is understandable, even justified. The vast majority of black women think that just publicly stating that these men are the enemy or identifying them as oppressors would do little to change the situation; they fear it could simply lead to greater victimization. Naming oppressive realities, in and of itself, has not brought about the kinds of changes for oppressed groups that it can for more privileged groups, who command a different quality of attention. The public naming of sexism has generally not resulted in the institutionalized violence that characterized, for example, the response to black civil rights struggles. (Private naming, however, is often met with violent oppression.) Black women have not joined the feminist movement not because they cannot face the reality of sexist oppression; they face it daily. They do not join feminist movement because they do not see in feminist theory and practice, especially those writings made available to masses of people, potential solutions.

So far, feminist rhetoric identifying men as the enemy has had few positive implications. Had feminist activists called attention to the relationship between ruling class men and the vast majority of men, who are socialized to perpetuate and maintain sexism and sexist oppression even as they reap no life-affirming benefits, these men might have been motivated to examine the impact of sexism in their lives. Often feminist activists talk about male abuse of women as if it is an exercise of privilege rather than an expression of moral bankruptcy, insanity, and dehumanization. For example, in Barbara Smith's essay, she identifies white males as "the primary oppressor group in American society" and discusses the nature of their domination of others. At the end of the passage in which this statement is made she comments: "It is not just rich and powerful capitalists who inhibit and destroy life. Rapists, murderers, lynchers, and ordinary bigots do too and exercise very real and violent power because of this white male privilege." Implicit in this statement is the assumption that the act of committing violent crimes against women is either a gesture or an affirmation of privilege. Sexist ideology brainwashes men to believe that their violent abuse of women is beneficial when it is not. Yet feminist activists affirm this logic when we should be constantly naming these acts as expressions of perverted power relations, general lack of control over one's actions, emotional powerlessness, extreme irrationality, and in many cases, outright insanity. Passive male absorption of sexist ideology enables them to interpret this disturbed behavior positively. As long as men are brainwashed to equate violent abuse of women with privilege, they will have no understanding of the damage done to themselves, or the damage they do to others, and no motivation to change.

Individuals committed to feminist revolution must address ways that men can unlearn sexism. Women were never encouraged in contemporary feminist movement to point out to men their responsibility. Some feminist rhetoric "put down" women who related to men at all. Most women's liberationists were saying "women have nurtured, helped, and supported others for too long—now we must fend for ourselves." Having helped and supported men for centuries by acting in complicity with sexism, women were suddenly encouraged to withdraw their support when it came to the issue of "liberation." The insistence on a concentrated focus on individualism, on the primacy of self, deemed "liberatory" by women's liberationists, was not a visionary, radical concept of freedom. It did provide individual solutions for women, however. It was the same idea of independence perpetuated by the imperial patriarchal state which equates independence with narcissim and lack of concern with triumph over others. In this way, women active in feminist movement were simply inverting the dominant ideology of the culture—they were not attacking it. They were not presenting practical alternatives to the status quo. In fact, even the statement "men are the enemy" was basically an inversion of the male supremacist doctrine that "women are the enemy"—the old Adam and Eve version of reality.

In retrospect, it is evident that the emphasis on "man as enemy" deflected attention away from focus on improving relationships between women and men, ways for men and women to work together to unlearn sexism. Bourgeois women active in feminist movement exploited the notion of a natural polarization between the sexes to draw attention to equal rights effort. They had an enormous investment in depicting the male as enemy and the female as victim. They were the group of women who could dismiss their ties with men once they had an equal share in class privilege. They were ultimately more concerned with obtaining an equal share in class privilege than with the struggle to eliminate sexism and sexist oppression. Their insistence on separating from men heightened the sense that they, as women without men, needed equality of opportunity. Most women do not have the freedom to separate from men because of economic inter-dependence. The separatist notion that women could resist sexism by withdrawing from contact with men reflected a bourgeois class perspective. In Cathy McCandless' essay "Some Thoughts About Racism, Classism, and Separatism," she makes the point that separatism is in many ways a false issue because "in this capitalist economy, none of us are truly separate" (1979). However, she adds:

> Socially, it's another matter entirely. The richer you are, the less you generally have to acknowledge those you depend upon. Money can buy you a great deal of distance. Given enough of it, it is even possible never to lay eyes upon a man. It's a wonderful luxury, having control over who you lay eyes on, but let's face it: most women's daily survival still involves face-to-face contact with men whether they like it or not. It seems to me that for this reason alone, criticizing women who associate with men not only tends to be counterproductive; it borders on blaming the victim. Particularly if the women taking it upon themselves to set the standards are white and upper or middle class (as has often been the case in my experience) and those to whom they apply these rules are not.

Devaluing the real necessities of life that compel many women to remain in contact with men, as well as not respecting the desire of women to keep contact with men, created an unnecessary conflict of interest for those women who might have been very interested in feminism but felt they could not live up to the politically correct standards.

Feminist writings did not say enough about ways women could directly engage in feminist struggle in subtle, day-to-day contacts with men, although they have addressed crises. Feminism is politically relevant to the masses of women who daily interact with men both publicly and privately, if it addresses ways that interaction, which usually has negative components because sexism is so all-pervasive, can be changed. Women who have daily contact with men need useful strategies that will enable them to integrate feminist movement into their daily life. By inadequately addressing or failing to address the difficult issues, contemporary feminist movement located itself on the periphery of society rather than at the center. Many women and men think feminism is happening, or happened, "out there." Television tells them the "liberated" woman is an exception, that she is primarily a careerist. Commercials like the one that shows a white career women shifting from work attire to flimsy clothing exposing flesh, singing all the while "I can bring home the bacon, fry it up in the pan, and never let you forget you're a man" reaffirm that her careerism will not prevent her from assuming the stereotyped sex object role assigned women in male supremacist society.

Often men who claim to support women's liberation do so because they believe they will benefit by no longer having to assume specific, rigid sex roles they find negative or restrictive. The role they are most willing and eager to change is that of economic provider. Commercials like the one described above assure men that women can be breadwinners or even "the" breadwinner, but still allow men to dominate them. Carol Hanisch's essay "Men's Liberation" (1975) explores the attempt by these men to exploit women's issues to their own advantage, particularly those issues related to work:

Another major issue is the attempt by men to drop out of the work force and put their women to work supporting them. Men don't like their jobs, don't like the rat race, and don't like having a boss. That's what all the whining about being a "success symbol" or "success object" is really all about. Well, women don't like those things either, especially since they get paid 40% less than men for working, generally have more boring jobs, and rarely are even allowed to be "successful." But for women working is usually the only way to achieve some equality and power in the family, in their relationship with men, some independence. A man can quit work and pretty much still remain the master of the household, gaining for himself a lot of free time since the work he does doesn't come close to what his wife or lover does. In most cases, she's still doing more than her share of the housework in addition to wife work and her job. Instead of fighting to make his job better, to end the rat race, and to get rid of bosses, he sends his woman to work—not much different from the old practice of buying a substitute for the draft, or even pimping. And all in the name of breaking down "role stereotypes" or some such nonsense.

Such a "men's liberation movement" could only be formed in reaction to women's liberation in an attempt to make feminist movement serve the opportunistic interests of individual men. These men identified themselves as victims of sexism, working to liberate men. They identified rigid sex roles as the primary source of their victimization and though they wanted to change the notion of masculinity, they were not particularly concerned with their sexist exploitation and oppression of women. Narcissism and general self-pity characterized men's liberation groups. Hanisch concludes her essay with the statement:

Women don't want to pretend to be weak and passive. And we don't want phony, weak, passive acting men any more than we want phony supermen full of bravado and little else. What women want is for men to be honest. Women want men to be bold—boldly honest, aggressive in their human pursuits. Boldly passionate, sexual and sensual. And women want this for themselves. It's time men became boldly radical. Daring to go to the root of the own exploitation and seeing that it is not women or "sex roles" or "society" causing their unhappiness, but capitalists and capitalism. It's time men dare to name and fight these, their real exploiters.

Men who have dared to be honest about sexism and sexist oppression, who have chosen to assume responsibility for opposing and resisting it, often find themselves isolated. Their politics are disdained by antifeminist men and women, and are often ignored by women active in feminist movement. Writing about his efforts to publicly support feminism in a local newspaper in Santa Cruz, Morris Conerly explains:

Talking with a group of men, the subject of Women's Liberation inevitably comes up. A few laughs, snickers, angry mutterings, and denunciations follow. There is a group consensus that men are in an embattled position and must close ranks against the assaults of misguided females.

Without fail, someone will solicit me for my view, which is that I am
100% for Women's Liberation. That throws them for a loop and they
start staring at me as if my eyebrows were crawling with lice.

They're thinking, "What kind of man is he?" I am a black man who
understands that women are not my enemy. If I were a white man with a
position of power; one could understand the reason for defending the
status quo. Even then, the defense of a morally bankrupt doctrine that
exploits and oppresses others would be inexcusable.

Conerly stresses that it was not easy for him to publicly support feminist
movement, that it took time:

. . . Why did it take me some time? Because I was scared of the negative
reaction I knew would come my way by supporting Women's Liberation. In my mind I could hear it from the brothers and sisters. "What
kind of man are you?" "Who's wearing the pants?" "Why are you in that
white shit?" And on and on. Sure enough the attacks came as I had
foreseen but by that time my belief was firm enough to withstand public
scorn.

With growth there is pain . . . and that truism certainly applied in
my case.

Men who actively struggle against sexism have a place in feminist movement.
They are our comrades. Feminists have recognized and supported the work of
men who take responsibility for sexist oppression—men's work with batterers, for example. Those women's liberationists who see no value in this
participation must re-think and re-examine the process by which revolutionary struggle is advanced. Individual men tend to become involved in feminist
movement because of the pain generated in relationships with women. Usually a woman friend or companion has called attention to their support of male
supremacy. Jon Snodgrass introduces the book he edited, *For Men Against
Sexism: A Book of Readings* (1977), by telling readers:

While there were aspects of women's liberation which appealed to men,
on the whole my reaction was typical of men. I was threatened by the
movement and responded with anger and ridicule. I believed that men
and women were oppressed by capitalism, but not that women were
oppressed by men. I argued that "men are oppressed too' and that it's
workers who need liberation! I was unable to recognize a hierarchy of
inequality between men and women (in the working class) not to attribute it to male domination. My blindness to patriarchy, I now think,
was a function of my male privilege. As a member of the male gender
case, I either ignored or suppressed women's liberation.

My full introduction to the women's movement came through a
personal relationship. . . . As our relationship developed, I began to
receive repeated criticism for being sexist. At first I responded, as part of
the male backlash, with anger and denial. In time, however, I began to
recognize the validity of the accusation, and eventually even to acknowledge the sexism in my denial of the accusations.

Snodgrass participated in the men's consciousness-raising groups and edited
the book of readings in 1977. Towards the end of the 1970s, interest in male

anti-sexist groups declined. Even though more men than ever before support the idea of social equality for women, like women they do not see this support as synonymous with efforts to end sexist oppression, with feminist movement that would radically transform society. Men who advocate feminism as a movement to end sexist oppression must become more vocal and public in their opposition to sexism and sexist oppression. Until men share equal responsibility for struggling to end sexism, feminist movement will reflect the very sexist contradictions we wish to eradicate.

Separatist ideology encourages us to believe that women alone can make feminist revolution—we cannot. Since men are the primary agents maintaining and supporting sexism and sexist oppression, they can only be successfully eradicated if men are compelled to assume responsibility for transforming their consciousness and the consciousness of society as a whole. After hundreds of years of anti-racist struggle, more than ever before non-white people are currently calling attention to the primary role white people must play in anti-racist struggle. The same is true of the struggle to eradicate sexism—men have a primary role to play. This does not mean that they are better equipped to lead feminist movement; it does mean that they should share equally in resistance struggle. In particular, men have a tremendous contribution to make to feminist struggle in the area of exposing, confronting, opposing, and transforming the sexism of their male peers. When men show a willingness to assume equal responsibility in feminist struggle, performing whatever tasks are necessary, women should affirm their revolutionary work by acknowledging them as comrades in struggle.

REFERENCES

Angelou, Maya. 1983. "Interview." In *Black Women Writers at Work*, edited by Claudia Tate. New York: Continuum Publishing.

Hanisch, Carol. 1975 "Men's Liberation," Pp. 60–63 in *Feminist Revolution*. New Paltz, NY: Redstockings.

Hornacek, Paul. 1977. "Anti-Sexist Consciousness Raising Groups for Men." In *A Book of Readings for Men Against Sexism*, edited by Jon Snodgrass. Albion: Times Change Press.

Leon, Barbara. 1975. "Separate to Integrate." Pp. 139–44 in *Feminist Revolution*. New Paltz, NY: Redstockings.

McCandless, Cathy. 1979. "Some Thoughts About Racism, Classism, and Separatism." Pp. 105–15 in *Top Ranking*, edited by Joan Gibbs and Sara Bennett. New York: February Third Press.

"Redstockings Manifesto." 1970. Page 109 in *Voices from Women's Liberation*, edited by Leslie B. Tanner. New York: Signet, NAL.

Smith, Barbara. 1979. "Notes for Yet Another Paper on Black Feminism, Or Will the Real Enemy Please Stand Up." *Conditions: Five* 2 (2):123–27.

Snodgrass, Jon (ed.). 1977. *A Book of Readings for Men Against Sexism*. Albion: Times Change Press.

Betty Friedan
THEIR TURN:
HOW MEN ARE CHANGING

I believe that American men are at the edge of a tidal wave of change—a change in their very identity as men. It is a change not yet clearly visible, not really identified or understood by the experts and not even, or seldom, spoken about by men themselves. Yet this change will be as basic as the change created for women by the Women's Movement, even though it is nothing like the Women's Movement. Nobody is marching or making statements. There is no explosion of anger, no enemy to rage against, no list of grievances or demands for benefits and opportunities clearly valuable and previously denied, as with women.

This is a quiet movement, a shifting in direction, the saying of no to old patterns, a searching for new values, a struggling with basic questions that each man seems to be going through alone. At the same time, he continues the outward motions that always have defined men's lives, making it (or struggling to make it) at the office, the plant, the ball park . . . making it with women . . . getting married . . . having children . . . yet he senses that something is happening with men, something large and historic, and he wants to be part of it. He carries the baby in his backpack, shops at the supermarket on Saturdays, with a certain showing-off quality.

It started for many men almost unwillingly, in response to the Women's Movement. The outward stance of hostility and bristling defensiveness that the rhetoric of the first stage of the Women's Movement almost demanded of men obscured the reality of the first changes among them, the real reasons those changes were threatening to some men, and the surprising relief, support—even envy—many men felt about the Women's Movement.

At first glance, all it looked like was endless arguments about his doing a fair share of the housework, the cooking, and the cleaning; and his responsibility for helping with the children, getting them to bed, into snowsuits, to the park, to the pediatrician. Because now it wasn't *automatic* that her job was to take care of the house and all the other details of life while his job was to support everyone. Now she was working to support them too.

But then, even if she didn't have a job outside the home, she suddenly had to be treated as a person too, as he was. She had a right to her own life and interests; at night, on weekends, he could help with the children and the house.

He felt wronged, injured. He had been working his can off to support her and the children and now he was her "oppressor," a "male chauvinist pig," if he didn't scrub all the pots and pans to boot. "You make dinner," she said. "I'm going to my design class."

He felt scared when she walked out like that. If she didn't need him for her identity, her status, her sense of importance, if she was going to get all that for herself and have a life independent of him, wouldn't she stop loving him? Wouldn't she just leave? He was supposed to be the big male oppressor, yeah? How could he admit the big secret—that maybe he needed her more than she needed him? That he felt like a baby when he became afraid she would leave.

That suddenly he didn't know what he felt, what he was *supposed* to feel—as a man.

I believe much of the hostility of men comes from their very dependence on our love, from those feelings of need that men aren't supposed to have—just as the excesses of our attacks on our male "oppressors" stemmed from our dependence on men. That old, excessive dependence (which was supposed to be natural in women) made us feel we had to be *more* independent than any man in order to be able to move at all. Our explosion of rage and our attacks on men masked our own timidity and fear at risking ourselves, in a complex and competitive world, in ways we never had had to before.

And the more a man was pretending to a dominant, cool, masculine superiority he didn't really feel—the more he was forced to carry the burden alone of supporting everyone against the rough odds of that grim, outside economic world—the more threatened and the more hostile he felt.

Sam, a foreman for an aerospace company in Seattle, Washington, believes that the period when his wife "tried to be just a housewife" was the worst time in his marriage. "If you decide you're going to stay home and be taken care of," he says, "and you have to depend for everything on this guy, you get afraid. *Can he do it?* It all depended on me, and I was in a constant panic, the way our business is now, but I'd say, 'Don't worry.'

"Susie was tired of her job anyhow," explains Sam. "It wasn't such a great job—neither is mine, if you want to know—but she had an excuse. She said she wanted to be home with the children. The pressure was on me. But it was crazy. Here I was, not knowing where the next paycheck was coming from after our government contract ran out, suddenly supporting a wife and children all by myself.

"It's better now that she's working and bringing some money in," Sam insists. "And I don't just help with the kids. She has to be at work before I do, so I give them breakfast and get them off to school. The nights she works late, I make dinner, help with homework, and get everyone to bed. But I don't feel so panicky now—and she isn't attacking me any more."

Phil Kessler, a young doctor who started out to be a surgeon but who now has a small-town family practice in New Jersey, talks to me as he makes pickles and his children run around underfoot in the country kitchen that is next to his office. "I was going to be a surgeon, super cool in my gleaming white uniform," he says, "—the man I was supposed to be but knew I wasn't. So I married a nurse and she stayed home to raise our chidren, and she was supposed to fulfill herself through my career. It didn't work for either of us.

"I went through torture before every operation," Phil explains. "Then Ellen started turning against me. I always said the children needed her at home full time. Maybe because I was so scared inside. Maybe she didn't have the nerve to do her own thing professionally. All she seemed to want was revenge against me, as if she were locked into some kind of sexual battle against me, playing around, looking elsewhere for true love.

"When Ellen finally got up the nerve to do her own thing—she's a nurse-midwife now—it was a relief," says Phil. "The other stuff stopped. She could come back to being my wife. And I'm *redefining myself*, no longer in terms of success or failure as a doctor, although I still am a doctor, and not as superior or inferior to her. It was a blow to my ego, but what a relief to take off my surgical mask! I'm discovering my own value to the family.

"Now that I'm not so hurt and angry and afraid that she'll leave me, I can see that it's a hell of a fight for a woman to be seen as a person. I think she was afraid of trying to accomplish something on her own, so she made me the villian. But it's as hard for me to feel like a person as it is for her. We couldn't—either of us—get that from each other."

The new questions are harder for men because men have a harder time talking about their feelings than women do. That's part of the masculine mystique. And after all, because men have the power and the top-dog position in society that women are making all the fuss about, why should men want to change—unless women make them?

"Maybe men feel more need to pretend," says a sales engineer in Detroit, Michigan, who is struggling to take "equal responsibility" for the children and the house, now that his wife has gone to work in a department store. "I don't think men thought much about what it was to be a man," he explains, "until women suddenly were talking about what it was to be a woman—and men were left out of the equation.

"In the '80s," this man says, "we're going to see more men dropping away from traditional male roles, partly because of the economy, partly because men are beginning to find other goodies at the table, like their children—areas from which men were excluded before. Being a daddy has become very important to me. When I used to see a man on the street with his children on a weekday, I assumed he was unemployed, a loser. Now it's so common— daddies with their children, at ease."

The truth is that many of the old bases for men's identity have become shaky. If being a man is defined, for example, as being *dominant, superior—as not-being-a-woman*—the definition gets shaky when most of the important work of society no longer requires brute muscular force. The Vietnam War probably was the beginning of the end of the old caveman-hunter, gun-toting, he-man mystique. The men I have been interviewing around the country these past months are the men who fought in Vietnam or who went to graduate school to stay out of the war.

Vietnam was somehow a watershed. If men stop defining themselves by going to war or getting power from jobs women can't have, what is left? What does it mean to be a man, except *not-being-a-woman*—that is, physically superior and able to beat up everyone else? The fact is, when a man admits to those "messy feelings" that men as well as women have, he can't *play* the same kind of man any more.

Tony Kowalski, of the Outer Banks of North Carolina, was a pilot in Vietnam when it started for him. "I was a captain, coming up for major," he says. "I had all the medals, and I would have gone on for twenty years in the Air Force. Sitting up there over Nam, the commander, under heavy fire, the guys screaming into the mikes, the bombers and fighters moving in, me giving the orders, I was caught up in it, crazy-wild, excited. And then I woke up one day, coming out of Special Forces camp, and found myself clicking my empty gun at civilians. I knew I had to get out."

Tony can fly any piece of machinery. He took a job with an airline. "All I wanted was security," he says. "After one year I was furloughed because the company was having financial difficulties. There was no security. So I came back to this town where I grew up and took a job as a schoolteacher, working with seventh and eighth graders who were reading at the second-grade level.

It was the 'reading lab,' the pits, the bottom—and traditionally a 'woman's job.' It's the hardest job I've ever done and it gets the least respect. Flying a three-hundred-twenty-three-thousand-pound Lockheed Starlifter can't compare." As a pilot Tony made $34,000 a year; as a teacher he makes $12,000.

"But maybe now," he says, "with the ladies moving in and picking up some of the financial slack—my wife works for a florist and as a waitress nights—a guy can say, 'I'm not going to get much of anywhere with the money anyhow. Why don't I do something really worthwhile from a human point of view?'"

Another man, a West Point graduate of the class of '68, whose father and grandfather were Army men, insists: "Men can't be the same again after Vietnam. It always defined men, as against women, that we went to war. We learned it in the locker room, young. The worst insult was to be called all the four- and five-letter words for women's sex. Now that women are in the locker rooms at West Point, how can that work?

"Women have a powerful advantage," this man adds, "because they aren't brought up to believe that if someone knocks you down, *he* has the courage, so you have to knock *him* down. Women aren't stuck with the notion that that kind of courage is necessary. It seems to me, ever since the Vietnam war more and more men are reaching a turning point, so that if they don't get beyond these games, they start to die. Women will make a mistake if they reach that turning point and start to imitate men. Men can't be role models for women, not even in the Army. We badly need some new role models ourselves."

At first it seems as if men and women are moving in exactly opposite directions. Women are moving out of the home and into the men's world of work and men are shifting toward a new definition of themselves *in* the home. As we move into the '80s, social psychologist and public-opinion analyst Daniel Yankelovich is finding that a majority of adult men in the United States no longer are seeking or are satisfied by conventional job success. Only one in every five men now says that work means more to him than leisure.

"Men have come to believe that success on the job is not enough to satisfy their yearnings for self-fulfillment," says Yankelovich. "They are reaching for something more and for something different."

Certain large signs of this movement are reported in the newspapers almost daily. Corporation heads complain that young executives refuse to accept transfers because of "the family." Economists and government officials bewail increased absenteeism and declining productivity among workers. In the past ten years, more than half of West Point's graduates have resigned as Army career officers. College and graduate-school enrollments are dropping among men (as they continue to increase among women), and not just because it isn't necessary for men to evade the draft any more.

In the book *Breaktime*, a controversial study of men "living without work in a nine-to-five world," Bernard Lefkowitz reports a 71-percent increase in the number of working-aged men who have left the labor force since 1968 and who are not looking for work. According to Lefkowitz, the "stop-and-go pattern of work" is becoming the predominant pattern, rather than the lifetime jobs and careers men used to pursue both for economic security and for their masculine identity.

"In the depression of the '30s," says Lefkowitz, "men were anxious because they were not working. In the '70s men became anxious because their work was not paying off in the over-all economic security they had expected."

Bob O'Malley, 33, quit his rising career in a big New York City bank to sell real estate on the tip of Long Island.

"I asked myself one day, if my career continued going well and I really made it up the corporate ladder, did I want to be there fifteen years from now, with the headaches of the senior executives I saw being pushed off to smaller offices, their staffs, secretaries, status taken away, or having heart attacks, strokes? Men who had been loyal to the company twenty-five years—it governed their whole lives—and to what end? I didn't want to live my life like that. I wanted to be more independent—maybe not making so much money but living more for myself."

The trouble is that once men disengage themselves from the old patterns of masculinity and success, they are just as lost for role models as women are. Moreover, if a man tries to get out of his own bind by *reversing roles* with his wife—if he yearns for a superwoman to support him as she used to yearn for a strong man who would take care of her—it makes his wife uneasy.

"My husband wants me to have another child, and he says he'll quit his job and stay home to take care of the children," a woman in Vermont tells me. "But why should that work for him when it didn't work for me? And maybe I don't want him to take over the family that much. Maybe I'd resent it—just working to support him."

It's a situation that didn't work when Dr. Phil Kessler, in the first flush of relief after dropping his surgical mask, tried reversing roles with his wife. In the first place, his wife couldn't make as much money as a nurse-midwife as he could make as a doctor. And somehow when she came home from work, the house was never "clean enough," the meat loaf wasn't seasoned "right" and he'd also forgotten to put the potatoes on. So she would rush around, tired as she was, doing everything over, making him feel just as guilty as she had in the old days.

"Then I began to feel like a martyr," he says. "Nobody appreciated how hard I worked, taking care of the house and the children. Now that I'm doing my own work again—and bringing money in—I don't have to feel guilty if the house isn't all that clean. And now that they're treating her like a professional at the hospital, she doesn't notice the dust on the windowsills so much, either."

It takes trial and error, of course, to work out the practicalities, the real trade-offs, of the new equality between the sexes when both try to share home and work responsibilities. And it might be harder for men because the benefits of the trade-offs for them aren't that obvious at first. Women, after all, are fighting for an equal share in the activities and the power games that are rewarded in this society. What are men's rewards for giving up some of that power?

Jimmy Fox, a blue-collar worker in Brooklyn, New York, won't admit that there are any rewards for him in the trade-offs he's been "forced" to work out with his wife. "In our community," says Jimmy, "men don't freely accept women's equality. It's got to be slowly pushed down their throats. Men are the ones who go to the bar on the corner, drink, come home when the heck they want, and expect supper to be on the table, waiting for them. When that starts changing, it scares them to death. It scared me."

"I didn't know what was going on," he says. "First thing I knew, my wife is going out to a women's organization, the National Congress of Neighborhood

Women, and she wants to go do this, do that. She's learning, letting me know that things are wrong with our marriage. What am I supposed to do? It took five years before we got to the point where she went out to work and found her own role."

Today Jimmy makes $9,000 a year and his wife makes $9,000. "And when she's out working," says Jimmy, "I'm taking care of the baby. It's no picnic. Any man who wants to change places with his wife when his wife stays home and takes care of the house and children has got to be a maniac. Her job in the house was twice as hard as mine at the plant. I work ten, twelve hours. She works from when she gets up in the morning until she goes to bed."

When Linda Fox first started working, she says, "there were many, many battles between Jimmy and me. I wanted equality, which I thought meant that if he put three hours and twenty-two minutes into housework, then I would put in three hours and twenty-two minutes. I wanted a blow-by-blow division and I was fanatical about it. Jimmy was so happy to be relieved of some of the burden of being the only one with the paycheck that he was willing to do that, although I know he was teased by the guys at the bar."

The first payoff for men then, obviously, is economic survival. Unfortunately, few of the other big trade-offs of equality can be measured as mechanically as men's and women's making exactly the same amount of money (women on the average still earn only 59 cents to a man's $1) or their spending exactly the same amount of time on housework.

"What I've gained," says Avery Corman, who wrote the novel *Kramer versus Kramer*, on which the movie was based, from his own experience of taking over the children when his wife started a business, "is the joy—and it is a joy—of having my children really rely on me. I've gained this real participation in their upbringing because I've been active in it on a daily basis."

Unlike the Kramers, the Cormans remain happily married, and he says, "what I've given up is being waited on myself. There are times when I'd really like to be the prince of patriarchs and sit around with my pipe and slippers with my wife and children tiptoeing around, but it sure isn't like that now and it never will be again. A secret part of me would sometimes like a less-equal marriage, would like to be catered to the way guys used to be."

"But the real payoff," he says, "is that men can begin to think about who they are as *men*. I can ask myself what I really want in life. With my wife out there earning, I don't have to be just a breadwinner."

Another big trade-off for men while women become more independent is more independence—more "space"—for them. An Atlanta cotton broker, now married at thirty to a woman with her own career, recalls his first marriage, to a woman who depended on him for everything.

"She made me feel suffocated," he says. "Living with a completely dependent woman is debilitating. You don't know why, but you just feel awful. She's breathing your air. She's passing her anxiety on to you. She's got no confidence in herself and she's looking to you for everything; but what she does is always put you down, make you feel you won't make it."

"She may be very sweet," he explains further. "She may be lovely, but all you know is that you don't have room to breathe. I never heard of any ruling class resigning, but as men realize that it's better to live with a nondependent woman, the change will come about because the payoff is real—economic and emotional."

Paradoxically, part of the trade-off is that when women share the economic burden—and declare themselves equal persons in other ways—men are able to put a new value on personal qualities once considered the exclusive domain of women. It's the new American frontier for men, this exploration of their inner space, of the "messy feelings" we all have but that for too long were considered awesome and mysterious and forbidden territory for men.

When women share the work burden and relieve men of the need to pretend to false strengths, men can open up to feelings that give them a real sense of strength, especially when they share the daily chores of life that wives used to shield them from. "It grounds me—I have to admit it," says a man named Bernie, who for the first time, after thirty years of his mother's and wife's doing it for him, is cooking, shopping, and washing clothes. "I like the relief from always thinking about my job, feeling like a disembodied head chained to a typewriter."

Or as a man named Lars Hendrix, of Oakland, California expressed it: "It makes me feel alive. I don't have to pretent to be so strong because I feel good. I feel grounded. The silence that most men live with isolates them not only from women but also from other men. My wife's assault on my silence was at first extremely painful. She made me share my feelings with her. It brought an incredible sense of liberation, and maybe for the first time in my adult life a sense of reality, that I can *feel* my feelings and share them with her."

"But there'll still be a loneliness, for me and for other men," says Lars, "until we can share our feelings with each other. That's what I envy most about the Women's Movement—the way women share their feelings and the support they get from each other. Do you know how isolated and lonely and weak a man feels in that silence, never really making contact with another man?"

There is another, major problem. As men seek for themselves the liberation that began with the Women's Movement, both men and women have to confront the conflict between their human needs—for love, for family, for purpose in life—and the demands of the workplace.

A family therapist in Philadelphia, Pennsylvania, the father of a three-year-old son, talks about the conflict in terms of his own profession and personal needs. "I was working at one of the top family-training centers in the country," he says. "There was constant theoretical discussion about getting the father back into the family, but the way the jobs were set up there, you had to work fifty, sixty hours a week. To really get anywhere you had to put in seventy hours and work nights, weekends. You didn't have time for your own family. I won't do that. My family is number one—my job is only to be a good therapist."

Recent managerial studies have shown that the long working hours and the corporate transfers that keep many men from strong daily involvements with their families or with other interests are not always necessary for the work of the company. But the long hours and the transfers do serve to keep a man *dependent* for his very identity, as well as his livelihood, on the corporation—dependent as a "company man."

Recently, at the National Assembly on the Future of the Family sponsored by the NOW Legal Defense and Education Fund, corporation heads and union leaders joined feminists and family experts in contronting the need for "practical and innovative" solutions to balancing the demands of the workplace and the family. The agenda for the '80s must include restructuring the institutions of work and home to make equality livable and workable—for women and men.

Women can't solve the problem alone by taking everything on themselves, by trying to be "superwomen." And women don't have the power to change the structure of the workplace by themselves. But while more and more men decide that they want some self-fulfillment beyond their jobs and some of the life-grounding that women always have had in the family—as much as women now need and want some voice and active power in the world—there will be a new combined force for carrying out the second stage of liberation for us all.

It seems strange to suggest that there is a new American frontier, a new adventure for men, in the struggle for *wholeness*, for openness to feeling, for living and sharing life on equal terms with women. But it is a new frontier where both men's and women's needs converge. Men need new role models now as much as women do.

Men also need to share their new questions and feelings about work and family and self-fulfillment with other men. To help each other. To begin to break out of their isolation and become role models for each other, as women are doing in the second stage of the struggle for liberation.

The dialogue has gone on too long in terms of women alone. Let men join women in the center of the second stage.

CONTRIBUTORS TO
THE SECOND EDITION

Anthony Astrachan is a New York writer with many specialties, among them Soviet affairs, health-care policy, and men's issues. He is the author of *How Men Feel: Their Response to Women's Demands for Equality and Power* (Doubleday/Anchor, 1986).

Maxine Baca Zinn is in the Department of Sociology at Michigan State University. She has written widely in the areas of family relations, Chicano studies, and gender studies, including, most recently (with D. Stanley Eitzen), *Diversity in Families* (1990) and *The Reshaping of America* (1989).

Tim Beneke, a writer living in the San Francisco Bay area, is the author of *Men on Rape*.

Jessie Bernard, a sociologist at Penn State University, has written and lectured widely on gender and family issues. Her influential writings include *The Female World*.

Harry Brod is Associate Professor of Women's and Gender Studies and Philosophy at Kenyon College. He is the editor of *The Making of Masculinities: The New Men's Studies* and *A Mensch Among Men: Explorations in Jewish Masculinity*. He was the Founding Editor of *Men's Studies Review* and Founding Chair of the National Men's Studies Association.

Susan Brownmiller is the author of numerous articles and books which examine feminist issues, including *Against Our Will: Men, Women, and Rape*, and *Femininity*.

John Ceeley lives in Madison, Wisconsin. He is the author of a book of poems, *The Country Is Not Frightening*.

James Chin is a clinical psychologist at the Holliswood Hospital, a clinical research consultant to the NYS Office of Mental Health, and in private practice. His areas of specialization include the prevention and treatment of addictive disorders, behavioral medicine, and health psychology.

Chris Clark graduated from New York University in 1985 and currently lives in New York.

David L. Collinson is in the Department of Management Sciences at the University of Manchester. His research focuses on the construction of masculinity in workplaces.

Bob Connell is Professor of Sociology at Macquarie University in Sydney, Australia. His most recent works include *Gender and Power* and *Staking a Claim: Feminism, Bureaucracy, and the State*, coauthored with Suzanne Franzway and Dianne Court.

Edward Donnerstein is Professor and Chair of the Communication Studies Program at the University of California, Santa Barbara. His major research interest is in mass-media violence and he has published widely in this area.

His books include *The Question of Pornography: Research Findings and Policy Implications* (with Dan Linz and Steve Penrod) and *Pornography and Sexual Aggression*.

Martin Duberman is Distinguished Professor of History at Herbert Lehman College of the City University of New York. Among his many books and plays are *In White America, About Time: Exploring the Gay Past, Paul Robeson,* and *Cures: A Gay Man's Odyssey*.

Wayne Ewing is Assistant Dean, Loretto Heights College, Denver, Colorado. He is author of *Violence Works/Stop Violence*.

Kathryn Ann Farr is Professor of Sociology at Portland State University.

Thomas J. Ficarrotto is a research associate with the Department of Psychiatry and Langley Porter Psychiatric Institute at the University of California in San Francisco. His areas of specialization include social psychology and health psychology. He writes on cross cultural aspects of homophobia and sex differences in mortality and health behaviors.

Jules Fieffer is a syndicated cartoonist and regular contributor to *The Village Voice*.

Gary Alan Fine is Chairman of the Department of Sociology at the University of Georgia. His most recent book is *With the Boys: Little League Baseball and Preadolescent Culture*.

Ben Fong-Torres is a journalist in the San Francisco Bay area.

Jeffrey Fracher is a psychotherapist who practices in Metuchen, New Jersey, specializing in the treatment of sexual disorders. He is adjunct Assistant Professor of Psychology at Rutgers University.

Clyde W. Franklin II is in the Department of Sociology at The Ohio State University. His research focuses largely on black masculinity. His numerous publications include *The Changing Definition of Masculinity*.

Jewelle Taylor Gibbs is Associate Professor in the School of Social Welfare at the University of California, Berkeley. She has numerous publications on the psychological problems and treatment of minority youth, and is the editor of *Young, Black, and Male in America: An Endangered Species*.

Barry Glassner is Chairman of the Department of Sociology at the University of Southern California. He is the author of *Bodies: Why We Look the Way We Do (and How We Feel About It)*, among other books.

Matt Groening is a cartoonist based in Los Angeles. He is the creator of the comic strip "Life in Hell" and the creator of *The Simpsons*.

Alan E. Gross is former Professor and Chair of the Department of Psychology at the University of Maryland. He currently lives in New York City.

Jeffrey P. Hantover is a freelance writer and consultant living in New York City. He has published articles on photography, film, and social issues. He is presently working on a novel.

Ian Harris is Chair of the Department of Educational Policy and Community Studies at the University of Wisconsin, Milwaukee, and author of *Peace Education*. He has been active in the men's movement since 1976.

James Harrison is a clinical psychologist and codirector of Harrison Associates, a holistic psychological consultation center in New York City. He currently writes and produces videos on psychological issues with a particular interest in gender studies.

Arlie Russell Hochschild is Professor of Sociology at the University of California, Berkeley. Her books include *The Managed Heart: Commercialization and Human Feeling* and *The Second Shift: Working Parents and the Revolution at Home*.

Bell Hooks is a writer and a teacher who speaks widely on issues of race, class, and gender. Her books include *Ain't I a Woman: Black Women and Feminism*, *Feminist Theory from Margin to Center*, and *Talking Back: Thinking Feminist, Thinking Black*. Her column, "Sisters of the Yam," appears monthly in *Zeta* magazine.

Patricia Horn is a staff editor for *Dollars & Sense*, a monthly socialist magazine on current economic affairs.

Barbara Katz Rothman is Professor of Sociology at Baruch College and the Graduate Center of the City University of New York. Her books include *In Labor: Women and Power in the Birthplace*, *The Tentative Pregnancy: Prenatal Diagnosis and the Future of Motherhood*, and *Recreating Motherhood: Ideology and Technology in a Patriarchal Society*.

Michael Kaufman is associated with the Faculty of Political Science at York University in Toronto, Canada. He is the editor of *Beyond Patriarchy: Essays by Men on Pleasure, Power and Change* (Oxford, 1987), and *Cracking the Armor* (Ballantine, forthcoming).

Michael S. Kimmel is Associate Professor of Sociology at the State University of New York at Stony Brook. He is editor of *Changing Men: New Directions in Research on Men and Masculinity* (Sage, 1987), *Men Confront Pornography* (Crown, 1990), and *Against the Tide: Pro-Feminist Men in America, 1776–1990* (Beacon, 1991). He is currently writing a history of manhood in America.

Gary Kinsman is an activist in the gay liberation and socialist movements in Toronto and is a member of the collective that publishes *Rites*, a magazine for lesbian and gay liberation. He is the author of *The Regulation of Desire*.

Seymour Kleinberg is the author of *Alienated Affections: Being Gay in America* and teaches at the Brooklyn Center of Long Island University.

John Krich is a writer whose books include *A Totally Free Man: An Unauthorized Autobiography of Fidel Castro* and a novel, *One Big Bed*.

Barbara Kruger is a graphic artist in New York City.

Ralph La Rossa is Associate Professor of Sociology at Georgia State University. He has published widely on the topics of men, parenting, and families.

Gregory K. Lehne is the author of "Homophobia Among Men: Supporting and Defining the Male Sex Role." He is Assistant Professor of Medical Psychology in the Department of Psychiatry and Behavioral Sciences at The Johns Hopkins School of Medicine.

Martin P. Levine is Associate Professor of Sociology at Florida State University and a Research Associate at Memorial Sloan Kettering Cancer Research Center. He has published extensively on the sociology of AIDS, sexuality, and homosexuality.

Charles J. Levy is the author of "ARVN as Faggots: Inverted Warfare in Vietnam."

Daniel Linz does research on the effects on males of exposure to various forms of media violence against women and other images of women. He currently teaches in the Department of Psychology at UCLA Center for the Study of Women.

Peter Lyman is Director of the Center for Scholarly Technology at the University of Southern California. His research on computing began when he was looking for a good field site to study anger, and a friend suggested the computer center. He is currently working on a study of how technical knowledge and hardware are "gendered," that is, founded in a masculine epistemology.

Richard Majors is Assistant Professor of Psychology at the University of Wisconsin, Eau Claire. He is the cofounder and chairman of the National Council of African American Men. He is the coauthor of *Cool Pose: The Dilemma of Black Malehood* (Free Press, 1991) and the upcoming *The American Black Male: His Present Status and Future* (Nelson-Hall, 1992).

Pip Martin is a psychologist who has also worked as an activist in the Australian environmental movement.

Michael A. Messner is Assistant Professor in the Department of Sociology and the Program for the Study of Women and Men in Society at the University of Southern California. He writes and speaks about men and masculinity and issues related to gender and sport. He co-edited (with Donald F. Sabo) *Sport, Men and the Gender Order: Critical Feminist Perspectives*. His book, *Power at Play: Sport, Men, and the Construction of Masculinity*, will be published in 1992.

Brian Miller is a psychotherapist in West Hollywood, California. He writes a popular advice column for the gay community called "Out for Good." Besides gay husbands and fathers, he has researched victims of anti-gay violence.

Peter M. Nardi is Professor of Sociology at Pitzer College. He has published articles on AIDS, anti-gay hate crimes and violence, magic and magicians, and alcoholism and families. He has recently edited *Men's Friendships* (Sage

Publications, 1991). He has also served as co-president of the Los Angeles chapter of the Gay and Lesbian Alliance Against Defamation.

Joseph H. Pleck is a Research Associate at the Wellesley College Center for Research on Women. He is the author of numerous articles and books on men and masculinity, including *The Myth of Masculinity* and *Working Wives, Working Husbands*.

Norm Radican has a background in public health education and in counseling about sexuality. He is active in The Australian Men's Movement.

Rex Reece is the author of "Coping With Couplehood."

M. Rochlin is the author of "The Heterosexual Questionnaire."

Ebet Roberts is a photographer in New York City.

Lillian Rubin is Alumni Professor of Sociology, Queens College, City University of New York, and a Research Associate at the Institute for the Study of Social Change, University of California, Berkeley. Her books include *Intimate Strangers: Men and Women Together*, *Just Friends*, *Erotic Wars*, and *Worlds of Pain*.

Don Sabo is in the Department of Sociology at D'Youville College in Buffalo, New York. He writes and speaks widely about gender and sport. He is editor (with Ross Runfola) of *Jock: Sports and Male Identity* and is currently editing a book (with Michael Messner) entitled *Sport, Men, and the Gender Order: Critical Feminist Perspectives*.

Jack Sattel is in the Department of Sociology of Normandale Community College in S. Bloomington, Minnesota. He was among the first people to research male inexpressivity.

Ruth Sidel is Professor of Sociology at Hunter College of the City of New York. She studies the role of women, the care of preschool children, and the provision of human services. Her books include *Women and Childcare in China: A Firsthand Report*, *Families of Fengsheng: Urban Life in China*, and *The World of Working Class Women*.

Martin Simmons was born and raised in Harlem, and he continues to reside in New York. He is a screenwriter, author, teacher, lecturer, and television producer. He is a former contributing editor to *Essence* magazine. His forthcoming novel is entitled *Blood at the Root*. He is a former member of the Harlem Writer's Guild and a founding member of New Renaissance Writers.

Robert Staples is in the Department of Sociology at the University of California, San Francisco. He has written widely on black families and gender issues, including his book, *Black Masculinity*.

Barrie Thorne is Streisand Professor of Intimacy and Sexuality in the program for the Study of Women and Men in Society and the Department of Sociology at the University of Southern California. She has written widely on feminist theory and gender issues, especially with respect to children.

Her works include *Rethinking the Family: Some Feminist Questions* (edited with Marilyn Yalom).

Leonore Tiefer has been engaged in research on human sexuality for the past 15 years, most recently as a staff psychologist in the Department of Urology, Beth Israel Medical Center, New York City.